The Principal's Legal Handbook

Fourth Edition

The Principal's Legal Handbook

Fourth Edition

Editors

Kenneth E. Lane
Southeastern Louisiana University, Hammond, LA

Mark A. Gooden
University of Cincinnati, Cincinnati, OH

Julie F. Mead
University of Wisconsin-Madison, WI

Patrick Pauken
Bowling Green State University, Bowling Green, OH

Suzanne Eckes
Indiana University, Bloomington, IN

EDUCATION LAW ASSOCIATION
DAYTON, OH

Disclaimer

The Education Law Association (ELA) is a private, nonadvocacy, nonprofit, international member association. The opinions expressed in this publication are those of the authors and do not represent official views of the Association.

300 College Park / Dayton, OH 45469-0528
p: (937) 229-3589 / f: (937) 229-3845
www.educationlaw.org

Printed in the United States of America
ISBN-10: 1-56534-134-1
ISBN-13: 978-1-56534-134-0

Dedications

Mandy Schrank, Jody Thornburg, Judy Pleiman, and Christine Wilson who as the staff of the Education Law Association make being a member of ELA and the editing of this book an enjoyable experience and relationship

- Kenneth E. Lane

Chantae Recasner, doctoral candidate at the University of Cincinnati, who proofread the chapters in the *Students and the Law* section

- Mark Gooden

Mark A. Paige, doctoral student at UW-Madison, for his tireless assistance

- Julie Mead

All of my students at BGSU, past and present, and my favorite future students—my niece Ryan and my nephew Jordan

- Patrick Pauken

Kelly Rapp, doctoral candidate at Indiana University, who assisted with the chapters in the *Schools and the Law* section

- Suzanne Eckes

Authors

Alexander, M. David
Department Chair and Professor, Department of Educational Leadership and Policy Studies, College of Human Resources and Education, Virginia Polytechnic Institute and State University, Blacksburg, Virginia

Bathon, Justin M.
Associate Instructor, Department of Educational Leadership and Policy Studies, Indiana University, Bloomington, Indiana

Beckham, Joseph C.
Allan Tucker Professor of Educational Leadership and Policy Studies, Florida State University, Tallahassee, Florida

Borreca, Christopher P.
Partner, Bracewell and Giuliani, LLP, Houston, Texas

Borreca, Elizabeth
Associate Professor & Director of Exceptionality, University of St. Thomas, Houston, Texas

Broe, Karen-Ann
Risk Manager for Education Programs, United Educators, Chevy Chase, Maryland

Camp, William E.
Professor, Teacher Education and Administration, University of North Texas, Denton, Texas

Chang, Tina
Assistant Professor, Educational Leadership, University of Nevada, Reno, Nevada

Clark, Susan G.
Assistant Professor, Educational Administration, Department of Educational Foundations and Leadership, College of Education, University of Akron, Akron, Ohio

Crockett, Jean B.
Associate Professor, Department of Special Education, University of Florida, Gainesville, Florida

Cummings, Jay
Dean, College of Education, Texas Southern University, Houston, Texas

Daniel, T. K. Philip
Professor of Educational Administration/Higher Education, Adjunct Professor of Law, The Ohio State University, Columbus, Ohio

Dayton, John
Professor of Educational Administration, Department of Lifelong Education, Administration, and Policy, University of Georgia, Athens, Georgia

Eckes, Suzanne
Assistant Professor of Educational Leadership and Policy Studies, Indiana University, Bloomington, Indiana

Ferrin, Scott Ellis
Associate Professor of Educational Leadership and Foundations and Adjunct Professor of Law, Brigham Young University, Provo, Utah

Fossey, Richard
Professor and Program Director in the Department of Teacher Education and Administration and Director of the Texas Higher Education Law Institute, University of North Texas, Denton, Texas

Frels, Kelly
Partner, Bracewell and Giuliani, LLP, Houston, Texas

Geisel, Richard T.
Assistant Professor of Educational Leadership, Grand Valley State University, Allendale, Michigan

Geraghty, Cathleen A.
School Psychologist, San Bernardino City Unified School District, San Bernardino, California

Gessford, James B.
Attorney, Perry, Guthery, Haase & Gessford, P.C., L.L.O., Lincoln, Nebraska

Gibbs, Jesulon S. R.
Assistant Professor of Education, South Carolina State University, Orangeburg, South Carolina

Gooden, John S.
Professor, Doctoral Program in Educational Leadership, Policy and Law, Alabama State University, Montgomery, Alabama

Gooden, Mark A.
Associate Professor and Program Director of Educational Leadership and Urban Educational Leadership, University of Cincinnati, Cincinnati, Ohio

Green III, Preston
Associate Professor of Education and Law, The Pennsylvania State University, University Park, Pennsylvania

Gunn, Kelly M.
Urban Educational Leadership Doctoral Student, University of Cincinnati, Cincinnati, Ohio

Horner, Jeffrey J.
Partner, Bracewell and Giuliani, LLP, Houston, Texas

Ingle, W. Kyle
Assistant Professor of Educational Administration and Leadership Studies, Bowling Green State University, Bowling Green, Ohio

Kallio, Brenda R.
Associate Professor of Educational Administration, University of North Dakota, Grand Forks, North Dakota

Kunzman, Robert
Assistant Professor of Education, Indiana University, Bloomington, Indiana

Lane, Kenneth E.
Professor of Educational Leadership, Department of Educational Leadership and Technology, Southeastern Louisiana University, Hammond, Louisiana and Professor Emeritus, California State University, San Bernardino, California

Mawdsley, Ralph D.
Professor of Educational Administration, Department of Counseling, Administration, Supervision and Adult Learning, Cleveland State University, Cleveland, Ohio

McCarthy, Martha M.
Chancellor's Professor, Chair of the Department of Educational Leadership and Policy Studies, Indiana University, Bloomington, Indiana

McNair, Jeff
Professor of Education, California Baptist University, Riverside, California

McNeal, Laura R.
Assistant Professor of Educational Policy Studies, Georgia State University, Atlanta, Georgia

***Mead, Julie* F.**
Associate Professor, Department of Educational Leadership & Policy Analysis, University of Wisconsin-Madison, Wisconsin

Miller, Margaret Bannon
Partner, Bose, McKinney & Evans, L.L.P., Indianapolis, Indiana

Osborne, Jr., Allan G.
Principal, Snug Harbor Community School, Quincy, Massachusetts

Otto, Doug
Superintendent, Plano Independent School District, Plano, Texas

Pauken, Patrick
Associate Professor in Educational Administration, Bowling Green State University, Bowling Green, Ohio

Perry, Gregory H.
Attorney, Perry, Guthery, Haase & Gessford, P.C., L.L.O., Lincoln, Nebraska

Potter, R. Lance
Research Associate, The Pennsylvania State University, University Park, Pennsylvania

Richardson, Michael D.
Professor and Endowed Chair of Educational Leadership and Department Head of Educational Leadership & Technology, Southeastern Louisiana University, Hammond, Louisiana

Risch, Judith
University of Wisconsin-Madison, Wisconsin

Russo, Charles J.
Joseph Panzer Chair in Education in the School of Education and Allied Professions and Adjunct Professor in the School of Law at the University of Dayton, Ohio

Schimmel, David M.
Professor of Education, University of Massachusetts, Amherst, and Visiting Professor, Harvard's Graduate School of Education

Scott, Lynn Rossi
Director, Brackett & Ellis, PC, Fort Worth, Texas

Sharp, Ralph
Associate Professor, Department of Education, East Central University, Ada, Oklahoma

Sparkman, William E.
Dean, College of Education, University of Reno, Reno, Nevada

Sughrue, Jennifer
Associate Professor of Educational Leadership, Florida Atlantic University, Boca Raton, Florida

Swartz, Stanley L.
Professor of Special Education, California State University, San Bernardino, California

Torres, Mario
Assistant Professor of Educational Administration, Texas A&M University, College Station, Texas

Vacca, Richard S.
Professor Emeritus of Education Law and Senior Fellow, Commonwealth Educational Policy Institute in the VCU Center for Public Policy, L. Douglas Wilder School of Government and Public Affairs, Virginia Commonwealth University, Richmond, Virginia

Van Berkum, Dennis W.
Associate Professor of Educational Administration, Minnesota State University at Moorhead, Moorhead, Minnesota

Williams, Verna L.
Represented the petitioner in *Davis v. Monroe County Board of Education,* Professor, University of Cincinnati College of Law, Cincinnati, Ohio

Wood, R. Craig
B. O. Smith Research Professor, Department of Educational Leadership, The University of Florida, Gainesville, Florida

Contents

Section 4:
Schools and the Law

Chapter 1

Introduction: The American Legal System

Charles J. Russo & Allan G. Osborne, Jr.

Introduction

Pursuant to the Tenth Amendment of the Federal Constitution, education in the United States is predominantly a function of the state. Even so, before any discussion of legal issues that arise in the public schools can take place, it is important to understand the legal framework under which our schools operate on both the federal and state levels. Accordingly, this introductory chapter examines the sources and types of laws in the American legal system while presenting information on how these laws affect the daily operations of public schools.

Sources of Law

There are four sources of law in the United States: constitutions, statutes, regulations, and judicial decisions. These sources of law exist at both the federal and state levels. A constitution is the fundamental law of a nation or state.[1] A statute, on the other hand, is an act of the legislative body, or a law enacted by Congress or a state legislature.[2] All statutes must be consistent with the controlling constitutions within their jurisdiction. Many statutes are accompanied by implementing regulations or guidelines written by officials in the agencies responsible for their execution and enforcement. Regulations are usually more specific than the statutes they are designed to implement because they construe legislative intent as to how laws should work in practice. Further, the numerous opinions issued by the courts interpreting the constitutions, statutes, and regulations comprise a body of law known as case, judge-made, or common law. Relying heavily on the notion of binding precedent—that is, a ruling of the highest court in a jurisdiction is binding on all lower courts in that jurisdiction—case law provides further insight into how constitutions, statutes, and regulations are to be applied to factual situations. While cases from other jurisdictions have no binding effect on courts outside of their jurisdictions, they are persuasive precedent. In other words, decisions of courts in one jurisdiction are not binding on those in other jurisdictions but may have some influence on how other courts may interpret the law.

Constitutions

As is common knowledge, the Constitution of the United States is the law of the land. Thus, all federal statutes and regulations, state constitutions, state laws and regulations, and ordinances of local governmental bodies, including school boards, are subject to the Constitution as it has been interpreted by the United States Supreme Court and other courts. Relatively few sections of the U.S. Constitution are implicated in school-related lawsuits. For the most part, the amendments protecting individual rights, such as the First, Fourth, Fifth, and Fourteenth Amendments, are the sections of the Constitution that impact the operation of the schools most dramatically. Similarly, a state's constitution is the supreme law of that state by which all of the state's other statutes, regulations, and ordinances must conform. State constitutions typically deal with many of the same matters as their federal counterpart.

Statutes and Regulations

As noted under the Tenth Amendment to the Constitution, education is reserved to the states.[3] Nevertheless, Congress has the authority to enact laws under the general welfare clause of Article I, Section 8, by offering funds for purposes that it believes will serve the public good. For example, Congress has enacted a series of statutes, such as the Civil Rights Act of 1964,[4] that subject public school systems to its anti-discrimination in employment provisions.

Federal statutes often make funds available to state and local governments conditioned on their acceptance of specific requirements for the use of the money. As discussed later in this paragraph, when states accept federal funds, educational officials are bound by whatever conditions Congress has attached to the legislation. If challenged, federal courts must be satisfied that those conditions pass constitutional muster. In 1987, Congress expanded its authority by defining a "program or activity" as encompassing "all of the operations of [an entity] any part of which is extended Federal financial assistance."[5] This broad general prohibition covers "race, color or national origin,"[6] "sex,"[7] and "otherwise qualified handicapped individuals,"[8] categories that have become increasingly important in school settings. For example, in order to receive funding for special education under the Individuals with Disabilities Education Act,[9] states, often through state and local educational agencies, must develop detailed procedures to identify children with disabilities and offer each qualified student a free appropriate public education in the least restrictive environment.

As another recent example of federal involvement in education, Congress enacted the No Child Left Behind Act (NCLB) in 2002.[10] States that receive federal financial assistance from NCLB must take steps to improve academic achievement among students who are economically disadvantaged; assist in preparing, training, and recruiting "highly qualified" staff; provide improved language instruction for children of limited English proficiency;

make school systems accountable for student achievement, particularly by imposing standards for annual yearly progress for students and districts; require school systems to rely on teaching methods that are research based and that have been proven effective; and afford parents better choices while creating innovative educational programs, especially if local school systems are unresponsive to their needs.

Regulations issued by the Federal Department of Education and other administrative agencies give the executive branch the means to implement statutes by carrying out their full effect. In other words, while statutes set broad legislative parameters, regulations allow administrative agencies to provide details to satisfy the requirements of the law. Regulations generally carry the full force of the law unless courts interpret them as conflicting with the legislation.

Most of the law affecting public schools comes from statutes enacted by state legislatures. Although state legislatures are subject to the limitations of federal law and of state constitutions, they are relatively free to establish their own systems of education. The law is well settled that state and local boards of education, administrators, and teachers have the authority to adopt and enforce reasonable rules and regulations to ensure the smooth operation and management of schools. Rules and regulations are subject to the same constitutional limitations as statutes passed by legislative bodies. As such, if it is unconstitutional for Congress or state legislatures to enact laws violating the free speech rights of children, it is also impermissible for teachers to do so by creating rules that apply only in their classrooms. It is also important to note that legislation or rule-making on any level, whether federal or state, cannot conflict with a higher authority.

Common Law

The duty of the courts is to interpret the law. When there is no codified law, or if statutes or regulations are unclear, courts apply common law. Common law is basically judge-made law, meaning that the courts may adjust the law to new or changing circumstances. The collective decisions of the courts make up the body of common law. When disputes involve legislation, the job of the courts is to uncover, as best they can, the intent of the legislative bodies that enacted statutes. To the degree that judicial decrees establish precedent, they have considerable weight in terms of providing guidance on how statutes and regulations are to be applied to everyday situations.

Judicial Systems

The federal court system and most state judicial systems have three levels. The lowest level in the federal system consists of trial courts that are known as district courts. Each state has at least one federal district court while larger states, such as California and New York, may have as many as four. District courts are the basic triers of fact in legal disputes; they review evidence and render decisions based on the evidence presented by the parties to disputes. Depending on the situation, trial courts may review the record of any administrative hearings that have been held, hear additional evidence, and/or hear the testimony of witnesses.

Parties not satisfied with the decision of a trial court may appeal to the federal circuit court of appeals within which their state is located. For example, a decision issued by a federal trial court in New York would be appealed to the Second Circuit which, in addition to New York, consists of the states of Connecticut and Vermont. There are thirteen federal judicial circuits in the United States.

Parties not satisfied with the decisions of circuit courts may appeal to the Supreme Court. Due to the sheer volume of cases appealed each year, the Supreme Court accepts less than one percent of the cases in which parties seek further review. Cases typically reach the Court in requests for a writ of certiorari, which literally means "to be informed of." When the Supreme Court agrees to hear an appeal it grants a writ of certiorari. At least four of the nine Justices must vote to grant certiorari in order for a case to be heard.[11] Denying a writ of certiorari has the effect of leaving a lower court's decision unchanged.[12]

Each of the fifty states and various territories has a similar arrangement to the federal scheme except that the names of the courts vary. In most states, there are also three levels of courts: trial courts, intermediate appellate courts, and courts of last resort. It is important to take great care with the names of state courts. For example, we generally think of a supreme court as being the highest court. Yet, in New York, the trial court is known as the Supreme Court while the state's top court is called the Court of Appeals.

When courts render their judgments, their opinions are binding only within their jurisdictions. It should be kept in mind that a court's jurisdiction can refer to either the types of cases that it can hear or the geographic area over which it has authority. However, in this situation, reference is made to the geographic area. Put another way, a judgment of the federal district court for Massachusetts is binding only in Massachusetts. The federal district court in Rhode Island might find a decision of the Massachusetts court persuasive, but it is not bound by its order. Nonetheless, a ruling of the First Circuit Court of Appeals is binding on all states within its jurisdiction, and lower courts in those states must rule consistently. A decision by the Supreme Court of the United States is, of course, enforceable in all fifty states and American territories.

As indicated above, the complex American judiciary operates at both the federal and state levels. The most common feature of these systems is a three-tiered system with trial courts, intermediate appellate courts, and courts of last resort, most commonly named supreme courts. Trial courts have general jurisdiction so that there are few limits on the types of cases that they may hear. Trial courts hear the facts behind the dispute, apply the law to the circumstances, and are generally presided over by a single judge or justice. Intermediate courts, generally known as appellate courts or courts of appeal, review cases when a party is dissatisfied with the decision of the lower court. Appellate courts are not triers of fact, but rather, review the lower court's application of the law. In rare cases an appellate court may throw out a lower court's interpretation of the facts of a case if it feels that it was clearly erroneous. Appellate courts usually consist of a panel of judges. For example, at the federal level, appeals are heard by a panel of three judges. Finally, issues may be appealed to a court of last resort. At the federal level, this is the Supreme Court. The Supreme Court has discretion to review rulings of lower federal courts and state high courts that involve federal constitutional, statutory, or regulatory issues.

Insofar as education is a state function and federal courts exist for federal matters, most educational disputes are resolved by state courts. Unless there is a substantial federal question, a case must be tried in a state court. If a substantial federal question is involved with a state question, a dispute may be litigated in either a state or federal court. When federal courts examine cases involving both state and federal law, they must follow interpretations of state law made by the state courts within which they sit because there is no such thing as federal common law.

Legal Resources

The written opinions of most courts are generally available in a variety of published formats. The official version of Supreme Court opinions are in the United States Reports, abbreviated U.S. The same opinions, with additional research aids, are published in the Supreme Court Reporter (S. Ct.) and the Lawyer's Edition, now in its second series (L. Ed. 2d). Opinions issued by the federal circuit courts of appeal are located in the Federal Reporter, now in its third series (F.3d) while federal district court decisions are published in the Federal Supplement, now in its second series (F. Supp. 2d). State court cases are published in a variety of publications, most notably West's National Reporter system, which divides the country up into seven regions: Atlantic, North Eastern, North Western, Pacific, South Eastern, South Western, and Southern. Most education-related cases are also republished in West's *Education Law Reporter*. Before being published in hard-bound volumes, most decisions are released in what are known as slip opinions, a variety of loose-leaf services, and electronic sources. There are also many commercial services available that publish decisions in a specialized area. For example, special education court decisions, as well as due process hearing decisions, are reproduced in a looseleaf format in the *Individuals with Disabilities Education Law Reporter* (IDELR) published by LRP Publications.

Statutes and regulations are also accessible in similar formats. Federal statues are published in the United States Code (U.S.C.), the official version, or the United State Code Annotated (U.S.C.A.), published by West Publishing

Company Agency regulations are published in the Code of Federal Regulations (C.F.R.). Copies of education statutes and regulations can be downloaded via links on the U.S. Department of Education's website. Legal materials are also available online from a variety of sources, most notably WestLaw and LexisNexis. State laws and regulations are commonly available online from the websites of their states.

Reading Legal Citations

Legal citations are fairly easy to read. The first number indicates the volume number where the case, statute, or regulation is located followed by the abbreviation of the book or series in which the material may be found. The second number indicates the page on which a case begins or the section number of a statute or regulation. The last part of a citation provides the name of the court, for lower court cases, and the year in which the dispute was resolved. For example, the citation for *Pennycuff v. Fentress County Board of Education*, 404 F.3d 447 (6th Cir. 2005) can be located in volume 404 of the Federal Reporter Third Series beginning on page 447. The case was decided by the Sixth Circuit Court of Appeals. Similarly, the citation for the Individuals with Disabilities Education Act, 20 U.S.C. §1400-1482 (2005) can be found in volume 20 of the United States Code beginning with section 1400 and continuing through section 1482.

Endnotes

[1] B. A. Garner, BLACK'S LAW DICTIONARY (8th ed.) (2004).
[2] *Id.*
[3] *See* Epperson v. State of Ark., 393 U.S. 97, 104, 89 S. Ct. 266, 21 L.Ed.2d 228 (1968).
[4] 42 U.S.C.A. § 2000e–2a.
[5] Civil Rights Restoration Act, 20 U.S.C.A. § 1687.
[6] 42 U.S.C.A. § 2000d.
[7] 20 U.S.C.A. § 1681.
[8] 29 U.S.C.A. § 794.
[9] 20 U.S.C.A.§§ 1400-1482.
[10] 20 U.S.C.A. §§ 6301 *et seq.*
[11] *Id.*
[12] Garner, *supra* n. 1.

Section I:

Students and the Law

Chapter 2

Student Discipline Law

Richard S. Vacca & Jeff Horner

Introduction

Most of today's public school systems have formal policies and rules specifically covering student discipline. Generally, such documents, often referred to as "Student Codes of Conduct," specify the nature and severity of the student offense and include the alternatives of punishment available for each. Generally written carefully to avoid vagueness, these documents typically enumerate the procedures to be followed in dealing with student offenders and often designate the person or persons responsible for enforcing each rule and implementing each procedure.

In enforcing a public school system's disciplinary code, the severity of the punishment of a student is an important factor to consider.[1] Generally, the more serious the punishment, the more formalized and extensive the requirements of procedural due process (e.g., an expulsion from school rather than a one-day suspension). For example, the Seventh Circuit Court of Appeals held that a high school senior who had been suspended from school because of drinking for three days and subsequently missed final exams and did not graduate was not entitled to the same level of due process as a student being expelled from school.[2] Courts have consistently held that confrontation and cross-examination of witnesses against a student, and a student's representation by counsel, may not be mandatory though "desirable when the possible discipline of a student is severe."[3] The age of the student or student group will affect the formality of the procedural due process to be afforded.[4] Additionally, whether a student has an educational disability will impact the nature of due process.[5]

Legal Issues

Basic fairness is the main precept of contemporary procedural due process. Fairness should undergird every decision made by a governmental entity, especially public schools. For more than thirty years, courts have been very active in extending procedural rights to public school students under the United States Constitution when they are involved in disciplinary situations.

Corporal Punishment

An age-worn mode of student punishment available in public schools is corporal punishment—the affliction of physical pain upon a student for misconduct. The legal justification for using corporal punishment is found in state statutes. Some states specifically allow it, while some states explicitly forbid it; at this time, more than twenty states forbid corporal punishment in public schools. The others do not mention it explicitly, but by implication, they authorize or allow it. The law on corporal punishment has not changed significantly in recent years, and both federal and state courts consistently uphold its reasonable use where the state allows it. However, due to liability concerns, a growing number of states and localities now forbid its use.

Where corporal punishment is used, it must conform to the laws of the state, local school board policy, and the common law standard of reasonableness. Courts have, over the years, spelled out nine general guidelines as to what constitutes reasonable corporal punishment. These guidelines suggest that corporal punishment

1. must be allowed by state statute (either directly or by inference);
2. must be implemented consistently with state statutory requirements;
3. must be used as a method of correction;
4. must not be cruel or excessive;
5. must not involve anger or malice;
6. must suit the age, gender, and physical condition of the child;
7. must involve use of an appropriate instrument; and
8. must not leave permanent or lasting injuries.
9. must be appropriate for the offense.[6]

Baker v. Owen[7] was the first case in this area to come before the United States Supreme Court. It allowed teachers to administer corporal punishment and did not require prior parent approval for such punishment. The following four procedural guidelines were approved in the decision: (1) students were warned in advance of the specific kinds of behavior that could result in their being corporally punished, (2) corporal punishment was not to be the "first-line" of punishment, (3) when corporal punishment was administered to a student, a second school official was present to witness the act, and (4) parents of a punished student were furnished with a written statement on request about the act including reasons for it and the names of the witnesses.

In *Ingraham v. Wright,*[8] the United States Supreme Court decided that the use of corporal punishment in a public school does not fall within the Eighth Amendment's prohibition regarding cruel and unusual punishment. The Eighth Amendment applies only to situations involving criminal punishments. The Court further held that a student is not entitled to notice and a hearing prior to corporal punishment. In the Court's opinion, if children are subjected to unreasonable applications of corporal punishment, they may obtain remedy by filing a civil suit.[9]

Hall v. Tawney[10] was a post-*Ingraham* case decided by the Fourth Circuit Court of Appeals. The court in *Hall* faced three basic issues: the legality of corporal punishment, the procedural due process guarantee of a hearing prior to the punishment, and the student's constitutional right to ultimate bodily integrity. In the Fourth Circuit, corporal punishment does not violate a child's protected rights. However, the force used by a disciplinarian must not be disproportionate to maintaining order and discipline in the school, nor should it be the product of malice, sadism, or brutality. The court believed that not every violation of state tort law or criminal assault law amounts to a violation of a constitutional right. In *Hall*, the court did address the substantive due process issue of a student's right to ultimate bodily integrity and held that this right applies to situations of corporal punishment.

Two years later, the Supreme Court of West Virginia addressed the procedural guarantees available to students in that state prior to the administration of corporal punishment. According to the court, the following minimal due process procedures should be utilized: a student should be given an opportunity to explain his or her version of the disruptive event, "as such an explanation may convince a fair-minded person that corporal punishment is not warranted," and absent some extraordinary factor, the administration of corporal punishment should be done in the presence of another adult "to protect both the student and the person administering corporal punishment by providing a neutral observer."[11]

Student Discipline Hearings and Due Process

Background

In general, students have the right to freedom from bodily restraint cognizable under the Fourteenth Amendment of the United States Constitution.[12] As stated earlier, this right does not extend so far as to implicate the Eighth Amendment prohibition on cruel and unusual punishment.[13] The courts have held that the Eighth Amendment applies only in the criminal context, not student discipline proceedings.[14] With respect to the Fourteenth Amendment concern, courts have recognized the rights of students to be informed of prohibited behavior and afforded certain procedural safeguards prior to the imposition of punishment. The extent of these procedural rights was the primary focus of *Goss v. Lopez*.[15] Decided in 1975, *Goss* has been the leading case in the student due process area for more than thirty years. *Goss* held that in the event of minor disciplinary infractions calling for suspensions of ten days or fewer, a student must only be afforded the opportunity to tell his or her side of the story before punishment is imposed. This opportunity is the "hearing" envisioned under *Goss* for minor disciplinary infractions. The scenario changes significantly for expulsions and long-term suspensions of eleven days or more. More thorough due process is required before imposing these punishments. The procedures for expulsions vary between states, and an administrator should consult his or her state statutes and school policies for precise requirements.

The Relevance of a *Miranda*-Type Warning

Currently, other possible elements of procedural due process are being clarified in the courts. One such element concerns whether a student is entitled to a *Miranda* warning prior to being questioned by school authorities. This element would require school authorities to advise a student of his or her rights as a police officer must do prior to arresting a criminal suspect. In *Boynton v. Casey*,[16] for example, a high school student was subjected to questioning by his school principal and vice-principal concerning the use of marijuana on school premises. During the one-hour questioning session, the student was denied permission to leave, was not informed of his right to not answer questions, and was not allowed to have his parents present at the questioning. Admitting that he used marijuana on school property, Boynton was immediately suspended.

Subsequently, in federal district court, Boynton and his parents alleged that by refusing their son permission to leave the initial questioning session, failing to advise him of his right to remain silent, failing to notify him that he had a right to have his parents present during questioning, and failing to notify his parents of the questioning, school officials denied him procedural due process. In dismissing the complaint for failure to state a federal constitutional claim upon which relief can be granted, the court held that the student was not entitled to *Miranda* warnings prior to being questioned by school authorities, and there was no requirement that the authorities notify the student and his parents of a right to have the parents present during questioning.[17]

Gathering of Information Concerning the Infraction

Generally, the first step in a student discipline case once a student is charged with an infraction involves securing information about the infraction. Most often, an allegation of student misconduct comes from a teacher, school administrator, or student. A teacher may see students fighting on the playground, for instance. The teacher would then report this incident to the proper authority. Any information gathered about a possible infraction should be communicated to the person in charge of discipline at that school, usually a principal or assistant principal. It then becomes incumbent upon that administrator to move forward with an investigation.

Completing the Investigation of the Allegations

After receiving a report of a possible disciplinary infraction, it is usually standard procedure for an administrator to conduct an investigation. One of the first parts of this investigation should be to talk to the accused student and determine if he or she committed the acts in question. The student should always be given the opportunity to relate his or her account of the allegations. The student may agree with the facts stated by the administrator, thereby essentially confessing to the wrongdoing. If this occurs, the administrator is in a position to immediately recommend the appropriate punishment for the infraction. In many cases, a student will disagree with the facts related by the administrator. The administrator should then question other witnesses to ascertain the facts concerning the event. If contradictory views of the incident in question exist, the administrator may believe whomever he or she feels is the most credible.

Ascertaining Whether the Misconduct Warrants Minor or Severe Punishment

Perhaps the most important step in the disciplinary process from a due process perspective is for the administrator to determine the nature of the punishment. If it is determined the incident warrants short-term suspension or other minor punishment, then such punishment can be immediately imposed by the administrator. The process of affording a student the opportunity to tell his or her side of the story is the only "hearing" contemplated in *Goss* for minor disciplinary infractions. Written notice should be sent to the student and the student's parents or guardians, describing the nature of the misconduct and the punishment to be imposed. Absent applicable state statutes or school administrative regulations, an appeals process is not legally required. However, to be fair to all involved, many school districts allow an appeal to a higher level, such as the superintendent or his designee.

In some instances, however, the investigation may reveal a more serious violation of school policy. If the proposed punishment for an infraction is expulsion or suspension for eleven days or more, a student is entitled to more thorough due process. The punishment cannot be immediately imposed. First, a letter should be sent to the student's parents outlining the charges against the student and informing them of the student's rights under the appropriate school policies and law. Copies of all applicable school policies should be attached. Next, it must be determined whether the student or parents desire a hearing on the charges. If such hearing is requested, a letter notifying them of the hearing date, the administration's witnesses, and the nature of the witnesses' testimonies in sufficient detail should be sent to the parents and student so that they can prepare a defense. All letters should be hand-delivered or sent by certified mail to make certain that the notice is received.

Preparing for the Hearing—Expulsion or Long-Term Suspension

Many state statutes require that expulsion or long-term suspension hearings be held before a school board. Statutes in other states allow designees of the school board, usually school administrators, to hear these cases. All parties are generally best served if the school principal or other administrator conducts the initial hearing. Several benefits are attained by having the initial hearing before a building administrator. First, such hearings are appropriate administrative functions. Second, holding the hearing before the administrator provides due process at the earliest time and at the lowest possible administrative level. Because a student is entitled to an impartial hearing, the administrator acting as "the judge" should avoid becoming overly involved in investigating the case prior to the hearing. If the administrator acting as a hearing officer becomes actively involved in the investigation, he or she should request that the superintendent appoint another administrator to hear the matter because the administrator could become a witness in the case.

Conducting the Hearing

At the expulsion or long-term suspension hearing, the administration has the burden of going forward and proving its case by a preponderance of the evidence. Because student disciplinary cases are not criminal actions, the higher burden of proof associated with criminal actions (beyond a reasonable doubt) does not apply. The administration must prove by a preponderance of the evidence that the student violated a school rule that warrants expulsion or long-term suspension. Generally, it is not necessary for a school district attorney to be present unless the student has an attorney. Also, the hearing should be tape recorded or transcribed by a court reporter to maintain a record for future use. Court reporters are much more expensive than tape recorders. In most instances, a good tape system will suffice to preserve a record of the hearing. A court reporter should be used only if the case is particularly complex and is likely to be appealed.

The first step of the hearing process is for the hearing officer to state the ground rules. He or she may read an outline of the proceedings, which should be provided to everyone in attendance so that all are apprised of the rules. The administration will begin the proceedings by presenting its case. The student or representative may be allowed to cross-examine witnesses presented by the administration. Time limits on cross-examination are generally not a good idea. Such limitations simply raise the specter of unfair treatment and violation of due process. The hearing officer may, however, require that the testimony be relevant and not repetitive or cumulative. Both the administration and the student may seek to sequester witnesses. This option simply means that each witness, other than parties to the case, may be required to remain outside of the hearing room until his or her testimony is given.

After the administration has presented its witnesses and documentary evidence, the student should then present his or her case. Again, time limits should not be placed on the student's presentation. After the student has presented his or her case, the hearing officer should allow rebuttal evidence and closing arguments. After the presentation of arguments, the administrator may render a decision at that time or may reserve the right to render the decision at a future date. The decision may have two parts. The first finding should state whether the student engaged in prohibited behavior, and the second finding—if necessary—should specify the appropriate punishment. Any decision made by the administrator should be confirmed in writing. This notification letter should inform the parents or guardians of the decision and the right of appeal to the next administrative level.

The Processing of the Initial Decision

After a student has been afforded a hearing, generally no further appeals process is legally required, except by statute. Many states require that such an appeals process be afforded to students. It is probably a good idea to allow an appeal so that the concept of fundamental fairness is observed. In most cases, an appeal of an expulsion or long-term suspension is directed to the local school district board or its designee. An appeal to the board can be based on either the record made before the school administrator or new evidence presented to the board. School policies and state law sometimes permit school boards to designate other parties, such as superintendents, to hear these appeals. To save time, expense, and repetitive testimony, an appeal based on the record is preferable. The board may then either listen to the tape recordings or read the transcript of the initial proceedings and review any documents. Each side should be given an equal amount of time to present oral arguments based on the record.

Based on a review of the record and the arguments of both parties, the board should make its ruling. The board should adopt specific findings of fact and conclusions of law similar to those made by the school administrator. It may make its decision either at the time of the hearing or at a later date. Any decision should be written and sent to the student and parents. The board should also pass a motion confirming its decision.

Further Appeal Outside the School District

If the punishment imposed by the board is an expulsion or long-term suspension, the student or parents may have the right of appeal to a body outside of the school district. This determination is normally dictated by state law. Some states afford an appeals route to the state education agency. Other states allow appeal directly to the state or federal court system. If a particular state allows appeal beyond the school board level, the student and parents should be informed of this right in the letter notifying the student of the expulsion or long-term suspension.

Suspension and Expulsion of Students with Disabilities

In 1988, the United States Supreme Court held, among other things, that the "stay put" provision of the Education of All Handicapped Children Act, retitled in 1990 as the Individuals with Disabilities Education Act (IDEA), prohibits state and local school authorities from *unilaterally* excluding disabled children from the classroom for dangerous or disruptive conduct growing out of their disabilities during the pendency of a review proceeding.[18] The Court stated that school authorities may use procedures—including a suspension for up to ten school days—to deal with students who pose immediate danger to themselves or others, or students who cause substantial disruption of classrooms or the school.[19] In 1997, the reauthorized IDEA added an option of placing a student in an interim alternative education setting (IAES) for forty-five days for such offenses as possession of weapons or drugs. A student may be placed in an IAES for more than forty-five days or have his or her program changed, but the procedural requirements of the IDEA must be followed.[20] Reauthorized again in 2004, the IDEA includes specific provisions detailing procedures required to ensure fairness in the discipline of students with disabilities.

Recommendations for Practice

Current public school administrators would be wise to adhere to the following guidelines from case law as they carry out their daily disciplinary routines.

1. The legal duty to control a school must be balanced with the procedural due process entitlements of students.
2. Due process is neither a fixed nor stagnant concept because it changes from situation to situation and is dependent upon a continuum of factors.
3. Fairness is the basic precept of contemporary procedural due process in public schools.
4. The technicalities of criminal procedure, including a *Miranda*-type warning, presence of an attorney, as well as confrontation and cross-examination of witnesses, do not automatically transfer into school disciplinary procedures.
5. Timely and adequate notice, an explanation of the charges against the student, and a chance to be heard are the minimal elements of procedural due process in student disciplinary episodes.
6. Procedural due process requires school administrators to be predictable and consistent and to exercise caution, thoughtful restraint, and common sense when disciplining students.

7. Student discipline must incorporate sanctions for misbehavior that were previously announced to students and their parents, directly linked to modes of misbehavior, and must follow the dictates of reasonableness.

Courts have recognized the rights of students to be informed of prohibited behavior and afforded certain procedural safeguards prior to the imposition of punishment. In discipline cases, several rules should be followed.

1. The administrator should move forward with an investigation by gathering additional information on any disciplinary infractions reported. Administrators should make further inquiry of other witnesses to ascertain the facts concerning the event.
2. The administrator must determine the nature of the punishment, as the necessary steps will be modified with increasing severity of punishment. The scenario changes significantly for long-term suspensions of eleven days or more and expulsions. More thorough due process is required before imposing these punishments.
3. A letter should be sent to the student's parents, outlining the charges against the student and informing them of the student's rights under the appropriate school policies and law for more severe punishments.
4. If the administrator acting as a hearing officer becomes actively involved in the investigation, he or she should request that the school district superintendent appoint another administrator to hear the matter.
5. Principals should become fully familiar with applicable state laws and regulations and school district policies impacting their schools.
6. Students who represent an imminent threat of harm to themselves or others or those who disrupt the school or its classrooms should be dealt with immediately with appropriate sanctions.
7. Students who are covered by the Individuals with Disabilities Education Improvement Act (2004) and whose misbehavior is a manifestation of their disability are not automatically subject to a school system's suspension and/or expulsion process as applied to general education students. These students have additional protection afforded under Section 504 of the Rehabilitation Act (1973) to ensure fairness and equity of treatment.
8. Suits for damages may result if administrators knew or should have known that their actions violate the procedural due process entitlements of their students.

Endnotes

[1] "In school discipline cases the nature of the sanction affects the validity of the procedure used in imposing it,..." *Schools*, 68 AM. JUR.2d § 269-291. More recently, a seventh-grade mathematics teacher found himself in court for using excessive disciplinary measures on a student who "coughed out loud" in class. Jones v. Witinski, 931 F. Supp. 364 (M.D. Pa 1996). *See also* Kolesmick By and Through Shaw v. Omaha Public Sch., 558 N.W.2d 804 (Neb. 1997) (where the court found no disparity between a two-semester expulsion and a student's knowing possession of a knife on school grounds). The reader is reminded that matters of academic discipline are treated differently from matters of discipline for misbehavior. *See, e.g.*, Moore v. Hyche, 761 F. Supp. 112 (N.D. Ala. 1991), and State v. McHenry, 915 S.W.2d 325 (Mo. 1995).

[2] Lamb v. Panhandle Cmty. Unit Sch. Dist. No. 2, 826 F.2d 526 (7th Cir. 1987). For another case concerning the issue of the severity of the expulsion as an "unfair punishment," *see* Adams v. City of Dothan Bd., 485 So. 2d 757 (Ala. Ct. Civ. App. 1986). *See also,* Bivens v. Albuquerque, 899 F. Supp. 556 (D.N.M. 1995); Donovan v. Ritchie, 68 F.3d 14 (1st Cir. 1995); and Obersteller v. Flour Bluff ISD, 874 F. Supp 146 (S.D. Tex. 1994) (for a case involving the lowering of a student's grade).

[3] *Schools, supra* note 1, at 597. *See also*, Newsome v. Batavia, 842 F.2d 920 (6th Cir. 1988) (it was held that an expelled student was not entitled, as a matter of right, to the names of student accusers; nor was he entitled to cross-examine the administrators who investigated his situation).

[4] *Id.* at 593. Coplin v. Conejo Valley, 903 F. Supp. 1377 (C.D. Cal. 1995) (the court held that a right to the names of females alleging sexual harassment did not exist in a pre-expulsion hearing).

[5] Honig v. Doe, 108 S. Ct. 592 (1988). 20 U.S.C. § 1415(k). For more recent cases on this point, *see* Magyar v. Tucson Unified, 958 F. Supp. 2d 1423 (D. Ariz 1997), Springer v. Fairfax County (Va.) Sch. Bd., 134 F.3d 659 (4th Cir. 1998), and Gadson City Bd. of Educ. v. B.P., 3 F. Supp. 2d 1299 (N.D. Ala. 1998).

[6] Portions of this chapter are adapted from the prior work of two well-known scholars on school jurisprudence, H. C. HUDGINS & R. S. VACCA, LAW AND EDUCATION: COMTEMPORARY ISSUES AND COURT DECISIONS, 345-351 (rev. 5th ed. 1999).

[7] Baker v. Owen, 395 F. Supp. 294 (M.D.N.C. 1975), *aff'd* 423 U.S. 907 (1975).

[8] Ingraham v. Wright, 430 U.S. 651 (1977). *See also,* Johnson v. Rosendez, 993 S.W.2d 723 (Tex. Ct. App. 1999), and Pomeroy v. Ashburnham Westminster Reg'l Sch. Dist., 410 F. Supp. 2d 7 (D. Mass. 2006).

[9] *Id. See also,* Harris v. Tate City, 882 F. Supp. 90 (N.D. Miss. 1995).

[10] Hall v. Tawney, 621 F.2d 607 (4th Cir. 1980). For another case showing the criminal prosecution of a private school principal for excessive paddling of a student *see* Commonwealth v. Douglas, 588 A.2d 53 (Pa. Super. Ct. 1991).

[11] Smith v. W. Va. State Bd., 295 S.E.2d 680 (W. Va. 1982). For more cases involving corporal punishment issues *see* Wise v. Pea Ridge Sch. Dist., 855 F.2d 560 (8th Cir. 1988); Lillard v. Shelby County, 76 F.3d 716 (6th Cir. 1996) (where it was said that a single slap does not rise to the level of a constitutional violation); Holbrook v. Commonwealth, 925 S.W.2d 191 (Ken. 1996) (where a teacher paddled a fourth-grade student for failing to complete an assignment); Spacek v. Charles, 928 S.W.2d 88 (Tex. Ct. App. 1996) (where athletic coaches were charged with using "excessive force);" Daniels v. Gordon, 503 S.E.2d 72 (Ga. Ct. App. 1998); and Saylor v. Bd. of Educ., 118 F.3d 507 (6th Cir. 1997).

[12] Ingraham v. Wright, 430 U.S. 651 (1977).

[13] *Id.*

[14] *Id.*

[15] Goss v. Lopez, 419 U.S. 565 (1975).

[16] 543 F. Supp. 995, (D. Me. 1982).

[17] *Id.* For additional cases *see* Keough v. Tate, 748 F.2d 1077 (5th Cir. 1984) (involving the issue of pre-suspension due process); Pollnow v. Glennon, 594 F. Supp. 220, *aff'd* 757 F.2d 496 (2d Cir. 1985) (involving the issue of whether a student would be advised that he can call his mother); Brewer by Dreyfus v. Austin Indep. Sch. Dist., 779 F.2d 260 (5th Cir. 1985) (involving the issue of whether criminal procedure is transferred into school procedure); New Jersey v. T.L.O., 105 S. Ct. 733 (1985) (where the Supreme Court held that a standard of "reasonable suspicion" applied to school searches of students and their belongings and not the police standard of "probable cause"); State v. Moore, 603 A.2d 513 (N.J.Super.Ct. App. Div. 1992) (for a case showing the reasonable suspicion standard as being a lesser standard than that of "probable cause"); and Davis v. Churchill County Sch. Bd., 616 F. Supp. 1310 (D. Nev. 1985) (concerning whether suspension hearing may be closed to the public). *See also,* S.A. v. Indiana, 654 N.E.2d 791 (Ind. Ct. App. 1995) (where the reasonable suspicion versus probable cause standards are compared); C.B. v. Driscoll, 82 F.3d 383 (11th Cir. 1996) (where the reliability of informants in a school search situation is an issue); and Farrell v. Gwinnett County Bd. of Educ., 2007 U.S. Dist. LEXIS 24297 (N.D.G. 2007) (where the court differentiates between School Resources Officers (SRO) and regular police officers).

[18] *See Honig*, 108 S. Ct. 592 (1988) (involving procedural issues in possible suspension or expulsion of students with disabilities in public schools).

[19] *Id.* at 605. *See also,* Kaelin v. Grubbs, 682 F.2d 595 (6th Cir. 1982), and *Gadson*, 3 F. Supp. 2d 1299 (N.D. Ala. 1998). Public school officials will be wise to review all changes in the revised IDEA (1997), at 20 U.S.C. § 601, *et. seq.* For two excellent articles on this point, *see* B. Dowling-Sendor, *Wiggle Room in IDEA*, 185 NAT. SCH. BD. J. 14 (March 1998), and B. Willams & A. Katsiyannis, *The 1997 IDEA Amendments: Implications for School Principals*, 82 NASSP BUL. 12 (January, 1998).

[20] 20 U.S.C. § 1415 *et. seq.* The reader is reminded to reference the reauthorized IDEIA, 20 U.S.C.A. 1400, *et. seq.* (2004) for any changes in the discipline mandates in the law.

Chapter 3

Freedom of Expression

David M. Schimmel

Introduction

For more than 175 years, it was assumed that the United States Constitution did not protect student freedom of speech or press. If students challenged school censorship during those years, courts would uphold the school's policy or disciplinary action unless the students could prove that the censorship was unreasonable. The task was nearly impossible, and the rare student who went to court almost always lost.

In 1969, however, in the landmark case of *Tinker v. Des Moines*,[1] the United States Supreme Court held that the First Amendment did protect student freedom of expression in the public schools. Most administrators have come to accept the *Tinker* ruling and have shaped their school policies accordingly. However, in a 1986 case about a controversial student speech,[2] a 1988 case concerning student newspapers,[3] and a 2007 case about a student banner,[4] the Supreme Court ruled in favor of administrative limitations on student expression. In view of these apparently conflicting decisions, this chapter clarifies the scope and limits of student freedom of expression in public schools. It also examines two emerging areas of concern: controversial message T-shirts and inappropriate use of the Internet.

Legal Issues

Protected Speech

In *Tinker v. Des Moines*, the Court ruled that students do not "shed their Constitutional rights to freedom of speech or expression at the schoolhouse gate."[5] In hundreds of cases since then, every state and federal court has reaffirmed this basic principle. Clearly, the First Amendment still protects a student's controversial opinions.

According to the Supreme Court, "Students in school as well as out of school are … possessed of fundamental rights which the State must respect, just as they themselves must respect their obligations to the State."[6] Since schools are "educating the young for citizenship," they should protect the "Constitutional freedoms of the individual, if we are not to strangle the free mind at its source and teach youth to discount important principles of our government as mere platitudes."[7] Thus, in *Tinker* the Court ruled that students had the constitutional right to wear black armbands in public schools to protest against American involvement in the Vietnam War.

The Court realized that protecting controversial speech might cause problems in schools. In fact, it recognized that "any word spoken, in class, in the lunchroom, or on the campus, that deviates from the views of another person may start an argument or cause a disturbance."[8] According to the Court, "our Constitution says we must take this risk; and our history says that it is this sort of hazardous freedom—this kind of openness—that is the basis of our national strength ... independence and vigor."[9]

Disruptive Speech

Despite the breadth of the *Tinker* decision, it also recognized that schools can legally limit student expression. In *Tinker*, the Court identified that limit when it wrote that any student conduct that "materially disrupts class work or involves substantial disorder or invasion of the rights of others" is not protected by the constitutional guarantee of freedom of speech.[10] Thus, a federal appeals court allowed administrators to enforce a "no-button" rule in a Cleveland high school because evidence indicated that such symbols led to serious fighting between black and white students and substantially disrupted the education process.[11]

Symbolic speech, however, cannot be prohibited merely because administrators are fearful or concerned about possible disruptions. As the Court stated, "Undifferentiated fear or apprehension of disturbance is not enough to overcome the right to freedom of expression."[12] To restrict such expression, administrators must justify their actions based on evidence, not just intuition, that the forbidden expression would substantially interfere with the work of the school or the rights of others. They cannot prohibit a particular opinion merely "to avoid the discomfort and unpleasantness that always accompany an unpopular view."[13]

Principals do not have to wait until a disruption takes place to limit speech. In a case concerning a student demonstration inside a school, a judge explained that a school official may restrict student expression when there is significant evidence of a "reasonable likelihood of substantial disorder."[14] A similar result was reached in an Indiana case in which several students were suspended for distributing leaflets calling for a "school walkout." The judge ruled that student expression is not protected where administrators can demonstrate any facts that lead them to reasonably forecast substantial disruption.[15]

Obscene or Vulgar Speech

Courts have never protected student speech or writing that is obscene. However, language is not legally obscene merely because it contains offensive, vulgar, or "dirty" words. To be legally obscene, material must violate three tests developed by the Supreme Court: (1) it must appeal to the prurient or lustful interest; (2) it must describe sexual conduct in a way that is "patently offensive" to community standards; and (3) taken as a whole, it "must lack serious literary, artistic, political, or scientific value."[16]

Can school administrators prohibit and punish vulgar and offensive speech that is not legally obscene or disruptive? In 1986, the Supreme Court answered this question in *Bethel v. Fraser.* The case involved a high school senior, Matthew Fraser, who was punished for giving a nominating speech at a school assembly that referred to his candidate using "an elaborate, graphic, and explicit sexual metaphor."[17] In *Bethel,* the Court ruled that school officials have broad authority to punish students for using "offensively lewd and indecent speech" in classrooms, assemblies, and other school-sponsored educational activities, even if the speech does not cause disruption and is not legally obscene. In addition, *Bethel* held that administrators have the discretion to define and determine what constitutes vulgar and offensive speech.[18]

In a related case, Emily Heller was suspended from an Indiana high school for shouting that she was not a "fucking bitch" at a student who called her one. Heller argued that the suspension violated her free speech rights since the name-calling was not in an academic setting. However, a federal court ruled that *Fraser* allowed schools to punish speech that is "plainly offensive," even if it does not occur during a school-sponsored event.[19]

School-Sponsored Curricular Publications

The First Amendment gives very little protection to student freedom of the press in school-sponsored, curricular publications. This was the ruling of the U.S. Supreme Court in *Hazelwood v. Kuhlmeier.* The case involved a St. Louis high school principal who objected to two stories in a student newspaper about pregnancy and divorce that were written and published as part of a journalism course. The Court ruled that a curricular newspaper was not a public forum and that "school officials were entitled to regulate the contents … in any reasonable manner."[20]

The Court explained that when a student expressed personal, controversial views on school grounds, the First Amendment protects such views and the principles of *Tinker* apply. However, in school-sponsored publications or theatrical productions that are part of the school curriculum, educators may exercise greater control and set higher standards for student speech. Thus, the Court wrote that in a curricular publication, educators have broad discretion to prohibit articles that are "ungrammatical, poorly written, inadequately researched, biased or prejudiced, vulgar or profane, or unsuitable for immature audiences."[21] In short, the Court held that neither teachers nor administrators violate the First Amendment by "exercising editorial control over the style and content of student speech in school-sponsored expressive activities so long as their actions are reasonably related to legitimate pedagogical concerns."[22] The Court concluded that the principal in *Hazelwood* acted reasonably in deleting the controversial articles because of his concern that the articles were not sensitive to the privacy interests of the students, boyfriends, or parents who were mentioned.[23]

Hazelwood, however, does not permit educators to censor school-sponsored publications unless they have a valid educational purpose. Similarly, the Supreme Court has ruled that school boards do not have unlimited discretion to censor library books, to deny students access to ideas for narrowly partisan or political reasons, or simply because the board dislikes the ideas contained in those books.[24] Thus, a federal court ruled in 2003 against an Arkansas school district that restricted access to Harry Potter books because of unfounded fears that they might promote disruption, witchcraft, and disobedience to parents.[25]

Students' Underground Publications

The Supreme Court decision in *Hazelwood* does not give school officials control over the style and content of underground student periodicals that are published without school sponsorship or support and are not part of the curriculum. Instead, *Tinker* governs such publications, and their distribution usually cannot be prohibited unless administrators have evidence to forecast that they will cause substantial disruption or interfere with the rights of others. Thus, underground publications cannot be banned for discussing unpopular, sensitive, or controversial topics, and students cannot be punished merely for criticizing school officials or administrative policies in such publications.

In a Texas case, for example, school officials banned an underground newspaper because of its "negative attitude" and its criticism of the administration. A court rejected this defense and explained that "aversion to criticism" is not a constitutional justification for restricting student expression. The First Amendment, wrote the court, protects freedom of the press precisely because those regulated "should have the right and even the responsibility" to criticize their regulators.[26]

On the other hand, a federal court upheld the expulsion of a Wisconsin student who wrote an article in an underground paper "to tell everyone how to hack the school's gay ass computers." The court rejected the student's First Amendment defense since administrators reasonably forecasted substantial disruption because the article encouraged "invasive and destructive" action involving the school's computers.[27]

Students may be required to submit their publications to administrators for review before distribution. The justification for allowing prior review of underground publications, explained one judge, is "to prevent disruption and not to stifle expression."[28] Several courts have prohibited schools from censoring publications through prior restraint without clear, objective standards and procedural safeguards.[29]

Further Developments

Hazelwood has led to a variety of interpretations in state and federal courts. Some judges have interpreted *Hazelwood* broadly and supported restrictions on school-sponsored expression that were not related to the curriculum. For example, a divided federal appeals court ruled in favor of the Nevada principals who refused to print an advertisement by Planned Parenthood not only in the school newspaper and yearbook, which were published as part of the curriculum, but also in the athletic programs, which were not.[30] According to the court, schools retain the right to disapprove of ads that might carry a school-sponsored message to readers and put their imprimatur on one side of a controversial issue. Furthermore, some judges have interpreted *Hazelwood* to grant administrators broader control over curricular decisions than they had in the past.[31]

Other judges have interpreted *Hazelwood* more narrowly. One example is a case concerning restrictions on a peace group's participation in Career Day in Atlanta schools. Administrators argued that *Hazelwood* permitted them to control the content of the curricular programs and ban any group that criticized opportunities presented by other participants. However, a federal appeals court struck down the ban. It acknowledged that schools could decline to discuss military careers. If such a topic is discussed, the *Hazelwood* decision does not justify "allowing educators to discriminate" against a particular viewpoint.[32]

Another federal decision that interpreted *Hazelwood* narrowly concerned a controversial student-written piece in a school-sponsored, non-curricular newspaper. The school argued that their authority to control the curriculum should include extracurricular or co-curricular activities such as the student paper, but the court disagreed. The judge declined to interpret *Hazelwood* broadly because it "opens the door to significant curtailment of cherished First Amendment rights." The court concluded that "educators may exercise greater editorial control over what students write for class than what they voluntarily submit to an extracurricular, albeit school funded, publication."[33]

Distribution Policies

A number of recent controversies involved student distribution of religious or political publications. Policies prohibiting distribution of such materials usually have been struck down. A Colorado case, for example, involved students who were suspended for giving out a Christian newspaper, *Issues and Answers,* in violation of a policy prohibiting distribution of "material that proselytizes a particular religious or political belief." The administrators argued that *Hazelwood* allowed them to prohibit distribution of such controversial publications, but the judge disagreed and explained: "Because students have a right to engage in political and religious speech," school policies that prevent students from discussing issues they feel are important inhibit their individual development and "defeat the very purpose of public education in secondary schools."[34] Similarly, a federal court ruled against a Massachusetts high school that punished members of a Bible club for distributing candy with a religious message.[35] Administrators claimed the controversial message violated the school's "responsible" speech code and its policy prohibiting student distribution of any printed material without administrative approval. However, the court ruled that the school could not totally prohibit students from distributing literature during non-instructional time that does not cause disruption, and it held that the policy giving administrators discretion to suppress any speech they feel is not responsible is unconstitutionally vague.

On the other hand, content-neutral policies that simply regulate the time, place, and manner in which students can distribute printed material are usually upheld. In another Colorado case that concerned *Issues and Answers*, students challenged school rules that prohibited distribution of newspapers in hallways. Since distribution was allowed in other school locations, and since the restrictions were applied equally to all students, were designed to maintain order, and were not based on the viewpoint of the publication, the court concluded that the policy did not violate student freedom of expression.[36] And in a recent New Jersey case, a federal court allowed an elementary school to prohibit a first-grade student from distributing pencils with religious messages to his classmates during a school-sponsored, in-class party.[37] The judge gave several reasons for supporting the school: the party was part of the curriculum; there were legitimate concerns that allowing the distribution during class time might lead young, impressionable students to think that the school endorsed the religious message; and the school allowed the student to distribute his gifts before and after school and during recess.

Equal Access

In a U.S. Supreme Court decision concerning the recognition of religious clubs, the Court upheld the Federal Equal Access Act, which prohibits public secondary schools from denying equal access to students who wish to meet on the basis of the "religious, political, philosophical, or other content" of the speech at such meetings. Concerning the fear that by permitting controversial speech, a school will appear to endorse it, the Court wrote: "We think that secondary students are mature enough and are likely to understand that a school does not endorse or support student speech that it merely permits."[38]

State Protection

Although no public school in any state can provide less protection for student speech than is required by the United States Supreme Court, individual states or school districts can provide more. Thus, in the aftermath of *Hazelwood*, a number of states—through statute or judicial interpretation—now have greater protection for student expression. In New Jersey, a state superior court ruled in favor of a student whose movie reviews for the school-funded extracurricular newspaper were censored because they reviewed R-rated films that the principal considered "inappropriate for junior high students." Judge Francis stated that, if he were to decide the case under the United States Constitution, he would be compelled to declare that the school's action was constitutional under the test laid down by the United States Supreme Court in *Hazelwood.* However, he ruled that the school violated the student's rights under the New Jersey Constitution, which is "more expansive than the First Amendment" and "indicates that free speech is an affirmative right."[39]

In other states, student expression is protected by statute. For example, the California Education Code states: "Students of the public schools shall have the right to exercise freedom of speech and of the press … whether or not such publications … are supported financially by the school."[40] As a result, a California court ruled in favor of a student who wrote a controversial article in a school newspaper. In explaining his decision, the judge wrote: "The broad power to censor expression in school-sponsored publications for pedagogical purposes recognized in *Kuhlmeier* is not available to this state's educators.[41] In Massachusetts, the law states: "The right of students to freedom of expression in the public schools of the Commonwealth shall not be abridged provided that such right shall not cause any disruption or disorder."[42] Similarly, Colorado law protects freedom of expression and prohibits prior restraint in student publications, regardless of whether such publication is school sponsored.[43]

While *Hazelwood* confirmed administrative control over curricula-related activities, *Tinker* continues to govern controversies concerning students' personal views. Thus, a federal appeals court ruled that high school students had the right to wear "antiscab" buttons to protest plans to replace striking teachers. In cases involving nondisruptive political speech, the judge wrote that courts must "insure that robust rhetoric … is not suppressed by prudish failures to distinguish the vigorous from the vulgar."[44] Similarly, a federal judge ruled that a policy allowing an elementary principal to prevent distribution of any material he considered controversial was unconstitutional.[45] The principal used the policy to prevent a student from giving classmates invitations to a church party. However, one 1996 decision questioned whether *Tinker* applies to elementary schools. "Age," wrote the judge, "is a critical factor in student speech cases" and the Court "has not suggested that fourth-graders have the free expression rights of high school students."[46]

Re-affirming *Tinker*

In 2007, the Supreme Court ruled on the case of an Alaska student who unfurled a banner at a school event that said "BONG HiTS 4 JESUS."[47] The principal believed that the banner was not protected speech since it encouraged the use of illegal drugs. In *Morse v. Frederick*, a divided Court agreed with the principal.

The Court ruled 6-3 that school officials may "restrict student expression that they reasonably regard as promoting illegal drug use."[48] However, Chief

Justice Roberts indicated that *Tinker* was still good law, and he rejected the broad interpretation of *Fraser* that would allow schools to prohibit any student speech that officials considered "plainly offensive."

In addition, a significant concurring opinion by Justices Alito and Kennedy emphasized the narrowness of the majority opinion and wrote that not all student messages advocating illegal activity can be punished if they comment on political or social issues and do not cause disruption. For example, these justices said they would protect student views that criticized the war on drugs or advocated the legalization of marijuana. Thus, *Morse* reaffirmed *Tinker* and perhaps expanded the rights of students to criticize current laws and promote controversial political or religious views.

Emerging Controversies

Message T-Shirts. In recent years, cases concerning controversial T-shirts have erupted throughout the country. In most cases, judges have applied the principles of *Tinker* and ruled that students should not be punished for wearing message T-shirts unless there is evidence that the message would substantially disrupt discipline or interfere with the rights of others. Three cases illustrate the way courts have ruled on this issue.

Just before the 2003 Iraq War, a high school student from Michigan wore a T-shirt with a picture of President Bush above the caption "International Terrorist." Administrators banned the shirt because it was "inappropriate" and might be disruptive. Since there was no evidence that the T-shirt caused or was likely to cause substantial disruption, a federal court ruled that the ban violated the student's First Amendment rights.[49]

In a related Virginia case, a middle school student was prohibited from wearing a National Rifle Association T-shirt that depicted three silhouettes holding firearms above the words "Shooting Sports Camp."[50] Administrators said the shirt violated the school's dress code that prohibited "messages related to weapons." The judge noted that the school certainly could prohibit messages that were violent, threatening, indecent, libelous, or disruptive. But in this 2003 case, the T-shirt message relating to weapons was nonviolent, nonthreatening, and caused no disruption. Therefore, the court ruled that the dress code's prohibition of all messages related to weapons was "overbroad" and the NRA T-shirt could not be banned. Similarly, another federal appeals court ruled in favor of a student who was suspended under the school's racial harassment policy for wearing a T-shirt inscribed with "redneck" jokes.[51] While past racial conflicts would justify banning any provocative racial message, it did not justify banning this T-shirt since administrators had no evidence it might threaten disruption.

Internet Controversies. The increasing use of computers in schools and homes raises the question of when administrators can punish students for their improper use. Administrators have broad discretion to restrict the use of school computers, and they can prohibit inappropriate uses such as violating copyright laws, harassing students or staff, commercial purposes, or transmitting pornography. In short, if students challenge policies that restrict Internet use in school, courts will probably uphold the restrictions if they have an educational purpose and are not arbitrary or ambiguous.

In contrast, recent cases have limited the authority of schools to restrict and punish students' offensive use of their home computers. In a 2003 Pennsylvania case, a student was disciplined for violating a school policy prohibiting the "use of computers to receive, create or send ... inappropriate material and/or messages" after he posted a controversial Internet message on his home computer.[52] The judge held this policy to be "unconstitutionally overbroad and vague" for two reasons: first, it allowed a school official to discipline a student for an undefined "offensive" or "inappropriate" expression outside of school; second, the policy was not limited to speech that "is likely to cause a substantial disruption with school operations."

Other courts also have ruled against schools for punishing students for controversial messages on their home computers. In a Missouri case, for example, a high school student was suspended for creating a webpage at home that used vulgar language and was critical of teachers and administrators. However, the court ruled that the need to maintain discipline does not outweigh a students' freedom of expression that causes no disruption.[53] Similarly, a Washington high school student was suspended for "intimidation and disruption" after he posted a webpage at home that asked viewers to vote on "Who Should Die" and be featured in a fictional obituary. Since the school had no evidence that the webpage caused any disruption or that anyone felt intimidated, the court ruled in favor of the student and noted that schools cannot prohibit distribution of student material "on the basis of undifferentiated fears of possible disturbances."[54]

In contrast, a Pennsylvania court upheld the expulsion of a middle school student who posted a website at home that harassed and threatened his algebra teacher and contained a picture of her with her head cut off.[55] Since the website had a profoundly disruptive effect that caused the teacher to suffer mentally and physically, the court ruled against the student. In sum, recent court cases indicate that students should not be punished for posting an offensive, insulting, or vulgar home page on the Internet unless it causes substantial disruption at school.

Cell Phones. An increasing number of students in grades 3-12 use cell phones in and after school. In some states, such as New Hampshire, many schools encourage students to use web-based cell phones to access homework and class assignments. Furthermore, many parents, especially in urban areas, want their children to carry cell phones to and from school for safety reasons.

On the other hand, concerns about inappropriate student use of cell phones have led ten states to prohibit such phones in school, and seventeen states have granted local districts explicit authority to prohibit them.[56] Even in states without such legislation, schools may prohibit cell phones that disrupt education or interfere with the rights of others. Although there is little case law on this topic, if administrators know of improper use (such as taking secret photographs) and do not try to stop it, they might be charged with negligent supervision.

Recommendations for Practice

Four Supreme Court decisions—*Tinker, Bethel, Hazelwood,* and *Morse*—have summarized and explained the constitutional principles that apply to student expression in the public schools. What emerges from these and more recent rulings is a sense that the First Amendment applies broadly to a student's personal views and narrowly in areas that are considered part of the curriculum.

1. When a student speaks or writes as an individual, such expression is protected by the First Amendment and cannot be restricted unless it causes substantial disruption or interferes with the rights of others. Students may not be punished for expressing their personal opinions about controversial political, religious, social, or educational issues—even if their views are unpopular and in conflict with the ideas of most students, teachers, and administrators.
2. Administrators have broad discretion in regulating student speech or writing that is part of the school curriculum. Supreme Court decisions have clarified the scope of such control. In *Bethel,* the Court ruled that educators can define and punish vulgar and offensive language in classrooms, assemblies, and probably in any other educational activity. In *Hazelwood,* the Court held that educators may exercise broad editorial control over curricular publications and plays when there are legitimate educational reasons for doing so. And *Morse* permitted schools to prohibit student speech that promotes illegal drug use, but not speech that advocates changes in drug laws.
3. Educators in most states can control student publications that are not part of the formal curriculum if they are school-sponsored, teacher-supervised, educational activities. However, some states provide greater protection for students' rights than *Hazelwood* requires. Therefore, principals should check relevant state statutes, regulations, judicial opinions, and district policies before developing school rules or imposing punishments that restrict student expression.
4. Administrators usually may control student speech in curricular activities, even if the student's views are not disruptive or obscene and do not interfere with the rights of others. In such cases, courts will tend to presume that administrative control is valid, and it will probably be upheld unless students can prove that the school's control or punishment of their views was unreasonable, arbitrary, or unrelated to legitimate educational goals.

5. It is not clear whether courts will apply the principles of *Hazelwood* or *Tinker* to school-sponsored extracurricular activities. Therefore, to be constitutionally safe, cautious administrators should follow *Tinker* more than *Hazelwood* in establishing policies governing school-sponsored publications that are not part of the curriculum.

6. The *Tinker* principles apply to students who wear controversial message T-shirts to school, and such shirts should not be banned unless they disrupt education or interfere with the rights of others.

7. Although administrators have broad discretion to restrict the use of computers in school, they should not punish students for posting offensive messages on their home computers unless they substantially disrupt school activities.

8. Related to the right to speak is the right to remain silent, especially in matters of conscience. Thus, schools may not require students to salute the flag or stand at attention while the flag is being saluted.[57]

9. Schools cannot ban student distribution of publications because they advocate a particular religion, political, or social view. However, administrators can establish policies that regulate the time, place, and manner for distributing materials in the schools. Such rules must be viewpoint neutral and cannot be so restrictive that they prevent the dissemination of student opinions.

10. Administrators should distinguish between what they have authority to do legally and what it is wise to do educationally. For example, *Hazelwood* allows schools to censor almost all articles in curricular publications. But this, of course, does not mean that censorship is the best way to train students to exercise their First Amendment rights in a fair and responsible manner.[58]

Endnotes

1 Tinker v. Des Moines, 393 U.S. 503 (1969).
2 Bethel Sch. Dist. No. 403 v. Fraser, 106 S. Ct. 3159 (1986).
3 Hazelwood Sch. Dist. v. Kuhlmeier, 108 S. Ct. 562 (1988).
4 Morse v. Frederick, 127 S.Ct. 2618 (2007).
5 *Tinker*, 393 U.S. 503, at 506 (1969).
6 *Id.* at 511.
7 *Id.* at 507.
8 *Id.* at 508.
9 *Id.* at 508–09.
10 *Id.* at 513.
11 Guzick v. Drebus, 431 F.2d 594 (6th Cir. 1970), *cert. denied,* 401 U.S. 948 (1971).
12 *Tinker*, 393 U.S. 503, at 508 (1969).
13 *Id.* at 509.
14 Karp v. Becken, 477 F.2d 171 (9th Cir. 1973).
15 Dodd v. Rambis, 535 F. Supp. 23 (S.D. Ind. 1981).

16 Miller v. California, 413 U.S. 15 (1973).
17 *Bethel,* 106 S. Ct. 3159 at 3160 (1986).
18 For more on *Bethel,* see D. Schimmel, *Lewd Language not Protected: Bethel School District v. Fraser,* 33 EDUC. L. REP. 999 (1986).
19 Heller v. Hodgin, 928 F. Supp. 789 (S.D. Ind. 1996).
20 *Hazelwood,* 108 S. Ct. 562, at 569 (1988).
21 *Id.* at 570.
22 *Id.* at 571.
23 Comments about *Hazelwood* in this chapter are based on D. Schimmel, *Censorship of School-Sponsored Publications: An Analysis of Hazelwood v. Kuhlmeier,* 45 EDUC. L. REP. 941 (1988).
24 Board of Educ., Island Trees Union Free Sch. Dist. No. 26 v. Pico, 457 U.S. 853 (1982).
25 Counts v. Cedarville Sch. Dist., 295 F. Supp. 2d 996 (W.D. Ark. 2003).
26 Boucher v. Sch. Bd. of Greenfield, 134 F.3d 821 (7th Cir. 1898).
27 Shanley v. Northeast Indep. Sch. Dist, 462 F.2d 960 (5th Cir. 1972).
28 Shanley v. Northeast Indep. Sch. Dist., 462 F.2d 960 (5th Cir. 1972).
29 In *Hazelwood,* 108 S. Ct. 562, at 571 (1988), the Supreme Court ruled that school officials could control school-sponsored publications without specific written regulations. But it declined to decide whether such regulations "are required before school officials may censor publications not sponsored by the school." Since several federal appeals courts have required that schools have written due process safeguards in reviewing underground publications, such regulations continue to be required in the absence of a Supreme Court ruling to the contrary.
30 Planned Parenthood v. Clark County Sch. Dist., 941 F.2d 817 (9th Cir. 1991).
31 Virgil v. Sch. Bd. of Columbia County, 862 F.2d 1517 (11th Cir. 1989).
32 Searcey v. Harris, 888 F.2d 1314, 1324 (11th Cir. 1989).
33 Romano v. Harrington, 725 F. Supp. 687 (E.D.N.Y. 1989).
34 Rivera v. E. Otero Sch. Dist., R-1, 721 F. Supp. 1189, 1194 (D. Colo. 1989).
35 Westfield High Sch. L.I.F.E. Club v. City of Westfield, 249 F. Supp. 2d 98 (D.C. Mass. 2003).
36 Hemry by Hemry v. Sch. Bd. of Colo. Springs, 760 F. Supp. 856 (D. Colo. 1991).
37 Walz v. Egg Harbor Township Bd. of Educ., 187 F. Supp. 2d 232 (D. N.J. 2002).
38 Board of Educ. of Westside Cmty. Sch. v. Mergens, 110 S. Ct. 2356, 2360 (1990).
39 Desilets v. Clearview Reg'l Bd. of Educ., Superior Court of New Jersey, Gloucester County No. C-23-90, May 7, 1991. Art. I, ¶ 5 of the New Jersey Constitution states: "Every person may freely speak, write, and publish his sentiments."
40 CAL. EDUC. CODE § 48907 (1991).
41 Leeb v. DeLong, 243 Cal. Rptr. 494, 498 (Cal. App. 1988).
42 General Laws of Mass., ch. 71, § 82 (1991).
43 COLO. REV. STAT. § 22-1-120(1) (1990).
44 Chandler v. McMinnville Sch. Dist., 978 F.2d 524 (9th Cir. 1992).
45 Johnston-Loehner v. O'Brien, 859 F. Supp. 575 (D.M. Fla. 1994).
46 Muller by Muller v. Jefferson Lighthouse Sch., 98 F.3d 1530 (7th Cir. 1996).
47 Morse v. Frederick, 127 S.Ct. 2618 (2007).
48 *Id.* at 2629.
49 Barber v. Dearborn Pub. Sch., 286 F. Supp. 2d 847 (E.D. Mich. 2003).
50 Newsom v. Albemarle County Sch. Bd., 354 F.3d 249 (4th Cir. 2003).
51 Sypniewski v. Warren Hills Reg'l Bd. of Educ., 307 F.3d 243 (3d Cir. 2002).
52 Flaherty v. Keystone Oaks Sch. Dist., 247 F. Supp. 2d 698 (W.D. Pa. 2003).
53 Beussink v. Woodland R-IV Sch. Dist., 30 F. Supp. 2d 1175 (E.D. Mo. 1998).
54 Emmett v. Kent Sch. Dist. No. 415, 92 F. Supp. 2d 1088 (W.D. Wa. 2000).
55 J.S. v. Bethlehem Area Sch. Dist., 757 A.2d 412 (Pa. Commw. Ct. 2000).

[56] A. Dean Pickett and Christopher Thomas, "21st Century Intrusion Into Learning," A Legal Memorandum, National Association of Secondary School Principals, Reston, VA, Summer, 2005.

[57] Lipp v. Morris, 579 F.2d 834 (3d Cir. 1978).

[58] This chapter is based on material from FISCHER, SCHIMMEL, & STELLMAN, Chapter 9 *in* TEACHERS AND THE LAW (6th ed. 2003).

Chapter 4

Searches in Public Schools

Joseph Beckham & W. Kyle Ingle

Introduction

The Fourth Amendment provides a right to privacy against "unreasonable searches and seizures" that extends to students in public schools.[1] Public school employees are state officers and are bound by the Fourth Amendment prohibition against unreasonable searches and seizures. However, perceptions of epidemic drug use and high profile instances of violence involving weapons in the nation's schools have led judges to grant considerable discretion to school officials in the conduct of student searches. If school officials articulate a reasonable suspicion justifying a search and limit the scope of a search to avoid excessive intrusion into personal privacy, judges typically find in favor of the state's interest in maintaining discipline and ensuring a safe learning environment.

Legal Issues

In *New Jersey v. T.L.O.*,[2] the United States Supreme Court established the standard of reasonable suspicion as a justification for the search of a student. In this case, a vice-principal sought evidence to confirm a teacher's statement that a student had been smoking in a restroom. After questioning the student and hearing her denials, the vice-principal searched the student's purse. The initial search resulted in the discovery of a pack of cigarettes and rolling papers. Knowing that rolling papers were often used with marijuana, the administrator continued to search the purse, discovering a pipe, empty baggies, a large quantity of money in small bills, an index card with names and amounts of money owed, and a small bag of marijuana. The marijuana was turned over to police, and when the student was subjected to a delinquency proceeding, she sought to have the marijuana excluded from evidence on the grounds that the administrator's search violated her Fourth Amendment rights.

The United States Supreme Court made two inquiries in order to determine the reasonableness of the school administrator's search. The first inquiry was whether the search was justified at inception given the totality of circumstances that led to suspicion of the student. The Court reasoned that the initial search was justified because the vice-principal had testimony from a reliable source that the student had violated school rules by smoking on school grounds, and the purse was an obvious place for the student to keep cigarettes. The second inquiry was whether the search was reasonable in its scope. Although the search was intended to confirm the student was in possession of cigarettes, the discovery of the rolling papers, which the vice-principal associated with the use of marijuana, justified the continued search of the purse. Thus, the search was deemed reasonable in scope.

Reasonable Suspicion

The search of a student is justified at inception "when there are reasonable grounds for suspecting that the search will turn up evidence that the student has violated or is violating either the law or the rules of the school."[3] Under this standard, a school official must determine whether a search is justified by evaluating evidence obtained prior to the conduct of the search. For example, in an Indiana case, a rash of school locker thefts and the discovery that the master locker combination book was missing led to an investigation in which a student informant specifically identified a student as having the combination book in a blue bookbag. The student who was suspected of having the combination book was removed from class and escorted to his locker where a blue bookbag was confiscated. Once in the school office, the bookbag was searched, the combination book was discovered, and the student was charged with theft. Finding that the search of the book bag was reasonable, a state appeals court emphasized that the search was justified at inception because school officials established individualized suspicion based on the testimony of an informant who provided specific identification of the student and detailed information concerning where the book could be found.[4]

When considering whether to conduct a search, the school official should assess what is sought, the degree of individualized suspicion that may implicate a particular student in misconduct, and the age, history, and background of that student. For example, a New Hampshire assistant principal received an anonymous phone call in which the caller said that a particular student at the high school would be carrying drugs to school that day. The caller identified the student by name, and the assistant principal knew of the student as a result of reports from teachers that implicated the student in a previous drug transaction at school. The administrator was also aware that the student had been arrested for drug possession in another state. The student, who reported late for school, was called into the principal's office and told to turn his pockets inside out. The contents of his pockets included a pipe and rolling papers. The principal then required the student to open his knapsack, which held several bags of marijuana and an unloaded semi-automatic pistol. The Supreme Court of New Hampshire held that the totality of circumstances justified the search. The telephone tip, which specifically identified the student, and the existing knowledge of the student's drug involvement were enough to establish individual suspicion for the search.[5]

A student's demeanor and conduct may contribute to individualized suspicion.[6] In one such case, a teacher reported that a student was sleeping in class, had glassy eyes, and complained of nausea. After reporting her concerns to the assistant principal, the student's parents were contacted, and the student, consistent with district policy, was transported by bus to a local hospital where a urine screen yielded a positive result for marijuana use. Although the parent challenged the district policy requiring urine screening as a violation of privacy, the federal district court found the district policy constitutional and held the search met the standard for reasonable suspicion.[7] In another case, when an Alaskan high school student was confronted for creating a disturbance in the school library, a school security officer noticed that the student swayed and bumped into objects as he walked, his eyes were glassy, and his face was flushed. Discovering the student was evasive in responding to questions and had improperly parked his automobile on school grounds, an assistant principal undertook a search of the automobile and discovered two grams of cocaine. A state appeals court ruled the search was constitutional, noting that evidence of individualized suspicion was initially established given the student's disorientation and finding that the improperly parked automobile added to a suspicion that the student was using drugs.[8]

In a similar case from Georgia, a police officer on special detail with the school district confronted a student after being informed by a school secretary that the student smelled of marijuana. The officer confirmed that the student smelled strongly of marijuana and undertook a pat down of his jacket. When he felt several packets in the student's jacket pocket, the student said to him, "Come on and let me slide." Viewing this as a confirmation that the student was in possession of contraband, the officer reached into the student's jacket pocket and removed wrapped bags of marijuana. When the student moved to suppress this evidence at a criminal trial, a state appeals court found that the totality of circumstances justified the search.[9]

It must be emphasized, however, that a generalized hunch may be insufficient evidence of reasonable suspicion. An observation that a male student was not "acting himself," together with an inference that "something was not right," would not justify a search unless additional information were adduced that would permit a reasonable inference of misconduct.[10] While the reasonable suspicion standard has been liberally interpreted to apply to a variety of suspicious student actions, judges insist that the school official explain why the search was reasonably related to the offense the student committed. For example, the discovery that a student lied about having driven a car to school would not justify a search of the vehicle absent evidence permitting a reasonable suspicion that the student had drugs or contraband in the vehicle.[11]

Individualized suspicion, the identification of a particular student alleged to be engaged in misconduct, strengthens the basis for a search. However, the standard of reasonable suspicion does not require individualized suspicion of a particular student, and more than one student may reasonably be implicated in misconduct that would justify a search. For example, administrators in a Hawaii high school observed a student and her companion leave school grounds without authorization and cross the street to an area called "the Tunnel," a culvert system off school grounds where students were known to gather to smoke tobacco and marijuana. A vice-principal and school security officer followed the students into the area, detected the odor of burning marijuana, and observed four students congregating near a grate. All four students exited when directed to do so, and two students were found to be carrying purses. The two students who were carrying purses were subjected to searches, and the marijuana was found when the students emptied the contents of their purses on the principal's desk. The state supreme court considered the totality of circumstances and found credible evidence supported the searches since the students were violating school policies by being in a restricted area and school officials detected the odor of marijuana.[12]

In a similar situation involving a student who was caught in possession of knives, the administrator responded to a complaint from a private citizen that students were congregating in a cul-de-sac on the way to school to smoke cigarettes. The administrator found a group of twenty students in a blue haze at that location, many of whom made furtive gestures as if discarding cigarettes. After ordering the students to a room at school, the administrator had each one searched. In the course of this search, knives were found. One student objected on the basis that the search was not based on individualized suspicion and brought a civil suit against the administrator, but the federal appeals court affirmed a lower court's rejection of the suit finding that there was nothing improper in the administrator's action.[13]

Investigation and articulation of all the evidence surrounding a search can be highly persuasive in influencing a judge to conclude the search was reasonable. In a case from Illinois, a school resource officer in an alternative school for students with discipline problems received reports from teachers that a student intended to sell drugs to students and planned to bring drugs to school that day. The student who was suspected of drug possession was standing at a locker with a student who was in possession of a flashlight. Both students were talking and giggling, and this aroused the officer's suspicions because the two students seemed to think they were deceiving him. Considering it unusual for a student to have a flashlight at school and knowing that both students were suspected of dealing drugs at school, the officer started a search and seized and flashlight in the possession of the second student and discovered a quantity of crack cocaine in the case. The student sought to avoid prosecution by contending that the search was unconstitutional, but the state appeals court ruled that the reasonable suspicion standard applied to the officer when performing duties in the school setting.[14] Finding that the totality of circumstances would lead a reasonable person to suspect that the student was carrying drugs in the flashlight, the seizure and search of the flashlight were regarded as reasonable. The court emphasized that this was an alternative school for students with behavioral problems and this context, coupled with the suspicious conduct of the students and their history of suspected drug activity, heightened the urgency of maintaining a safe and secure learning environment.[15] The court was persuaded by the school official's intuitive judgment about the behavior of the students,[16] as well as his effort to develop the totality of circumstances implicating the student, including details of the context of the search, the age and history of the student, and the nature of that which was sought.

Permissible Scope of a Search

Once the totality of circumstances supports reasonable suspicion for a search, the school administrator, in making a determination about how far the search should go, must balance the student's expectation of privacy against the legitimate need to maintain a safe learning environment. As the *T.L.O.* decision emphasized, "[a] search will be permissible in scope when the measures adopted are reasonably related to the objectives of the search and not excessively intrusive in light of the age and sex of the student and the nature of the infraction."[17]

As a general rule, the closer the search is to the person, the more evidence a school official must provide in order to establish a reasonable basis for the scope of the search. Judges grant little expectation of privacy in a school locker, particularly when school board policy or state statute makes it clear that lockers are the property of the school and subject to inspection at any time.[18] An expectation of privacy would apply to a student's car,[19] but that expectation has been diminished when the vehicle is on school grounds and school policy makes clear students must register their cars and vehicles may be routinely searched.[20] A student's bookbag or purse carries an expectation of privacy, requiring evidence of reasonable suspicion,[21] but touching the outside of the bookbag or purse would be less intrusive than opening and examining the contents.[22] A minor medical examination in the form of a vital-signs check involving limited contact would be sufficiently invasive to require reasonable suspicion of drug use, usually manifest in the student's uncharacteristic behavior and evasiveness.[23] In addition, requiring students to remove caps or jackets to permit examination of pockets appears permissible particularly when there is a reasonable suspicion that the student is in possession of a weapon or drugs.[24]

Pat-Down Searches

Concerns for safety in the school setting justify the use of pat-down searches,[25] and judges grant substantial flexibility in the conducting of pat-down searches when weapons are suspected.[26] In a representative case involving the use of a frisk for a weapon, a school security officer in a New York high school observed a youth entering the school in a restricted area and demanded identification. When the youth failed to produce identification, the officer sought to escort the youth to the school office. As he took the youth's elbow, the guard testified that his hand brushed against a metal object in the student's waistband. An immediate pat down resulted in the recovery of a pistol. The court reasoned the officer was justified in frisking the student based on his suspicion that the student was carrying a weapon.[27]

Even when the pat down may be regarded as highly intrusive, judges have affirmed these searches when weapons are implicated. In a case from Wisconsin, several informants told the school principal that a fourteen-year-old was carrying a weapon on school grounds. The principal called the school security officer, and the officer interviewed one of the informants, who corroborated the story. After identifying the student, the officer and an administrator removed the suspected student from class. The officer explained to her that they had received information that she may have a weapon. He did a quick pat-down search of her jacket and had the student empty and display the contents of her backpack. She was then taken to an office, and the officer initiated a second pat down. In this second pat down, which included visual inspection of her waistband, the officer discovered and removed a nine-inch knife. The Supreme Court of Wisconsin ruled that the search was justified in scope despite its highly intrusive nature.[28]

However, a school official's failure to articulate a reasonable fear or apprehension that the student has a weapon may defeat a pat-down search. In a case from Indiana, a school security officer's decision to search a student who was late in arriving at a school-sponsored academic program was regarded as an "improvisational" search not justified by the evidence of misconduct. The search was undertaken because the school had a policy of searching program participants with a hand-held wand in order to check for weapons. At the time the student arrived at school, the metal detector had been locked in the principal's office, and the officer elected to conduct a pat-down search of the student, which included placing his hands in her pants' pockets. Two partially smoked marijuana cigarettes, a wooden pipe, and a package of rolling papers were discovered in the student's pockets. Reasoning that notice of a metal detector search would not automatically imply consent to a more intrusive physical search, the reviewing state court found that the search could not be justified solely by the student's tardiness.[29]

Strip Searches

Strip searches constitute the most intrusive form of search and create the greatest risk of legal liability for school districts and their employees.[30] There have been instances in which judges have upheld such searches, but only in circumstances in which a strong evidentiary basis supported individualized suspicion and the items sought were either drugs or weapons.[31] For example, in a case involving an Illinois high school student enrolled in a behavioral-disorder program, school administrators acted on observations by teachers and administrators of an unusual bulge in the crotch area of the student's sweatpants. The student had been rumored to have smoked marijuana on the school bus and was known to have failed to complete an off-campus drug rehabilitation program. Teachers and students had previously reported that the student had been in possession of drugs at school. Believing that the student was hiding drugs in the crotch of his underwear, two male administrators accompanied the student to a locker room, locked the door after determining that no other persons were in the area, and observed the student after directing him to remove his street clothes and put on a gym uniform. In the course of the observation, no drugs were discovered.

A federal appeals court found that the administrators based their decision to conduct the search on a number of factors that justified the intrusive procedures. Given the reports by various teachers and aides, the student's history, and the administrator's observations, the totality of circumstances created a reasonable suspicion that the student was concealing drugs. The search was regarded as reasonable in scope because the search was conducted in the privacy of the locker area by persons of the same sex as the student, the student was allowed to change into gym clothes while his street clothing was physically examined, and the administrators stood a discrete distance from the student to undertake a visual inspection.[32]

A high school administrator who was supervising a student participating in an after-school smoking cessation program conducted a less-intrusive strip search. The student had been caught smoking at school on two previous occasions and was required to attend the after-school program. During the program, he was noisy and distracting. The administrator noticed that the student's eyes were bloodshot and dilated and his handwriting appeared erratic. The administrator suspected the student was using drugs and confronted him with this accusation. The student denied that he was using drugs, and the administrator took the student to the office of the school nurse for her evaluation of the student. The nurse noted that the student's blood pressure and pulse were high and confirmed that the student's eyes appeared dilated. Although the nurse could not conclude that the student had been using drugs, the administrator took the student to a private room and required him to remove his shirt, hat, shoes, and socks. At all times, the student continued to wear his undershirt and pants. No drugs were discovered during the search.

In response to a civil suit against the administrator and the school district, a federal appeals court ruled that the search did not deny the protections of the Fourth Amendment. The court regarded the student's behavior and condition to be an appropriate basis on which to ground a suspicion of drug use and held that the search was both justified at its inception and reasonably related to its objective. While recognizing that the more intrusive the search the greater the standard of reasonable suspicion required, the court did not regard this search as unreasonably intrusive, particularly since the search was less intrusive than requiring the student to strip off all clothing.[33]

The testimony of informants may be sufficient to justify a highly intrusive strip search, provided that school officials find corroborating evidence that would substantiate the informant's reliability before ordering the search.[34] In *Redding v. Safford Unified School District*,[35] the principal relied on a student informant's face-to-face testimony implicating another student in possession of prescription drugs. The student informant had been discovered in possession of the illegal drugs at school. That student then implicated another student, indicating that she had received the illegal drugs from the student along with a black planner that contained knives, a lighter, and a cigarette. At this point, the principal questioned the newly implicated student. She denied any knowledge of illegal prescription drugs, but acknowledged her friendship with the informant and her ownership of the planner. She also admitted that her intention in loaning the planner to the informant was to permit her friend to hide contraband, although she contended she was ignorant of what that contraband might be. The principal then asked the student if she objected to being searched for illegal drugs. The student did not object, and, after an initial search of her backpack, she was taken into the school nurse's office for a strip search conducted by a female administrator while the school nurse served as a witness.[36] Emphasizing that there was sufficient evidence to support the veracity of the informant and corroborating evidence implicating the student prior to the search, the federal appeals court ruled that the search was justified at inception.[37]

In assessing whether the search was reasonable in scope, the court emphasized the school's "strong interest both in safeguarding students entrusted to their care from the harm posed by the misuse of prescription drugs and in enforcing the school's official policy, which prohibited the use, possession, and distribution of such drugs without permission."[38] The size of what was sought also supported the more intrusive search: prescription drugs in the form of pills would necessitate the more intrusive search because of the potential to hide them on the body. Finally, the court approved of the protocol used in searching the student. The search had been conducted in the privacy of the school nurse's office, by two employees of the same gender as the student. The door to the office had been securely locked, and the student was not touched at any time during the search. She was not asked to remove her undergarments.

The facts of a Michigan case are instructive on the question of consent to a search as well as the permissibility of a strip search. Four students reported to the assistant principal that a fourteen-year-old with attention deficit hyperactivity disorder had a dime roll of marijuana, which they had either seen or heard the student acknowledge. The student, who had a long history of minor disciplinary infractions but no history of drug possession, admitted he had shown a dime roll to students during class, but denied that he had told them it contained marijuana. No marijuana was found in an initial search of the student's gym bag and pockets. Later that day, the four students reported to the assistant principal that the student had hidden the dime roll of marijuana between his buttocks. The assistant principal was aware that this student was regularly teased and bullied by the four students in class, that all four of the students were to be disciplined with a detention for damaging his property while at school, and that one of the students had been previously searched and found to be in possession of marijuana. The assistant principal and a school resource officer were present when the student was asked about the marijuana and repeatedly asserted that he had nothing to hide. The assistant principal requested that the student "drop his drawers." Both the officer and the assistant principal testified that they advised the student he did not have to comply and the search had to be entirely voluntary. They testified that the student seemed relaxed and eager to comply with the request. The student did lower his undershorts, and the officer pulled back the waistband to examine the space between the student's buttocks.

In rejecting the contention that the assistant principal and the school resource officer were protected by qualified immunity, the federal district court found the search highly intrusive and unaccompanied by the extensive investigation and careful accumulation of information that might justify a strip search. The court ruled that the student's repeated statement that he had nothing to hide was not consent to a search and reasoned that consent is never to be presumed. Considering the "consent" in light of the totality of circumstances, the student's vulnerability, youth, and behavioral conditions affecting his impulse control and decision-making capacity militated against an informed and willing waiver of his privacy rights. As to the search, the court held it was neither justified at inception nor reasonable in scope. The court noted that the students who provided evidence all had a potential vendetta against the student, and that diminished their reliability and credibility.[39]

When a strip search is involved, judges are likely to place heightened scrutiny on the elements justifying a search at its inception. In a case involving a pre-announced search of all student bags prior to an off-campus trip, a lighter and cigarettes were found in a student's purse. Another student on the trip told a teacher that the student had voiced the intention to hide marijuana down her pants during the bag search. School personnel brought the student's mother to school and directed her to undertake a strip search of the student under the supervision of the school nurse, predicating reasonable suspicion on what they viewed as a reliable informant, the student's past history of discipline problems, her denial of the allegation she possessed marijuana, and possession of the lighter and cigarettes. The strip search, which included having the student drop her skirt to the floor and pull her underpants away from her body to demonstrate nothing was hidden, did not reveal any marijuana. In rejecting an award of summary judgment for the school officials and the district, the federal appeals court insisted on a stringent standard of reasonable suspicion when strip searches are involved, reasoning that the factors on which school officials relied were suspect because there was insufficient evidence establishing the reliability of the informant, the student's discipline problems were not related to drug use, school personnel did not explain why the student's denial was suspicious, and the contraband was not demonstrated to be related to illegal drug use.[40]

In the absence of individualized suspicion, school officials should be particularly wary of undertaking strip searches. Six seventh-grade girls from

Indiana sued the school district and school employees for violating their rights under the Fourth Amendment in the conducting of a strip search. The search was initiated when it was reported that four dollars and fifty cents were missing from the girls' locker room at the end of a physical education class. The school principal directed that a search of the lockers and the students be undertaken. The search began with an inspection of lockers and bookbags, and then each of the girls was brought into the locker room to determine whether the missing money might be hidden in a bra. All of the searches were conducted in a similar fashion, although the searches varied in that in some instances the girls removed blouse and bra for inspection, and in other instances, the bra was inspected by lifting it up.

The federal district court ruled that strip searching the seventh-grade girls was not reasonable and rejected the claim of the principal and teachers that their actions were protected under the doctrine of qualified immunity. Under this doctrine, school officials would be immune from liability if their conduct did not violate clearly established rights of which a reasonable official would have been aware at the time of the conduct. In the court's view, conducting a strip search in an effort to recover the "grand sum" of four dollars and fifty cents from young students was clearly a violation of the Fourth Amendment right to privacy.[41]

While some courts have granted immunity to public school employees who undertook strip searches in the absence of individualized suspicion,[42] a case from New Mexico illustrates the prevailing view of liability for these searches. In that case, students who were strip searched down to their undergarments to locate another student's missing ring were granted compensatory and punitive damages against school officials who violated their right to privacy. Ironically, the school employees involved in planning and conducting the searches had participated in a similar search some years before. That search had brought a substantial amount of public criticism and a promise from the district that such searches would not be permitted in the future. In this case, a student reported that her diamond ring was missing, and the fourteen and fifteen-year-old students were detained for another class period. Students were subjected to highly intrusive searches when they exited the detention classroom to use toilet facilities. Two school employees would observe students through open stall doors while they urinated; then each student would be directed to leave pants and underwear down for inspection after urinating. Following this inspection, students were told to lift their shirt or blouse, and female students were directed to lift their bras, exposing their breasts.

The Supreme Court of New Mexico refused to grant qualified immunity to the school employees for their conduct in initiating the highly intrusive searches.[43] The court quoted from a Seventh Circuit Court of Appeals decision that stated, "It does not require a constitutional scholar to conclude that a nude search of a thirteen-year-old child is an invasion of constitutional rights of some magnitude."[44] The state supreme court first emphasized that no individualized suspicion accompanied the searches of students. Finding that the searches were not justified at inception, the court went on to note that such a highly intrusive search "was excessive in light of (the student's) youth, the significant possibility that the ring was simply lost and no infraction had occurred, and the non-dangerousness of the hypothesized infraction."[45]

One exception to the general rule to avoid the conducting of a strip search may apply to investigations involving victims of sexual abuse. In one case involving the visual examination of a child's body, a federal appeals court ruled that school officials are entitled to qualified immunity when investigating whether a child has been abused, particularly when the investigation is initiated after the student has complained of pain in an area and is evasive about the circumstances that led to a suspected abuse injury.[46] In another case in which a sixth-grader alleged that a classmate had sexually assaulted her, a school resource officer who interviewed the student and a nurse who conducted a brief physical examination of the student to verify scratches on her back and arms were insulated from liability. The federal district court applied the two-pronged test of *T.L.O.* in determining that the search was justified at inception and reasonable in scope, reasoning that the school had a "great, even overwhelming" interest in the conduct of a sexual assault investigation involving a student.[47] In response to the parent's contention that no investigation should have been conducted without parental presence and consent, the court acknowledged parental concerns for potential emotional trauma but found the school's compelling need to promptly investigate incidents of student-on-student violence must prevail.[48]

Searches Off School Grounds

Just as judges have become increasingly supportive of school search policies when school officials can point to a past history of problems involving drugs or weapons, situations in which students will be supervised off school grounds during school-sponsored trips or programs have led judges to approve extraordinary measures involving student searches. Under one junior high school's policy, students who participated in a voluntary field trip and picnic were subjected to a search of hand luggage before boarding the trip bus. School officials required parental approval, using a permission slip that included a statement that hand luggage would be searched. A New Jersey appeals court concluded that the interest of school officials in ensuring that students did not bring prohibited contraband on a field trip justified the policy. Although there was no evidence of individualized suspicion for the search, the court rationalized the general search policy by pointing to its deterrent potential in discouraging students from bringing prohibited items. The court also noted the special duty of supervision that was created in the context of a field trip in which supervising teachers would not have the level of control over students available in the school setting.[49]

A similar rationale guided the Eighth Circuit Court of Appeals in a case in which a seventeen-year-old student was subjected to a search by school resource officers (SROs) while attending a shop class at a local body shop. On the way to the shop, the supervising teacher observed a student using a folding knife but did not know that the student had borrowed the knife from another student to open an orange juice can. After the bus arrived at the body shop, the teacher notified school authorities, who decided that the eight students on the bus should be searched. School officials and two SROs went to the body shop. After searching the bus, they asked if any of the students had a knife, and the student who had brought the folding knife on the bus handed it over. Thereafter, all the students were subjected to a pat-down search, and the student who had used the knife on the bus was discovered to be in possession of an expandable baton. The school initiated expulsion proceedings based on possession of the knife and the baton. When the parents sued the school district for violation of the student's Fourth Amendment rights to privacy, a federal district court granted qualified immunity to the SROs and summary judgment to the school district.

The federal appeals court affirmed this immunity, noting that the search was justified at inception on the basis of a reasonable suspicion.[50] The court determined that the search off school grounds did not elevate the standard beyond reasonable suspicion because the nature of the administrator and teacher's supervisory responsibilities for the students dictated the Fourth Amendment standard. The SROs were justified in continuing the search even though a knife had been discovered because they had no way to verify that the confiscated knife was the one that had been seen earlier and they were aware that the student who handed over the knife had not been seen previously with a knife. Given these facts, the officers had reasonable cause to believe that there was another knife in the possession of one of the student participants.

An interesting comparison case involved a school principal/chaperone's decision to search student motel rooms during a class trip to Disney World. Prior to the trip, students were given a brochure that specifically warned they would be subjected to "room checks." Parents signed a form accepting responsibility for the costs of travel if their child were sent home early from the trip based on misconduct. The notice to parents also included a statement that possession or use of drugs or alcohol would result in early departure. The administrator and his wife were returning to their room when they detected the strong odor of marijuana in the hallway adjacent to student rooms. The principal contacted the hotel representative and was told it was the policy of the resort to give adult chaperones access to student rooms. The principal and a hotel representative entered the rooms of students on the floor where the marijuana had been detected and also accessed the safes in those rooms. Marijuana and alcohol were found in the safe. The federal district court ruled that the search was reasonable under all the circumstances, noting that the students and parents were cautioned about the use of drugs or alcohol on the trip and students had been informed of the likelihood of room checks. This information reduced the student's expectation of privacy on the trip. More to the point, however, the court emphasized that school trips often present greater challenges to school personnel trying to maintain order and discipline than in-school settings. As a consequence, the school administrator's actions were regarded as reasonable, and to hold otherwise would subject him to a greater risk of liability for injury to students while at the same time denying him the authority necessary to lessen the risk of injury.[51]

Special Needs

In some instances, a search by school authorities may take place absent evidence of reasonable suspicion. A public school district may undertake such searches if it can demonstrate that a special need justifies the search. However, even if such a special need were present, it must be balanced against the nature of the student's privacy interest and the degree of intrusion into that interest. Courts have recognized that public school districts have an essential responsibility to deter weapons possession and drug use in order to maintain a safe learning environment and protect students. When searches are unaccompanied by reasonable suspicion, they may still be constitutional if special needs can be articulated, the nature of the proposed search is not regarded as highly intrusive, and concerns for the health and well-being of students can be established.

As the cases involving strip searches of students illustrate, special needs searches have been difficult to justify when the searches are highly intrusive.[52] As a case from the Eighth Circuit Court of Appeals illustrates, a school district practice of conducting random searches in secondary school classrooms may be vulnerable to a Fourth Amendment challenge. Under the search protocol, students were directed to exit the classroom after removing all the contents from their pockets and placing all of their belongings, including backpacks and purses, on their desks. While waiting in the hall outside the classroom, a student's purse was searched, and marijuana was discovered in a container. The federal appeals court acknowledged that a student's legitimate expectation of privacy in personal belongings is limited in the school setting but held that the school district's practice of subjecting students to full-scale, suspicionless searches effectively eliminated privacy in a student's personal belongings and was unaccompanied by any compelling justification.[53] In assessing the intrusiveness of the search against the student's expectation of privacy under the Fourth Amendment, the court emphasized:

> While the line separating reasonable and unreasonable school searches is sometimes indistinct, we think it plain enough that the (school district's) search practice crosses it. In light of the government's legitimate interest in maintaining discipline and safety in the public schools, the privacy that students in those schools are reasonably entitled to expect is limited. The (district's) search practice, however, effectively reduces these expectations to nothing, and the record contains no evidence of unique circumstances that

> would justify significant intrusions. The mere assertion that there are substantial problems associated with drugs and weapons in its schools does not give the (district) *carte blanche* to inflict highly intrusive, random searches upon its general student body.[54]

Even when searches do not involve the investigation of wrongdoing, the intrusive nature of a general search may implicate the Fourth Amendment. For example, the Tenth Circuit Court of Appeals reasoned that physical examinations required under provisions of a Head Start program could not be undertaken by school officials absent express parental consent. The examinations were performed on preschool students by registered nurses who relocated the children to an empty classroom and used desks as examining tables. Children were required to remove their underclothes and submit to a genital examination and blood test. The federal appeals court concluded that the examinations were searches within the meaning of the Fourth Amendment and found that none of the forms provided by the defendants gave explicit authorization to conduct the examination. Although the school district contended that a "special need" justified the search, the court held that school officials had acted out of carelessness and neglect rather than recognition that compliance with Fourth Amendment requirements would be impracticable.[55]

On the other hand, judges have also reasoned that the magnitude and immediacy of a potential threat in the school setting may permit the school's use of a general search, such as a pat-down search, when school officials have exhausted all reasonable alternatives to such a search. For example, when a kitchen knife was reported missing following a middle school lunch period in which pizza had been served, school officials first searched the cafeteria area and then asked students in the cafeteria to come forward if they had information concerning the missing knife. When no student came forward, the school's vice-principal obtained permission from the principal to conduct a pat down of students. The students were divided into two groups, male and female, and were patted down by staff of the same sex. The pat down consisted of touching the areas around the student's pockets and their ankles. The knife was not found, and a ten year-old student filed suit alleging a denial of Fourth Amendment rights to privacy. In rejecting the suit, a federal district court found the search was conducted in the least intrusive manner possible consistent with its purpose and was justified by urgent and immediate concerns for the safety and welfare of students.[56]

In balancing student privacy and the immediate need for a general search, a state appeals court affirmed the permissibility of a pat-down search of all middle school students. School officials instituted the search in order to prevent the repetition of a Halloween tradition involving an egg-throwing melee. The egg throwing had, in a previous year, led to damage of school property and injury to students. The school principal directed staff to pat down the outer garments of students as they entered the building. In the course of the pat down, one student was discovered to have a handgun in his waistband. In a criminal adjudication, the student sought to suppress the evidence on the basis that the pat down was an illegal search. The state appeals court ruled that the pat down of outer clothing by school personnel was the least intrusive, most practical means of locating the concealed eggs and represented a reasonable balance between the privacy expectation of students and the interests of school officials in maintaining order.[57]

Metal Detectors and "Sniff" Dogs

In contrast to intrusive general searches, which receive heightened judicial scrutiny, judges have emphasized that the use of drug and weapon detection dogs[58] and metal detectors[59] is clearly permissible as part of a general search policy. School districts have characterized these approaches as screening devices rather than searches. When the screening procedures are minimally intrusive and used in deterring drugs and weapons possession, judges have affirmed the legitimacy of the practices. For example, when a Texas school district adopted a policy of random searches using sniff dogs trained to look for drugs, alcohol, firearms, and other contraband in student automobiles parked on school property, a federal appeals court sustained the policy. The court emphasized that if it could be demonstrated that the dog had been proven reliable in detecting drugs, then the search of an automobile parked on school property is justified once the dog alerts.[60] Similarly, when a trained drug-detection dog alerted that a student's truck parked on school grounds might contain drugs, school officials had reasonable grounds to search the vehicle. The fact that a machete was found in the toolbox of the vehicle instead of drugs did not invalidate the search. The federal district court reasoned that the school official was legally in a position to view the contents of the toolbox when he discovered the machete, and taking possession of the machete constituted a valid plain-view seizure.[61]

While the use of drug-detection dogs to sniff lockers, automobiles, desks, and backpacks does not constitute an intrusive a search, federal courts appear divided on whether the use of a drug-detection dog to sniff a student would constitute a search requiring individualized suspicion. The Fifth Circuit Court of Appeals took the position that using a dog to sniff a student was "indecent and demeaning" and held the use would only be permissible if reasonable suspicion was established.[62] Given nearly identical factual circumstances, the Seventh Circuit ruled otherwise, taking the view that the use of sniff dogs to screen students is not a search that would require reasonable suspicion.[63] The Ninth Circuit Court of Appeals addressed this question in the context of a high school search in which local law enforcement officials cooperated with school officials to arrange for the use of drug-detection dogs to inspect classrooms. As students exited the classroom, they walked by the dog, and in some instances, the dog alerted. The federal appeals court ruled that this protocol constituted a search of the students and concluded that the search was highly intrusive because it was involuntary and the use of dogs could engender fear.

The court concluded that the public school's interest in deterring student drug use would not have been placed in jeopardy by a requirement of individualized suspicion prior to the use of drug detection dogs on students.[64]

Whenever weapons are implicated, the degree of flexibility in the conduct of blanket student searches appears to increase. For example, a New York high school with an on-going problem of violence and weapons possession among students set up metal detector scanning posts in the main lobby of the building. Students were told to remove all metal objects before passing through the posts, and when crowding became a problem, a random procedure was used to select students who would pass through the metal detector. If a student activated the device, he or she was told to remove all metal objects and cross through the posts a second time. If the student activated the detector a second time, a pat-down search was conducted. Using this procedure, a female student was discovered with a switchblade knife. When the student sought to suppress the weapon in a later criminal prosecution, the court ruled that the search was permissible and emphasized that the use of a metal detector was a minimally intrusive search, and the more intrusive pat down was only undertaken after the scanning device was twice activated.[65]

A Pennsylvania urban high school enforced its policy forbidding drugs or weapons on school property by employing police officers to conduct metal detector scans and bag searches of students. Signs were posted warning of the search policy, and parents were notified of the policy periodically during the year. The procedure for conducting the searches involved bringing students into the gym where they formed lines and stepped up to a table. At the table, students emptied their pockets, surrendered jackets or any bags in their possession, and were scanned by an officer using a metal detector. When a student surrendered a knife while emptying his pockets, he was arrested for possession of a weapon on school property. The Supreme Court of Pennsylvania held the search was justified given the high rate of violence in the district's public schools.[66]

Florida secondary school students were subjected to random, hand-held metal detector scans conducted in classrooms. Under the protocol, a classroom would be randomly selected, and students would be segregated by gender and directed to remove all metal objects from their clothing. If a detector sounded, the student would be asked to remove the metal object before a second scan. If the detector sounded a second time, the area would be patted down. During the search process, a student was observed taking off his jacket and moving it to the back of the room while the scanning procedure was taking place. The jacket was patted down, and a handgun was discovered. A state appeals court found that the search policy minimized the intrusion into students' privacy while meeting the school district's immediate concern to deter the presence of weapons in schools and promote a safe learning environment.[67]

Random Urinalysis Testing

The United States Supreme Court has concluded that a school district's interest in deterring drug use and the desirability of reducing the risk of injury associated with drug use among students engaged in athletic programs and extracurricular activities justifies random urinalysis testing. In the first of two decisions, the high court affirmed an Oregon high school's policy requiring random drug testing of student-athletes. [68] Granting that the drug testing of student-athletes was a search under the Fourth Amendment, the Court noted the results of the tests remained confidential and were neither released to law enforcement nor used for disciplinary purposes. The Court majority balanced the intrusiveness of the search against the school district's legitimate interest in discouraging drug use, reasoned that the process of obtaining urine samples was not highly intrusive, and held that any compromise of the students' privacy interest was justified by the school district's substantial and important interest in fighting drug abuse among student athletes.[69]

In a later decision, the United States Supreme Court upheld a school district's requirement that all middle and high school students participating in extracurricular activities consent to a drug-testing program.[70] The Court majority once again balanced the student's interest in privacy against the school district's "custodial and tutelary responsibility," reasoning that students who participate in extracurricular activities voluntarily subject themselves to intrusions that lessen any expectation of privacy that might apply to the student body as a whole. The Court ruled that the government's interest outweighed the student's privacy rights. In reaching its decision, the Court majority noted that urinalysis testing was an insubstantial interference with privacy and the school district's interest was sufficient even if there was no evidence of a pervasive drug problem at the school or among students participating in extracurricular programs.

Other federal courts decisions have been receptive to a school district's proposed extension of mandatory drug testing. For example, a federal appeals court approved a school district policy requiring mandatory urinalysis testing, not only for students participating in extracurricular activities, but also for those students who drove an automobile on school grounds.[71] The appeals court emphasized that the school district had established sufficient evidence of a governmental need to test students using automobiles on campus for alcohol and marijuana use solely because the danger of even one student driving on school property while impaired was substantial.[72]

However, the application of random drug testing to students participating in the regular school curriculum remains suspect. For example, the Seventh Circuit has rejected a school district policy requiring drug and alcohol testing for students suspended for fighting.[73] In this case, a student suspended for fighting received another suspension when he refused the drug-testing requirement. The appeals court ruled the policy violated the student's Fourth Amendment rights because the search could not be justified on the basis of either a reasonable suspicion or a special need that would permit suspicionless testing. In the appeals court's view, the student's violent behavior would not justify a reasonable suspicion of drug use, and a district special need for drug testing could not be supported. The federal appeals court distinguished the case from other "special need" situations by noting that the voluntary participation of students in extracurricular activities involves a conscious decision to submit to policies that reduce the student's expectation of privacy, while a student's "unauthorized participation in disfavored activities"[74] (fighting) does not permit the same inference.[75]

Similarly, a federal district court in Texas struck down a school board policy in which a student's or parent's refusal to consent to drug testing was construed as the equivalent of a "positive" test. The student's first offense subjected him to suspension from participation in all extracurricular activities for twenty-one days and removal to in-school suspension for a minimum of three days. Continued refusal by a parent to consent to the child's being tested for drugs would, as with continued positive test results, result in escalation up to placing the child in an alternative school and disqualifying him from participating in any activity or receiving any honors for the year. Considering the students' increased expectation of privacy in the regular school setting and the dearth of evidence demonstrating a need to be met by the search, the federal court ruled that the district's drug testing program was unreasonable and, hence, unconstitutional under the Fourth Amendment.[76]

Seizure

Although most "seizures" involve the seizing of evidence obtained in a search, a relatively recent development in the area of Fourth Amendment jurisprudence applicable to public schools has to do with the seizure of a student. In the public school context, these seizures involve removal of a student from the regular school setting in order to protect the health and safety of others[77] or investigate allegations of misconduct.[78] The student is regarded as "seized" when a reasonable person under the same or similar circumstances would feel that they were not at liberty to leave.[79] While *T.L.O.* involved the search of a student and the seizure of materials found in her purse, the same two-pronged standard applied in that case appears appropriate to the seizure of a student. For example, in *Edwards v. Rees*,[80] a student removed from class for questioning related to a bomb threat challenged a "seizure" that involved twenty minutes of questioning by a vice-principal. The federal appeals court concluded that the seizure was justified at inception because two students who had reported the threat implicated the student as the person responsible. The seizure was reasonable in scope because the questioning by the vice-principal related directly to the bomb threat.

Other courts have applied the reasonableness standard, informed by the two-pronged analysis in *T.L.O.*, to cases involving seizure of a student.[81] In *Mislin v. City of Tonawanda School District*,[82] allegations of racial and homosexual harassment were brought to the attention of the superintendent and school administrators. A student's complaint specifically named one student as engaging in the harassment and charged that school officials were allowing students to get away with the misconduct. The superintendent determined the allegations were serious and ordered an investigation. In the course of the investigation, interviews with several students pointed to one student as a perpetrator of the harassment. He was removed from class and questioned for approximately twenty minutes about his involvement in the harassment. Although the student later brought suit, at the time of the interview he was compliant with requests for information and did not lose his composure. He never asked to leave the room or call his parents. School officials used no physical force to restrain the student, and the student did not ask to leave prior to the conclusion of the interview.

The student contended that the seizure was not justified at its inception because he had been previously disciplined for the harassment in the complaint and the actual interview took place some six weeks after the initial complaint. However, the federal district court reasoned that the interview was justified because the complaint of harassment also alleged that school officials had not taken appropriate steps to address it after the student was initially disciplined. In response to the contention that the interview was impermissible in scope because there were questions related to anti-homosexual and anti-Semitic animus, the court emphasized that the original complaint had alleged this animus and there was no impermissible "straying" from that complaint in the course of investigation. Finding for the school district and its administrators, the district court rejected the contention that there was a violation of the Fourth Amendment and granted summary judgment to school officials.[83]

While seizures involving removal from class and questioning have seldom led to liability,[84] concerns arise when the seizure involves excessive use of force. In a case addressed by the Eleventh Circuit Court of Appeals, a nine-year-old student in a gym class threatened to strike a teacher when she was removed from an exercise activity. A school resource officer who witnessed the insubordinate conduct intervened, forced the student against a wall, and handcuffed her. The student wore the handcuffs for approximately five minutes, crying and complaining of the pain. Neither of the coaches who were present felt threatened by the child, and one testified that the conduct wasn't "major" and that he would have simply warned the child of the misconduct.

The federal appeals court affirmed a district court's summary judgment for the school district and the local law enforcement agency, but remanded the case after denying qualified immunity to the school resource officer. While the deputy may have acted reasonably in intervening and stopping the student, the court concluded that handcuffing was an unreasonable action because there was no indication that the student posed a threat to anyone's safety. The "seizure" was regarded as a punishment that clearly violated the student's rights under the Fourth Amendment.[85]

Recommendations for Practice

In cases involving student searches, the historic challenge for judges is how to strike the appropriate balance between the public school district's legitimate interest in maintaining a safe and appropriate learning environment and the student's reasonable expectation of privacy protected by the Fourth Amendment. Although the legality of a search will depend on a standard of reasonable suspicion given all the circumstances relating to the search, the gradual erosion of the student's privacy rights has been a trend in judicial opinions. While students may contend that they have an expectation of privacy in the public school setting, the state's custodial and supervisory authority over the student coupled with judicial perceptions of epidemic drug use and unprecedented violence in public schools continue to overwhelm whatever expectation of privacy the student might once have assumed. Courts continue to apply a standard of "reasonable suspicion" in the context of student searches, but that standard has weighed heavily in favor of school officials in recent decisions. In light of those applications, we have provided some recommendations below.

1. It remains true that searches are more likely to be permissible when there is evidence implicating a particular student. School officials must continue to evaluate the totality of circumstances justifying a search, giving consideration to the weight and credibility of evidence implicating an individual student, the age and previous history of the student, and the nature of that which is sought. However, when searches for drugs or weapons are involved, judges have shown extraordinary deference in permitting student searches, even when that search may be highly intrusive.

2. In deciding how intrusive a search to undertake, school officials must recognize that the more intrusive the search, the greater the degree of individualized suspicion required. A student's expectation of privacy in a locker, desk, automobile, bookbag, or purse has been significantly reduced in recent decisions and is likely to become more attenuated in the future.

3. Highly intrusive searches, such as strip searches, continue to require a substantial degree of individualized suspicion based on specific and reliable evidence and should never be undertaken unless serious infractions, such as possession of drugs or weapons, are suspected.

4. In the limited cases in which strip searches have been addressed, courts have required a high degree of individualized suspicion, often involving the corroboration of more than one reliable informant and other credible evidence tending to confirm drugs or weapons possession. Such a standard approximates the requirement of probable cause for a search and suggests that any strip search in the public school

setting should best be left to the discretion of local law enforcement rather than school officials.

5. General, suspicionless searches continue to require that school officials document the nature and immediacy of the school district's "special need" to provide security and safety.

6. Blanket pat-down searches have been justified when concerns about weapons possession are paramount and evidence of a danger is particularized. Less intrusive searches, involving drug detection dogs and metal detectors, have been authorized by courts on the basis that these activities are not true "searches" and involve little genuine intrusion on the student's expectation of privacy. However, federal courts are divided on the extent to which searches of this type require documentation of serious drug or violence problems in the particular school setting. Policies on the use of urinalysis testing have been validated in application to students involved in extracurricular activities, but students must be given adequate notice of the drug-testing policies, and the procedures should be followed carefully to ensure that the initial search involves a minimal intrusion on the student's privacy. These drug-testing policies should emphasize the deterrent potential of the search as a means of discouraging drug use and should be limited to students engaged in extracurricular activities.

7. An emergent area of litigation involves student "seizures" in school settings. When a student is removed from a classroom setting, school officials must be able to articulate a reasonable suspicion justifying the removal, and any interviews should be limited to an inquiry that is within the scope and authority of school officials.

8. School policies may permit local law enforcement to participate in an investigation, but unauthorized persons should not be permitted carte blanche to undertake investigations that are beyond the authority of school officials.

Endnotes

1 The Amendment reads, in pertinent part, "The right of the people to be secure in their persons, houses, papers, and effects, against unreasonable searches and seizures, shall not be violated …" U.S. Const. Fourth Amendment.

2 469 U.S. 325, 105 S. Ct. 733, 83 L.Ed.2d 720 (1985).

3 *Id.* at 341-42, 105 S. Ct. at 743, 83 L.Ed.2d at 735.

4 S.A. v. State, 654 N.E.2d 791 (Ind. App. 1995). *See also* C.B. v. Driscoll, 82 F.3d 383 (11th Cir. 1996) in which reliance on a student informant resulted in the discovery of a look-alike drug that was located in a student's coat pocket.

5 State v. Drake, 139 N.H. 662, 662 A.2d 265 (N.H.1995).

6 *See* Rinker v. Sipler, 264 F. Supp. 2d 181, 188 (M.D. Pa. 2003) in which a search was justified at inception on the basis that a school administrator and a security officer observed that the student "looked stoned, smelled of marijuana, and was somewhat incoherent."

7 Gutin v. Washington Township Bd. of Educ., 467 F. Supp. 2d 414 (D. N.J. 2006). In this case, the parent claimed there was a lack of consent, contending this made drug testing based on reasonable suspicion unconstitutional, but the court rejected this contention.

8 Shamberg v. State, 762 P.2d 488 (Alaska App. 1988). A Florida appeals court has also found that a search of a student's car is justified where a teacher's aide patrolled the parking lot and saw drug paraphernalia in a student's car. State v. D.T.W., 425 So.2d 1383 (Fla. D.C.A. 1983).

9 Patman v. State, 244 Ga. App. 833, 537 S.E.2d 118 (Ga. App. 2000).

10 A.N.H. v. State, 832 So. 2d 170 (Fla. D.C.A. 2002). *See also* A.H. v. State, 846 So. 2d 1215 (Fla. D.C.A. 2003) in which search of a student's wallet was not supported by sufficient facts when the sole basis for the search was that a teacher had difficulty understanding the student and advised the administrator that the student might be "on something."

11 Coronado v. State, 835 S.W.2d 636 (Tex. App. 1992).

12 In Interest of Doe, 77 Haw. 435, 887 P.2d 645 (Haw. 1994).

13 Smith v. McGlothlin, 119 F.3d 786 (9th Cir. 1997). *See* People v. Alexander B., 220 Cal. App. 3d 1572, 270 Cal. Rptr. 342 (Cal. App. 1990) in which a school search was reasonable where suspicion focused on a group of five or six students, rather than one student alone.

14 People v. Dilworth, 169 Ill. 2d 195, 210, 661 N.E.2d 310, 319 (Ill. 1996). *See* State v. N.G.B., 806 So.2d 567 (Fla. D.C.A. 2002) in which a school resource officer's search of a student was justified on the basis of reasonable suspicion when the investigation was initiated by a school administrator who then listed the officer's assistance; James v. Unified Sch. Dist., 959 F. Supp. 1407 (D. Kan. 1997) in which a police officer was granted qualified immunity for the conduct of a search of a vehicle on school grounds on the basis that it was not established that an officer must meet a probable cause standard when accompanying school officials in a search on school grounds; and S.A. v. State, 654 N.E.2d 791 (Ind. App. 1995) in which a search of a student's bookbag by a school liaison officer met the reasonable suspicion standard, and, when acting in his capacity as security officer for the school district, the officer's conduct was governed by the standard of reasonable suspicion. *See also* State v. D.S., 685 So. 2d 41 (Fla. D.C.A. 1996) in which the presence of a school resource officer in the conduct of a search on school grounds does not heighten the standard of reasonable suspicion for a search. *But see* State v. Tywayne H., 123 N.M. 42, 933 P.2d 251 (N.M. App. 1997) in which police acting as security for a school dance were held to a standard of probable cause for a search of a student.

15 *Id.*

16 *But see* A.S. v. State, 693 So. 2d 1095 (Fla. App. 1997) in which an assistant principal's observation that one student in a group was "fiddling" in his pockets while another was holding money in his hand would be insufficient to establish reasonable suspicion for a search of the student's wallet.

17 469 U.S. 341-42, 105 S. Ct. at 743, 83 L.Ed.2d at 735.

18 *See In re* Patrick Y., 358 Md. 50, 746 A.2d 405 (Md. App. 2000); Commonwealth v. Cass, 551 Pa. 25, 709 A.2d 350 (Pa. 1998); and *In re* D.E.M., 727 A.2d 570 (Pa. Sup. 1999). *But see* State of Iowa v. Jones, 666 N.W.2d 142 (Iowa 2003), in which the court recognized that a student has a legitimate expectation of privacy in the contents of his or her school locker, but ruled that the discovery of marijuana as part of an end-of-year school locker clean-out search was reasonable.

19 *See* Commonwealth v. Williams, 749 A.2d 957 (Pa. Sup. 2000) in which school security officers violated the Fourth Amendment when they searched a student's car parked on a city street off school grounds.

20 Myers v. State of Indiana, 839 N.E. 2d 1154 (Ind. 2005), *cert.denied*, Myers v. State of Indiana, 126 S. Ct. 2295 (2006). *See* People v. Williams, 339 Ill. App. 3d 956, 791 N.E.2d 608 (Ill. App. 2003) in which a school security officer's search of a student's car based on a student's

testimony that a gun was in the car was permissible; Covington County v. G.W., 767 So. 2d 187 (Miss. 2000) in which a vehicle search was justified because informants advised school officials that the student had been observed drinking beer at his vehicle while it was parked on school grounds and school administrators discovered beer cans when the car was inspected; and F.S.E. v. State, 993 P.2d 771 (Okla. Crim. App. 1999) in which a school official's search of a student's vehicle was justified because the vehicle was parked on school grounds, the school administrator smelled marijuana on the student, and the student alleged that a stranger had left a marijuana cigarette in the car.

[21] *In re* Murray, 136 N.C. App. 648, 525 S.E.2d 496 (N.C. App. 2000) in which the school administrator had a reasonable suspicion to search a student's book bag based on a reliable informant's tip that the student had something in the bag that "he shouldn't have" and on the student's initial evasiveness in stating he did not have a bookbag. Greenleaf *ex rel.* Greenleaf v. Cote, 77 F. Supp. 2d 168 (D. Me. 1999) in which a student's tip that four students had discussed drinking alcohol at school provided a reasonable suspicion justifying a requirement that a student shake out her bookbag in order to discover evidence of alcohol possession.

[22] Matter of Gregory M., 184 A.D.2d 252, 585 N.Y.S.2d 193 (App. Div. 1992). In this case, a school security officer patted down the exterior of a student's bookbag when the metallic thud of the bookbag on the desk alerted the officer to the possibility of a weapon. The outline of a gun led the officer and a school administrator to search the bag, and they discovered a handgun. In a subsequent juvenile court proceeding, the court ruled that the search was reasonable and the weapon was properly admitted in evidence.

[23] *See, e.g.,* Ineirghe v. Bd. of Educ. of E. Islip, 2007 U.S.Dist. LEXIS 61841 (E.D.N.Y. 2007) (nurse's examination and salvia drug test were warranted when student had been found in parking lot during school hours in violation of school rules, exhibited anxious behavior, continued to wipe his eyes and nose during questioning); Hedges v. Musco, 204 F.3d 109, 117 (3d Cir. 2000) (nurse's vital signs examination, a urinalysis, and a blood test did not constitute unreasonable searches when the student had exhibited uncharacteristic behavior consistent with drug use); and Bridgman v. New Trier High Sch. Dist., 128 F.3d 1146, 1149 (7th Cir. 1997) (medical assessment was reasonably calculated to uncover further evidence of suspected drug when the student was "giggling and acting in an unruly fashion," "had dilated and bloodshot eyes" and provided "flippant" answers).

[24] *See In re* L.A., 21 P.3d 953 (Kan. 2001) in which removing a student's cap to check the headband was justified by an informant's tip that the student was hiding marijuana in the headband and D.B. v. State, 728 N.E.2d 179 (Ind. App. 2000) in which minimally intrusive pat down of student's clothing was justified by evidence student had been smoking in school bathroom and was unresponsive to questioning.

[25] *See, e.g.,* C.S. v. State, 735 N.E.2d 273 (Ind. App. 2000) in which pat down by school resource officer was justified by concern for her safety in removing student from classroom.

[26] *See, e.g., In re* Randy G., 18 Cal. App. 3d 1023, 96 Cal. Rptr. 338 (Cal. App. 2000) in which detaining a student for suspicious behavior resulted in a pat down that yielded a knife; *In re* Josue T., 128 N.M. 56, 989 P.2d 431 (N.M. App. 1999) in which the student was suspected of having used marijuana, but after he was isolated, an unusually large bulge in his pants pocket led to an apprehension that he might have a weapon and a school resource officer's search at the direction of school officials was justified by a reasonable suspicion; and J.A.R. v. State, 689 So. 2d 1242 (Fla. D.C.A. 1997) in which reasonable suspicion based on student informer's testimony that student had a gun permitted either the school resource officer or the administrator to isolate the student and conduct a pat down;

[27] In the matter of Kevin P., 186 A.D.2d 199, 587 N.Y.S.2d 730 (App.Div.1992).

[28] In Interest of Angelia D.B., 211 Wis. 2d 140, 564 N.W.2d 682 (Wis. 1997) the court also concluded that the reasonable suspicion standard should apply to trained law enforcement officers assisting administrators in the public school setting. *See also* People v. Butler, 725 N.Y.S.2d 534 (N.Y. Sup. 2001) in which reasonable suspicion existed to support a pat down given a school safety officer's concern that the defendant was wearing gang colors and could not produce student identification.

[29] D.I.R. v. State, 683 N.E.2d 251 (Ind. App. 1997).

[30] In addition to a risk of liability for a constitutional tort under 42 U.S.C Section 1983, at least one federal district court has indicated employee liability may be predicated on negligent infliction of emotional distress. Higginbottom *ex rel.* Davis v. Keithly, 103 F. Supp. 2d 1075 (S.D. Ind. 1999). *But see* Beard v. Whitmore Lake Sch. Dist., 2007 U.S. App. LEXIS 14749 (6th Cir. 2007), in which a federal appeals court rejected school district liability for "failure to train" in a case in which the school district acknowledged that teachers had improperly strip searched students in a gym class to locate money missing from a student's purse. The appeals court reasoned that the district had a clear policy prohibiting such searches and the plaintiffs failed to show the district was deliberately indifferent to the students' interests in being free from unreasonable searches and seizures.

[31] *See* Beard v. Whitmore Lake Sch. Dist., 402 F.3d 598, 605 (6th Cir. 2005), in which the federal appeals court invalidated a strip search on the basis that the governmental interest in finding missing money is less weighty "than a search undertaken for items that pose a threat to the health or safety of students, such as drugs or weapons" and State *ex rel.* Galford v. Mark Anthony B., 189 W. Va. 538, 433 S.E.2d 41 (W.Va. 1993), in which a strip search of a student to locate money missing from a teacher's purse was unreasonable in scope and excessively intrusive.

[32] Cornfield v. Consol. High Sch. Dist. No. 130, 991 F.2d 1316 (7th Cir. 1993).

[33] Bridgman v. New Trier High Sch. Dist. No.203, 128 F.3d 1146 (7th Cir. 1997).

[34] *See* Williams v. Ellington, 936 F.2d 881 (6th Cir. 1991) in which the Sixth Circuit upheld a highly intrusive search based on a confidential tip from a fellow student, finding that it was justified at its inception given the particularized suspicion of the student and reasoning that the scope of the search was reasonable because of the size of the object sought (a small glass vial), the suspected nature of the object (suspected narcotics), and the previous searches of the student's locker and purse.

[35] 2007 U.S. App. LEXIS 22521 (9th Cir. 2007).

[36] The strip search began with the student removing her jacket, shoes and socks, then her pants and shirt. She was directed to pull her bra out and to the side and shake it, exposing her breasts. She was then directed to pull her underwear out at the crotch and shake it, exposing her pelvic area. School official made no attempt prior to or during the search to contact the student's parents.

[37] *Id.* at 17. *But see* Phaneuf v. Fraikin, 448 F.3d 591 (2d Cir. 2006) in which the federal appeals court noted that while the student informant made the tip "face-to-face," claimed that her knowledge was based on a "direct conversation" with the plaintiff, and gave "relatively specific" information, her tip was nevertheless inadequate because there was no concrete evidence of her reliability, and the defendants had failed to make any effort to "investigate, corroborate, or otherwise substantiate [the tip] prior to ordering the strip search." *Id.* at 598.

[38] *Id.* at 19-20.

[39] Fewless *ex rel.* Fewless v. Bd. of Educ. of Wayland, 208 F. Supp. 2d 806 (W.D. Mich. 2002).

[40] Phaneuf v. Fraikin, 448 F. 3d 591 (2d Cir. 2006). Finding that the search, on the basis of the totality of circumstances, did not meet the justified-at-inception test, the appeals court declined to determine whether the search was reasonble in scope. (*Id.* at 601.) On remand, a federal district court granted qualified immunity to the school employees involved in the search on the grounds that the student's rights were not clearly established at the time the strip search was conducted. Phaneuf v. Cipriano, 2007 U.S. Dist. LEXIS 5963 (D. Conn. 2007).

[41] Oliver by Hines v. McClung, 919 F. Supp. 1206 (N.D. Ind. 1995). *See also* Bell v. Marseilles Elementary Sch., 160 F. Supp. 2d 883 (N.D. Ill. 2001), in which a school resource officer's strip search of thirty students in a gym class to find missing money violated privacy rights and the officer was not entitled to immunity.

[42] Jenkins v. Talladega City Bd. of Educ., 115 F.3d 821 (11th Cir. 1997). *See also* Thomas *ex rel.* Thomas v. Roberts, 323 F.3d 950 (11th Cir. 2003), in which strip searches of male fifth-grade students to locate the sum of $26 missing from a student's desk was ruled unreasonably excessive, but the appeals court affirmed the district court's grant of qualified immunity, insulating school officials from liability. *But see* H.Y. v. Russell Cty. Bd. of Educ., 490 F. Supp. 2d 1174 (E.D. Ala. 2007) in which school officials were not entitled to qualified immunity in a strip search of middle school students to find $12 stolen from a teacher's purse. Konop v. Northwestern Sch. Dist., 26 F. Supp. 2d 1189 (D.S.D. 1998) in which the federal district court found a strip search of female students participating in a gym class was unreasonable in light of the nature of the infraction, which involved locating missing $200 allegedly taken from a student's locker.

[43] Kennedy v. Dexter Consol. Schs., 129 N.M. 436, 10 P.3d 115 (N.M. 2000).

[44] *Id.* at 441, 10 P.2d at 121, *citing* Doe v. Renfrow, 631 F.2d 91, 92-93 (7th Cir. 1980).

[45] *Id.* at 444, 10 P.2d 123.

[46] Landstrom v. Ill. Dep't of Children and Family Servs., 892 F.2d 670 (7th Cir. 1990). *See also* Tenenbaum v. Williams, 193 F.3d 581 (2d Cir. 1999) in which qualified immunity applied to child's removal from school and medical examination for signs of sexual abuse.

[47] Wilson v. Cahokia Sch. Dist., 470 F. Supp. 2d 897, 911-912 (S.D.Ill.2007). The district court also rejected the parent's contention that the school resource officer should be subject to the probable cause standard, determining that a sheriff's deputy serving as a school resource officer is a school employee under the direction of school authorities in the course of investigating a disciplinary infraction.

[48] *Id.* at 912. *See also* Villanueva v. San Marcos Consol. Indep. Sch. Dist., 2007 U.S. LEXIS 17208 (5th Cir. 2007) in which the federal appeals court affirmed a grant of summary judgment to a school nurse and school district after finding that a student's subjective belief that she was required to complete a pregnancy test at school and her unsubstantiated speculation that to refuse to take the test would have resulted in punishment did not constitute competent summary judgment evidence.

[49] Desilets v. Clearview Bd. of Educ., 265 N.J. Super. 370, 627 A.2d 667 (N.J. Super A.D. 1993). *But see* Kuehn v. Renton Sch. Dist., 694 P.2d 1078 (Wash. 1985) in which a blanket policy requiring the search of student luggage before a class trip were unreasonable because there was no individualized suspicion for a search.

[50] Shade v. City of Farmington, Minn., 309 F.3d 1054 (8th Cir. 2002). The court also emphasized that the *T.L.O.* test of reasonable suspicion applies to SROs while in the scope of their duties in the school context.

[51] Rhodes v. Guarricino, 54 F. Supp. 2d 186 (S.D.N.Y. 1999)

[52] *See* Kennedy v. Dexter Consol. Schs., 129 N.M. 436, 10 P.3d 115 (N.M. 2000); Burnham v. West, 681 F. Supp. 1160 (E.D. Va. 1987); and Bellnier v. Lund, 438 F. Supp. 47 (N.D.N.Y. 1977).

[53] Doe v. Little Rock Sch. Dist., 380 F.3d 349 (8th Cir. 2004).

[54] *Id.* at 357.

[55] Dubbs v. Head Start, 336 F.3d 1194 (10th Cir. 2003).

[56] Brousseau v. Town of Westerly, 11 F. Supp. 177 (D.R.I. 1998).

[57] Matter of Haseen N., 251 A.D.2d 505, 674 N.Y.S.2d 700 (App. Div. 1998)

[58] *See, generally,* Bundick v. Bay City Indep. Sch. Dist., 140 F. Supp. 2d 735 (S.D. Tex. 2001) drug detection dog's alert to student's parked car justified search that led to discovery of machete in toolbox; Commonwealth v. Cass, 551 Pa. 25,709 A.2d 350 (Pa. 1998) canine sniffing of student lockers justified by danger of drug use and limited expectation of privacy in school lockers; and State v. Barrett, 683 So. 2d 331 (La. App. 1996) Use of drug detection canine permissible to sniff selected classes consisting of "problem students" given concern for drug use and minimal intrusion on student privacy.

[59] *See, e.g., In re* Latasha W., 60 Cal. App. 4th 1524, 70 Cal.Rptr.2d 886 (Cal. App. 1998) (metal detector used to discover knife); State v. J.A., 679 So. 2d 316 (Fla. D.C.A. 1996) (metal detector followed by pat-down and discovery of a handgun); *In re* S.S., 452 Pa. Super. 15, 680 A.2d

1172 (Pa. Sup. 1996) (boxcutter knife discovered during scan of students and pat down of coat); and People v. Pruitt, 278 Ill. App. 3d 194, 662 N.E.2d 540 (Ill.App.1996) (walk-through detector resulted in pat-down and discovery of handgun).

[60] Jennings v. Joshua Indep. Sch. Dist., 877 F.2d 313 (5th Cir. 1989). *See also* Horton v. Goose Creek Indep. Sch. Dist., 690 F.2d 470 (5th Cir. 1982).

[61] Bundick v. Bay City Indep. Sch. Dist., 140 F. Supp. 2d 735 (S.D. Tex. 2001).

[62] Horton v. Goose Creek Indep. Sch. Dist., 690 F.2d 470, 479 (5th Cir. 1982).

[63] Doe v. Renfrow, 631 F.2d 91 (7th Cir. 1980).

[64] B.C. v. Plumas Unified Sch. Dist., 192 F.3d 1260, 1268 (9th Cir. 1999). In this case, the court granted qualified immunity to the defendants on the basis that it was not clearly established at the time of the searches that the use of dogs to sniff students in a school setting constituted a search.

[65] People v. Duke, 183 A.D.2d 936, 583 N.Y.S.2d 850 (App. Div. 1992).

[66] *In re* Interest of F.B., 555 Pa. 661, 726 A.2d 361 (Pa. 1999). *See* In Interest of S.S., 452 Pa. Super. 15, 680 A.2d 1172 (Pa. Super. 1996) in which a blanket search that included a pat-down of a student's coat was reasonable though not based on individualized suspicion. On entering the school, students placed their coats on a table and were subject to a metal detector scan. In patting down the student's coat, a box cutter was discovered and the student was subject to a juvenile court prosecution. The state court found that the search was reasonable given the uniformity of the search process and documentation of a high rate of violence in area schools. *See also* People v. Pruitt, 278 Ill. App. 3d 194, 662 N.E.2d 540 (Ill. App. 1996) in which a student passing through the metal detector set off the alarm and was subject to a pat-down by a police officer who discovered of a handgun. When the student sought to suppress this evidence in a criminal trial, a state appeals court held that the screening was minimally intrusive since no touching occurred unless the detector alerted, and, once the detector reacted, the facts were sufficient to justify a pat-down.

[67] State v. J.A., 679 So. 2d 316 (Fla. D.C.A. 1996).

[68] Vernonia Sch. Dist. v. Acton, 515 U.S. 646, 115 S. Ct. 2386, 132 L. Ed. 2d 564 (1995).

[69] *Id.*

[70] Board of Educ. of Indep. Sch. Dist. No. 92 v. Earls, 536 U.S. 822, 122 S. Ct. 2559, 153 L. Ed. 2d 735 (2002)

[71] Joy v. Penn-Harris-Madison Sch. Corp., 212 F.3d 1052 (7th Cir. 2000).

[72] *Id.* at 1065. The policy could not be extended to testing for the use of nicotine, as the school district could not demonstrate a sufficient governmental need to justify this intrusion.

[73] Willis by Willis v. Anderson Comm. Sch. Corp., 158 F.3d 415 (7th Cir. 1998), *cert. denied*, 119 S. Ct. 1254, 143 L.Ed.2d 351 (1999). *See also*, Gruenke v. Seip, 225 F.3d 290 (3d Cir. 2000) in which a mandatory pregnancy test required by a high school swimming coach violated the student's right to privacy and her Fourth Amendment rights against unreasonable search and seizure.

[74] *Id.* at 422.

[75] The use of urinalysis testing in a case of reasonable individualized suspicion is illustrated in Hedges v. Musco, 204 F.3d 109 (3d Cir. 2000) in which a student who appeared to be under the influence of drugs was evaluated by a school nurse and, as a consequence, a school requirement that the student submit to a drug test before being readmitted to school was reasonable under all the circumstances.

[76] Tannahill *ex rel.* Tannahill v. Lockney Indep. Sch. Dist., 133 F. Supp. 2d 919 (N.D. Tex. 2001).

[77] *See* Johnson v. City of Lincoln Park, 434 F. Supp. 2d 467 (E.D. Mich. 2006) (student's violent conduct in struggling with police officers justified removal from school setting and charge of assaulting a police officer and resisting arrest) and Valentino v. Sch. Dist. of Phila., 2003 U.S. Dist. LEXIS 1081 (E.D. Pa. 2003) (student removed from classroom and held in police custody following threatening gesture toward an apprentice teacher).

[78] In one unique case, the school district implemented a policy of allowing police interviews with students during school hours and without parental consent. In the course of a police

investigation, a student was subject to four such interviews and a DNA sample was taken during one of the interviews. The federal appeals court granted a motion for summary judgment for the school principal, ruling that his peripheral participation in obtaining the DNA sample did not violate the student's Fourth Amendment rights. Burrelson v. Barnesville Sch. Dist., 434 F. Supp. 2d 588 (W.D. Wis. 2006).

[79] Gorthy v. Clovis Unified Sch. Dist., 2006 U.S. Dist. LEXIS 6271 at 3 (E.D. Cal. 2006).

[80] 883 F.2d 884 (10th Cir. 1989).

[81] *See* Shuman v. Penn Manor Sch. Dist., 422 F.3d 141, 148-149 (3d Cir. 2005); Doe v. Haw. Dep't of Educ., 334 F.3d 906, 908 (9th Cir. 2003); and Hassan v. Lubbock Indep. Sch. Dist., 55 F.3d 1075, 1079 (5th Cir. 1995).

[82] 2007 U.S. Dist. LEXIS 23199 (W.D.N.Y. 2007).

[83] *Id.*

[84] *But see* Howard v. Yakovac, 2006 U.S. LEXIS 27253 (D. Idaho, 2006) in which a principal agreed to allow a parent, who was also a local magistrate, to question individual students about a flyer implicating his daughter in sexual activities. The district court found there were genuine issues of material fact regarding whether Fourth Amendment rights were violated by the interviews since it was not clear that students knew they were free to leave if they did not want to answer questions, the evidence suggested that the parent threatened prosecution of at least one of the students, and some of the questions may have been beyond the scope of the school's interest or authority.

[85] Gray v. Bostic, 458 F.3d 1295 (11thCir. 2006).

Chapter 5

Student Records

John S. Gooden

Introduction

In an effort to protect the rights and privacy of students' educational records, Congress enacted the Family Education Rights and Privacy Act (FERPA)[1] in 1974. FERPA, sometimes referred to as the "Buckley Amendment," was signed into law by President Gerald Ford on August 21, 1974, and has since been amended nine times. Congress used its enumerated authority to provide for the general welfare under the General Welfare Clause of the U.S. Constitution when enacting the act. FERPA is a "spending clause statute," which means that public and private educational institutions or agencies who receive federal dollars must implement policies outlined in the act. If a state education agency (SEA) or local education agency (LEA) does not follow FERPA policies, it can lose federal dollars. According to the statute, the U.S. Department of Education has the authority to terminate federal financial assistance to those who fail to comply with the act.[2]

FERPA requires schools to protect the privacy and confidentiality of personally identifiable information by giving parents some discretion over the educational records of their minor children. The act gives parents the right to access their children's records, inspect and review them, challenge their accuracy, and have incorrect or erroneous information removed or amended.[3] Parents are also afforded some discretion over what personally identifiable information is disclosed in records.[4]

When a student reaches eighteen years old or enrolls in a postsecondary school at any age (eligible student), FERPA rights are transferred from the parents to the student.[5] Although the rights are transferred to the eligible student, the school may still disclose the student's educational records if the student is claimed as a dependent for income tax purposes.[6] If the student is not a dependent, consent must be given for the parents to access the student's records. If the student is enrolled in both a high school and postsecondary school, the two schools may exchange information about the student. If a student is under eighteen years old, the high school may share any information received from the postsecondary institution with parents because they retain their FERPA rights at the high school. However, the parents do not have the same rights at the postsecondary institution unless the eligible student is a dependent for tax purposes[7] or the student gives parents permission to access his or her educational records.

Legal Issues

Definitions

Educational Records. FERPA defines educational records as any record maintained by an institution or a party representing the institution that will personally identify an individual student.[8] Placement documents, progress reports, financial aid information, and cumulative academic records are just some examples of records normally maintained by schools that include information considered confidential. If released, a violation of a student's privacy would occur. These documents or files may be digital, handwritten, print, tapes, disks, film, microfilm, or microfiche.[9] Transcripts and other records obtained from schools in which the student was enrolled are also covered under FERPA.[10] However, to release these records, the school must have written permission from the parents or eligible student.

Under FERPA, an education record does not cover sole possession notes made by school officials or teachers that are in the exclusive possession of the individual and will not be shared with others. It excludes records created and maintained by a law enforcement unit of a school or district for law enforcement purposes. The law does not cover the medical records that are created, maintained, or used in the treatment of an eligible student who is eighteen years old by a physician, psychiatrist, psychologist, or other recognized professional or paraprofessional acting in his or her professional capacity.[11] The law also indicates that FERPA does not pertain to information concerning a student who is no longer with the institution or agency.[12]

In 2002, the United States Supreme Court was asked to determine whether peer grading was a violation of FERPA. Peer grading is when the teacher allows students to score each other's quizzes, tests, or other assignments while the teacher is reviewing the correct answers with the entire class. The Court upheld the practice by concluding that peer-graded assignments are not an education record covered under FERPA until the teacher has collected them and recorded them in his or her grade book. The Court concluded that although parents may contest the accuracy of their child's record under FERPA, Congress would never have established such a complex system so that parents would be able to challenge grades on spelling tests or art projects.[13]

Directory Information. Information that is not harmful or an invasion of privacy and may be disclosed without the permission of the parent or eligible student is known as directory information.[14] It includes the student's name, address, telephone number, email address, photograph, date and place of birth, major field of study, participation in officially recognized activities and sports, weight and height of members of athletic teams, dates of attendance, grade level, and enrollment status.[15] It may also include honors and awards received and the most recent educational agency or institution attended.[16] According to FERPA, dates of attendance include the overall time that a student attends a school, such as academic years or semesters. However, it does not include the student's daily attendance records.

The educational institution or agency making directory information available to the public must give public notice of the categories of information that have been designated.[17] It must also allow a reasonable period after such notice is given for parents to notify the institution or agency in writing that any or all of the information designated should not be released.[18] If an institution does not define the scope of the directory information, give public notice, or seek parental consent as required by FERPA, it is not permitted to release the information.[19] School districts must give parents or eligible students the opportunity to prevent the release of directory information. This is an important feature of FERPA because schools may release directory information in yearbooks, honor roll and other recognition lists, graduation programs, playbills, and athletic information (e.g., height and weight). The reader is cautioned to check applicable state laws that may contain a different definition of what constitutes directory information in that state.

Under no circumstance may an agency or institution release directory information that includes social security numbers; student identification numbers; the nationality, race, or ethnicity of the student; gender; transcripts; grade point average; or grade reports. This information must not be released to anyone without prior written consent of the parents or eligible student. School officials, faculty, and staff can access this information only if they have a legitimate need.

Personally identifiable information. This information includes, but is not limited to, directory information, the name of the student's parents or other family members, a social security number or student number, or a list of personal characteristics that would make the student's identity easily traceable.[20] Disclosure of standardized test scores in a scrambled order with the name of students deleted would suffice to safeguard the privacy of the student. If an education record of a student contains information on more than one student, the parent or eligible student may inspect and review or be informed of only the specific information about that student.[21]

Parent means a natural parent, a guardian, or a person acting as a parent in the absence of a parent or guardian.[22] Thus, foster parents who are acting as a child's parent would have the rights afforded natural parents under FERPA with respect to the child's education records.

Disclosure means to permit access to or the release, transfer, or other communication of personally identifiable information contained in an education record to any party, by any means, including oral, written, or electronic means.[23]

Implications

Under FERPA, prior written consent is not required to release information to other school officials who have "legitimate educational interests," or to officials of another school or school system that the student seeks or intends to enroll. However, notification of the transfer to parents is required, and they must receive a copy of the record if desired and have an opportunity to challenge the records' contents. Written consent is also not necessary when providing educational records to federal, state, and local education authorities for the purpose of an educational program audit, evaluation, or compliance. Officials processing student financial aid, institutions involved in organizing and conducting studies and improving instruction, and accrediting organizations are not required to have written consent as long as personally identifiable information is not disclosed. Also, officials complying with a judicial order or a Federal Grand Jury subpoena or proceeding are not required to have written consent. Those officials requiring access to educational records for law enforcement purposes and in judicial proceedings in cases when a school institutes legal action involving the parent or student do not need written consent. This is true even if the school has been ordered not to disclose the existence of the records. Finally, written consent is not necessary when appropriate individuals are dealing with an emergency and the release of information is necessary to protect the health or safety of the student or others or when state and local authorities need information that is specifically allowed to be reported by state statute.

FERPA normally would not apply to records of an SEA. However, the statute does give parents the right to inspect and review education records maintained by the SEA pertaining to their children, for instance, state assessments administered by LEAs and maintained by the SEA. The educational records must be made available to the parent by the SEA, or the SEA may send them to the LEA for inspection and review by the parent within forty-five days of the receipt of the request.[24]

Personal information can only be released to a third party under the express condition that the information will not be disclosed to anyone else without the written consent of the student or parent.[25] Two federal laws require LEAs receiving assistance under the Elementary and Secondary Education Act of 1965 (ESEA) to provide directory information upon request to military recruiters in the following three categories: names, addresses, and telephone listings. An eligible student or parent may request that the information not be disseminated unless with prior written permission, and the school or agency must comply with the request.[26] These statutes also indicate that schools provide military recruiters the same access to secondary students that is generally given to postsecondary institutions and prospective employers.[27]

Each institution must maintain a record that indicates all individuals who have requested and/or obtained access to students' education records and the specific legitimate interest for requesting the information.[28] This record of access is available only to parents or eligible students, school officials, records custodians, and those authorized by law.[29] The record of disclosures and requests must be kept as long as the institution retains the record.[30]

Access by Noncustodial Parents

Because FERPA does not distinguish between custodial and noncustodial parents, an educational agency or institution must give full rights to either parent. However, if the agency or institution has been provided with evidence that there is a court order, state statute, or legally binding document relating to a divorce, separation, or custody that specifically revokes these rights, information cannot be disclosed to the noncustodial parent.[31] A signed statement alone by one parent will not serve to bar the other parent from access to student records.[32]

Access to information by noncustodial or joint custody parents with whom a child is not living during the school year often presents a challenge for schools, particularly if that information must be mailed to each parent. FERPA permits a school to "charge a fee for a copy of an education record which is made for the parent or eligible student," unless the imposition of the fee effectively prevents a parent or eligible student from inspecting the record.[33] A noncustodial parent may be placed on a school's mailing list and receive the same information that is mailed to the custodial parent.[34] The custodial and/or noncustodial parent may be charged a fee for actual expenses incurred by the school for providing such records.[35]

Special Education Students

State education agencies and institutions must afford special education students the same privacy rights as other students.[36] Addressing the confidentiality of special education students presents a different challenge for school officials because the Individuals with Disabilities Education Act (IDEA) has its own requirements concerning the disclosure of student information. Parents must consent to the disclosure of student information and be notified when personally identifiable information "is no longer needed to provide educational services to the child." The same exceptions to parental consent apply if the information is disclosed to "other school officials who have legitimate educational interests."[37] Thus, IDEA issues of access to student information are not significantly different from those encountered under FERPA generally—i.e. both accommodate the desire to prevent the student from being "stigmatized and humiliated if sensitive information in the record is made public."[38] Documents used in the placement of children with disabilities in specialized classes are considered personally identifiable records, thus prohibiting release of such records except by subpoena or with prior parental release.[39]

Health and Safety Emergency

The secretary of education has not issued definitive regulations specifying what constitutes a "health or safety emergency."[40] There must be a need for the information to protect the health or safety of the student or other persons.[41] Therefore, great caution should be used when an emergency is declared. Educational records may only be shared with parties who need the information to avert the emergency, i.e. those with legitimate purposes for the information.[42] Some examples of such incidents may include on-campus disruptions involving criminal acts, especially those involving controlled substances or weapons, or off-campus situations that affect campus or public safety.

Law Enforcement and Homeland Security Exceptions

FERPA specifically exempts from the definition of "education records" those records that a law enforcement unit of a school or school district creates and maintains for a law enforcement purpose.[43] FERPA defines a law enforcement unit as "an individual, office, department, [or] component" of a school or school district that is officially authorized or designated by the school district to enforce federal, state, or local law or that maintains the physical safety and security of the school district.[44] Nothing in FERPA prohibits an educational agency or institution from contacting its law enforcement unit, orally or in writing, to investigate a possible violation of or to enforce state, local, or federal laws.[45]

FERPA allows an exchange between schools of information in a student's education record concerning disciplinary action taken against a student for conduct that posed a "significant risk to the safety or well-being of the student, other students, or other members of the school community."[46] Under FERPA, schools may disclose such information to teachers and school officials, including those in other schools, who have legitimate educational interests in the behavior of the student.[47] The regulations give individual schools the discretion to determine the circumstances that are appropriate to disclose information.

State law may grant public access to law enforcement records; however, FERPA does not require nor prohibit the disclosure by any educational agency or institution of its law enforcement unit records.[48] Schools may receive and use information from law enforcement, courts, and other justice agencies in order to maintain a safe learning environment. Once information is received and maintained by the school, it becomes subject to FERPA and any applicable exceptions.[49] Education records in an attorney's file relating to a student's juvenile proceedings may also be deemed education records.[50]

State law may authorize an administrator to share education records with juvenile justice authorities in order to help at-risk students; those involved with the juvenile justice system; or those students who have been apprehended for a crime, but who have not yet been adjudicated a delinquent.[51] The juvenile justice agency must agree in writing not to disclose the records to anyone other than a juvenile justice agency official.[52] The disclosure should relate to the juvenile justice system's ability to serve the minor prior to an adjudication of delinquency.[53]

After the 2001 terrorist attacks, Congress amended FERPA to permit the release of student records for homeland security purposes.[54] This provision allows the U.S. Attorney General or a designee to seek an ex parte court order requiring an educational agency or institution to permit the attorney general to collect, retain, disseminate, and use the educational records for the investigation or prosecution of terrorist acts.[55]

When applying for a court order, the attorney general is required to "certify that there are specific and articulable facts" suggesting the educational records are likely to contain information related to terrorist acts.[56] If the court finds such certification, it is required to issue the order.[57] An educational agency or institution that is subject to a court order to produce education records is not required to maintain a record of the request for, or release of, the records.[58] An agency or institution that in good faith produces education records pursuant to a court order also "shall not be liable to any person for that production."[59]

Challenging Records' Accuracy

FERPA provides a right on the part of the eligible student or parents to inspect and review the student's education record, to challenge the accuracy of the information contained within, and to prevent the dissemination of the record in certain instances. Requests for access to education records must be granted within a reasonable period.[60] They have the right to request that records that are inaccurate, misleading, or in violation of their privacy rights be corrected. Parents or legal guardians of students may establish their right to review an eligible student's records provided the parents or guardians can document the student's dependency as defined by the Internal Revenue Code.

The remedy that the statute provides is that the parents or eligible student may request that the institution amend the record. Once the parent or eligible student has made the request, the district must respond within a reasonable period, but in no case more than forty-five days. If the institution agrees to amend the record, nothing further needs to be done. If the institution refuses, the parents or eligible student must be notified of their right to a hearing on the matter.[61] The educational institution or agency must provide notice of the date, time, and place in reasonable advance of the hearing.[62] Then the hearing, if requested, must take place within a reasonable time.[63]

The hearing may be conducted by any person, including an official of the institution who does not have a direct interest in the outcome.[64] The parents or eligible students must be given an opportunity to present all evidence relevant to the issues and may be assisted or represented by an individual at his or her own expense, including an attorney.[65] The final decision as to whether to amend or delete the material at issue belongs to the institution. The decision must be made based upon evidence presented at the hearing and must include a written summary of the evidence and reasons for the decision.[66] If the parent or eligible student still disagrees with the institution, he or she may put a statement to that effect in the education record.[67] This statement of dispute must be kept in the education record as long as it is retained.[68]

Enforcement of FERPA

Enforcement of FERPA is the responsibility of the Family Policy Compliance Office of the U.S. Department of Education. The office provides assistance on FERPA to education agencies and institutions, state and local officials, parents, and eligible students. The office also investigates alleged violations of the law.[69] Parents and eligible students have the right to file a written complaint with the U.S. Department of Education concerning an alleged failure to comply with the requirements of FERPA.[70] A written complaint alleging specific violations of the act must be filed within 180 days of the date of the alleged violation, absent good cause.[71] The office then notifies the parent and the educational agency of its decision to begin an investigation of the complaint.[72] The notice to the educational agency includes the substance of the alleged violation and asks the agency to submit a written response to the complaint.[73] The complainant will also be notified when the office does not initiate an investigation if a complaint fails to meet certain requirements.[74]

After an investigation of the complaint, the office will provide the educational agency and the complainant written notice of its findings, which will include the basis for reaching its conclusion.[75] If the educational agency has not complied with FERPA, the office will include a statement of the specific steps that must be taken for the institution to comply and must allow a reasonable time for compliance.[76] If the institution or educational agency does not comply either voluntarily or within a reasonable time, the secretary may withhold further payments, issue a cease and desist order, or terminate eligibility to receive funding under any applicable program.[77]

Protection of Pupil Rights Amendment

Like FERPA, the Protection of Pupil Rights Amendment (PPRA) applies to programs that receive funding from the U.S. Department of Education. The law was enacted to make certain that schools and contractors give parents the opportunity to inspect instructional materials that are used in conjunction with Department of Education funded surveys, analysis, or evaluations in which their children are participants. It was also designed to ensure that schools and contractors obtain parental consent before minor children are required to participate in any Department of Education funded survey, analysis, or evaluation that reveals information concerning the following: political affiliations; mental and psychological problems potentially embarrassing to the student and his or her family; sex behavior and attitudes; illegal, anti-social, self-incriminating, and demeaning behavior; critical appraisals of other individuals with whom respondents have close family relationships; legally recognized privileged or analogous relationships, such as those with lawyers, physicians, and ministers; or income (other than that required by law to determine eligibility for participation in a program or for receiving financial assistance under such a program).[78]

Under PPRA, parents must receive notice and be given an opportunity to opt their children out of any protected information survey, regardless of the funding, or activities involving collection, disclosure, or use of personal information obtained from students for marketing purposes to sell or distribute to others. They must also be given the opportunity to opt-out of any non-emergency, invasive physical examination or screening required as a condition of attendance that is administered by the school or its agent, if it is not to protect the immediate health and safety of the student or others. The exception is those instances when it is required by state law or for any routine physical examinations and hearing, vision, or scoliosis screenings.

Parents should be afforded the opportunity to inspect before the administration, or use, of protected information surveys; instruments used to collect personal information from students for marketing, sales, or other distribution purposes; and instructional material used as part of the education curriculum. Like FERPA, the rights of parents transfer to a student who is eighteen years old or who is an emancipated minor under state law.

Recommendations for Practice

1. FERPA and PPRA may supersede state law where federal and state law conflict. Laws vary by state. The laws of some states specify what will be considered directory information. It is important to look at the state's open records and freedom of information laws for additional guidance. School officials may also find protection from liability when acting pursuant to state law.
2. FERPA no longer imposes a requirement that schools have a student records policy at all. Nevertheless, it is highly recommended that you maintain a student records policy. Instead of requiring a local policy, the regulations now require that you provide an annual notice to parents and students.
3. Educational institutions are required to advise parents of their rights under the federal law and regulations to inspect student records. Eligible students and parents must be notified annually of the categories of personally identifiable information that the institution has designated as directory information and will release without written consent. The notice must also inform parents and students of their right to refuse to permit the disclosure of directory information from their files and the time period for submitting a written statement refusing to allow the release of directory information.

4. The annual notice must contain the foregoing information and should set forth the procedures for exercising the right to inspect and review education records and for requesting an amendment of student records. The notice must state whether you have a policy of disclosing student records to other school officials within your district. If so, the notice must list your criteria for deciding who is a school official and what constitutes a legitimate educational interest that permits such officials to review student records.
5. Administrators are required to transmit annual FERPA and PPRA notices to disabled persons and parents who have a primary or home language other than English in an "effective way." This may mean the use of alternate formats for the annual notice, such as audiotape, Braille, computer diskette, large-print documents, or information written in their native language.
6. In light of the technology revolution, the use of computerized record keeping is ever increasing. These data will replace most paper documents. Keep in mind, however, that the same principle of confidentiality must be applied to electronic data as to paper documents.
7. Many records will contain information about more than one student. A requesting parent, however, is entitled to see information relating to only his or her child. In this situation, redaction of information about other students must be done by the school district prior to making the documents available to a parent. Copying techniques or blackening of information can be used to accomplish this objective.
8. The school system's records custodian must be aware that custodial and noncustodial parents have equal rights of access to their child's records, absent a court order limiting those rights. A parent who asserts a desire to limit records access to the other parent should be informed that the school district is unable to do so unless the parent produces a valid court order so specifying.
9. School districts are urged to develop comprehensive student records policies to provide guidance to parents and to school personnel. Such policies may be developed with guidance from the district's legal counsel.

Endnotes

1 The FERPA statute is 20 U.S.C. 1232g, and the subsequent regulations are: 34 CRF Part 99.
2 20 U.S.C. § 1232g.
3 20 U.S.C. § 1232g (a)(1)(A); 34 C.F.R. § 99.7.
4 20 U.S.C. § 1232g(a)(2); 34 C.F.R. § 99.7.
5 20 U.S.C. § 1232g(d).
6 34 C.F.R. § 99.31(a)(8).
7 *Id.*

[8] 20 U.S.C. § 1232g(a)(4)(B); 34 C.F.R. § 99.3(a).
[9] 20 U.S.C. § 1232g; 34 C.F.R. § 99.3.
[10] 20 U.S.C. § 1232g(a)(4).
[11] 20 U.S.C. § 1232g(a)(4)(B); 34 C.F.R. § 99.3.
[12] 20 U.S.C. § 1232g(a)(4); 34 C.F.R. § 99.3.
[13] Owasso Indep. Sch. Dist. No. I-011 v. Falvo, U.S. 2002; 122 S. Ct. 934; 534 U.S. 426; 151 L.Ed.2d 896.
[14] 20 U.S.C. § 1232g(a)(5)(A); 34 C.F.R. § 99.3.
[15] *Id.*
[16] *Id.*
[17] 20 U.S.C. § 1232g(a)(5)(B).
[18] *Id.*
[19] Brent v. Paquette, 567 A.2d 976 (N.H. 1989).
[20] 20 U.S.C. § 1232g; 34 C.F.R. § 99.3.
[21] 20 U.S.C. § 1232g(a)(1)(A); 34 C.F.R. § 99.12(a)
[22] 20 U.S.C. § 1232g; 34 C.F.R. § 99.3.
[23] 20 U.S.C. § 1232g(b)(1); 34 C.F.R. § 99.3.
[24] 20 U.S.C. § 1232g(a)(1)(A); 34 C.F.R. § 99.10.
[25] 20 U.S.C. § 1232g(b)(1).
[26] 20 U.S.C. § 7908; 10 U.S.C. 544.
[27] 20 U.S.C. § 7908.
[28] 20 U.S.C. § 1232g(b)(4)(A); 34 C.F.R. § 99.32.
[29] *Id.*
[30] *Id.*
[31] 20 U.S.C. § 1232g; 34 C.F.R. § 99.4.
[32] Page v. Rotterdam-Mohansen Cent. Sch. Dist., 441 N.Y.S.2d 323 (1981).
[33] 20 U.S.C. § 1232g(a)(1); 34 C.F.R. § 99.11.
[34] Fay v. S. Colonie Cent. Sch. Dist., 802 F.2d 21 (2d Cir. 1986).
[35] *Id.*
[36] 34 C.F.R. §§ 300.560–577 (contain requirements regarding the confidentiality of information relating to handicapped children who receive benefits under the IDEA).
[37] *See* M.R. by R.R. v. Lincolnwood Bd. of Educ. Dist. 74, 843 F. Supp. 1236 (N.D. Ill. 1994), *reconsideration denied, aff'd* 56 F.3d 67, *rehearing denied.*
[38] Webster Groves Sch. Dist. v. Pulitzer Publ'g Co., 898 F.2d 1371, 1375 (8th Cir. 1990).
[39] Mattie T. v. Johnston, 74 F.R.D. 498 (N.D. Miss. 1976).
[40] 20 U.S.C. § 1232g(b)(1)(I); 34 C.F.R. § 99.36.
[41] *Id.*
[42] 20 U.S.C. § 1232g(b)(1)(A); 34 C.F.R. § 99.36(b)(3).
[43] 20 U.S.C. § 1232g(a)(4)(B)(ii); 34 C.F.R. § 99.8.
[44] 20 U.S.C. § 1232g(a)(4)(B)(ii); 34 C.F.R. § 99.8.
[45] 20 U.S.C. § 1232g(a)(4)(B)(ii); 34 C.F.R. § 99.8(c)(1).
[46] 20 U.S.C. § 1232g(h)(1).
[47] 20 U.S.C. § 1232g(h)(2).
[48] 34 C.F.R. § 99.8(d).
[49] 34 C.F.R. § 99.8(c)(2).
[50] Belanger v. Nashua, N.H. Sch. Dist., 856 F. Supp. 40 (D.N.H. 1994).
[51] 20 U.S.C. § 1232g(b)(1)(J); 34 C.F.R. § 99.38.
[52] *Id.*
[53] *Id.*
[54] 20 U.S.C. § 1232g(j).
[55] 20 U.S.C. § 1232g(j)(1).
[56] 20 U.S.C. § 1232g(j)(2)(A).
[57] 20 U.S.C. § 1232g(j)(2)(B).
[58] 20 U.S.C. § 1232g(j)(4).

[59] 20 U.S.C. § 1232g(j)(3).
[60] 20 U.S.C. § 1232g(a)(1)(A).
[61] 20 U.S.C. § 1232g(a)(2); 34 C.F.R. § 99.21.
[62] 20 U.S.C. § 1232g(a)(2); 34 C.F.R. § 99.22(b).
[63] 20 U.S.C. § 1232g(a)(2); 34 C.F.R. § 99.22(a).
[64] 20 U.S.C. § 1232g(a)(2); 34 C.F.R. § 99.22(c).
[65] 20 U.S.C. § 1232g(a)(2); 34 C.F.R. § 99.22(d).
[66] 20 U.S.C. § 1232g(a)(2); 34 C.F.R. § 99.22(f).
[67] 20 U.S.C. § 1232g(a)(2); 34 C.F.R. § 99.21(b)(2).
[68] 20 U.S.C. § 1232g(a)(2); 34 C.F.R. § 99.21(c).
[69] 20 U.S.C. § 1232g(f); 34 C.F.R. § 99.63.
[70] 20 U.S.C. § 1232g(g); 34 C.F.R. § 99.63.
[71] 20 U.S.C. § 1232g(g); 34 C.F.R. § 99.64.
[72] 20 U.S.C. § 1232g(g); 34 C.F.R. § 99.65.
[73] *Id.*
[74] 20 U.S.C. § 1232g(g); 34 C.F.R. § 99.65.
[75] *Id.*
[76] 20 U.S.C. § 1232g(f); 34 C.F.R. § 99.67(a).
[77] Ohio Rev. Code § 3319.321.
[78] 20 U.S.C. § 1232h.

Chapter 6

Promotion, Retention, and Graduation

Patrick Pauken

Introduction

A discussion of the legal issues surrounding promotion, retention, and graduation of students is deceptively easy. One may think that decisions to promote or retain students are primarily curricular, left to the teachers and administrators, and rarely challenged legally. One may think that the criteria, activities, and events surrounding graduation and commencement are so established and time-honored that due deference is offered to school boards without question. Much of this is true; state and local policies for promotion, retention, and graduation have not seen too much litigation over the years, and the decisions of school leaders in these areas have been afforded great judicial deference, even in light of the accountability movement and high-stakes testing of children. Nevertheless, discussion of the legal issues surrounding these topics is difficult. All areas of the legal work of school principals and other educational leaders draw their energy from a wide variety of local, state, and federal laws and regulations, and promotion, retention, and graduation is no exception. But the law of promotion, retention, and graduation in schools has few long-standing guiding principles. Mostly, this discussion consists of several loosely connected judicial statements and local statutes and regulations that vary slightly from state to state. Many of the issues that arise here can also be discussed in the contexts of the other chapters in this book. For purposes of this chapter, however, some attention will be paid to policies made and challenged at the building and district levels, as well as policies and practices made and challenged at the state and/or federal level, such as legislation governing high-stakes testing, academic credits and courses needed for the receipt of a diploma, community service requirements, rules and regulations regarding commencement ceremonies, due process rights to earn a diploma and participate in commencement, the effects of disciplinary penalties on receipt of credits and diplomas, and special considerations given to children with disabilities.

Legal Issues

Promotion and Retention

Promotion and retention policies are directed by state statutes and regulations and developed by boards of education. State departments of education are obligated to formulate and prescribe minimum promotion standards for elementary and secondary schools, and in compliance, schools and school districts are required to adopt promotion and retention policies for their students.[1] Despite the judicial deference paid to the decisions of school administrators, state statutory and regulatory provisions may direct promotion and retention decisions when certain factors are present or not present. This direction may be for the entire curriculum, or it may be for an individual student. For example, in Ohio, each school and school district must include at least one year's study of American history as a requirement for promotion from eighth grade to ninth grade.[2] Promotion factors affecting individual students include passage of courses, accumulation of sufficient credits or units, excessive truancy,[3] and passage of standardized tests.

Judicial and Legislative Deference to Promotion and Retention Decisions and the Rational Basis Standard

In the United States, the conventional norm in grade-level placements and promotion is to enroll and educate children in grades K-12. As stated by the New York Supreme Court:

> After a child is admitted to a public school, the board of education has the power to provide rules and regulations for promotion from grade to grade, based not on age, but on training, knowledge, and ability.[4]

The first questions that arise with promotion and retention often arise with the initial admission to school. Initial admission to school is guided by compulsory attendance, the birth date of the child, and the local policies governed by the school district and state. Courts are hesitant to interfere in these decisions, as they do not typically implicate constitutional due process or equal protection rights. Some state statutes have built-in case-by-case flexibility on the required birth date for initial admission. If a state has such flexibility built in to its statutes, school districts are advised to abide.[5]

As is the theme for much of this chapter, there is great legal deference afforded the academic decisions of school teachers and administrators when it comes to promotion and retention. Naturally, promotion and retention decisions are difficult to make and must be handled with great care. Much of the philosophical debate over the goodness of promotion and retention is beyond the scope of this chapter. But suffice it to say, the debate is a heated one, with very few arguments falling in the middle of the road. Despite the controversial nature of promotion and retention decisions, the legal rule of thumb is a confident one: as long as promotion and retention decisions are made with solid evidence of academic progress and social growth, made consistently with established policies, practices, and state regulations, and made with some rational basis, the courts will not intervene.[6] The rational basis standard for promotion and retention decisions is, effectively, the standard governed by the Equal Protection Clause, where state actors must justify the classifications they make in order to continue the practice.[7] In support of a school district's decision to retain students, the court in *Sandlin v. Johnson* stated:

> Defendants [school administrators] here classified plaintiffs [students] according to their attained reading level. The stated purpose for the classification was to enable the school to provide students with the level of instruction most appropriate to their abilities and needs. The objective was to further the education, the preparation for life of the plaintiffs. The governmental end is a permissible one, and defendants' classification is clearly related to achieving it.[8]

For the related due process claim, courts have held that there is no property or liberty interest in promotion to the next grade.[9]

On the deference to the decisions of educators, the *Sandlin* court made the following comments:

> Decisions by educational authorities which turn on evaluation of the academic performance of a student as it relates to promotion are peculiarly within the expertise of educators and are particularly inappropriate for review in a judicial context.[10]

A more recent example provides evidence of the long-lasting power of these standards. In *Erik V. v. Causby*, the parents of several students challenged the retention policy in the Johnston County Schools wherein students in grades 3-8 who fail one or more of the statewide standardized exams will be retained, with only one retention possible during those years.[11] The court rejected the parents' due process, equal protection, and Title VI claims and their motion for an injunction with some powerful statements on deference to school policy making:

> The most severe consequence [of an injunction to the defendants] would be the effect of having a carefully engineered promotion/retention policy superseded by a federal court, outweighing the policy decisions made by an elected school board in a deliberative process. The administrators and teachers would also suffer a lapse of credibility from the sudden overturning of a policy they have been enforcing in their classrooms, as well as from the disruptive effect of having students deemed unready for promotion being mixed in with others ready for the challenges of a new grade.[12]

Similar legally to the decisions to retain students in the same grade for another year and to promote students one grade level are the decisions and/or requests to promote a student more than one grade level. In other words, if the school district can articulate a reasonable justification for either granting or denying a parent's request to promote a student more than one grade level—or to permit a student to join an accelerated program—then courts will not intervene.[13]

Contrary to the deference courts show to promotion and retention decisions, at least one case shows that a decision to demote a student is cause for some judicial intervention.[14] This, however, may be due to the circumstances of the demotion and may not give rise to a rule of thumb. In *Gant v. Wallingford Board of Education*, a student entered his public school's first-grade class during winter but was in that placement only three days before his teacher told his parents that he was not ready for first-grade work and would be demoted to kindergarten. In vacating and remanding the case, the court of appeals asserted that there were substantive and qualitative differences between kindergarten and first grade. "In the absence of a record on this subject, we have no difficulty accepting the idea that a student who has already mastered kindergarten will learn less by repeating it than by being promoted to the next grade."[15] According to the court, demotion in this case could cause permanent delays in meeting ultimate educational goals.

Denial of Academic Credit in Discipline

It is widely known that students have protected property and liberty rights in their public education.[16] And for discipline purposes, particularly suspensions and expulsions, school districts may not deprive students of these rights without due process of law, usually in the form of written notice and an opportunity for a hearing. It is also widely known and practiced that students who are suspended or expelled from school do not typically have the opportunity to make up missed schoolwork. This policy and practice are generally recognized as part of the penalty associated with the exclusion. But schools should be careful not to abuse their discretion in this regard. *South Gibson School Board v. Sollman* provides the example.[17] On December 17, 1998, three days before the first semester of the school year ended, high school student Trent Sollman was suspended and later expelled after school officials found marijuana in the glove box in his car. The search was precipitated by a drug dog sweep of the school's parking lot. Trent's suspension began on December 17. He did not complete any assignments or exams that remained that semester. At the expulsion hearing in January of 1999, the examiner voted to expel Trent for the remainder of the first semester, all of the second semester, and summer school. Trent was permitted to return in the fall of 1999 but was denied all credit earned during the fall semester in which the search occurred. The board of education upheld the expulsion. However, the trial court struck down the expulsion, and the court of appeals affirmed. The court found that the denial of academic credit for Trent's first semester courses was arbitrary and capricious. Generally, loss of credit is to be expected when a student is expelled for an entire semester (or nearly all of a semester). But in this case, Trent was expelled with only three days left in the first semester. "Under these circumstances, we discern no reasonable basis for requiring that Trent forfeit all first semester credit merely because he was expelled during that semester. Such a loss of credit would be reasonable only under circumstances where expulsion causes the student to miss so much coursework that an award of credit would be impossible."[18]

A more recent case illustrates a similar deference principle to promotion decisions, but the court held in favor of the school district, albeit reluctantly.[19] In *B.W.S. v. Livingston Parish School Board*, an eighth-grade student was expelled for a year. The expulsion was imposed in November of her eighth-grade year. The school offered no educational alternative during the year; meanwhile, the parents educated their daughter at home, and she passed the state's proficiency exam required under law for promotion to the ninth grade. The following August, the parents requested an evaluation to have their daughter placed in the ninth grade. The school denied the request and the ninth-grade placement because the expulsion had not yet expired. The parents filed for an injunction to order the school to promote the student to ninth grade. After protracted litigation that lasted almost the entire school year, the state court of appeals denied the parent's motion. The court offered a few reasons. First, the court has no jurisdiction to review a school's promotion and placement decision. Second, while the decision not to place the student in ninth grade appeared arbitrary, the remedy of ordering the placement was not viable in that the school year was almost over.[20]

Promotion and Retention: High-Stakes Accountability Testing

Several states have enacted laws requiring students to pass certain exams, usually in reading and/or math, before promotion to certain grades. The Ohio General Assembly, for example, enacted the "fourth grade guarantee," which mandates, subject to a couple exceptions, that schools retain any third graders who do not reach a certain level on a statewide standardized reading test. The school may promote a student who has failed the exam only if the student's principal and teachers feel he or she is academically prepared for fourth-grade work, or if the student is provided with intensive interventions while in the fourth grade.[21] See also the discussion of *Erik V. v. Causby*, presented above, in which the court denied a parent's motion to enjoin the use of high-stakes promotion exams. Despite the presentation of social science research arguing otherwise, the court held that the students who fail the exams and are then subject to retention would not suffer irreparable harm without the injunction. Under the policy, students who are retained are given remedial attention and an opportunity to learn material in advance of moving on to higher grades.

Promotion and Retention: Students with Disabilities

Readers of this handbook are encouraged to consult the chapters on special education law for full discussions of free appropriate public education (FAPE), individualized education programs (IEPs), least restrictive environment (LRE), and their impact on the education of children. In this chapter, much of the discussion of the legal issues surrounding promotion, retention, graduation, and children with disabilities is presented in the sections on graduation. But with respect to promotion and retention, it must be mentioned that students with disabilities are, for lack of a better phrase, expected to live under two sets of rules: one for standardization (credits toward graduation, state curriculum benchmarks and required subject matter, state and local standardized examinations) and one for individualization (a FAPE in the LRE, governed by special education services, related services, goals and objectives in an IEP). Therefore, promotion decisions may be based on whether the student meets *all* of the requirements of both sets.[22] In addition to the substantive and procedural decisions required under the Individuals with Disabilities Education Act (IDEA), school administrators are also advised to be careful not to make discriminatory retention decisions based solely on the student's disability. For example, despite outstanding grades and acceptance into the state's prestigious Regents program for eighth graders, a seventh-grade student who had missed several weeks of school due to a serous illness was retained in the seventh grade for another year. As a result of the illness, the student completed the remainder of her seventh-grade year as a homeschooled student. The public school system refused to accept the grade report from the homeschool instructor, despite the student's acceptance into the Regents program. The district court dismissed all of the student's legal claims, but the Court of Appeals for the Second Circuit reversed and held that there were viable claims under Section 504 of the Rehabilitation Act, the Americans with Disabilities Act, and the IDEA.[23]

Graduation

"A graduate is one who has honorably passed through the prescribed course of study and received a certificate to that effect."[24] As simple as that phrase sounds, the number of legal issues arising from graduation is indeed high. This section of the chapter presents several of them and provides examples from the case law.

Diplomas and the Earning of Academic Credit

A diploma is a document or certificate awarded to a student who has completed all requirements for a degree or a course of study. Generally, these requirements consist of a certain number of academic credits or units in several subject areas, such as English and language arts (reading and writing), mathematics, social studies, science, foreign language, the arts, physical education, and electives. In addition, requirements for a diploma often include passing scores on one or more statewide and/or district-wide examinations. In some instances, participation in a community service program or internship is required. Diploma requirements vary by state and are typically codified in legislation or in regulations from the state department of education. Readers are encouraged to consult their local laws. In Ohio, for example, every high school graduate is required to earn twenty academic units in grades 9-12.[25] Generally, the units required for graduation are earned in high school. However, it may be possible for students younger than grade 9 to earn credits toward graduation, as long as the courses are taught by teachers who hold a valid teaching license or certificate in the area being taught.[26] In addition, several states are now granting high school credit for courses taken at colleges and universities, in what is often called a "post-secondary option."[27] States also award diplomas to adults beyond the age of compulsory attendance, often called general equivalency diplomas or adult education diplomas.[28]

A high school diploma varies not only from state to state, but often among students within each state. For example, states may offer more than one type of diploma, depending on the program or track the students complete. A regular high school diploma, for example, is awarded to students meeting the minimum requirements of GPA, credits earned, and examinations passed. Several states also offer honors diplomas,[29] or diplomas designed for students with disabilities who complete the goals and objectives of an IEP.[30] There may also be separate diplomas for those students who earn the required number of academic credits at the required GPA but who fail to pass all of the required statewide or districtwide exams.[31] Ohio has added a special provision where a regular or standard diploma may be granted to a student who satisfies all course work and credit requirements and passes all but one of the required graduation exams.[32] In order for a student to take advantage of this provision, he or she must fail the one exam by ten points or less, must maintain a 97 percent attendance rate during the previous four years, must have no expulsions in the previous four years, must maintain a GPA of at least 2.5 out of 4.0, and must complete the high school curriculum as prescribed by state law. In addition, the student must have taken advantage of the interventions provided for exam preparation and must acquire a letter of recommendation from the high school teachers in the subject matter at issue.

The Constitutional Right to a Diploma

Great deference is afforded to the work of state legislatures and departments of education in the development and enforcement of diploma and graduation requirements. However, once a student has completed all of the requirements for the diploma, a constitutional property right attaches, protected by the Due Process Clause of the Fourteenth Amendment. Courts will intervene rarely in graduation issues, but will do so when a school attempts to deny a diploma to a student who has met the requirements. In *Valentine v. Independent School District of Casey*, for example, the Supreme Court of Iowa held that a school may deny participation in a commencement ceremony for refusal to wear a cap and gown but may not deny the diploma in such a case.[33] The constitutional property right in a diploma does not attach until the student meets all of the legitimate requirements, such as completion of course work and sufficient numbers of credits,[34] completion of a reasonable community service program,[35] and passage of graduation exams.[36]

Schools that suspend or expel a student close to the end of his or her senior year and then allow that student to complete the schoolwork necessary for graduation have allowed the due process property right to manifest itself and will not be able to deny the diploma. In *Shuman v. Cumberland Valley School District Board of Directors*, the Cumberland Valley School District expelled high school senior David Shuman for selling LSD to some of his classmates.[37] The infraction was discovered on May 16; notice of expulsion and hearing was sent on May 21; and the hearing was to be held on May 30. Due to Shuman's illness, the hearing was held on June 3, the last day of school for seniors. In the meantime, the school allowed Shuman to sit for final exams. The board voted to expel Shuman permanently. As Shuman's graduation was three days later, the board also voted to deny him his diploma. The board argued that Shuman was not a "student" under the law at the time of graduation; therefore, it did not have to award him the diploma. But Shuman had completed all requirements for the diploma. The board continued and argued that issuing a diploma would wreak "havoc and chaos" in the school and that the schools would not be permitted to discipline seniors. The court disagreed. The school had already allowed Shuman to sit for senior finals, allowing him to complete the requirements for the diploma. The court stated, "we hold only that a student may not be denied a high school diploma where he has successfully completed all the course-work required for graduation and is expelled after successful completion of his courses."[38] The decision was not about the authority to maintain discipline; it was about the right to withhold an earned diploma.[39]

The Grant or Denial of Academic Credits

Before the onset of widespread graduation exams, the most common reasons for a student's failure to graduate were the failure of a required course and the failure to earn sufficient academic credits toward graduation. Courts, as is typical in these areas, will afford school boards great deference in their academic decision making and their compliance with applicable state laws and regulations. The board must only be careful of abusing its discretion and violating the rights of students and parents. Parents may find a particular course objectionable, but the courts may not be the proper forums for voicing those objections. If the student fails the course, he or she may not graduate:

> The courtroom is not the proper forum for resolution of personal conflicts arising from the State Board of Educa-

> tion's ... decision to include sex education in the public school curriculum, the district's program to comply with that decision, nor the pupil's failing grade on a test of that subject matter.[40]

Some objections to required coursework are based on legitimate constitutional claims and will act as limits to school board and/or state curricular authority. For example, a school may not deny a diploma to a student who has sincerely held religious objections to a required ROTC course.[41] There is no compelling governmental interest in a course that trumps the free exercise of religion, particularly when the course is not integral to the curriculum and the board of education denies any request for exemption or reasonable accommodation. In such cases, boards of education may not force the student to choose between his religious beliefs and earning a high school diploma.

Seemingly, the most litigious area in the discussion of a school district's grant or denial of academic credit, aside from exclusionary discipline and due process claims, involves denial of credit for attendance problems. The primary words of caution to school leaders in this regard are that almost regardless of the attendance of the student, if the student has met all requirements for the diploma, then a school district may not violate the property interest the student has in that diploma without due process. In *Miller v. McLeod*, a high school senior quit school during the second semester of her senior year to take a job in a local factory.[42] She was one-half credit away from graduating, and the school refused to issue her a diploma. But school policy permitted students to graduate after only seven semesters of high school, provided sufficient credits had been earned. Under the policy, three of the credits were allowed to be earned through on-the-job training. The trial court held that the school should have granted the student academic credit sufficient to graduate and earn a diploma; the court ordered the school district to award the diploma. The court of appeals affirmed this finding.

Similarly, a student who missed one-fourth of his junior year due to disciplinary infractions, but still managed to take the required courses and earn the appropriate number of credits, must be granted his diploma.[43] In fact, the student in *Sageser v. Ledbetter* was permitted to return to school for his senior year and was treated as a senior. The school district wanted to enroll the student for the exact number of days he had missed, even though he had already earned the credits to graduate. The court declined to approve this exercise in futility:

> Within reasonable limits a school board may determine graduation requirements but where, as here, a rule is applied or enforced unreasonably, capriciously, arbitrarily or inequitably to deny a diploma to a qualified candidate, [ordering the diploma] is an appropriate remedy.[44]

Schools must also beware of arbitrary, capricious, and unreasonable attendance policies. Truancy laws, when properly enforced, may legitimately and reasonably deny a student credit and cause retention or failure to graduate. But a policy that makes no distinction between excused and unexcused absences could be applied to harm a student who has genuinely earned her diploma. In *Barno v. Crestwood Board of Education*, a school policy required students to achieve a 93 percent attendance rate to earn academic credit.[45] This translated into a loss of credit at fourteen days absent, including excused and unexcused absences. Jennifer Barno missed 18.5 days of school her senior year, all but two of which were excused. She filed for an extenuating circumstances exception, and her request was denied. In holding for the student, the court found three errors in the policy. First, the policy makes attendance a prerequisite for academic credit. Accordingly, granting or denying credit based on attendance makes attendance curricular. The curriculum statute in Ohio, which outlines the subject areas and credits one must earn in each area to earn a diploma, does not list attendance among the requirements. And the court chose not to write such a requirement into the law. "Attendance is not a subject of study in the same sense as are geography, history, or mathematics. There is no textbook for it, there are no lectures on it, and students cannot be tested by a traditional examination of questions and answers."[46] Second, the policy counted excused and unexcused absences identically when calculating academic penalties. If the goal is to encourage attendance and to teach responsibility among young adults, making a distinction between excused and unexcused absences and requiring students to request permission for an excused absence does not harm this goal. Third, the policy failed to define "extenuating circumstances." The parties subject to the policy were not adequately prepared to follow it.

Finally, schools should be careful not to further harm a student who has already been victimized at school. Heidi McLaughlin was a victim of rape at the hands of three classmates, and she missed a month of school as a result.[47] The alleged perpetrators returned to school pending their trial, and the school made no effort to accommodate Heidi. At least three months after the rape, she began attending the local Catholic high school at the city's expense. Heidi attended the Catholic high school for her senior year, but maintained a spot on her public school's cheerleading squad. It was not until the spring of her senior year that she learned she would not have enough credits to graduate. She quickly enrolled in a course at the local community college to make up for the lost credits. Even though that course would not be complete before the high school's graduation, the McLaughlins understood that Heidi would still get to participate in graduation and receive a blank diploma. However, school officials told the McLaughlins that Heidi could not participate because she was not a Lowell High School student. The McLaughlins filed and maintained several tort law and constitutional claims against individual school district officials.

Participation in Graduation Ceremonies

The constitutional right to a diploma, once all requirements have been met, does not include a similar constitutional right to attend the commencement ceremony. There have been challenges, however, to school district decisions to deny attendance, whether the denial is due to failure to meet academic requirements, unrelated misconduct, or failure to comply with commencement rules and regulations. Applying these constitutional due process principles, a court has held that there is no violation of a constitutional right when a school district holds its commencement ceremony on a day of the week that conflicts with the religious practices of one of its graduates.[48]

Valedictorians and Salutatorians

Consistent with the primary message of this chapter, policies and practices associated with the selection of valedictorians and salutatorians are afforded due deference. Naturally, judicial deference for the work of administrators does not halt the competition among students (and their parents) to win the race. Typical of this competition is the story in *Jeffrey v. Board of Trustees of the Bells Independent School District*.[49] The controversy brewed over the competition between Jessica Jeffrey and Vanessa Novak and the scheduling of Spanish III. The controversy grew when the two girls, the Spanish teacher, and the principal searched for a period to teach the course, a weighted course for GPA purposes. Both students were taking electives fourth period and could drop them to make room for Spanish III. But Jeffrey's elective was an agriculture science course—one that would help her earn an agriculture science scholarship. Moore, the school's principal, offered to move the agriculture course to the zero hour (7:30 A.M.). Jeffrey requested that Spanish class be moved to another period. Her request was denied. The Jeffreys then requested a hearing with the principal and asked that the course not be offered at all. Moore denied the request, and the Jeffreys took their claim to the superintendent. The superintendent upheld Moore's denial. Jeffrey dropped the Spanish course, took the agriculture course, and Novak was named valedictorian. The Jeffreys filed suit alleging due process violations over the school's scheduling of courses and the handling of the hearings. They claimed that the schedule was set so that their daughter could not take the weighted courses necessary to earn valedictorian status. The court held for the school. There are no property or liberty interests in a particular course offered at a particular time. The court stated, "Put simply, Ms. Jeffrey's parents do not have a constitutional right to direct, control, or determine what classes or curriculum the Bells ISD will offer its students."[50] Similarly, there was no violation of substantive due process. Jeffrey was fully accommodated in the scheduling of courses and Novak was not accommodated to Jeffrey's detriment.

The controversy over the valedictorian does not diminish when the competitors include students with disabilities. In *Hornstine v. Township of Moorestown*, the board of education and high school administrators got caught up in the politics of valedictorian competitions and were pressured into amending the valedictorian and salutatorian policies to offset what some parents believed was a competitive advantage for students with disabilities, in that those students may take courses that are not as challenging and/or may receive modifications and accommodations on assignments and tests.[51] The amended policy gave the board of education subjective discretion to name multiple valedictorians. Throughout the school year, the district's superintendent fought on behalf of a non-disabled student, treating that student much better than he treated Hornstine, the student with the disability (chronic fatigue) who took half of her classes in home instruction. In response, Hornstine filed suit alleging violations of the IDEA, section 504, and the Americans with Disabilities Act (ADA). The court addressed only the ADA and section 504 claims and held for the student, enjoining the school from implementing the new policy. The terms of the policy itself were generally applicable, regardless of disability status. However, in application, the policy did harm Hornstine in benefiting from the activities and programs of the school, namely the valedictorian competition.

When Students Have Not Earned Sufficient Credits

Students who have not earned enough academic credits do not earn their diplomas, and will very rarely be invited to participate in commencement ceremonies. Most often, courts will hold that there are no property or liberty interests in the walk across the stage at a commencement ceremony until all requirements have been met.[52] This is the case even in situations where the failure to meet all requirements is purely technical. In *Swany v. San Ramon Valley Unified School District*, a student submitted a required participation log for an independent study physical education course three days late and did not receive credit for the course, even though all substantive requirements were filled on time.[53] He was not permitted to participate in graduation. His parents pleaded with the school to allow him to participate anyway (even with a later diploma). The school rejected the request. The student attended the ceremony anyway, in full cap and gown. An administrator warned him not to join the other graduates and threatened him with a call to the security officers if he tried to join them. The student did not join them. The student received his diploma in time to begin college that fall. His parents filed suit alleging a violation of due process, in that the decisions and actions of the school district were arbitrary, capricious, and an abuse of discretion. The court held for the district on all counts. The lateness of his diploma and his preclusion from the commencement ceremony have not deprived him of his reputation, good name, honor, or future opportunities.

In contrast to the decision in *Swany* is the much older case of *Sweitzer v. Fisher*.[54] In *Sweitzer*, the plaintiff earned insufficient grades to earn his diploma, but the school permitted him to march in the commencement ceremony anyway. The student's name was listed in the program as well. The court held that the permission to participate in the ceremony was made to respect the feelings of the student, but did not furnish the right to the diploma itself, nor did it actually confer a graduation on the plaintiff. "Mere permission to one to take part in the ceremonials, with the understanding that is was to save him and his family from humiliation, does not, to our mind, entitle him to a certificate of graduation."[55]

Dress and Grooming Codes

Dress and grooming policies are typical for commencement ceremonies and are upheld regularly, just as other rules and regulations that guide voluntary extracurricular activities. In *Fowler v. Williamson*,[56] Hickory High School's dress code required boys to wear "dress pants as opposed to jeans; shirts and ties; shoes and socks." The plaintiff came to school in expensive brushed denim pants, but was asked to go home and change. He went home to change clothes, but when he returned, the assistant principal denied him admission to the ceremony as the graduates had already entered. The graduate filed suit and asked for $500,000 in compensatory damages. He had received his diploma. The court held for the school district.

Violation of a dress code, however, does not warrant the denial of a rightfully earned diploma, only the denial of the opportunity to participate in the ceremony.[57] Similar deference is granted to school districts for policies on hair length for boys who are graduating.[58]

Penalty for Disciplinary Infraction Includes the Denial of Attendance

Perhaps surprisingly, the courts are mixed on the question of whether students who have been punished for conduct unrelated to the graduation ceremony and who are currently serving suspensions or expulsions at the time of the ceremony are, nonetheless, permitted to attend and participate in the graduation. The decisions vary on a few factors: the proximity in time between the conduct and the graduation, the reasonableness of the threat of disruption the student's attendance might have on the ceremony, and how well the school district handled the procedures surrounding the imposition of the penalty. The most standard of the representative cases is *Bundick v. Bay City Independent School District*,[59] where a senior was barred from the graduation ceremony after a random search revealed an illegal knife in a toolbox in the student's truck. The student still received his diploma, and the punishment was upheld. Similarly, in *Posthumus v. Board of Education of the Mona Shores Public Schools*, the court rejected a graduate's claim that he was unreasonably barred from participating in his commencement ceremony after he was suspended for ten days after an infraction at a senior honors assembly.[60] Like the student in *Bundick*, the student in *Posthumus* received his diploma on time and suffered no long-term consequences.

In *Ladson v. Board of Education, Union Free School District No. 9,*[61] the court struck down a school's decision to bar a graduating senior from her commencement ceremony, even though she had been expelled since March after participating in a bomb threat. She was under home instruction for the remainder of her high school career and completed all requirements for graduation. According to the court, if there had been a threat of disruption or danger, then the school's action would have been permissible. However, there was no evidence of such threat.

School administrators must be careful when imposing penalties on high school seniors close to the ends of their careers. Piling on a punishment to make a statement often backfires. In *Mifflin County School District v. Stewart,* a high school senior was suspended for three days after a fight with classmates.[62] On the third day of the suspension, a hearing was held, after which the school extended the suspension by four days. The second suspension prevented the student from attending his graduation. The student's parents sued to reinstate their son and allow him to attend the ceremony. The court held that the additional days of suspension were imposed without the proper written notification. The court held for the student.

The recent case of *Herrmann v. Board of Education of Unified School District No. 256* provides the most provocative scenario.[63] The plaintiff was one of several students suspended from the school for the remainder of the school year, following a prank committed during the senior class trip off campus. The plaintiff, apparently the primary actor, defecated into an empty can of Pringles and had intended to give it to a classmate because, according to the plaintiff, "he had been a turd throughout the day." The turn of events led the contents of the can to be placed into the shoe of another classmate. The notice of disciplinary exclusion included the prohibition of participation in all extracurricular activities for the rest of the year, including the graduation ceremony. The plaintiff's parents agreed that she should be punished, but appealed the suspension to the disciplinary committee, claiming that it was too harsh. The disciplinary committee decided to suspend the students for five days and that they would be able to attend commencement only after a conference with the principal. On appeal to the school board, the board upheld the suspension and disallowed the students to attend graduation. The plaintiff in this case then filed suit seeking an injunction that would allow her to participate in graduation. The court upheld the suspension, granted the injunction, and she participated in the graduation.

Graduation and Students with Disabilities

Age and graduation limits; change in placement. Basically, the IDEA requires no more services for children with disabilities who successfully graduate as would be provided children without disabilities under similar post-graduation situations.[64] Federal regulations under the IDEA provide that if a state offers education to students without disabilities who are between the ages of three to five or eighteen to twenty-one, then the state must also provide education to students with disabilities who are in these age ranges. Whether or not the child is capable of earning the diploma is irrelevant.[65] In other words, students with disabilities who are under the age of twenty-two and who desire to continue their education and who have not yet completed their high school education must be given this opportunity in furtherance of the FAPE requirements of the IDEA.[66]

Graduation from high school with a regular diploma constitutes a change in placement.[67] FAPE is not required for students who have graduated, but the graduation must be with a *regular* high school diploma. A student with a disability who has received a special diploma for completion of his or her IEP still has the right to receive FAPE at public expense as long as the student continues to qualify as a child with a disability.[68]

A family challenging a district's decision to graduate their child with a disability may invoke the stay-put provision while due process hearings are pending. Most often, the current placement for purposes of the stay-put provision will be the school at which the student was receiving special education and related services pursuant to a current and valid IEP.[69] As with any change in placement, decisions to graduate a child with a disability must not be made unilaterally. A school must provide parents with written notice of its decision to graduate the student and an opportunity to challenge the decision.[70] In *Kevin T. v. Elmhurst Community School District No. 205*, the district's decision to graduate a student with a disability was struck down due to several procedural violations.[71] The district failed to consider or provide assistive technology to help him overcome poor academic performance, did not permit the student to participate in state academic assessment tests, and failed to properly implement transition plans. For students on IEPs, graduation is not based on credits and grades alone. The district must assess whether the student makes progress on IEP goals and objectives before appropriately graduating the student. In such cases, reimbursement for educational expenses incurred by parents in the meantime will be warranted, as will compensatory education.

Graduation and free appropriate public education are not equivalent. One can occur without the other. Grade advancement is an important factor in the FAPE determination, but is not the only factor. "Compensatory education is a legal term used to describe future educational services that are awarded to compensate for a school district's failure to provide a free appropriate public education in the past."[72] Compensatory education is a judicially constructed form of relief designed to remedy past educational failings for students who are no longer enrolled in public school due to their age or graduation. As such, defenses that the student's demands are moot due to graduation often fail.[73] For compensatory education, the court reviews past violations and compensates the associated loss. School districts may be ordered to provide educational services past his or her twenty-first birthday to make up for any earlier deprivation of an appropriate education.[74] As long as a free appropriate public education has been conferred, no award of compensatory education is warranted, even if the claim is not technically moot.[75] Naturally, students with disabilities who graduate from high school with a regular diploma will still have special needs. However, graduation with a regular diploma ends the public school district's obligations to provide special education and related services.[76] As the popular FAPE standard from *Board of Education v. Rowley* articulates, the FAPE provision of the IDEA does not guarantee any substantive level of education, only an IEP that is designed to meet the individual needs of the student and is reasonably calculated to confer some educational benefit.[77] In such instances where FAPE has been provided and the student has graduated, parents are not entitled to continued special education and related services, including non-academic services such as psychiatric, social, and emotional services.[78] In at least one case, a court held that parents were not entitled to post-graduation compensatory education even where there was no IEP. The parents presented no evidence that the student suffered, and she graduated without assistance, despite her disability.[79]

Participation in graduation ceremony. There is no language in the IDEA that requires or grants a child with a disability the right to participate in a graduation ceremony where the student has not yet met the requirements for graduation. Graduation ceremonies are designed to celebrate and acknowledge the achievements of those students who have met the requirements of their instructional programs. And such policies apply to all students, regardless of disability status. In *Woodland Hills v. S.F.*, the student plaintiff had enough credits to graduate, but the IEP was not entirely satisfied. The court held that the student did not have the right to participate in the ceremony, even to receive a blank diploma.[80] Here is another example of the often uncomfortable bridge between individualization and standardization. Federal and state law requires school districts to draft and implement an IEP for each child with a disability. The IEP must contain statements of present levels of performance, annual goals, short-term learning objectives, specific special education and related services designed to help the student meet those goals and objectives, and appropriate criteria and assessment procedures designed to measure progress toward those goals. "Thus, both federal and state law mandates that [a student with a disability] is entitled to an individualized educational plan which may result in [the student] being required to complete more criteria than non-disabled students before being able to graduate and receive a diploma."[81]

High-Stakes Accountability Testing

With the No Child Left Behind Act and the accompanying state statutes, one of the most significant issues affecting promotion, retention, and graduation today is the existence of high-stakes standardized testing, where students must pass a certain number of exams in various subject areas in order to graduate or in order to move on to the next grade. The legality of the use of such exams is not in question today, as these exams have been administered in many states for decades and receive great deference from the courts in that the exams are designed to make a local high school diploma a meaningful credential of the graduate. The validity, enforcement, and effect of these exams, however, have raised questions of due process violation (notice and exposure to the exam material), race and national origin discrimination, free appropriate public education violations when the tests are required of students with disabilities and diplomas are denied, and disability discrimination when the exams are required without the accommodations and modifications outlined in IEPs.

The seminal case on high-stakes competency testing is *Debra P. v. Turlington*.[82] In *Debra P.*, students challenged the constitutionality of graduation exams under due process and equal protection. They claimed that the tests were racially biased. The district court agreed with the plaintiffs, and the court of appeals affirmed and enjoined the use of the exams; it did, however, hold that it is permissible to deny a diploma for failure to pass such exams, but only if the exams were instructionally valid. On the due process claim, the *Debra P.* court, in its 1981 decision, held that due process is deeper than the number of years' notice the students had in preparation for the tests:

> We believe that the state administered a test that was, at least on the record before us, fundamentally unfair in that it may have covered matters not taught in the schools of the state .... If the test is not fair [in content], it cannot be said to be rationally related to a state interest.[83]

In an important finding, the *Debra P.* court also stated that past discrimination on the basis of race or national origin was at the root of the huge disparities in pass rates on the exams. Consequently, the court enjoined the use of the tests until they could be shown to be free of discriminatory impact.[84] On remand, four years into the initial injunction halting the use of the tests, the Court of Appeals for the Eleventh Circuit upheld the tests.[85] For a more recent decision on the issue of racial discrimination in testing, see *GI Forum v. Texas Education Agency*, in which the court upheld the use of the Texas Assessment and Academic Skills (TAAS) against due process and equal protection claims.[86] The TAAS tests have also been subject to the same fairness and validity challenges as the tests examined in *Debra P.*[87] In 2004, a Massachusetts state court upheld the use of tenth-grade mathematics and language arts graduation exams.[88]

The most recent litigated challenges to graduation exams occurred in two separate cases in California, both attacking aspects of the California high school exit exam. In the first case, the state court of appeals granted the state superintendent's request to vacate a trial court's issuance of a preliminary injunction against enforcement of the exam requirement. The public interest in raising academic standards in California public schools outweighed the students' alleged irreparable injury.[89] In the second case, the court of appeals noted that the statute establishing the exam requirement obligated the state board of education to complete a study of alternatives to the exit exam. However, the court held that the statute did not require the study to be completed before the exit exam was enforced against the first class of seniors.[90]

In many states, there is a debate over whether high-stakes testing requirements must be met by nonpublic school and public school (including charter school) students alike. Early decisions in this body of law have held that the distinction between public and nonpublic school students is permissible and that the requirement to pass the exams belonging to only the public school students does not violate the Equal Protection Clause.[91] More recently, however, state statutes have required all students to pass proficiency examinations.[92] Similar arguments have been made regarding charter schools.[93]

Not surprisingly, much of the law-related discussion of high-stakes accountability testing has involved children with disabilities. In fact, federal law requires each IEP to contain a statement as to the participation or nonparticipation of students with disabilities in district-wide and statewide assessments. This discussion again highlights the struggle between standardization (e.g., requiring the exams) and individualization (exemptions, allowance of accommodations and modifications). In large part, courts have held true to the *Debra P.* analysis and rationale and upheld the administration of the tests to children with disabilities. In *Brookhart v. Illinois State Board of Education*, students with disabilities challenged a school district policy that required all students to pass a "minimum competency test" (MCT) to graduate.[94] On the due process claim, the court held for the plaintiffs: the notice in advance of the exam was insufficient for adequate preparation. Addressing the struggle between individualized education programs and standardized graduation tests, the court stated, "[T]he plaintiffs' programs of instruction were not developed to meet the goal of passing the MCT, but were instead geared to address individual educational needs."[95] The parents had only twelve to eighteen months to prepare for the exams. On a free appropriate public education claim, the court held that the denial of a high school diploma for failure to pass a required graduation exam does not amount to a denial of FAPE. The Supreme Court, in *Board of Education v. Rowley*,[96] held that a free appropriate public education guarantees no maximum level of academic performance. Instead, it guarantees special education and related services designed to meet the unique needs of the child and to provide access to a meaningful education that confers some educational benefit for the student. Accordingly, the court in *Brookhart* held that the "some educational benefit" standard does not guarantee the grant of a diploma.

The court in *Board of Education of Northport-East Northport Union Free School District v. Ambach*[97] addressed many of the same concerns as the court did in *Brookhart*, finding no violations of FAPE or due process because three years' notice in advance of the exams was adequate. The court in *Ambach* also rejected the plaintiffs' equal protection claim. The state articulated a rational basis for the exams (concern over decreasing college board scores and reports that increased numbers of students were graduating from high school without basic skills). Finally, the *Ambach* court also addressed the important claim under Section 504 of the Rehabilitation Act. Emphasizing the "otherwise qualified" language of section 504, the court held that the denial of a diploma to students who fail to pass state competency exams required for graduation is not a violation of section 504. Under section 504, the student must be able to meet the program's requirements *in spite* of his or her disability. Note, though, that a recent California opinion held that the administration of statewide graduation exams to students with disabilities is unlawful unless the students are offered the accommodations outlined in their section 504 plans.[98]

In *Rene v. Reed*, students with disabilities filed a class action suit, claiming that the Indiana State Superintendent violated their state and federal due process rights by requiring them to pass the Graduation Qualifying Examination (GQE).[99] They had previously been exempted from the tests and had not been taught some of the material on the test. In addition, they claimed that their rights under the IDEA had been violated when the exams were administered without accommodations and adaptations required by their IEPs. Using analysis similar to that seen in *Debra P.* and *Ambach*, the court rejected all claims. First, the appeals court held that the students had at least three years' notice that they had to pass the exams. Second, the students argued that, even with three years, their disabilities required more time and coverage before the exams. Furthermore, they argued that their curriculum had been modified away from the test material. The court of appeals disagreed and held that the students had sufficient coverage of the material in advance of the exam; some of the material was even concentrated in remedial interventions. Third, the court rejected a claim that the students had insufficient opportunities for remediation. The court, instead, held that three to five years of remedial opportunities were enough to satisfy the plaintiffs' due process rights. On the IDEA claim, the students argued that the state failed to provide adequate testing accommodations and modifications. According to the plaintiffs, the students were required to take the exams with no modifications or accommodations at all. The trial court held that the too many accommodations and modifications for students with disabilities would be unreasonable, as they would undermine the graduation tests and their validity.

Community Service as a Graduation Requirement

Several states have enacted statutes and regulations granting schools and school districts the discretion to adopt community service requirements for its graduates. Ohio's discretionary program holds that if high school credit toward graduation will be offered for participation in community service programs, then approximately half of the program must be devoted to classroom study of such topics as volunteerism, civic responsibility, and training.[100] Community service programs usually require students to serve a certain number of hours (e.g., forty-five or sixty) over a specified number of semesters or years. There have been only a few legal challenges to mandatory community service programs. In these cases, the programs have been upheld against challenges that the programs violate the First (free speech and/or religion), Thirteenth (involuntary servitude), and Fourteenth (due process) Amendments. In *Steirer v. Bethlehem Area School District*, the court held that there was no involuntary servitude in violation of the Thirteenth Amendment because the students themselves are among the beneficiaries of the service; there is no legal or physical coercion employed. The court also held that there is no First Amendment violation here, as the school is not engaging in expressive conduct by requiring students to engage in community service as an academic requirement.[101]

Recommendations for Practice

The laws and regulations of promotion, retention, and graduation vary by state. Check your jurisdiction for the applicable laws.

1. Administrative decisions regarding promotion, retention, and graduation are given great judicial deference. In the drafting and implementation of policy, exercise discretion wisely, objectively, and consistently. Prepare to defend the academic decisions you make.
2. Respect the difference between the individualization emphasized by the Individuals with Disabilities Education Act and the standardization required by federal, state, and local laws on proficiency examinations and graduation tests.
3. Watch the impact the disciplinary exclusions may have on the earning of academic credit. Be careful not to impose excessive punishments.
4. Watch also the impact that disabilities and other impairments or extenuating circumstances may have on the earning of academic credit. There is a distinction between excused and unexcused absences.
5. Articulate your commencement ceremony regulations well so that they are clear to those who must follow them.
6. Valedictorian and salutatorian policies should be clear in writing and consistent in application.
7. Barring students from participation in graduation ceremonies, even for violations of student codes, is not a slam-dunk. Courts vary on this, but there may need to be some connection between the misconduct and the ceremony itself for the punishment to hold.
8. For students with disabilities under the IDEA, graduation is a change in placement and requires written notice to the parents and an opportunity for the parents to request a hearing. The stay-put provision will apply.

9. For students with disabilities under the IDEA, only rightful graduation with a regular diploma will end the school district's obligation to provide special education and related services.

10. For accountability tests to be fair, students must be taught the material that is covered on the tests. And they must have sufficient notice of the exams and adequate opportunity to prepare for them.

Endnotes

1 OHIO REV. CODE ANN. § 3313.609.

2 *See,* OHIO REV. CODE ANN. § 3313.60.

3 OHIO REV. CODE ANN. § 3313.609. In Ohio, if a student is truant (absent without excuse) for more than 10 percent of the required attendance days and fails more than two of the required subject areas in the current grade, then that student will not be promoted to the next grade unless the student's principal and teachers feel the student is academically prepared to move on to the next grade.

4 Isquith v. Levitt, 137 N.Y.S.2d 497, 498 (N.Y. App. Div. 1955). For a more complete discussion of gradation and promotion, and the other issues discussed in this chapter, see also SPERRY, D.J., DANIEL, P.T.K., HUEFNER, D.S. & GEE, E.G., EDUCATION LAW AND THE PUBLIC SCHOOLS: A COMPENDIUM (1998).

5 Blessing v. Mason County Bd. of Educ., 341 S.E.2d 407 (W. Va. 1985).

6 *See, e.g.,* Sandlin v. Johnson, 643 F.2d 1027 (4th Cir. 1981).

7 Killion v. Burl, 860 F.2d 306 (8th Cir. 1988).

8 *Sandlin,* 643 F.2d at 1029. *But see* Doe v. Nashoba Reg'l Sch. Dist., No. 05-0932-C, 2005 Mass. Super. LEXIS 477, 20 Mass. L. Rep. 131 (Mass. Super. Ct. Oct. 12, 2005) (following a sexual assault committed by one kindergartner against another one, the school district promoted the assailant to first grade but retained the victim and cited no educational reasons for doing so; the court denied the district's motion to dismiss the parents' negligence claim).

9 *Killion,* 860 F.2d 306. *See also* Bester v. Tuscaloosa City Bd. of Educ., 722 F.2d 1514 (11th Cir. 1984).

10 *Sandlin* at 1029.

11 977 F. Supp. 384 (E.D.N.C. 1997).

12 *Id.* at 389.

13 *See* Board of Educ. of Sycamore v. Ohio, 88 N.E.2d 412 (Ohio 1909); and Ackerman v. Rubin, 231 N.Y.S.2d 112 (N.Y. Sup. Ct. 1962).

14 Gant v. Wallingford Bd. of Educ., 69 F.3d 669 (2d Cir. 1995).

15 *Id.* at 675.

16 *See* Goss v. Lopez, 419 U.S. 565 (1975).

17 728 N.E.2d 909 (Ind. Ct. App. 2000).

18 *Id.* at 914.

19 B.W.S. v. Livingston Parish Sch. Bd., 960 So. 2d 997 (La. Ct. App. 2007).

20 *Id.* The court noted that the child might have a damages claim relating to the school's refusal to provide her with alternative education during the expulsion.

21 OHIO REV. CODE ANN. § 3313.608. The statute also requires districts to adopt programs and policies for students in the first and second grade so that schools may identify students who need help in advance of the tests.

22 *See, e.g.,* Gabel v. Bd. of Educ. of Hype Park Cent. Sch. Dist., 368 F. Supp. 2d 313 (S.D.N.Y. 2005), in which the court held that the private school placement of a child with a severe communication speech disorder was appropriate, despite an age difference between the child and her classmates.

23 Weixl v. Bd. of Educ. of the City of New York, 287 F.3d 138 (2d Cir. 2002).

[24] Sweitzer v. Fisher, 172 Iowa 266, 274, 154 N.W. 465, 467 (1915).
[25] Ohio Revised Code Ann. § 3313.603. There is a provision in this statute that permits students who reside in correctional institutions to earn a diploma. *See* Ohio Rev. Code Ann. § 3313.603(F).
[26] Ohio Rev. Code. Ann. § 3313.603(G).
[27] Note, though, that this option is likely not available to students who have been expelled from school. Ohio Rev. Code Ann. § 3313.613.
[28] *See, e.g.,* Ohio Rev. Code Ann. § 3313.611.
[29] *See, e.g.,* 14 Del. Code § 151–52; Ohio Rev. Code Ann. § 3301.61.
[30] *See, e.g.,* Ga. Code Ann. § 20–2–281 (a special education diploma for those who complete the IEP, but who fail one or more of the required standardized exams); Miss. Code Ann. § 37–16–3, 37–16–7.
[31] *See, e.g.,* Alaska Stat. 14.03.075; Tex. Educ. Code § 28.025, 29.025; Va. Code Ann. 22.1–253.13:4.
[32] Ohio Rev. Code Ann. § 3313.615.
[33] 183 N.W.2d 434 (Iowa 1921).
[34] Swany v. San Ramon Valley Unified Sch. Dist., 720 F. Supp. 764 (N.D. Cal. 1989).
[35] Steirer v. Bethlehem Area Sch. Dist., 987 F.2d 989 (3d Cir. 1993).
[36] Debra P. v. Turlington, 644 F.2d 397 (5th Cir. 1981); Rene v. Reed, 751 N.E.2d 736 (Ind. Ct. App. 2001).
[37] 536 A.2d 490 (Pa. Commw. Ct. 1988).
[38] *Id.* at 492.
[39] For a case with similar facts and conclusion, see Ream v. Centennial Sch. Dist., 765 A.2d 1195 (Pa. Commw. Ct. 2001).
[40] Aubrey v. Sch. Dist. of Phila., 63 Pa. Commw. 330, 334, 437 A.2d 1306, 1308 (1981).
[41] Spence v. Bailey, 325 F. Supp. 601 (W.D. Tenn. 1971).
[42] 605 S.W.2d 160 (Mo. Ct. App. 1980).
[43] Sageser v. Ledbetter, 559 S.W.2d 230 (Mo. Ct. App. 1977).
[44] *Id.* at 234.
[45] 134 Ohio App. 3d 494, 731 N.E.2d 701 (1998).
[46] 134 Ohio App. 3d at 505, 731 N.E.2d at 709.
[47] McLaughlin v. City of Lowell, 8 Mass. L. Rep. 343 (Mass. Super. Ct. 1998).
[48] Smith v. N. Babylon Union Free Sch. Dist., 844 F.2d 90 (2d Cir. 1988).
[49] 261 F. Supp. 2d 719 (E.D. Tex. 2003), *aff'd,* 96 F. App'x 248, 2004 U.S. App. LEXIS 9004 (5th Cir. May 7, 2004).
[50] *Id.* at 727.
[51] 263 F. Supp. 2d 887 (D.N.J. 2003).
[52] *See, e.g.,* Nieshe v. Concrete Sch. Dist., 129 Wn. App. 632, 127 P.3d 713 (2005).
[53] 720 F. Supp. 764 (N.D. Cal. 1989).
[54] 172 Iowa 266, 154 N.W. 465 (1915).
[55] 172 Iowa at 274, 154 N.W. at 467.
[56] 448 F. Supp. 497 (W.D.N.C. 1978).
[57] Valentine v. Indep. Sch. Dist. of Casey, 191 Iowa 1100, 183 N.W. 434 (1921).
[58] Christmas v. El Reno Bd. of Educ., 313 F. Supp. 618 (W.D. Okla. 1970).
[59] Posthumus v. Bd. of Educ. of the Mona Shores Pub. Sch., 380 F. Supp. 2d 891 (W.D. Mich. 2005).
[60] 140 F. Supp. 2d 735 (S.D. Tex. 2001).
[61] 323 N.Y.S.2d 545 (N.Y. Sup. Ct. 1971).
[62] 503 A.2d 1012 (Pa. Commw. Ct. 1986).
[63] No. 01–4019–RDR, 2002 U.S. Dist. LEXIS 21700 (D. Kan. Oct. 16, 2002).
[64] Similarly, the requirement that schools conduct periodic evaluations for continued eligibility for special education services does not apply when the student graduates. 34 C.F.R. § 300.534.
[65] 20 U.S.C. § 1412(2)(B).

[66] Evans v. Tuttle, 613 N.E.2d 854 (Ind. Ct. App. 1993). The court struck down an Indiana law that made education for students with disabilities age 18 or older discretionary.

[67] 34 C.F.R. § 300.122(a)(3)(iii).

[68] Barnett v. Memphis City Sch. Sys., 294 F. Supp. 2d 924 (W.D. Tenn. 2003).

[69] Bell v. Educ. in the Unorganized Territories, Civ. No. 00-CV-160-B, 2000 U.S. Dist. LEXIS 15262 (D. Me. Oct. 16, 2000).

[70] Kevin T. v. Elmhurst Cmty. Sch. Dist. No. 205, No. 01-C-0005, 2002 U.S. Dist. LEXIS 4645 (N.D. Ill. Mar. 20, 2002).

[71] *Id. See also* Somoza v. New York City Dep't of Educ., 475 F. Supp. 2d 373 (S.D.N.Y. 2007), in which the court remanded a matter involving family's claim that a student's graduation and diploma were shams, in that the student's academic abilities were no where near twelfth-grade level.

[72] Brett v. Goshen Cmty. Sch. Corp., 161 F. Supp. 2d 930, 942 (N.D. Ind. 2001).

[73] *See, e.g.,* Jessie v. Bullitt County Bd. of Educ., No. 3:04CV-306-H, consolidated with 3:04CV-365-H, 2005 U.S. Dist. LEXIS 7270 (W.D. Ky. Apr. 26, 2005); and Sammons v. Polk County Sch. Bd., No. 8:04-cv-2657-T-24, 2005 U.S. Dist. LEXIS 45838 (M.D. Fla. Oct. 7, 2005).

[74] *See* Barnett v. Memphis City Sch. Sys., 294 F. Supp. 2d 924 (W.D. Tenn. 2003); Hall v. Knott County Bd. of Educ., 941 F.2d 402 (6th Cir. 1991); Pihl v. Mass. Dep't of Educ., 9 F.3d 184 (1st Cir. 1993).

[75] Brett v. Goshen Cmty. Sch. Corp., 161 F. Supp. 2d 930 (N.D. Ind. 2001). Brett was twenty-four years old, had an IQ of 133, and scored 1430 on his SAT. He earned his diploma in 1996. Brett also had anxiety disorder with depressive features. Brett alleged that the diploma was wrongfully conferred and that the school district denied him FAPE. The court held otherwise.

[76] Howell v. District of Columbia, No. 07-1066, 2007 U.S. Dist. LEXIS 81749 (D.D.C. Nov. 6, 2007).

[77] *See* 458 U.S. 176 (1982).

[78] Daugherty v. Hamilton County Schs., 21 F. Supp. 2d 765 (E.D. Tenn. 1997).

[79] Puffer v. Raynolds, 761 F. Supp. 838 (D. Mass. 1988).

[80] 747 A.2d 433 (Pa. Commw. Ct. 2000).

[81] *Id.* at 436. *See also* Frank S. v. Sch. Comm. of the Dennis-Yarmouth Reg'l Sch. Dist., 26 F. Supp. 2d 219 (D. Mass. 1998).

[82] 644 F.2d 397 (5th Cir. Unit B 1981), *rev'd on remand*, 564 F. Supp. 177 (M.D. Fla. 1983), *aff'd*, 730 F.2d 1405 (11th Cir. 1984).

[83] 644 F.2d at 404–06.

[84] *See also,* Anderson v. Banks, 520 F. Supp. 472 (S.D. Ga. 1981) (a state must show that vestiges of past discrimination in a segregated system of public education have been eliminated before high-stakes exams may be administered).

[85] 730 F.2d 1405 (11th Cir. 1984).

[86] 87 F. Supp. 2d 667 (W.D. Tex. 2000).

[87] Williams v. Austin Indep. Sch. Dist., 796 F. Supp. 251 (W.D. Tex. 1992) (student was provided with adequate notice of the exams, and the material covered on the exams was taught in his school); Crump v. Gilmer Indep. Sch. Dist., 797 F. Supp. 552 (E.D. Tex. 1992) (court granted a motion for preliminary injunction allowing plaintiffs to participate in graduation, despite failing the TAAS exams, and held that the district had not yet made a showing that the material covered on the tests was taught in the school).

[88] Student No. 9 v. Bd. of Educ., 440 Mass. 752, 802 N.E.2d 105 (Mass. 2004).

[89] O'Connell v. The Super. Ct. of Alameda County, 141 Cal. App.4th 1452, 47 Cal. Rptr.3d 147 (Cal. Ct. App. 2006).

[90] Californians for Justice Educ. Fund v. State Bd. of Educ, No. A114190, 2006 Cal. App. Unpub. LEXIS 8832 (Cal Ct. App. Sept. 29, 2006).

[91] Debra P., 644 F.2d 397 (5th Cir. 1981); Rankins v. La. State Bd. of Elementary and Secondary Educ., 637 So. 2d 548 (La. Ct. App. 1994).

[92] OHIO REV. CODE ANN. § 3313.612.

[93] International High Sch.: A Charter Sch. at LaGuardia Cmty. Coll. v. Mills, 715 N.Y.S.2d 490 (N.Y. App. Div. 2000).
[94] 697 F.2d 179 (7th Cir. 1983).
[95] *Id.* at 187.
[96] 458 U.S. 176 (1982).
[97] 458 N.Y.S.2d 680 (N.Y. Sup. Ct. 1982).
[98] Chapman v. Cal. Dep't of Educ., No. C 01–01780 CRB (N.D. Cal. 2002).
[99] 751 N.E.2d 736 (Ind. Ct. App. 2001).
[100] OHIO REV. CODE ANN. § 3313.605.
[101] 987 F.2d 989 (3d Cir. 1993). *See also* Herndon v. Chapel Hill-Carrboro City Bd. of Educ., 899 F. Supp. 1443 (M.D.N.C. 1995).

Chapter 7

Child Abuse

James B. Gessford & Gregory H. Perry

Introduction

> [T]he … prevention of child abuse is of the highest priority, and all instances of child abuse must be reported to the proper authorities who should diligently and expeditiously take appropriate action.[1]

The above quote clearly sets forth our Nation's policy as it pertains to child abuse and reporting. The scope of this policy was recently tested before the Supreme Court of New Jersey in *Hardwicke v. American Boychoir School.*[2]

The Court in *Hardwicke* was called upon to analyze and determine the contours of this basic policy when John Hardwicke, a second student victim[3] of Donald Hanson, the school's music director, sued Hanson and the school for damages. For about two years, from the fall of 1969 to April of 1971, Hanson sexually abused Hardwicke "on an almost daily basis and sometimes several times a day … at the School, on School-sponsored field trips and in [the Music Director's] car, among other places." At the time, Hardwicke was twelve years old. When Hardwicke filed suit, he was forty-three years old. As is common with many abuse cases, the suit asserted numerous state law claims against the school including intentional infliction of emotional distress, negligent infliction of emotional distress, breach of the duty to disclose, active concealment of the abuse, assault and battery, negligent hiring and supervision, and false imprisonment.[4]

The Court in *Hardwicke* allowed Hardwicke's case to continue to trial.[5] To a large extent, the court decided the case based on the principle of furthering "the important public policies of protecting those who are especially vulnerable from the unlawful exercise of authority … [which] considerations apply equally to claims based on child abuse, whether brought under [child abuse statutes] or the common law, where the goal is to protect children from victimization."

Such a principle allows for ever-expanding parameters of institutional liability in the child abuse area.[6] Guided by this principle, the court held that the school was a "person" standing in loco parentis under the New Jersey Child Sexual Abuse Act, and as such, the school could be held vicariously liable for the acts of its employees in common-law child abuse claims. One point of note here is that the court ruled that the child abuse liability of public and private schools are essentially the same. Thus, even though the Boychoir School was a private institution, the court found "no principled distinction between the two cases."[7]

Child abuse and neglect issues have existed for decades, and schools, to a degree, have always been involved with the problem.[8] Today, however, schools seem to be involved with the subject more than ever before. Cases abound on the topic, and new areas of concern have evolved. The issues are more varied and intricate, and all aspects of the problem are being examined. Principals can help protect their students, themselves, and their schools if they are vigilant and stay current about legal developments with the child abuse topic.

Legal Issues

Child Abuse Basics

To have any sort of meaningful understanding or discussion about the issue of child abuse, definitional terms are critical. *Child abuse* and *neglect* are, unfortunately, common terms. They are also terms that mean vastly different things to different people. "The definition of child abuse can range from a narrow focus, limited to intentional inflicted injury, to a broad scope, covering any act that adversely affects the developmental potential of a child."[9] It is thus imperative that schools and administrators are familiar with the definitions in their particular state.

As a general matter, there are some commonly accepted definitions for abuse and neglect,[10] along with mandatory reporting requirements in effect in all states.[11] There are also lists that include the *cluster of indicators,* or more common signs of abuse.[12]

A recent Oklahoma decision cautions that child abuse is something more than inappropriate or unprofessional conduct. In *Hagen v. Independent School District No. I-004,*[13] a majority of the Oklahoma court recently reinstated a terminated teacher who pushed a special education student through the front doors of the elementary building and then slapped him twice on his left cheek, leaving it reddened. The majority found that contrary to the school board's determination, the teacher had not committed "child abuse" since the board failed to prove a specific intent by the teacher to harm the child. The teacher testified that he did not intend to injure the student when he slapped him, but that his intention was to try to get the student's attention and find out what was wrong. The teacher further testified that he later went to the student's home and apologized to the student, his grandmother, and his brother. Both the grandmother and brother testified that they bore no ill-will toward the teacher and would be comfortable having him teach the student again. The grandmother, who was the student's caregiver, testified that she had occasionally slapped the student and that she felt it was appropriate.

Once the relevant definitions of child abuse are in place, the following must be understood: duty to protect students from child abuse, duty to report child abuse, when the duty to respond to possible child abuse arises (the "knew or should have known" standard), and the statute of limitations for school liability.

Duty to Protect Students

The New Jersey court in *Hardwicke v. American Boychoir School,*[14] citing *Frugis v. Bracigliano,*[15] stated that "[a] board of education must take *reasonable measures* to assure that the teachers and administrators who stand as surrogate parents during the day are educating, not endangering, and protecting, not exploiting, vulnerable children."[16] More recently, the same court in *L.W. ex rel. L.G. v. Toms River Regional School Board of Education,*[17] reiterated and expanded the reasonable measures standard from adult abuse cases to those involving student-on-student abuse and harassment. The court stated:

> Educators have "[n]o greater obligation … than to protect the children in their charge from foreseeable dangers, whether those dangers arise from the careless acts or intentional transgressions of others." Although *Frugis* involved the need to protect children from adults, its rationale applies to the present circumstances. That is, a school district's "first imperative must be to do no harm to the children in its care. A board of education must take reasonable measures to assure that the teachers and administrators who stand as surrogate parents during the day are educating, not endangering, and protecting, not exploiting, vulnerable children."[18]

On the question of the reasonableness of the safety measures employed by the school in meeting the duty to protect, the *Frugis v. Bracigliano* decision is instructive. The court reasoned that in light of several observed acts of questionable and deviant behavior by the principal, the failure to report "standing alone was evidence of negligence, vicariously imputable to the board."[19] It determined that paper covering the principal's office-door window in violation of administrative regulations, the frequent click of a camera, the pop of flashbulbs from behind the closed door after students entered the office, the door always being locked even when students visited, the strange matter of the elementary principal's attendance at the weigh-ins of naked athletes on the high school's varsity wrestling team, and the superintendent's "superficial" written evaluations reflecting "an absolute absence of oversight" were telltale signs that should have prompted inquiry.[20] The court held that the lack of reporting protocols and staff training in their use were the primary reason "the Board failed to put together the varied strands of [the principal's] strange and aberrant behaviors that were known by teachers, staff, and administrators."[21]

Finally, it "encourage[d] school districts to promulgate policies that will guide school staff in reporting the abuse of students by anyone, at any level in the educational hierarchy and to implement training programs to ensure the effectiveness of a zero-tolerance-of-abuse policy."[22]

Though grounded on various different legal theories, schools clearly have a legal duty to protect students from child abuse.

Duty to Report

The New Jersey statutory scheme under review in *Hardwicke v. American Boychoir School* is typical of that in most states, i.e., "[a]ny person having reasonable cause to believe that a child has been subjected to child abuse or acts of child abuse shall report the same immediately."[23] In this regard, the recent West Virginia case of *Barbina v. Curry*[24] cites with approval *Arbaugh v. Board of Education.*[25] *Arbaugh* addressed the subtle question of what level of knowledge is necessary to require a report; that is, what is "reasonable cause" to suspect child abuse which triggers the reporting duty? The victim in *Arbaugh* claimed that he was sexually abused by a teacher and sued the board of education, a former superintendent of schools, and others, alleging that individuals who had a duty to report suspected incidents of child abuse, and had reason to believe he was being abused, failed to report their suspicions to authorities.

The *Arbaugh* court first distinguished between cases where a school official is an eyewitness to or has direct knowledge of child abuse and the typical situation, where school officials learn of possible child abuse. In the typical situation, the court noted the need for exercising individual judgment because in most cases the reporter becomes "aware of a possible case of child abuse only through rumors, innuendo or second-hand reports." The *Arbaugh* court refused to extend liability to a non-reporter stating "[n]onetheless, we hesitate to extend a private cause of action by implication to any child injured by a non-reported abuser against the person responsible for reporting since substantial questions of causation are raised," and the failure to report "would not in the direct sense be a proximate cause of the injury to the child."[26]

Along these same lines is *P.R. v. Commonwealth, Department of Public Welfare*,[27] which addressed the fine line between corporal punishment and child abuse, and noted that the task of determining when that line has been crossed is not easy. In reaching its decision, the court focused on the two prevailing interests at stake: (1) the interests of the parents or others in retaining the right to administer corporal punishment and (2) the interest of the child in being protected from abuse.[28] The court determined that the best way to maintain both interests was to impose a criminal negligence standard for non-reporting, rather than a foreseeability test or a focus on intent alone.[29]

In addition, the line between harassment and abuse is also less than clear. In *Gabrielle v. Park Forest - Chicago Heights*,[30] the Seventh Circuit found that the school district was not liable under Title IX for the sexual harassment of a kindergarten girl by one of her classmates. The court held that the district's response to the inappropriate conduct was not unreasonable in that after each reported or observed instance, the offending student was disciplined and steps were taken to prevent future inappropriate conduct. The conduct at issue involved the boy jumping on the girl's back, kissing her, pulling his pants down, and having their hands inside of each others' clothes. While in other circumstances this conduct could just as easily have been characterized as child abuse, in the context of peer harassment between five-year-olds, this court characterized it as indicative of nonactionable teasing and name calling rather than as potentially actionable harassment.[31]

In Arizona, two administrators faced the loss of their teaching licenses for failing to report an incident of sexual abuse. The incident, in which a football player shoved a girl's face into his crotch during class, was classified as sexual harassment, not sexual abuse, by the school's athletic director and assistant principal and was dealt with accordingly. Noting that "[s]warms of school administrators have been calling the Arizona School Boards Association (ASBA) on how to report suspected incidents of either abuse or harassment," the ASBA attorney stated that "it is better to overreport than to underreport, even though he acknowledges that too much reporting could overwhelm police" and that "[e]ven if an incident can be considered 'horseplay,' if it involves touching, the law says to let police handle it."[32]

In *Brown v. Town of E. Haddam*,[33] a child told a school official that the bruise on her eye was a result of an argument she had had with her mother, and her mother had swung her right arm backward in the daughter's direction. School officials reported the mother for the suspicion that her daughter was physically abused. The mother filed suit against the board of education, claiming a violation of her right to family integrity and intentional infliction of emotional distress. The Sixth Circuit affirmed a ruling in favor of the board of education because it found that there was a reasonable basis for the finding of abuse.

School officials who do report suspected child abuse can be pleased to know that reporting helps children who are being abused. Two cases out of Nebraska illustrate this fact, although there are of course many others throughout the country.

The facts in the *McPherson* case[34] involved a father (Roger) in Lincoln who was sexually abusive and a mother (Donna) who allowed the abuse to continue. The children were two girls, "S.M.," age 12, and "M.M.," age 11. The abuse of the girls was discovered and reported by school officials:

> In February 2001, M.M. approached school officials concerning her situation at home. She told officials that Roger had recently announced a new rule which would require the girls to "go around the house" naked on the weekends. She also alleged that Roger made her engage in fellatio with him. After talking with both girls, school officials called the police to report the incidents of sexual abuse.

> The police took the girls to the Child Advocacy Center to be interviewed. The girls were placed in protective custody after the interviews.

The girls later testified that

> they had engaged in fellatio with Roger and that Donna had watched and participated on some occasions. They also testified that Roger sexually touched their vaginas. According to S.M., on at least one occasion, Donna actively participated in the sexual activity when Roger sexually touched S.M.'s vagina. Both girls further testified that they had watched Donna engage in fellatio with Roger. According to the girls, Donna often went about the house nude and Roger went about the house partially nude. Their testimony also revealed that Roger took nude photographs of both girls.

Roger and Donna were convicted of first degree sexual assault, aiding and abetting sexual assault, and child abuse.

The *Phyllisa B.*[35] case took place in Omaha. The case involved Phylissa, who was then not quite seven years old. Phyllisa's elementary school teacher asked her why she was falling asleep in class. Phyllisa said that her father would come into her room late at night and "stick something in her mouth." The school officials reported this to police department, who further learned from Phyllisa that "her father came into her room and laid on top of her and 'humped her.'" Phyllisa also later reported that her brother, who is approximately two years older than Phyllisa, had sexual contact with her. The parents' parental rights to Phylissa were terminated after school officials reported what Phyllisa's parents had been doing to her.

Knew or Should Have Known

Another emerging issue discussed in *Hardwicke v. American Boychoir School*, is to what extent must a school have knowledge of a reason to take action to a threat of possible child abuse before it can be held liable? While persons who inflict child abuse (or what New Jersey calls "active abusers") are individually liable for their civil wrongs, and are often sued,[36] the clear trend is to also seek compensation from supervising officials, administrative personnel, and their institutions. New Jersey calls this latter group "passive abusers," defined generally as those who stand in loco parentis, who know of the abuse, and who fail to protect the child.[37]As such, many of the allegations in *Hardwicke* centered around issues involving the so-called passive abusers and what they "knew or should have known" of the abuse. It was alleged, for example, that the school should have known because, among other things, the teacher's "homosexuality was known to some when hiring occurred [and] while employed, [he] maintained a homosexual relationship with a senior staff member."[38]

One problem for schools and supervisory personnel under this analysis is that they will always be deemed to stand in loco parentis or at least as occupying some form of special relationship triggering a heightened duty of care.[39] They will thus face potential liability in almost all cases that arise, regardless of best practice or due diligence. A second problem with this analysis is with the "knowing" requirement. This component of child abuse jurisprudence is becoming especially troublesome for educators, as courts are taking a "relaxed" view on what a school must know before a child abuse cause against it or its supervisory personnel becomes viable.

Even in *Hardwicke*, the knowledge requirements for passive-abuser-type liability to attach was variously stated as *knew or should have known* or even a broader notion as alleged in the student's pleadings that the school had "acquiesced in" the conduct. In *U.S. Bank v. Board of Education*,[40] the Illinois Federal Court was faced with a passive abuser liability issue when a math teacher sexually assaulted a student after class. The court in reviewing the 42 U.S.C. Section 1983 portion of the claim refused to dismiss the case in part because "[a]lthough [the student] falls short … of specifically asserting that [the school or its officials] knew of the sexual assaults and failed to take action, the [student does] allege that [they] knew *or should have known* of allegations of sexual assault, sexual misconduct, or inappropriate touching of female students" by the employee. The *U.S. Bank* court assessed this issue by citing the Seventh Circuit Court's decision in *Hildebrandt v. Illinois Department of Natural Resources,*[41] which spoke of liability attaching in even broader terms than *should have known*, such as when a school or its officials "facilitate it, approve it, condone it, or turn a blind eye."[42]

A Pennsylvania federal court recently reiterated that school officials must take prompt legal action if they know or suspect that a teacher or other staff member is abusing a child with a disability. In *Kimberly F. v. Northeastern Education Intermediate Unit 19,*[43] a parent sued on numerous federal and state law grounds, alleging that the teacher hit, grabbed, stepped on, verbally abused, and physically restrained her child and that two teacher's assistants had notified the supervisors, but the supervisors purportedly failed to investigate or report the teacher's alleged conduct to child welfare authorities as required under state law. Instead, the parent claimed that the supervisors accused the assistants of "breaking a silent code" and transferred them to another district. "[The parent has] alleged facts—particularly [the assistants'] communications—sufficient to give rise to the reasonable inference that [the supervisors] were on notice about [the teacher's] alleged abusive acts and knew or should have known that their nonfeasance would allow the abuses to continue," the court wrote. As such, the court concluded that the supervisors could not assert qualified immunity as a defense to the parent's claims.

Another recent case involving the *knew or should have known* standard is *Hertzel v. Palmyra School District*[44] Robert Hertzel and another student, John Doe, were in the same kindergarten class. There were two alleged incidents of John Doe inappropriately touching Robert in the bathroom at school. The first occurred in February or March. Robert told his babysitter that he had been touched in the bathroom at school on his private area. Robert's mother called the school guidance counselor to report what her son had said. The counselor told her "kids 'explore,' it was 'normal,' there was nothing to be worried about, and [the mother] should not make an issue out of it."

On the last day of school, Robert told his babysitter that John Doe inappropriately touched him again that day at school. Robert's mother called John's mother, who told her that John was in counseling for a non-school-related incident in which he had inappropriately touched a child and that John Doe had admitted to touching Robert.

Robert and his mother then filed a lawsuit against the school and school officials. The suit claimed that the school "*knew or should have known* that John Doe was likely to cause bodily harm to others if he was not controlled." Evidence from both the kindergarten teacher and the elementary school principal was clear that they had no reason to have known that John Doe was a threat to sexually abuse other students. No reports had been made to them and there was nothing in John Doe's behavior that in any way indicated that he might abuse children or inappropriately touch them. On these facts, the trial court dismissed the suit, finding "no evidence which demonstrates that [the school district] knew" of the incidents.

In reversing the lower court decision and allowing the case to proceed, the Nebraska Appellate Court pointed out that the guidance counselor had reason to know of John Doe's potential to abuse other students because she had been told of the first incident. Relying on the *know or should know* language in both Sections 319 and 320 of the Restatement (Second) of Torts the court stated:

> Thus, while the record shows that [the school], the actor in this case, did not know that John Doe was the child molesting Hertzel until after the second incident … at the end of the school year, it is the "should know" portion of the two Restatement sections which is crucial.
>
> * * *
>
> [T]he knowledge the counselor acquired … can be seen as being such that a reasonable person should have known of the threat that John Doe posed to other children—had she investigated. We do not believe that the Restatement envisions no duty when one fails to acquire the precise knowledge necessary to prevent the harm when the necessary knowledge is available, if one seeks it out. Put another way, "ignorance may be bliss," but ignorance is not always a defense, because as the Restatement makes clear, sometimes one "should know." Whether the counselor and, by imputation, [the school district] should have known that John Doe

> had molested Hertzel and thus needed to be controlled to prevent further harm is a factual question for trial.

The lesson from *Hertzel* is that all staff should be instructed to forward reports of concern about a student's potential to abuse or harm others to the administration so that the administration can share the information with the student's pertinent supervising staff.

The liberalized trend of imputing knowledge of an employee to a school district and its officials is concerning. It almost assures liability under recent analysis if anyone in the district knew and didn't tell. As recently stated in *Baumgardt v. Wausau School District Board of Education*,[45] "[a]lthough the determination that a child is being abused involves discretionary acts, ... once a school administrator *is aware* of abuse, all discretion is stripped away: a school administrator 'shall' report abuse of which he is aware to authorities."

Statute of Limitations

The statute of limitations insures schools and school officials against the inevitable prejudice and injustice that is created when a lawsuit is filed long after the events in question. In the area of child abuse, however, the courts have relaxed the statutes of limitation.

The abuse in *Hardwicke v. American Boychoir School*, for example, occurred in the late 1960s and early 1970s. The student victim did not file suit until 2001, some thirty years later. One might ask: Aren't there statutes of limitations? How can a suit like this be filed for something that occurred that long ago?

Under the law in many states, if the potential plaintiff is a minor when the cause of action first accrues, the action is extended for a certain period after the minor reaches the age of majority, or the statute is tolled until the minor reaches majority.[46] Even so, assuming the age of majority in *Hardwicke* was twenty-one, the statute of limitations would have run sometime in the late 1970s. On the limitations issue, the court detailed the following facts:

> For limitations purposes, then, plaintiff would have been considered a minor and, hence, the relevant limitations period would have been tolled until plaintiff achieved "the age of 21 years." N.J.S.A. 2A:14-21. Plaintiff, however, did not bring this action until more than thirty-one years after he first entered the School, more than thirty years after plaintiff alleges the sexual assaults he endured started, almost thirty years after plaintiff alleges the sexual assaults ended, and at least twenty-two years after plaintiff reached the age of majority. At first blush, then, plaintiff's statutory and common-law claims should be time-barred.[47]

In New Jersey, prior to 1992, victims of child abuse were limited to common-law theories of recovery and constrained by a two-year statute of limitations for tort actions. In 1990, however, the court in *Jones v. Jones*[48] directly confronted the question of whether the mental trauma suffered by [a child victim of sexual abuse] serves to toll the statute of limitations. *Jones* highlighted the difficulties victims then faced when bringing claims against their abusers. The Appellate Division panel found "that factual questions were presented" and whether a child abuse victim's mental condition prevented them from asserting their rights, thereby tolling the statute of limitations, either because they lacked the capacity to do so or because of duress sufficient to prevent the exercise of freedom of will.[49] The New Jersey Legislature responded to the concerns raised in *Jones* with the passage of the Child Sexual Abuse Act (CSAA), N.J.S.A. 2A:61B-1. In effect, the statute codified and amplified the holding in *Jones* by essentially granting a limitations exception in the circumstances of an abuse victim.[50]

The *Hardwicke* court further interpreted this new legislative exception or what it characterized as a "relaxed statute of limitations" in the CSAA to apply to "any civil action" including any common-law claims based on conduct falling within its definition of abuse. It stated that on remand, the trial court must hold a hearing and determine whether the two-year statute of limitations was tolled by this exception on both the statutory and common-law child abuse claims. This holding appears to be in line with an increasing number of state laws and court decisions, which in recent years have been enacted or found exceptions for child abuse victims as ways to delay or toll running of the various statutes of limitation on civil actions against both the perpetrators of such wrongs and their employers.[51]

Emerging Trends in Child Abuse Law

While knowledge of the basics is critical,[52] it is no longer enough to be knowledgeable only about the basics. The issues now range from the traditional problems of reporting possible abuse by a parent, school supervisor, or teacher, to concerns about volunteers,[53] teacher suicide over false reporting,[54] teacher privacy rights connected with mandatory fingerprinting,[55] slander actions for false reporting,[56] personal protective orders (PPOs),[57] the acquitted abuser, HIPAA questions, cyber bullying, and various and sundry federal cyber laws.

As to false reporting, it has been recognized that "there is no more deplorable badge of infamy a person can wear than that of being a child abuser..."[58] While school officials have a duty to report suspected child abuse, it is important that reports be founded on a reasonable basis.

As to the acquitted abuser, authorities commonly face the issue of the legality of discharging a school employee who is accused but then acquitted of criminal charges of abuse. In *Boguslawski v. Department of Education*,[59] the Pennsylvania court affirmed the Standards and Practices Commission's action that revoked a teacher's teaching certificate. The teacher appealed on the basis that a criminal jury trial had found him not guilty of all charges, and he had denied all charges consistently. In upholding the commission's actions, the court stated: "[R]esolution of criminal charges in favor of a criminal defendant does not bar subsequent civil or administrative proceedings concerning the same underlying conduct."[60]

On the HIPAA question, some schools may be "covered entities" under the new Health Insurance Portability and Accountability Act (HIPAA). As such, legitimate concerns exist about disclosure of child abuse information as possibly violating HIPAA privacy regulations.[61] These regulations generally prohibit disclosure of protected health information (PHI) without a special written HIPAA authorization. The definition of PHI is very broad, encompassing any past, present, or future medical condition, which could certainly include child abuse information.[62] Schools should be aware, however, that the regulations specifically permit disclosure of PHI without authorization when reporting suspected abuse, neglect, and domestic violence.[63]

Finally, the issue of student abuse of a teacher was recently addressed by the Delaware court in *Mongelli v. Red Clay Consolidated School District Board of Education*[64] *Mongelli* involved JW, a male special education student's, conduct towards Ms. Mongelli, JW's female teacher. The facts are rather graphic as to JW's conduct which included among other things:

> 6) May 6, 2004: "[JW] got out of his seat, came up to Ms. Mongelli's desk, and stared directly at [her]. Then, [JW] sang a rap song stating, 'How's your p y?' He sang the word 'p y' several times during his rap song. When I told him to go to [the time out room], he continued singing even louder. After [JW] sang, he made 'sucking' noises with his mouth."
>
> 7) May 7, 2004: "[JW] got out of his seat and walked over to Ms. Mongelli. Then [he] sang a rap song stating, 'Ms. Mongelli gives h d.' He sang this four times. As he was singing, [JW] pointed to his p s three times."[65]

Recognizing the problems it was dealing with and the various competing interests in the case, the court stated:

> [This] scenario involves competing public interests, namely, a school's duty to protect teachers from abusive students versus its obligation to teach those students how to conduct themselves in a socially acceptable way. Unlike cases involving abusive co-workers or customers, a school district cannot easily "terminate" a student or permanently ban him from the premises; instead, the district must attempt

> to deal with the abusive student using the limited tools and resources at its disposal... The court next turns its attention to whether such claims may arise when the abuse is perpetrated by a special education student. The competing public interests discussed above become even more pronounced (and a district's options are even more limited) in cases involving harassment by special education students, whom school districts are obligated under federal law to teach.[66] As [Ms. Mongelli] has acknowledged, special education students are prone to disruptive behavior by virtue of their disabilities; even so, defendants are essentially asking the court to "immunize" schools from liability for harassment of a teacher by a special education student, no matter what the circumstances or how severe the harassment. Such a blanket prohibition would do a disservice to teachers, who deserve a working environment free from abuse, and would provide schools with no incentive to remedy incidents of harassment in their special education classrooms. Therefore, while the requisite threshold of abuse will necessarily be higher than with students lacking developmental disabilities, the court finds that harassment of teachers by special education students can constitute a hostile work environment for Title VII purposes.

The court ultimately ruled for the school district in *Mongelli*, finding the conduct did not satisfy Title VII's "severe or pervasive" requirement because JW's actions occurred over a short period of time, after which he was permanently removed from Ms. Mongelli's classroom. While not a child abuse case per se, *Mongelli* does serve to illustrate the various difficult and competing legal interests along with the variety of related issues principals now face on almost a daily basis.

Safety Plans

Many states have adopted statutes requiring that schools have safety plans to address child abuse and the growing incidence of violence in schools. One such example is a Georgia statute, which states:

> Every public school shall prepare a *school safety plan* to help curb the growing incidence of violence in schools, to respond effectively to such incidents, and to provide a safe learning environment for Georgia's children, teachers, and other school personnel. Such plan shall also address preparedness for natural disasters, hazardous material or radiological accidents, acts of violence, and acts of terrorism. *School safety plans* of public schools shall be prepared

> with input from students enrolled in that school, parents or legal guardians of such students, teachers … , community leaders, other school employees and school district employees, and local law enforcement, fire service, public safety, and emergency management agencies.[67]

In *Murphy v. Bajjani*,[68] a Georgia student was assaulted by a fellow student and suffered severe injuries as a result. The parents sued the school district, the board of education and the individual members thereof, the superintendent, the principal, the assistant principal, and the clinic nurse. The claim was based on negligent performance of the statutory duty to create a school safety plan that addressed security issues and negligence *per se* for failing to report immediately to the district attorney and the police the name of the student believed to have committed an aggravated battery on school property. In dismissing the suit as to the safety plan issue, the court held that the actions complained of were discretionary functions rather than ministerial acts, thus entitling the school defendants to statutory immunity. The court stated:

> [T]he statutory mandate that a school safety plan be created calls for the plan's creator to exercise a discretionary duty—"the exercise of personal deliberation and judgment, which in turn entails examining the facts, reaching reasoned conclusions, and acting on them in a way not specifically directed" … and is prepared with input from a variety of persons ("students enrolled in that school, parents or legal guardians of such students, teachers in that school, community leaders, other school employees and school district employees, and local law enforcement, fire service, public safety, and emergency management agencies"). GA (1) (1) We conclude that the mandated action set forth in OCGA § 20-2-1185 is a discretionary duty rather than a ministerial duty.[69]

The court also dismissed the failure to report claim, noting it was a penal statute and that the failure to report was a misdemeanor. It reasoned that "[w]here the breach of a statutory duty can result in criminal liability, the statute is penal in nature and 'the violation of a penal statute does not automatically give rise to a civil cause of action on the part of one who is [purportedly] injured thereby.'" The court then held "[w]hile [the reporting statute] establishes Georgia's public policy concerning the need to report timely to the appropriate authorities the identity of students who commit certain proscribed acts on school grounds, *it does not create a civil cause of action for damages* in favor of the victim or anyone else for the purported failure to report timely."

Investigating Child Abuse—Child Suggestibility

School officials are permitted to interview students to investigate suspected child abuse, including abuse that may be occurring at home. "When a parent sends her child to school, she delegates some of her parenting responsibilities to school officials ... [and] should reasonably expect that school officials will speak with her child if the child raises serious concerns about her home life."[70]

Interviewing for possible child abuse is tricky business. Once child abuse is suspected, school officials should not interview or question the child further. Instead, they should report it to law enforcement or child protection services and let their child abuse interviewer experts do the interviewing.

The trickiness is that "child suggestibility" may be inferred if the interview is not videotaped or if the questioning is inappropriate for any number of reasons, including asking leading or repetitive questions, conducting repeated interviews, the interviewer's suggestive body language, etc. The New Jersey court set out factors that may result in the results of a suspected child abuse interview being subject to a charge of child suggestibility, thereby making the results of the interview inadmissible in court:

> The *Michaels* court further advised trial judges to consider the following factors to determine if there is some evidence to authorize a pretrial hearing: The absence of a taped initial interview; an inability to control familial influences; lack of spontaneous recollection on the part of the alleged victim(s); apparent bias on the part of the interviewer; the use of leading questions; the use of repeated questioning; the use of multiple interviews; the use of incessant questioning; instances of vilification of the alleged abuser; the use of bribes, threats, or cajoling; the appearance of suggestiveness through voice and body language; positive or negative reinforcement; or other influences. If any of these factors are present, the Court held they "constitute more than sufficient evidence to support a finding that the interrogations created a substantial risk that the statements and anticipated testimony are unreliable, and therefore justify a taint hearing."[71]

Criminal Background Checks

When a student is the victim of child abuse at the hands of a school employee or school volunteer, the school may be held responsible on the basis of a "negligent hiring" theory. One way to combat such liability is to do criminal background checks on employees and volunteers.

There is no such thing as a complete, nationwide criminal history. However, in the summer of 2006, Congress passed the Schools Safely Acquiring

Faculty Excellence Act (SAFE) as part of the Adam Walsh Child Protection and Safety Act of 2006. This law opens up the FBI database to school districts in all states.[72]

Further, most schools use and need the services of volunteers. In *C.L.C. v. Minneapolis Public School*,[73] the school was sued under the Minnesota Child Abuse Reporting Act by the mother of a physically and cognitively disabled child who was sexually assaulted by a volunteer at school. The volunteer was also the parent of another student. This volunteer/parent had an extensive criminal history, and the suit claimed the school was negligent for failure to conduct a background check. The Minnesota federal court did not rule the claim was frivolous. Rather, in dismissing the claim, the federal court stated "[t]hese claims present complex and sensitive issues concerning the extent to which state law will subject a school district to liability for the actions of its volunteers [and] [s]uch issues are best addressed by a state court in the first instance ..."[74]

Child Abuse and the Computer Age

Principals are facing challenges as they struggle to adapt policies and rules connected with use of the Internet and email in order to attempt to comply with federal laws, such as the Children's Internet Protection Act (CIPA).[75] Among other things, these abuse-related developments call on administrators to protect students from harmful material by the use of filter software and other means along with balancing student and employee privacy while monitoring Internet and email usage.[76]

Congress first attempted to protect children from exposure to pornographic material on the Internet by enacting the Communications Decency Act of 1996 (CDA). The CDA prohibited the knowing transmission of obscene or indecent messages over the Internet to any recipient less than 18 years of age.[77] In 1997, the U.S. Supreme Court in *Reno v. ACLU*,[78] struck down two provisions of the CDA that regulated speech on the Internet. In response to that decision, Congress passed the Child Online Protection Act (COPA) that was narrower than its predecessor yet still attempted to target pornography on the World Wide Web by prohibiting material "harmful to minors." In *Ashcroft v. American Civil Liberties Union*,[79] the Supreme Court upheld COPA's reliance on "community standards" to identify what material is considered harmful to minors, but left other issues regarding the law unanswered.

Then in *Ashcroft v. Free Speech Coalition*,[80] the Supreme Court held that the ban on virtual child pornography in the Child Pornography Prevention Act of 1996 (CPPA), 18 U.S.C.S. Section 2251 *et seq.*, abridged free speech and was unconstitutionally overbroad since it proscribed speech that was neither child pornography nor obscene and thus abridged the freedom to engage in a substantial amount of lawful speech. Finally, Congress abandoned the idea of censorship and turned to a more time-tested approach—impose obligations on recipients of federal funding. Among other things, this act requires K-12 schools receiving federal funding to filter against material that is obscene, involves child pornography, or is harmful to minors; create Internet safety policies; and conduct at least one public meeting to collect input from community members. In *United States v. American Library Association*,[81] the Supreme Court held that the Children's Internet Protection Act (CIPA) did not impose an unconstitutional condition on public libraries[82] because the use of Internet filtering software did not violate their patrons' First Amendment rights and was a valid exercise of Congress's spending power. Confident over this approach to the problem, Congress also included a similar requirement in the No Child Left Behind Act of 2001 (NCLB).[83]

Personal Protective Orders (PPOs)

One more recent phenomenon to muddle the principal's desk is responding to various types of abuse protective restraining orders.[84] These orders, referred to by many as Personal Protection Orders (PPOs) are closely akin to the child abuse topic. As an off-shoot of the child abuse issue, educators must become enlightened about the PPO and problems it presents in the public school setting.

PPOs are issued to victims of abuse, harassment, or threatening conduct, and typically restrict contact or communication between two individuals. Presently, PPOs can be obtained with relative ease, often without a lawyer, and are issued ex parte in many states. In the school setting, PPOs may be issued between coworkers, classmates, parents, board members, or visitors. For example, the Washington Education Association advises its members that an option "to counteract student violence against school employees is to file an anti-harassment injunction keeping the student (or parent who is harassing an employee) from any contact with the employee."[85] In fact, they have become so popular in the school context that even school districts as entities consider them an option for handling abuse or unruly conduct.[86] Presently, almost all states have PPO laws that emanate from statutes prohibiting harassment, domestic-abuse, or stalking.[87]

There are few reported cases dealing with the topic and while at first blush, it might seem that schools have no responsibility for administering or enforcing PPOs, the concept that public schools act as surrogate parents or in loco parentis, along with expanding theories of premises liability and a school's duty to protect students, it is likely schools do owe a duty to take reasonable steps to protect against foreseeable acts of violence and the harm that naturally flows.[88] In other words, if schools have notice of PPOs and fail to respond, even though they are not parties to the proceeding, liability may follow. Administrators will need to learn how to respond to PPOs as they enter the schoolhouse gate, and the Recommendations for Practice section of this chapter offers some guidelines.

Recommendations for Practice

Child Abuse Generally

Case law and statutory provisions on child abuse involving schools and educators continue to proliferate, and many aspects of the issue remain unclear. What is clear, however, is that school officials and school districts have responsibilities in the area and are perceived by courts and law makers as the first line of defense against abuse and neglect.[89] There are many specific procedures and useful behaviors that do contribute to a safe school environment for children, and some of those recommendations follow.

1. Know the *cluster of indicators* of abuse and train others who have a duty to report suspected abuse. Indicators that occur repeatedly and/or in combination with each other should be red flags to the educator. Do not fail to investigate an abuse complaint or make a decision to delay or ignore the necessary action out of concern for confidentiality or employee loyalty. Some commentators even recommend that schools "[d]o not attempt to confirm your suspicions of child abuse yourself before making a report... [Noting] [c]hildren are awfully pliable, and can be happy one day and troubled the next... [L]eave it up to law enforcement to do an investigation ... [and] focus on how to get information to family services, how they're going to document their report to the agency, and how they're going to work with the agency once it has intervened..."[90]

2. Maintain a clear policy on the principal's role and the teacher's role in reporting. Teachers, especially beginning teachers, say they are not always certain about the expectations of the principal regarding procedures. They need to know where and who to call or submit written reports to if they are required. Communicate teacher's duties in teacher handbooks.[91]

3. Collaborate with local child protective services. Use them to train staff and to work with the school in the interest of high-risk children. Also, to ensure that everyone understands the proper process for and consequences of child abuse reporting, offer comprehensive training. There should be annual training of all school employees on how to recognize symptoms of abuse and their obligation to make a prompt report to school principals or other appropriate parties of all facts known to them. Involve district social workers, school counselors, and principals as you determine what information staff needs to spot signs of abuse. Involving these parties in training preparation can ensure participants get a comprehensive understanding of proper reporting protocol, including how to avoid overreporting, which can damage relationships between districts and parents. Other points:

a. Share state specifics. Your state law will offer specific guidance on mandatory reporting requirements for school employees and define which employees this covers.

b. Train on internal reporting policy. Let staff members know to whom they should report regarding issues of suspected abuse. Provide detailed information about whether you and the school principal should be notified first, or if reporters should contact law enforcement directly under local policy.

c. Stress confidentiality. While reporting suspected abuse to a designated official will not violate a student's Family Educational Rights and Privacy Act protections, sharing information with other unrelated parties might. That means employees should avoid asking coworkers questions about whether they have noticed symptoms of abuse in particular students. A better rule of thumb is for staff to make judgments based on their own observations, then report abuse through the proper channels.

d. Be safe, not sorry. If you think abuse may be occurring, it is better to report concerns and allow an investigator to take a closer look at the case.

e. You should also let your staff know they are not responsible for "investigating" any suspected incidents of abuse. They should, however, rely on red flags they have observed or heard when working with the child.

f. Share promise of anonymity. It's important to make sure your staff members understand that if they report suspected abuse through the proper channels, their names will not be mentioned as the source of the report.[92]

4. Have a clear policy on how to proceed when an abuse investigator comes to school.
5. Inform parents regularly of the school's policy regarding child abuse and the procedures followed by the school in the event of potential child abuse allegations.
6. Provide training for parents so that they, too, can recognize the signs of abuse and know where to go or whom to contact for assistance.
7. Use legal screening methods to keep abusers out of the schools through the hiring process. Be vigilant in checking employment references.
8. Do not "pass on" abusing staff members to other school districts.[93]
9. Adopt and publish an anti-harassment policy, which includes grievance procedures providing for prompt and equitable resolution of sex discrimination or harassment complaints.[94]

10. Beware of the fine lines between corporal punishment versus child abuse and harassment versus child abuse, and over-report rather than under-report. If corporal punishment is allowed within the state and school district, follow policy scrupulously in administering it; establish clear rules and expectations for the staff regarding it; and train faculty in more effective alternatives for disciplining students.[95]
11. Practice prevention: educate children in problem-solving, in how to deal with crisis, and self-protection.[96]

Computers and Internet[97]

1. Most educational institutions have adopted policies governing the use of the Internet. Because of the potential for student access to inappropriate materials and possible misuse of the Internet, these policies serve to provide helpful instruction to those provided access.[98]
2. Many policies require that parental consent must be provided for students to utilize the Internet at school. For religious or other reasons, some parents object to their children having access to such technology. A written consent from parents would be ideal, but is impractical in many circumstances. Accordingly, most schools now disseminate a policy and specifically provide that parents may elect to prevent access to the Internet by their children.
3. An opt-out, rather than opt-in, procedure is utilized. Reasonably informed parents are well aware that students are provided access to the Internet and should be expected to inform school officials if they object to their children having that access.
4. Policies usually contain a listing of prohibited conduct with regard to the Internet, violation of copyrights, and access to obscene material.
5. Schools are usually well-advised to make clear that access to all data on, taken from, or compiled using school computers is subject to inspection and discipline, but encourage self-regulation rather than attempt to over-regulate usage.
6. A school is well advised to encourage responsible use of the Internet away from school. However, the authority of a school to regulate home use of the Internet is more limited in the absence of some clear nexus to the school setting such as a reasonable likelihood of disruption.

Responding to PPOs

So how does an administrator respond as PPOs will enter the schoolhouse gate? The following recommendations[99] are offered as guidelines. They are by no means all inclusive, nor will some be appropriate for all circumstances.

1. ***Get a copy of the order.*** If anyone states he or she has a PPO, the principal should ask to see it. A photocopy should be made and kept in the appropriate school file. It can be referred to by staff or shown to the police if needed.
2. ***Verify the order.*** Make sure the PPO is genuine. The order should be signed and dated by a judge. Call the issuing court and give the court clerk the case number listed. Confirm the name of the case, the expiration date, and the names of the victim and perpetrator. Or send a copy to the school attorney to confirm its validity and to get advice on what it means.
3. ***Photo and description.*** Depending on the case, ask for a photograph and detailed description of the harasser, and distribute it as appropriate to school personnel.
4. ***Alert school employees.*** Notify all school building staff and any security personnel of the PPO. Provide details and an explanation of its meaning.
5. ***Emergency protocols.*** Establish emergency procedures and protocols with school security personnel and local law enforcement. A close working relationship with local law enforcement is imperative.
6. ***Intervention.*** Consider intervening in the PPO proceedings for specific court guidance or direction on how to respond or accommodate the order at school. In proper cases, courts might consider including an incidental contact exception.

Endnotes

[1] Doe v. Corp. of the President of Church of Jesus Christ of Latter-Day Saints, 2007 Wash. App. LEXIS 2656 (Wash. Ct. App. 2007)

[2] Hardwicke v. Am. Boychoir Sch., 188 N.J. 69, 902 A.2d 900 (N.J. 2006).

[3] "The School reportedly settled [an earlier] suit for $ 875,000." *Id.*

[4] The court in *Hardwicke* addressed primarily state law claims. For recent cases addressing abuse claims under federal law, *see* U.S. Bank v. Bd. of Educ., 2007 U.S. Dist. LEXIS 35722 (D. Ill. 2007) (violation 42 U.S.C. § 1983 (section 1983) based upon violation of the minor's right to be free from sexual abuse; discrimination in violation of Title IX of the Education Amendments of 1972 (Title IX), and violation of 20 U.S.C. § 1681 et seq.); and Allen v. Susquehanna Twp. Sch. Dist., 2007 U.S. App. LEXIS 9394 (3d Cir. 2007) (violations of section 1983 based on the Due Process Clause of the Fourteenth Amendment of the United States Constitution, liability under the Individuals with Disabilities Education Act (IDEA) for failure to provide a free appropriate public education; violation of the child's rights under

Section 504 of the Rehabilitation Act, and violations of the child's rights under the Americans with Disabilities Act).

5 In a somewhat complicated procedural history, the trial court in *Hardwicke* had granted the school's motion for summary judgment and dismissed the case. On appeal, a divided panel of the Appellate Division reversed in part. The Supreme Court then agreed to hear the case and ultimately allowed it to proceed by affirming the judgment of the Appellate Division and remanding it to the trial court for further proceedings.

6 *Compare Hardwicke with* Larson v. Miller, 76 F.3d 1446 (8th Cir. 1996), where even though the school van driver was ultimately convicted of sexual abuse and sentenced to jail, the court held that "[t]he jury's verdict [against the school officials] in this case appears to have been the product of pure speculation and understandable sympathy for a little girl who was undisputably harmed." *Miller* was a featured case in the "Child Abuse" chapter from the 2000 Principal's Legal Handbook; see J.B. Gessford, J.L. Curcio, & T.W. Curtis, *Child Abuse*, Principal's Legal Handbook, (2d ed. 2000).

7 *See* Hardwicke v. Am. Boychoir Sch., 368 N.J. Super. 71, 77 (App. Div. 2004). While this specific finding was made in the Appellate Division's opinion, the Supreme Court's analysis is not inapposite.

8 C. C. Tower, The Role of Educators in the Protection and Treatment of Child Abuse and Neglect (1992).

9 James A. Monteleone & Armand E. Brodeur, *Identifying Physical Abuse,* Recognition of Child Abuse for the Mandated Reporter (1994).

10 Tower, *supra* note 8.

11 Tower, *supra* note 8, at 32.

12 Tower, *supra* note 8, at 15–19; *see also* Lane J. Velktkamp & Thomas W. Miller, Clinical Handbook of Child Abuse and Neglect, 13–16 (1994).

13 Hagen v. Indep. Sch. Dist. No. I-004, 157 P.3d 738 (Okla. 2007). The dissenting opinion challenged the majority's holding stating: "I respectfully dissent for three reasons. First, the district court's finding that the school district board failed to prove that this special education teacher ... inflicted mental and physical abuse on a child is clearly erroneous. Second, the district court's and this Court's injection of a specific intent to harm requirement into the definition of child abuse in the Oklahoma Child Abuse Reporting and Prevention Act is contrary to the plain terms of the Act and inconsistent with the criminal assault and battery statutes. Third, this Court's construction of provisions in the Teacher Due Process Act as placing in the district courts the final discretionary authority to fire a career teacher is contrary to the plain terms of the Act."

14 *Id.* at note 2.

15 Frugis v. Bracigliano, 177 N.J. 250 (N.J. 2003). *Frugis* was a featured case in the "Child Abuse" chapter from the 2005 Principal's Legal Handbook and remains an important case in providing guidance to principals in the child abuse area; *see* J.B. Gessford & G.H. Perry, *Child Abuse*, The Principal's Legal Handbook, (3rd ed. 2005).

16 The court's use of the "surrogate parents" language is a reference to the *in loco parentis* doctrine. "The law itself recognizes the [school's] responsibilities [to act in place of the parent when the child is under the school's authority and control] with the phrase *in loco parentis*." Board of Educ. of Indep. Sch. Dist. No. 92 of Pottawatomie County v. Earls, 122 S. Ct. 2559, 2565 (2002) (Brennan, J. concurring). The United States Supreme Court has "acknowledged that for many purposes 'school authorities act in loco parentis,' with the power and indeed the duty to 'inculcate the habits and manners of civility.'" Vernonia Sch. Dist. 47j v. Acton, 515 U.S. 646, 655 (1995). "Through the legal doctrine of *in loco parentis*, courts upheld the right of schools to discipline students, to enforce rules, and to maintain order ... Applying *in loco parentis*, the judiciary was reluctant to interfere in the routine business of school administration, allowing schools and teachers to set and enforce rules and to maintain order.... The doctrine of *in loco parentis* limited the ability of schools to set rules and control their classrooms in almost no way." Morse v. Frederick, 127 S. Ct. 2618 (2007) (Thomas, J., concurring).

[17] L.W. ex rel. L.G. v. Toms River Reg'l Sch. Bd. of Educ., 189 N.J. 381 (2007).

[18] *Id.* It must be noted that the New Jersey "reasonable measures to protect" standard, grounded on one legal theory or another, has essentially been adopted by the courts in most states. *See, e.g.,* Dutra v. Eagleson, 146 Cal. App. 4th 216 (Cal. Ct. App. 2006); Pritchard v. Von Houten, 960 So. 2d 568 (Miss. Ct. App. 2007); Hertzel v. Palmyra Sch. Dist., 15 Neb. App. 538 (Neb. Ct. App. 2007); Baumgardt v. Wausau Sch. Dist. Bd. of Educ., 475 F. Supp. 2d 800 (D. Wis. 2007) ("[t]he Wisconsin legislature ... has specifically imposed on school officials an affirmative duty to protect students from actual or threatened abuse by reporting such conduct to the authorities."); Guda v. Commonwealth, 42 Va. App. 453 (Va. App. 2004); Doe v. Warren Consol. Schs., 2004 U.S. App. LEXIS 6037, 17–18 (6th Cir. 2004) and Jane Doe A v. Green, 298 F. Supp. 2d 1025 (D. Nev. 2004). *But see* Lee v. Pine Bluff Sch. Dist., 472 F.3d 1026 (8th Cir. 2007) (holding that school had no constitutional duty of care with respect to students participating in voluntary school-related activities where the student became ill on an out-of-town band trip and died).

[19] Frugis v. Bracigliano, 177 N.J. 250, 827 A.2d 1040, 1052 (N.J. 2003).

[20] *Id.* at 1052.

[21] *Id.* at 1052.

[22] *Id.* at 1053.

[23] N.J. Stat. § 9:6-8.10 (2007).

[24] Barbina v. Curry, 2007 W. Va. LEXIS 4 (2007).

[25] 591 S.E.2d 235 (W. Va. 2003).

[26] *Id.* at 240.

[27] 801 A.2d 478 (Pa. 2002). *See also* Maryfrances T. Behney, Annual Survey of Pennsylvania Administrative Law: Public Welfare: *P.R. v. Commonwealth*, Department of Public Welfare: "The Supreme Court of Pennsylvania Changes the Standard for Expunging a Record of Child Abuse," 12 Widener L.J. 355 (2003).

[28] *Id.* at 483.

[29] Kirkland v. Greene County Bd. of Educ., 347 F.3d 903 (11th Cir. 2003) (principal's conduct of repeatedly striking a student with a metal cane, including once on the head as he was doubled over protecting his chest, when he was not armed or physically threatening in any manner, fulfilled the criteria that the principal engaged in abuse rather than use of valid corporal punishment and established a constitutional violation).

[30] Gabrielle M. v. Park Forest-Chicago Heights, II. Sch. Dist. 163, 315 F.3d 817, 828 (7th Cir. 2003).

[31] *Id.* at 822.

[32] *See* Justin Juozapavicius, The Arizona Republic (Mar. 31, 2004), *2 Mesa Administrators Could Lose Licenses* (because the administrators viewed the incident only as harassment or "horseplay" and not abuse, they did not report the incident).

[33] 2000 U.S. App. LEXIS 8802 (U.S. App. 2000).

[34] State v. McPherson, 266 Neb. 715 (2003).

[35] *In re* Interest of Phyllisa B., 265 Neb. 53 (2002).

[36] For example, while the male teacher-perpetrator in *Hardwicke* was named as a defendant in the suit, by the time it was filed in 2001 he had moved to Canada and did not even bother to file a responsive pleading. *Id.* at 902 A.2d 906.

[37] *Id.* at 902 A.2d 910.

[38] Hardwicke v. Am. Boychoir Sch., 368 N.J. Super. 71, 79 (App. Div. 2004).

[39] *See* J.B. Gessford & G.H. Perry, *Child Abuse*, in The Principal's Legal Handbook, (3rd ed. 2005).

[40] 2007 U.S. Dist. LEXIS 35722 (D. Ill. 2007).

[41] 347 F.3d 1014, 1039 (7th Cir. 2003).

[42] 2007 U.S. Dist. LEXIS 35722 (D. Ill. 2007) at 20.

[43] Kimberly F. v. Northeastern Educ. Intermediate Unit 19, 2007 U.S. Dist. LEXIS 35778, and 2007 U.S. Dist. LEXIS 71394 (motion for reconsideration), (D. Pa. 2007).

[44] 15 Neb. App. 538 (Neb. Ct. App. 2007).

45 Baumgardt v. Wausau Sch. Dist. Bd. of Educ., 475 F. Supp. 2d 800 (D. Wis. 2007).

46 51 Am Jur 2d *Limitation of Actions* § 224.

47 *Id.* at 902 A.2d 926.

48 *Jones v. Jones*, 576 A.2d 316 (N.J. App.Div.), *certif. denied*, 585 A.2d 412 (N.J. 1990).

49 *Id.* at 198, 205, 208-09, 576 A.2d 316.

50 As reported by the Senate Judiciary Committee in its Statement to Senate Bill No. 257, at 1 (Feb. 24, 1992) "Because of the unique nature of sexual abuse, which may only be discovered by an adult victim after years of repression, ... [a]ny such action must be brought within two years after reasonable discovery." The bill allows a court to find that the statute of limitations in a particular case was suspended ("tolled") because of the plaintiff's condition. The judge would conduct a hearing, and would be able to order an independent psychiatric evaluation of the victim, in order to make this determination." The Statement has been reproduced at N.J.S.A. 2A:44 to 2A:65A (West 2000) at 717-19.

51 *See*, "Running of limitations against action for civil damages for sexual abuse of child," 9 A.L.R.5th 321. *See also* C.R.G. v. Brunty, 38 Va. Cir. 431 (Va. Cir. Ct. 1996) (a former student who had recently been released from a psychiatric hospital in Missouri, allegedly recovered *repressed memories* that that teacher had sexually assaulted her in 1982. The court stating "there is no more deplorable badge of infamy a person can wear than that of being a child abuser ..." reversed Department of Social Services ("DSS") findings of "Sexual Abuse-Level 1" to be maintained in the Child Abuse and Neglect Information System (CANIS) central registry for lack of evidence).

52 For a more detailed treatment of the basics of child abuse, *see* J.B. Gessford, J.L. Curcio, & T.W. Curtis, *Child Abuse*, in The Principal's Legal Handbook, (2d ed. 2000).

53 S.J. v. Kan. City Mo. Pub. Sch. Dist., 294 F.3d 1025 (8th Cir. 2002) (a student challenged summary judgment for school district and its officials in the student's action under 42 U.S.C. § 1983, claiming that they failed to receive, investigate, or act on complaints of constitutional violations and that they failed to properly train a minister who volunteered for the school district). For a detailed analysis of legal concerns with school volunteers, *see* Gregory H. Perry, *Volunteers Enter the Schoolhouse*, 79 Neb. L. Rev. 998 (2000).

54 T. Dwyer, The Washington Post, Thurs., Feb. 12, 2004, at B01.

55 Christina Buschmann, *Mandatory Fingerprinting of Public School Teachers: Facilitating Background Checks or Infringing on Individuals' Constitutional Rights?*, 11 Wm. & Mary Bill of Rts. J. 1273 (Apr. 2003).

56 Rhone v. Dickerson, 2003 Del. C.P. LEXIS 43 (Del. C.P. 2003) (holding that false accusations of child abuse are slander per se because child abuse is considered a crime of moral turpitude, and while most states grant immunity to a mandatory reporter, in the event the court finds that the report of child abuse was not made in good faith, the reporter will be found guilty of slander per se even when the report is made to a government agency dealing with the protection of children).

57 James B. Gessford, *Personal Protective Orders (PPOs) Enter the Schoolhouse Gate*, 79 Neb. L. Rev. 828 (2000).

58 C.R.G. v. Brunty, 38 Va. Cir. 431, 438 (Va. Cir. Ct. 1996), *quoting* Jackson v. W., 14 Va. App. 391 (Va. Ct. App. 1992). The *Brunty* case involved a teacher who was accused of sexual abuse of a child. He established that the accusation was unfounded. *See also*, FN 51.

59 837 A.2d 614 (Pa. Commw. 2003).

60 *Id.* at 617.

61 45 C.F.R., Parts 160 and 164.

62 45 C.F.R. § 160.103.

63 45 C.F.R. § 164.512.

64 Mongelli v. Red Clay Consol. Sch. Dist. Bd. of Educ., 491 F. Supp. 2d 467 (D. Del. 2007).

65 *Id.*

66 This was the court's footnote: "Under the Individuals with Disabilities Education Act, 20 U.S.C. §§ 1400 et seq. ("IDEA"), "[a] free appropriate public education is available to all children with disabilities residing in the State between the ages of 3 and 21, inclusive,

including children with disabilities who have been suspended or expelled from school." *Id.* § 1412(a)(1)(A). The Code of Federal Regulations states that "[s]chool personnel ... may remove a child with a disability who violates a code of student conduct from his or her current placement to an appropriate interim alternative educational setting, another setting, or suspension, for not more than 10 consecutive school days ... , and for additional removals of not more than 10 consecutive school days in that same school year for separate incidents of misconduct (as long as those removals do not constitute a change of placement ...)" 34 C.F.R. § 300.530(b)(1). *See also Id.* § 300.536(a) (defining "change of placement" as a suspension lasting ten or more consecutive school days or a "series of removals that constitute a pattern" of disruptive behavior).

Within ten school days of any decision to change the placement of a child with a disability because of a violation of a code of student conduct, the [local education agency ("LEA")], the parent, and relevant members of the child's [Individualized Education Program ("IEP")] Team ... must review all relevant information in the student's file ... to determine ... [i]f the conduct in question was caused by, or had a direct and substantial relationship to, the child's disability....

Id. § 300.530(e)(1)(i). Barring the existence of any '[s]pecial circumstances,' *see id.* § 300.530(g), if it is determined "that the conduct was a manifestation of the child's disability, the IEP Team must ... return the child to the placement from which the child was removed, unless the parent and the LEA agree to a change of placement as part of the modification of the behavioral intervention plan.' *Id.* § 300.530(f)(2)."

67 OCGA § 20-2-1185 (a).

68 Murphy v. Bajjani, 647 S.E.2d 54 (Ga. 2007).

69 *Id.*

70 United States v. Hollingsworth, 2007 U.S. App. LEXIS 18178 (7th Cir. 2007).

71 State v. Michaels, 642 A.2d 1372 (N.J. 1994). Justice Scalia discussed the problem of child suggestibility in a dissenting opinion. The majority of the Court allowed the State to exclude an accused child abuser from the courtroom while the child victim testified, with the accused able to view the testimony only via a one-way video. Justice Scalia felt that this violated the Confrontation Clause. He stated: "The 'special' reasons that exist for suspending one of the usual guarantees of reliability in the case of children's testimony are perhaps matched by 'special' reasons for being particularly insistent upon it in the case of children's testimony. Some studies show that children are substantially more vulnerable to suggestion than adults, and often unable to separate recollected fantasy (or suggestion) from reality. *See* Lindsay & Johnson, Reality Monitoring and Suggestibility: Children's Ability to Discriminate Among Memories From Different Sources, in Children's Eyewitness Memory 92 (S. Ceci, M. Toglia, & D. Ross eds. 1987); Feher, *The Alleged Molestation Victim, The Rules of Evidence, and the Constitution: Should Children Really Be Seen and Not Heard?*, 14 AM. J. CRIM. L. 227, 230-233 (1987); Christiansen, *The Testimony of Child Witnesses: Fact, Fantasy, and the Influence of Pretrial Interviews*, 62 WASH. L. REV. 705, 708-711 (1987). "The injustice their erroneous testimony can produce is evidenced by the tragic Scott County investigations of 1983-1984, which disrupted the lives of many (as far as we know) innocent people in the small town of Jordan, Minnesota ... There is no doubt that some sexual abuse took place in Jordan; but there is no reason to believe it was as widespread as charged." Maryland v. Craig, 497 U.S. 836 (1990) (Justice Scalia, dissenting). *But see* State v. Campbell, 2007 NMCA 51 (N.M. Ct. App. 2007) (allowing a child expert's testimony of child abuse). *See also*, Ceci & Friedman, *The Suggestibility of Children: Scientific Research and Legal Implications*, 86 CORNELL L. REV. 33 (2000).

72 This pertinent section of this law is referred to as the "Schools Safely Acquiring Faculty Excellence Act of 2006." It provides that "[t]he Attorney General of the United States shall, upon request of the chief executive officer of a State, conduct fingerprint-based checks of the national crime information databases ... pursuant to a request submitted by ... a private or public elementary school, a private or public secondary school, a local educational agency, or State educational agency in that State, on individuals employed by, under consideration

for employment by, or otherwise in a position in which the individual would work with or around children in the school or agency." 42 USCS § 16962 (b).

73 C.L.C. v. Minneapolis Pub. Sch., 2007 U.S. Dist. LEXIS 44869 (D. Minn. 2007).

74 *Id.*

75 114 Stat. 2763A-335. See also The Communications Decency Act of 1996 (CDA) 47 U.S.C. § 223; Child Online Protection Act (COPA) 47 U.S.C. § 231, the Child Pornography Prevention Act of 1996 (CPPA) 18 U.S.C. § 2251 et seq., and the Neighborhood Children's Internet Protection Act (NCIPA), 47 U.S.C. § 254.

76 Kathleen Conn, *Protecting Children From Internet Harm (Again): Will the Children's Internet Protection Act Survive Judicial Scrutiny?,* 153 Educ. L. Rep. 469, 470 (2001) (providing a helpful discussion and overview of this area).

77 *See* 47 U.S.C. § 223 (a).

78 521 U.S. 844 (1997).

79 535 U.S. 564 (2002).

80 535 U.S. 234 (2002).

81 539 U.S. 194 (2003).

82 Presumably, this ruling will relate to schools as well.

83 20 U.S.C. § 6777, § 2441, Pub. L. 107–110, No Child Left Behind Act.

84 *See* Anand Vaishnav & Doreen Iudica Vigue, *Restraining Orders Illustrate Greater Focus on School Safety*, The Boston Globe, May 15, 2000, at B01 ([T]he idea of students obtaining restraining orders against classmates—and the Challenge school administrators face in enforcing them—raises new questions: …). *See also* "Difficult Parents—Six Steps to Deal with Parent's Restraining Order," School Policy Insider, July 1998, at 7.

85 http://www.wa.nea.org/publicat/Legal/prvntsv2.htm at p. 21.

86 *See, e.g.*, Lathrop & Clark, *Harassment Injunctions*, Wisc. Sch. News, Apr. 1998, at 27 (suggesting schools themselves consider securing protective orders to deal with unruly students, parents or visitors); Tigerton v. Minniecheske, 565 N.W.2d 586 (Wis. Ct. App. 1997) (reference to "persons" in harassment injunction statute includes municipalities as an entity within its scope).

87 *See*, Neb. Rev. Stat. § 42–924 (Reissue 1998) and Neb. Rev. Stat. § 28–311.09 (1998 Cum. Supp.).

88 For a detailed analysis of this topic, *see* James B. Gessford, *Personal Protective Orders (PPOs) Enter the Schoolhouse Gate*, 79 Neb. L. Rev. 828 (2000).

89 W. B. Crenshaw, L. M. Crenshaw, & J.W. Lichtenberg, *When Educators Confront Child Abuse: An Analysis of the Decision to Report*, 19 Child Abuse & Neglect 1095.

90 See *Let authorities carry out investigations*, Today's School Psychologist, Vol. 11 No. 1 (August 1, 2007).

91 The importance of teacher handbooks to communicate child abuse duties to staff is reflected in the court's decision in *P.H. v. The Sch. Dist. of Kan. City, Mo.*, 265 F.3d 653 (8th Cir. 2001). A high school teacher had engaged in sexual relations with a male student, including oral sex almost daily throughout a two-year time period, oftentimes at school during school hours or at hotels and other places. The student filed a lawsuit against the district claiming (among other things) a civil rights violation based on a failure to train staff. The court rejected the claims against the district, noting that "the school had developed and implemented policies prohibiting sexual abuse of students and procedures for handling complaints of sexual abuse. The [district] required employees to report all suspected cases of child abuse. The teacher handbooks state policies prohibiting sexual abuse and harassment, procedures were in place for remedying such abuse, and in-service meetings were held to educate administrators and staff … [The teacher] had notice that this was prohibited conduct by reason of the handbook … [and] simply chose to disregard the handbook and all common sense."

92 Adapted from *Share protocol for reporting suspected child abuse*, School Law Bulletin Vol. 10 No. 12 (April 1, 2007).

93 An example of the need to not provide employee reference letters that falsely portray a former teacher is provided in *Shrum ex rel. Kelly v. Kluck*, 249 F.3d 773 (8th Cir. 2001). A boy was

molested by a teacher in a Texas school district. The teacher had been hired in part based on a recommendation letter from a Nebraska superintendent of a school district where the teacher had worked before. The letter was written as part of a confidential settlement that terminated the teacher's employment in that district, after the Nebraska school had become aware of possible inappropriate conduct by the teacher involving students. The boy's mother sued the Nebraska school district, claiming the molestation of her boy would not have occurred if the Nebraska superintendent had given an honest, complete reference letter. The court ultimately ruled in favor of the Nebraska school district, since the reference letter was neutral in tone and content.

The misconduct of teacher Kluck recently led to a jury verdict against a Nebraska school district, where Kluck had worked before leaving to Texas. An August 10, 2007, Associated Press news article entitled "*Jury awards $1.2 million to former student in sex abuse case,*" reports:

A North Platte jury on Thursday awarded $1.2 million to a former student who says he was sexually abused by a teacher after other students made numerous complaints to the school about the teacher's behavior. The former student, who is now 25 and identified only as John Doe in the lawsuit, said he was sexually assaulted in 1993 by the teacher, Michael Kluck, but told no one of the assault. In 2003, the Elwood Public School District, its insurance company and a guidance counselor pressured the former student into signing a form to keep him from suing, even after the teacher confessed to the assault, according to the lawsuit filed in U.S. District Court in North Platte. Kluck died of a heart attack in 2000. The school district, guidance counselor David Blessing and the Allied Insurance Co. were defendants in the lawsuit.

94 Office of Civil Rights, "Revised Sexual Harassment Guidance: Harassment of Students by School Employees, Other Students, or Third Parties" (Jan. 2001).

95 http://childlaw.law.sc.edu/usermanual/educator/section6.htm (last visited July 1999).

96 *Id.*

97 For further detail on internet laws, *see* James A. Rapp, Education Law, § 11.02, Matthew Bender & Company, Inc., 2007.

98 *See, e.g.*, Lynch, *School Districts and the Internet: Practice and Model Policy*, 122 Educ. L. Rep. 21 (1998).

99 Adapted from "Difficult Parents—Six Steps to Deal with Parent's Restraining Order," School Policy Insider, July 1998, at 7.

Chapter 8

Student-to-Student Sexual Harassment

Verna L. Williams

Introduction

This chapter[1] examines the legal issues surrounding student-to-student sexual harassment under Title IX of the Education Amendments of 1972[2] and discusses briefly some policy recommendations for principals to consider. Title IX prohibits sex discrimination in any federally funded educational program or activity. Because most schools—public or private—receive money from the federal government, Title IX's proscription against sex discrimination extends broadly. Principals should be aware that their state laws may also impose various obligations regarding sex discrimination; however, this chapter deals only with the law under Title IX. It is also important to note that Title IX imposes liability upon educational institutions that receive federal funds[3] and not upon individual school officials.[4]

Legal Issues

Background

Title IX liability for sexual harassment in schools is grounded in the statute's mandate that "no person … be excluded from participation in, be denied the benefits of, or be subjected to discrimination" on the basis of sex.[5] The first Supreme Court cases interpreting the statute read that proscription very broadly, recognizing a need to give Title IX "a sweep as broad as its language."[6] Accordingly, over the past thirty-five years that Title IX has been on the books, courts have understood the statute to prohibit a wide range of sex discrimination, from policies excluding pregnant and parenting students from participating in honor societies,[7] to disparities in athletics opportunities.[8] Following the Supreme Court's direction, lower courts have looked to the law governing Title VII of the Civil Rights Act of 1964 to discern the meaning of sex discrimination in this context.[9] As a result, just as Title VII requires educational institutions to address sexual harassment of employees, Title IX imposes a similar obligation on schools with respect to students, irrespective of whether the harassers are teachers or fellow students.[10]

The Supreme Court's decision in *Davis v. Monroe County Board of Education*[11] established the standard of damages liability under Title IX for school districts when students sexually harass one another. Building upon numerous cases that had come before, the Court held that school districts could be held legally responsible when:

1. the alleged harassment was based on sex;
2. it was sufficiently severe and pervasive to interfere with the student's ability to get an education;
3. appropriate school officials had actual knowledge of the harassment; and
4. they responded with deliberate indifference.

The following explains how the courts have interpreted these factors after *Davis*.

Actionable Sexual Harassment in the Title IX Context

Far from childish pranks, sexual harassment in the school setting consists of serious misconduct that can have a devastating effect on students at the receiving end. Harassment occurs at all levels of schooling, among students of all ages. It can take many forms, from verbal taunts and abuse or inappropriate touching, to criminal misconduct, such as rape.[12] The reasons students engage in sexual harassment are not altogether clear;[13] however, in some cases, misconduct that is of a sexually precocious nature[14] may suggest child abuse that state law may require school officials to address.[15] As the following will explain, school districts can be held financially liable for failing to address student-to-student sexual harassment of which they are aware. The law that has developed in this area provides some guidance to ascertaining when misconduct rises to the level of actionable harassment. Generally speaking, harassment must be "based on sex" and "sufficiently severe and pervasive" in order to result in damages liability. It should be noted, however, that school officials would be wise to intervene as soon as possible to prevent harassment from escalating and, in turn, to mitigate the harm to targeted students.[16]

Based on Sex

In general, "based on sex" means that *but for* the targeted student's sex,[17] she[18] would not have been harassed. In other words, the target was selected for harassment because she was female. As explained below, "based on sex" includes harassment that is of a sexual nature, based on hostility to a particular sex, or based on stereotypes assigned to a particular sex, which may also be referred to as gender-based harassment. Additionally, "comparative evidence about how the harasser treated both males and females in a mixed-sex workplace" also could constitute conduct that is "based on sex" for Title IX purposes.[19]

Courts generally have no trouble concluding that misconduct of a sexual nature is "based on sex" when the harassment is between males and females.

For example, in *Fitzgerald v. Barnstable School Committee*,[20] a third-grade boy allegedly forced a kindergarten girl to pull up her dress, remove her underwear, and spread her legs, which the court concluded "constituted severe, pervasive, and objectively offensive harassment."[21] Similarly, when two boys made gestures asking for sexual favors, grabbed a girl's buttocks, and "made lewd comments such as 'you are a slut,' 'you want to f--- me,' 'give me head,' and 'let me touch your ass,'" the court assumed with no discussion that the conduct was "based on sex."[22] This aspect of the test for sexual harassment is frequently presumed when the misconduct is sexual in nature, particularly when the victim and the aggressor are of different sexes. As a result, at least one school district has tried to defend against a Title IX lawsuit by arguing that because the alleged misconduct was not "'motivated by sexual desire' or spouted by the opposite sex," it was not "based on sex."[23] In that case, the defendant school district argued that the alleged harassment, consisting of other students calling the target a "slut" and a "whore," occurred because of a past rape that the victim had suffered and reported.[24] The court rejected that argument, recognizing that the "based on sex" inquiry is not contingent upon sexual desire.[25] In that case, the harassment reflected gendered stereotypes about the targeted student's sexual conduct, which the court deemed was based on sex.[26]

Indeed, as the Supreme Court emphasized in *Oncale v. Sundowner Offshore Services,*[27] because the "based on sex" element means simply that the harassment would not have occurred *but for* the victim's sex.[28] As a result, the harasser's sexuality or desire may be one way of making that showing, but it is not the only way. Similarly, the fact that the harasser and the target may be of the same sex should not, per se, bar a finding that the misconduct was in fact based on sex; rather, courts must engage in a more searching inquiry to determine whether the misconduct occurred on account of sex as a legal matter. Thus, as discussed briefly above, evidence that the harasser was hostile to the victim because of sex would satisfy this part of the standard, as would evidence that the misconduct was a premised on the victim's failure to adhere to a gender stereotype.[29] Making such a determination is, as the Court noted, a fact-based inquiry that calls for "[c]ommon sense, and an appropriate sensitivity to social context."[30]

Theno v. Tonganoxie Unified School District No. 464[31] provides a useful illustration of this analysis in the Title IX setting. During a timeframe spanning four years, Dylan Theno was the target of comments, rumors, drawings, and written notes questioning his sexual orientation, using terms such as "faggot," "jack-off boy," "flamer," "queer," and "banana boy."[32] The court concluded that the harassment at issue was driven by his classmates' "stereotyped expectations for gender" and designed to "disparage his perceived lack of masculinity."[33]

Severe and Pervasive

The *Davis* Court noted, "[s]chools are unlike the adult workplace and … children may regularly interact in a manner that would be unacceptable among adults … students often engage in insults, banter, teasing, shoving, pushing, and gender-specific conduct that is upsetting to the students subjected to it. Damages are not available for simple acts of teasing and name-calling among school children."[34] Thus, in order to be actionable, harassment must be sufficiently "severe, pervasive, and objectively offensive that it can be said to deprive the victims of access to the educational opportunities or benefits provided by the school."[35] As a result, not every instance of misconduct will rise to the level of actionable harassment. It is worth pointing out, however, that even minor instances of teasing can mushroom into actionable harassment if they are ignored. For example, in *Vance v. Spencer County Public School District*, the alleged harassment began with first-grade students calling the plaintiff gay. It escalated over the course of two years to groups of students touching her buttocks and chest, hitting her, stabbing her hand with a pen, among other things, and a jury verdict of $220,000 in favor of the plaintiff.[36] Accordingly, school officials should take steps to address and ameliorate, where necessary, instances that might not be harassment as a legal matter to avoid the potential for more serious and possibly actionable misconduct to arise.

Courts typically examine the "type, frequency, and duration of the conduct,"[37] among other things, to determine whether the alleged harassment may be characterized as sufficiently severe and pervasive. Courts review this evidence within the context of the totality of the circumstances to determine whether Title IX has been violated, recognizing that "some behavior would be abusive in one setting, but not abusive in another."[38] In this connection, determining whether alleged misconduct is sufficiently severe and pervasive requires the court to critically examine the form the harassment takes, the ages of the victim and the perpetrators, the location of the harassing incidents, the gender of the harasser/s, and the frequency of the misconduct, among other things.

When a student is subjected to a campaign of harassment that includes a myriad of offensive misconduct, courts typically conclude that the severe and pervasive requirement has been met. Thus, for example, the court found actionable misconduct that included anti-gay remarks, defacement of the targeted student's locker, and physical abuse, including being urinated upon.[39] In another case, more than a dozen students harassed a classmate almost daily over the course of three years, during, between, and after classes and during meetings with the school counselor.[40] The harassment was primarily verbal, with students threatening the plaintiff and calling her such names as "bitch," "dyke," "freak," "lesbian," and "gothic."[41] The combination of multiple harassers and the protracted nature of the abuse persuaded the court to conclude that the harassment was sufficiently severe and pervasive to be actionable.[42]

The Supreme Court in *Davis* noted that a single incident of sexual harassment rarely rises to the level of severe and pervasive conduct.[43] The Office for Civil Rights for the Department of Education (OCR) has clarified this part of the standard, drawing upon the substantive law of sexual harassment in the Title VII context. Specifically, OCR has explained that when the conduct at issue is particularly severe, there is less of a need to show a series of harassing incidents, particularly when the harassment is physical.[44] As one court explained, one incident could be construed as actionable harassment if it "were vile enough and the institution's response, after learning of it, unreasonable enough to have the effect of denying access to a scholastic program or activity."[45] Rape is the prototypic "vile" misconduct that need only occur once in order to be actionable. Thus, for example, the Eleventh Circuit noted that allegations that three basketball players gang raped a young woman "differ[ed] markedly from the rarely actionable, theoretical single incident mentioned in *Davis*...The [alleged] incident involved a ringleader who lured the victim to his territory and then conspired with two friends to commit two separate acts of sexual assault and so constitute[d] a continuous series of events."[46] Because of the severity of the assault, coupled with multiple assailants, the court suggested that in this case, the single incident had a sufficiently significant effect on the plaintiff's educational experience to satisfy the legal standard.[47]

Similarly, courts have found actionable claims involving a single incident that occurred off school premises under certain circumstances. For example, in *Doe ex rel. Doe v. Derby Board of Education,*[48] a female middle school student was sexually assaulted by a high school male during the summer break off campus.[49] When classes resumed in the fall, the targeted student and her assailant attended school in the same building. Doe testified that seeing him almost daily "was very upsetting"[50] and "made the school year hard."[51] The court concluded that "even absent actual post-assault harassment...the fact that [the assailant] and plaintiff attended school together could be found to constitute pervasive, severe, and objectively offensive harassment."[52]

As the foregoing suggests, sexual harassment may be characterized as "severe, pervasive, and objectively offensive" when the totality of the circumstances demonstrates a pattern of systemic and abusive conduct. The more egregious the misconduct, the more likely it will be deemed sufficiently severe and pervasive, even if it occurred only once. This standard reflects the notion that Title IX is intended to reach sex discrimination that systematically interferes with a student's educational opportunities, a concern that is additionally manifest in the requirement that it must rise to a level that deprives students of the education program and benefits a recipient provides. The next section further explains this issue.

Deprivation of Educational Opportunities

The Court in *Davis* held that actionable harassment must "effectively den[y] students equal access to an institution's resources and opportunities."[53]

In this regard, the severity of the harassment must interfere with students' access to available educational opportunities. To illustrate, the Court likened the effects of ongoing harassment in school to "a case in which male students physically threaten their female peers every day, successfully preventing the female students from using a particular school resource—an athletic field or a computer lab."[54] In so doing, the Court recognized that, although sexual harassment may not present a physical impediment to a specific educational resource, it nonetheless may present an almost impregnable sex-based barrier to the targeted students' learning experience overall, which is antithetical to the letter and spirit of Title IX.[55]

Thus, courts have found peer sexual harassment claims actionable when there has been evidence that the targeted student was prevented from fully accessing the resources of an educational institution in a variety of respects. For example, a student's decision to transfer to another school to escape further harassment was deemed to be actionable.[56] Similarly, a district court held that sexual harassment had interfered in the student's educational experience because she had missed several days of school, refused to ride the bus, or participate in gym class due to the harassment.[57] In the context of remedying harassment, the failure of school officials to ensure that the targeted student was not at risk during mediation sessions was construed as a deprivation of an educational resource.[58] Because of the harassing student's persistent physical and verbal aggression during school-sponsored mediation sessions, the plaintiff decided, instead, to see the school counselor on an individual basis.[59]

A student's grades also may be relevant to determining whether sexual harassment has deprived the targeted student of educational opportunities. More specifically, the Supreme Court stated that academic performance has some bearing on determining whether the requisite showing has been made; however, grades alone are not conclusive to this part of the analysis.[60] In some cases, students' grades were unaffected by the harassment, but the court nonetheless has found an actionable deprivation when there was other evidence of deprivation. For example, when a plaintiff allegedly cried every day at school because of her classmates' harassment of her and was repeatedly absent from school, the court concluded that she had been deprived of educational opportunities.[61] The plaintiff's grades had not suffered during the course of the harassment; however, the court noted that the key factor for this part of the *Davis* standard is whether the harassment "created a disparately hostile educational environment relative to her peers."[62] Because some students may be able to persevere academically notwithstanding such misconduct, assessing the totality of the circumstances is essential to determine whether the harassment created an adverse hostile educational environment for the targeted students to which other students were not subjected.

Notice of Harassment

In order to prevail in an action for damages, plaintiffs must demonstrate that the school had notice of the harassment,[63] which, in this context, means actual knowledge on the part of a person with the authority to correct the discrimination.[64] Only where a funding recipient possesses a sufficient level of awareness and adequate authority to address allegations of sexual harassment may the school be held legally responsible for its own failure to respond. This holding was premised on Title IX's implementing regulations, which require the enforcing agency to notify recipients of noncompliance with the statute and allow them to remedy the situation before taking the most severe sanction of withdrawing federal funds.[65] Since the regulatory scheme contemplated notifying recipients before penalizing them for noncompliance, the Court reasoned that actual notice should be required in an action for damages.[66] As the following section will discuss, some key issues regarding notice include the content of the notice and the appropriate official to be notified.

Substance of Notice

For purposes of damages liability, the content of the notice is significant. Specifically, under *Gebser* and *Davis*, notice that results in damages liability must put school officials on notice that the particular form of discrimination being complained of is occurring. Thus, for example, in *Gebser,* school officials had notice that the harassing teacher frequently made inappropriate comments of a sexual nature; however, because these complaints did not put the school on notice that the teacher was engaging in an inappropriate sexual relationship, the school was not liable in damages for the harassment.[67] In contrast, in *Davis*, the plaintiff's claim that she notified school officials repeatedly about the same or similar misconduct by the same student satisfied the notice requirement and obligated school officials to remedy the discrimination.[68]

Based on these holdings, courts have examined the content of the notice carefully in determining whether it triggered an obligation on the part of school officials to address the complained of misconduct. Thus, for example, when a student provided only a generalized report of harassment—stating that boys were "bothering her"—school officials were not deemed to be placed on notice that the boys had coerced her into engaging in sexual behavior.[69] In that case, the plaintiff was an eighth-grade student with the mental capacity of a seven- or eight-year-old.[70] The next year, when the child was due to enroll in high school, her mother met with the principal,[71] having received no response from the middle-school officials, seeking school intervention.[72] The principal removed the girl from the special education class and assigned her an aide to assist with school coursework. The plaintiff then informed a guidance counselor that a boy had been "calling and bothering her by asking her for sexual favors."[73] The counselor asked the school resource officer to question the girl, and at that time, she explained the full nature of the harassment.[74] The police then investigated the matter, but no prosecution resulted.[75] Thus, in this case, the fact that the high school acted appropriately upon learning the full extent of the misconduct may have remedied the failure of the middle school officials to pursue the girl's complaints more thoroughly, particularly given her developmental deficiency and given the repeated requests of the child's mother. Indeed, the court noted that "[i]n retrospect, it is unfortunate that the eighth grade counselor did not follow through on Ms. Rost's requests to talk with K.C. to try to learn what had caused her to change her attitude about attending school...At any rate the duty of the District to take some action does not arise until some school official has actual knowledge of harassment."[76] Once the district officials received notice of harassment, the court concluded it "acted appropriately in deferring the matter to law enforcement personnel and it could do nothing for K.C. after she left school."[77] As this case suggests, the content of the notice is important because it triggers the institution's obligation to act; additionally, it provides a baseline for assessing the nature of the institution's response, which is discussed later.

This principle supports holding schools financially responsible when they learn of prior instances of harassment, even those not involving the plaintiff. In this context, such knowledge places the institution on notice to take action to prevent future occurrences of harassment. For example, a university's recruitment of a student-athlete in the face of known allegations of sexual assault constituted actual knowledge, for purposes of damages liability, that other students at the institution would be at risk of attack.[78] Specifically, in *Williams v. Board of Regents of the University System of Georgia*, the university president and director of the athletic association actively recruited a male basketball player to the university, fully aware that the student had been dismissed from two other colleges for committing sexually related offenses.[79] The court found that the institution could be held liable for a subsequent rape of a female student, observing that its knowledge of the player's misconduct obligated officials to take action—such as supervising him and other student-athletes and informing them of the institution's sexual harassment policy—to ensure that he would not repeat this history.[80] Similarly, in *Michelle M. v. Dunsmuir Joint Union School District*,[81] the court found that school officials' knowledge of a student's "proclivity to obsessive behavior toward other students"[82] obligated the institution to take some preventive action—in this case, notifying parents of the school sexual harassment policy.[83] In contrast, the fact that a harasser had a history of more generalized disciplinary problems or that a school, as a whole, had a reputation for undisciplined students, is not sufficient to constitute actual notice of the harassment.[84]

Nevertheless, the "actual notice standard does not set the bar so high that a school district is not put on notice until it receives a clearly credible report of sexual abuse from the plaintiff-student."[85] In *Doe ex rel. Doe v. Derby Board of Education*, a female middle school student was sexually assaulted by a high school male off campus during the summer break . When school resumed in the fall and both students were in the same building, the plaintiff alleged that this situation created a hostile environment because of the assailant's presence.[86] In addition, his friends made matters worse by taunting her about the rape.[87] The court found that the school had notice of the discriminatory environment, in part, because the local newspaper widely publicized the arrest of the male assailant; therefore, it was obliged to respond appropriately under the circumstances.[88]

Appropriate School Official

In addition to the substance of the notice, *Gebser* and *Davis* make clear that an appropriate official must be notified in order for damages liability to attach.[89] That person is defined as "an official who at a minimum has authority to address the alleged discrimination and to institute corrective measures on the recipient's behalf."[90] Because the standard of damages liability is not based upon agency principles,[91] courts must examine each given circumstance to determine whether a particular school official had the authority to act. In light of the disparate roles that school officials take, there exists a myriad of persons who may be empowered to act, as the Tenth Circuit has observed:

> school districts contain a number of layers below the school board: superintendents, principals, vice-principals, and teachers and coaches, not to mention specialized counselors such as Title IX coordinators. Different school districts may assign different duties to these positions or even reject the traditional hierarchical structure altogether.' Because officials' roles vary among school districts, deciding who exercises substantial control for the purposes of Title IX liability is necessarily a fact-based inquiry.[92]

The OCR further explains that a responsible employee for purposes of notice may include "a principal, campus security, bus driver, teacher, affirmative action officer, or staff in the office of student affairs."[93] It also advises that "even if a responsible employee does not have the authority to address the discrimination and take corrective action, he or she does have the obligation to report it to appropriate school authorities."[94] Accordingly, to determine whether a given official is "appropriate" for purposes of determining damages liability may require examining a variety of sources: from state law to determine how schools are organized,[95] to individual school policies, to identify the persons the district has designated as responsible for addressing sexual harassment. With regard to the latter, a court found the notice prong satisfied where the plaintiff reported the harassment to her teachers, guidance counselor, and vice principals in compliance with the school's sexual harassment policy, which directed students to contact "the building principal or other administrator, a faculty member, the nurse, or other responsible adult."[96]

Deliberate Indifference

Davis explains that, in order to be liable in damages for peer harassment, the institution must have responded to the misconduct with deliberate indifference,[97] which, in this context, means that the school's response was "clearly unreasonable" under the known circumstances.[98] Integral to this element of the damages liability test is the notion that the funding recipient must have "substantial control over both the harasser and the context in which the known harassment occurs,"[99] consistent with the statute's proscription against "subjecting" persons to sex-based discrimination. Thus, the recipient must, as a threshold matter, have authority to "take remedial action."[100] In this regard, the Court noted that liability is not based on agency principles; rather, it is based on the institution's own failure to respond to known misconduct when it had the authority to do so.[101] By failing to respond, the recipient thus "subjects" the harassed student to discrimination in violation of the statute.

This aspect of the holding is most clearly illustrated by the *Davis* fact pattern, involving two students attending the same institution in the defendant school district. The harassment occurred "during school hours and on school grounds… [that is] 'under' the 'operation' of a funding recipient…In these circumstances, the recipient retains substantial control over the context in which the harassment occurs. More significantly, however, in this setting, the Board exercises significant control over the harasser."[102] In this regard, the *Davis* standard echoes the Court's jurisprudence in school context, where it repeatedly has recognized the significant authority officials have to maintain order and discipline.[103] Additionally, however, because the standard focuses on the issue of school authority, institutions may be obliged to respond in the myriad contexts where they control, such as school buses and athletic arenas, in addition to classrooms. In this regard, school authority may extend not only to students attending that institution, but also to visitors on campus, such as players from an opposing football or debating team.[104]

Assuming the institution has "substantial control over both the harasser and the context of the harassment,"[105] the deliberate indifference inquiry examines the institution's response to determine whether it was "clearly unreasonable in light of the known circumstances."[106] Calibrated to provide recipients with the requisite flexibility to respond as needed,[107] this standard is intended to "account both for the level of disciplinary authority available to the school and the potential for liability arising from certain forms of disciplinary action."[108] Thus, the standard provides institutions with the leeway to determine what response is most fitting under the circumstances, allowing them to take into consideration the age and maturity of students, since Title IX applies to institutions serving elementary-age children as well as post-graduate adults. Against this reality, the Court's standard accounts for the fact that the degree of control and the appropriate disciplinary action will vary greatly across the board.[109]

Building upon *Davis*, courts thus have hewn closely to the requirement that the recipients not respond in a manner that is "clearly unreasonable" under the known circumstances. Thus, as the First Circuit Court of Appeals has observed, "Title IX does not require educational institutions to take heroic measures, to perform flawless investigations, to craft perfect solutions."[110] Rather, it requires them not to be "so deficient as to be clearly unreasonable,"[111] which would include actions that were "so lax, so misdirected, or so poorly executed as to be clearly unreasonable under the known circumstances."[112]

These principles suggest that deliberate indifference must be determined on a case-by-case basis, assessed in the light of the circumstances known by school officials, and measured against their capacity to discipline in a given instance. As will be discussed below, courts may find deliberate indifference when school officials repeatedly fail to respond to complaints of harassment, fail to take common sense measures to address the misconduct—e.g., removing the harasser from the targeted student—take actions that facilitate the harassment, or fail to follow their own policies with respect to such misconduct. Thus, for example, in *Davis,* school officials' failure to respond to five months' worth of complaints of harassment, including the target's request to simply change seats could satisfy the deliberate indifference requirement for purposes of a motion to dismiss.[113]

Similarly, in *Doe v. East Haven Board of Education,* a district court found deliberate indifference when school officials ignored repeated complaints of harassment and disregarded the suggestions of the child's parent for remedying the harassment in violation of its own policy.[114] In this case, two students sexually assaulted a high school girl, A.N. After she reported the assault to school authorities, students verbally harassed her daily, calling her "slut, a liar, a bitch, a whore," among other things.[115] A.N.'s mother reported this misconduct many times, contacting a myriad of administrators, including the East Haven superintendent, the high school principal, and the guidance counselor.[116] She suggested to school officials that two of the harassers be removed from A.N.'s classroom; she also sent school administrators a memo asking them to refrain from discussing the sexual assault and the attendant investigation.[117] In response, school officials removed A.N. from the classroom and placed her in the guidance office.[118] In addition, school officials distributed the local newspaper containing a front-page story about the assault; a substitute teacher even read it aloud in class.[119] Finally, the school's "Discipline Policy...stated that harassment or discriminatory behavior directed to a victim's gender was punishable by out of school suspension and possible expulsion."[120] However, none of the harassing students apparently was punished.[121] According to the defendant school district, officials met with the harassing students and their parents in the presence of East Haven police officers.[122] In addition, school officials argued that they responded appropriately to the harassment because they provided A.N. with a private room in the guidance office where she could retreat if she felt uncomfortable.[123] On appeal, the Second Circuit affirmed. It observed that the school "acted in a clearly unreasonable fashion, where the alleged victim of a rape complained of verbal harassment based on her sex and related to the rape for five weeks before authorities took concrete action to get the perpetrators of the harassment to stop."[124] In affirming the district court, the Second Circuit's analysis appeared to emphasize the time it took for school officials to act and the fact that they failed to take actions other than talking to the harassers.

Deliberate indifference also examines the institutional response after taking action, namely whether it assesses the remedial action to ensure that it appropriately addresses the misconduct. For example, in *Annamaria M. v. Napa Valley Unified School District*,[125] two boys harassed the eighth-grade plaintiff for a period of six to seven weeks, during which "she lost twenty-two pounds, dropped out of school and attempted suicide."[126] Teachers sent the boys to the principal's office "for the same harassing conduct on multiple occasions."[127] Even though school officials eventually contacted the police about the misconduct, the fact that they persisted with the same ineffective remedy of talking to the harassers for six or seven weeks before they modified their response meant that, for purposes of the motion to dismiss, the plaintiff had satisfied the deliberate indifference requirement.[128]

The "known circumstances" for purposes of evaluating an institution's response also may include the school disciplinary or sexual harassment policy. For example, in *Michelle M. v. Dunsmuir Joint Union School District*,[129] Jordan S., a male high school student, requested that the plaintiff, another male student, "expose his penis on numerous occasions through messages typed into a graphing calculator, and through several follow up entreaties"; when the plaintiff refused, Jordan continued to harass him physically and verbally.[130] After the plaintiff's mother complained about Jordan's conduct, school officials met with the students, informed teachers, and kept the two boys from sharing classes when possible.[131] Officials did not take any action against Jordan; the plaintiff's parents demanded that the boy be removed from school.[132] The local juvenile court issued a restraining order against Jordan because his behavior had escalated to including stalking and threats against the plaintiff's life.[133] The school did not remove the boy until the plaintiff left the school for "an at-home independent study program."[134] The district court concluded that the school's response was deliberately indifferent under the circumstances because there was evidence that Jordan had harassed other students; at least one other parent had complained to school officials about Jordan's misconduct.[135] In addition, the court noted, "Despite school personnel's knowledge of Jordan's apparent proclivity to obsessive behavior towards other students of the same sex, the school refrained from including within the parent handbook its own previously adopted sexual harassment policy."[136] The policy required that it be disseminated at the start of each academic year; yet, the school failed to comply "for budgetary reasons."[137] Accordingly, the court determined that summary judgment for the school district was not appropriate; given the "[d]efendants' knowledge of prior behavior, this Court cannot say as a matter of law that this shortcoming does not amount to deliberate indifference giving rise to Title IX liability."[138] In this case, the court observed that unlike *Gebser,* which rejected damages liability for recipients that failed to implement and disseminate sexual harassment policies in accordance with the Department of Education's directive,[139] the school failed to follow its own policy, "in violation of both the policy itself and California law,"[140] when there was a clear problem with harassment in the school.

Recommendations for Practice

Preventing harassment based on sex—and, indeed, other bases—is critical to assuring that all students have an environment conducive to learning. There are many resources for sexual harassment that can help schools develop curricula and policies to address harassment, including the National Education Association, American Federation of Teachers, Wellesley College Center for Research on Women, and the American Association of University Women,[141] among others.

Some recommendations to consider include the following:

1. School districts should provide training for educators on a regular basis about harassment and the myriad ways it manifests, how to address it, and strategies for preventing it.
2. School administrators and educators should have regular training on their school's sexual harassment policy and have facility in using it.
3. Schools should develop protocols for addressing harassment that are consistent with the policy and make certain that students and educators alike understand it.
4. Schools should distribute their sexual harassment policies to students' families at the start of every academic year.
5. Schools should develop and distribute age-appropriate materials explaining the sexual harassment policy, identifying the persons students should contact if they believe they have been harassed.
6. Policies and protocols should be reviewed and revised periodically to make certain that they are appropriate for use in this context. Getting input from educators, administrators, and parents can help ensure that the entire school community supports the effort.

Endnotes

[1] At the outset, I must thank my research assistant, Danielle Anderson, without whom this work would never have been completed. Any errors or omissions are mine.

[2] 20 U.S.C.A. §§ 1681 *et. seq.*

[3] 20 U.S.C.A. § 1681(a).

[4] In *Doe v. Omaha Public School District*, for example, the plaintiff was sexually assaulted by a classmate and reported the incident to her principal. After the principal concluded that the encounter was consensual and suspended both students, the plaintiff filed suit against both the school district and the principal under Title IX. The court ultimately dismissed the claims against the principal, concluding that Title IX claims are not actionable against individual defendants.

[5] 20 U.S.C.A. § 1681(a).

[6] North Haven Bd. of Educ. v. Bell, 456 U.S. 512, 521 (1982).

7 *See, e.g.,* Chipman v. Grant Co. Sch. Dist., 30 F. Supp. 2d 975 (E.D. Ky. 1998) (temporarily enjoining policy excluding pregnant girls from the National Honor Society as violative of Title IX).

8 *See, e.g.,* Cohen v. Brown Univ., 101 F.3d 155 (1st Cir. 1996) (finding that Brown had violated Title IX by eliminating athletic opportunities for female athletes).

9 *See, .e.g.,* Franklin v. Gwinnett Co., 503 U.S. 60, 75 (1992) (applying Title VII to conclude that when a teacher sexually harasses a student, he discriminates based on sex).

10 Davis v. Monroe Co. Bd. of Educ., 526 U.S. 629, 645 (1999) (observing that damages liability is based on institution's failure to remedy known harassment when it had the authority to do so).

11 526 U.S. 629 (1999).

12 *See, e.g.,* Kathleen Conn, *Peer Sexual Harassment in Elementary Schools: Is Title IX the Answer,* 219 Educ. L. Rep. 25, 27 (2007) (describing the many forms harassment takes).

13 *See id.* (suggesting that heightened exposure to sexuality in the media and popular culture at a minimum facilitates the ability of very young children to engage in sexual harassment).

14 Conn cites a survey the Mayo Clinic, finding that "[a]bused children consistently demonstrated more explicit behaviors, including imitating intercourse." *Id.*

15 In most states educators who suspect child abuse are obligated to report such misconduct to state authorities.

16 *See, e.g.,* Vance v. Spencer Co. Pub. Sch. Dist., 231 F.3d. 253, 256-257 (6th Cir. 2000) (describing harassment that began with name-calling and escalated to daily propositions for sex and inappropriate touching).

17 *See, e.g.,* Riccio v. New Haven Bd. of Educ., 467 F. Supp. 2d. 219, 226 (D. Conn. 2006).

18 Research shows that female students are more likely to report sexual harassment; male students also are subjected to it, but are reluctant to complain about it. *See, e.g., Thirty-Five Years of Title IX: Hearing before H. Subcomm. on Higher, Education, Lifelong Learning and Competitiveness of the Comm. on Education and Labor,* 2007 WLNR 11497465 (June 19, 2007) (testimony of Lisa M. Maatz, Director, American Association of University Women).

19 Oncale v. Sundowner Offshore Servs., 523 U.S. 75, 81 (1998).

20 504 F.3d 165 (1st Cir. 2007).

21 *Id.* at 172.

22 Annamaria M. v. Napa Valley Unified Sch. Dist., No. C03-0101VRW, 2006 U.S. Dist. LEXIS 38641 (N.D. Cal. May 30, 2006) [hereinafter *Annamaria M.*].

23 *See, e.g.,* Doe v. E. Haven Sch. Dist., 430 F. Supp. 2d 54, 60 (D. Conn. 2006) [hereinafter *E. Haven I*], *aff'd Doe v. E. Haven Bd. of Ed.,* 200 F. App'x 46 (2d Cir. 2006) (hereinafter *E. Haven II*).

24 *E. Haven I,* 430 F. Supp. at 60.

25 *Id.*

26 *Id.* at 48.

27 523 U.S. 75, 80, 82 (1998).

28 *See, e.g., Riccio,* 467 F. Supp. 2d at 226 (concluding that plaintiff, a female, would not have been subjected to other females' slurs "implying she [was] a female homosexual" but for her sex).

29 Cf. Price Waterhouse v. Hopkins, 490 U.S. 228 (1988).

30 *Id.* at 61, citing *Oncale*, 523 U.S. at 80, 82.

31 *Theno*, 377 F. Supp. 2d at 963-65.

32 *Id.* at 955-961.

33 *Id.* at 964-965.

34 *Davis*, 526 U.S. at 651-52.

35 *Id.* at 650.

36 *Vance*, 231 F.3d at 255-257.

[37] Revised Sexual Harassment Guidance: Harassment of Students by School Employees, Other Students, or Third Parties, Dept. of Educ. Office for Civil Rights, 6 (Jan. 19, 2001), http://www.ed.gov/about/offices/list/ocr/docs/shguide.html. (hereinafter OCR Guidance).

[38] No. Civ.A. 8:04-23001RBH, 2006 WL 1473853, 8 (D.S.C. May 25, 2006), *citing* Jennings v. Univ. of N.C., at Chapel Hill, 444 F.3d 255, 270 (4th Cir. 2006) (overturned on other grounds).

[39] The court similarly concluded in *Doe v. Perry Community School District* that the plaintiff had "some likelihood of success" in establishing severe and pervasive conduct after he was targeted with anti-gay comments, had his locker defaced, was urinated on, and was physically assaulted and threatened. citation

[40] Riccio v. New Haven Bd. of Educ., 467 F. Supp. 2d 219, 227(D. Conn. 2006).

[41] *Id.* at 222.

[42] *Id.*

[43] *Davis,* 526 U.S. at 652-53.

[44] OCR Guidance, *supra* note 37, at 6.

[45] *Fitzgerald*, 2007 U.S. App. LEXIS 23620, at *13.

[46] Williams v. Bd. of Regents, 477 F.3d 1282, 1298 (11th Cir. 2007).

[47] *Id.*

[48] 451 F. Supp. 2d 438, 444 (D. Conn. 2006) (hereinafter *Derby*).

[49] *Id.* at 440.

[50] *Id.* at 442.

[51] *Id.*

[52] *Id.* at 444.

[53] *Davis,* 526 U.S. at 651.

[54] *Id.* at 650-51 (citation omitted).

[55] *Id.* at 651.

[56] *Derby,* 451 F. Supp. 2d at 445.

[57] Hunter *ex rel.* Hunter v. Barnstable, 456 F. Supp. 2d 255, 261, 264 (D. Mass. 2006).

[58] *Riccio*, 467 F. Supp. 2d at 223, 228.

[59] *Id.*

[60] *Davis*, 526 U.S. at 652 (observing that lowered grades may suggest deprivation of educational opportunities).

[61] *E. Haven I,* 200 F. App'x at 48.

[62] *Id., quoting* Hayut v. State Univ. of N.Y., 352 F.3d 733, 748. 750 (2d Cir. 2003).

[63] *Gebser,* 524 U.S. at 285; *Davis*, 526 U.S. at 643.

[64] *See Davis*, 524 U.S. at 290.

[65] *Id.* at 289.

[66] *Id.*

[67] *Id.* at 292.

[68] *Davis* at 633-35, 654.

[69] Rost v. Steamboat Springs RE-2 Sch.Dist., Civ. Action No. 04-cv-02302-RPM, 2006 U.S. Dist. LEXIS 82041 (D. Colo. Nov. 9, 2006)

[70] *Id.* at *2.

[71] *Id.* at *5.

[72] *Id.*

[73] *Id.* at *6.

[74] *Id.*

[75] *Id.* at *6.

[76] *Id.* at *8-*9.

[77] *Id.* at *8.

[78] Williams v. Board of Regents, 477 F.3d 11282 (11th Cir. 2007).

[79] *Id.* at 1290.

[80] *Id.* at 1296. *See also* Doe v. Omaha Pub. Sch. Dist., No. 8:04CV295, 2005 WL 2347284, *2 (D. Neb. Sept. 26, 2005) (denying motion to dismiss where plaintiff alleged that school officials knew alleged assailant had a history of sexual harassment).

[81] No.2:04cv-2411-MCE-PAN, 2006 U.S. Dist. LEXIS 77328 (E.D. Cal. Oct. 12, 2006) (hereinafter *Michelle M.*).

[82] *Id.* at *7.

[83] *Id.* at *8.

[84] *See, e.g.,* Peer *ex rel.* Doe v. Porterfield, 2006 WL 3899263, *9 (W.D. Mich. Jan. 8, 2007); Soriano v. Bd. of Educ. of N.Y., 2004 U.S. Dist. LEXIS (E.D.N.Y. 2004).

[85] 451 F. Supp. 2d 438, 446 (D. Conn. 2006), quoting Doe v. Sch. Admin. Dist. No. 19, 66 F. Supp. 2d 57, 63 (D. Me. 1999).

[86] *Doe*, 451 F. Supp. at 440.

[87] *Id.*

[88] *Id.* at 446.

[89] *Gebser,* 524 U.S. at 290.

[90] *Id.*

[91] *Id.* at 288.

[92] 186 F.3d 1238, 1247 (10th Cir. 1999), citing Rosa H. v. San Elizario Indep. Sch. Dist., 106 F.3d 648 (5th Cir. 1997).

[93] OCR Guidance, *supra* note 37, at 13.

[94] *Id.*

[95] *See, e.g.,* Annamaria M., 2006 LEXIS 38641 at *11, *quoting,* Hawkins v. Sarasota County Sch. Bd., 322 F.3d 1279, 1286 (11th Cir. 2003) (noting the need to consult state law for such purposes).

[96] Jones v. Indiana Area Sch. Dist., 397 F. Supp. 2d 628, 644 (W.D. Penn. 2005); *see also Williams*, 477 F.3d at 1294 (holding that appropriate levels of authority were established where the plaintiff reported harassment to the president of the university and athletic association and the athletic director, who were aware of basketball recruit's past sexual misconduct and criminal charges at other colleges and who was authorized to address sexual harassment among student-athletes); Bruning *ex rel.* Bruning v. Caroll Cmty. Sch. Dist., 486 F. Supp. 2d 892, 914 (N.D. Ia. 2007) (concluding that principal is in position of sufficient authority to address allegations of sexual harassment under Title IX); Peer *ex rel.* Doe v. Porterfield, No. 1:05-cv-769, 2006 WL 3898263, 2, 9 (W.D. Mich. Jan. 8, 2007) (holding that school principal who had authority to suspend students accused of harassment occupied sufficient position of authority to establish substantial control where female kindergarten student reported sexual assault to teacher, who subsequently informed the principal).

[97] *Davis,* 526 U.S. at 644-45.

[98] *Id.* at 643.

[99] *Id.* at 645.

[100] *Id.* at 644.

[101] *Id.*

[102] *Id.* at 646.

[103] *Id.*, citing Tinker v. Des Moines Ind. Comm. Sch. Dist., 393 U.S. 503, 507 (1967); New Jersey v. T.L.O., 469 U.S. 325, 342 n.9 (1985)(quotations omitted).

[104] *C.f.* OCR Guidance, *supra* note 37, at 12 (discussing school responsibility with regard to third-party harassers).

[105] *Davis*, 526 U.S. at 645.

[106] *Id.* at 649.

[107] *Id.* at 648.

[108] *Id.* at 649.

[109] *See id.*

[110] *Fitzgerald*, 504 F.3d at 174.

[111] *Id.*

[112] *Id.* at 175.

[113] *Davis,* 526 U.S. at 654.
[114] *E. Haven I.*, 430 F. Supp. 2d at 63-65.
[115] *Id.* at 59.
[116] *Id.* at 62.
[117] *Id.* at 63.
[118] *Id.*
[119] *Id.* at 63-64.
[120] *Id.* at 64.
[121] *Id.*
[122] *E. Haven II,* 200 F. App'x 46 (2d Cir. 2006).
[123] *Id.* at 49.
[124] *Id.*
[125] *Annamaria M.,* 2006 U.S. Dist. LEXIS 28641.
[126] *Id.* at *8.
[127] *Id.* at *13.
[128] *Id.* at *14-*15. *See also* Vance v. Spencer County Sch. Dist., 231 F.3d 253 (6th Cir. 2000) (finding deliberate indifference where recipient persists with the same ineffective remedy).
[129] *Michelle M.,* 2006 U.S. Dist. LEXIS 77328.
[130] *Id.* at *3.
[131] *Id.* at *6.
[132] *Id.*
[133] *Id.* at *7, *9.
[134] *Id.* at *9.
[135] *Id.*at *8.
[136] *Id.* at *8.
[137] *Id.* at*8-*9.
[138] *Id.* at *20.
[139] *Gebser,* 524 U.S. at 291-92.
[140] *Michelle M.,* 2006 U.S. Dist. LEXIS 77328 at *20 n. 12.
[141] Each of these organizations maintains a website from which users can download materials about sexual harassment: the NEA site is www.nea.org; AFT's is www.aft.org; the site for Wellesley College Center for Research on Women is http://www.wcwonline.org/joomla/; the AAUW site is www.aauw.org (last visited December 13, 2007). These sites also have links to other resources. In addition, publications about the legal issues regarding sexual harassment are available at the websites for the National Women's Law Center site, www.nwlc.org, and Legal Momentum, www.legalmomentum.org.

Chapter 9

Civil Liberties in Cyberspace: Some Rights and Responsibilities in an Evolving Era of Technology

Mark A. Gooden & Kelly M. Gunn

Introduction

The Bill of Rights was seldom referenced in pre-1969 constitutionality cases of student-contested school rules. The courts applied a reasonableness test to judge school policies. Judges upheld a school rule if they determined a reasonable relationship existed between the rule and some educational purpose. This custom was followed even if judges believed a rule was unwise, unnecessary, or unfairly restrictive of the rights of students and/or teachers. Since judges regarded school officials as the experts on education, they held that wide discretion should be tolerated in the creation and implementation of school policies. Accordingly, the courts were reluctant to substitute their judgment for that of the school officials.[1]

This hands-off inclination of the courts changed with the decision handed down in the *Tinker v. Des Moines Independent School District*[2] case. For more than thirty years, *Tinker* has been the standard established by the Supreme Court for how school officials should address free speech issues in schools. Although the advancements in technology have somewhat changed the way courts look at schools in the context of Internet cases, clearly the landmark case that establishes the foundation of such decisions on student speech is still *Tinker*. This was evidenced in a federal district court ruling that addressed the issue of off-campus student speech in 1998. This chapter will explore this case and others like it that offer guidance on how best to approach this relatively new entity, the Internet, and its connection to the more established phenomenon of the First Amendment jurisprudence in schools.

Legal Issues

Pure Speech

In *Tinker*, three students planned to wear black armbands as a symbol of protest against the Vietnam War. On the day before they were to wear the armbands in a silent protest, administrators, as a result of finding out about the plan, met and adopted a policy forbidding the wearing of such armbands. Although the students knew of the consequences, they wore the bands in protest anyway and were suspended. The Supreme Court held that the prohibition of wearing of the armbands violated the students' First Amendment rights.[3]

In this landmark case, the Supreme Court moved beyond the reasonableness test by ruling that students do not lose their constitutional rights to freedom of expression when they enter the schoolhouse. In considering the First Amendment rights of students, the courts will balance a school's need to maintain discipline against a student's right to free expression.[4] The *Tinker* ruling did not license students to say or write anything they wish, but it did broaden the boundaries of student expression.

Lewd, Vulgar, and Indecent Student Speech

Matthew Fraser, a student at Bethel High School, delivered a speech nominating a fellow classmate for student-elected office. Approximately six hundred high school students, many of whom were fourteen-year-olds, attended the school-sponsored assembly, which was part of an educational program in self-government. Students who elected not to attend the assembly were required to report to study hall. During the entire speech, Fraser referred to his candidate in terms that were considered to be "an elaborate, graphic, and explicit sexual metaphor."[5]

Despite prior warnings from teachers not to give the "lewd" speech, Fraser delivered it anyway and was suspended for three days and removed as a candidate for commencement speaker as punishment for his decision. Fraser unsuccessfully challenged the school's decision. The school had an extant policy clearly prohibiting the use of obscene language that materially and substantially interfered with the educational process. The Supreme Court upheld the disciplinary actions stating that officials have the authority to regulate vulgar, indecent, or obscene speech.

School-Sponsored Speech

In *Hazelwood School District v. Kuhlmeier*,[6] the U.S. Supreme Court upheld a principal's decision to remove two articles from a school-sponsored student newspaper. The Court held that where the school sponsors an activity in such a way that the speech bears the imprimatur of the school, the official has the right to restrict student speech.

In analyzing First Amendment rights of public school students Sperry, Daniel, Huefner, and Gee,[7] the Court connected the three landmark cases of *Tinker, Bethel*, and *Hazelwood* in this way:

> First, "vulgar or plainly offensive speech (*Fraser*-type speech) may be prohibited without a showing of disruption or substantial interference with the school's work. Second, school-sponsored speech (*Hazelwood*-type speech) may be restricted when the limitations reasonably related to legitimate educational concerns. Third, speech that is

> neither vulgar nor school-sponsored (*Tinker*-type speech) may only be prohibited if it causes a material disruption of the school's operation.[8]

The three landmark cases above clearly illustrate that school administrators are agents of the state and, as a result, are required to grant students their First Amendment rights to freedom of speech. On the other hand, they are also responsible for maintaining order in schools. The conflict between these competing responsibilities has been more pronounced in recent years, thus increasing the necessity for school officials to write clear school policies.

These three important Supreme Court cases together establish a starting point and a framework for dealing with First Amendment free speech cases involving the rights of students. Any new cases involving free speech issues of students in schools will likely guide courts through an analysis that involves at least one of these important cases, which together will be referred to here as the TBH (*Tinker, Bethel, Hazelwood*) framework. This development has been seen so far in cases that involve students' Internet speech. Although there are only a few Internet free speech cases that have been decided to date, it appears that administrators can benefit significantly from employing the TBH framework established by courts in this trio of cases when considering what steps to take when students get involved in these matters.

Free Speech and the Internet

Although the *Tinker* speech took place on campus, it opened the door for students to express unpopular speech as long as that expression did not upset the smooth operation of school. The Supreme Court described the student protest in *Tinker* as "pure speech" because it was "a silent, passive, expression of opinion, unaccompanied by any disorder or disturbance."[9] The type of analysis employed in this landmark, free speech decision applies in the case of *Beussink v. Woodland R-IV School District*,[10] in which Brandon Beussink, a high school student, was suspended for ten days because he posted his homepage on the Internet. On his webpage, he used vulgar language to criticize his high school, its webpage, and schools officials. He created the page on his home computer. Beussink's friend viewed the page at his home and, after becoming angry with him on another matter, decided to show the page to school officials. As a result, the principal suspended Beussink for ten days, even though he did not show the page to anyone at school. The suspension caused Beussink, who had already missed eight days of school, to be "dropped" a letter grade in each class pursuant the school's absenteeism policy, and he consequently failed the semester. He filed suit.

Citing *Tinker*, the court found that Beussink's page did not materially and substantially interfere with the operation of the school.[11] The page was not created at school, and it was not created using school resources. In fact, Beussink did not intend for his website to be viewed at school, and he did not access it there until asked to do so by school officials. *Tinker* offers guidance here in the sense that Beussink's Internet speech was silent and passive prior to being accessed by another student. The principal testified that he was upset by the homepage and that he decided to discipline Beussink immediately after seeing the page and before investigating whether the page had actually interfered with the smooth operation of the school. The court noted that the principal disciplined Beussink because of the content of his speech, not because that speech interfered with the smooth operation of the school.[12] Courts seem to indicate the latter path is a wiser one for principals to take.

Applying the TBH framework above, a principal may decide if a webpage is visited an inordinate amount of times, perhaps due to obscene material on the page such as in a *Bethel*-type speech situation, and created on campus, then the student can be punished. If the page is not created on campus but causes a material and substantial disruption in school, then the student may also be punished. The most poignant point for the school administrator here is that the *Beussink* court sends the message that the punishment must not be meted out simply because of the content of the Internet speech or expression on the webpage.

In *Dustin Mitchell v. Rolla High School District No. 31*,[13] a junior honor student, Mitchell, participated in a teens-only chat room five days after the Littleton, Colorado shooting. He responded "Yes" to the question of whether such a tragedy could happen at his school, and he did so using his own computer after hours and away from school. Mitchell used the name of another student known for wearing a black trench coat, like the school shooters at Columbine. Consequently, Mitchell was initially suspended for ten days. The punishment was later reduced to four days and forty-two hours of community service. The court found that Mitchell's speech was protected, the suspension violated his First and Fourteenth Amendment rights, and the rules in the school handbook were constitutionally void-for-vagueness and overbroad. Moreover, the school officials failed to provide adequate notice that his behavior was punishable. The court noted that school officials were allowed "unfettered discretion" in disciplining the student for "off-campus misconduct." This case emphasizes the need to write specific policies clearly defining the parameters of administrator authority and student conduct, including policies outlining Internet use in schools, to avoid violating students' due process rights. It is important to see that the court limited the authority of school officials to on-campus expression, but recognized that the administrators were clearly reacting to what they may have understood to be a potential Columbine situation. However, the court held, the decision to punish cannot go beyond the bounds of student free speech rights.

In another Internet case, Nick Emmett, an eighteen-year-old high school student with a 3.95 GPA and no prior disciplinary infractions, created a website at his home and posted it to the Web. The page was entitled the unofficial homepage of his high school, and on it he posted at least two mock obituaries of friends and allowed visitors to vote on who would "die" next in this mock obituary list. Emmett was suspended for five days as a result of the content on his website. The principal claimed that he was placed on emergency expulsion for intimidation, harassment, and disruption to the educational process, and in violation of Kent School District copyright policy. Emmett sued for a restraining order to prevent the school district from enforcing the suspension.[14] The court sided with Emmett because it found that the school presented no evidence "that the mock obituaries or voting on this website were intended to threaten anyone, did actually threaten anyone or manifested any violent tendencies whatsoever."[15] Hence, the school district was enjoined from enforcing the short-term suspension.

In *Mahaffey v. Aldrich*,[16] a student named Mahaffey was initially suspended for contributing to the creation of a webpage constructed off campus with another student in the district. The site was entitled "Satan's Web Page" and Mahaffey claimed it was fashioned "for laughs" because he and the other student were bored and wanted something to do. Mahaffey stated that he "may have" used the school's computers to create part of the page in question but the school district offered no evidence on this point. On the page, the students posted a list of people they wished would die as well as people they thought were cool. The site also contained Satan's mission instructing viewers to kill someone, but it included a request that viewers should not go out and really do this. A fellow student reported the site to the police who then contacted the school officials who, in turn, recommended expulsion. The school based its decision on admitted and alleged violation of three categories of misconduct: Behavior Dangerous to others, Internet Violations, and Intimidation and Threats. After a breakdown in communication at the hearing between the school director and Mahaffey's attorney, the director re-classified the violation in the third category dealing exclusively with intimidation and threats.[17]

Mahaffey's parents sued the board of education and the school director after he was suspended for contributing objectionable material to the website. A federal district court held that his suspension violated his First Amendment rights because there was no proof of disruption to the school by the website or a determination that it was created on school property. Citing *Tinker*, the court determined that even if the page had not been created on campus, the school district could punish the student for his speech on the website if that speech "substantially interfere[d] with the work of the school or impinge[d] upon the rights of other students."[18] Furthermore, Mahaffey's statements on the website did not constitute threats as the school officials had charged in his suspension; thus, the speech was protected by the First Amendment. The court found that the student's due process rights were violated when he was suspended for one semester for publishing the material on the website without being able to cross-examine witnesses, as required by the school district's code of conduct.[19]

In another case, Jon Coy, a middle school student, created a personal website at his home on his own time that contained crude humor and profanity. For example, the site contained a "loser" section with pictures of three fellow students with unflattering captions below the pictures. At the beginning of the school year, Coy's parents signed the school district's computer network/Internet acceptable-use policy that outlined the appropriate behavior for students who accepted the privilege of using school computers. The policy prohibited students from, among other things, "[h]acking into unauthorized computers, sites, or information databases" and "[d]isplaying offensive messages or pictures."[20] Additionally, the Internet-use policy informed students that discipline as outlined by the student conduct code may be applied for violations of the policy.

On July 26, 2001, the Coys filed their complaint alleging in their first of four claims that the school district violated Jon Coy's First Amendment rights by disciplining him for creating, publishing, and maintaining an off-campus website. In a second claim, they asserted that Jon Coy's First Amendment rights were violated when he was disciplined under the unconstitutionally vague and overbroad sections of the student conduct code. In the third claim, the Coys say the principal and the superintendent chilled Jon Coy's speech by causing a police officer to visit his home and causing the Web-hosting service to discontinue hosting the website. In the fourth and final claim, the plaintiffs say the defendants' actions violated the Ohio Constitution.

Because material issues of fact still existed with respect to the school district's motivation for disciplining Jon Coy, the court denied both parties' motions for summary judgment with respect to the Coy's first and fourth claims. The Coys alleged he was disciplined for the content of the webpage, and the school district claimed he was disciplined for viewing the webpage at school. After determining that the *Tinker* standard was the proper standard to analyze the student's claims, the court opined:

> Although implausible, some evidence exists that the defendants expelled Coy, a student who had no previous disciplinary action, for accessing an unauthorized website and not for the content on that website. If true, the defendants could properly discipline Coy for violating the school district's Internet policy. Given the parties' demand for a jury, that jury should decide whether the defendants were motivated by the website's content or, as defendants claim, motivated solely by the accessing of an unapproved site.[21]

Citing *Beussink* and *Kent*, the court pointed out that if Coy was disciplined for content, then he should prevail at trial. If, in fact, he was disciplined for viewing the site in violation of the Internet use policy, then the school may discipline him. However, the court commented that in order to prevail, the school district must justify disciplining Coy and that would mean it must show, consistent with *Tinker*, that his expressive activity "materially and substantially interfere[d] with the requirements of appropriate discipline in the operation of the school."[22] The court ended the point by stating that so far, no evidence suggested that Coy's acts in accessing the website had any effect upon the school district's ability to maintain discipline in the school.

The court also granted the Coys' motion for summary judgment on their facial challenge to section 21, one of three sections in question, of the school district's student conduct code, which was found to be impermissibly vague because it failed to give students any indication of what actions or behavior would lead to discipline.[23] The court granted the school district summary judgment on the plaintiffs' third claim because even though a school official contacted the webpage host asking them to remove the site, Jon voluntarily decided not to repost his site. Summary judgment was also denied on the fourth claim because it was related to the first claim on the First Amendment.

In another case, Zachariah Paul, a high school student, brought a section 1983 action alleging violations of his First Amendment and due process rights by a school district and administrators who tried to suspend him after he wrote a "top ten list" ridiculing the school's athletic director. Paul created the list at home and emailed it from his computer to his friends. The list essentially mocked the athletic director's weight and genitals. Another student printed the list and took it to school and distributed it.

When school officials found out days later, they called Paul to the office and requested that he bring the original email to school the next day. The next day, he was called to the office again and telephoned his mother because he thought he might be disciplined.[24] During the meeting he and his mother were told that he was suspended for ten days. The district mailed a certified letter the following day informing him that he was being suspended for "verbal/written abuse of a staff member."[25] A U.S. district court held:

> Because Paul did not receive any written communication from defendants until the day after the ten-day suspension had been imposed, and then only because Mrs. Killion insisted on such notice. The deficient notice further translated into a due process violation because plaintiffs did not have an opportunity to prepare for the hearing, including the right to summon and cross examine witnesses.[26]

The court also found that the student's list that was created off campus did not disrupt the school environment or interfere with anyone's substantial rights, and the district's policy against abuse of teachers and administrators was unconstitutionally vague and overbroad. The court pointed out that "an overbroad statute is one that is designed to punish activities that are not constitutionally protected, but which prohibits protected activities as well."[27] Moreover, the rule was considered void because "under the 'void for vagueness doctrine,' a governmental regulation may be declared void if it fails to give a person adequate warning that his conduct is prohibited or if it fails to set out adequate standards to prevent arbitrary and discriminatory enforcement."[28]

In *Layshock v. Hermitage School District,*[29] Justin Layshock, a seventeen-year-old senior, created a parody profile of his principal on a website called "MySpace," a popular Internet social-networking site where users can share photos, journals, personal interests, and other information with other users on the site. He created the parody off campus using his grandmother's computer during non-school hours. He used MySpace's template for profiles, which make it easy for novice users to complete a basic page by inputting answers to specific questions. Layshock's parody answers included immature responses, some with crude and vulgar language and allusions to excessive alcohol use. For example, the website template asks, "Do you drink?" and the parody response was, "big keg behind my desk."[30] The parody also reflected that the principal was "too drunk to remember" the date of his birthday. Finally, the parody included a photo image of the principal, which he copied from the school's website. Layshock told a few close friends at school about the site, and eventually word of it reached most of the student body. In addition, a few other parodies (which were described as more crude and vulgar) of unknown origin appeared on the Internet and were spread throughout the cyber community of the school.

In a meeting that included Layshock and his mother, the district superintendent, and the co-principal, Layshock admitted to creating the parody. Though no disciplinary action was taken at that time, nearly three weeks later, Layshock and his parents received a letter advising them that an informal hearing would be held to consider disciplinary action against the student. The specific violations of the school's code of conduct included disruption of the normal school process; disrespect; harassment of a school administrator via computer/Internet with remarks that have demeaning implications; gross misbehavior; obscene, vulgar, and profane language; and computer policy violation (use of school pictures without authorization). At the hearing, Layshock received a ten-day, out-of-school suspension. Additionally, he was to be placed in the Alternative Curriculum Education Program for the remainder of the school year, he was banned from attendance and participation in any events in which the school district sponsored or participated, and he was prohibited from participating in the graduation ceremony.[31]

Though the case began with purely out-of-school conduct, the Internet parody subsequently carried over into the school setting as students retrieved the site on school computers and school officials sought to show that the normal operations of the school day were disrupted while Layshock sought a temporary restraining order (TRO). After the TRO hearing, the court concluded that his actions appeared to have substantially disrupted school operations and interfered with the rights of others.

In cases involving off-campus speech, such as this one, "the school must demonstrate an appropriate nexus."[32] The school argued that Layshock's website parody, along with others of unknown origin, was constantly accessed by students, causing the school to shut down its computer system to student use for five days.[33] The lack of computer access resulted in the cancellation of several classes and interfered with the students' ability to use the computers for their school-intended purposes. Consequently, the school district's technology coordinator devoted nearly 25 percent of his time to deal with the disruption caused by the profiles on MySpace, and the school principal testified at the TRO hearing that he had to spend at least 25 to 30 percent of his time dealing with the disruptions and the investigation into the source of the website parodies.[34]

Though they made a seemingly strong case, the school officials failed to make a causal link between Layshock's off-campus conduct and any material and substantial disruption of operations in the school. Most notably, the school district was unable to connect the alleged disruption to Layshock's conduct insofar as there were three other MySpace profiles of the principal that were available during the same timeframe. Moreover, the school did not demonstrate distinctly that the discussions were caused by his profile as opposed to the reaction of administrators. Indeed, according to the court, Layshock and his parents showed instances in court in which students objected to the investigation, rather than the profile. Thus, the school district was unable to demonstrate that a material disruption had taken place.

In *J.S. v. Blue Mountain School District*,[35] a case with a similar fact pattern, J.S. and a fellow student created a profile for their principal on MySpace. In the profile, students indicated that Principal McGonigle was a married, bisexual man whose interests include "f-----g in [his] office" and "hitting on students and their parents." It also indicated that he was a "sex addict" who loved children and any kind of sex.[36] The profile also made disparaging comments regarding the principal's wife and children and contained his photograph, which the students copied from the school district's website. J.S. and his parents sought a temporary restraining order against the school, but the court denied it, finding that they did not have a likelihood of success on the merits and that at this juncture, it is in the public interest to allow the school the ability to discipline its students. It is important to make clear that in the first *Layshock* case, the court denied Layshock's TRO, just like in the *J.S.* case. Also, both cases are from Pennsylvania, perhaps making the outcomes a bit perplexing.

Beussink, Mitchell, Kent, Mahaffey, Coy, and *Layshock* all have several commonalities in addition to being free speech cases involving student rights, the Internet, and a perceived relationship to school violence and/or disrespect of school officials. All of the cases involved situations where the students participated in off-campus conduct that was protected speech. In each case, the student was punished by school officials who were using ambiguous or poorly defined policies that remotely applied to the infractions, thus contributing violations of students' first amendment and/or due process and rights. The school officials in *Layshock* built the strongest case as they attempted to demonstrate that the conduct was disruptive; however, this was to no avail. Still, the *Layshock* case is instructive, as the cases are below, to school officials looking to build defensible arguments against student off-campus Internet conduct.

In *Doninger v. Niehoff*,[37] Avery Doninger—an intelligent and articulate senior at Lewis S. Mills High School in Burlington, Connecticut—became frustrated at school officials over developments regarding a music festival she had been planning. Avery posted a public message to her fellow students on a social-networking site called LiveJournal. Though the site allowed for the author to make the text private, Avery decided to make it public and invite others to respond to her criticisms of the superintendent and her principal. Avery expressed her frustration using offensive and inappropriate language, for example, referring to school officials as "douchebags in central office."[38] Additionally, her message contained misleading and false information regarding the planning of the music festival and the action of the school officials. Specifically, Avery alleged that school officials had cancelled the festival when in fact they had given her the option to change the venue and/or date. Avery's blog called on students and their parents to write the school superintendent in order to "piss her off more."[39]

When school officials—who had advised Avery before she made her blog posting about the proper way for student leaders to address issues of concern with the administration—discovered the message, they disqualified her from running for class secretary for her senior year. They thought Avery's conduct in posting the blog message failed to display the qualities of civility and citizenship that the school expected of class officers and leaders. Avery's mother disagreed, arguing this was too harsh and asked for another type of punishment, but the officials refused. That was Avery's only punishment as she was not suspended from school and did not receive any other written discipline in her permanent school file. Moreover, she continued as a member of student council and as a leader of her student music class. Despite the Doningers' arguments, the court found that Avery did not have a First Amendment right to run for a voluntary extracurricular position as a student leader while engaging in uncivil and offensive communications regarding school administrators. The punishment was not excessive and was not meted out based on school officials being upset with the student.

In *Wisniewski v. Board of Education of the Weedsport Central School District,*[40] Aaron, a middle school student, created an instant messenger (IM) icon that suggested a named teacher at the school should be shot and killed. Aaron shared his IM icon with fifteen of his friends and fellow classmates over three weeks. The school district's hearing officer found that Aaron's icon posed a threat to his teacher and a disruption of the educational environment. Although he created the icon on his home computer, the court stated that "[t]he fact that Aaron's creation and transmission of the IM icon occurred away from school property does not necessarily insulate him from school discipline."[41] He was suspended, and his parents brought a section 1983 action against the school board and superintendent, alleging that his suspension violated the First Amendment. A United States District Court granted summary judgment in favor of school district, and his parents appealed. However, the Second Circuit Court of Appeals affirmed the district court holding that Aaron's actions posed reasonably foreseeable risk that the drawing would come to attention of school authorities and would materially and substantially disrupt work and discipline of school. School officials had clear policies against threatening teachers, no matter the medium. These cases demonstrate that reasonable rules and sanctions do much to strengthen principals' arguments in the First Amendment and Internet cases.

Cyberbullying

Bullying is perhaps an all too common part of the school experience. In an effort to discourage bullying, school officials typically create and enforce rules that encourage students to be respectful of one another and also urge them to be good citizens. Naturally, merely establishing rules is not a panacea to a problem that has likely been in existence as long as schools. Moreover, advancements in technology have given rise to a new category of bullying that is facilitated through its use. The new type of bully may not be a kid who uses his massive size to intimidate others but instead may spread nasty messages via the Internet using weblogs[42] or through text messaging on cell phones. More than 80 percent of American school-age children have access to computers[43] and the Internet, and more than 60 percent of teenagers have cellular phones;[44] thus, modern technology has made it easy for bullies to harass others day and night with the dexterity of their fingers, rather than the power of their fists.

This new form of bullying, which can take place anytime and anywhere, has been termed *cyberbullying,* and it is formally defined as "[b]ullying which is carried out through an Internet service such as email, chat room, discussion group, instant messaging or web pages. It can also include bullying through mobile phone technologies such as SMS (Short Message Service [Text Messaging])."[45] Cyberbullies commit offenses such as stealing other students' passwords and sending false messages to others from the victim's account or sending hateful, anonymous messages. Cyberbullies may create and participate in bashing websites where students can vote for the "fattest" or "ugliest" kid. Offline, cyberbullies may use their cell phones to send harassing text messages or to text rumors to others. Cyberbullying can take on a variety of different forms and is only limited by the bandwidth and imagination of the bully.[46]

Cyberbullying increases the number of students willing to become bullies because perpetrators feel comfortable or even safe participating as doing so does not require them to be face-to-face with the potential victims.[47] Accordingly, some students do not really consider the consequences or the detrimental effect of posting malicious or threatening messages on the Internet about schoolmates. Moreover, such behavior can and often does lead rather easily to sending such threats directly to peers and/or school personnel. Cyberbullying is difficult for parents and teachers to regulate because oftentimes kids are more technologically advanced than adults.

Because cyberbullying is a recent phenomenon, much of the research to date on the subject is still in development, but new occurrences ensure that there is rapid growth. However, studies on the correlate of traditional bullying provide assistance in comprehending the reality and growth of cyberbullying, which can similarly cripple the self-esteem of a child or adolescent.[48] Thus, cyberbullying can become just as problematic as traditional bullying, particularly with society's increasing reliance on technology.

There have been few cases dealing directly with cyberbullying, and a Canadian case that was expected to provide parameters around the growing phenomenon was settled out of court.[49] Nonetheless, principals can still use this case in efforts to be proactive. In 2003, a fifteen-year-old Canadian student filmed himself imitating a scene from the movie *Star Wars,* which was intended to be private. Apparently, the two-minute film did not show the student in his best light and quickly became the object of hundreds of online criticisms when three of the student's classmates obtained possession of the video clip without the owner's permission.[50] The video was revised at least thirty-five times by online users and was edited to include unflattering commentary and additional sound and visual effects. The teasing that the student endured as a result was so tormenting that the student dropped out of school and completed the year at a children's psychiatric ward. The victim's parents sued the parents of the pranksters for $351,000 in damages. The statement of claim included long excerpts, allegedly from Internet chats among the three student perpetrators, showing that they lacked remorse and bragged of their attempts to avoid being caught by school officials.

School administrators can consider several points from this case to formulate proactive solutions for dealing with cyberbullying. For example, does the school's code of conduct include a definition of cyberbullying along with specific consequences for violations? Has the school taken steps to block controversial websites or sites that do not promote the academic goals of the school? Do students and parents clearly understand the computer-use policies? Taking preventative steps can help school administrators avoid potential legal action.

Threats

In the *Mahaffey v. Aldrich*[51] case, the school district characterized the student's Internet speech as a threat but was unable to convince the court of this assertion.[52] In crafting their arguments, the school officials cited two important cases: *Lovell v. Poway* and *Doe v. Pulaski*. These cases are from the Ninth and Eighth Circuit courts, respectively, and in each, (not surprisingly) the judges reached the same conclusion: threats are not protected speech. Each case is instructive for different reasons discussed below.

In the first case, Sarah Lovell, a student, brought action against her high school, claiming free speech and due process violations after she received a three-day suspension for allegedly threatening to shoot her school guidance counselor in connection with a proposed schedule change.[53] A United States district court held that Lovell's speech was entitled to First Amendment protection because a California statute enlarged her First Amendment rights by ensuring that "a student shall have the same right to exercise his or her right to free speech on campus as he or she enjoys when off campus."[54] However, the Ninth Circuit Court of Appeals overruled the decision, finding that the statements made by Lovell to her guidance counselor constituted a threat. The court found that the district court erroneously conflated the student's federal and state free speech rights. However, the court determined that threats are not protected speech, regardless of the context, and as such the school district "did not violate Lovell's First Amendment right to free expression under either federal or state law when it suspended her for threatening a school guidance counselor"[55] because threats are not protected by the First Amendment.

In the second case that involved student expression directed at another student, an eighth grader brought action against his school district, claiming his expulsion based on two letters he composed—which the court described as "violent, misogynic, and obscenity-laden rants expressing a desire to molest, rape, and murder"[56] his former girlfriend—violated his First Amendment rights. He wrote the letters at home during the summer prior to the start of his eighth-grade year. Although he told the former girlfriend of the letters over the phone, he never showed them to her directly. His best friend stole the letters at the behest of the ex-girlfriend and delivered them to her. She read them aloud in the presence of some fellow students in her gym class. One of those students reported the contents to school officials who investigated and found the content of the letters constituted a threat to the female student. Making threats violated school policy, and as a result of the content, they expelled the author of the letters. A U.S. district court concluded that the composition in the letters was not a true threat and voided the expulsion, finding no proof that the young author communicated or intended to communicate a threat in writing them. The Eighth Circuit Court of Appeals affirmed. However, upon rehearing, the Eighth Circuit held that the student intended to communicate the letter and is therefore accountable because a reasonable recipient would have viewed the letter as a threat.[57] Hence, the court found that the expulsion of student did not violate the student's First Amendment rights.

In *Pulaski,* the court points out that the Supreme Court has determined "that threats of violence also fall within the realm of speech that the government can proscribe without offending the First Amendment."[58] However, even if expression is not found to be a threat, the school may still regulate it if it is found to disrupt the environment or interfere with the rights of others. For example, in the following case, a student created a website off campus that contained expression that did not fall within the protection of the First Amendment. In *J.S. v. Bethlehem*, a middle school student and his parents sought review of school district's decision to permanently expel him based on his off-campus creation of an Internet website containing threatening and derogatory comments about a teacher and the principal. The decision was affirmed, and J.S. and his parents appealed.[59]

Eventually, the state's highest court held that the student's website did not constitute a "true threat," even though on it he asked why a teacher should die, displayed a picture of her head severed from her body, and solicited funds to hire a hit man to kill the teacher. The court found that the website was a crude and highly offensive attempt at humor or parody but did not reflect a serious expression of intent to inflict harm, despite the actions taken by the teacher and the fear she experienced after viewing website. The teacher actually took a leave of absence because she was so shocked by the page and its contents.[60] Even though it was not found to be a threat, the speech expressed by the student on the website was considered on-campus speech with respect to the school environment because he had accessed the site at school, had shown it to another student, and had discussed it with others. Moreover, the court concluded that the website had the potential to cause a disruption of the entire school community because it was aimed at two school officials, and "where speech that is aimed at a specific school and/or its personnel is brought onto the school campus or accessed at school by its originator, the speech will be considered on-campus speech."[61] Hence, expelling the student did not violate his First Amendment rights.

Lovell and *Pulaski* are illustrative of the fact that threats will not be protected for the purpose of the First Amendment if they are connected to the school environment. In *J.S. v. Bethlehem,* we see reasoning similar to that in *Tinker* being applied to an Internet case after the threat question is resolved. The difference in *Bethlehem* is that the speech is disruptive, but it was also created off campus. However, this is off-campus speech that is considered by the court to be on-campus because it materially disrupted the school environment, thus making the school's case compelling enough for the court to uphold the expulsion of the student.

Searches of Computers

The landmark case of *New Jersey v. T.L.O.*[62] defines conduct of school officials for searches and seizures of students. In *T.L.O.,* a student was accused of smoking in the lavatory, which led to a search of her purse for cigarettes. The search produced evidence of smoking but also turned up rolling papers and a list of names, which administrators believed pointed to drug trafficking. The student claimed a violation of her Fourth Amendment rights because school personnel did not have probable cause, which required a warrant for the search. Although the United States Supreme Court noted that students have an expectation of privacy in schools, it determined that school officials are not police officers and, therefore, are not bound by the same strictures for search and seizure purposes in the school atmosphere. The high court concluded that the warrant is ill suited for searches in school environments as it would interfere with the need to carry out swift and informal disciplinary procedures.[63]

Consequently, the Court determined that a reasonableness standard is more suitable for school purposes and it essentially states that a search of a student by a teacher or other school official will be "justified at its inception" when there are reasonable grounds for suspecting that the search will turn up evidence that the student has violated either the law or the rules of the school.[64] Such a search will be permissible in its scope when the measures adopted are "reasonably related to the objectives of the search and not excessively intrusive in light of the age and sex of the student and the nature of the infraction."[65] Hence, searches in schools should be governed by the lower standard of reasonableness rather than probable cause. There is a scant number of cases on searches and seizures of computers relative to students in the K-12 environment, but the following three cases offer some guidance.

In *Herzog v. Wills,* a senior high school student, Joshua Herzog, edited and published a non-school-sponsored underground newspaper entitled "The Sub Station."[66] The paper was loaded with vulgarities, misspellings, grammatical errors, poor usage of English, and unflattering language about fellow students.[67] The principal and the assistant principal found copies of the publication at the school and consequently questioned the student regarding his role in its preparation. He confessed and signed a purported consent to a search of the Herzog residence by the Monticello Police Department. School officials and police escorted Joshua to his residence and entered his parents' bedroom, where the computer on which he prepared the newspaper was located. Joshua then downloaded onto a disc a copy of the Sub Station data stored on the computer's hard drive, which also contained private documents belonging to his parents. He was arrested and faced criminal charges but was released the same day.

Joshua Herzog and his parents brought a section 1983 action against the school board and school officials, alleging violations of their constitutional rights as protected by the First, Fourth and Fourteenth Amendments arising from school disciplinary action taken against Joshua Herzog, his arrest, and an alleged illegal search of the Herzog residence. The school officials moved for summary judgment requesting that the court grant qualified immunity. However, the court found that there were too many questions to grant immunity. For example, it was unclear whether Joshua actually did anything on school grounds in connection with the distribution of the paper and whether any school officials had reasonable grounds to believe he had done so. Moreover, the court concluded that the status of the principal in the student's home along with the arresting officers was highly ambiguous. The court also noted that school persons possessed no authority to search a student's home, and the seizure of the computer disks was improper as they in no way represented school property.

The second search case is *Ianson v. Zion-Benton Township High School,* which was decided in 2001.[68] Students at a high school were detained and questioned at school by administrators and a security guard in connection with possibly pirated or pilfered school software and/or computer programs. The students were then allegedly coerced into giving statements that implicated themselves and others in this theft. Later that day, the school security guard accompanied students to their respective homes, supposedly under the instruction of school officials. The security guard entered the students' homes without a warrant and seized their personal computers and software. Students were then suspended for five days by the principal, and afterwards, they claimed to have received neither notice nor a statement of the charges against them.

The students brought several charges against the district, in addition to a claim that their Fourth Amendment rights to be free from searches and seizures had been violated when they were detained for questioning and by the search of their respective homes and the seizure of their computers without a warrant. Citing *T.L.O.*, the court found that in light of the special relationship between teachers and students, the diminished protection of the Fourth Amendment for public schoolchildren and the need to maintain discipline and order in the schools, the individuals' actions in detaining and interrogating the students was reasonable,[69] given that they were questioned in connection with the pirated software.

The students further alleged that the security guard violated their Fourth Amendment right to be free from unreasonable searches and seizures when she, without a warrant, accompanied them to their respective homes, entered each home and seized their personal computers. She argued that the protection from Fourth Amendment claims laid out in *T.L.O.* should apply to this situation. The court disagreed and refused to extend the protections of *T.L.O.* beyond the walls of the school and into the homes of the students. It noted, "In light of the fact that the opinion in *T.L.O.* turned on the need for 'maintaining security and order in the schools,' this court declines defendant's invitation to extend the protection of *T.L.O.* out from the schoolyard and into the home."[70]

A third case that does not deal with the K-12 environment directly but is instructive nonetheless is *U.S. v. Butler*.[71] In *Butler*, a college student enrolled in the University of Maine had access to a college computer lab as a student. On one occasion, he left a frozen image on a university computer screen that a university employee considered to be child pornography. That incident prompted university authorities to investigate, and as part of their inquiry, they examined session logs and hard drives in the computer labs. The investigation revealed more such images on the lab's hard drives, and the officials then contacted the police. The student wanted the images and session logs suppressed, claiming that the items were products of illegal searches in violation of his Fourth Amendment rights.

The court expressed some difficulty in addressing the issues of the case because the "rapidly changing technology and provisions of service."[72] However, the court started the analysis by examining the student's expectation of privacy. It noted that "to assert a right under the Fourth Amendment, a defendant must demonstrate both a subjective expectation of privacy and an expectation that society judges as objectively reasonable."[73] The difficulty of deciding the case was simplified because the student failed to present even a minimal showing that he had a reasonable expectation of privacy in either his session logs or the hard drives of these university-owned computers. The court noted the logs were kept for university purposes and that the student had received no privacy policy or representation that the information on the hard drives was private. Hence, the court concluded there was no expectation of privacy in shared computer usage, and the student failed to establish an expectation of privacy in the school computers. Without that, he cannot challenge the university's decision to search the computers.

Internet safety policies should address the fact that computers are school property and are akin to lockers when it comes to searches. For instance, many schools include in their general policies or student handbooks that lockers can be searched anytime because they are school property. As in *Butler*, a policy such as this establishes up front that students have no expectation of privacy or at least a diminished one in the shared usage of the computers. The policy should state that the machines are to be used for curricula purposes and may be searched at all times, including floppy disks, hard disk drives, or portable flash drives. At a minimum, students should understand that unauthorized use is prohibited. It is wise to require that students store documents on a server—if possible—for two reasons. Doing so reduces the probability of students bringing in disks that they can use to infect the individual computers and/or the network with viruses, inadvertently or intentionally, and secondly, this undergirds the policy's focus that students have a lesser expectation of privacy because all searches then will be conducted on school-purchased equipment rather than personal devices such as diskettes used to store and transport data.

Internet-Use Policies and Due Process

A common theme in the foregoing cases has been a lack of clear Internet use policies for guidance. Recent laws have made it necessary for schools and libraries to have some type of policy in place. In December of 2000, the Children's Internet Protection Act (CIPA) was signed into law.[74] CIPA requires that schools and libraries receiving E-rate federal funding adopt and implement "technology protection" measures on all computers with Internet access as a condition of receiving those funds. Specifically, each schools or library must verify that it has adopted and implemented an Internet safety policy and that it has installed filters that are used to block Internet access to obscenity, child pornography, and material harmful to minors.[75] To comply with CIPA requirements, the policy of each school or library shall address:

1. access by minors to inappropriate matter on the Internet;
2. the safety and security of minors when using electronic mail, chat rooms, and other forms of direct electronic communications;
3. unauthorized access, including so-called "hacking," and other unlawful activities by minors online;

4. unauthorized disclosure, use, and dissemination of personal identification information regarding minors; and
5. measures designed to restrict minors' access to materials harmful to minors.[76]

The school, school board, or educational agency with the responsibility for administration of the school shall provide reasonable public notice and hold at least one public hearing or meeting to address the proposed Internet safety policy.[77]

The purpose of the E-rate is to assist schools and libraries in obtaining telecommunications and Internet access at discounted rates. CIPA provides that a school having computers with Internet access may not receive services at discount rates unless the school, school board, local educational agency, or other authority with responsibility for administration of the school submits certifications with respect to minors and adults that officially verify that an Internet safety policy has been adopted and implemented for the school and ensures the use of such computers in accordance with the certifications.[78]

To receive certification with respect to minors, a school or library must verify that it is enforcing an Internet safety policy for minors and monitoring their online activities through the operation of a technology protection measure. The term "technology protection measure" means software that blocks or filters Internet access to the material.[79] The blocking software should prevent minors from accessing visual depictions via the Internet that are obscene, contain child pornography, or are harmful to minors.[80] Moreover, the school or district must also verify that it is enforcing the operation of blocking technology during the use of its computers by minors.[81]

Similarly, a school or library will receive certification with respect to adults when it verifies that it is enforcing an Internet safety policy using blocking software that prevents access to visual depictions that are obscene or depicting child pornography and that it is enforcing the operation of such technology protection measure during any use of such computers.

If a school or library does not receive E-rate funds, it may still be required to comply if it receives funds under some other federal statute, which typically cajoles schools districts to comply through the "threat of a lawsuit, the lure of federal money, or a threat of a cutoff of federal funds."[82] For instance, libraries that receive funds under Section 224 of the Museum and Library Services Act must comply.[83] In 2003, the American Libraries Association challenged the constitutionality of CIPA requirements, charging that if they installed filters on their computers that it would force them to abridge the First Amendment rights of their patrons. The Supreme Court disagreed, holding that CIPA did not impose an unconstitutional condition by requiring filters on public library computers and it did not violate First Amendment free speech rights of patrons. In addition, the Court held that the requirement was not an abuse of Congress' spending power.[84] The No Child Left Behind Act has incorporated the requirements of CIPA, ensuring that an Internet safety policy is adopted and that filters are used by schools that are receiving funds.[85] This ensures that those schools receiving Title I money instead of E-rate funds will be obligated to comply.

Because of CIPA, many school districts have implemented some form of an Internet safety policy or what is sometimes referred to as an Acceptable Use Policy. However, such policies vary in adequacy and ability to address issues associated with student use of the Internet. Although typically such policies cover the basics of rules and regulations of Internet use in schools, a common problem is that authors offer no guidance relative to students who have attained the age of seventeen, i.e., those individuals who are considered adults for the purpose of the statute.[86] Many administrators fail to disable filters during adult use or to inform them that this is within their rights to have it done under the statute. CIPA provides that an administrator, supervisor, or other person authorized by the certifying authority may disable the technology protection measure during use by an adult to enable access for bona fide research or other lawful purpose.[87] For this reason, it is a good idea to include this in your Internet safety policy.

Parents, and sometimes students, are required to sign Internet-use policy forms before students are permitted to use the school's computers to access the Internet. Some districts decide against this and make policies part of the general handbook, or they send a policy to parents that presents the opt-out provision, which gives access to all students unless parents say otherwise. Policies often include what has come to be known as *netiquette,* or etiquette when surfing the Internet. These are just behaviors that give students recommendations on how to be good citizens when using the Internet. Guidance for construction of such policies can be found on the Internet.[88]

Several of the cases above illustrate the importance of granting students' due process and highlight the frequency at which such rights are overlooked in cases involving student speech over the Internet. For example, the *Mitchell, Mahaffey,* and *Killion* decisions emphasized the importance of writing good policies in the process of granting due process and enforcing rules. In *Mitchell,* the court roundly criticized district officials for policies that permitted "unfettered discretion" in punishing students. In *Mahaffey*, the school failed to escape a violation because it did not allow the student to cross-examine witnesses, as required by the school district's code of conduct. In *Killion*, the student was suspended for creating an email list and was notified after the hearing, thus violating his due process rights.

In the final Internet case, Jack Flaherty, a high school student, was disciplined for posting messages to a website message board about an upcoming volleyball game. He used vulgar language and profanity in the postings. Three of the messages were posted at home and one at school.[89] His parents sought a declaration that portions of the

> Student Handbook are unconstitutionally overbroad and vague because particular portions allow for punishment of speech that school officials deem to be "inappropriate, ha-

> rassing, offensive or abusive" without defining those terms or limiting them in relation to geographic boundaries (at school or school sponsored events) or to speech that causes a material and substantial disruption to the school day.[90]

The court found that, in addition to being separate from abuse, discipline, and harassment sections, which were at issue in the case,

> the freedom of expression provision does not require or put a school official on notice that his authority to discipline under a school policy is limited to those instances where a student's abusive, offensive, harassing or inappropriate behavior causes or is likely to cause a substantial disruption to school operations.[91]

Moreover, the court found that the handbook did not limit restrictions on speech to those that caused a substantial disruption as required by *Tinker*, so they found the policies to be overbroad and vague because several terms like "abuse" lacked definitions and did not provide the students with adequate warnings of the conduct that is prohibited. Policies were also vague in application because they could lead to arbitrary enforcement.[92] Another problem with the policies is that they did not geographically limit school official's authority to discipline expression that occurred on school premises or at school-related activities.

In the formulating policies, school districts should consciously avoid creating policies that are vague and overbroad. A description of these terms is found in the summary of the *Killion* case above. Writing good Internet safety policies is also connected to granting students due process because good ones give notice to students and staff of the types of behaviors that are acceptable when accessing the Internet using the school's computers.

Conclusion

The cases above outline court action regarding issues involving student expression and the Internet. *Beussink*, followed by other decisions, points to the fact that personal student expression will be protected unless it causes a substantial and material disruption. Moreover, expression that is found to be a threat, causes a material and substantial disruption, or interferes with the rights of others will not be protected for the purposes of the First Amendment. Other speech that is created in school on district computers can be restricted more, especially if the purpose of the machine relates to the curriculum in some fashion, which is common of school computers. An Internet safety policy helps to define approved and prohibited activity for students using computers in schools. Filters can facilitate this responsibility of school officials and allow for flexibility in application to avoid violating the rights of older students who are "adults" who need to have filters disabled to do legitimate research. Recommendations are given below.

Recommendations for Practice

1. First Amendment speech expressed on the Internet via a webpage or other medium, like *Tinker* speech, cannot be punished unless it significantly interferes with a school function, causes a disruption, or interferes with the rights of others. Students cannot be punished for such expression merely because it is disrespectful or unpopular. This will likely be true regardless of where the speech is created.
2. CIPA mandates, among other things, creating an Internet safety policy and adding filters to school computers. It is likely that your school has some form of Internet use policy. If not, check with your district. Some districts may not have filtering software in place because of cost or other reasons. Whether they have filters or not, districts should have some form of an Internet use policy. This may include non-CIPA school districts.
3. Administrators employing such filters should be aware that this blocking software is not infallible and that it likely will over- or under-block. Make this fact known to students and parents. Compensate for the shortfall of the software with the Internet safety policy.
4. When creating Internet safety policies, be sure to avoid vague language in the actual rules of use. It is important to spell out in clear, unambiguous language the purpose of your Internet safety policy and what actions are permitted and prohibited when students are using the schools' computers. This includes using email, instant messages, and material posted on webpages or weblogs ("blogs"). Be sure to define all terms. Include language in Internet safety policies about social networking sites and cell phones.
5. Administrators should include in the Internet safety policy when blocking software may be disabled. Even schools with policies usually fail to address when and why filtering software may be disabled. There are cases when "adults" or older minors need to do bona fide or legitimate research and this is permitted by CIPA. A minor is defined as anyone who has not attained the age of seventeen, which means he or she may still be in high school.[93]
6. Have students and parents sign the Internet safety policy. Such signed agreements should be kept on file. Students without signed policies should not be permitted to use the Internet at school. If you decide to do an opt-out policy, make sure parents understand the terms.

7. Make sure students receive due process. Discipline for inappropriate Internet use should be fair and fit the infraction. The other side of the coin of having specific, well-defined policies is having clear and fair punishment for breaking rules. Examples of first time infractions may include suspension of privileges for a period of time. Define threats and cyberbullying for students and encourage students to be good citizens when using the Internet and not engage in these activities. Students should be warned that serious infractions bring about serious penalties that may result in punishment beyond the school's discipline decision.
8. Make sure students understand that computers belong to the school and are to be used primarily for curricular purposes only. School officials often use computers for other purposes that may further the mission of the school.
9. Inform students that computers are school property and can be searched at anytime. Therefore, there is a diminished expectation of privacy and that means computers are analogous to lockers that can be searched. This is important in light of the fact that recent virus creators have been high school-age students who use school computers and networks.[94] Requiring students to store data on a server is a possible solution to this problem.
10. Promote positive computer experiences by teaching students to be good citizens when using the Internet.

Endnotes

1 Louis Fischer, David Schimmel, & Cynthia Kelly, Teachers and the Law (5th ed. 1999).

2 393 U.S.503 (1969).

3 *Id.*

4 David J. Sperry, Philip T.K. Daniel, Dixie Snow Huefner, & E. Gordon Gee, Education Law and the Public Schools: A Compendium (2d ed. 1998).

5 Bethel Sch. Dist. No. 403 v. Fraser, 478 U.S. 675 (1986).

6 Hazelwood Sch. Dist. v. Kuhlmeier, 484 U.S. 260 (1988).

7 Sperry et al., *supra* note 4.

8 *Id.* at 521.

9 Tinker v. Des Moines Indep. Sch. Dist., 393 U.S. 503, 508 (1969).

10 Beussink v. Woodland R-IV Sch. Dist., 30 F. Supp. 2d 1175 (E.D. Mo. 1998).

11 *Id.*

12 *Id.*

13 Dustin Mitchell v. Rolla High Sch. Dist. No. 31(Missouri) (E.D. Mo. 1999) *available at* http://archive.aclu.org/court/Mitchell_brief.html.

14 Emmett v. Kent Sch. Dist. No. 415, 92 F. Supp. 2d. 1088 (W.D. Wash. 2000).

15 *Id.* at 1090.

16 236 F. Supp. 2d 779, 781 (E.D. Mich.2002).

17 *Id.* at 783.

18 *Id.* at 784.

19 *Id.*

[20] Coy v. Bd. of Educ. of the N. Canton City Schs., 205 F. Supp. 2d 791, at 795 (N.D. Ohio 2002).

[21] *Id.* at 800.

[22] *Id.* at 801.

[23] *Id.* at 802.

[24] Killion v. Franklin Reg'l Sch. Dist., 136 F. Supp. 2d 446 (W.D. Pa. 2001).

[25] *Id.* at 449.

[26] *Id.* at 451.

[27] *Id.* at 458.

[28] *Id.* at 459.

[29] Layshock v. Hermitage Sch. Dist., 496 F. Supp. 2d 857 (W.D. Pa. 2007)

[30] *Id.* at 591.

[31] *Id.*

[32] *Id* at 599.

[33] Layshock v. Hermitage Sch. Dist., 412 F. Supp. 2d 502 (W.D. Pa. 2006).

[34] *Id.*

[35] 2007 WL 954245 (M.D. Pa. 2007).

[36] *Id* at *1.

[37] 514 F. Supp. 2d 199 (D. Conn. 2007).

[38] *Id* at 207.

[39] *Id* at 206.

[40] 494 F.3d 34 (2d Cir. 2007).

[41] *Id* at 39.

[42] *See, e.g., What is a Blog (aka Web log /Weblog)?, available at* http://weblogs.about.com/cs/weblogs101/f/whatisablog.htm.Weblog: The word *blog* is short for web log (weblog). It is used both as a noun and a verb. As a noun, a blog is also known as an online journal or web diary, as well as a content management system or an online publishing platform. As a verb, "to blog" means to write on one's weblog. Essentially, a weblog is a chronologically organized site with the latest entry appearing at the top of the page. It is updated by an individual (or a group of individuals) using these main items in each entry or post: a) Main Body - where personal commentaries, ideas, and/or stories are typically written in the first person ("I"). b) Date/Time Stamp - to show the day and/or time the entry. c) Title - to give a general idea or gist of what the entry is all about. Not all bloggers (people who keep weblogs) use this format. Students use them as online diaries and post things—messages, sometimes malicious, about classmates.

[43] Susan Patrick, *Invited Commentary: Children, Schools, Computers, and the Internet: The Impact of Continued Investment in Educational Technology Under NCLB*, 5 Educ. Statistics Quarterly, No.4 (2004). http://nces.ed.gov/programs/quarterly/Vol_5/5_4/2_4.asp

[44] Center on Media and Child Health (2007) http://www.cmch.tv/mentors/hotTopic.asp?id=70

[45] *See, e.g., Net Alert: What is Cyber Bullying?, at* http://www.netalert.net.au/01023-What-is-Cyber-Bullying.asp. *See, also, e.g., Cyberbullying* Basics at http://www.aftab.com/Cyberbullying%20Basics%20FAQs_files/frame.htm. Note that Parry Aftab, an expert in cybercrime and Internet safety for kids, defines cyberbullying as when a child, preteen, or teen is tormented, threatened, harassed, humiliated, embarrassed, or otherwise targeted by another child, preteen, or teen using the Internet, interactive and digital technologies, or mobile phones. It has to have a minor on both sides, or at least have been instigated by a minor against another minor.

[46] *Id.*

[47] For a discussion of Cyber Bullying, see e.g., *Cyber bullying Stalks Students, at* http://www.detnews.com/2003/editorial/0311/09/a13-319592.htm.

[48] Justin W. Patchin & Sameer Hinduja, *Bullies Move Beyond the Schoolyard: Preliminary Look at Cyberbullying,* Youth Violence and Juvenile Justice, Apr. 2006, at 149

[49] Allison Lampbert, *Stars Wars Kid Settles Lawsuit,* THE GAZETTE (Quebec), 2006. http://www.canada.com/globaltv/quebec/news/story.html?id=e93a2a11-11c9-4d97-82ed-221d6cfa1ef2&k=14313
[50] Teresa Haykowsky, *Star Wars Kid Cyberbullying Lawsuit Offers Lessons to School Boards,* EDUC. L. EMAIL ALERT, Apr. 20, 2006. http://www.mross.com/law/Publications/Email+Alerts?contentId=887
[51] Mahaffy v. Aldrich, *supra* note 16.
[52] *Id.*
[53] Lovell v. Poway Unified Sch. Dist., 90 F.3d 367 (9th Cir. 1996).
[54] *Id.* at 371.
[55] *Id.* at 373.
[56] Doe v. Pulaski, 306 F.3d. 616, at 619 (8th Cir. 2002).
[57] *Id.* at 624.
[58] *Id.* at 622.
[59] J.S. v Bethlehem Area Sch. Dist., 807 A. 2d 847 (Pa. Super. Ct. 2002).
[60] *Id.*
[61] *Id.* at 864.
[62] 469 U.S. 325 (1985).
[63] *Id.*
[64] *Id.*
[65] *Id.*
[66] Herzog v. Wills, 931 F. Supp. 276 (S.D.N.Y. 1996).
[67] *Id.*
[68] Ianson v. Zion-Benton Township High Sch., 2001 WL 185021 (N.D. Ill.).
[69] *Id.* at 4.
[70] *Id.* at 4.
[71] U.S. v. Butler, 151 F. Supp. 2d 82 (2001).
[72] *Id.* at 84.
[73] *Id.*
[74] Pub. L. 106-554, codified at 20 U.S.C. § 9134 and 47 U.S.C. § 254 (h).
[75] 47 U.S.C. § 254(h).
[76] 47 U.S.C. § 254(l).
[77] 47 U.S.C. § 254(h)(5)(A)(iii).
[78] 47 U.S.C. § 254(h)(5)(A)(i).
[79] 47 U.S.C. § 254(h)(7)(I).
[80] 47 U.S.C. § 254(h)(5)(B)(i).
[81] 47 U.S.C. § 254(h)(5)(B)(ii).
[82] MICHAEL W. LAMORTE, SCHOOL LAW: CASES AND CONCEPTS 10 (2005).
[83] 20 U.S.C. § 9134(b).
[84] United States v. Am. Libraries Ass'n, 123 S. Ct. 2297 (2003).
[85] 20 U.S.C. § 6777, § 2441, Pub. L. 107–10, No Child Left Behind Act.
[86] 47 U.S.C. § 254(l)) A minor is defined by the statute as "someone who has not attained the age of 17."
[87] 47 U.S.C. § 254(h)(5)(D).
[88] *See, e.g., Virginia Department of Education Acceptable Internet Use Policies: A Handbook, at* http://www.pen.k12.va.us/go/VDOE/Technology/AUP/home.shtml.
[89] Flaherty v. Keystone Oaks Sch. Dist., 247 F. Supp. 2d 698 (W.D. Pa. 2003).
[90] *Id.* at 702.
[91] *Id.* at 703.
[92] *Id.*
[93] 47 U.S.C. § 254(h)(7)(D); 47 U.S.C. § 254(h)(6)(D).
[94] *PC viruses: Never Open Your Door to Strangers, at* http://www.usatoday.com/tech/news/2002/05/02/virus-ordeal.htm.

Chapter 10

Truancy

Laura R. McNeal

Introduction

Historically, the emergence of compulsory attendance laws began in 1852, when Massachusetts became the first state to enact a compulsory attendance statute.[1] Compulsory attendance laws make sure that educational services are provided and that children participate in those services. By 1918, every state had adopted a compulsory education law.[2] In 1925, the landmark *Pierce v. Society of Sisters* Supreme Court case crystallized the important role of education in preparing our nation's children for good citizenry. This case solidified compulsory education attendance laws as a valid exercise of state power provided by the U.S. Constitution. More than seventy-five years after the *Pierce* case, many states still struggle to ensure that every child receives an education as a result of increasingly high truancy rates in America's schools. The realization that a high school diploma and postsecondary degree are critical for full participation in today's workforce has resulted in an influx of truancy-prevention programs throughout the country. As school leaders address truancy incidents, it is imperative that they are well informed about their legal responsibilities in addressing truancy.

Legal Issues

Compulsory attendance laws are the primary legal tool for ensuring that children receive the training they need to become self-sufficient adults. Compulsory attendance laws are shaped and formed through state statutes. State statutes require parents or legal guardians of children between specific age ranges to attend school on a regular basis. The maximum age range in which children are required to attend school varies among states. Currently, sixteen states require children to attend school until the age of 18; nine states require attendance until age 17; twenty-six states require attendance until age 16.[3] There are also stark differences among states regarding the minimum age in which children are required to begin schooling. Presently, two states require children to attend school starting at age 8, seventeen states at age 7, twenty-three states at age 6, and nine states at age 5.[4] For example, in California, students must begin to attend school at age 6 and continue until age

18, whereas students in Michigan are required to attend school beginning at age 6 and must continue until age 16.[5] Typically states that require students to attend school until age 17 or 18 will permit students to withdraw at age 16 with parental consent.[6]

Enforcement of Compulsory Attendance Laws

Federal Role

The No Child Left Behind Act (NCLB) attempts to increase school accountability for truancy by requiring school districts to submit attendance data to the state government as a requisite for receiving federal funding.[7] Although NCLB's data-reporting mandate is intended to provide an accurate assessment of the prevalence of truancy in America's schools and increase school accountability for truancy, there are several limitations within the law that prohibit its effectiveness. For example, the law fails to distinguish between excused and unexcused absences, thus allowing schools to create their own individual guidelines to differentiate between the two. In addition, states are allowed to define their own formulas for calculating truancy rates.[8] As a result, there is a lack of uniformity in state truancy data, making it difficult for stakeholders in education to obtain an accurate picture of the extent of truancy in schools. Lastly, although NCLB requires states to submit their data to their state government, there is currently no requirement to submit truancy data to any federal agency, therefore minimizing the degree of local and state accountability.

State Role

The legal definition of truancy is defined as chronic unexcused absenteeism. School officials are required to address students who are habitual truants. Each individual state attendance law specifies the number of unexcused absences necessary for a student to be designated a habitual truant. For example, Colorado's compulsory attendance law characterizes a student as a habitual truant for ten unexcused absences during the school year or four unexcused absences in one month.[9] In Arizona, a student is considered a habitual truant for five or more unexcused absences in a school year. Since state attendance laws vary in how they define the parameters of what constitutes chronic truancy, it is imperative that school leaders familiarize themselves and school staff with their state's truancy guidelines.

The current legal milieu encourages schools to employ all available strategies to remediate truancy prior to filing court charges. Many states have statutory requirements that schools must employ prior to filing truancy charges in court.[10] These strategies include, but are not limited to, counseling, student psychiatric evaluations, parental intervention meetings, and alternative education placements. Ideally, the court system is intended to be the final stop for chronic truants who have failed to respond to school intervention efforts.[11]

For example, the school district in Ramsey County, Minnesota, employs the following three-tiered Truancy Intervention Program: (1) an informational meeting with the parents and truant student to explain the laws and legal consequences of truancy; (2) collaboration of school officials (including counselors), parents, the assistant county attorney, and students to develop an attendance contract; and (3) a petition filed to the juvenile court if the truancy continues after the first two intervention efforts.[12] Other states have alternative schools for habitually truant students, such as the Dekalb Truancy School in Dekalb County, Georgia, which utilizes a specialized curriculum designed to intervene and stop truancy before initiating court involvement.[13]

The court system has the authority to order a range of consequences for habitually truant children such as placing the child on probation; ordering the child to undergo evaluation or treatment for chemical dependency; performing community service; placing the child on house arrest, which makes the child unable to leave home except to attend school or when accompanied by a parent; removing the child from the home and placing the child in a shelter, foster care, group home, or short-term residential facility; placing the child in long-term residential treatment; or imposing any other activities or treatment programs that are deemed appropriate. The Juvenile Justice and Delinquency Prevention Act also permits judges to issue a court order to compel truant students to attend school. If a truant student fails to comply with the court order, he or she may be sentenced to juvenile detention for a period of time specified by the court.[14] According to data from the Census of Juveniles in Residential Placement Databook, habitual truants collectively spend approximately 286,160 days in a juvenile detention center in a given year.[15]

States also have a myriad of criminal and civil sanctions that may be imposed upon the parents of habitually truant students that fail to respond to school intervention efforts. More specifically, the parents of a habitually truant student are subject to criminal and civil liability for failing to remedy the child's truancy upon notice by school officials. The severity of parental sanctions are often dependent upon the state of residence, age of the child, student attendance records, and the court philosophy regarding the most effective way to address truancy. The most common sanctions are monetary fines, which can range anywhere from $100 to $1,000. More severe truancy cases can result in jail time or in rare cases parental loss of custody.

In recent years, some states have revised existing compulsory attendance laws to include innovative sanctions for parents and students that do not involve the legal system. For example, in Georgia, a student's ability to maintain or obtain a driver's license is suspended for one year if the student has ten or more unexcused absences.[16] Additionally, other state attendance laws require parents to participate in parenting classes, attend school with their child for a specified period of time, or perform community service.

Truancy Defenses

School authorities may use their discretion in determining what constitutes a sufficient excuse for absence from school. However, school officials must balance their discretionary power within the limits of their state's statutory guidelines, which distinguish between excused and unexcused absences. As a general rule, courts will not infringe upon a school official's discretionary power to determine what constitutes an approved absence from school unless such power has been substantially abused.[17] Common defenses to truancy are child illness, family emergency, funeral, religious holiday, and inaccurate attendance records. It is recommended that school officials investigate all cases of student truancy prior to filing legal charges. This is evidenced by the *S.H. v. State* case in which a student appealed a lower court decision adjudicating her as a truant on the basis that the school principal failed to follow statutory procedures by not investigating the truancy charge before filing a formal complaint with the court.[18] Although the court held that the Alabama state compulsory attendance statute required the county or city attendance officer, not the principal, to investigate truancy cases, it does highlight the importance of school leaders understanding their statutory duties regarding student truancy. Although Alabama's state compulsory law does not affirmatively place a duty on school principals to investigate all cases of nonattendance, it is important to remember that each state attendance law has its own unique requirements. Therefore, as a general rule, it is advisable for school principals to thoroughly investigate truancy cases before filing a formal complaint with the court to avoid possible legal liability.

Legal Exemptions to Compulsory Attendance Laws

Although states can compel children to attend school within a certain age range, the state cannot compel children to attend public schools.[19] In *Norwood v. Harrison*, the Supreme Court held that state compulsory attendance statutes must permit children to attend private, public, or parochial schools.[20] In recent years, the legal system has also provided clarity regarding the application of state compulsory attendance laws to parents who choose to educate their children at home as opposed to a traditional private or public school setting. In the United States, homeschooling is legal in all fifty states. Although the Supreme Court has never directly addressed homeschooling, the landmark Supreme Court case, *Wisconsin v. Yoder*, upheld the rights of Amish parents to keep their children out of schools for religious reasons.[21] Thus, it is well established through the *Wisconsin v. Yoder* decision and other court rulings that parents may satisfy state compulsory attendance requirements through home instruction.[22] In Kentucky, a fifteen-year-old high school student withdrew from public school and started a homeschooling program due to poor health. Despite her participation in a homeschooling program, a county district judge found the high school student guilty of truancy and ordered her to attend public school until she turned eighteen years of age. A circuit court appeals judge overruled the lower court decision stating, "parents have a fundamental right to direct the education and upbringing of their children. This includes the right of parents to choose an alternate education in lieu of public schools."[23]

The degree and scope of truancy monitoring of students who are homeschooled varies with each state attendance law. Some states, such as North Carolina, require parents of children who are homeschooled to maintain attendance records, whereas states such as Tennessee require parents to actually submit attendance records to the local superintendent at the end of each school year.[24] States such as Ohio require parents to sign a document verifying that their children will receive 900 hours of instruction per year as opposed to maintaining yearly attendance data.[25]

Conclusion

With the increased pace and scope of truancy incidents across the United States, ensuring that every child is educated has become a formidable task for many school officials.[26] Research studies have shown strong correlations between student attendance and academic success.[27] It is also well established that students are less likely to engage in delinquent or destructive behaviors if they attend school on a regular basis. In summary, "Education is perhaps the most important function of state and local government...in these days, it is doubtful that any child may reasonably be expected to succeed in life" without receiving an education.[28] Given the prevalence of truancy in secondary schools it is imperative that school officials both understand their legal responsibilities and fully enforce their state's compulsory attendance law to reduce truancy and ensure that every child is educated.

Recommendations for Practice

1. Submit truancy data to the state government on an annual basis as mandated by the No Child Left Behind Act.
2. A school attendance policy should be aligned with state attendance law guidelines and should clearly delineate between excused and unexcused absences. It is imperative that school leaders consistently follow their school district's attendance policy when evaluating student truancy and provide students with due process when bringing truancy charges to avoid potential legal challenges by parents and students.
3. Ensure that school staff is trained on the proper procedures that should be followed in addressing student truancy in relation to intervention efforts and at what stage parents, social services, and law enforcement should be notified.

4. Any school district policy that which permits excused absences for field trips and other extracurricular activities should not be arbitrary or capricious.
5. School officials should require parents or legal guardians to provide a doctor's certificate as a means of verifying a child's medical condition for an excused absence.
6. Remember that accountability for school attendance is shared among school officials and parents. Parents are responsible for ensuring their children attend school every day, and schools are responsible for developing and maintaining thorough record-keeping procedures for student attendance to ensure that attendance records are accurate.

Endnotes

[1] Charles Russo, *Conflicts Over Directing the Education of Children: Who Controls, Parents or School Officials?,* J. OF EDUC., 186(2), 27-40 (2005).

[2] *See* Trujillo, *supra* note 1 at 19.

[3] Anthony DeSouza, Report issued by the Education Commission of the States (ECS). (2007), *available at* http://www.ecs.org (last visited September 20, 2007).

[4] *Id.*

[5] *Id.*

[6] Claire Shubik & Jessica Kendall, *Rethinking Juvenile Status Offense Laws: Considerations for Congressional Review of the Juvenile Justice and Delinquency Prevention Act*, 45 FAM. CT. REV. 384 (2007).

[7] L. Abrams & W. Haney, Accountability and the grade 9-10 transition, in Orfield, G. (ed), Dropout in America, 181-206. Cambridge, MA: Harvard Education Press.

[8] *Id.*

[9] Kathy Christie, Counting the Truants. Phi Delta Kappan, p. 485-486, (March, 2006).

[10] Julius Menacker, *Legal Policy Affecting School Truancy*, 119 EDUC. L. REP. 763 (1997).

[11] *Id.*

[12] Charles Walls, *New Approaches to Truancy Prevention in Urban Schools*, Eric Clearinghouse on Urban Education, 1-6, (2003).

[13] Gary McGiboney, *Truants are Welcome Here*, AM. SCH. BD. J., 1888 43-45 (2001).

[14] Howard Synder & Melissa Sickmund, *Juvenile Offenders and Victims: 2006 National Report* (U.S. Department of Justice, Office of Justice Programs, Office of Juvenile Justice and Delinquency Prevention) 2006, at 158, 203-05, *available at* http://www.ncjrs.gov/html/ojjdp/nationalreport99/frontmatter.pdf (last visited October 4, 2007).

[15] *See* Shubrik et al., *supra* note 3

[16] Kelderman, Eric, *Truant Teens Lose Licenses in Georgia and Other States, available at* http://www.stateline.org (last visited September 23, 2007).

[17] Latimer v. Bd. of Educ. of City of Chi., 68 N.E. 2d 305 (1946).

[18] S.H. v. State, 868 So. 2d 1110 (2003).

[19] Norwood v. Harrison, 413 U.S. 455 (1973).

[20] *Id.*

[21] *See supra note 22.*

[22] Wisconsin v. Yoder, 406 U.S. 205 (1972); Meyer v. Nebraska, 262 U.S. 390 (1923); Troxel v. Granville, 530 U.S. 57 (2000).

[23] *See* Home School Legal Defense Association, *Ohio Homeschooling Law, available at* www.hslda.org/legal/state/ky/20001227SarahD/ (last visited September 23, 2007).

[24] Kathryn S. Richtman, *The Truancy Intervention Program of the Ramsey County Attorney's Office: A Collaborative Approach to School Success*, 45 FAM. CT. REV. 421 (2007).

[25] *Id.*

[26] Lorenzo A. Trujillo, *Truancy in Colorado: A Truancy Reduction Model in the Public Schools*, 34-NOV COLO. L. 19 (2005).

[27] Joe D. Nichols, *Prediction Indicators for Students Failing the State of Indiana High School Graduation Exam*, REV. OF EDUC. RESEARCH, 72, 549-576, (2003); *See also* Douglas Lamdin, *Evidence of Student Attendance as an Independent Variable in Education Production Functions*, J. OF EDUC. RESEARCH, 89, 155-162 (1996).

[28] Brown v. Bd. of Educ., 347 U.S. 483, 493 (1954).

Chapter 11

Homeschooling and the Law

Robert Kunzman

Introduction

Homeschooling has grown rapidly in recent years. The National Center for Education Statistics (NCES) estimates that 1.1 million students were being homeschooled in the United States in spring of 2003.[1] This represents a 29 percent increase from the NCES survey just four years earlier. Some researchers assert that more than two million students are being homeschooled in the United States today, with an annual growth rate of at least 7 percent.[2] Although the total number of homeschooled students remains disputed, what seems clear is the rapid relative increase of homeschooling. Even using the more conservative NCES figures, the number of homeschooled students nationally increased at a rate ten times that of public school students during the last survey period.

The NCES survey also queried parents about their motivations for homeschooling. The three most common reasons were concerns about schools' environment (85 percent), desire to provide religious or moral instruction (72 percent), and dissatisfaction with schools' academic instruction (68 percent). These survey data also suggest that, compared with the public school population, homeschoolers are more likely to be white and have larger families.[3]

While the demographics of homeschoolers appear to be increasingly diverse,[4] most observers acknowledge that conservative Christians constitute the largest subset of homeschoolers. The most prominent and politically active national homeschool advocacy group, the Home School Legal Defense Association (HSLDA), describes itself as a Christian organization and estimates that conservative Christians comprise as much as 60 percent of the nationwide homeschool population.[5] Other homeschool organizations such as the National Home Education Network (NHEN), however, believe this number is lower. It appears that the majority of homeschooling occurs in the elementary years, although estimates vary widely concerning how many students continue homeschooling through high school.[6] Regardless of the percentages, homeschooling is becoming a big business. The HSLDA estimates the current homeschool curriculum market as approaching $1 billion in sales.[7]

While such data are worth considering, any empirical claims about homeschooling across the United States should be viewed with at least some skepticism. This uncertainty can be traced in part to the widely varying practices of data collection among states and the general reluctance of homeschoolers to provide any more information than is required by law. This caution holds true not only for estimating the homeschool population and its demographics, but—as detailed below—claims about academic achievement and other quality indicators. In short, virtually no comprehensive data exist about homeschooling numbers, practices, and outcomes.

History and Background

The modern homeschooling movement began to gain momentum in the 1970s, inspired by two different schools of thought. One was progressive in nature and critical of standardized education; the practice of "unschooling," where children are encouraged to pursue their own interests in a self-directed, unstructured environment, grew from this philosophical approach. The other strand of modern homeschooling focused more on the centrality of the parent in schooling and was frequently religious in nature, emphasizing the inculcation of Christian values against the secular world of public education and broader society.

During the 1970s, however, only a few states permitted homeschooling; it wasn't until 1993 that all fifty states recognized homeschooling as legal.[8] While the United States Supreme Court has never reviewed the right to homeschool specifically, several high court cases underscore parental rights to shape their child's education, while also acknowledging that states have the authority to regulate basic matters such as attendance and the broad scope of the curriculum.[9]

Research on the Effectiveness of Homeschooling

Since data collection on homeschoolers varies so widely among states, with some even having no idea how many homeschoolers there are within their borders, it is impossible to generate a comprehensive, empirical picture on homeschoolers' academic performance. Because of this, the most frequently cited research studies have used nonrepresentative samples without controlling for variables, such as household income; in addition, many of them have been sponsored by homeschool advocacy groups.

Advocates point to homeschooling as the ultimate in educational flexibility, efficiency, and customization to meet the individual needs of learners. While occasional reports do appear in the media about instances of severe educational (and physical) neglect among children being homeschooled, we do not have data revealing whether the frequency is greater than in families whose children are educated in institutional settings. Nevertheless, some public school officials and other education professionals are skeptical that homeschooling provides a quality education for students. These misgivings generally focus on two specific areas of concern: academic achievement and socialization.

Academic Achievement of Homeschoolers

The question of how homeschool students compare academically with their public school peers remains a matter of dispute. Homeschool advocates can point to high-achieving individuals who win national spelling and geography bees, debate competitions, art contests, and so on. Even stalwart critics of homeschooling acknowledge that the "high end" of academic homeschooling performance compares favorably with other forms of schooling; certainly the nation's elite colleges and universities have come to think so, with many admissions departments welcoming homeschooler applications and some assigning a liaison specifically for homeschool applicants.[10]

In terms of empirical research, the most frequently cited study by homeschool advocates confirms that at least a segment of homeschool students score two to four grade levels and 20 percentage points higher on a nationally recognized achievement test (either the Iowa Tests of Basic Skills or Tests of Achievement and Proficiency).[11] But the study's author himself acknowledges that participants were an unrepresentative sample of homeschoolers and the study was not a controlled experiment; therefore, it prevents us from making reliable extrapolations to the general homeschooling population or comparing homeschoolers' performance with the broader student population.[12] Similar limitations occur in a separate study of SAT scores.[13]

Socialization of Homeschoolers

Critics of homeschooling often argue that homeschoolers lack sufficient opportunity for socialization apart from the institutional schooling setting. It seems clear, however, that for many families, the "home" in homeschooling is only part of the picture. Homeschool community groups abound, mixing educational activities (such as student presentations on research topics, theatre productions, and study groups) and more informal, social-recreational activities. Local colleges and universities frequently welcome advanced homeschool students into their classrooms. Museums, libraries, and other educational organizations are increasingly oriented toward providing programming for homeschool families. Extracurricular opportunities for homeschoolers continue to grow as well. Formal homeschool athletic leagues offer competition from the local level up through national championships in sports such as basketball, soccer, volleyball, and softball.

Again, however, comprehensive empirical evidence is lacking. Homeschool advocates routinely cite one particular study, commissioned by the Home School Legal Defense Association, as evidence that homeschool graduates are engaged citizens, involved in their communities, and leading fulfilling lives.[14] But this study examined a small, homogeneous group of homeschoolers without controlling for parent income, education, or other variables, so neither definitive statements about homeschoolers nor reliable comparisons with the general U.S. population can be made.

Another study explored whether homeschoolers and other private schoolers were engaged in broader civic life. Sociologists Christian Smith and David Sikkink used data from the 1996 National Household Education Survey (NHES) to argue that religious school and homeschool families are consistently *more* involved in civic activities than families with children in public schools.[15] They used homeschooling as a prime example of the rich array of networks, support groups, and political advocacy efforts that privatized schooling can foster and claim that this civic participation strengthens public life. But it would seem that the *nature* of this participation, and the degree to which it includes acknowledgement of the reasonableness of diverse perspectives within the public realm, matters a great deal as to whether our public is the better for it.

Much of the debate on this issue seems to hinge on the question of what constitutes healthy socialization. Advocates point out that homeschoolers are likely to have a greater opportunity to interact with the full range of ages—rather than almost exclusively with their peers—in a greater variety of learning settings throughout the community. Medlin sought to bring greater precision to the question in his review of dozens of studies focused on homeschooler socialization. He concluded that the evidence, while still preliminary, suggests that homeschooled children are engaged in their community, acquire necessary rules of behavior, and demonstrate social maturity and leadership skills. Medlin emphasized, however, that more and better research is needed before definitive conclusions about homeschooler socialization can be drawn.[16]

Homeschooling Regulations

As mentioned above, homeschool regulations vary widely from state to state (see Figure 1 for details). Seventy-six percent of states mandate some sort of initial notification or enrollment, and 39 percent require parents to keep attendance records (although not necessarily submit them unless asked). A much larger percentage (69 percent) identify certain subjects as required in homeschool curricula, but only half (51 percent) mandate some form of regular—not necessarily yearly—assessment of homeschooler academic achievement. These evaluations are most frequently in the form of standardized tests, but occasionally states provide the option for homeschoolers to submit a portfolio of work for review by a "qualified" individual (typically, a licensed teacher). Eleven states specify required levels of parents' educational attainment. Finally, several states also have a "religious freedom" component to their legal code; in two of them, Alabama and Virginia, this extends specifically to homeschooling regulations, meaning families are exempt from some or all homeschooling requirements if they claim a religious exemption.

Figure 1: State-by-State Regulations for Homeschooling[1]

STATE	category option(s)[2]	notification or registration with state required	annual notification required	parent/instructor educational requirements	minimum instruction time	required to keep attendance records	required to submit attendance recs. regularly	state-mandated subjects	required to maintain curriculum records[3]	required to maintain test scores and/or student work[3]	evaluation/assessment required by state	evaluation/assessment options	eligible for part-time public school enrollment	eligible for public school extracurricular participation[4]	state required to provide special education services[5]	state statutes located within these code sections
Alabama[6]	RSS	Y	N	N	N	Y	N	N	N	N	N	--	N	N	N	16-28
Alaska	HS	N	--	N	N	N	--	N	N	N	N	--	Y	Y (DD)	Y	14.20-14.45
Arizona	HS	Y	N	N	N	N	--	Y	N	N	N	--	Y (DD)	Y	Y	15-802, 15-828
Arkansas	HS	Y	Y[7]	N	N	N	--	N	N	N	Y	ST (3-9)	Y (DD)	Y (DD)	Y	6-15, 6-18
California	HPS	Y	Y[7]	N	N	Y	Y	Y	Y	N	N	--	Y (DD)	Y (DD)	Y	48200-48410,
	PSS	N	N	N	N	Y	N	Y	Y	N	N	--	Y (DD)	Y (DD)	Y	51745-51749
Colorado	HS	Y	Y	N	Y	Y	N	Y	N	Y	Y	ST (3,5,7,9,11) or PE	Y (DD)	Y	N	22-33-104
	PSS	N	--	N	N	N	--	Y	N	N	N	--	Y (DD)	Y	Y	
Connecticut	HS	N	--	N	Y	N	--	Y	N	N	N	--	Y(DD)	Y (DD)	N	10-184, 10-220[8]
Delaware	HS	Y	Y	N	N	Y	Y	Y	N	N	N	--	N	Y (DD)	N	14.1.27.2703A

Figure 1: State-by-State Regulations for Homeschooling *(continued)*

STATE	category option(s)[2]	notification or registration with state required	annual notification required	parent/instructor educational requirements	minimum instruction time	required to keep attendance records	required to submit attendance recs. regularly	state-mandated subjects	required to maintain curriculum records[3]	required to maintain test scores and/or student work[3]	evaluation/assessment required by state	evaluation/assessment options	eligible for part-time public school enrollment	eligible for public school extracurricular participation[4]	state required to provide special education services[5]	state statutes located within these code sections
Dist. Columbia	PI	N	--	N	Y	Y	N	N	N	N	N	--	Y (DD)	Y (DD)	N	38.202-38.205
Florida	HS	Y	N	N	N	Y	N	N	Y	Y	Y	ST or PE	Y	Y	N	1002-1003
Georgia	HS	Y	Y	Y	Y	Y	Y	Y	N	Y	Y	ST (3,6,9,12) + PR[9]	Y (DD)	Y (DD)	Y	20-2-690
Hawaii	HS	Y	N	N	N	N	--	N	Y	N	Y	ST or PR[10]	N	N	Y	8-12, 302A-1132
Idaho	AI	N	--	N	Y	N	--	Y	N	N	N	--	Y	Y	Y	33-202
Illinois	HPS	N	--	N	N	N	--	Y	N	N	N	--	Y (DD)	Y (DD)	Y	105 ILCS 5
Indiana	HPS	N	--	N	Y	Y	N	N	N	N	N	--	Y(DD)	Y (DD)	Y	20-33-2
Iowa	HS	Y	Y[7]	N	Y	N	--	N	N	N	Y	ST or PE	Y	Y	Y	299A, 281-31
Kansas	HPS	Y	N	N	Y	N	--	N	N	N	N	--	Y (DD)	Y(DD)	Y	72-53, 72-1101-1111
	PSS	N	--	N	Y	N	--	N	N	N	N	--	Y(DD)	Y (DD)	Y	
Kentucky	HPS	Y	Y	N	Y	Y	N	Y	Y	Y	N	--	Y (DD)	Y (DD)	Y	158-159

Figure 1: State-by-State Regulations for Homeschooling *(continued)*

STATE	category option(s)[2]	notification or registration with state required	annual notification required	parent/instructor educational requirements	minimum instruction time	required to keep attendance records	required to submit attendance recs. regularly	state-mandated subjects	required to maintain curriculum records[3]	required to maintain test scores and/or student work[3]	evaluation/assessment required by state	evaluation/assessment options	eligible for part-time public school enrollment	eligible for public school extracurricular participation[4]	state required to provide special education services[5]	state statutes located within these code sections
Louisiana	HS	Y	Y[7]	N	Y	N	--	Y	Y	Y	Y	ST or PE	N	Y (DD)	N	17.221-17.268
	HPS	Y	Y	N	Y	N	--	Y	N	N	N	--	N	N	Y	
Maine	HS	Y	Y	N	Y	N	--	Y	N	N	Y	ST or PE	Y	Y	Y	20-A 5001-A
Maryland	HS	Y	Y	N	N	N	--	Y	Y	Y	Y	PE[11]	N	N	N	7-301(a),
	RSS	Y	Y	N	N	N	--	Y	Y	N	N	--	N	N	N	13A 10.01
Massachusetts	HS	Y	Y[7]	N	Y	N	--	Y	N	N	Y	negotiated[12]	Y	Y	Y	76-1
Michigan	HS	N	--	N	N	N	--	Y	N	N	N	--	Y	Y (DD)	N	380.1561-380.1578
Minnesota	HS	Y	Y	Y[13]	N	Y	N	Y	Y	Y	Y	ST **and** HV or PE	N	Y	Y	120A.22-120A.26
Mississippi	HS	Y	Y	N	N	N	--	N	N	N	N	--	Y (DD)	Y (DD)	N	37-13-91
Missouri	HS	N	--	N	Y	Y	N	Y	Y	Y	N	--	Y (DD)	Y (DD)	Y	167.031

Figure 1: State-by-State Regulations for Homeschooling *(continued)*

STATE	category option(s)[2]	notification or registration with state required	annual notification required	parent/instructor educational requirements	minimum instruction time	required to keep attendance records	required to submit attendance recs. regularly	state-mandated subjects	required to maintain curriculum records[3]	required to maintain test scores and/or student work[3]	evaluation/assessment required by state	evaluation/assessment options	eligible for part-time public school enrollment	eligible for public school extracurricular participation[4]	state required to provide special education services[5]	state statutes located within these code sections
Montana	HS	Y	Y[7]	N	Y	Y	N	Y	N	N	N	--	Y (DD)	Y (DD)	N	20-5
Nebraska	HPS	Y	Y[7]	N	Y	N	--	Y	N	N	N	--	Y	Y (DD)	Y	79-201, 79-1601
Nevada	HS	Y	Y[7]	N	N	N	--	Y	N	N	N	--	Y	Y	Y	385, 392
New Hampshire	HS	Y	Y	N	N	N	--	Y	Y	Y	Y	ST or PE	Y	Y	Y	193A
New Jersey	HS	N	--	N	N	N	--	N	N	N	N	--	Y (DD)	Y (DD)	N	18A:38-25
New Mexico	HS	Y	Y	Y	Y	Y	N	Y	N	N	N	--	Y (DD)	Y (DD)	N	22-1-2
New York	HS	Y	Y[7]	N	Y	Y	Y	Y	Y	Y	Y	ST (4,6,8,9-12)[14]	N	Y(DD)	N	100.10, 3204-3212
North Carolina	HS	Y	N	Y	Y	Y	N	N	N	Y	Y	ST	Y	Y (DD)	N	115C-547-1115C-565
North Dakota	HS	Y	Y	Y	Y	Y	N	Y	Y	Y	Y	ST (4,6,8,10)	Y (DD)	Y (DD)	Y[15]	15.1-23

Figure 1: State-by-State Regulations for Homeschooling *(continued)*

STATE	category option(s)[2]	notification or registration with state required	annual notification required	parent/instructor educational requirements	minimum instruction time	required to keep attendance records	required to submit attendance recs. regularly	state-mandated subjects	required to maintain curriculum records[3]	required to maintain test scores and/or student work[3]	evaluation/assessment required by state	evaluation/assessment options	eligible for part-time public school enrollment	eligible for public school extracurricular participation[4]	state required to provide special education services[5]	state statutes located within these code sections
Ohio	HS	Y	Y[7]	Y	Y	N	--	Y	N	N	Y	ST or PE	Y (DD)	Y (DD)	N	3321.04, 3301-34
Oklahoma	AI	N	--	N	N	N	--	N	N	N	N	--	Y (DD)	N	N	70 10-105(A)
Oregon	HS	Y	N	N	N	N	--	N	N	N	Y	ST (3,5,8,10)	Y (DD)	Y	N	339.030, 581-021
Pennsylvania	HS	Y	Y[7]	Y	Y	N	--	Y	Y	Y	Y	ST (3,5,8) **and** PE	Y (DD)	Y	Y	24 PS 13-1327
	RSS	N	--	N	Y	N	--	Y	N	N	N	--	Y (DD)	Y	Y	
Rhode Island	HS	Y	Y	N	Y	Y	N	Y	N	N	Y	ST or other[16]	Y (DD)	Y (DD)	Y	16-19
South Carolina	HS	N	--	Y	Y	Y	Y	Y	Y	Y	Y	ST **and** PR	Y (DD)	Y (DD)	Y	59-65
	PSS	N	--	Y	Y	Y	N	Y	N	N	N	--	Y (DD)	Y (DD)	Y	
South Dakota	HS	Y	Y	N	Y	Y	N	Y	N	Y	Y	ST (2,4,8,11)	Y (DD)	Y (DD)	N	13-27

Figure 1: State-by-State Regulations for Homeschooling *(continued)*

STATE	category option(s)[2]	notification or registration with state required	annual notification required	parent/instructor educational requirements	minimum instruction time	required to keep attendance records	required to submit attendance recs. regularly	state-mandated subjects	required to maintain curriculum records[3]	required to maintain test scores and/or student work[3]	evaluation/assessment required by state	evaluation/assessment options	eligible for part-time public school enrollment	eligible for public school extracurricular participation[4]	state required to provide special education services[5]	state statutes located within these code sections
Tennessee	HS	Y	Y[7]	Y	Y	Y	Y	Y	N	N	Y	ST (5,7,9)	Y (DD)	Y (DD)	N	49-6
	RSS	N	--	N	Y	N	--	N	N	N	N	--	Y (DD)	Y (DD)	N	
Texas	HPS	N	--	N	N	N	--	Y	N	N	N	--	Y (DD)	Y (DD)	Y	25.086(a)(1)
Utah	HS	Y	Y	N	Y	N	--	Y	N	N	N	--	Y	Y	Y	53A--11
Vermont	HS	Y	Y[7]	N	N	N	--	Y	N	N	Y	PE or ST	Y	Y	N	16 11(a)(21), 16 166b
Virginia[6]	HS	Y	Y[7]	Y	N	N	--	N	N	N	Y	ST or PE	Y (DD)	Y (DD)	N	22.1-254
Washington	HS	Y	Y	Y	Y	N	--	Y	N	Y	Y	ST or PE	Y	Y	N	28A.225.010,
	PSS	N	N	N[17]	Y	N	--	Y	N	N	N	--	Y	Y	Y	28A.200.010
West Virginia	HS	Y	Y[7]	Y	N	N	--	N	N	N	Y	ST or PE	Y (DD)	N	Y	18-5, 18-8
Wisconsin	HS	Y	Y	N	Y	N	--	Y	N	N	N	--	Y (DD)	Y (DD)	N	118.15, 118.165
Wyoming	HS	Y	Y[7]	N	Y	N	--	Y	N	N	N	--	Y (DD)	Y	N	21-4-101, 21-4-102

Figure 1 key: RSS=religious school satellite; HS=home school; HPS= home as private school; PSS=private school satellite; PI=private instruction; AI=alternative instruction; ST(#)=standardized testing (if not yearly, applicable grade levels for testing indicated); PE=portfolio evaluation of student's work by "qualified" person (see state code for qualifications); PR=progress report at end of each year; HV=home visit; DD=district discretion

Figure 1 Endnotes

1 Since homeschooling regulations change periodically and legal interpretations may vary, these data should be verified with state or district legal counsel as well.

2 Private (including religious) schools may be responsible for meeting certain state requirements themselves, but such details are not reflected in this chart if the state does not require them directly of homeschoolers. Also, many states have additional "homeschooling" options not listed here that impose further regulation (e.g., private tutoring that requires a certified instructor, or state-approved correspondence curricula) and are thus less popular choices for homeschoolers. In many instances, however, these options have correspondingly fewer demands in terms of assessment and ongoing state oversight. Consult individual state statutes for details.

3 Unless indicated by PE (portfolio evaluation), PR (progress report), or ST (standardized testing) in "evaluation/assessment options" category, these records do not need to be submitted regularly, but must be available for inspection (see specific state statutes for details on what information is required and access rules).

4 Some states that allow many forms of extracurricular participation will still restrict high school interscholastic athletic competition to full-time students.

5 In many states, however, districts can choose to offer special education services even when not required by law.

6 State law includes a "religious freedom" component which may allow qualifying families to avoid some or all homeschool regulations.

7 Notification must also include information about intended curricula and planned instructional schedule (Arkansas also requires information about educational qualifications of parents).

8 Also includes "suggested procedures" for home instruction which include state notification and annual portfolio review.

9 While these assessments are mandated, homeschoolers do not need to submit them (just have them available for possible inspection).

10 Standardized tests are required in addition to portfolio evaluation for grades 3, 5, 8, and 10.

11 Portfolio of "relevant materials" must be available for review by local superintendent, who has the option to do so up to three times per year.

12 Home education plans—detailing proposed curriculum, instructor competency, and proposed assessments—must be reviewed and approved by local districts.

13 If parent-instructor does not meet qualification requirements, he or she must submit quarterly progress reports in required subjects to local superintendent.

14 An Individualized Home Instruction Plan must be submitted to the school district at the start of each year, as well as progress reports on a quarterly basis; during grades 1-3, 5, and 7, parents may submit either standardized test results or a portfolio review by a "qualified" person.

15 Parents of children with developmental disabilities in North Dakota must follow strict guidelines in order to be permitted to homeschool them (15.1-23-14 and 15.1-23-15).

16 Assessment is not mandated, but school district has the option of requiring it; if so, parents may choose standardized testing or some other form of assessment.

On the whole, the regulatory climate surrounding homeschooling has shifted toward less state oversight and fewer requirements for those wishing to homeschool their children. Homeschool advocacy groups, especially the HSLDA, are seen by friend and foe alike as powerful and effective lobbyists. Periodic attempts to increase state regulation frequently meet with determined homeschooler opposition, and HSLDA continues its efforts to have existing regulations lessened or eliminated.

As a result, state regulation of homeschooling remains a shifting landscape. Two areas of recent or ongoing change that merit attention involve special education law and the opportunity for homeschoolers to access public school classes and/or extracurricular activities.

Special Education

Although no comprehensive research exists on the subject, homeschool advocates contend that the customized, individual attention inherent in homeschooling can be of particular benefit to students with special needs.[17] In fact, nearly one-third (29 percent) of homeschool parents in the 2003 NCES survey pointed to their child's special needs as a motivation for their choice to homeschool.[18]

The Individuals with Disabilities Education Act (IDEA) requires school districts, or local education agencies (LEAs), to locate and evaluate both public school and private school children in the district who may have special education needs. Whether homeschoolers are considered private school students—and thus eligible for special education services—varies from state to state (see Figure 1 for details). In *Hooks v. Clark County School District*, the Ninth Circuit Court of Appeals ruled that this "Child Find" provision of the IDEA does not apply in states who categorize homeschools as distinct from private schools.[19] A year later, however, a New Jersey court judgment in *Forstrom v. Byrne* highlighted an exception to this distinction, ruling that school districts may still be responsible for providing special education services to homeschooled students even when they are not considered private schools. Because the student in question was willing to come to the school to receive speech therapy in a group setting, the court ruled that there was no basis for treating him differently than other private school students willing to do the same.[20]

In recent years, the HSLDA has sought to clarify IDEA regulations involving homeschoolers, especially the right to refuse evaluation for services. The final regulations issued in 2006 for the reauthorized IDEA indicate that "if a parent of a child who is home schooled or placed in a private school by the parents at their own expense does not provide consent for the initial evaluation or reevaluation, or the parent fails to respond to a request to provide consent, the public agency may not use the consent override procedures" that are applicable in the public school context, and "the public agency is not required to consider the child as eligible for services."[21] In short, school districts may not evaluate homeschool students for disabilities if the parent refuses consent.[22]

Homeschooler Access to Selected Classes and Extracurricular Activities

While separate homeschool-support programs may not fall under a principal's purview, the issue of homeschoolers wishing to enroll in selected public school classes and extracurricular activities often does. Again, laws governing such participation vary by state, and frequently policies are left up to the discretion of local school districts. As Figure 1 indicates, fourteen states have legislation mandating that homeschoolers be permitted to enroll as part-time public school students, and only seven states prohibit this option outright; the remaining thirty appear to leave it to the discretion of each school district. Regarding participation in extracurricular activities, sixteen states have legislation ensuring homeschooler access, only five states prohibit it, and thirty appear to leave it up to the local district.[23]

A growing number of school districts throughout the United States now offer programs designed to support homeschool families in their efforts, often providing facilities (e.g., science labs), teaching resources (both curricula and professional consultation), or supplemental courses. These services frequently have a distance-education component to them as well. In addition to helping homeschoolers, these programs frequently trigger additional state funding for the district based on student enrollment.

While receiving additional state support in exchange for homeschooler participation is certainly desirable, good reasons exist for welcoming homeschooler involvement in public school classes or extracurricular activities regardless, when logistics will permit. Such arrangements help foster positive relationships and regular communication between homeschool families and public schools; in addition, they provide opportunities for homeschoolers to engage with the broader school population, and vice versa, even if in a limited capacity. The promise of public schools as preparation for social diversity is best realized when as much of the public is involved as possible.

Administrators should be aware, however, that not all homeschoolers view access to public school resources as a welcome development. Several homeschool organizations (such as HSLDA) warn their members to be wary of such involvement, as they fear it will lead to greater state control over not only these public school activities, but ultimately will open a door for encroachment on their private homeschool efforts as well.

Recommendations for Practice

Some public school organizations have formulated official position statements on homeschooling. The National Education Association, for instance, is generally critical of homeschooling. They call for greater regulation, asserting that homeschoolers should be required to meet all state curricular and testing requirements, and that instruction should be provided only by those with a state teaching license. They also argue against homeschooler participation in public school extracurricular activities. Finally, they contend that local public school systems should have the authority to determine grade placements and school credits for homeschoolers transferring into public schools.[24] The National Association of Elementary School Principals also expresses concern with the growth of homeschooling and urges that "those who exercise these options are held strictly accountable for the academic achievement and social/emotional growth of children."[25]

Although some public school officials remain suspicious and even critical of homeschooling as an educational option, the admittedly limited research evidence does suggest that homeschooling can and does provide a rich learning experience for many children. As some public school administrators have experienced, there are some parents who choose to homeschool for dubious reasons (e.g., to sidestep disciplinary consequences or attendance issues for their children), and some homeschool environments neglect children's basic educational interests. But it is worth considering that many administrators may have disproportionate exposure to these negative examples and relatively little contact with families who homeschool their children with great skill and dedication.

The relationship between homeschoolers and state authorities has been, at times, contentious and adversarial. While some homeschoolers do view public schools (or any institutional schooling, for that matter) as "the enemy," many others acknowledge public schools as both important and necessary—just not how they choose to educate their own children, at least at the present time. In this regard, their motivations may not differ greatly from parents who choose to enroll their children in private schools. From some homeschoolers' perspectives, public school administrators and social service agencies sometimes overstep legal boundaries—for example, asking for more information about a homeschool curriculum than is legally required, or demanding a home visit and interviews with children without following appropriate legal procedures. Public school and other state officials obviously have certain legal and moral obligations to protect children's welfare, but it should not automatically be assumed that homeschool parents' refusal to provide any more information than is required by law means that they have something to hide.

The National School Boards Association (NSBA) does not have an official policy position on homeschooling, but a recent NSBA publication offers sage advice:

> A comprehensive home schooling policy that is up to date, based on state law, mindful of ambiguities and concerns of home schooled parents, and applied evenhandedly will go a long way in averting legal trouble before it begins. Moreover, cultivating positive relationships with homeschooling parents will lessen the possibility of conflict and

> lead to a better education for home-schooled students—a goal public schools and parents share.[26]

Clear, thoughtful policies regarding the relationship between homeschoolers and the public schools are vital. In addition, while perhaps obvious, it bears emphasis that public school policies are not permitted to make distinctions between homeschoolers who claim religious reasons for their homeschooling decisions and/or practices versus those who don't.

But the second part of the NSBA recommendations deserve close consideration as well. Instead of viewing all homeschoolers with immediate suspicion, school administrators should strive to maintain open lines of communication with parents and perhaps consider ways in which the public schools can partner more with homeschool parents, as suggested above. Done well, homeschooling requires tremendous commitment on the part of parents, and to the extent that public schools can assist in those efforts, the better off their children—and our public—will be.

Endnotes

1 National Center for Education Statistics, *1.1 Million Homeschooled Students in the United States in 2003.* NCES Publication No. 2004115 (2004) ["NCES"].

2 Brian Ray, *A Homeschool Research Story, in* HOME SCHOOLING IN FULL VIEW: A READER, 1-19 (Bruce Cooper ed., 2005). Ray contends that many homeschool parents are reluctant to identify themselves because of their resistance to any form of governmental regulation; *see also* Kevin M. Welner, *Exploring the Democratic Tensions within Parents' Decision to Homeschool.* Occasional Paper No. 45. New York: National Center for the Study of Privatization in Education (2002). Although some critics have questioned Ray's objectivity—he homeschooled his own children and has been funded by the Home School Legal Defense Association—other analysts have questioned the NCES sampling methodology and small sample size (11,994 surveyed, revealing 239 homeschoolers) and similarly suggest that actual numbers are likely higher (see, *for example*, Clive Belfield, *Home-schooling in the U.S.* Occasional Paper No. 88. New York: National Center for the Study of Privatization in Education (2004).

3 *NCES, supra* note 1.

4 Kariane M. Nemer, *Understudied Education: Toward Building a Homeschool Research Agenda.* Occasional Paper No. 48. New York: National Center for the Study of Privatization in Education (2002).

5 Ian Slatter, HSLDA Director of Media Relations, personal communication, November 2007.

6 Lawrence M. Rudner, *Scholastic Achievement and Demographic Characteristics of Home School Students in 1998.* Education Policy Analysis Archives*,* 7(8) (1999), *at* http://epaa.asu.edu/epaa/v7n8/.

7 *Slatter, supra* note 5.

8 Scott W. Somerville, *Legal Rights for Homeschool Families, in* HOME SHCOOLING IN FULL VIEW: A READER, 135-149, (Bruce S. Cooper ed., 2005).

9 *See, e.g., Meyer v. Nebraska*, 262 U.S. 390 (1923); *Pierce v. Society of Sisters*, 268 U.S. 510 (1925); *Prince v. Massachusetts*, 321 U.S. 158 (1944); *Wisconsin v. Yoder*, 406 U.S. 205 (1972); *Troxel v. Granville*, 530 U.S. 57 (2000).

10 Joyce A. Marean, Marc F. Ott, & Matthew J. Rush, *Homeschooled Students and the Ivy League, in* HOME SHCOOLING IN FULL VIEW: A READER, 179-197, (Bruce S. Cooper ed., 2005);

Paul Jones & Gene Gloeckner, *A Study of Admission Officers' Perceptions and Attitudes Toward Homeschool Students*, THE JOURNAL OF COLLEGE ADMISSION, 184, 12-21 (2004).

[11] *Rudner, supra* note 6.

[12] Kariane M. Welner, & Kevin G. Welner, *Contextualizing Homeschooling Data: A Response to Rudner*, Education Policy Analysis Archives, 7(13) (1999), *at* http://epaa.asu.edu/epaa/v7n13/.

[13] Clive R. Belfield, *Home-schooling in the US.* Occasional Paper No. 88. New York: National Center for the Study of Privatization in Education (2004).

[14] Brian D. Ray, *Home Educated and Now Adults: Their Community and Civic Involvement, Views about Homeschooling, and other Traits.* Salem, OR: National Home Education Research Institute (2003).

[15] Christian Smith & David Sikkink, *Is Private School Privatizing?* First Things 92, 16-20 (1999).

[16] Richard G. Medlin, *Home Schooling and the Question of Socialization*, Peabody Journal of Education, *75*(1&2), 107-123 (2000).

[17] Jacque Ensign, *Defying the Stereotypes of Special Education: Home School Students.* Peabody Journal of Education, *75*(1&2), 147-158 (2000).

[18] *NCES, supra* note 1, this reason was listed as a separate choice from "child has a physical or mental health problem," which itself was mentioned by 16% of homeschool parents.

[19] Hooks v. Clark County Sch. Dist., 228 F.3d 1036 (9th Cir. 2000).

[20] Forstrom v. Byrne, 775 A.3d 65 (N.J. Super. Ct. App. Div. 2001).

[21] 34 CFR 300.300(d)(4); 20 U.S.C. 1414(a)(1)(D) and 1414(c).

[22] This addition to the regulations was prompted in part by *Fitzgerald v. Camdenton R-III School District*, 439 F. 3d 773 (8th Cir. 2006) (ruling that school districts cannot override a homeschool parent's refusal to consent for evaluation).

[23] Some states that permit homeschoolers to access extracurriculars still prohibit access to interscholastic high school sports, however.

[24] National Education Association 2007-08 Resolutions, B-75, p. 36.

[25] National Association of Elementary School Principals 2007-08 Platform, section F, #4, page 38. Unlike its elementary-level counterpart, the National Association of Secondary School Principals does not have an official position statement on homeschooling.

[26] Lisa Soronen, *Home-schooling and the Law*, Leadership Insider: Practical Perspectives on School Law and Policy. Alexandria, VA: National School Boards Association, 8 (2006).

Section 2:
Special Education and the Law

Chapter 12

Fundamentals of Federal Disability Law

Julie F. Mead & Judith Risch

Introduction

In today's world of site-based management, principals must have a working knowledge of a number of topics. Without question, a firm grasp of federal disability law should number among those competencies. Knowledge of federal disability law bears strong connections to the principal's focus on providing instructional leadership for a diverse teaching staff and an even more diverse student body, while at the same time championing equity in all workings of the school.[1] The precepts of Section 504 of the Rehabilitation Act of 1973,[2] the Individuals with Disabilities Education Act,[3] and the Americans with Disabilities Act[4] affect classroom instruction, student discipline, hiring and supervision of staff, and relationships with parents. All three acts are premised on the notion that in order for individuals with disabilities to enjoy equal educational or employment opportunities, sometimes difference of treatment must be applied. For example, equity requires that some deaf children be furnished with a sign language interpreter in order to access the learning of the classroom. Likewise, equity may necessitate that a worker who uses a wheelchair for mobility be allowed to rearrange his office space in order to allow for better accessibility to the files and equipment necessary to do his job. Understanding the boundaries formed by these three federal disability statutes empowers the principal both by helping to specify what is required and by elucidating the degrees of freedom available for creative use of building and district resources. This chapter is designed to explore the major precepts of these important laws and to serve as an introduction to the more detailed chapters on the subject that follow.

Legal Issues

Section 504 of the Rehabilitation Act of 1973

Of the three laws under focus here, Section 504 of the Rehabilitation Act of 1973 is the oldest and in some ways the simplest. As a civil rights statute, its purpose is straightforward; it bars discrimination on the basis of disability by any recipient of federal funds.[5] As such, it applies to all public schools in the United States and private schools that also receive federal monies. Accordingly, schools and school districts must ensure that all the programs offered are accessible to persons with disabilities. As an anti-discrimination statute, its coverage extends from birth to death. Therefore, it has implications for students, employees, parents, and members of the general public who wish to access the benefits created by a school.

Principals are probably most familiar with its application to students. Those students who have a "physical or mental impairment which substantially limits one or more of such person's major life activities"[6] must receive an education comparable to that of their nondisabled peers.[7] Major life activities include, among others, walking, talking, hearing, seeing, breathing, and learning.[8] The disability may be permanent (e.g., a visual impairment, cerebral palsy, or attention deficit disorder) or temporary.[9] In the case of temporary disabilities, the issue is whether the disability substantially affects the person for a sufficient period of time. As the Office for Civil Rights (OCR) explains, "[t]he issue of whether a temporary impairment is substantial enough to be a disability must be resolved on a case-by-case basis, taking into consideration both the duration (or expected duration) of the impairment and the extent to which it actually limits a major life activity of the affected individual."[10] Section 504 also applies to students with acquired immune deficiency syndrome (AIDS).[11] In addition, care must be taken so that personnel do not discriminate against a person based on a perceived disability where one does not exist.[12] Although some argue these last two eligibility categories (has a history of a disability or is regarded as having a disability) extend the protections of section 504 to nearly everyone, the point is that discrimination is no less abhorrent simply because the person or persons discriminating jumped to erroneous conclusions. Whether or not the disability actually exists, section 504 protects individuals from discriminatory treatment based on the status characteristic of disability.

Once a child with a disability is identified, section 504 requires that he or she receives meaningful access to the educational program provided by a school. Providing an education comparable to that of nondisabled peers means that school personnel may be required to make reasonable accommodations in order that the student's disability does not serve as a barrier to how the child can access information or demonstrate learning.[13] Reasonable accommodations may be physical (e.g., Braille, preferential seating, a notetaker, assistance with carrying supplies) or instructional (e.g., a sign language interpreter, extended time on a test, vocabulary assistance) and may include special education and related services.[14] Accommodations are determined by staff members in consultation with the parents[15] and are outlined on an accommodation plan. Although regulations do not require it, most schools prudently use written accommodation plans.[16]

Section 504 also has implications for hiring and working with staff. Again, those protected by the act have mental or physical impairments that substantially limit them or have a history of such impairments or are regarded as having such.[17] And just as students must be reasonably accommodated in order to access educational opportunities, employees' disabilities must be reasonably accommodated in order to access employment opportunities.[18] Reasonableness has its bounds, however, and employers are not required to substantially alter the qualifications or essential requirements of a job in order to accommodate a worker's disability.[19] In addition, the employer is not expected to bear undue administrative or financial burdens when considering accommodations.[20]

Parents with disabilities also enjoy protection under section 504. In this case, the school must ensure that parents with disabilities, through reasonable accommodations when necessary, have access to parent-teacher conferences and any meetings concerning the child's progress and behavior in school.[21] For example, a teacher planning to meet with a parent who utilizes a wheelchair for mobility would have to be sure the meeting place was accessible to the parent.

Chapter 13 provides a detailed discussion of section 504 and the obligations it places on schools.

Americans with Disabilities Act

Using its Constitutional power to regulate interstate commerce,[22] Congress enacted the Americans with Disabilities Act (ADA) in 1990.[23] The ADA extends the non-discrimination protections of section 504 beyond recipients of federal financial support to private employers and commercial establishments.[24] The law is divided into five titles:

1. Title I – prohibits employment discrimination.[25]
2. Title II – applies to all subdivisions of state and local government, regardless of whether they receive federal financial assistance.[26] Students in public schools are protected under this title.
3. Title III – prohibits discrimination by businesses that serve the public (e.g., stores, restaurants, hotels and motels, etc.).[27] Title III's provisions also apply to non-sectarian private schools, although private schools are not held to the same programmatic accessibility standards as are public schools. Private schools need only accommodate those children with disabilities that can be served with minor adjustments to the academic program.
4. Title IV – applies to telecommunications services such as telephone and television companies.[28]
5. Title V – contains several miscellaneous, but important, provisions including a statement that the ADA should not be read to require lesser standards than those of section 504;[29] that a state's immunity from suit under the Eleventh Amendment is abrogated by the ADA;[30] that ADA's provisions apply to Congress and all agencies of the legislative branch;[31] that the term "individual with a disability" does not include active drug users[32] or transvestites;[33] and that ho-

mosexuality and bisexuality are not "impairments" under the ADA and that various other "conditions" are not included under the term "disability."[34]

Because Title II of the ADA largely mirrors the requirements of section 504, requirements of both acts are often jointly referred to as "section 504/ADA."[35] For public schools, then, additional ADA requirements often relate to construction and renovation requirements associated with physical accessibility. Chapter 14 details the requirements for creating barrier-free schools.

Individuals with Disabilities Education Act

The Individuals with Disabilities Education Act (IDEA) is without doubt the most prescriptive of the three acts with regards to the educational experience of children with disabilities. First enacted in 1975 under the title the Education for All Handicapped Children's Act (EAHCA),[36] Congress renamed the EAHCA the Individuals with Disabilities Education Act (IDEA) in 1990 at the same time it enacted the ADA. Unlike section 504 and the ADA, the IDEA is a funding statute, rather than a civil rights statute.[37] It provides funds to assist states to meet the needs of students with disabilities whose disabilities "adversely affect[] educational performance"[38] such that special education is needed.[39] This piece of child welfare legislation serves as a complement to section 504. You might say that section 504 is the "stick" (punishing those who violate it by termination of federal funds), while the IDEA is the "carrot" (providing financial incentives for the appropriate delivery of special education[40] and related services[41]).

Therefore, a student with disabilities enjoys protection against discrimination under section 504, but may not meet the more narrow definitions of disability to be able to qualify for services under the IDEA. Those served under the IDEA are a subset of those protected under section 504. For example, children with life-threatening food allergies or temporary impairments may not qualify under the IDEA. In addition, a child could have an impairment (e.g., a visual impairment or health related issue) that is not severe enough to "adversely affect[] educational performance" as defined under the regulations to qualify for services under the IDEA.[42] However, that child may still be entitled to accommodations under section 504 in order to receive an education comparable to students who are not disabled.[43]

The IDEA is an extremely detailed law that requires school districts to document and justify the services provided to eligible children with disabilities. The IDEA creates a federal statutory right or an entitlement for each student with a disability. That entitlement is a free appropriate public education (FAPE) that consists of special education and related services designed to address the unique needs of the individual child.[44] The law creates an affirmative obligation on the part of the state and its local school districts to identify and serve all eligible students with disabilities within their geographic boundaries.[45] This obligation to find children with disabilities also extends to those children whose parents have chosen to enroll them in private schools.[46] Students may be referred for evaluation by any school personnel or by parents. Once referred, the school district must review the child's records and design a series of assessments in order to determine whether the suspicions of a disability are founded.[47] Parents must be provided notice of their rights under the law and must consent in writing to any evaluation before any testing may commence.[48] Once the evaluation is complete, the school personnel meet with the parents as an "IEP team" to determine eligibility together.[49] To be eligible, the student's profile of needs and abilities must match the definition of one or more disability categories specified by the IDEA.[50] These disability categories are "mental retardation, hearing impairments (including deafness), speech or language impairments, visual impairments (including blindness), serious emotional disturbance ..., orthopedic impairments, autism, traumatic brain injury, other health impairments, and specific learning disabilities."[51] As mentioned before, the mere presence of a disability does not qualify a child for services under the IDEA.[52] Rather, eligibility is dependent on whether the disability adversely affects educational performance, the degree to which may be further specified in the state's plan of service.[53]

Once eligibility is determined, the IEP team, which includes the parents, collaborates to produce an individualized education program (IEP).[54] The IEP is a document that delineates measurable annual goals for the child and specifies the kind and nature of services to be provided to or on behalf of the child.[55] As such, the IEP is the document by which FAPE is defined for an individual child—an individualized equity plan, if you will. Note that FAPE does not have a unitary definition under the law. That is, what is FAPE for one child may not be for another. A child's unique needs dictate the goals, objectives, and services defined by the IEP. This fact reveals a foundational characteristic of the IDEA. All decisions must be based on individualized determinations of need, as opposed to considerations of group instruction or programmatic design. You might say the "I" looms large in the IDEA.

In 1982, the Supreme Court provided further explanation of FAPE and what it requires. The Court explained that FAPE does not require that a child's potential be maximized, but rather that the IEP be "reasonably calculated to enable the child to receive educational benefits."[56] FAPE is a "floor of opportunity," a minimum level of service below which a district may not go.[57]

Once the IEP team determines the child's IEP goals and objectives,[58] the team must determine the issue of placement.[59] The IDEA[60] requires that children with disabilities be educated in the least restrictive environment (LRE), another central principle of the IDEA. LRE requires that children be educated with their nondisabled peers to the "maximum extent appropriate."[61] The 1997 amendments to the IDEA re-asserted this principle and created a strong presumption in favor of educating children with disabilities in traditional classroom settings.[62] That is, the IEP team must first consider how the child's needs can be met in the regular class environment. This consideration must include a discussion of the curricular adaptations and supports, supplemental aids and services that may make it possible to deliver the child's IEP in the general classroom.[63] However, even given that strong presumption of regular class placement with support, the LRE for some students will require placement in other than the regular classroom for part or all of the school day. It is incumbent upon school personnel to show why, given the "nature and severity of the [child's] disability,"[64] and even with the addition of supplementary aids and services as well as curricular adaptations and supportive services, FAPE cannot be achieved in the regular class setting for part or all of the child's school day. To that end, the law requires that school districts make available a "continuum of alternative placements" (e.g., resource rooms, special classes, special schools)[65] but that these other placements only be used when equity demands such a difference.

If a child's poor performance in the regular class motivates the IEP team to re-examine the appropriateness of a placement, it is helpful to note that the provisions of the IDEA essentially offer two explanations for such a problem: either the child is inadequately supported in the traditional classroom or the child is inappropriately placed in that setting. The law requires that the IEP team carefully examine the first question before considering the second.

It is also important for all staff to comprehend that LRE is related to, but is not synonymous with, "inclusion." Inclusion is an educational philosophy defined as "providing all students within the mainstream appropriate educational programs which are challenging and yet geared to their capabilities and needs as well as any support and assistance they and/or their teachers may need to be successful in the mainstream."[66] Some even argue that all students with disabilities should be included at all times regardless of the nature and severity of their disabilities. This stance, often referred to as "full inclusion," is inconsistent with the IDEA. The IDEA does not require that students with disabilities be included as much as *possible*. It requires that students with disabilities be included as much as *appropriate*.[67] The IDEA is predicated on the principle that sometimes appropriateness (read equity) requires something other than what is traditional to meet the unique needs of an individual child. However, it is certainly true that for most students with disabilities, an individualized examination of the needs of the child and the appropriate settings to address those needs will result in an "included" placement for all or part of the school day. Chapter 15 addresses provisions in the law regarding IEPs, least restrictive environment, and placement; chapter 16 discusses related services; chapter 17 details requirements for transition services; and chapter 18 delineates requirements for assessing children with disabilities.

The final core component of the IDEA is procedural protections. In order to protect the child's entitlement and to ensure that all decision-making occurs in the proper context, the IDEA mandates detailed procedural requirements and safeguards. If parents believe that the school is not providing at least an appropriate education for their child, they can challenge the district through a "due process" hearing.[68] This hearing is presided over by an impartial hearing officer supplied by the state. The hearing officer makes findings of fact and then applies the law to the facts of the situation.[69] Parents may challenge any decision relative to the process (e.g., evaluation, eligibility, appropriateness, placement). Likewise, if the district believes that parents are obstructing the school's ability to meet its obligation of FAPE for the child by refusing to consent to an evaluation, the district may request a due process hearing to settle the dispute.[70] Hearing decisions may be appealed in federal district court.[71] Provisions also require school districts to make available mediation as a mechanism for resolving any dispute with parents and avoiding the more adversarial hearing process.[72] Chapter 19 describes parental rights in detail.

Another major addition to the law in 1997 and preserved in 2004 includes the creation of provisions detailing procedural safeguards for children with disabilities facing disciplinary sanctions.[73] These provisions essentially codify earlier case law and require disciplinarians to ensure that children with disabilities are treated equitably by the process.[74] The particulars of the discipline provisions are detailed in chapter 18.

Finally, case law has established that parents who prevail at the hearing or in court may be entitled to remedies under the court's broad authority to fashion "such relief as the court determines is appropriate."[75] These remedies include recovery of attorney fees;[76] reimbursement of costs, including tuition costs borne by the parent; [77] and compensatory education.[78]

Recommendations for Practice

This chapter has provided an overview of federal disability law as it applies to public schools today. Subsequent chapters will further elaborate on these themes. They include the following:

Chapter 13: Discrimination Under Section 504 of the Rehabilitation Act

Chapter 14: Barrier-Free Facilities

Chapter 15: IEPs, Least Restrictive Environment, and Placement

Chapter 16: Related Services under the IDEA

Chapter 17: Transition: Individuals with Disabilities

Chapter 18: Disciplining Students with Disabilities

Chapter 19: Parental Rights

Chapter 20: Assessing Students with Disabilities under the IDEA and NCLB

Considering the issues related to this topic, the savvy principal would do well to consider the following recommendations for practice:

1. Develop a full understanding of federal disability law and its application to schools.

2. Develop a firm grasp of state laws and regulations that complement these federal laws. Particular attention should be paid to provisions that heighten the standards or requirements set by federal law.
3. Fully examine local policies and procedures that have been created to fulfill the obligations created by these laws.
4. Periodically review local policies to be certain they are current and accurately reflect the federal and state laws upon which they are founded.
5. Determine who can serve as a network of support within the school, the district, and the community to help all staff understand these laws and to help keep abreast of changes in the law.
6. Provide staff development opportunities so that all staff members understand their responsibilities under the law.
7. Cultivate relationships with disability advocacy groups in the area, particularly parent groups. Doing so allows the district to establish the kind of cooperative relationships envisioned between parents and school personnel in the IDEA.
8. Find a mechanism for remaining current with the developments in this rapidly evolving area of school law. There are numerous commercial newsletters that serve this function. In addition, school districts may utilize a law firm that provides such updates on either a regular or as-needed basis. Be sure to be on the "routing list" for any such publications received by the district.

Endnotes

1 This chapter builds, in part, on sections of Julie Mead, "The Legal Foundations of Equity: Protecting Access to Education." Chapter 8 in FOUNDATIONS OF DEMOCRATIC EDUCATION, O'Hair, M.J., McLaughlin, J., & Reitzug, U.C. (Belmont, CA: Wadsworth/Thomson Learning, 2000).

2 29 U.S.C. 794: 34 C.F.R. 104 *et seq.*

3 20 U.S.C. 1400 *et seq.*; 34 C.F.R. 300 *et seq.*

4 42 U.S.C. 12101 *et seq.*

5 29 U.S.C. 794.

6 34 C.F.R. 104.3(j)(1)(i).

7 34 C.F.R. 104.3(k)(2).

8 34 C.F.R. 104.3(j)(2)(ii).

9 See for example: *Davis (CA) Joint Unified Sch. Dist.* 31 IDELR 186 (OCR 1999).

10 Office for Civil Rights, PROTECTING STUDENTS WITH DISABILITIES, *Frequently Asked Questions about Section 504 and the Education of Children with Disabilities,* http://www.ed.gov/about/offices/list/ocr/504faq.html#protected *(last visited February 8, 2008).*

11 *See, e.g.*, Martinez v. Hillsborough County Sch. Bd., 861 F.2d. 1502 (11th Cir. 1988). (The court found AIDS to be a disability within the definition of a disability in section 504 because AIDS is a physical impairment that substantially limits a major life activity.)

12 34 C.F.R. 104(j)(2)(ii) (Section 504 provides coverage for persons with "a record of such an impairment" meaning the person "has a history of or has been misclassified as having"

a disability. This would include a student who in the past fell within the category of severe learning disability, but no longer possesses the necessary deviation discrepancy to qualify under the IDEA would fall under section 504). (DIXIE SNOW HUEFNER, GETTING COMFORTABLE WITH SPECIAL EDUCATION LAW: A FRAMEWORK FOR WORKING WITH CHILDREN WITH DISABILITIES 41 (2000)). 34 C.F.R. 104(j)(2)(iv); (Section 504 also extends its coverage to a person who "is regarded as having an impairment" such as a person with HIV, whose condition could be perceived to interfere with their education, when it does not.)

13 34 C.F.R. 104.34(a).

14 34 C.F.R. 104.32(b).

15 34 C.F.R. 104.35(c).

16 SUSAN GORN, WHAT DO I DO WHEN… THE ANSWER BOOK ON SECTION 504, 3:29 (2000).

17 34 C.F.R. 104.3.

18 34 C.F.R. 104.11(a)(1).

19 34 C.F.R. 104.12(a).

20 Southeastern Cmty. Coll. v. Davis, 442 U.S.397, 99 S.Ct. 2361, 60 L.Ed.2d 980 (1970).

21 Rothschild v. Grottenthaler, 907 F.2d. 286 (2d 1990).

22 United States Constitution, Article 1, Section 8, Clause 3 ("Congress shall have Power… to regulate Commerce with foreign Nation, and among the several States…").

23 Public Law 103-336.

24 42 U.S.C. 12111.

25 42 U.S.C 12112(a).

26 42 U.S.C 12132.

27 42 U.S.C 12181.

28 47 U.S.C. 225 *et seq.*

29 42 U.S.C. §12201.

30 42 U.S.C. §12202.

31 42 U.S.C. §12209.

32 42 U.S.C. §12210.

33 42 U.S.C. §12208.

34 42 U.S.C. §12211; conditions enumerated under paragraph (b) of this section include, among others, pedophilia, exhibitionism, voyeurism, compulsive gambling, kleptomania, and pyromania.

35 *See, e.g.*, Council of Administrators of Special Education, Inc., SECTION 504 AND THE ADA PROMOTING STUDENT ACCESS: A RESOURCE GUIDE FOR EDUCATORS (2d ed. 1999); PERRY ZIRKEL & JEANNE KINCAID, SECTION 504, THE ADA AND THE SCHOOLS (1995).

36 Public Law 94-142.

37 20 U.S.C. § 1401 (d)(1).

38 34 C.F.R. §300.8 (2006).

39 20 U.S.C. §1402(3)(A)(ii).

40 20 U.S.C. §1402(29) (2006), ("The term `special education' means specially designed instruction, at no cost to parents, to meet the unique needs of a child with a disability, including—(A) instruction conducted in the classroom, in the home, in hospitals and institutions, and in other settings; and (B) instruction in physical education.")

41 20 U.S.C. §1402(26) (2006) ("The term `related services' means transportation, and such developmental, corrective, and other supportive services (including speech-language pathology and audiology services, interpreting services, psychological services, physical and occupational therapy, recreation, including therapeutic recreation, social work services, school nurse services designed to enable a child with a disability to receive a free appropriate public education as described in the individualized education program of the child, counseling services, including rehabilitation counseling, orientation and mobility services, and medical services, except that such medical services shall be for diagnostic and evaluation purposes only) as may be required to assist a child with a disability to benefit from special education, and includes the early identification and assessment of disabling conditions in children.")

42 34 C.F.R. §300.8 (2006).

43 Chapter 13 provides a number of examples of this phenomenon.

44 20 U.S.C. 1402(9).

45 20 U.S.C. 1412(a)(3). The law uses the terms state education agency (SEA) and local education agency (LEA) (20 U.S.C.). It should be noted that

46 20 U.S.C. 1412 (a)(3)(A); 34 C.F.R. 300.111. The rights afforded children enrolled by their parents in private settings are not coextensive with those of children in the public setting. These students enjoy only a group entitlement as opposed to an individual one and must be served "consistent with [their] number and location" (20 U.S.C. 1412 (a)(10)(A); 34 C.F.R. 300.132). In addition, the IDEA now only requires LEAs to expend federal dollars on those children in private schools and makes no requirements for the expenditure of state or local funds (20 U.S.C. 1412 (a)(10)(A)(i)(I); 34 C.F.R. 300.133). Of course, states may impose additional requirements through state statutes.

47 20 U.S.C. 1414 (b)(2).

48 20 U.S.C. 1414 (a)(1)(D).

49 IEP refers to the Individualized Education Program (20 U.S.C. 1402(14)). The law specifies that the IEP team must include at a minimum: "(i) the parents of a child with a disability; (ii) not less than 1 regular education teacher of such child (if the child is, or may be, participating in the regular education environment); (iii) not less than 1 special education teacher, or where appropriate, not less than 1 special education provider of such child; (iv) a representative of the local educational agency who—(I) is qualified to provide, or supervise the provision of, specially designed instruction to meet the unique needs of children with disabilities; (II) is knowledgeable about the general curriculum; and (III) is knowledgeable about the availability of resources of the local educational agency; (v) an individual who can interpret the instructional implications of evaluation results, who may be a member of the team described in clauses (ii) through (vi); (vi) at the discretion of the parent or the agency, other individuals who have knowledge or special expertise regarding the child, including related services personnel as appropriate; and (vii) whenever appropriate, the child with a disability" (20 U.S.C 1414(d)(1)(B); 34 C.F.R. 300.321). Note that all decisions under the IDEA must occur in a context of group decision-making including an opportunity for full parental participation in all determinations.

50 20 U.S.C. 1402(3); 34 C.F.R. 300.8.

51 20 U.S.C. 1402(3).

52 Although mere presence of a disability does qualify a child for *protection from discrimination* and an education comparable to that of non-disabled peers under section 504.

53 34 C.F.R. 300.100.

54 20 U.S.C. 1414(d).

55 The IEP should also specify any curricular adaptations, supports, supplementary aids, and services (20 U.S.C. 1414 (d)(1)(A); 34 C.F.R. 300.320).

56 Board of Educ. of the Hendrick Hudson Cent. Sch. Dist. v. Rowley, 458 U.S. 176, 177 (1982). However, state law may place requirements for a higher level of service on its LEAs.

57 *Id.*, at 200 (internal citations omitted).

58 Chapter 15 examines the IEP process in depth including the requirements for who must be on an IEP team and the content required of each IEP; chapter 16 discusses related services requirements; and chapter 17 focuses on a particular requirement of IEPs, the transition plan to help children matriculate from school to postsecondary or post-school employment opportunities (20 U.S.C. 1414(d)(1)(A)(vii); 34 C.F.R. 300.347 (b)).

59 20 U.S.C. 1414 (e); 34 C.F.R. 300.327.

60 And section 504/ADA, for that matter.

61 20 U.S.C. 1412 (a)(5).

62 Senate Committee Report on P.L. 105-17, p. 26. *See also* Julie Mead, *Expressions of Congressional Intent: Examining the 1997 Amendments to the IDEA*, 127 Educ. L. Rep. (West) 511(Sept. 17, 1998).

63 20 U.S.C. 1414(d)(1)(A)(iii); 34 C.F.R. 347(a)(3).

64 20 U.S.C. 1412(a)(5).

[65] 34 C.F.R. 300.115.

[66] William Stainback & Susan Stainback, Support Networks for Inclusive Schooling 3 (1990).

[67] 20 U.S.C. 1412(a)(5).

[68] 20 U.S.C. 1415(f).

[69] 20 U.S.C. 1415(h).

[70] 20U.S.C. 1414(a)(1)(D)(ii)(I).

[71] 20 U.S.C. 1415(i)(2).

[72] 20 U.S.C. 1415(e).

[73] 20 U.S.C. 1415(k).

[74] *See also* Mead, note 61. "Essentially these provisions, like the judicial interpretations from which they stem, demonstrate that when school officials consider the discipline of students with disabilities they must ask three critical questions to ensure that the disciplinary sanction does not result in discrimination on the basis of disability and to ensure equity: (1) Is the behavior a manifestation of the disability? (2) Does the disciplinary consequence result in a change of placement thereby invoking the procedures of the IDEA? and (3) Was the child receiving an appropriate programming [sic] at the time the misbehavior occurred?" (p. 524).

[75] 20 U.S.C. 1415(i)(2)(B).

[76] 20 U.S.C. 1415 (i)(3).

[77] School Comm. of Town of Burlington v. Dep't of Educ. of Mass., 471 U.S. 359, 105 S. Ct. 1996, 85 L. Ed. 2d 385 (1985); Florence County Sch. Dist. Four v. Carter, 510 U.S. 7, 114 S. Ct. 361, 126 L. Ed. 2d 2846 (1993).

[78] See for example: Meiner v. Missouri, 800 F.2d 749 (8th Cir. 1986); Jefferson County Bd. of Educ. v. Breen, 853 F.2d 853 (11th Cir. 1988); Lester H. v. Gilhool, 916 F.2d 865 (3d Cir. 1990); Parents of Student W. v. Puyallup Sch. Dist., 31 F.3d 1489 (9th Cir. 1994).

Chapter 13

Discrimination under Section 504 of the Rehabilitation Act

Allan G. Osborne, Jr.

Introduction

Section 504 of the Rehabilitation Act of 1973, as amended, provides that "[n]o otherwise qualified individual with a disability ... shall, solely by reason of her or his disability be excluded from participation in, be denied the benefits of, or be subjected to discrimination under any program or activity receiving [f]ederal financial assistance...."[1] Section 504 in effect prohibits any recipient of federal funds from discriminating against individuals with disabilities in the provision of services or employment. Section 504 applies to any agency that receives federal funds; thus, it applies to all public schools and many private schools.

A person is considered to have a disability under section 504 if he or she has a physical or mental impairment that substantially limits one or more of his or her major life activities, has a record of such an impairment, or is regarded as having such an impairment.[2] Major life activities are "functions such as caring for oneself, performing manual tasks, walking, seeing, hearing, speaking, breathing, learning, and working."[3] The Supreme Court has held that a person is otherwise qualified for purposes of section 504 if he or she is capable of meeting all of a program's requirements in spite of the disability.[4] If a person is otherwise qualified, a recipient of federal funds is expected to make reasonable accommodations for his or her disabilities unless doing so would create an undue hardship.[5]

An individual is not considered to have a disability for purposes of section 504 if his or her major life activities are not substantially limited by the condition.[6] Furthermore, short-term conditions,[7] or those that can be mitigated, are not considered to be impairments under section 504.[8] For example, the Sixth Circuit affirmed that a surgical resident who suffered from depression did not have a disability covered by section 504 because any restrictions on job performance were temporary and could be mitigated by medication.[9] Another court determined that an individual with poor eyesight did not have a disability because his vision could reasonably be corrected with glasses.[10]

Students with disabilities at the elementary and secondary level are protected by and have rights under section 504 as well as the Individuals with Disabilities Education Act (IDEA).[11] Any student covered by the IDEA would also be covered under section 504; however, the reverse is not always true.

Many students who are not eligible under the IDEA are still entitled to the anti-discrimination protections of section 504. For example, a student with a physical disability who does not require special education and related services would not be entitled to the provisions of the IDEA but would be entitled to accommodations under section 504.

Under section 504, schools may not discriminate against parents who are disabled. Thus, schools must provide accommodations to parents with disabilities to allow them to participate in activities that are essential to the education of their children. For example, schools must provide reasonable accommodations to allow a parent with a disability to participate in a parent-teacher conference.

School employees are entitled to the protections of section 504. An employer is required to provide reasonable accommodations to an otherwise qualified disabled employee. However, as will be discussed later in this chapter, there are limits as to how far an employer must go to provide reasonable accommodations.

Legal Issues

Students

As stated above, students with disabilities are entitled to the protections of section 504 as well as the IDEA. A student is entitled to a free appropriate public education (FAPE) under both statutes. Like the IDEA, section 504 does not require a school board to provide students with disabilities with an education that maximizes potential. Section 504 only requires reasonable accommodations that will give a student with disabilities the same access to the benefits of a public education that is provided to all students.[12] Usually compliance with the IDEA will translate into compliance with section 504. Thus, if a school district provides a FAPE under the provisions of the IDEA, the school district also will meet its obligations under section 504.[13] In fact, the same process may be used to determine if a student is eligible to receive services under either statute.[14] When a student with disabilities is not entitled to services under the IDEA, a school board still may be required to provide educational services under section 504 so that the student's needs can be met as adequately as the needs of nondisabled students.[15]

A school board cannot exclude a student from any of its programs simply because the student has a disability. For example, courts have ruled that schools cannot exclude a student who has AIDS absent evidence that the student poses a health risk to his classmates or teachers.[16] Similarly, schools may not exclude students who have other health impairments[17] or other disabilities such as mental retardation,[18] learning disabilities,[19] or attention deficit hyperactivity disorder (ADHD).[20] Public schools may not exclude students with disabilities for behavior that is a manifestation of their disabilities; however, disruptive or dangerous students may be moved to more restrictive environments.[21]

Students with disabilities may not be subjected to differential treatment because of their disabilities or because of the accommodations they receive. In one high profile case, a court issued an injunction to prevent a school board from adopting a new policy that would allow for multiple valedictorians.[22] The court found that the proposed policy was intended and designed to have a particular exclusionary effect on a student with disabilities who earned the valedictorian honor under the former policy. In the court's view, the new policy was being implemented solely because the student had received accommodations due to her disability.[23]

Schools must provide reasonable accommodations so that students with disabilities may access its programs. This may involve alterations to the physical plant, such as building wheelchair ramps or removing architectural barriers, so that students may physically enter and get around the school building.[24] In some situations schools also must allow students to bring service dogs into the classroom as an accommodation, particularly if use of the service dog is necessary for the student to have a degree of independence.[25] If the student is quite independent, or if the presence of a service dog could present a health risk to others, the school may not be required to allow the student to be accompanied by the dog.[26]

Schools are not required to provide accommodations that go beyond what would be considered to be reasonable. Accommodations that are excessively expensive, expose the school's staff to excessive risk, or that require a school to substantially modify the mission or purpose of a program are not mandated.[27] In this regard, school boards are not necessarily required to make alterations to or provide accommodations in the student's home school. School districts may enroll a student with disabilities in another school that is accessible or that has the appropriate accommodations available. In the interests of economy, school boards may centralize programs rather than offer duplicative programs in each of its schools.[28] However, school boards must provide students with disabilities with facilities that are comparable to those provided to students who are not disabled.[29]

A school board is not required to fundamentally alter a program to allow participation by a student with disabilities who is not otherwise qualified for the program. For example, if a student with disabilities does not meet the basic requirements for participation in an academic program, school officials are not required to accept the student into the program just because he or she has a disability. As long as the school's participation requirements are neutral and are not specifically designed to exclude students with disabilities, a student's exclusion from the program due to failure to meet entrance requirements is not discriminatory.[30]

Many school districts currently have a school choice policy whereby parents may elect to send their children to a school other than the neighborhood school. Although these policies cannot be used to exclude a student with disabilities solely because of the disability, students with disabilities may be excluded due to other considerations. For example, the Sixth Circuit found that a student with disabilities whose application for school choice was denied was not subject to discrimination because the denial was a function of his residence and the funds associated with his education and not solely because of his disability.[31] Most school choice policies require the parents to provide their own transportation if they elect to send their children to a distant school. If the child has a disability, a school board is not required to provide that student with special transportation to the school of choice as long as the board has offered an appropriate program at the student's home school.[32] Even so, if under the school choice policy the board provided transportation to students without disabilities, it would also be required to provide transportation to students with disabilities.

Health-related services are among the most common accommodations schools provide to students with disabilities. Under section 504 schools are required to provide students with disabilities with basic health services such as catheterization[33] and administration of medication. However, a school nurse is not required to administer medication if the prescription exceeds the normal recommended dosage.[34]

The requirements for testing accommodations recently have taken on new interest among school administrators as many states now require students to pass an examination to graduate from high school.[35] Again, section 504 requires accommodations that would allow a student with disabilities to take a test on an equal footing with peers who are not disabled but would not require a fundamental alteration in the content of the test itself. In other words, school boards may be required to modify how a test is administered but are not required to modify the actual content of the test. Thus, section 504 would require schools to give a Braille version of the test to a blind student or provide assistance in recording answers to a physically challenged student but would not require that easier test items be administered to a student with learning disabilities. Basically, school officials are required to provide modifications that will allow the student to take the test but do not need to modify the item content or compromise the validity of the test.[36]

Recently, many questions have arisen regarding the participation of students with disabilities in extracurricular or athletic programs. Some students, due to their disabilities, do not meet the usual requirements for participation. In many cases, school boards and athletic associations are required to waive the normal requirements for participation unless doing so would fundamentally alter the program or impose an excessive burden on the agency. Thus, schools or athletic associations may be required to waive grade point average requirements, but may not be required to waive age limitation[37] or eight-semester rules.[38] This issue is very controversial, however, and the outcome of a lawsuit frequently depends on the particular circumstances. If a student transfers from one school to another in order to receive special education services, the school may be required to waive any rules requiring the student to sit out a period of time before being eligible for athletics.[39] Nevertheless, a school board may not be required to waive its requirement that student-athletes adhere to a specific code of conduct to participate in sports.[40] Also, school officials may justifiably exclude a student if there is evidence that the student is at an increased risk of serious injury, or could put others at risk, due to his or her disability.[41] In such an instance, school administrators may seek medical direction and clearance for physical activities from the student's doctor.[42]

Just as students are entitled to accommodations so that they can participate in the school's academic program, they also may be entitled to accommodations to allow them to participate in the school's extracurricular programs. One court wrote that a hearing-impaired student was entitled to the services of a sign-language interpreter so that she could understand the directions of her basketball coach.[43]

Parents

School districts also may be required to supply reasonable accommodations so that parents who have disabilities are able to participate in activities essential to their child's education. One court required a school to provide a sign-language interpreter so that parents who were hearing impaired could participate in school-initiated conferences regarding the academic and disciplinary aspects of their child's educational program.[44] Under this ruling, school boards would not be required to provide accommodations for other school functions in which parental participation is not necessary, such as school plays or even graduation ceremonies. The school would, however, be required to allow parents to provide their own accommodations. For example, the school could not prevent parents from bringing their own sign language interpreter to a graduation ceremony.

Employees

School districts may not refuse to hire an applicant who has a disability, or in any way discriminate against an employee with a disability, as long as the applicant or employee is otherwise qualified for the position. An employer must, however, provide reasonable accommodations that will allow the employee or prospective employee to perform the job in question.

Discrimination Claims. Generally, in order to maintain a discrimination claim under section 504 an employee must show that he or she was treated differently than nondisabled employees or that an adverse employment decision was made because of the individual's disability. For example, a part-time worker with a disability could not maintain a discrimination claim when he was laid off after he had worked the maximum number of hours allowed for part-time workers when part-time employees who were not disabled were laid off for the same reason.[45]

In another lawsuit, a former high school principal, who was a recovering alcoholic, was unable to show that a school district discriminated against him when it abolished his position and did not appoint him to the newly created position of combined elementary and high school principal.[46] For economic reasons, the school district had combined the two positions but offered the new job to the former elementary principal because he was certified for grades K-12, whereas the former high school principal was not.

Employees with disabilities cannot maintain a discrimination claim if they do not have the skills to perform the job in question, even when provided with accommodations. Courts will not uphold a discrimination claim if the school district can show that an adverse employment decision was made for nondiscriminatory reasons. For example, one court held that an employee with a disability was not discriminated against when the employer was able to show that the employee was not promoted because his work performance was not up to standards and it had not improved when he was provided with accommodations.[47] Another court maintained that a school board did not discriminate against a paraprofessional who was not re-appointed after being given poor evaluations, in part, because she had never submitted any documentation to indicate that she had an impairment.[48]

An employee also cannot maintain a discrimination claim if the employee's alleged disability is not covered by section 504. One court held that the term "individual with disabilities" does not include an individual with sexual behavior disorders.[49] In that case, an instructor had been fired for violating the school's sexual harassment policy but alleged that he was wrongfully terminated because he had a sexual addiction that was a mental disability under section 504. Similarly, another court held that a professor who had suffered a stroke was not discriminated against when he received smaller salary raises than other faculty members.[50] First, the court held that the professor was not disabled as defined by section 504 since his stroke had not substantially limited a major life activity.[51] Secondly, the court found that the reasons why the professor's salary raise was not comparable to other professors were related to his overall performance.

Employers are permitted to take appropriate disciplinary action against an employee who commits egregious or criminal misconduct, regardless of whether the employee is disabled. One court upheld the termination of a coach who had been arrested for driving under the influence of alcohol and public intoxication.[52] The court posited that the employer could hold an alcoholic employee to the same performance and behavior standards as other employees, even if the unsatisfactory performance was due to the employee's alcoholism. Similarly, employees can be terminated for excessive absenteeism even if the absences are related to the disability because being present is considered to be an essential requirement of any job.[53]

Otherwise Qualified Individual with a Disability. The Supreme Court has indicated that an individual with a disability is otherwise qualified if that person can perform all essential requirements of the position in question in spite of the disability.[54] Thus, if the individual cannot perform essential functions of the position, even with reasonable accommodations, the individual is not otherwise qualified.

An essential requirement of most positions, especially those in school systems, is regular attendance. An employee who is unable to attend the workplace in a reliable and predictable manner is not otherwise qualified.[55] Section 504 does not protect excessive absenteeism, even when it is caused by a disability.[56] Similarly, a classroom teacher is expected to be able to be physically present in a classroom and to be able to interact with students. A teacher who, due to a disability, is unable to interact with students may not be entitled to an assignment that does not involve sustained contact with large groups of students. Classroom teaching would generally be considered an essential function of a teacher's job, and an inability to teach in a classroom in most situations would mean that the individual could not meet all requirements of a teaching position in spite of his or her disability. However, if non-classroom positions are available, the teacher may be entitled to a reassignment to one of those positions.[57]

Failure to meet teacher certification requirements may disqualify an individual even if the failure is allegedly due to a disability. A teacher who claimed to be learning disabled and had not passed the communications portion of the National Teachers Examination after numerous attempts was not considered to be otherwise qualified for teacher certification.[58] The court found that the skills measured by the communications portion of the examination were necessary for competent performance as a classroom teacher. Thus, the court said that the teacher was not otherwise qualified because she could not perform the essential functions of the position.

Similarly, an employer can expect an individual to be able to perform his or her duties in a safe manner.[59] For example, bus drivers who are poorly controlled diabetics are not otherwise qualified since they pose an unpredictable risk of developing hypoglycemia or the complications of hypoglycemia.[60] The complications may include a sudden loss of vision or consciousness. On the other hand, if the diabetes can be controlled and the bus driver's fitness to operate the vehicle easily monitored, the driver would be considered otherwise qualified.[61] The same would be true for drivers who have other medical conditions such as a seizure disorder[62] or a heart condition. The employee in question must be individually assessed for fitness to perform the duties of the job. Before refusing to hire an individual with a disability due to perceived risk, an employer must determine the nature, duration, and severity of the risk; the probability that the potential injury will actually occur; and the possibility that reasonable modifications of policies, practices, or procedures will mitigate the risk.[63]

Section 504 also does not protect misconduct, even when it can be attributed to a disability.[64] One court upheld the dismissal of an alcoholic employee who had repeatedly reported to work intoxicated and unable to perform his duties.[65] The court found that the employee was dismissed because of his misconduct, not his alcoholism, and that relief was not available under section 504 for misconduct. Similarly, another court upheld the dismissal of a teacher who had been arrested and charged with possession of cocaine.[66] The court declared that his criminal conduct undermined his ability to work as a teacher.

Reasonable Accommodations. Under section 504 an employer must provide reasonable accommodations so that an otherwise qualified employee with disabilities can work and compete with his or her nondisabled colleagues.[67] The purpose of providing an accommodation is so that the employee with a disability can lead a normal life.[68] Accommodations may include alterations to the physical environment, adjustments to an employee's schedule, or minor changes in the employee's job responsibilities. What is, and is not, a reasonable accommodation has been the subject of much litigation.

An employer is not required to supply an accommodation if doing so would place an undue burden on the employer. Minor accommodations, however, are generally not held to be excessively burdensome. For example, one court held that monitoring a diabetic's ability to operate a school bus on a daily basis would not place an undue burden on the school system.[69] Generally, it is the school board's responsibility to show that requested accommodations would create an undue financial or administrative burden.[70]

An employer also is not required to make accommodations that would essentially change the nature of the position. However, an employer may be required to re-assign an employee with a disability to another position. This may be required when the employee is unable to perform the essential functions of his or her current job even with reasonable accommodations, and there exists, or soon will exist, a vacant position that the employee is able to perform.[71] In the case of classroom teachers, re-assignment to a non-teaching position could be required if such positions existed in the district.[72] Re-assignment is not required, however, when there is no other position available for which the employee is qualified.[73] An employer also is not required to create a new position or accommodate an employee with a disability by eliminating essential aspects of his or her current position.[74]

As indicated in the previous section, regular attendance is considered to be an essential requirement of most jobs. An employer is not required to let an employee with a disability work only when his or her condition allows.[75] For example, one court held that a requested accommodation of being allowed to work when the employee's illness permitted would result in an undue hardship to the employer.[76] An employee who cannot report to work on a consistent basis may not be considered to be otherwise qualified.[77] On the other hand, in another situation, a court determined that a school board had adequately accommodated a teacher whose illness caused frequent absences when it hired a long-term substitute to work alongside the teacher.[78]

State Immunity under Section 504

The issue of whether a state is immune from a lawsuit under section 504 has resulted in mixed opinions from the courts even though Congress has amended Title VI of the Civil Rights Act to affirm that states are not immune to lawsuits filed in federal courts under a variety of civil rights statutes including section 504.[79] Most courts reviewing the question have been convinced that states do not enjoy Eleventh Amendment immunity from lawsuits brought on the basis of section 504. The First,[80] Third,[81] Fifth,[82] Sixth,[83] Eighth,[84] and Tenth[85] Circuits have ruled that the states of Puerto Rico, New Jersey, Louisiana, Texas, Ohio, Arkansas, and Kansas, respectively, have waived their immunity under section 504 by accepting federal funds.[86] Conversely, the Eleventh Circuit has ruled that suits in federal court by state employees to recover money damages under section 504 are barred by the Eleventh Amendment.[87]

Damages

An individual may be entitled to damages if he or she is able to show that his or her rights under section 504 were egregiously disregarded. For example, a Wyoming court stated that to be entitled to compensatory damages under section 504 a plaintiff must prove that the defendant intentionally discriminated against her on the basis of her disability.[88] A New York court also stated that allegations that school officials failed to provide special education services, if proven, could constitute a deliberate indifference to the fact that a student's rights were being violated and could entitle the student to damages.[89] However, a school board will not generally be held liable as long as a good faith effort was made to address the student's or employee's disabilities.[90]

Individual school officials may be held personally liable for their actions under section 504 if an individual can show that they acted with bad faith or gross misjudgment.[91] An individual teacher could be held liable for flagrant failure to abide by the terms of a student's IEP or section 504 service plan.[92] A federal trial court in Pennsylvania saw no difficulty in holding individuals liable for violations of section 504.[93]

Recommendations For Practice

1. Students with disabilities may not be excluded from public schools or denied services simply because they are disabled.
2. Students with disabilities may not be subjected to differential treatment because of their disabilities or because they receive accommodations for their disabilities.
3. If a student with disabilities does not qualify for special education and related services under the IDEA, school officials should determine if the student requires reasonable accommodations under section 504 to access the schools' services and programs.
4. School authorities should make an individualized determination regarding waivers of participation requirements for student-athletes

with disabilities who may not meet usual requirements because of their disabilities.

5. School administrators may request medical clearance before allowing a student with disabilities to participate in sports if they have reason to believe that the student has an increased risk of injury.
6. Accommodations must be provided to parents with disabilities so that they can participate in school functions essential to their child's education such as parent-teacher conferences.
7. To maintain a discrimination claim under section 504 an employee must show that the disability is covered under section 504, that an adverse employment decision was made because of the disability, and that the employee has the skills to perform the job in question.
8. An employee is not otherwise qualified if that employee cannot perform the essential functions of the position even with reasonable accommodations.
9. Employees must be individually assessed for fitness to perform the job in question.
10. An employer is not required to provide an accommodation if doing so would create an undue financial or administrative burden.
11. If an employee is no longer able to perform the essential functions of his or her job, the employer must transfer an employee with a disability to another vacant position if one exists and the employee is qualified for the position; however, an employer is not required to create a new position for the employee with a disability.
12. In most jurisdictions, sovereign immunity cannot be used as a defense in a lawsuit under section 504.
13. School employees can be held personally liable for damages if an act of discrimination is egregious and intentional.

Endnotes

[1] 29 U.S.C. § 794.

[2] 29 U.S.C. § 705(20)(B).

[3] 34 C.F.R. § 104.3(j)(2)(ii).

[4] School Bd. of Nassau County v. Arline, 480 U.S. 273 (1987); Southeastern Cmty. Coll. v. Davis, 442 U.S. 397 (1979).

[5] 34 C.F.R. § 104.12(a).

[6] Welsh v. City of Tulsa, 977 F.2d 1415 (10th Cir. 1992); Mackie v. Runyon, 804 F. Supp. 1508 (M.D. Fla. 1992).

[7] Paegle v. Dep't of the Interior, 813 F. Supp. 61 (D.D.C. 1993).

[8] Sutton v. United Air Lines, 527 U.S. 471 (1999); Murphy v. United Parcel Serv., 527 U.S. 516 (1999); Albertson's, Inc. v. Kirkingburg, 527 U.S. 555 (1999). Although these cases were decided under the Americans with Disabilities Act, the principle that corrective or mitigating

measures should be considered in determining whether an individual is disabled applies to section 504 due to the similarities in both statutes' definitions of an individual with a disability.

9 Swanson v. Univ. of Cincinnati, 268 F.3d 307 (6th Cir. 2001).

10 Pacella v. Tufts Univ. Sch. of Dental Med., 66 F. Supp. 2d 234 (D. Mass. 1999).

11 20 U.S.C. § 1400 *et seq.*

12 J.D. v. Pawlet Sch. Dist., 224 F.3d 60 (2d Cir. 2000).

13 *See, e.g.* Wenger v. Canastota Cent. Sch. Dist., 961 F. Supp. 416 (N.D.N.Y. 1997); McGraw v. Bd. of Educ. of Montgomery County, 952 F. Supp. 248 (D. Md. 1997); D.F. v. W. Sch. Corp., 921F. Supp. 559 (S.D. Ind. 1996); Cordrey v. Euckert, 917 F.2d 1460 (6th Cir. 1990); Puffer v. Raynolds, 761 F. Supp. 838 (D. Mass. 1988).

14 N.L. *ex rel.* Ms. C. v. Knox County Sch., 315 F.3d 688 (6th Cir. 2003).

15 Lyons v. Smith, 829 F. Supp. 414 (D.D.C. 1993).

16 Doe v. Dolton Elementary Sch. Dist. No. 148, 694 F. Supp. 440 (N.D. Ill. 1988); Thomas v. Atascadero Unified Sch. Dist., 662 F. Supp. 376 (C.D. Cal. 1987).

17 Thomas v. Davidson Acad., 846 F. Supp. 611 (M.D. Tenn. 1994); Jeffrey S. v. State Bd. of Educ. of State of Ga., 896 F.2d 507 (11th Cir. 1990).

18 Oberti v. Bd. of Educ. of the Borough of Clementon Sch. Dist., 801 F. Supp. 1393 (D.N.J. 1992), *aff'd* 995 F.2d 1204 (3d Cir. 1992).

19 I.D. v. Westmoreland Sch. Dist., 788 F. Supp. 634 (D.N.H. 1992).

20 *See, e.g.* Bercovitch v. Baldwin Sch., 964 F. Supp. 597 (D.P.R. 1997).

21 *See, e.g.* S-1 v. Turlington, 635 F.2d 342 (5th Cir. 1981); Sherry v. N.Y. State Educ. Dep't, 479 F. Supp. 1328 (W.D.N.Y. 1979).

22 Hornstine v. Township of Moorestown, 263 F. Supp. 2d 887 (D.N.J. 2003).

23 *See also* Weixel v. Bd. of Educ. of the City of New York, 287 F.3d 138 (2d Cir. 2002), where the court found that school officials failed to make reasonable accommodations for a student who could not attend school due to documented illness so that she did not receive educational services for most of one school year.

24 *See, e.g.* Begay v. Hodel, 730 F. Supp. 1001 (D. Ariz. 1990).

25 Sullivan v. Vallejo City Unified Sch. Dist., 731 F. Supp. 947 (E.D. Cal. 1990).

26 Cave v. E. Meadow Union Free Sch. Dist., 480 F. Supp. 2d 610 (E.D.N.Y. 2007).

27 Eva N. v. Brock, 741 F. Supp. 626 (E.D. Ky. 1990); Kohl v. Woodhaven Learning Ctr., 865 F.2d 930 (8th Cir. 1989).

28 *See, e.g.* Barnett v. Fairfax County Sch. Bd., 927 F.2d 146 (4th Cir. 1991).

29 Hendricks v. Gilhool, 709 F. Supp. 1362 (E.D. Pa. 1989).

30 St. Johnsbury Acad. v. D.H., 240 F.3d 163 (2d Cir. 2001).

31 Clark v. Banks, 193 F. App'x 510 (6th Cir. 2006).

32 Timothy H. v. Cedar Rapids Cmty. Sch. Dist., 178 F.3d 968 (8th Cir. 1999).

33 Irving Indep. Sch. Dist. v. Tatro, 468 U.S. 883, 104 S. Ct. 3371, 82 L. Ed. 2d 664 (1984).

34 DeBord v. Ferguson-Florissant Sch. Dist., 126 F.3d 1102 (8th Cir. 1997); Davis v. Francis Howell Sch. Dist., 104 F.3d 204 (8th Cir. 1997).

35 In fact, the IDEA requires the participation of students with disabilities in state testing programs. 20 U.S.C. § 1412(a)(17), 34 C.F.R. § 300.138.

36 Brookhart v. Ill. State Bd. of Educ., 697 F.2d 179 (7th Cir. 1983). Many of the lawsuits concerning testing accommodations are at the collegiate level, and some were filed under the Americans with Disabilities Act (42 U.S.C. § 12101 *et seq.*), but can be instructive. *See, e.g.*, Rush v. Nat'l Bd. of Med. Examiners, 268 F. Supp. 2d 673 (N.D. Tex. 2003) (learning disabled student given additional time to take medical exam); Stern v. Univ. of Osteopathic Med. and Health Scis., 220 F.3d 906 (8th Cir. 2000) (student failed to show that requested accommodations were related to his dyslexia); Biank v. Nat'l Bd. of Med. Examiners, 130 F. Supp. 2d 986 (N.D. Ill. 2000) (medical student failed to show that his dyslexia would significantly limit his ability to pass an exam unless given additional time); D'Amico v. N.Y. State Bd. of Law Examiners, 813 F. Supp. 217 (W.D.N.Y. 1993) (additional time granted to a visually impaired student to take state bar exam).

37 M.H. v. Mont. High Sch. Ass'n, 929 P.2d 239 (Mont. 1996); Sandison v. Mich. High Sch. Athletic Ass'n, 64 F.3d 1026 (6th Cir. 1995); Pottgen v. Mo. State High Sch. Activities Ass'n, 40 F.3d 926 (8th Cir. 1994). *But see* Dennin v. Conn. Interscholastic Athletic Conference, 913 F. Supp. 663 (D. Conn. 1996), *dismissed as moot* 94 F.3d 96 (2d Cir. 1996); Johnson v. Fla. High Sch. Activities Ass'n, 899 F. Supp. 579 (M.D. Fla. 1995), *vac'd and rem'd with instructions to dismiss as moot* 102 F.3d 1172 (11th Cir. 1997); Univ. Interscholastic League v. Buchanan, 848 S.W.2d 298 (Tex. Ct. App. 1993).

38 McPherson v. Mich. High Sch. Athletic Ass'n, 119 F.3d 453 (6th Cir. 1997); Rhodes v. Ohio High Sch. Athletic Ass'n, 939 F. Supp. 584 (N.D. Ohio 1996).

39 Crocker v. Tenn. Secondary Sch. Athletic Ass'n, 735 F. Supp. 753 (M.D. Tenn. 1990), *aff'd sub nom.* Metropolitan Gov't of Nashville and Davidson County v. Crocker, 908 F.2d 973 (6th Cir. 1990) (mem.).

40 Long v. Bd. of Educ., Dist. 128, 167 F. Supp. 2d 988 (N.D. Ill. 2001) where the court stated that a waiver of the application of the code of conduct would be unreasonable as it would send the message to others that a challenge in federal court could thwart the enforcement of rules.

41 Pahulu v. Univ. of Kan., 897 F. Supp. 1387 (D. Kan. 1995); Kampmeier v. Nyquist, 553 F.2d 296 (2d Cir. 1977); *but see* Pace v. Dryden Cent. Sch. Dist., 574 N.Y.S.2d 142 (N.Y. Sup. Ct. 1991) (order issued on the basis of state law); Grube v. Bethlehem Area Sch. Dist., 550 F. Supp. 418 (E.D. Pa. 1982); Wright v. Columbia Univ., 520 F. Supp. 789 (E.D. Pa. 1981).

42 Doe v. Woodford County Bd. of Educ., 213 F.3d 921 (6th Cir. 2000).

43 State *ex rel.* Lambert by Lambert v. W. Va. State Bd. of Educ., 447 S.E.2d 901 (W. Va. Ct. App. 1994).

44 Rothschild v. Grottenthaler, 725 F. Supp. 776 (S.D.N.Y. 1989), *aff'd in part, vac'd and rem'd in part* 907 F.2d 286 (2d Cir. 1990).

45 Spells v. Cuyahoga Cmty. Coll., 889 F. Supp. 1023 (N.D. Ohio 1994).

46 Pierce v. Engle, 726 F. Supp. 1231 (D. Kan. 1989).

47 Adrain v. Alexander, 792 F. Supp. 124 (D.D.C. 1992).

48 Curcio v. Bridgeport Bd. of Educ., 477 F. Supp. 2d 515 (D. Conn. 2007).

49 Winston v. Me. Technical Coll. Sys., 631 A.2d 70 (Me. 1993).

50 Redlich v. Albany Law Sch. of Union Univ., 899 F. Supp. 100 (N.D.N.Y. 1995).

51 *See also* Harris v. Adams, 873 F.2d 929 (6th Cir. 1989) where an applicant was unable to show that his asthma substantially limited a major life activity.

52 Maddox v. Univ. of Tenn., 62 F.3d 843 (6th Cir. 1995).

53 Walders v. Garrett, 765 F. Supp. 303 (E.D. Va. 1991); Linares v. City of White Plains, 773 F. Supp. 559 (S.D.N.Y. 1991).

54 *See* Sch. Bd. of Nassau County v. Arline, 480 U.S. 273 (1987); Southeastern Cmty. Coll. v. Davis, 442 U.S. 397 (1979).

55 Santiago v. Temple Univ., 739 F. Supp. 974 (E.D. Pa. 1990).

56 Carr v. Reno, 23 F.3d 525 (D.C. Cir. 1994); Jackson v. Veterans Admin., 22 F.3d 277 (11th Cir. 1994); Linares v. City of White Plains, 773 F. Supp. 559 (S.D.N.Y. 1991).

57 Mustafa v. Clark County Sch. Dist., 876 F. Supp. 1177 (D. Nev. 1995), *aff'd in part, rev'd in part and rem'd* 157 F.3d 1169 (9th Cir. 1998).

58 Pandazides v. Va. Bd. of Educ., 804 F. Supp. 794 (E.D. Va. 1992), *rev'd on other grounds* 13 F.3d 823 (4th Cir. 1994).

59 Chiari v. City of League City, 920 F.2d 311 (5th Cir. 1991).

60 Wood v. Omaha Sch. Dist., 25 F.3d 667 (8th Cir. 1994).

61 *See, e.g.* Commonwealth, Dep't of Transp., Bureau of Driver Licensing v. Tinsley, 564 A.2d 286 (Pa. Commw. Ct. 1989).

62 Commonwealth, Dep't of Transp., Bureau of Driver Licensing v. Chalfant, 565 A.2d 1252 (Pa. Commw. Ct. 1989).

63 Bombrys v. City of Toledo, 849 F. Supp. 1210 (N.D. Ohio 1993).

64 Wilber v. Brady, 780 F. Supp. 837 (D.D.C. 1992).

65 Gonzalez v. Cal. State Pers. Bd., 39 Cal. Rptr. 2d 282 (Cal. Ct. App. 1995).

[66] Gedney v. Bd. of Educ. of the Town of Groton, 703 A.2d 804 (Conn. Ct. App. 1997).

[67] Fink v. New York City Dep't of Pers., 855 F. Supp. 69 (S.D.N.Y. 1994).

[68] McWright v. Alexander, 982 F.2d 222 (7th Cir. 1992).

[69] Commonwealth of Pa. v. Tinsley, 564 A.2d 286 (Pa. Commw. Ct. 1989).

[70] Byrne v. Bd. of Educ., Sch. Dist. of W. Allis - W. Milwaukee, 741 F. Supp. 167 (E.D. Wis. 1990).

[71] Ransom v. State of Ariz. Bd. of Regents, 983 F. Supp. 895 (D. Ariz. 1997).

[72] Mustafa v. Clark County Sch. Dist., 157 F.3d 1169 (9th Cir. 1998).

[73] Black v. Frank, 730 F. Supp. 1087 (S.D. Ala. 1990).

[74] Alexander v. Frank, 777 F. Supp. 516 (N.D. Tex. 1991).

[75] Huber v. Howard County, 849 F. Supp. 407 (D. Md. 1994).

[76] Walders v. Garrett, 765 F. Supp. 303 (E.D. Va. 1991).

[77] Ramirez v. New York City Bd. of Educ., 481 F. Supp. 2d 209 (E.D.N.Y. 2007).

[78] Nichols v. Harford County Bd. of Educ., 189 F. Supp. 2d 325 (D. Md. 2002).

[79] 42 U.S.C. § 2000d-7.

[80] Nieves-Marquez v. Commonwealth of P.R., 353 F.3d 108 (1st Cir. 2003).

[81] A.W. v. Jersey City Pub. Sch., 341 F.3d 234 (3d Cir. 2003).

[82] Bennett-Nelson v. La. Bd. of Regents, 431 F.3d 448 (5th Cir. 2005); Miller v. Tex. Tech Univ. Health Scis. Ctr., 421 F.3d 342 (5th Cir. 2005); Pace v. Bogalusa City Sch. Bd., 403 F.3d 272 (5th Cir. 2005).

[83] Carten v. Kent State Univ., 282 F.3d 391 (6th Cir. 2002).

[84] Jim C. v. United States, 235 F.3d 1079 (8th Cir. 2000).

[85] Robinson v. Kansas, 295 F.3d 1183 (10th Cir. 2002).

[86] *See also* Shepard v. Irving, 204 F. Supp. 2d 902 (E.D. Va. 2002); Patricia N. v. LeMahieu, 141 F. Supp. 2d (D. Haw. 2001); Patrick and Kathy W. v. LeMahieu, 165 F. Supp. 2d 1144 (D. Haw. 2001); Werner v. Colo. State Univ., 135 F. Supp. 2d 1137 (D. Colo. 2000).

[87] Garrett v. Univ. of Ala. at Birmingham, 261 F.3d 1242 (11th Cir. 2001), *on remand sub nom. from* Bd. of Trs. of the Univ. of Ala. v. Garrett, 531 U.S. 356, 121 S. Ct. 955, 148 L. Ed. 2d 866 (2001). *See also* Biggs v. Bd. of Educ. of Cecil County, 229 F. Supp. 2d 437 (D. Md. 2002).

[88] Swenson v. Lincoln County Sch. Dist. No. 2, 260 F. Supp. 2d 1136 (D. Wyo. 2003).

[89] Butler v. S. Glens Falls Cent. Sch. Dist., 106 F. Supp. 2d (N.D.N.Y. 2000). *See also* Patricia N. v. Lemahieu, 141 F. Supp. 2d 1243 (D. Haw. 2001).

[90] *See e.g.* Finn *ex rel.* Steven P. v. Harrison Cent. Sch. Dist., 473 F. Supp. 2d 477 (S.D.N.Y. 2007); Sellers v. Sch. Bd. of the City of Mannassas, 141 F.3d 524 (4th Cir. 1998).

[91] Bradley v. Ark. Dep't of Educ., 301 F.3d 952 (8th Cir. 2002).

[92] Doe v. Withers, Civ. No. 92-C-92, 20 IDELR 422 (W.Va. Cir. Ct. 1993).

[93] McCachren v. Blacklick Valley Sch. Dist., 217 F. Supp. 2d 594 (W.D. Pa. 2002).

Chapter 14

Barrier-Free Facilities

Ralph D. Mawdsley

Introduction

Until 1991, the Architectural Transportation Barriers Compliance Board (ATBCB) Establishment had the sole responsibility for the maintenance of barrier-free schools. Created in 1973 by Section 502 of the Handicapped Act,[1] the ATBCB used Section 504 of the Vocational Rehabilitation Act[2] to resolve violations of the Architectural Act.[3] Prior to passage of the Americans with Disabilities Act (ADA),[4] the Architectural Barriers Act of 1968 was the medium for declaring and standardizing accessibility standards. With the passage of the ADA, the agency that was empowered to promulgate regulations and enforce the ADA became the Department of Justice (DOJ).[5] However, the ATBCB has statutory authority to "establish and maintain … minimum guidelines and requirements for the standards issued pursuant to" the ADA, which then can be adopted by the DOJ.[6] In addition, since the ADA did not invalidate other federal laws,[7] the ATBCB can still conduct investigations, hold public hearings, and issue orders to insure compliance with the provisions of the Architectural Barriers Act.[8]

The ADA has imposed exhaustive requirements for accommodating the needs of persons with disabilities in terms of all new construction after January 26, 1993, and alterations to existing facilities after January 26, 1992. The ADA has three separate divisions. Title I of the ADA deals with discrimination in private sector employment.[9] Title II of the ADA,[10] which applies to public entities, covers all public schools,[11] while Title III,[12] which applies to public accommodations, covers all private schools,[13] except those controlled by religious organizations.[14] The ADA places responsibility for enforcement of the act on the Attorney General and the DOJ,[15] although the DOJ has been criticized for its inability to adequately investigate the increasing number of complaints.[16]

Legal Issues

Section 504 of the Vocational Rehabilitation Act requires that federally assisted programs and activities be readily accessible to and usable by individuals with disabilities. Under the ADA, Congress adopted two distinct systems: one to apply to existing facilities (designed and constructed before January 26, 1993) and another to apply to later-constructed facilities. Whereas the grandfathered facilities must remove barriers to accessibility only to the extent that such removal is "readily accessible,"[17] new facilities must be "readily accessible and usable to individuals with disabilities."[18] However, the ADA does not off-set the obligations under other federal or state laws, and state tort claims conferring greater remedies are clearly not preempted by the ADA.[19] The ADA applies to all new construction where the first occupancy occurred after January 26, 1992, or to alterations of existing facilities after January 26, 1993, but the statute does not apply to claims that arose prior to those dates.[20]

Generally, new construction must meet all of the ADA requirements except where full compliance would be "structurally impracticable,"[21] a term that will apply "only in those rare circumstances when the unique characteristics of terrain prevent the incorporation of accessibility features."[22] Regarding alterations, the ADA uses two important concepts, "primary function" and "accessible route," to determine the applicability of the statute. A primary function is a major activity for which the facility is intended[23] and an accessible route is a continuous unobstructed path connecting all accessible elements and spaces of a building or facility and includes both interior and exterior routes.[24]

An alteration that affects or could affect the usability of or access to an area of a facility that contains a primary function shall be made so as to ensure that, to the maximum extent feasible, the path of travel to the altered area as well as restrooms, telephones, and drinking fountains serving the altered area, are readily accessible to and usable by individuals with disabilities, unless such alterations are disproportionate in terms of the cost and scope (as determined under criteria established by the Attorney General).[25] However, if a particular type of facility is not required, then an accessible route is required under the ADA for only "a reasonable number, but at least one" of the facilities.[26]

The ADA imposes responsibilities on anyone in interstate commerce to make alterations to existing facilities that make them readily accessible to and usable by individuals with disabilities. Alterations include, but are not limited to, remodeling, renovation, rehabilitation, reconstruction, historic restoration, changes or re-arrangement in structural parts or elements, and changes or re-arrangement in the plan configuration of walls and full-height partitions. Normal maintenance, re-roofing, painting or wall papering, asbestos removal, and changes to mechanical and electrical systems are not alterations unless they affect the usability of the building or facility.[27]

Both the ADA and the Architectural Barriers Act reference the standards published by the American National Standards Institute (ANSI). The ANSI standards are the basis for the Uniform Federal Accessibility Standards (UFAS) published in the Federal Register.[28] ANSI is a private, national organization that has published recommendations on a wide range of subjects.

The basic ANSI standards for barrier-free design are ANSI A117.1-1980, with the most recent modifications found in ANSI A117.1-1987. The ANSI standards are entitled "American National Standards for Buildings and Facilities – Providing Accessibility and Usability for Physically Handicapped People."[29] The ADA has published its own complete set of standards and, generally, these standards are the same as those of ANSI A117.1-1980.[30] For the purposes of educational institutions, the exceptions deal with accessibility in new and altered construction for such items as parking places, toilets, telephones, and assembly areas.[31] When ADA standards differ from ANSI, the ADA standards prevail.

Specifications

Even with some differences between ADA and ANSI standards, ANSI is still the single most important and complete document of facility accessibility, in part because the ADA regulations follow ANSI, and in part because ANSI minimum guidelines are referenced in most state building codes.[32] ANSI standards have essentially achieved uniformity with UFAS, although ANSI "is basically a resource for design specifications and leaves to the enforcing agency the application of criteria such as where, when, and to what extent such specifications apply."[33] The purpose of the ANSI standards is to enable "persons with disabilities to achieve independence... [so they] can live, study, work, and participate in other community activities, fully developing their human potential...."[34] ANSI standards represent the collaborative effort of fifty-three different organizations as diverse as the American Association of Retired Persons, American Foundation for the Blind, American Hotel/Motel Association, American Society of Plumbing Engineers, Builders Hardware Manufacturers Association, National Conference of State on Building Codes and Standards, National Restaurant Association, and nine different federal agencies and cabinet-level departments.[35]

ANSI standards have been designed to deal with a wide range of physical disabilities, such as "the inability to walk, difficulty walking, reliance on walking aids, blindness and visual impairment, deafness and hearing impairment, incoordination, reaching and manipulation disabilities, lack of stamina, difficulty interpreting and reacting to sensory information and extremes of physical size."[36] The specifications remain the same "whether they are applied to new construction, remodeling alteration or rehabilitation"[37] and will be the appropriate standard to the extent they have not been modified by the ADA. ANSI standards are intended to be used in conjunction with other American National Standards, including Safety Code for Elevators and Escalators,[38] Power Operated Pedestrian Doors,[39] and Power Assist and Low Energy Operated Doors.[40] A complete, comparative listing of all topics addressed in graphics and dimensions in ANSI standards and the ADA reveals that the concern of accessibility in both, despite some differences, is one of function rather than location, be it a school, hotel, or manufacturing plant.[41] Other topics include space allowances and reach ranges (e.g., wheel chair turning space, forward reach, side reach); accessible route (e.g., passing space, headroom, slope, egress); protruding objects; ground and floor surfaces; parking spaces and passenger loading zones; curb ramps; stairs; elevators; platform lifts; windows; doors; entrances; drinking fountains and water coolers; water closets; toilet stalls; urinals; lavatories; sinks and mirrors; bathtubs; shower stalls; storage; grab bars and tub shower seats; control and operating mechanisms; alarms and detectable warnings; signage; telephones; seating, tables, and work surfaces; auditorium and assembly areas; and dwelling units.[42]

In addition, states can and have made valuable contributions to ANSI standards.[43] Modifications of the standards to suit children is one area of interest. Specifications in both ANSI and the ADA "are based upon adult dimensions and anthropomorphics,"[44] but federal regulations permit modifications "concerning the age groups of the individuals who will use the buildings or equipment."[45] The areas of UFAS affected by the standards for children are:

1. space allowance and reach range of twenty inches;
2. parking and passenger loading zones with the loading zones protected from weather;
3. ramps with handrails the same height as ramps;
4. elevators with changes in the distance of hall call buttons, car controls, and emergency communications above the floor;
5. drinking fountains and water closets with varying distances for grab bars, toilet seats, flush controls, and dispensers;
6. urinals placed thirty-two inches above the floor;
7. shower stalls with modified height of seats and controls;
8. storage including shelves and hooks placed a maximum of thirty-six inches above the floor;
9. signs placed forty inches above the floor;
10. telephones at a thirty-six-inch maximum above the floor;
11. seating, tables, and work surfaces with varying heights for chairs, knee clearance. and work surfaces;
12. restaurants and cafeterias with a percentage of fixed seating or tables for handicapped and height of tray slides;
13. libraries with a maximum reach of thirty-six inches for card catalogs, magazine displays, dictionary stands, and reference stacks;
14. locker rooms and gymnasium lockers with locker shelves and hooks at a maximum of twenty-six inches above the floor and lockers with minimum twenty-eight-inch openings;

15. and classrooms including wall-mounted objects like pencil sharpeners, light switches, and blackboards having a centerline maximum height of thirty-six inches above the floor.[46]

Enforcement

The ADA provides a private cause of action as well as investigations by the Department of Justice and suits by the Attorney General.[47] However, architects cannot be held liable for failure to design and construct in accordance with the ADA.[48] Even with enforcement of the rights of the disabled under the ADA, a significant remedy continues to exist under Section 504 of the Vocational Rehabilitation Act.[49] Since the ADA is based on the Interstate Commerce Power[50]—while section 504 applies only to institutions, organizations, or persons receiving federal assistance[51]—the ADA has become the major enforcement device for private institutions not receiving federal assistance.[52] Both section 504 and the ADA have broad provisions prohibiting denial of the enjoyment of benefits, goods, services, privileges, advantages, or accommodations.[53]

In program accessibility, both section 504 and the ADA distinguish between existing facilities and new construction. Alterations under the ADA have been discussed earlier.[54] Under section 504, existing facilities can be "viewed in [their] entirety... [as to whether they are] readily accessible to and usable by handicapped persons."[55] It is not necessary in making alterations "to make each of its existing facilities or every part of a facility accessible to and usable by handicapped persons."[56] Structural changes are not required to existing facilities "where other methods are effective in achieving compliance...."[57] In new construction, "[e]ach new facility constructed by, on behalf of, or for the use of a recipient shall be designed and constructed in such manner that the facility is readily accessible to and usable by handicapped persons...."[58] Where alterations are made to existing facilities, they shall "to the maximum extent feasible, be made in an accessible manner."[59]

Litigation can arise in a variety of settings where facilities do not meet the requirements of section 504 or the ADA. In many cases, lawsuits have arisen because school districts have failed to take steps to make certain that existing facilities being used by the districts are barrier-free. Two cases illustrate the kinds of violations that can be litigated. A public school district violated both section 504 and the ADA where an existing theater at which the district's graduation programs were conducted was not accessible to and usable by persons with disabilities. The district had also failed to provide notice ensuring that interested persons, including those with impaired visions or hearing, could obtain information as to the existence and location of graduations services, activities, and facilities that would be accessible to and usable by persons with disabilities.[60] Another school district violated both statutes when it conducted programs and activities on an elementary school's existing stage and playground that were inaccessible to and unusable by persons with disabilities insofar as the only route to the stage was by stairs; there were no wheelchair-traversable routes connecting the school building's exit doors to the roadway adjacent to the playground; and there was no surface area within the playground that was accessible to or usable by a student using a wheelchair.[61]

Both section 504 and the ADA are clear that alterations to existing facilities need not be made if they would be too expensive. The issue of cost, however, is an affirmative defense for the educational institution. In an action by a disabled high school student, alleging that the school was inaccessible to her, the school district was not required to incur expenses to demonstrate that facility alterations would result in undue financial burdens but, rather, was entitled to raise the financial burden in remedying architectural barriers to make the school accessible to students with wheelchairs as an affirmative defense.[62] However, once the school district entered into a consent decree, a court could order that the school district issue a report addressing the following safety hazards:

1. ramp slopes in excess of 10 percent;
2. cross-slopes greater than 3 percent on ramps;
3. ramps lacking handrails that meet the specifications of [federal and state law];
4. ramps lacking level areas at the top, middle, and bottom of ramps where required by the specifications of [federal and state law];
5. gratings parallel to the direction of travel;
6. gaps larger than 1.5 inches in gratings; and
7. any other conditions that the parties agree constitute safety hazards.[63]

Employee complaints of any form of disability discrimination are handled by the Equal Employment Opportunity Commission (EEOC) and can result in litigation if a negotiated settlement is not possible.[64] Under the ADA, the Department of Justice can also investigate discrimination.[65] In the case of accessibility for students or employees under the Architectural Barriers Act, investigations are handled by the ATBCB, which can hold administrative hearings and issue compliance orders as well as withhold or suspend federal funds.[66]

Litigation involving public schools under Title II of the ADA or under section 504 permits injunctive relief, attorney fees, and compensatory damages under certain conditions. Title II borrows the intentional discrimination standard for damages from section 504, but proof of intent can be inferred from a school's deliberate indifference. Thus, where a school district built a new high school that did not comply with requirements regarding parking lot signage, resulting in signs being covered with snow in the winter and disability spaces being occupied by other vehicles, a federal court opined that failure of school officials to address the problem when they knew the school was not in compliance with the ADA can be evidence of deliberate indifference.[67] However, punitive damages are not available under Title II of the ADA or under section 504.[68]

Since all states now have barrier-free legislation, the responsibility for ensuring accessibility has been a state and local matter.[69] Enforcement of disability accessibility can include review of all building designs by state building officials[70] and refusal to issue a certificate of occupancy.[71] Unfortunately, state enforcement of accessibility requirements can be erratic, inconsistent, and perhaps even nonexistent.[72] Remedies under state laws may vary, and damage awards may be prohibited in certain situations where enforcement is permissible only by government officials.[73] More viable remedies for physically disabled persons would be filing a complaint with the state's Human Rights Commission or filing a lawsuit seeking injunctive relief to compel compliance, damages, and attorney fees.[74] If the state Human Rights Commission is not effective in addressing complaints, other state remedies may be curtailed or be illusory if the Human Rights Act prohibits private causes of action to enforce the statute.[75]

In addition to state and federal standards, some larger cities may have separate accessibility guidelines. A state may leave enforcement to local officials,[76] a practice that can create problems of enforcement by those without experience or expertise[77] or with differing interpretations of identical code sections.[78] However, if the facility has been built with federal funds, another and perhaps better option would be to file a complaint with the ATBCB.[79]

Recommendations for Practice

School officials are well advised to check their statewide building code, as well as the ADA, regarding disability accessibility before altering existing facilities or constructing new ones. Alarmist fears of excessive escalation in building costs to achieve accessibility have largely been just that—unsubstantiated fears.[80] School officials need to examine building codes carefully for key elements to determine whether

1. the scope of renovations requires compliance with accessibility;
2. the standard for accessibility has been published;
3. the district has an established approval process for determining compliance with accessibility;
4. a variance is necessary for intended alterations or new construction; and
5. employees are adequately instructed in the importance of maintaining an "accessible route" under the ADA.

Endnotes

1 29 U.S.C. § 792(b)(1).

2 29 U.S.C. § 794.

3 42 U.S.C. §§ 4151-4171. For a discussion of early cases under this Act, *see* Goldman, *Architectural Barriers: A Perspective on Progress*, 5 W. NEW ENG. L. REV. 466 (1983).

4 42 U.S.C. §§ 12101-12213.

5 42 U.S.C. § 12206(a)(1).

6 42 U.S.C. § 12204(a)-(b); 29 U.S.C. § 792(b)(3)(B).

7 56 Fed. Reg. 35547 (§ 36.103(b)) (July 26, 1991) .

8 29 U.S.C. §§ 792(d)(1) and 792(e)(2)(3).

9 42 U.S.C. §§ 12111-12117.

10 42 U.S.C. §§ 12131-12150, 12161-12165.

11 42 U.S.C. § 12131(1).

12 42 U.S.C. §§ 12181-12189. The categories covered under Title III include the following: Places of lodging; Establishments serving food or drink; Places of exhibition or entertainment; Places of public gathering; Sales or rental establishments; Stations used for specified public transportation; Places of public display or collection; Places or recreation; Places of education; Social service center establishments; Places of exercise or recreation. 42 U.S.C. § 12181(7).

13 42 U.S.C. § 12182(a).

14 28 C.F.R. § 36.102(e).

15 56 Fed. Reg. 35602-35603 (§§ 36.501-503) (July 26, 1991).

16 *See* D. Russell Hymas & Brett R. Parkinson, *Architectural Barriers Under the ADA: An Answer to the Judiciary's Struggle with Technical Non-Compliance*, 39 CAL. W. L. REV. 349 (2003).

17 42 U.S.C. § 12182(b)(2)(A)(iv).

18 42 U.S.C. § 12183(a)(1).

19 *See* Gaither v. Barron, 924 F. Supp. 134 (M.D. Ala. 1996) (in dismissing an ADA claim of harassment, the court observed that the plaintiff may have had state civil and criminal claims).

20 *See* State *ex rel.* Human Servs. Dep't v. Penny J., 890 P.2d 389 (N.M. Ct. App. 1994).

21 *See* Long v. Coast Resorts, Inc., 267 F.3d 918 (9th Cir. 2001) where the defense of structural impracticability was not available to a hotel where the terrain had no unique characteristics that would make changes to width of all bathroom doors unusually difficult to achieve.

22 36 C.F.R. Pt. 1191, App. A, ADA Accessibility Guidelines for Buildings and Facilities 4.1.1(5).

23 56 Fed. Reg. 35600 (§ 36.403(b)) (July 26, 1991).

24 36 C.F.R. Pt. 1191, App. A, ADA Accessibility Guidelines for Buildings and Facilities 3.5.

25 36 C.F.R. Pt. 1191, App. A, ADA Accessibility Guidelines for Buildings and Facilities 4.1.6.(K)(2).

26 Title III Technical Assistance Manual III – 5.300.

27 36 C.F.R. Pt. 1191, App. A, ADA Accessibility Guidelines for Buildings and Facilities 3.5.

28 *See* 56 Fed. Reg. 35408-35756 (July 16, 1991).

29 49 Fed. Reg. 31528-31617, August 7, 1984.

30 36 C.F.R. § 1191.1 and 49 C.F.R. § 37.9.

31 *See* 36 C.F.R. Pt. 1191, App. A, ADA Accessibility Guidelines for Buildings and Facilities 4.1.1-4.1.7.

32 *See* Note, *Access to Buildings and Equal Employment Opportunities for the Disabled: A Survey of State Statutes*, 50 TENN. L.Q. 1067 (1977).

33 American National Standard for Buildings and Facilities-Providing Accessibility and Usability for Physically Handicapped People 3 (ANSI A117.1-1986).

34 *Id.*

35 For complete list, see *Id.* at 4.

[36] *Id.* at 11.

[37] *Id.* at 12.

[38] ANSI/ASME A117.1-1984.

[39] ANSI/BHMA A156.10-1985.

[40] ANSI/BHMA A156.19.1984.

[41] ADA regulations 5-14 are different from ANSI A117.1 in their entirety and address the following areas: Restaurants and Cafeterias, Medical Care Facilities, Business, Mercantile and Civic, Libraries, Accessible Transient Lodging, Transportation Facilities, Judicial, Regulatory and Legislative Facilities, Detention and Correctional Facilities, Accessible Residential Housing, and Public Rights-of-Way.

[42] *See generally* the ADA regulations at 36 C.F.R. Pt. 1191, App. A, ADA Accessibility Guidelines for Buildings and Facilities 4.2-4.35, which are identical with ANSI A117.1-1980.

[43] ADA regulations are clear that Congress did not intend to displace any of the rights or remedies provided by federal or state law that provide greater or equal protection to individuals with disabilities. 56 Fed. Reg. 35593 (§ 36.103), July 26, 1991.

[44] Providing Accessibility at 12 (ANSI A117.1-1986); 36 C.F.R. §2.1 (ADA).

[45] 24 C.F.R. § 304.50.

[46] OSEP-86-14, Recommendations For Accessibility to Serve Physically Handicapped Children In Elementary Schools 2-23.

[47] 56 Fed. Reg. 35602 (§ 36.501-508) (July 26, 1991).

[48] Paralyzed Veterans of Am. v. Ellerbe Becket Architects & Engineers, 945 F. Supp. 1 (D.C. 1996); Kuchmas v. Towson Univ., 2007 WL 2694186 (D. Md. 2007).

[49] 28 C.F.R. § 41.1 Executive Order 12250, which had empowered the Justice Department to coordinate the implementation of section 504 along with Title VI and Title IX, has been merged into the ADA.

[50] *See* Fed. Reg. at 35593 (§36.104-Definitions), July 26, 1991.

[51] 28 C.F.R. § 41.3(d).

[52] 56 Fed. Reg. 35554 (July 26, 1991). "Private schools, including elementary and secondary schools, are covered by the rules as places of accommodation."

[53] 28 C.F.R. § 41.3(d); 56 Fed. Reg. at 355595 (§§ 36.201, 36.202), July 26, 1991.

[54] *See supra* notes 15-19.

[55] 28 C.F.R. § 45.521(a).

[56] *Id.*

[57] *Id.* at § 42.531(b). For example, in an older multi-story building, it is not necessary to install an elevator if the entire program is on the first floor. 28 C.F.R. §§ 41-56, 41.58; 45 C.F.R. § 4.23. The ADA has an elevator exemption for any altered building that has less than three stories. 36 C.F.R. § 4.1.3(5)(a). *See* Association for Disabled Americans v. Concorde Gaming Corp., 158 F. Supp. 2d 1353 (S.D. Fla. 2001) where installation of elevator not required on gaming ship where it would cost $200,000 and result in ship being in dry-dock for two months.

[58] 28 C.F.R. § 45.522(a).

[59] *Id.*

[60] *In re* West Warwick Pub. Sch. Dist., 4 ADD 390 (Dept. of Educ. 1993).

[61] *In re* Whitman-Hanson Reg'l Sch. Dist., 4 ADD 399 (Dept. of Educ. 1993).

[62] Putnam v. Oakland Unified Sch. Dist., 15 ADD 1361 (N.D. Cal. 1995).

[63] Putnam v. Oakland Unified Sch. Dist., 980 F. Supp. 1094, 1097 (N.D. Cal. 1997).

[64] 28 C.F.R. §§ 46.601-42.613. Remedies can include damages, injunctive relief, and attorney fees. 29 C.F.R. § 794a; 42 U.S.S. § 2000e-5(f)-(k).

[65] 56 Fed. Reg. 36.501-505 (July 26, 1991). Remedies can include injunctive relief, other equitable relief, and damages.

[66] *See* 29 U.S.C. § 792(d).

[67] *See* Swenson v. Lincoln County Sch. Dist., 260 F. Supp. 2d 1136 (D. Wyo. 2003).

[68] *See* Barnes v. Gorman, 536 U.S. 181 (2002).

[69] *E.g., see* CAL. CIV. CODE § 54.

[70] *E.g., see* OHIO REV. CODE ANN. § 378.111.

[71] Tex. Civ. Stat. Ann. Art. 601b. *See* Granny's Cottage v. Town of Occuquan, 352 S.E.2d 10 (Va. Ct. App. 1987) (whenever a part of a building is enlarged, extended or altered in Virginia, the Uniform Stateside Building Code prohibits occupancy until a certificate of use and occupancy has been issued).

[72] *See generally*, White, *Washington State's barrier-Free Code: Still Misunderstood After All These Years*, 20 GONZAGA L. REV. 229 (1984-85). *See also*, R. Burgdorf, The Legal Rights of Handicapped Persons 465 (1980) (local enforcement may be in the hands of persons possessing limited or no experience in the fields of architectural barriers and with persons with disabilities).

[73] *See, e.g.*, Donald v. Café Royale, Inc., 266 Cal. Rptr. 804 (Cal. Ct. App. 1990) where enforcement of part of state statute limited to county attorney, city attorney, or attorney general. *See also* Urhausen v. Longs Drug Stores, 65 Cal., Rptr. 3d 838 (Cal. App. 1 Dist. 2007).

[74] For an explanation of the State of Washington's experience, *see* White at 243-44.

[75] *See* CODE OF VIRGINIA § 2.1-725 (prohibits private causes of action and tort actions "instituted instead of or in addition to the current statutory actions for unlawful discrimination.") Cf. 56 Fed. Reg. at 35602 (§ 36.501) where ADA expressly provides for private causes of action.

[76] *See* N.Y. Pub. Bldgs. Law § 52.

[77] *See* White and Burgdorf, *supra* note 72.

[78] *See* White, *supra* note 72 at 242.

[79] Architectural Barriers Act of 1968, 42 U.S.C. §§ 4151-4157 (1981); 36 C.F.R. § 1190.1-240 (1980); Rehabilitation Act of 1973, 29 U.S.C. §§ 791-796 (1982); 34 C.F.R. §§ 104.21-104.30 (1984).

[80] *See* Goldman, *supra* note 72 at 486-88; White, *supra* note 72 at 233.

Chapter 15

IEPs, Least Restrictive Environment, and Placement

Jean B. Crockett

Introduction

The Individuals with Disabilities Education Act (IDEA)[1], originally authorized as The Education for All Handicapped Children Act (EAHCA) in 1975, began as a remedy for excluding millions of children from public instruction based solely upon their disabilities. The IDEA went beyond the limits of traditional civil rights legislation in affirming the guarantee of a free appropriate public education (FAPE) through an individualized education program (IEP) for each eligible student with a disability. From its enactment to its most recent reauthorization, the law has required that decisions about special education programming and placements be team-based and child-centered. The least restrictive environment (LRE) principle guides placement decisions so that students can be taught in regular classes, to the maximum extent appropriate to their individual needs and in alternative settings when teams of parents and professionals determine that they cannot make satisfactory progress in regular classes, even with specialized supports.

Although legal procedures guide its delivery, special education is not about law; it is about educating students with disabilities in specialized ways that build upon their strengths and strengthen their weaknesses. Special education is not about *where* students are educated but about *how* young people are prepared for their futures through far-sighted programming and personalized supports. If students with disabilities were just like everyone else, there would be no need for special education. If schools were not accountable for the learning of every student, there would be less urgency to treat some students differently in order to ensure their success. Special education continues to rely on law because justice has not been blind to students whose learning needs are exceptional or to the extraordinary efforts required by school systems in providing their education. In this chapter, the interplay among IEPs, the least restrictive environment, and placements is explained and illustrated with examples drawn from the IDEA Amendments of 2004, the 2006 Federal Regulations, and relevant case law. References are made to recent guidance from the U.S. Supreme Court addressing IEP disputes and the shared responsibility of school officials and parents to improve outcomes for students with disabilities.

Legal Issues

School principals are critical to ensuring effective special education in schools that are challenged to provide all students with a high-quality education as required by the No Child Left Behind Act of 2001 (NCLB).[2] NCLB expects most students with disabilities to learn the same academic content as nondisabled students. The IDEA 2004, although aligned with NCLB, expects educators to teach special education students differently and sometimes to teach them different things in ways that are ensured through a personalized IEP. Some educators and members of society prefer students with disabilities to perform in the same way as typically developing students, even though doing things differently would lead to more efficient performance.[3] Special education, in contrast, addresses individual differences head-on, providing students who learn differently with more intensive and specialized instruction so they can learn appropriately and participate in their communities.

Defining Special Education and the Purpose of the IDEA

According to the statute, the purpose of the IDEA is clear: "to ensure that all children with disabilities have available to them a free appropriate public education that emphasizes special education and related services designed to meet their unique needs, and prepare them for further education, employment and independent living."[4] All children with disabilities ages 3-21 who need special education have the right to FAPE, including children with disabilities who have been suspended or expelled from school, as well as children who are advancing from grade to grade who have not failed or been retained in a course or grade.[5]

The provision of FAPE, in the wording of the purpose statement, emphasizes special education and related services. As defined in the statute, special education has an instructional mission meaning "specially designed *instruction,* at no cost to parents, to meet the unique needs of a child with a disability including instruction conducted in the classroom, in the home, in hospitals and institutions, and in other settings."[6] The term *specially designed instruction* was defined for the first time in the regulations to the IDEA Amendments of 1997 in the following way:

> Specially-designed instruction means adapting, as appropriate to the needs of an eligible child under this part, the content, methodology, or delivery of instruction-
>
> (i) To address the unique needs of the child that result from the child's disability; and
>
> (ii) To ensure access of the child to the general curriculum, so that he or she can meet the educational standards within the jurisdiction of the public agency that apply to all children.[7]

The sequence of these requirements indicates that ensuring genuine access to the general curriculum depends upon first addressing a student's unique needs. The primary directive for school officials is to provide special education—specially designed instruction—that addresses the specific disability-related needs of each student. Special education, with its related services and specialized supports, is the vehicle through which the IDEA delivers the individualized "in-puts," or "the counter-impairment' interventions," designed to help students by reducing the effects of their disability.[8] When appropriate techniques are delivered effectively, the likelihood is increased that each student will benefit and be able to adjust to the demands of the schoolhouse. The secondary imperative is to ensure that special education students have access to the general curriculum. School officials must ensure that all students have access to the same opportunities because if appropriate special education is being provided to them, more students with disabilities should be able to benefit from the experiences available to typically developing students.

It is also important to note that participation in the general curriculum does not mean the same thing as inclusion in general education classes. "Inclusion in a regular classroom concerns the setting where a student with a disability is educated.... Participation in the general curriculum concerns what a student learns."[9] The IDEA has never required that students receive inclusive instruction, but the law expects that students for whom the LRE is not the general classroom will be taught the general curriculum to the maximum extent appropriate to their learning needs wherever they receive instruction.

In providing students with FAPE, the IDEA requires school personnel to follow a proper sequence: finding a student eligible to receive special education, developing the student's IEP, and then determining the instructional placement that, for this particular student, constitutes the LRE.[10] In order to ensure educational benefit for individual students and to protect their civil rights in the process, decisions regarding IEPs and instructional placement must never be made by one individual—either a parent or a school official. Instead, programming and placement decisions are to be made by the consensus of a team comprising the child's parents and school personnel.[11]

IEPs: Prescribing an Appropriate Education

A free appropriate public education remains the centerpiece of the IDEA 2004, and the concept of FAPE is still assured through the IEP process. The IDEA defines the term *free appropriate public education* as special education and related services that are provided at public expense, under public direction, and that meet the standards set by the state's department of education. School officials must provide FAPE across the grade levels for school-aged youth in preschools, elementary schools, or secondary schools, and the special education and related services students receive must be provided in conformity with their IEPs.[12] An IEP is a written document that describes a child's educational needs, details the special education and related services the district will provide to meet those needs, and stipulates the goals that will serve to assess whether the student's needs were, indeed, met.[13]

Failure to develop and implement an IEP correctly is considered by courts as a denial of FAPE and a violation of law. Although formats will vary across school systems, each IEP must include the following information for the following reasons:

1. ***Performance Data***. The IDEA 2004 directs that an IEP must address the student's "present levels of academic achievement and functional performance."[14] The description must include how the disability affects the student's participation and progress in the general curriculum (or, for preschoolers, appropriate activities). This statement provides the starting point from which progress will be assessed, and it is recommended that performance data be stated measureably.

2. ***Measureable Annual Goals***. Measurable annual goals are required in IEPs. The IDEA 2004 stipulates the inclusion of academic and functional goals, eliminating mandatory short-term objectives for most students. A description of benchmarks or short-term objectives must be included only for significantly disabled students taking off-level assessments, or what the statute refers to as "alternate assessments aligned to alternate achievement standards."[15]

   Traditionally, benchmarks or short-term objectives have been included in IEPs so that personnel would know how to meet the student's disability-related needs and how to enable involvement and progress in the general curriculum. Measureable goals have always been required so that the effectiveness of the district services could be evaluated.[16] Meeting each of the student's educational needs that result from the disability is critically important because disabled students often need intensive instruction in curricular areas not addressed by the general education curriculum such as social skills, self advocacy, cognitive strategies, and independent living.

3. ***A Means to Measure Progress***. A statement is required to show how the child's progress toward the annual goals will be measured. The IDEA 2004 allows school systems to use "quarterly or other periodic reports, concurrent with the issuance of report cards" that delineate the progress the child is making toward meeting the annual goals.[17] The parents of special education students should be informed at least as often as they are informed about the progress of their nondisabled children so they might evaluate the extent to which the progress is sufficient to enable their child to achieve the goals by the end of the year.[18]

4. ***Services and Modifications***. A statement must address the special education, related services, and supplementary aids and services that are to be provided to the student. The IDEA 2004 requires that these practices are to be "based on peer-reviewed research to the extent practicable."[19] The statement must also address specific program modifications or supports for personnel so that the student can progress toward annual goals, progress in the general curriculum, and be educated and participate in extracurricular and nonacademic activities with other students, both those with disabilities and those without disabilities.[20] The regular educator on the IEP team is expected to help in determining the appropriate classroom services and modifications necessary for teaching the student appropriately.[21]

5. ***Instructional Placement***. An explanation must address the extent, if any, to which the student will not participate with nondisabled students in regular classes and in non-academic activities. As a result, the percentage of time a student spends in special settings for special purposes can be linked directly to the measurable goals, services, and modifications that the IEP team determined to be most appropriate for the student. This practice prevents teams from determining placements by disability category or by administrative convenience and promotes placements that foster the delivery of appropriate instruction.[22]

6. ***Individually Appropriate Testing Accommodations***. The IDEA 2004 shifts the emphasis from modifying test administration so that students with disabilities might participate in assessments to addressing accountability for results. New language requires a statement of "any individual appropriate accommodations that are necessary to measure the academic achievement and functional performance of the child on State and districtwide assessments." If the IEP team determines that the student will take an alternate assessment of achievement, a statement must address why he or she cannot participate in the regular assessment and why the alternate assessment is individually appropriate.[23]

7. ***Initiation Date and Service Delivery Details***. The projected date for the beginning of the services and modifications prescribed for the student and the anticipated frequency, location, and duration of those services and modifications must be included in the IEP. Indicating dates and details helps personnel know when to start and under what circumstances they are to provide service delivery.[24]

8. ***Transition Services***. The IDEA 2004 emphasizes accountability for transition services promoting post-school employment or education for students with disabilities. New provisions require that a statement of appropriate, measurable, postsecondary goals and transition

> services be formulated no later than the first IEP in effect when a student turns sixteen years old, and then be updated annually. Specific, measurable goals must be based upon age-appropriate transition assessments related to training, education, and employment, and, when appropriate, independent living skills. The transition services to be provided (including the prescribed courses of study) must be necessary to assist the student in reaching those goals. At least one year before the student reaches the age of majority under state law, a statement must be included in the IEP signifying that the student has been informed of the rights that would transfer to him or her upon reaching the age of majority.[25]

Additional considerations come into play as teams develop each student's IEP. Teams must consider the strengths of the student and the parents' concerns for enhancing the education of their child. Documentation that the team has considered these issues is recommended practice. IEPs should also reflect the results of the initial or most recent evaluation of the student and, as appropriate, the results of the student's performance on any general state or district-wide assessment programs.[26]

In certain circumstances, special factors must be considered by the team and documented in the IEP.[27] In the case of a student whose behavior impedes his or her learning or that of others, IEP teams must consider, if appropriate, strategies to address that behavior, including positive behavioral interventions, strategies, and supports. It is important to note that this requirement is not just for students with emotional disturbance. In the case of students with limited English proficiency, IEP teams must consider language needs as they relate to the IEP. For students who are blind or visually impaired, IEP teams must provide for instruction in Braille and the use of Braille unless the team determines, after an evaluation of the student's reading and writing skills and needs, that instruction in Braille or the use of Braille is not individually appropriate.[28]

IEP teams must also consider the communication needs of students. In the case of a student who is deaf or hard of hearing, the team must consider language and communication needs; opportunities for direct communications with peers and professional personnel in the student's language and communication mode; academic level; and full range of needs, including opportunities for direct instruction in the student's language and communication mode. IEP teams must consider whether students require assistive technology devices and services. If, in considering any of these special factors, the team determines that a student needs a particular device or service (including an intervention, accommodation, or other program modification) in order to receive FAPE, the team must include a statement to that effect in the student's IEP.[29]

The IDEA 2004 adds provisions designed to reduce the number of meetings and the amount of paperwork associated with IEPs. These provisions address attendance at meetings, changes to the IEP, multi-year IEPs, and programming for transfer students. In addition to providing for the excusal of participants from meetings, the IDEA 2004 states that after the student's annual review meeting, parents and school personnel may agree to modify the IEP and to document changes in writing without holding a formal meeting. The new law also prescribes a pilot program allowing school systems in fifteen states to offer parents the option of a multi-year IEP, not to exceed three years, that would coincide with natural transition points throughout their child's schooling. In addition, if the parents agree, IEP teams may use an Individual Family Service Plan (IFSP) for young children up to age 5 making the transition from early intervention services to school-aged special education. In a significant departure from prior practice, the IDEA 2004 requires school systems to ensure FAPE to students with IEPs transferring from other states within the same academic year. Services comparable to those in the previous IEP must be provided, in consultation with parents, until the school system conducts an evaluation and, if appropriate, develops a new IEP. Students with an IEP transferring from schools within the same state within the same academic year are also to be provided with comparable services to the prior IEP until the receiving school system adopts the prior IEP or develops and implements a new one.[30]

In reviewing the critical components and special factors to be included in developing IEPs, it becomes clear how the IEP document is intended to carry out the stated purpose of the IDEA. An IEP is not a simple plan of action; an IEP is a specific program designed to achieve results for a specific student. Educational programs of any kind are designed to address learning targets by setting measureable goals and developing ways to evaluate whether the services provided to the recipients were sufficient to meet the goals. Individualized education programs are no exception. To address the kinds of educational benefit a student might receive, the IEP process must rely on an analysis of performance data enhanced by the thoughtful consideration of the transition supports necessary to guide a special education student toward his or her future.

Determining the Extent of Educational Benefit

School officials might well ask the question, what is the proper measure of educational benefit for special education students in this era of standards-based reform?[31] The basic right to learn is the centerpiece of the accountability movement, and the proof of learning is now assumed to rest in positive results, not perfectly executed procedures. Program improvements and educational progress for typically developing students are being assessed against standard measures. However, assessing the progress of special education students is complicated by the nature of the disability and the type of assessments used by most states. Accommodations can conflict with the construct validity of tests, and research has yet to provide assurance that these assessments are accurately measuring what students really know and are able to do. There are also major concerns with whether these assessments are broad enough to capture the various ways that special education students demonstrate their capabilities rather than their disabilities.[32]

A fixed standard of *appropriate* has never been set by Congress nor established by the courts.[33] However, as early as the 1980s, courts determined that *appropriate* meant tailored to a child's individual needs, not to the needs of the school system, and that access to public schooling for children with disabilities fell short of requiring schools to provide the very best in programming.[34] Since the 1982 Supreme Court case of *Board of Education v. Rowley,*[35] cases addressing a free appropriate public education have hinged on the provision of an IEP designed to address a student's unique educational needs. Educational benefit was not substantively defined by the Supreme Court as an opportunity equal to that of non-disabled children, nor did the justices establish a test that would determine the adequacy of the benefits special education students should receive. However, the court provided guidance in the form of a two-part inquiry to determine if the programming designed for a student was appropriate. First, has the program embodied in the IEP been developed by the school system in a manner procedurally consistent with the law, and second, is the IEP based on a student's unique educational needs and reasonably calculated to confer educational benefit? If this two-part analysis has been met, the school system has complied with the obligations imposed by Congress, and "the courts can require no more."[36]

Most states define an appropriate education according to the federal standard set by the Supreme Court, and in some cases, colorful language has illustrated its meaning. For example, the Sixth Circuit used an automotive metaphor in noting that school systems are required to provide "the educational equivalent of a serviceable Chevrolet" to each student, rather than a Cadillac. The court noted that "the Chevrolet offered to [the student] is in fact a much nicer model than that offered to the average student," suggesting that a customized model offers special value in driving students with special needs toward successful outcomes.[37] This last concept is important to note because the benefit conferred by an IEP must be more than de minimis or trivial.

Some courts have struggled to be more explicit in relating the concept of appropriateness to an individual student's needs, taking into consideration the child's capacity to learn.[38] In recent years, experts have called for defining *appropriate* by linking the contents of the IEP with empirical data about student outcomes. Increased attention to academic performance, especially for students with learning disabilities, characterizes some decisions in which passing grades in regular classes were seen as indicators of FAPE for students pursuing a regular high school diploma.[39] Good grades may provide some evidence of compliance with the IDEA, but as a matter of law, they do not determine whether a school district provided FAPE. In some cases, good report card grades were seen as encouragements rather than as achievements reflecting a student's progress.[40] In *Hall v. Vance County Board of Education,*[41] the Fourth Circuit discounted grades and turned to standardized test scores and independent evaluations to determine that a student with severe learning disabilities had been denied FAPE, despite passing grades and promotion to the next grade level. The Supreme Court in *Florence Country School District Four v. Carter*[42] emphasized that the appropriate amount of regular education progress depends upon the abilities of each individual special education student. Some students, because of the extent of their disabilities, will not be able to perform at grade level or will take more time than typical to do so.

In the case of *Cypress-Fairbanks Independent School District v. Michael F.*,[43] the Fifth Circuit added to the calculus by determining that an appropriate IEP must provide educational benefits that are likely to produce meaningful progress for a student, rather than regression or minimal educational advancement. In finding that the school system's IEP provided an appropriate education to Michael, a student with attention deficit hyperactivity disorder (ADHD) and Tourette Syndrome, the court applied a four-point test: (1) was the program individualized on the basis of the student's assessment and performance; (2) was the program administered in the least restrictive environment; (3) were the services provided in a coordinated and collaborative manner by the key stakeholders; and (4) were positive academic and nonacademic benefits demonstrated?[44]

The circuit court determined that the district's seventh-grade IEPs were specifically designed to address Michael's individual needs and placed him in the least restrictive educational environment consistent with those needs. The court relied on testimony provided by individuals who had direct and frequent contact with Michael, including personnel who coordinated his academic and behavioral services when he attended district schools. Accordingly, Michael was achieving passing grades in classes, as well as managing his behavior well enough to eat lunch and travel through the building without a chaperone. Using the four-point test, the court determined that the IEP "was reasonably calculated to, and in fact did, produce meaningful educational benefits both academically and behaviorally."[45] In this case, the court denied tuition reimbursement to Michael's parents for enrolling him in private school because the district had met its obligation to provide an appropriate IEP. The court also ordered his parents to pay the costs of the litigation.[46]

The Fifth Circuit similarly defined *appropriate* as being demonstrated by student outcome data in the case of *Houston Independent School District v. Bobby R.*, in which parents were also denied reimbursement for their son's private school tuition.[47] In deciding whether the IEP for Caius, a student with dyslexia and attention deficit disorder, had conferred demonstrable academic and non-academic benefits, the court again applied the four-point test. In this case, the court used grade-level test scores from the Woodcock-Johnson cognitive and achievement test batteries as objective evidence of Caius's progress. In explaining its decision, the court made several things clear:

1. A student's academic and non-academic development should be measured against that individual student's prior performance and not by his relation to the rest of the class.

2. Declining percentile scores do not necessarily represent a lack of educational benefit, rather the student's inability to maintain the same level of academic progress achieved by his non-disabled peers in regular classes.
3. It is not necessary for the student to improve in every area in order to obtain educational benefits from the IEP.
4. The party challenging the IEP must show more than a trivial failure to implement all elements of the IEP and instead must demonstrate that the school system failed to implement substantial or significant provisions of the IEP.

The Fifth Circuit referred to the Supreme Court's definition of *appropriate* in stating that whether Caius might have received a greater benefit under different circumstances was not the proper consideration because the IDEA does not require maximization of a disabled student's educational potential. The court noted that although school officials have some flexibility in implementing IEPs, they are held accountable for material failures and for providing a child with meaningful educational benefits.

The *Rowley* court clarified that once an IEP has been determined to be appropriate, deference is to be extended to professionals, and courts are not to substitute their judgments for those of experts with regard to educational methodologies. However, recent increases in litigation addressing private school tuition reimbursement, and cases involving students with autism, suggest that methodology is not escaping scrutiny as relevant to FAPE.[48] In *Nein v. Greater Clark County School Corporation*,[49] the court determined that Lucas, an illiterate twelve-year-old with severe learning disabilities and a full-scale IQ of 95, was making insufficient progress in the county's Milestones reading program. Even though he was being promoted and making good grades, Lucas could not even read restroom signs. The court drew on the Sixth Circuit's metaphor, finding that the county's insufficiently intensive reading instruction from grade 1-4 provided him "a Chevrolet without a transmission—even if the engine might run, no power ever reached the wheels."[50]

In confronting the question of whether using eclectic methods was unsound practice in educating a young child with autism, the Sixth Circuit in *Deal v. Hamilton Board of Education* [51] noted that when different methodologies result in vastly different outcomes, providing a lesser program results in a denial of FAPE. What approach constituted the lesser program for Zachary Deal was remanded to the district court to decide by determining the substantive appropriateness of his IEP. The lower court found the hearing officer in error for passionately espousing one methodology for educating an autistic child like Zachary, despite the contrary evidence of educational professionals.[52] In holding for the district, the judge clarified that "whether an approach used in any particular case 'qualifies' as a sound educational practice is fact-specific." [53] The court referred to the reasoning in *J.P. v. West Clark Community Schools*,[54] in which these criteria were applied: can school officials explain the specific benefits of using the methods with the particular child; do local educators have the experience and expertise to use them successfully; and do qualified educational experts consider the methods to be at least adequate under the circumstances?[55] Affirmative answers to questions about methodology, along with the judgment of the hearing officer, were enough to provide the court with guidance in deciding whether FAPE had been denied.

New provisions in the IDEA 2004 add a more stringent criterion to the analysis: school officials must now be able to defend their use of scientifically based, peer-reviewed instructional practices that improve student achievement.[56] This requirement should result in strengthening the effectiveness of methods offered by school districts, increasing the probability that a given approach "works," and is reasonably calculated to result in educational benefit.[57]. In science, researchers enhance their credibility when their work is reviewed by other experts and published in scholarly journals. In schools, educators enhance their effectiveness when they use validated methods in the ways they were intended, and with the group of students for whom they were designed. The demand for peer-reviewed research currently exceeds its supply, yet justifying the validity of selected practices is a serious concern for school officials in providing FAPE.[58]

When districts deny FAPE, the IDEA allows for remedies and related expenses,[59] including attorney fees but not costs for expert witnesses.[60] Awarding compensatory education in the form of specialized training for teachers to implement a student's IEP is one remedy.[61] Reimbursing parents for private school enrollment is another remedy that relies on the analysis of an IEP.[62] In *Board of Education of the City Sch. Dist. of the City of New York v. Tom F.,*[63] the Supreme Court addressed the question of whether parents of a child with specific learning disabilities who never received services from the school district could obtain reimbursement for a unilateral private placement. The Court failed to provide a definitive ruling in its 4-4 vote,[64] and the favorable decision for the parents and child stands in the Second Circuit.[65] The high court recently provided surer guidance in other cases characterized as pro-school or pro-parent.

The IDEA is silent as to which party bears the burden of proving an IEP appropriate, but in *Schaffer v. Weast,*[66] the Supreme Court decided for the district that in an administrative proceeding, the burden of persuasion rests with the party seeking relief. In effect this means that parents who challenge an IEP must prove to a hearing officer that the district denied their child FAPE, unless state laws suggest otherwise.[67] In the pro-parent decision of *Winkelman v. Parma,*[68] the Court held that the IDEA grants parents independent, enforceable rights, not limited to procedural and reimbursement-related matters, but extending to the substantive formulation of their child's educational program. Justice Kennedy, in writing for the Court, concluded that parents have the right to represent their children's interests in special education cases and are not required to hire a lawyer before going to court. Collectively, these Supreme Court decisions underscore the shared responsibility throughout the

IEP process for professional diligence in meeting a child's individual needs, and parental vigilance in ensuring those needs are met appropriately.

The IEP was referred to by the Supreme Court in *Rowley* as a written record of reasonable expectations. However, educators have too often focused IEPs on expectations for what a student will achieve, including lengthy lists of goals, instead of emphasizing expectations for what the school system will provide. From the perspective of distributed leadership, IEPs are tools that communicate to members across various professional communities what needs to be done, specifically and intensively, to help a child learn.[69] From the perspective of law, IEPs secure the right to an individually appropriate education, prompting one advocate to remark, "[Y]ou can fight over placement all you want, but if you want to win, you need to control the content of the IEP."[70]

LRE: Utilizing the Principle of the Least Restrictive Environment

Not all cases determining the appropriateness of an IEP involve disputes over placement, but all disputes over placement are determined by the appropriateness of an IEP. The most contentious of these disputes have centered on issues of placement in the LRE. The least restrictive environment requirements of the IDEA set out the factors to consider in educating students with and without disabilities together to the maximum extent appropriate.[71] In the language of law, the LRE principle is considered to be a rebuttable presumption. In other words, the law presumes that the least restrictive placement for any student to receive appropriate instruction is the regular class. Presumptive placement in the regular class is rebutted by convincing evidence that an alternative placement would provide a particular student with an appropriate education. For this reason, school officials are legally required to make a full continuum of alternative learning environments available across the system that range from regular classes, special classes, separate schools, residential facilities, hospitals, to home settings.[72]

The IDEA's federal regulations set out the requirements that school officials must follow in order to prevent the troubling practice of placing special education students in general education classes without regard to their specific learning needs. The regulations set out fact-specific guidelines stipulating that placement decisions must be made by a group of people, including the student's parents and others who are knowledgeable about the child, the meaning of the evaluation data, and the placement options. Placement decisions are also to be made in conformity with the LRE provisions.[73] Placement decisions must be made annually, must be based on the IEP, and must give consideration to any potential harmful effect on the child or to the quality of the required services. Unless their IEPs require otherwise, students with disabilities are expected to attend a school as close to home as possible or the school they would attend if they were not disabled. A special education student must not be removed from education in age-appropriate regular classrooms solely because of needed modifications in the general curriculum[74]

Under the IDEA, the least restrictive environment is not a specific location but the outcome of a procedural process in which a greater weight is given to the standard of FAPE than to the factors that determine the places in which instruction occurs. In making placement decisions, courts carefully compare the student's educational benefits with the statute's overall preference for placement in the regular classroom. Parents and professionals, less familiar with the law's presumptive language, often confuse the terms mainstreaming, inclusion, and LRE, but these terms do not have interchangeable meanings. Mainstreaming implies that special education and general education students will be educated together as appropriate but not exclusively. Full inclusion implies that students with disabilities have an absolute right to regular class placement. The term LRE is not synonymous with inclusion, but rather requires that placement decisions for students be made on the basis of an appropriate IEP. LRE is a legal principle embodied in the IDEA statute and mandated in the federal regulations. In contrast, the practices of mainstreaming and inclusion are not required by law but are educational strategies used to make the LRE principle operational in schools. The concept of LRE means that when school officials cannot provide a beneficial education to a student with disabilities in the same way they do for typically developing students, they must meet their obligation to provide FAPE using the *least* restrictive alternative to usual practices.[75]

In making LRE placement decisions, school officials should keep the issue of place in perspective by remembering that *where* a student receives instruction is only one component of an appropriate education. Some students may need instruction that cannot be provided in regular classes because they need to learn something different than general education students, such as Braille, American Sign Language, or specific technologies that are more efficiently taught in other settings. Some students may need to learn things differently, such as students with severe learning disabilities who need intensive reading instruction in more private learning environments, or students with cognitive disabilities whose job training and life skills curriculum requires them to spend time in community-based settings. The LRE requirements compel school systems to make a continuum of options possible so that IEP teams can make appropriate student-centered placement decisions across a range of viable alternatives.[76]

In making legally correct placement decisions, what might be *possible* for the system to provide should not be construed as synonymous with what would actually be *appropriate* for a particular student to receive because some possibilities can cause harm. For this reason, school officials need to tally the benefits of regular classes for each special education student, but also calculate the risks. Educational harm can result when decisions about students are based on stereotypes instead of individual strengths; when students are miss-placed and left in separate settings that do not match their needs; or when they are included in regular classes without receiving services that comport with their IEPs. The word *harm* is mentioned only once in the IDEA, and that is in the LRE requirements of the federal regulations.[77]

Placement: Determining Appropriate Educational Settings

Currently, there is no national framework employed by courts in making placement decisions. The Supreme Court has denied hearing any placement cases to date, so each circuit uses its preferred strategy in deciding cases related to LRE. Several circuit courts have devised judicial tests, or analytic frameworks, to evaluate whether a student in a regular class placement is achieving satisfactorily.[78] Circuits not relying on analytic frameworks balance the benefit of special education and general education in determining if a student can be educated satisfactorily in regular classes. These judicial tests illustrate critical components to consider in making placement decisions.

The framework derived from the 1983 case of *Roncker v. Walter*[79] considers keeping the student in a general education placement. This framework uses a feasibility test, or a portability test, to determine whether services that make a specialized placement superior could be feasibly provided in a typical setting. Feasibility is defined by whether any marginal benefits of typical settings are outweighed by the benefits of the special setting; whether the student is disruptive in a typical setting; and whether the costs of serving one student in a typical setting are excessive, depriving other students from getting the services they need. This analytic framework requires school systems to be proactive by considering if specialized services might be transported to typical educational settings. If it is feasible to replicate services that are critical to an individual student's appropriate education, then the special setting is not the least restrictive environment.[80]

The framework derived from the 1989 case of *Daniel R. R. v. State Board of Education*[81] considers the benefits of supplementary aids and services and the non-academic as well as academic benefits of a general education placement. In this case, the Fifth Circuit rejected the portability standard, viewing the feasibility of transporting services to more integrated settings as dependent on contextual circumstances and reliant on the judgments of school officials, not of courts. This framework requires a child-centered and fact-specific inquiry that asks two questions: whether education in the regular classroom, with the use of supplementary aids and services, can be achieved satisfactorily for a given student, and if not, whether the school has included the student to the maximum extent appropriate. In making this determination, school officials must balance whether the student can benefit more from general or from special education. In doing so, school officials must consider more than token attempts at modifying instruction, but they need not offer every conceivable service nor completely alter the standard program. Undue teacher time and undue curricular modification are not required. According to the court, this inquiry focuses on the student's ability to grasp the essential elements of the general curriculum. As in the *Roncker* analysis, school officials can consider the effect this child will have on other children and the quality of their education.[82]

The analysis derived from the 1994 case of *Sacramento City Unified School District v. Rachel Holland*[83] is clearly related to the previous two frameworks. However, the *Holland* test differs from the others by not balancing the benefits of special or general education but considering only if a student can receive education satisfactorily in regular classes. This analysis addresses four issues: (1) the educational benefits of placing the student in a full-time regular education program; (2) the non-academic benefits of such a placement; (3) the effect the student would have on the teacher and other students in the regular classroom; and (4) the costs associated with this placement.

Although the circumstances surrounding each student were different in these cases, the analytical frameworks used to determine placements for them continue to guide school officials and to inform judges in making decisions that comport with both the standard of FAPE and the principle of LRE. For example, the *Roncker* and *Daniel R. R.* frameworks were put to the test in a case addressing the disputed placement of Beth, a thirteen-year-old student with Rett Syndrome, a rare neurological condition that severely impairs both cognitive and physical functioning. In this case, *Beth B. v. Van Clay,* [84] the district court, noting that neither the Supreme Court nor the Seventh Circuit has indicated a preference among these judicial tests, provided detailed illustrations of how they could be used in analyzing evidence. Before applying its analysis, the court discussed the merits of each framework, finding the *Daniel R. R.* test superior to the others in tracking the statutory language of the IDEA. In addition, the court determined that the standard of feasibility in the *Roncker* analysis placed too much emphasis on what services could be delivered but not enough on what the student actually learned.

In its first illustration, the district court analyzed Beth's current regular class placement using the *Daniel R. R.* test, determining that the school system made adequate attempts to accommodate her with the individualized services of two teacher-aides, an inclusion facilitator, and a customized curriculum using laminated books with embossed pictures and modified text. The district also provided a variety of assistive technologies and trained personnel and others students to use them in communicating with Beth. Although Beth received services that were described by her parents as inadequate and by the school system as Herculean efforts, the court determined that Beth's progress in the inclusive regular class setting was best described as inconsistent. The court commented on its hopes that she could learn much more in a setting that offered more intensive special education.

In relying on the *Daniel R. R.* analysis, the court noted that the IDEA does not require changes so extensive that the standard curriculum becomes unrecognizable. Significant alterations were made in the seventh-grade classroom to adjust to Beth's cognitive delays, which some experts placed at the ability level of a twelve-to-eighteen-month-old infant and others estimated as being at the ability level of a four-to-six-year-old child. Because of her disability, Beth frequently dozed in school, took twenty-to-thirty-minute scheduled toilet breaks, and was frequently absent. The court commented on how these factors inhibited Beth's gains, even given her parallel curriculum; when the class moved on to the next unit, so did Beth regardless of her progress. The record, according to the court, revealed that as Beth advanced in grade levels, her interactions with other class members diminished.

The court next considered Beth's effect on both students and teachers in the learning environment, finding that only on occasion were her outbursts or needs distracting to other students. As for her effect upon her teachers, the court noted that Beth's middle school teachers could not work with her and with other students simultaneously because of the significantly modified nature of her curriculum. Determining that Beth could not be satisfactorily educated in a regular classroom, the court turned to the second prong of the *Daniel R. R.* analysis, finding the district's plans for reverse mainstreaming—and for inclusion in non-academic activities including art, music, lunch, and field trips—acceptable opportunities for social integration. Using the *Daniel R. R.* analytical framework, the court determined that the statutory presumption for regular class placement was overcome.

The court next analyzed Beth's placement using the *Roncker* test. The court first considered what made specialized programming superior to regular programming for Beth. In this case, the court found that the specialized setting provided her with more direct contact with teachers trained and experienced in educating students with cognitive disabilities. The court noted that in either placement, Beth was accompanied by an aide, but that such a service is no substitute for contact with a teacher. In the smaller, more specialized setting, Beth could receive close attention from the teacher without detracting from other students. Not only were the teachers specially trained to work with students like Beth, the program's administrator had previous experience with students with Rett Syndrome. Although other personnel could be trained to communicate with Beth, such training was not viewed as equivalent to the specialized preparation and experience of special education teachers. According to the court, "special education is also more conducive to systematic instruction. Rather than attempting to keep pace, even in modified form, with her non-disabled classmates' lessons, Beth can repeat skills until she learns them."[85] In turning to the second prong of the test, the court found that these advantages could not feasibly be duplicated in a regular education setting. The district court determined that despite the IDEA's preference for regular class placement, the law does not require such placements if the result would be the student's unsatisfactory education. Beth's parents appealed the decision and invoked the IDEA's stay-put provision allowing Beth to remain in the regular class pending the resolution of the placement dispute.

Upholding the judgment of the lower court, the Seventh Circuit Court characterized the FAPE-IEP determination as being the threshold for any placement inquiry.[86] In making its decision, the court of appeals first considered the appropriateness of the IEP developed for Beth and determined that the FAPE mandate was not at issue. The court warned that "the FAPE provision and LRE provision are two sides of the same IEP coin,"[87] but that confusion about placement ensues when language from the FAPE analysis is misapplied to LRE inquires. In this case, the court expressed concerns that Beth's parents had confused the FAPE side of the coin with the LRE side by arguing that, as long as Beth received *some* educational benefit in the regular class, the school could not remove her from the setting. The court instructed that "the *Rowley* holding applies only to the school district's responsibility to provide a FAPE—a requirement that analyzes the appropriateness of the district's placement—not the appropriateness of its alternative, in this case the regular setting."[88] According to the court, misapplying the *Rowley* standard to placement decisions instead of correctly applying it to decisions about an appropriate IEP "turns the 'some educational benefit' language on its head."[89]

The court declined to adopt a formal framework for use in the Seventh Circuit but relied on a fact-specific inquiry in finding that the school system's placement represented "an acceptable point along the continuum of services between total integration and complete segregation."[90] As long as the special program included opportunities for interaction with non-disabled peers, the placement satisfied the requirement that Beth be mainstreamed to the maximum extent appropriate.

The Supreme Court denied Beth's parents' request for certiorari.[91] Although the Supreme Court established the standard of appropriateness in 1982, the attendant principle of instructional placement in the least restrictive environment continues to be left to members of the professional community and the courts to decide. Over the past two decades, legal analysts have developed sets of questions to guide LRE decision making[92] and established sequenced formats to ensure full consideration of the LRE placement requirements.[93] Although the IDEA prefers inclusion, it does not require inclusion; however, courts give careful scrutiny to decisions that place students in more restrictive settings. Placement decisions require thoughtful analysis because the law acknowledges a rational basis for determining, on a case-by-case basis, that a child's FAPE might be provided in specialized settings using differing treatments.

Changing Placements and Protecting Individual Rights

Fiscal resources and due process protections support the special education process, and the assurance of both funding and civil rights commands the attention of school administrators. FAPE is at risk when inadequate funding threatens the provision of costly but appropriate services. The IDEA places the fiscal burden for educating students with disabilities on school systems, and cost may not be a factor in providing a particular student with needed services. In a few cases, usually related to placements where an appropriate education can be provided in more than one setting, school officials are permitted to select the less expensive option.

FAPE is also at risk when inadequate safeguards fail to ensure a student's right to receive an individually appropriate education. The IDEA is a child-centered law, and procedural protections surround decisions about IEPs, LRE, and placements.[94] Parents, on behalf of their child, and students at the age of majority have the right to receive prior written notice and to participate in all meetings regarding identification, evaluation, programming, or placement. Informed consent is only required for an initial evaluation to determine if services are necessary and then only to initiate those services if the child is found eligible to receive special education. Some states have additional requirements for parents to sign annual IEPs before services for the year can begin. If parents whose children are receiving special education refuse to sign consent at any point, school officials may seek an order from a hearing officer to proceed without consent, if that action seems to be in the student's best interests. Dangers arise when school officials appease parents at the child's expense—keeping the peace but abandoning the child's best interests.

Prior written notice is also required when school officials propose any change in educational placement, including the proposal of a student's graduation with a regular education diploma.[95] In addition, the IDEA allows parents to pursue a due process hearing when they contest a change in placement for their child. However, courts are hesitant to grant hearings in cases where parents seek to prevent school officials from making organizational or fiscal decisions that affect more than their own child, such as closing or consolidating schools.[96] In these instances, it is important for school officials and for parents to understand the differences in meaning between a "program" and a "placement" under the IDEA. Students with disabilities can be transferred from schools or classes without these transfers being regarded as changes in placement, as long as the educational program offered in each setting is comparable and equally appropriate. Only when the services prescribed in a student's current IEP cannot be implemented in the new setting has a change in placement occurred that substantially affects a student's rights to an appropriate education.

Educating students in placements that support the delivery of appropriate instruction is a critical component of the IDEA, reinforcing the supportive role of placement in providing a student with FAPE. The percentage of time indicated on a student's IEP for the receipt of special education and related services outside the regular class is presumed to result from procedures that were legally correct and considerations that were student-specific. Educational placements that result from team-based decisions are presumed to comport with the delivery of services required by the IEP. Consequently, the IDEA's "stay put" provision prevents school officials from disrupting the provision of FAPE by removing students from placements over parental objections, pending the resolution of due process review proceedings.[97] In the case of *Hale v. Poplar Bluff R-I School District,*[98] the Eighth Circuit held that the stay put provision is to be rigorously enforced to stop schools from using the unilateral authority they once employed to exclude students with disabilities from school. A district court in Maine relied on the stay put provision in determining that graduation was grounds for a disputed change in placement. In *Bell v. Education in the Unorganized Territories,*[99] parents challenged the district's proposal that their son with autism graduate from high school with his class. Finding that the district failed to overcome the law's strong preference for preserving the educational status quo, the court determined that the student remain in his current placement attending to the curriculum prescribed in the previous year's IEP during the pendency of further proceedings. The decision in *C.P. v. Leon County School Board*[100] clarified for states in the Eleventh Circuit that the stay put provision does not require annual updating of an IEP.

Suspension and Expulsion

The only exception to the stay put provision occurs when a hearing officer finds substantial evidence to indicate that it would be dangerous for the student to remain in the current placement.[101] The IDEA 2004 permits school officials to remove students who inflict serious bodily injury to another person while at school, and students who bring weapons or illegal drugs to school or to school functions, for forty-five days if they attend an interim alternative educational setting. The discipline setting, not the pre-dispute setting, will be the stay-put placement during contested disciplinary actions.[102] With regard to suspension and expulsion, the IDEA again employs the legal strategy of a rebuttable presumption, favoring the student's placement in the present setting but allowing the presumption to be overcome by evidence that harm or danger might ensue. Suspending special education students for more than ten days or expelling them from school both represent changes of placement that trigger the use of procedural safeguards. In these cases, the IDEA is clear: there is to be no cessation of educational services when students are removed to alternative settings.[103] FAPE cannot be denied once it has been guaranteed through eligibility and initiated through an IEP. School officials must continue to provide services that allow special education students to have access to the general curriculum and to make progress toward their goals.

Although the disciplinary procedures of the IDEA affect student placement, they are essentially issues related to the principle of zero-reject, which stipulates that a student who has a disability cannot be denied an equitable educational opportunity.[104] The IDEA's requirements that IEPs for students whose behaviors impede their learning include behavioral intervention plans are essentially issues related to the provision of an appropriate education.[105] The U.S. Department of Education has provided strong guidance to school officials, recommending that proactive measures be taken to address misconduct as soon as it appears to prevent more drastic measures from being taken at a later point. Functional behavioral assessments could be conducted to determine if the present programming for a student who engages in misconduct is sufficiently specialized to provide appropriate support.[106] A detailed examination of the IDEA's disciplinary procedures exceeds the scope of this chapter. But consideration of proactive measures to address the misconduct of students through the IEP process, ensuring that individuals with disabilities are educated appropriately, brings this discussion of IEPs, least restrictive environment, and placement full circle.

The delivery of high-quality special education, that ensures the delivery of FAPE, relies on school principals who understand that the IDEA views a student's disability as "a distinction that usually justifies a different approach."[107] Greater alignment of the IDEA with the NCLB is viewed by some as the critical link enabling students with disabilities to achieve higher standards in higher performing schools. Given the differing perspectives of these public policies, such an alignment could mean significant changes for many students with disabilities and their parents. The IDEA focuses on the performance of individuals by mandating an IEP with placements that hinge on its appropriateness and by requiring school officials to provide appropriate programming to a personalized standard. The NCLB focuses on the performance of schools, mandating once-a-year standardized tests in reading and math and aiming for a common standard of academic performance, without assurance of appropriate benefit or of due process protections. In assessing the risks and benefits of a policy fusion, one advocate cautioned that "laws alone cannot create good administrators, or good teachers, or good schools, but they certainly can take away very hard won rights."[108]

Recommendations for Practice

In making IEP and placement decisions for students with disabilities, there is no substitute for implementing the IDEA with integrity. In making decisions with confidence, school principals should anchor their actions in the law's conceptual foundations. The following recommendations are grounded in the trinity of FAPE, LRE, and validated practices so that principals might guide the delivery of effective special education in their schools.

1. Make ethical and legally defensible decisions. Promote professional behavior that pays more than lip-service to providing equity, quality, and opportunity for all learners. Schools are now enrolling record numbers of students whose learning differences would have once excluded them from receiving a public education. But for some special education students, functional exclusion is still a reality when schools fail to deliver specially designed instruction or teachers fail to follow the prescriptions of an IEP. As a result, these students "experience a different kind of segregation—the exclusion from the basic right to learn."[108]

2. Directly address individuality and exceptionality in learning. School leaders are in strong positions to articulate that special education is for students with disabilities who need to learn something different

or who need to learn the same thing as everyone else but in a different way. Special education is not for any student who fails in the general curriculum but for students who, because of the extent of their disability-related needs, require different ways to learn and to demonstrate what they know in order to meet with school success. Special education, with its guarantee of an appropriate public education in the least restrictive environment, is for individuals whose disabilities threaten to handicap their future if left unnoticed and unaddressed.

3. Ensure the delivery of special education that is legally correct and educationally meaningful. Communicate to stakeholders the statutory purpose of the IDEA and the legal meanings of its critical components, including a free appropriate public education, special education, and placements made in accordance with the principle of the least restrictive environment. Although these are familiar terms to most educators, they are often used incorrectly, leading to imprecision, which, in turn, leads to violation of the law and nullification of FAPE.
4. Provide IEPs that address the procedural and substantive requirements of the IDEA. Serious procedural violations have been viewed by courts as violations of FAPE if they result in harmful disruption to the delivery of appropriate instruction and educational services.
5. Develop IEPs that rely on current and relevant data about the unique educational needs of each student, not on the prerogatives of the school system or on the availability of services.
6. Avoid filling IEPs with details about content standards. Focus, instead, on the necessary adjustments to be made in providing intensive and specific instruction in academics and desirable behavior so that students can appropriately access and participate in the general curriculum, and meet their disability-related goals.
7. Do not make policies of "full inclusion" in substitution for the IDEA's requirement for school systems to make available a full continuum of alternative placements. Use student-specific IEP data, not philosophical arguments about inclusion, in making legally correct decisions about placements that constitute the LRE for each student.
8. Remember that services to students are not to cease because of suspension or expulsion from school. Any change of placement, for any reason, requires that parents be notified of the school's intent to remove their child from the current setting. Remember, too, that the IDEA has a strong preference for the placement that represents the status quo.
9. Support high expectations for positive results. Ensure that professionals use effective instructional methodologies and assessment systems

that have a demonstrated record of being successful for students with disabilities. Ensure that special and general educators balance a student's need to be successful in the general curriculum with the need to learn from a specialized curriculum in other areas.

10. Establish productive partnerships with parents. Notify parents in writing before taking any action regarding their child's programming or placement. Give parents a copy of procedural safeguards before IEP meetings and provide them with genuine opportunities to participate in any meetings regarding their child. Involve parents as full partners but do not appease them by forsaking professional judgment about the best interests of their child.
11. Remember, schools have the best hope for meeting state standards and national goals adequately when they are vigilant in meeting the needs of their students with disabilities appropriately.

Endnotes

1 *The Individuals with Disabilities Education Improvement Act of 2004*, P. L. 108-446 (Dec. 3, 2004), codified at 20 U.S.C. Sec 1400, *et seq.*

2 *No Child Left Behind Act of 2001,* Pub. L. No. 107-110, 115 Stat. 1425 (2002), codified at 20 U.S.C. §§ 6301-6777.

3 Thomas Hehir, New Directions in Special Education, 49 (2005).

4 20 U.S.C. § 1400(d)(1)(A). Congress added new wording to include further education as an outcome along with employment and independent living.

5 20 U.S.C. § 1412(a)(1); 34 C.F.R. § 300.101(c)).

6 20 U.S.C. § 1401(29)(A), emphasis added.

7 34 C.F. R. §300.39 (b)(3)

8 H. Rutherford Turnbull, & Ann P. Turnbull, Free Appropriate Public Education: The Law and Children with Disabilities, 52 (2000).

9 Steven E. Lake, John Norlin, Karen Glasser Sharp, & Vicki M. Pitasky, The Current Legal Status of Inclusion, 1 (2006).

10 See Barbara D. Bateman & Mary Anne Linden, Better IEPs (2006), for an extended discussion of special education programming and placements.

11 IEP teams must include the following seven items: (1) the parents of the child; (2) at least one regular education teacher (if the child is, or may be, participating in the regular education environment); (3) at least one special education teacher of the child, or if appropriate, at least one special education provider of the child; (4) a representative of the public agency who is qualified to provide, or supervise the provision of, specially designed instruction to meet the unique needs of children with disabilities; is knowledgeable about the general curriculum; and is knowledgeable about the availability of resources of the public agency; (5) an individual who can interpret the instructional implications of evaluation results, who may already be a member of the team; (6) at the discretion of the parent or the agency, other individuals who have knowledge or special expertise regarding the child, including related services personnel as appropriate; and (7) if appropriate, the child (20 U.S.C.§1414(d) (1)(B); 34 C.F.R. §300.321(a)).

12 Authority: 20 U.S.C. § 1401(9); 34 C.F.R. §300.17

13 This document is developed, reviewed, and revised in a meeting in accordance with 34 C.F.R. §§ 300.320-300.324.

[14] This new wording replaces prior language requiring a statement of "present levels of educational performance" describing the student's unique learning needs in areas to be addressed by special services.

[15] 20 U.S.C. § 1414(d)(1)(A)(i)(I); 34 C.F.R. 300.320(a)(2)(B)(ii).

[16] Bateman & Linden, *supra* note 10, at 170.These authors advise districts against dropping short-term objectives because they serve a progress monitoring function.

[17] 20 U.S.C. § 1414(d)(1)(A)(i)(III).

[18] 34 C.F.R. § 300.320(a)(3).

[19] 20 U.S.C. § 1414(d)(1)(A)(i)(IV).

[20] 34 C.F.R. §300.320(a)(4). Including extensive lists of standards in IEPs is inappropriate. Instead, the IEP must indicate goals illustrating how professionals will enable the student to acquire the access skills necessary to address the standards considered by the team to be most relevant to the student.

[21] 34 C.F.R. § 300.324(a)(3). The role of the regular education teacher on the team is to assist in the development, review, and revision of the IEP with particular attention to the appropriate positive behavioral interventions and strategies for the child; and the supplementary aids and services, program modifications, or supports for school personnel that will be provided for the child to be successful in meeting individual goals, accessing the general curriculum, and being educated and participating with other students with and without disabilities.

[22] 20 U.S.C. § 1414(d)(1)(A)(i)(V); 34 C.F.R. § 300.320(a)(5).

[23] 20 U.S.C. § 1414(d)(1)(A)(i)(VI); 34 C.F.R. § 300.320(a)(6).

[24] 20 U.S.C. § 1414(d)(1)(A)(i)(VII); 34 C.F.R. § 300.320(a)(7).

[25] 20 U.S.C. § 1414(d)(1)(A)(i)(VIII); 34 C.F.R. § 300.320(a)(7)(b)(1)(2)(c).

[26] 34 C.F.R. § 300.324.

[27] Authority: 20 U.S.C. § 1414(d)(3) and (4)(B) and (e); 34 C.F.R. § 300.324(a)(2)

[28] 34 C.F.R. § 300.324(a)(2)(iii).Teams must also evaluate the appropriate reading and writing media for the student, including an evaluation of the student's future needs for instruction in Braille or the use of Braille.

[29] 34 C.F.R. § 300.320(a)(6)(i).

[30] 20 U.S.C. § 1414(d)(1)(B)(C)(2)(5); 34 C.F.R. § 300.324(a)(4). The IDEA 2004 modifies the requirements for team members to attend IEP meetings. When parents agree in writing, members may be excused who have provided input into the IEP prior to the meeting, or whose areas of curriculum or related services are not being modified or discussed at the meeting. The law also requires that school systems invite appropriate early intervention service providers to initial IEP meetings if requested by parents to smooth the transition from preschool (20U. S.C.§1414(C)(D); 34 C.F.R. § 300.321(f)). Parents and professionals may also agree to meet using alternative means, such as telephone and video conferences, 34 C.F.R. § 300.328.

[31] Scott F. Johnson, *Reexamining Rowley: A New Focus in Special Education Law*, 2003 BYU Educ. & L.J. 561-585. Johnson argues that the concept of FAPE is newly aligned with high expectations established in state education standards, although school systems must address more than academic needs.

[32] Hehir, *supra* note 3, at 131-136.

[33] Some theorists think this lack of firm definition has caused school officials to make decisions leading to costly conflicts and litigation with parents. Others caution that a fixed standard of appropriate would be undesirable and antithetical to the individualized nature of the IDEA.

[34] Allan G. Osborne, *Legal Standards for an Appropriate Education in the Post-Rowley Era.* Exceptional Chidren 488-494 (1992).

[35] Board of Educ. v. Rowley, 458 U.S. 176 (1982).

[36] *Id.* at 206-07.

[37] Doe v. Bd. of Educ. of Tullahoma City Sch., 9 F.3d 455 (6th Cir. 1993).

[38] In *Polk v. Central Susquehanna Intermediate Unit 16*, 853 F.2d 171, 182, 184 (3d Cir. 1988), the Third Circuit held that an IEP must be calculated to offer "meaningful benefit" by providing educational services in a way that a student can best achieve success in learning. In *Hall*

v. Vance County Board of Education, 774 F.2d 629, 636 (4th Cir. 1985), the Fourth Circuit allowed courts to make decisions regarding the substantive standard of an appropriate IEP on a case-by-case basis, taking into consideration the child's capacity to learn. In *J.S K. v. Hendry County School Board*, 941 F2d 1563, 1573 (11th Cir. 1991), the Eleventh Circuit required public schools to provide educational benefit greater than a trifle and defined an appropriate education in terms of "making measurable and adequate gains in the classroom" based on the child's needs, potential, and efforts.

39 Gaston Sch. Dist, 24 IDELR 1052 (SEA Or. 1996).

40 Fayetteville-Perry Local Sch. Dist., 20 IDELR 1289 (SEA Ohio 1994); Tucson Unified Sch. Dist., 30 IDELR 478 (SEA Ariz. 1999).

41 Hall v. Vance County Bd. of Educ., *supra* note 37.

42 Florence Country Sch. Dist. Four v. Carter, 510 U. S. 7 (1993).

43 Cypress-Fairbanks Indep. Sch. Dist. v. Michael F., 118 F.3d 245 (5th Cir. 1997).

44 *Id.* at 253. The court noted that each of the four factors comport with the federal regulations implementing the IDEA. *See* 34 C.F.R. §300.324 (academic and functional needs); 34 C.F.R. §§ 300.114-120 (least restrictive environment); 34 C.F.R. § 300.321 (team approach); and 34 C.F.R. § 300.320 (demonstrated outcomes).

45 *Id.* at 254.

46 This action preceded the provision of the IDEA 2004 allowing courts to levy a fee against parents for filing actions brought for improper purposes (20 U.S.C. § 1415(i)(3)(A)); 34 C.F.R. § 300.517.

47 Houston Indep Sch. Dist. v. Bobby R., 200 F.3d 341 (5th Cir. 2000).

48 Dixie Snow Huefner, Getting Comfortable with Special Education Law, 186 (2006). The IDEA's recent emphasis on adapting the content, methodology, or delivery of instruction has increased the interest of the courts in different methodologies and increased the need for educators to select teaching methods responsive to a student's unique educational needs. If a student needs a particular device, service, intervention, accommodation, or modification, then that information must be placed in the IEP. If FAPE can be provided without using a specific method, then the decision to include methodology on the IEP rests with the IEP team.

49 Nein v. Greater Clark County Sch. Corp., 95 F. Supp. 2d 961 (2000).

50 *Id.* at 977.

51 Deal v. Hamilton County Bd. of Educ., 392 F3d 840 (6th Cir. 2004)

52 Tessie E. Rose & Perry Zirkel, *Orton-Gillingham Methodology for Students with Reading Disabilities: 30 Years of Case Law*, 184, J. Special Educ., 171-185 (2007). In *Deal v. Hamilton County*, the ALJ characterized the Lovaas method as showing "extraordinary results," although its research base was not peer reviewed and of questionable rigor. Rose and Zirkel point out that although educators are expected to provide them, parents and judges may lack the expertise to recognize validated instructional practices.

53 Deal v. Hamilton County Dep't of Educ., 46 IDELR,45 (E.D. Tenn. 2006) at 72.

54 J.P. v. W. Clark Cmty. Sch., 230 F. Supp. 2d 910 (2002).

55 *Id.* at 936.

56 20 U.S.C. § 1414(d)(1)(A)(i)(IV); 34 C.F.R. § 300.320(a)(4).

57 Congress did not define peer-reviewed research, but usage of the term is consistent with *scientifically-based instruction* in NCLB, as practices tested and validated through systematic, rigorous, and objective methods; see 34 C.F.R. § 300.35.

58 *See* Bateman & Linden, *supra* note 10, at 175. In identifying and selecting practices, school officials should carefully review claims for the research base of publishers' curricular materials; pursue guidance from professional development; provide practitioner journals that publish practical articles for teachers and related service providers; consult personnel at state departments of education; and utilize professional websites that publish valid data on evidence-based practices.

59 A review of recent case law suggests that courts failed to find a denial of FAPE when procedural violations resulted in harmless error. *See* Gray v. O'Rourke, 48 F. App'x 899 (4th Cir.

2002); MS. S. v. Vashon Island Sch. Dist., 336 F3d 260 (9th Cir. 2003); N.L. v. Knox County Schs., 315 F.3d 688 (6th Cir. 2003); Lesesne v. District of Columbia, 447 Fed 828 (D.C. Cir 2006).

60 Arlington Cent. Sch. Dist. Bd. of Educ. v. Murphy, 45 IDELR 267 (U.S. 2006)

61 Park v. Anaheim Union High Sch. Dist., 45 IDELR 178 (9th Cir. 2006).

62 34 C.F.R. § 300.148.

63 Board of Educ. of the City Sch. Dist. of the City of New York v. Tom F, *ex rel.* Gilbert F., 48 IDELR 239 (U.S. 2007).

64 Justice Kennedy did not participate in the decision.

65 This dispute predates new provisions in the IDEA 2004 that require parental consent before a school district implements an initial IEP. The issue of whether districts have any obligation to offer services if a parent rejects an initial IEP was not argued in this case.

66 Schaffer v. Weast, 44 IDELR 150 (U.S. 2005).

67 For an extended discussion of this decision, see Charles J. Russo, & Allan G. Osborne, *The Supreme Court Clarifies the Burden of Proof in Special Education Due Process Hearings: Schaffer ex rel. Schaffer v. Weast.* Educ. L. Rep., 208, 705-717 (2006).

68 Winkelman by Winkelman v. Parma City Sch. Dist., 47 IDELR 281 (U.S. 2007).

69 For a discussion of how the tools used by educators are more than representative of intentions but are constitutive of their practice, see James P. Spillane, Richard Halverson, & John B. Diamond, *Investigating School Leadership Practice: A Distributed Perspective,* 30 Educ. Researcher, 23-28 (2001).

70 Jeffrey Champagne, *LRE: Decisions in Sequence*, Symposium at the Annual Conference of the National Association of Private Schools for Exceptional Children, 14 (1992).

71 20 U.S.C. § 1412(a)(5).

72 34 C.F.R. § 300.115

73 The regulations to the IDEA set out fact-specific guidelines stipulating that placement decisions must be made by a group of people, including the student's parents, and others who are knowledgeable about the child, the meaning of the evaluation data, and the placement options. Placement decisions are also to be made in conformity with the LRE provisions of the federal regulations at §§34 C.F.R §§ 300.114-120).

74 34 C.F.R. § 300.116.

75 See Crockett & Kauffman, The Least Restrictive Environment: Its Origins and Interpretations in Special Education (1999), for a full discussion of the origins and interpretations of the LRE principle in special education.

76 Jean B. Crockett. *The Least Restrictive Environment and the 1997 IDEA Amendments and Federal Regulations,* 8 J.L. & Educ., 1-22 (1999).

77 34 C.F.R. § 300.116(d): "In selecting the LRE, consideration must be given to any potential harmful effect on the child or on the quality of services that he or she needs."

78 The major frameworks include the *Roncker* standard, the *Daniel R. R.* two-pronged test, and the four-pronged *Holland* test.

79 Roncker v. Walter, 700 F.2d 1058 (6th Cir. 1983). This test is used in the Fourth, Sixth, and Eighth Circuits.

80 In developing the feasibility standard, the Sixth Circuit acknowledged that a student's need for an appropriate education might conflict with preferences for integration and that certain factors, including marginal benefits, disruption, and cost, could be considered in determining whether education in regular settings could be provided satisfactorily.

81 Daniel R. R. v. State Bd. of Educ., 874 F 2d. 1036 (5th Cir. 1989). This test is used in the Third, Fifth, Tenth, and Eleventh Circuits.

82 The *Daniel R. R.* two-pronged analytic framework influenced the 1997 amendments to the IDEA and has had a broad impact on courts deliberating placements in the LRE. This framework requires school systems to consider more than academic achievement in placement decisions and to ensure that access to general education settings will not be denied solely because the progress of the special education student will not equal that of a general education student.

[83] Sacramento City Unified Sch. Dist v. Rachel H., 14 F.3d 1398 (9th Cir. 1994). This test is used in the Ninth Circuit.
[84] Beth B. v. Van Clay, 211 F. Supp. 2d 1020.
[85] *Id.* at 1034.
[86] Beth B. v. Van Clay, 282 F.3d 493 (7th Cir. 2002).
[87] *Id.* at 498.
[88] *Id.* at 497.
[89] *Id.* at 498.
[90] *Id.* at 498.
[91] Beth B. v. Van Clay, 282 F.3d 493 (7th Cir. 2002), *cert denied*, 537 U.S. 948 (2002).
[92] *See* MITCHELL L. YELL, THE LAW AND SPECIAL EDUCATION, 326 (2006). The following questions address the components embodied in the LRE frameworks and rely on student-centered data collected throughout the LRE determination process.

1. Has the school taken steps to maintain the child in the general education class: What supplementary aides and services were used? What interventions were attempted?
2. What are the benefits of placement in a general education setting with supplementary aids and services versus the benefits of placement in a special education setting: What are the academic benefits? What are the nonacademic benefits such as social communication and interactions?
3. What are the effects on the education of other students: If the student is disruptive, is the education of other students adversely affected? Does the student require an inordinate amount of attention from the teacher, and, as a result, adversely affect the education of others?
4. If a student requires a separate setting, are appropriate opportunities for integration available? In what academic settings is the student integrated with nondisabled students? In what nonacademic settings is the child integrated with nondisabled students?
5. Is the full continuum of alternative services made available across the system from which to choose an appropriate placement?

[93] *See* Jeffrey Champagne, *supra* note 59. Decisions about placement can be addressed by using a sequential format that begins by considering whether the appropriate educational services written in the IEP can be delivered in the regular class if modified through the use of supplementary aids and services. If the answer is yes, then the regular class is the primary placement. If not, the team would move along the continuum of alternative placements one step at a time, from regular class to resource room to separate class to separate school residential setting hospital or home, considering whether the appropriate educational services might be delivered with appropriate supports until the answer *yes* is obtained.
[94] 34 C.F.R. §§ 300.500-520.
[95] 20 USC 1415(b)(1)(C); 34 C.F.R. § 300.503.
[96] Powell v. Studstill, 441 S.E.2d 52 (Ga. 1994).
[97] 34 C.F.R. § 300. 518.
[98] Hale v. Poplar Bluff R-I Sch. Dist., 280 F. 3d 831 (8th Cir. 2002).
[99] Bell v. Educ. in the Unorganized Territories, 2000 WL (D. Me. 2000).
[100] C.P. v. Leon County Sch. Bd., 46 IDELR 182 (11th Cir. 2006).
[101] 34 C.F.R. § 300.530.
[102] 20 U.S.C. § 1415(k)(1)(G)(H); 34 C.F.R. § 300. 533.
[103] 34 C.F.R. § 300. 530. A special education student removed from the current placement for more than ten consecutive days must continue to receive educational services and behavioral interventions whether or not the offending behavior is a manifestation of the disability.
[104] TURNBULL & TURNBULL, *supra* note 8, at 83.
[105] 34 C.F.R. § 300.324(a)(2)(i).
[106] 34 C.F.R. § 300.530.
[107] TURNBULL & TURNBULL, *supra* note 8, at 122.
[108] Jean S. Schumm et al., *General Education Teacher Planning: What Can Students With Learning Disabilities Expect*? 61 EXCEPTIONAL CHILDREN, 335 (1995).

Chapter 16

Related Services under the IDEA

Jennifer A. Sughrue

Introduction

Since the enactment of the Individuals with Disabilities Education Act (IDEA), the federal courts have attempted to bring clarification to the congressional intent of the law and to its implementation in public education, which is no small feat in view of the number of key provisions within the law and the subsequent passage of No Child Left Behind (NCLB). This chapter is focused on the related services provision and examples of the contexts in which it has been litigated. It covers the statutory definition of related services, as well as the judiciary's application of that definition, and finishes with a discussion of the implications for school leaders.

Legal Issues

Definition of Related Services

The definition of related services remained unchanged under the 2004 reauthorization. They are those support services that students with disabilities require in order to access and profit from special education. These encompass "transportation, and such developmental, corrective, and other supportive services … as may be required to assist a child with a disability to benefit from special education, and includes the early identification and assessment of disabling conditions in children."[1] Several examples of such services are included in the statutory definition, among them speech and audiology services, psychological services, rehabilitation therapies, recreation, therapeutic recreation, social work services, and counseling services. Medical services are to be provided if they are for the purpose of diagnosis and evaluation of the disability in relation to qualifying for and receiving special education.

Although the statutory language seems clear on related services, the nature and extent to which these services apply are sometimes called into question as school personnel, parents, and eligible students negotiate individual educational programs. For this reason, the courts have had to further characterize related services and their function.

The U.S. Supreme Court provided guidance by indicating that related services were those that were necessary for a child with disabilities "to remain at school during the day" in order to have "meaningful access to education."[2] This conclusion was a part of a decision that centered on whether a procedure known as clean intermittent catheterization (CIC) was a related service or an excluded medical service. CIC can be can be performed by non-medical personnel who have received basic instruction on the procedure. The student, Amber Tatro, was an eight-year-old child with spina bifida. In order to avoid damaging her kidneys, Tatro required CIC every four hours. This meant that this procedure had to be administered during school hours.

In a two-part analysis, the Supreme Court held that CIC clearly fell within the statutory definition of related services. The Court considered CIC as functionally the same as transportation inasmuch as it allowed Tatro to attend school and to benefit from special education. "Services like CIC that permit a child to remain at school during the day are no less related to the effort to educate than are services that enable the child to reach, enter, or exit the school."[3]

In the second half of the analysis, the Court distinguished eligible from non-eligible medical services under the IDEA. Federal implementation regulations stated that those school health services that could be performed by a school nurse or other qualified person would be considered related services.[4] Excluded medical services were those that required the services of a physician and in which cost might be a factor. Inasmuch as the CIC procedure did not require a physician, the Court held that it was clearly a related service.

The Supreme Court later discounted cost as a primary factor in determining what an excluded medical service is.[5] This conclusion stemmed from a case in which the parents requested the school district bear the financial responsibility for a nurse during the school day for their quadriplegic son who was ventilator dependent. Garret F. required continuous one-on-one nursing care in order to stay in school. He needed assistance with urinary bladder catheterization and with the suctioning of his tracheotomy tube, among other procedures. Also, it was essential that someone be available who could respond to a problem with the ventilator or in the event Garret was to experience autonomic hyperreflexia, an "uncontrolled visceral reaction to anxiety or a full bladder … [during which] blood pressure increases, heart rate increases, and flushing and sweating may occur."[6]

The school district did not dispute the lower court's conclusion that the kinds of assistance that Garret required were related services under the first prong of the *Tatro* analysis. It also acknowledged that other students in the district were receiving similar services. The district, however, contended that the scope of services that Garret required was beyond the school district's obligation under the IDEA.

The district proposed a multifactor test that would be employed on a case-by-case basis to determine whether a school district would be responsible for an extensive collection of related services for individual students. These factors included "[1] whether the care is continuous or intermittent, [2] whether existing school health personnel can provide the service, [3] the cost of the service, and [4] the potential consequences if the service is not properly performed."[7]

The Court rejected the school district's proposed test, arguing that the test was unsubstantiated by any legal authority and that there was no reasonable explanation as to why "one service [would be] any more 'medical' than another."[8] As it regarded each of the factors, the Court noted that the test more accurately assessed the potential cost to a school district than it assessed whether needed procedures were excluded medical services. It concluded that the district was attempting to establish an "undue burden exemption."[9] In rejecting this strategy, the Court asserted that the services that Garret required were necessary to his access to free appropriate public education (FAPE) and re-affirmed its earlier conclusion in *Tatro* that the single best determinant of an excluded medical service is one that requires the services of a physician.

Nature and Scope of Related Services

Although the Supreme Court has established a clear, two-step analysis on what constitutes related services under the IDEA, questions yet arise as to the nature and scope of such services. Decisions in recent lower court cases illustrate the breadth of the controversies.

Transportation

The first question centered on the matter of transportation: Is the school district responsible for transportation outside the boundaries of the school to programs unrelated to the student's IEP? The IDEA plainly states that transportation is a related service. However, in this instance, there was a challenge to a school district's refusal to provide after-school transportation for a student with epileptic seizures to a daycare center that was outside the school district's boundaries.[10] The Eighth Circuit held for the school, stating that the daycare program was not a part of providing FAPE to the child. The school was providing the necessary transportation for the child to and from home in order for the child to receive special education services, as required by the IDEA. The daycare center program was one of personal choice by the parents.

Another transportation dispute involved a question of whether or not a school district is responsible for reimbursing the parents of a special needs student for their travel to and from their child's residential treatment center.[11] This controversy involved an autistic boy, Aaron, who was in residence at Boston Higashi. This facility was chosen because of its unique twenty-four-hour "milieu therapy." The therapy is designed to teach autistic children independent living skills and to provide parents with the training necessary to help their children when they are at home and in the public.

The school district agreed to the placement as well to reimbursing the parents for travel to and from the center for training and for picking up and returning Aaron during school breaks. The per-trip reimbursement covered airfare, hotel accommodations for two days, airport parking, rental car, and two-days' per diem for meals. The district also covered the cost of the parental training, which was considered "vitally important if Aaron is ever to return to his home and family."[12]

For four years, the district had agreed to reimburse up to twelve trips per year. At the 1999 IEP meeting, however, the district offered to reimburse for no more than six trips per year and asked the treatment center to arrange to have the parental training sessions just prior to or immediately following a school break. The district did not ask the center to alter its training in any form.

The parents objected to this change and asked for a due process hearing. The impartial hearing officer (IHO) ruled in favor of the school district, noting that the number of trips were appropriate to providing FAPE under the IDEA. The parents appealed the IHO's decision.

The federal district court agreed with the IHO. It emphasized the IHO's finding that the parents had never taken as many as twelve trips each year, yet the Boston Higashi staff reported that Aaron was making good progress and that the parents were better able to control him when he was at home. The Boston Higashi staff never indicated that they would be unable to implement Aaron's IEP with the reduced number of trips. Lastly, the court drew attention to the fact that the IDEA does not require the school district to provide transportation for parents if it is unrelated to a child's access to special education. The school district was only obligated to provide parental transportation for the training sessions, which were essential to Aaron's social development needs.

Disputed Medical Services

There are a couple of examples in which parents and school districts were in dispute over what constitutes excluded medical services. The first example focuses on a parental request for reimbursement for hospitalization of a high school student.[13] The federal district court was reviewing an appeal by a school district that was ordered to reimburse parents for the cost of the hospitalization of their daughter, Cari Rae, during which time she was diagnosed with "oppositional defiance disorder" and drug dependency. This diagnosis was followed by a psychological evaluation and other tests that concluded Cari Rae was emotionally impaired.

The hospital stay and the subsequent evaluations preceded any action by the school district to identify Cari Rae as a student requiring special education, even though she always had struggled in high school and had been habitually absent. The administrative hearings officer ruled that the school district had breached the "child find" provision of the IDEA and, therefore, was responsible for reimbursing the parents for the hospitalization. Citing a Third Circuit Court of Appeals ruling, the federal district court agreed with the administrative hearing officer regarding the "child find" violation, stating that the "'child find' duty requires children to be identified and evaluated 'within a reasonable time after school officials are on notice of behavior that is likely to indicate a disability.'"[14]

In the second half of the analysis, the court then explored the question of whether requiring the school district to pay for the hospitalization was the appropriate remedy. The school district argued that the hospitalization was an intervention to an emotional crisis during which Cari Rae had locked herself in a bathroom and threatened her mother. Cari Rae's mother called the police who then referred Cari Rae to the acute care center at the hospital. The school district believed the cost should not be recoverable because it was a medical service, not a diagnostic or evaluative stay mandated by an IEP.

The court reasoned that while the emotional crisis led to the hospital stay, the result was the identification of Cari Rae's disability. "The stay at Queen's Hospital was—as the hearings officer found—the beginning of, if not an integral part of, the 'evaluation and diagnosis' of the Student."[15] In fact, the court went so far as to hypothesize that Cari Rae may never have been identified had it not been for her hospitalization.

Finally, the court remarked that the IDEA and case law provided courts with considerable discretion in determining an appropriate remedy to a substantive infringement of the IDEA.[16] Specifically, the court cited a Sixth Circuit Court of Appeals ruling in which reimbursement to parents for a unilateral private placement was appropriate when the district had failed to identify a student under "child find" who was later eligible for IDEA services.[17] The court concluded that reimbursement for the hospitalization was a "pre-placement"[18] expense and, therefore, should be reimbursed.

A second case involves a parental request for reimbursement for insurance co-payments for the services of an audiologist and for transportation costs incurred when taking their son to the audiologist.[19] Hunter was born deaf, although both parents and his siblings had normal hearing. He was initially fitted with acoustical hearing aids, but it soon became evident that he was not benefiting from them. On the advice of a physician, they chose to have Hunter fitted with a cochlear implant that would help him perceive sound that, in turn, would assist him in acquiring oral language skills.

Programming the speech processor, referred to as "mapping," was essential to the proper functioning of the implant and could be performed only by a specially trained audiologist. The school staff checked daily to test if Hunter was able to perceive a range of sounds. If he did not respond as expected, they referred him to the audiologist so that the processor could be adjusted.

Although Hunter's IEP included objectives that were based on the use of the cochlear implant and that he was expected to learn to hear, it neither included reimbursement for the co-payments nor the cost of taking him for "mapping" visits to the audiologist whose office was located in a neighboring city. His parents sought to have these expenses reimbursed and to have the audiologist services included in the IEP as related services.

At the due process hearing, the school district asserted that the cochlear implant was not an acoustical hearing device and, therefore, not covered under the IDEA. It also argued that "mapping" and other procedures related to the implant were excluded medical services, so the audiologist services should not be included in the IEP. The administrative hearing officer disagreed and ruled in favor of the parents.

The federal district court upheld the administrative hearing officer's decision. It was clear from the IEP that the implant was considered necessary to Hunter's language acquisition. Without it, he would not achieve some of the IEP's stated goals nor would he have meaningful access to special education services. "The IEP ... confirms that the educational methodology chosen for Hunter includes the use of the conchlear [sic] implant as a necessary part of the free appropriate public education provided to him. Under these circumstances, the mapping services necessary for the use of Hunter's cochlear implant are 'related services' within the meaning of the IDEA."[20]

Alternative Therapies

Not unlike disputes over specialized instructional approaches, parents have sought to have their choice of related services take precedence over those offered by the school. And, as in other cases, unless the parents can demonstrate that the proffered services are inadequate to ensuring FAPE, the courts will uphold a school district's right to choose the programs and services it provides at public expense.

One such example concerned a child, C.M., with profound hearing loss whose parents opted for cochlear implants for her when it was evident she was having no success with hearing aids.[21] After the devices were activated, C.M.'s parents sought "an 'educational program that maximizes exposure to meaningful sounds ... [particularly] exposure to spoken language every day,'"[22] as recommended by the company that created the implants. While the manufacturer made no specific recommendation as to which program to follow, the head of the Health Services' Department of Otolaryngology at the University of Miami encouraged them to continue with auditory-verbal therapy (AVT), the very same program they had chosen for their daughter while she was using hearing aids.

As a preschooler, C.M. was enrolled in a year-round program at her family's synagogue. Concurrently, she participated in the Miami-Dade County Early Intervention Program (EIP), until she was three years old, during which time her AVT was paid for by the county. After she turned three, her educational dossier from the EIP was forwarded to the school district so that it could determine whether she would be eligible for special education services.

Once it was determined that C.M. was eligible, the parents expressed their wish to continue her schooling at the synagogue but wanted the school district to pay for the AVT that she was still receiving. The district indicated that it had trained its personnel in the verbotonal (VT) approach, a recognized and well-established program in which hearing-impaired students learned how to communicate orally. The parents objected to the change in therapies and requested a due process hearing.

In denying the family's request to be reimbursed for tuition and AVT sessions, the administrative law judge (ALJ) ruled for the school district, indicating that "VT is an accepted and proven therapy and that '[i]t is the School Board's prerogative, not the Parents', to choose which of these accepted and proven methodologies will be provided at public expense.'"[23] Subsequently, after the district court ruled it did not have jurisdiction on the matter, the Eleventh Circuit Court of Appeals agreed with the ALJ.

> C.M.'s parents may be correct that VT would confuse C.M. and that the classroom dynamics offered by the School Board would not be most suitable for C.M. However, C.M.'s parents never challenged the School Board's assertion, or the ALJ's conclusion, that VT is a well-recognized means by which to teach hearing-impaired children to speak. While C.M.'s parents may not want such a program, the IDEA does not grant them a right to select among various programs. Rather, the School Board offered C.M. what was required under the IDEA—a free *appropriate* public education.... The IDEA does not permit them to challenge an IEP on the grounds that it is not the best or most desirable program for their child.[24]

Tort Claims

Another focus of related services litigation has been on claims of negligence. Several circuit courts have concluded that the IDEA does not provide for a private right of action for "tort-like money damages."[25] By way of example, a suit was filed by the parent of a deceased four-year-old developmentally delayed boy alleging that the school district was negligently responsible for his death. The child died by asphyxiation when his tracheotomy tube became dislodged while he played. His mother claimed that the "School District ... violated the IDEA by failing to have a person capable of reinserting Antione's tracheotomy tube ... at the time of the incident in question."[26]

While noting that it was a tragic case, the court granted summary judgment for the school district.

> Although the IDEA is silent about the availability of tort-like damages, "[t]ort-like damages are simply inconsistent with IDEA's statutory scheme." [citation omitted] "The purpose of the IDEA is to provide educational services, not compensation for personal injury, and a damages remedy-as contrasted with reimbursement of expenses-is fundamentally inconsistent with this goal." [citation omitted] "The IDEA's central mechanism for the remedying of perceived

> harms is for parents to seek changes to a student's program." [citation omitted][27]

The court emphasized that the only private right of action under the IDEA was that available to parents to force public education agencies to pay for educational services due under the IDEA.

Implications for Educational Leaders

The above discussions instruct principals and other educational leaders involved with the development of IEPs and with the delivery of special education services to follow the lead of the courts and ask two questions. The first question is *Does the requested service provide the student meaningful access to special education services?* While the statutory definition and federal regulations enumerate several examples of related services, those examples are not to be viewed as all inclusive. The IEP team must consider what services the student needs to go to, remain at, and return home from school, and to benefit from the education being provided.

The second question is *Does the requested service fall under the definition of an excluded medical service?* The IDEA specifies excluded medical services as those that are not for the purposes of student evaluation or diagnosis related to special education eligibility. The U.S. Supreme Court has provided a "bright line" test by defining an excluded medical service as one that requires the services of a physician. As was illustrated above, parents are likely to receive reimbursement for medical and other related costs if such expenses are the result of inaction by the school district and if the medical services provide evaluation and diagnosis that result in a child being identified as eligible for special education services. Furthermore, school district officials are unlikely to be successful in arguing that the cost associated with a student who requires extensive related services is an undue financial burden on the school district.

Essentially, the U.S. Supreme Court continues to emphasize the intent of Congress—to give students with disabilities access to a free appropriate public education and to do so in a manner that is reasonably calculated to provide them with educational benefit—through its rulings on all provisions of the IDEA, including related services. In this regard, school leaders will prevail in court challenges if they provide the supportive services students need to reach school, to stay in school, and to participate in the special education programs designed to give them meaningful educational experiences.

Endnotes

1 20 U.S.C. 1402 (26) (2004).

2 Irving Indep. Sch. Dist. v. Tatro, 468 U.S. 883, 891, 104 S. Ct. 3371, 3376 (1984).

3 *Id.*

4 34 C.F.R. § 300.13(b) (1983).

[5] Cedar Rapids Cmty. Sch. Dist. v. Garret F. *ex rel.* Charlene F., 526 U.S. 66, 119 S. Ct. 992 (1999).

[6] *Id.* at 69, note 3.

[7] *Id.* at 75.

[8] *Id.* at 75-76.

[9] *Id.* at 77.

[10] Fick *ex rel.* Fick v. Sioux Falls Sch. Dist. 49-5, 337 F.3d 968 (8th Cir. 2003).

[11] Aaron M. v. Yomtoob, 2003 WL 223469 (N.D. Ill. 2003)

[12] *Id.* at 2.

[13] Deptartment of Educ., State of Haw. v. Cari Rae S., 158 F. Supp. 2d 1190 (D. Haw. 2001).

[14] *Id.* at 1194, citing W.B. v. Matula, 67 F.3d 484, 501 (3d Cir.1995).

[15] *Id.* at 1199.

[16] *Id.* at 1199. "As a remedy for a substantive violation, the Court is authorized to 'grant such relief as the court determines is appropriate,'" citing 20 U.S.C. § 1415(i)(2)(B)(iii). "The statute thus 'confers broad discretion' on the Court and allows for reimbursement for costs of pre-eligibility private placements (e.g., private schools), if an IDEA violation is found and a child is subsequently determined to be eligible for IDEA services," at 1199-1200, citing *Burlington Sch. Comm. v. Mass. Dep't of Educ.,* 471 U.S. 359, 369, 105 S. Ct. 1996, 85 (1985).

[17] *Id.* at 1200. "Similarly, authorities have approved reimbursement for costs of private placements for 'child-find' violations, if a child is subsequently determined to be eligible for IDEA services … 'In cases where the lack of dialogue stems from the school district's failure to conduct sufficient 'child-find,' reimbursement may be appropriate,'" citing Doe v. Metro. Nashville Public Schs., 133 F.3d 384, 388 (6th Cir.1998).

[18] *Id.*

[19] Stratham Sch. Dist. v. Beth P., 2003 WL 260728 (D.N.H. 2003).

[20] *Id.* at 5.

[21] M.M. *ex rel.* C.M. v. Sch. Bd. of Miami-Dade County, Fla., 437 F.3d 1085 (11th Cir. 2006).

[22] *Id.* at 1099.

[23] *Id.* at 1094.

[24] *Id.* at 1103.

[25] Ortega v. Bibbs County Sch. Dist., 397 F.3d 1321, 1324 (11th Cir. 2005). *See also* Nieves-Marquez v. Puerto Rico, 353 F.3d 108 (1st Cir. 2003); Witte v. Clark County Sch. Dist., 197 F.3d 1271(9th Cir. 1999); Charlie F. v. Bd. of Educ. of Skokie Sch. Dist., 98 F.3d 989 (7th Cir. 1996); Heidemann v. Rother, 84 F.3d 1021(8th Cir. 1996); Gean v. Hattaway, 330 F.3d 758 (6th Cir. 2003); Babicz v. Sch. Bd. of Broward County, 135 F.3d 1420 (11th Cir. 1998).

[26] Ortega, at 1323.

[27] *Id.* at 1325.

Chapter 17

Transition: Individuals with Disabilities

Stanley L. Swartz, Jeff McNair, & Cathleen A. Geraghty

Introduction

The Individuals with Disabilities Education Act (IDEA) extended mandatory public education to include planning and programs to ensure a successful transition from K-12 educational experiences to community integration, including meaningful employment. The reauthorization of the IDEA in 2004 revised the definition of secondary transition services. Transition services are now defined as a

> coordinated set of activities for a child with a disability that is designed to be within a results-oriented process, that is focused on improving the academic and functional achievement of the child with a disability to facilitate the child's movement from school to post-school activities, including postsecondary education, vocational education, integrated employment (including supported employment); continuing and adult education, adult services, independent living, or community participation; is based on the individual child's needs, taking into account the child's strengths, preferences and interests; and includes instruction, related services, community experiences, the development of employment and other post-school adult living objectives, and, if appropriate, acquisition of daily living skills and functional vocational.[1]

Furthermore, the word *student* has been replaced with *child*. The emphasis of current legislative authority has developed from a growing research base indicating the need for coordination of agencies serving individuals with disabilities.

The National Council on Disability[2] made recommendations that included many of the elements that had gained recognition as needs that must be addressed, such as the transition from school to adult life. Their findings included:

1. Upon leaving school, students with disabilities and their families have a difficult time accessing appropriate adult services.

2. Effective transition planning for high school students with disabilities can facilitate their success in adult life.
3. Graduates with disabilities are more likely to be employed following school if comprehensive vocational training is a primary component of their high school programs and they have jobs secured at the time of graduation.
4. There are insufficient partnerships between the business community and schools for the purpose of enhancing employment opportunities for students with disabilities.
5. Parent participation during high school facilitates the successful transition of students with disabilities from school to adult life.

Support for the transition process can be provided on the three different levels. All students receiving special education under the IDEA must have transition services discussed in their individualized education program (IEP) at age 16. Secondary transition requirements may be added into an IEP before the child turns 16 if it is determined appropriate by the IEP team. Regardless of when the transition requirements are added into the IEP, it will be updated annually thereafter. In addition, the Rehabilitation Act Amendments of 1992[3] make clear that students eligible under section 504 are also eligible for transition planning. Services for transition to adult living range from no or limited support to time-limited, to specific and on-going support. Students with mild/moderate disabilities, such as specific learning disabilities, may not require adult services, or they may benefit from context-specific accommodations such as extended time to complete college and university course examinations, which are determined by services offered by the institution's Office of Student Disabilities. Second, students may need time-limited services including specific training such as on-the-job support or support in finding independent living arrangements. However, the assumption is that this support will only be needed for a specific period of time. Third, some individuals will need a specific type of support on an ongoing basis including specialized services permitting the individual to live normally within the community. Individuals with severe disabilities might be expected to need various levels of support throughout their lifetimes including ongoing support of an extensive nature. The outcome for each of these types of support is different. For individuals needing no support, time-limited support, or specific ongoing support, the outcomes are typically competitive employment and independent living. For individuals with severe disabilities that need ongoing support of an extensive nature, the expected outcomes are usually supported employment and supported living. In some cases, individuals with severe disabilities who need extensive and ongoing support may live independently and work in competitive employment.

Legal Issues

Transition Program

A successful school transition program can be conceptualized as a four-step procedure: (1) foundation, (2) process, (3) culmination, and (4) follow-up. The transition foundation includes all education, training, and experience that prepare an individual for adult life. An educational program is designed to develop functional skills, defined as skills that have a high probability of being required of someone as an adult. A foundation for children with mild educational disabilities will include academic skills that can be built upon with post-secondary vocational training or college training. For children with more severe educational disabilities, the curriculum will be more basic and functional. For all children, however, the curriculum should include training in social and vocational survival skills.

Survival skills are those that generalize across social and vocational settings. For example, social survival skills include behaviors such as responding appropriately, expressing needs such as the location of a restroom, and appropriately interacting with others in social settings. Vocational survival skills include reporting to work on time, working at one's workstation for a continuous period of time, and asking for clarification if an instruction is not understood. The need for these types of skills is not specific to individuals with disabilities but is expected of all adults. The IDEA 1997[4] amendments re-emphasize that transition to independent living and working is very much the goal of special education intervention. While the IDEA 2004[5] does not require formal transition planning earlier than age 16, the elementary IEP process should include some goals that build a foundation for secondary school transition planning. IEP decisions should be made in the context of how planning may affect the child's future school or post-school experiences. Section 300.43 of the IDEA[6] regulations defines transition services as a coordinated set of activities for a student with a disability that:

1. Is designed within a results-oriented process, that is focused on improving the academic and functional achievement of the child with a disability to facilitate the child's movement from school to post-school activities, including postsecondary education, vocational training, integrated employment (including supported employment), continuing and adult education, adult services, independent living, or community participation;

2. Is based on the individual child's needs, taking into account the child's preferences and interests;

3. Includes instruction; related services, community experiences, the development of employment, and other post-school adult living objectives; and, if appropriate, acquisition of daily living skills and functional vocational evaluation.

The transition plan should include the roles and responsibilities of teachers, agency personnel, parents, and students. Some examples include:

1. Assessing student needs, interests, or preferences for future education, employment, and adult living and devising goals in these areas;
2. Identifying, exploring, and trying out transition placements that match the student's assessment and vision and providing community experiences;
3. Instructing the student in the academic, vocational, and adult-living skills needed to achieve transition goals, including self-determination and independent living;
4. Identifying and providing the accommodations, supports, or related services the student needs to achieve the highest level of independent living possible;
5. Coordinating with adult services and organizations while helping families identify resources and natural supports; and
6. Providing or planning follow-up or follow-along support and activities once the student develops independence in a transition activity or graduates.

The IDEA requires that the child must be invited to the IEP team meeting if the purpose of the meeting is to discuss postsecondary goals for the child. Furthermore, the parent/guardian, child's special education teacher or related services provider, regular education teacher, and local educational agency representative are required to attend IEP meetings. If the child is sixteen years old or older and unable to attend the meeting, the law requires that steps are taken to ensure the child's preferences and interests are considered. Emphasis is placed on the child's involvement in transition planning while empowering the family to guide their child with a disability into adult living. With consent from parents and the child with a disability, appropriate adult-service organizations that provide or pay for transition services should be invited to attend the IEP. If the adult-service organization does not attend the meeting, the local education agency (LEA) is not required to take other steps in continuing to include the participating agency in transition planning. Other constituents such as guidance counselors, vocational educators, college counselors, related service providers, and administrators have a potential place in designing transition plans and may be invited to transition planning depending on the goals and needs of the student. If the aforementioned individuals will contribute to the transition plan, the teacher or administrator should invite those individuals. The 2004 reauthorization of the IDEA has allowed for state-level funds reserved under section 300.704 to be used when developing and implementing transition programs.

The 1997 amendments added two significant changes that related to transition. The definition of transition was changed to emphasize that related services are to be included and that every IEP must consider whether the student requires assistive technology devices and assistance. Therefore, every IEP meeting about transition must examine related services, determine the student's needs regarding technology, and consider assistive technology and services.

Goal development must be based on an individual child and take into account the interests and preferences of that child. Minimally, goals must address instruction (including all types of education); community experiences (community services including transportation, recreation, etc.); when appropriate, employment and their post-school daily living objectives (not only does this include community based work experiences, but also functional adult activities including voting, paying taxes, and utilizing Social Security or other government benefit programs); acquisition of daily living skills (self-care, budgeting, etc.); and functional vocational evaluation (vocational skill, interest or aptitude assessments). The 2004 reauthorization of the IDEA also stipulates that goals addressing graduation and dropout rates must also be established.

Additionally, the team must provide an explanation within the IEP if a determination is made that one or more of the goal areas are deemed unnecessary. These goals are part of the results-oriented process that considers all post-school activities, not exclusively employment. Often there are related services that must also be described in order for a student to access attainable outcomes (i.e. benefits from special education).

A critical component of transition goal development is personal choice. In order to facilitate lasting outcomes, student buy-in is critical. Developing choice-making skills through early student involvement in the IEP process will assist when students are later in the position of making decisions about their own lives. The law also facilitates this process by requiring LEAs to begin informing students of their rights one year prior to the age of majority under state law. Students in special education programs are not required to remain in school until age 22, and cannot be coerced into doing so by agencies unwilling to take them onto their caseloads and thereby begin paying for adult services. These decisions are an important part of the transition planning process.

Transition culmination occurs with the actual movement from secondary school to adult life. The transition team is charged with the responsibility of ensuring a smooth change from school to community service agencies and the provision of the activities described in the IEP. Finally, a transition follow-up is the last step. By evaluating results, school administrators can adjust the program and the process to ensure the most appropriate outcomes.

Special Education Legislation

The importance of the transition from public school educational programs to appropriate postsecondary experiences for individuals with disabilities and the necessary support services to successfully accomplish this transition has a history that can be traced through public policy reflected in legislation and changing professional practices. That the IEP must now include a specific statement of the needed transition services is a result of research demonstrating that the absence of such planning diminishes the likelihood of student success.[7] Additionally, political activism directed toward establishing the need for a follow-along plan for all children with disabilities has resulted in legislation hopefully facilitating a continuum of services for individuals with disabilities throughout their lives[8].

The need for transition services has been addressed in special education, vocational education, and rehabilitation legislation. Culminating in P.L. 94-142, the Carl Perkins Vocational Education Act, and the Rehabilitation Act of 1973, and refined in the Individuals with Disabilities Education Act and the Americans with Disabilities Act, a summary of this history is instructive to the understanding of changing public attitudes and awareness and changing public policy.

The Education of All Handicapped Children Act of 1975 (P.L. 94-142) required that children with disabilities have available to them a free and appropriate public education; protected the rights of children with disabilities and their parents to procedural due process; and required safeguards in the evaluation and placement process. Central to this legislation was making increased federal funds available to the states for the purpose of assuring the implementation of this law. Key to the eventual recognition of the need for transition services was the provision that the effectiveness of these programs be evaluated.

P.L. 94-142 marked the first consideration that special education programs for children with disabilities were a right and therefore mandated. The key provisions of the law included the provision of an IEP in the least restrictive environment (LRE). The IEP is a planning document that attempts to ensure an appropriate, results-based education. LRE is a requirement that children with disabilities be educated in an environment that is as close to the general education setting as possible where students with disabilities are having their educational needs met.

Further legislation in 1983[9] addressed the need to coordinate the education and training of youth with disabilities to assist in the transitional process from school to employment and postsecondary education. Major emphases included the design of vocational programs to increase the potential for youth with disabilities to gain competitive employment and to encourage the development of cooperative training models between educational and adult service agencies. This law marked the emergence of the transition process as a major focus in programs for children with disabilities.

A number of important revisions in secondary education and transitional services were included in 1986.[10] Programs were expanded not only for who can be served but also the nature of the services to be provided. Services could now be provided to children recently graduated or exited from the public schools. Reflecting Brown, Nietupski, and Hamre-Nietupski's (1976) "criterion of ultimate functioning," transition was reconceptualized as an educational theme throughout a child's school.[11] The IDEA expanded the concept of transition to include independent living and full participation of youth with disabilities in community programs as appropriate goals.[12] This change represents a movement from education as a means to competitive employment to a broader goal of full community integration. Requirements for IEP development include a statement of needed transition services by age 16, or age 14 when appropriate, and any necessary interagency responsibilities after school exit. Programs are expanded to address the development of job skills for transition to the workplace and social skills to enable full participation in community life.

The reauthorization of the IDEA in 2004 clarified that all students eligible under the IDEA must be considered for transition services and that transition must be considered as part of the IEP process beginning at age 16. Transition became one of the required statutory elements of an IEP after age 16. Under the IDEA 1997, the definition of transition was expanded to emphasize that related services must be included and required that every IEP meeting must consider whether the child requires assistive technology devices and services. Finally, the IDEA 1997 served to strengthen the belief that transition to independent living and working is the primary goal of all special education interventions.

Vocational Education

The Carl Perkins Vocation Education Act[13] allocated federal funds for equipment, staff, and buildings. Ten percent of funds available under this act were earmarked for children with disabilities and 22 percent for the disadvantaged. This act provided for assessment of interests and abilities related to vocational education programs; special services, including adaptation of curriculum, instruction, equipment, and facilities; guidance, counseling, and career development activities conducted by professionally trained counselors; and counseling services designed to facilitate the transition from school to post-school employment opportunities. By its very inclusion in Carl Perkins, vocational education for children with disabilities was legitimized. The focus of programming from education in the traditional academic sense to programs that emphasized employment and necessary functioning for adult life was made possible with the requirement that a portion of the funds authorized under this act be reserved for use by programs designed to benefit individuals with disabilities.

Rehabilitation Legislation

Building on a long history of the progressive expansion of services to individuals with disabilities, the Rehabilitation Amendments marked the entry of the Department of Rehabilitation into training for expanded employment outcomes.[14] Though earlier establishment of sheltered workshops had employment as a goal, this legislation concentrates on integrated community settings. The Rehabilitation Act of 1973[15] provided the statutory foundations for the Rehabilitation Services Administration and established priority for rehabilitation services to those with the most severe disabilities. It also initiated and expanded programs for individuals previously being underserved, including homebound and institutionalized clients; expanded employment opportunities for individuals with disabilities; included section 503, which eliminated architectural and transportation barriers impeding citizens with disabilities in public governmental buildings; required an individualized written rehabilitation plan (IWRP) with an annual review, which outlines, in the form of a contract developed in conjunction with the client, the conditions and responsibilities under which services will be provided; funded research and demonstration projects concerned with the rehabilitation of individuals with severe disabilities; and included section 504, which prohibits discrimination against an individual solely by reason of the disability in any program or activity receiving federal funds.[16]

Important to the eventual emphasis on transition for school-aged children was the inclusion of education for children with disabilities as one of the major features of the Rehabilitation Act. Children served by the public schools were guaranteed similar protections as adults served by rehabilitation and other service agencies. P.L. 94-142 was specifically referenced in the language of the law. This inclusion of school-aged children in the language of the act set the stage for the eventual coordination of services of various agencies because of the wide authority of this act.

Rehabilitation Comprehensive Services and Development Disabilities Amendments of 1978[17] continued and enlarged the existing trends of rehabilitation legislation. The law,

1. increased the commitment to rehabilitation research by expanding its research provisions and by stipulating the need and the means for ensuring coordination in the research enterprise;
2. continued the movement from a focus on preparation for employment to a focus on preparation plus affirmative action for enlarging opportunities for competitive employment for individuals with disabilities;
3. continued the attempt to provide services to underserved populations, especially the individuals with developmental disabilities and other severe disabilities;[18]
4. authorized the expansion of rehabilitation to include independent living as an objective for individuals served under the act;
5. and it provided employer incentives for training and hiring individuals with disabilities.[19]

Programs that required an affirmative action-type push were encouraged by this act. Transition at its inception was this type of an effort. This act authorized the use of funds to provide a variety of support mechanisms that allowed transition programs to be mounted.

The Vocational Rehabilitation Amendments of 1986[20] made notable changes to include the use of supported employment (defined as employment in an integrated setting with ongoing support services) as an acceptable outcome for the rehabilitation program.[21] Much of the historical emphasis of the state/federal rehabilitation agencies had been in rehabilitation that resulted in almost total independence of functioning for clients. This had the obvious effect of excluding serious efforts on behalf of individuals with moderate and severe disabilities. This act legitimized and authorized funding for services that were supportive in nature and expected to be ongoing.

The Americans with Disabilities Act[22] was federal civil right legislation that barred job discrimination against individuals with physical or mental disabilities. Access for individuals with disabilities to mass transportation, public buildings and transportation (defined as commonly used by the public), and governmental services was assured.[23] This act is considered an important extension of the Rehabilitation Act of 1973 because of the dramatically increased number of employers (those employing more than fifteen) that are affected. This act is seen as a last step in a process designed to ensure the integration of individuals with disabilities into the vocational mainstream of American society. The recognition that many individuals with disabilities will need support throughout their lives is carefully included in the provisions of the law.

Employment-Related Legislation

The Job Training Partnership Act of 1982[24] was designed to shift training away from the public sector to the private sector. Individuals with disabilities are targeted as a special population for services under this act. Incentives were made available to employers to accommodate individuals with disabilities in community-based employment settings.

The Supplemental Security Income Improvement Act of 1986 removed work disincentives by allowing recipients to work without loss of benefits.[25] It allowed participation in a variety of training programs, including supported employment, while still receiving income assistance.

Taken together, these pieces of legislation chart the evolution of programming for individuals with disabilities from traditional programs to a continuum of services beginning in the public schools and extending to community integration via adult service agencies. Such a movement was a public recognition of the need to coordinate efforts on behalf of individuals with disabilities as various governmental agencies assumed responsibility for service provision. It is important to remember that new initiatives built into legislation do not develop in isolation. Research demonstrating program efficacy and professional practice evolved because of field-based experience. One good example of this influence can be seen in the review of the Education for the Handicapped Act implementation mandated by Congress. In both the Eleventh[26] and Twelfth[27] Annual Reports to Congress, the importance of transition services to the success of students as adults are highlighted.

Trends and Upcoming Legislation

About every five years, Parts C and D of the IDEA must be reauthorized by Congress. Part B was permanently authorized, but changes are usually made to Part B during reauthorization. On December 3, 2004, President Bush signed into law PL 108-446, the Individuals with Disabilities Education Improvement Act of 2004. Most changes were effective as of July 1, 2005. The primary changes were in the areas of qualified teachers and discipline. Few of the changes directly affect transition issues. However, the following are the major changes regarding transition from PL 105-17 to the IDEA Improvement Act of 2004:

1. **IEP** – The transition process for a student with a disability now begins at age 16. The plan is not only a plan for transition. Parents should request that the IEP include a statement of inter-agency responsibilities and include links whenever appropriate. This is needed because this language is no longer in the statute.
2. **Transfers** – For students transferring between districts, comparable services described in the IEP that are in effect before the student's transfer must be provided by the new district. Those services must continue until that IEP is adopted or a new IEP is developed, adopted, and implemented. This is true of in-state and out-of-state transfers and is designed to help transferring families know what to expect from their new schools.
3. **Team transition** – At the initial IEP meeting, parents of a child transitioning from early childhood (Part C) to school age services (Part B) can request that representatives of the Part C system attend to assist with transition of services. This provision does not mandate a Part C representative to attend. It does however encourage collaboration.

In brief, with the passage of the Assistive Technology Act of 2004,[28] each state will receive additional money for technology programs, client protection, and advocacy services. New emphasis is placed on device demonstration and equipment loan, and there is an increased focus on training to ensure service providers have information on assistive technology. Supplemental grants are provided for equipment loan programs, and the act authorized a comprehensive national study of the assistive technology industry.

Recommendations for Practice

The focus on transition represents an important milestone in the history of efforts to serve individuals with disabilities. Past efforts were basically designed to guarantee access. Current efforts focus on the outcomes of special education. Do public school programs target eventual adult status and community participation? Have agencies with programming responsibility for individuals with disabilities developed agreements that will ensure continuous service during the transition from school to work and community living? Have the community agencies developed agreements with regard to the agency that will take primary responsibility with regard to case management? Current legislation suggests some practices that can be recommended for site-level program administration.

1. An IEP must be developed for each student. This plan must include descriptions of services and who will be responsible for providing the services. It is important to note that this plan will include a wide variety of activities that are other than traditional academic programming. Efforts will include cooperation with other service agencies.
2. The IEP should be carefully developed to ensure that all necessary information is included. Service recommendations will not be needed for each individual in all areas. The IEP should include consideration of each of the following areas: instruction, community experiences, employment and other post-school living objectives, acquisition of daily living skills, and functional vocational evaluation. Any area of which there is a recommendation must also include a statement of who will take responsibility for carrying out the action. If goals are not written in each of these areas, a statement must be provided as to why goals were not written in a particular area. The transition goals should be the school district's attempt to anticipate the transition needs of students in as many areas as possible. In the early stages of transition goal development, goals will be generic and exploratory. As students approach graduation, they should become more specific to the interests, needs, and desires of each student.
3. Cooperative relationships and agreements should be established with adult service agencies such as the Department of Rehabilitation, Mental Health, and Developmental Disabilities. Agencies should be invited to participate on an as-needed basis. Collaborative programs should be initiated to ensure that the transition from school to work or postsecondary programs will be a smooth one. An individual should be appointed with specific responsibility to serve as a liaison with community services agencies.
4. School curricula should be focused on the development of functional skills, those skills necessary for successful adult life. Programming

for youth with disabilities should include some balance of attention to vocational, independent living, and recreation and leisure activities. It must be recognized that appropriate programming for students with disabilities will not, in the vast majority of cases, be parallel to the regular academic programs. The law, however, requires that the least restrictive environment be enforced. Students who are able to be successful in the general education program, with support, must be provided the opportunity to do so. Decisions about inclusion must *not* be made exclusively on the basis of philosophy. Rather student performance data should guide these determinations.

5. Schools must make renewed efforts to involve families in the program development process. Parents who are full participants in program planning are less likely to initiate legal challenges that are costly both in time and resources.
6. Because transition is an outcome-based process, data collection is of increased importance. Follow-up studies of program graduates should be initiated. These data can be used to make any necessary program modifications.
7. Transitional programming for youth with disabilities should be viewed as a proactive process. Program opportunities that will enhance the likelihood of student success should be identified and supported. Schools need to take the initiative in developing community-based vocational programs. School programs that have the greatest potential for practical application in adulthood should be developed. Programs that have no demonstrable adult applications should be abandoned.
8. Efforts to educate school personnel and the public to the fact that appropriate programs for youth with disabilities are functional rather than academic should be initiated. The function of schooling for this group of children is to prepare for successful adulthood, and this information should be established and communicated.
9. A final area is for transition planners to develop an awareness of community-based existing natural supports. Increasingly, these resources are receiving attention in the research literature. Exemplified by groups, including churches and economic organizations, social or athletic groups, and business clubs, there is great potential in facilitating community integration through these voluntary attachments.[29]

Endnotes

[1] Individuals with Disabilities Education Act, 20 U.S.C. § 1401 *et. seq*

[2] *The education of students with disabilities: Where do we stand?* National Council on Disability. (1989).

[3] Public Law 102-569, the Rehabilitation Act Amendments of 1992.

[4] Individuals with Disabilities Education Act, P.L. 105-17, 1997

[5] Public Law 108-446 Individuals with Disabilities Education Improvement Act of 2004

[6] 34 C.F.R. 300.29. This regulation was promulgated prior to the 2004 Amendments. It is possible it may be amended when new regulations are created to implement the changes made.

[7] Individuals with Disabilities Education Act, 20 U.S.C. § 1400 *et.seq.*

[8] Americans with Disabilities Act, P.l. 101-336 (1990).

[9] Education of the Handicapped Amendments of 1983-Secondary Education and Transitional Services for Handicapped Youth, P.L. 99-199.

[10] Education of the Handicapped Act Amendments of 1986, P.L. 99-457.

[11] Brown, L., Nietupski, J. & Hamre-Nietupski, S. (1976). Criterion of ultimate functioning. In M.A. Thomas (ed.) *Hey don't forget about me!: Education's investment in the severely, profoundly, and multiply handicapped: A report.* Reston, VA: Council for Exceptional Children.

[12] Individuals with Disabilities Education Act of 1990 supra, note 3.

[13] Carl Perkins Vocational Education Act of 1984, P.L. 98-524.

[14] Vocational Rehabilitation Amendments of 1968, P.L. 90-391.

[15] Rehabilitation Act of 1973 P.L. 93-112.

[16] *See,* R.M. Garguilo, *Litigation and legislation for exceptional children: A historical perspective.* ICEC Q., 29 (1) (1980), and G.N. Wright, Total rehabilitation.

[17] Rehabilitation, Comprehensive Services, and Developmental Disabilities Amendments of 1978, P.L. 95-602.

[18] L. DESTAFANO & SNAUWAWERT. A VALUE-CRITICAL APPROACH TO TRANSITION POLICY ANALYSIS. (1989)

[19] Individuals with Disabilities Education Act of 1990, *supra,* note 3.

[20] Rehabilitation Act Amendments of 1986, P.L. 99-506.

[21] D. Braddock & G. Fujjura, *Federal Foundations for Transitions to Adulthood.* In B. Ludlow, A. Turnbull, & R. Likasson. Transitions TO ADULT LIFE FOR PEOPLE WITH MENTAL RETARDATION-PRINCIPLES AND PRACTICES. (1988).

[22] Americans with Disabilities Education Act of 1990, P.L. 101-336.

[23] C. Baird ADA – *Bridges, Not Barriers for People with Disabilities.* THE SPECIAL EDGE, 5(1) (1990).

[24] Job Training Partnership Act of 1982, P.L. 97-300.

[25] Supplemental Security Income Improvement Act of 1986, P.L. 99-643.

[26] *Eleventh Annual report to Congress on the Implementation of the Education of the Handicapped Act. U.S. Department of Education. (1989).*

[27] *Twelfth Annual Report to Congress on the Implementation of the Education of the Handicapped Act. U.S. Department of Education. (1990).*

[28] The Assistive Technology Act of 2004 (H.R. 4278)

[29] McNair, J. (1997). *A Discussion of Networks Supporting Adults with Disabilities in the Community.* The Center for the Study of Religion and Disability. Available at http://www.jeffmcnair.com/CSRD/networks.htm

Chapter 18

Disciplining Students with Disabilities*

Margaret Bannon Miller

Introduction

In June of 1997, Congress passed the long awaited reauthorization of the Individuals with Disabilities Education Act (IDEA).[1] Although the reauthorization contained a number of amendments, the most eagerly awaited and controversial were the amendments dealing with the discipline of students with disabilities. In its previous incarnations, the IDEA had never mentioned the word discipline and application of the principles of the act of disciplinary matters had been left to the courts and the Office of Special Education Programs (OSEP) of the United States Department of Education. In the 1997 reauthorization, Congress prescribed in considerable detail the requirements that schools must follow in applying school rules and disciplinary measures to students with disabilities. More recently, in December of 2004, the Individuals with Disabilities Education Improvement Act was signed into law by President George W. Bush. The discipline sections grant local education agencies increased unilateral authority and reconfigure requirements for making a manifestation determination. The regulations were revised in 2006, adding further clarity to the implementation of the newly tooled provisions.

Legal Issues

Discipline and the IEP

Even before the 1997 reauthorization, OSEP had issued a memorandum concerning the discipline of students with disabilities, which recommended the incorporation of a behavioral intervention plan into the individualized education programs (IEP) of students who were experiencing behavioral difficulties that interfered with their ability to function appropriately in the school setting.[2] Such a plan is now a requirement at any time when a student with a disability is removed from his or her program for more than ten school days in the same school year. This would encompass a suspension for more than ten consecutive days, a series of shorter suspensions at the point they accumulate to more than ten days in a school year, the removal of a student to an interim alternative educational setting for longer than ten school days, or an expulsion.[3]

Even though the law only requires conducting a functional behavioral assessment and devising a behavioral plan for a student at these specific times, the law requires IEP teams to consider intervention for a child whose behavior impedes learning whether or not the child has been excluded and whether or not the child has a "behavior disability."[4] It is a wise IEP team that explores how the student is doing behaviorally as well as academically at the annual meeting to review the student's placement. This kind of inquiry allows the student's IEP team to discover problem behaviors and, if necessary, conduct a functional behavioral assessment and formulate or modify a behavioral plan. Such a practice may allow the school to deal with problem behaviors early enough to avoid more serious misbehaviors by defining frequent systematic steps that the staff will use to deal with the student's behavior. This allows the staff to implement a consistent approach, which is generally much more successful in modifying a student's behavior, and such planning can facilitate the deliberation necessary to determine whether a student's behavior is a manifestation of his or her disability.

Suspension in its Various Forms

The treatment of suspension in both the IDEA and the implementing regulations appears to be a continuation of the differentiation between suspensions of less than ten school days and suspension of more than ten school days first made by the Office for Civil Rights (OCR) and adopted by the Supreme Court. In *Honig v. Doe,* the Supreme Court defined "change of placement" as "a suspension in excess of ten (10) days."[5] A suspension of less than ten school days was not seen as a change in placement triggering procedural safeguards including the need for a manifestation determination.

That distinction is now a part of the IDEA regulations that defines a change of placement as removal of the student from the current educational placement for more than ten consecutive days or a series of removals that constitute a "pattern" exceeding ten school days in a school year due to the length of each removal, the total amount of time the student is removed, and the proximity of the removals to one another.[6] "[I]t is the actual implementation of a 'change of placement,'" or the suspension itself, "which triggers the IDEA's requirements."[7] If a suspension is for ten school days or less, the school need not provide a student with educational services unless the suspension, when combined with previous suspensions, would take the student beyond ten cumulative suspension days in that school year. Further, a functional behavioral plan is not required as long as the student remains at the level of ten suspension days or less in a school year. Since a suspension of ten days or less is not a change in placement, neither a manifestation determination nor any of the other procedural safeguards in the act are required.[8] If the student is being suspended for ten school days or less, and has not previously been suspended during the school year so that the student's suspension days will not exceed the ten school-day mark, the school need not provide services during the period of suspension, nor is there a need for a behavioral plan, a manifestation determination, or other procedural safeguards.[9] The discipline protections apply to every school day, including summer school programs, regardless of whether the program is voluntary.[10]

Although there was some confusion about multiple suspensions when the discipline section was first created, the regulations allow school officials to impose additional suspensions, beyond ten cumulative school days in the same school year, for separate incidents of misconduct.[11] However, there is a caveat to this seeming flexibility. If the additional removals constitute a "pattern of exclusion," they are transformed from an allowable suspension to a change in placement requiring procedural safeguards. As previously mentioned, the regulations contemplate that when certain factors converge (the total cumulative days exceeds ten, the length of each removal, and the close proximity of one removal to another) a change of placement has occurred.[12] Again, this approach is similar to the longstanding analysis of suspension done by the OCR. In determining whether a series of suspensions created a pattern amounting to a change in placement, the OCR used the same three factors, which are now part of the IDEA regulations. As an example of a pattern of suspensions that would clearly amount to a significant change in placement, the OCR described a student being suspended "several times during a school year for eight or nine days at a time."[13]

Unlike a single suspension of ten days or less, suspensions that are each less than ten days but amount cumulatively to more than ten days in a school year do require a continuation of educational services. Under these circumstances, the student must be provided services that enable him or her to "continue to participate in the general education curriculum, although in another setting, and to progress toward meeting the goals set out in the child's IEP."[14] The extent to which these services are necessary during the period of suspension, beginning at the tenth cumulative day of suspension, is decided by school personnel in consultation with the student's special education teacher.[15]

Further, whenever a child's removal exceeds the ten cumulative school days in a school year for misbehavior related to the child's disability , the student's IEP team must conduct a functional behavioral assessment if one has not been completed. The team must also reconvene to develop a behavioral intervention plan.[16] If the development of the plan is a result of a series of suspensions, the plan should provide strategies calculated to lessen or eliminate those behaviors for which the suspensions were assigned. If the student has a behavioral plan prior to the suspension that takes him or her beyond the ten cumulative school days, the student's IEP team would convene within ten school days of that suspension to review the behavioral plan and make any necessary changes.[17]

A Word About In-School Suspension

A topic of much debate has been whether in-school suspension is to be counted when figuring the number of days a student has been suspended from school. In the analysis and comment that accompanied the publication of the 2006 IDEA Regulations,[18] the U.S. Department of Education reiterated its earlier stance[19] that in-school suspension would not be considered a part of the suspension days addressed in the regulations as long as the student is given the opportunity to: continue to appropriately progress in the general curriculum;[20] continue to receive the specific services in the student's IEP; and continue to participate with non-disabled students to the extent that the student would in his or her current placement.[21] Although this approach allows schools greater flexibility in dealing with disciplinary problems, it may not be achievable given the current structure of some in-school suspension programs. In order to ensure that the use of in-school suspension meets these three conditions, the IEP team may want to include in the student's behavioral plan a description of exactly what will happen when the student is placed in an in-school suspension so as to guarantee that he or she is continuing to receive access to the general curriculum, is receiving the services in the IEP, and is with non-disabled children. For example, the behavioral plan could specify that when the student reports to the in-school suspension room (which may contain a number of non-disabled students), the student's special education teacher will be notified so that the teacher will know where the student is located when it is time to provide certain services contained in the student's IEP. The plan should also indicate that the student will continue working on assignments from the various classes during the time he or she is in the in-school suspension so as to be considered separately from suspensions that must be counted towards the ten cumulative school days in a school year.

Whether the school must count suspension from the school bus as a day of suspension from school depends upon several factors. If transportation is listed in the student's IEP as a related service, meaning the school has deemed transportation necessary for the student's special education, a day of suspension from the bus would count as a day of suspension from school unless the school provided an alternate method of transportation. However, if transportation is not listed as a related service in the student's IEP, suspension from the bus would not be a suspension from school, and the student's parents would have to find a way for the student to get to school.[22]

Pattern of Suspensions

Finally, if a series of suspensions of ten school days or less forms a pattern so as to amount to a change of placement, the school would need to follow the steps delineated below under "Expulsion:" provide notice to the student's parents of all other necessary procedural safeguards; hold a manifestation determination conference to decide whether the student's disability directly caused the misbehavior(s) that brought about the suspensions: and if related, develop a functional behavioral assessment plan, conduct the assessment, and formulate a behavioral intervention plan.[23] Because it may be impossible to determine the exact point at which a series of suspensions forms a pattern, school administrators would be wise to establish a schedule by which a student's IEP team would automatically reconvene once a certain number of suspension days is reached. For example, as the student is assigned a suspension of less than ten days, but one which will take him or her beyond the ten cumulative school days in a school year, the IEP team would meet to discuss the reason for the current and past suspensions and to look at the number of days the student has been suspended as well as the proximity of those days to each other. A meeting would have to be held in any event to formulate an assessment plan or to review an already existing behavioral plan. If the IEP team decides that existing suspensions do not form a pattern, it could authorize the further use of suspensions up to a certain number, at which point the team would reconvene to again examine the behavioral plan and the nature, frequency, and number of suspensions. Some kind of periodic review will be absolutely necessary in order to avoid suspensions becoming a change of placement without the procedural safeguards.

Use of Forty-Five-Day Interim Alternative Educational Setting

Presumably, a student's IEP team could fashion and move the student to an interim alternative educational setting (IAES) at any time school personnel and the student's parents agree that such a placement is appropriate. For example, if the school placement has become inappropriate and the IEP team, including the student's parents, agree upon the need for residential placement, the team might choose to create an IAES to serve the student's needs while arrangements for the residential placement were being made. However, the IDEA and its implementing regulations address the use of IAES under only two circumstances: (1) when triggered by a student bringing a weapon to school,[24] knowingly possessing or using illegal drugs or soliciting the sale of a controlled substance at school or a school function, or inflicting serious bodily injury upon another person at school or a school function; and (2) when ordered by an independent hearing officer upon a determination that the student is a danger to self or others.[25]

A student who brings a weapon to school may have his placement unilaterally changed to an IAES for up to forty-five school days: the change can be ordered by the school without the consent of the parent. For purposes of the IDEA regulations, *weapon* has the same meaning as *dangerous weapon* in the United States Code:

> A weapon, device, instrument, material or substance, animate or inanimate that is used for or is readily capable of causing death or serious bodily injury, except that such

> term does not include a pocket knife with a blade of less than 2 1/2 inches long.[26]

A school may also impose a unilateral move to an IAES for a student who knowingly possesses or uses illegal drugs or sells or solicits the sale of a controlled substance. The regulation defines controlled substance as "a drug or other substance identified under Schedules I, II, III, IV or V in Section 202(c) of the Controlled Substances Act." *Illegal drug* is also defined as a controlled substance that is "legally possessed or used under the supervision of a healthcare professional or under any provision of federal law."[27]

In addition, under the 2004 amendments, a school may unilaterally remove a student to an IAES for no more than forty-five school days if he or she has inflicted "serious bodily injury" upon another person. The term *seriously bodily injury* in the IDEA regulations has the same meaning as defined elsewhere in the United States Code:

> the term "serious bodily injury" means bodily injury which involves—
>
> (a) a substantial risk of death;
>
> (b) extreme physical pain;
>
> (c) protracted and obvious disfigurement; or
>
> (d) protracted loss or impairment of the function of a bodily member, organ, or mental faculty."[28]

Even though a student may be ordered to an interim alternative educational setting by school officials, the setting itself must be determined by the student's IEP team.[29] The team must design the IAES so as to enable the student to continue to participate in the general education curriculum and to progress toward meeting the IEP goals. The plan for the IAES must also include a functional behavioral assessment, behavioral intervention services, and modifications that address the student's behavior and are designed to prevent the behavior from recurring.[30] Presumably, unless the school has already created a pattern of suspensions that precludes its use of any further suspensions that school year, the student could be suspended for a few days to allow the IEP team to meet and design the IAES.

No later than the date on which the decision is made to place the student in the IAES, the school must provide the student's parents notification of this decision and a copy of the notice of procedural safeguards. Within ten school days of the decision to move the student to an IAES, the IEP team must meet to conduct a manifestation determination review following the same set of procedures described in the "Expulsion" section below. If the student's behavior is not found to be a manifestation of his or her disability, the school may continue on with the normal expulsion procedure that it employs for students without disabilities unless the student's parent disagrees with the manifestation determination and asks for a due process hearing to decide the question. In the event of a hearing request, the student would stay in the IAES for the duration of the forty-five school-day period or until the independent hearing officer renders his or her decision, whichever occurs first.[31] Even if the student's behavior is judged to be a manifestation of his or her disability, the student may still remain in the IAES for the remainder of the forty-five school day period before returning to the original placement or moving to another placement that the IEP team, including the student's parent, feels better meets the student's needs.

Another use of the IAES is as a temporary placement for students who are a danger to themselves or others. Although placing such a student in an alternative setting can be decided upon by agreement of the student's IEP team, including the student's parent, the procedures in the regulation address the situation in which the parties cannot agree, and the decision is turned over to an independent hearing officer.[32] An IAES for a dangerous student cannot be unilaterally assigned by school officials without parental consent. Like any hearing about a forty-five-school-day IAES, this hearing is held on an expedited basis. In order to grant a school's request to place a dangerous student in an IAES, the independent hearing officer must determine that keeping the student in the current placement is substantially likely to result in injury to the student or others.[33] It is interesting to note that the IAES, which the school asks an independent hearing officer to impose in the case of a dangerous student, may be, but need not be, the work of the IEP team. Instead, it may be something that the school proposes after consultation with the student's special education teacher, although the U.S. Department of Education encourages schools to develop the IAES through use of the IEP team.[34]

It is important for schools to remember that under *Honig v. Doe*, school officials still have the ability to go directly to court to seek injunctive relief in order to immediately remove a student who is dangerous to self or others.[35] Obtaining injunctive relief from the court precludes the necessity of obtaining the decision of an independent hearing officer, and unlike a hearing officer, a judge may choose to order an IAES of longer than forty-five school days. It is reasonable to assume that a judge has the power to order a student out of the current placement and into an IAES for whatever period of time the judge deems appropriate, although this point is not discussed in either *Honig* or in the IDEA regulations.

Expulsion or Other Change of Placement for Disciplinary Reasons

An expulsion or other change of placement for disciplinary purposes (including a pattern of suspensions) requires procedures[36] in addition to the steps that must accompany suspensions beyond ten cumulative school days. For example, on the day an administrator decides to expel the student, he or she must supply the student's parent with notice of the decision as well as a notice of procedural safeguards.[37] Within ten school days after the decision to initiate expulsion proceedings, the "relevant members" of the student's

IEP team[38] must conduct a review of the relationship between the student's disability and the misbehavior.[39] There is, however, no obligation to conduct the review before the decision to move for expulsion of the student.[40] In conducting this manifestation determination, the IEP team must consider all relevant information in terms of the student's misbehavior. This information includes: relevant information supplied by the parent; teacher observations of the student; and the student's IEP and any other relevant information in the child's file.[41] Based upon that information, the IEP team now makes two determinations: (1) that the student's disability caused or had a direct and substantial relationship to the conduct in question and (2) that the conduct in question was the direct result of the school's failure to implement the IEP.[42] Prior to the 2004 amendments, IEP teams making a manifestation determination had to consider whether the IEP was appropriate; whether the IEP was implemented as written; whether the "child's disability did not impair the ability of the child to understand the impact and consequences of the behavior;" and whether "the child's disability did not impair the ability of the child to control the behavior."[43] In addition, the 2004 amendments eliminated a legal presumption that the behavior and the disability were related unless the IEP team determined the opposite.

If the student's IEP team determines that the student's disability directly caused the conduct in question, the team must find that the behavior was a manifestation of the student's disability. Likewise, if the student's IEP listed certain modifications for a particular class, and those modifications were not made, and if as a direct result, the student's behavior in that class deteriorated, the student cannot be expelled for his actions in that particular class. Such a result may seem to remove students' responsibility to come to class and act appropriately despite an inappropriate IEP.[44] However, the school must first fulfill its obligations toward the student, and then it may hold the student responsible. Given a finding that the behavior is a manifestation of the student's disability, the IEP team must remedy deficiencies, if any, in the IEP[45] and determine what measures are necessary to assist the student in changing the behavior.[46] This may include a change of placement if the IEP team determines that such a change is necessary. However, the parent must agree to the change, or the school must move to mediation or request a hearing to decide the matter. In addition, if the team determines that the misbehavior is a manifestation of the disability, the IEP team must formulate a functional behavioral assessment to review and, if necessary, revise an already existing behavioral intervention plan. The plan should be focused on helping the child understand the misbehavior that caused the consideration of expulsion and in devising positive supports and strategies such that the misbehavior will not recur.[47]

Should the IEP team decide that the student's misbehavior is not a manifestation of the disability, the school must provide the parent with a notice of the decision, including a notice of procedural safeguards, and may proceed with expulsion or other disciplinary change of placement.[48] The school would then transmit the student's special education and disciplinary records to the person or persons making the final determination on the disciplinary action.[49] During a period of expulsion or other disciplinary change of placement, the student must continue to receive services as designed by the student's IEP team. In designing the services, the team must determine the extent to which they are necessary to enable the child to appropriately participate in the general education curriculum and progress towards meeting the goals in the student's IEP.[50]

Under a requirement that is not in the IDEA regulations, but is a mandatory part of any change of placement under the regulations implementing section 504,[51] a student must have a recent evaluation that yields information appropriate for the IEP team to use in making its manifestation determination. In a 1989 memorandum to senior staff, the OCR describes the kind of information it believes necessary to make a manifestation determination: "the information considered would include psychological evaluation data related to behavior [and] the relevant data would be recent enough to afford an understanding of the child's current behavior."[52] Thus, a recent evaluation that yields relevant behavioral data would be necessary before proceeding to the manifestation determination review since every student eligible under the IDEA is also covered by section 504.

If the student's parent wishes to challenge the manifestation determination, the parent may request a hearing, which is to be held on an expedited basis.[53] In reviewing the IEP team's decision, the hearing officer must "determine whether maintaining the current placement is substantially likely to result in injury to the child or others."[54] However, the hearing officer's task is not simply to review the findings of the IEP team. "Rather, he is to take the place of the IEP [t]eam and make his own independent determination of whether the agency has shown that the child's behavior was a manifestation of his or her disability."[55] The officer can therefore consider evidence, including a new diagnosis, not available to the IEP team during its manifestation determination.[56] Until the hearing officer makes a final determination, and during any period that a state might provide for appeal of a hearing officer's decision, the student must stay in the educational placement he was in when the misbehavior occurred unless the school and the student's parent agree to a different placement, or unless the student has been unilaterally assigned to a forty-five-school-day IAES due to weapons, drugs, or serious bodily injury.[57] Again, it should be noted that a student who is considered too dangerous to remain on school premises while the expulsion process and possibly a due process hearing are unfolding, can be removed through an expedited due process hearing or the injunctive process allowed by *Honig*. The length and complication of the procedures that surround expulsion or other disciplinary changes of placement should encourage administrators to adopt the periodic review of suspensions suggested in a previous section of this chapter, since a series of suspensions that form a pattern would invoke every single one of these procedures.

Application to Students Not Yet Eligible For Special Education

In any situation where the school can be determined to have knowledge of a student's disability prior to misbehavior that triggers expulsion, the student may receive all of the IDEA protections prior to the disciplinary action being carried out.[58] Knowledge of a student's disability is imputed to the school under any one of three circumstances:[59] (1) the student's parent has expressed concern in writing to appropriate supervisory or administrative school personnel or a teacher of the child that the student is in need of special education and related services; (2) the student's parent has requested an evaluation and has followed formal evaluation procedures; or (3) the student's teacher or other school personnel have expressed specific concerns about a pattern of behavior demonstrated by the student directly to either the director of special education or other supervisory personnel in accordance with the school's "child find" or special education referral procedure.[60]

A mere expression of concern by a teacher, which is not related to whether the student has a disability, would not form a basis for knowledge that the student has a disability. Similarly, a parent's verbal request that the school do something for the child's poor behavior and performance is not alone enough to impute knowledge, especially where the behavior and performance is typical of the average adolescent.[61] Further, if an expression of concern about the student's behavioral performance is followed by responsible school action to address that behavior, the expression of concern does not amount to knowledge that the student has a disability.[62] Also, the school is not deemed to have knowledge if it has conducted a special education evaluation and determined that the student is not eligible or if the school determines that an evaluation is unnecessary and provides the student's parent with this determination and notice of procedural safeguards.[63] Lastly, the school is not deemed to have knowledge if the parent has not allowed an evaluation of the child or has refused services.

Even if the school did not have prior knowledge of a student's disability, but during the period of an expulsion or other disciplinary change of placement the student's parent requests an evaluation, that evaluation must be done on an expedited basis.[64] During the evaluation period, the student would be in an educational placement determined by school officials. This placement can include suspension or expulsion without educational services.[65] In other words, services need not be provided to an expelled or suspended student while the expedited evaluation is taking place. Should the evaluation show that the student is eligible for special education and related services, the IEP team would conduct a manifestation determination review. If the student's behavior is not a manifestation of his or her disability, the expulsion or other disciplinary change of placement could continue with services designed by the IEP team, including a behavioral plan.[66]

The possibility of imputing knowledge of a student's disability based upon the three circumstances delineated in the act make it imperative that school administrators familiarize staff members with the special education "child find" and referral procedures of their local school district. In the past, many have thought that unless a student's behavior substantially interfered with educational progress, the behavior should not be looked upon as a possible sign of a need for special education services. The amendments added during the 1997 reauthorization and retained in 2004, with their emphasis on behavior, make such thinking outmoded. Expulsion of a student, even for egregious behavior, could be substantially delayed if it can be credibly contended that the district ignored its child find obligations.

Referral to Law Enforcement/Judicial Authorities

Because of a somewhat interesting court decision, which held that referral to a law enforcement agency had to be an IEP team decision if such a referral could result in a change of the student's placement,[67] the IDEA was amended in 1997 to explicitly address the issue of school officials' authority to refer students who engaged in criminal or delinquent conduct to the proper authorities. The IDEA now makes it clear that the school retains the right to report a crime committed by a student with a disability to the same extent that such crimes are reported when committed by students without disabilities. Both law enforcement and judicial authorities may exercise their responsibilities under federal or state law when a crime is committed by a student with a disability.[68]

The IDEA is not clear as to when the records must be provided. Courts considering the issue determined that the purpose of providing the records is to "help determine what disciplinary action or educational placement changes should be made if a child commits a crime that has been reported to authorities."[69] Records therefore need only be transmitted before the delinquency proceedings to "the persons making the final determination regarding the disciplinary action."[70]

When a referral to law enforcement or the courts is made by the school, copies of the student's special education and disciplinary records are to be transmitted for consideration by the authorities to whom the crime is reported. However, such a transmission can only take place if it meets the requirements of the Family Educational Rights and Privacy Act (FERPA).[71] In order to release any personally identifiable information, the school must receive consent from the student's parent, release the information in response to a judicial order or lawfully issued subpoena, or release the information because there exists a health or safety emergency.[72] In the absence of parental permission, the school would be unable to transmit the student's disciplinary and special education records to a law enforcement agency or court unless the school received a court order or subpoena to do so or unless the situation fulfilled the requirements of a health or safety emergency as described in the FERPA regulations. However, the fact that the records cannot be transferred does not prevent the school district from reporting the crime.

Recommendations for Practice

Suspension

1. Under a suspension,[73] no services are required unless the student has already been suspended for ten cumulative days in that school year, repeated suspensions constitute a change in placement, or behavior is determined to impede learning. However, any existing behavioral intervention plans should be followed.
2. When repeated suspensions total ten days or less, services must be provided to the extent necessary for the student to participate in the general education curriculum and progress toward meeting his or her IEP goals. The extent of necessary services is determined by school personnel in consultation with the student's special education teacher.
3. A change of placement occurs for removal for more than ten consecutive days or if a series of suspensions forms a pattern based on the length of each suspension, the total amount of time the student is removed and the amount of time between suspension. A manifestation determination, other procedural safeguards, and previous steps for less than ten-day suspensions must be implemented.
4. Schools can unilaterally assign the student to an IAES designed by the student's IEP team when the student brings a weapon to school or a school function; possesses, uses, or sells drugs at school or a school function; or inflicts serious bodily injury on another person at school or a school function. The student may be suspended for ten days or less while the team designs the IAES. The parents must be notified "no later than the date on which the decision is made" that the school is placing the student in an IAES, and the notice of procedural safeguards must be provided within ten business days of the suspension. Within ten days of the decision to initiate the IAES, the student's IEP team must convene to conduct a manifestation determination review as in cases of expulsion. If the behavior is not a manifestation of the disability, the school may continue with the expulsion proceeding, and the IEP team would determine services to be provided once the student is expelled. If the behavior is a manifestation of the disability, the student may remain in the IAES for the forty-five school days and then would be returned to his original placement unless a change of placement has been agreed upon by the school and the student's parents.

5. When triggered by dangerous behavior, the school can seek a judicial order to move the student to an IAES or can reach an agreement with the student's parents. Otherwise, the school must seek an expedited due process hearing. To change the placement, the hearing officer must determine that the current placement is likely to result in injury to the child or to others.

Expulsion

1. When a school seeks an expulsion[74] or a move to an IAES for a period of more than ten school days, the school must notify the parent on the day the decision is made and provide notice of procedural safeguards. The student can be suspended for no more than ten consecutive school days (or forty-five in IAES if drug or weapon related).
2. Within ten school days of making the decision to expel or remove the student to an IAES, the IEP team must conduct a manifestation determination conference to consider relevant information provided by the parent, teacher observations of the student, the student's IEP, and other relevant information in the file. They must determine whether the student's disability caused or had a direct and substantial relationship to the conduct in question and whether the conduct in question was the direct result of the school's failure to implement the IEP.[75]
3. If the act was a manifestation of the disability, the case conference determines whether a change in services and/or placement is warranted and remedies any deficiencies in the IEP. The team must also conduct a functional behavioral assessment and formulate a behavior intervention plan.[76]
4. If it is not a manifestation of the disability, the school sends notice of the decision and procedural safeguards to the parents, proceeds with the expulsion, and sends records to the expulsion examiner. If the parent files for a special hearing, the students stays in the IAES until the forty-five school-day period expires, moves to another placement with the agreement of the school personnel and parents, or returns to the last placement under the current IEP.[77]

Endnotes

* This chapter appears with only minor revisions from the chapter published in the 3rd Edition of the *Principals Legal Handbook*. Mark A. Paige contributed to the updates relating to the 2006 regulations. Victoria J. Maslow and Michelle A. Turner also contributed to the earlier version of this chapter.

1 20 U.S.C. § 1400 *et seq.*

2 OSEP Memorandum, 13 EHLR 372 (1987).

3 20 U.S.C. 1415(k)(1)(F)(i); 34 C.F.R. § 300.536

4 20 U.S.C. 1414(d)(3)(B)(i); 34 C.F.R. § 300.530(d)(ii)

5 Honig v. Doe, 484 U.S. 305 at 325 (1988).

6 34 C.F.R. § 300.536.

7 Orlando C. v. Ysleta Indep. Sch. Dist., 34 IDELR 172 (W.D. Tex. 2001).

8 20 U.S.C. 1415(k)(1)(B); 34 C.F.R. § 300.530(e)

9 *Id.*

10 L.I.H. v. New York City Bd. of Educ., 103 F. Supp. 2d 658 (E.D.N.Y. 2000).

11 *Id.*

12 *Id.*

13 OCR Senior Staff Memorandum, 14 EHLR 307.05 (October 28, 1988).

14 20 U.S.C. 1415(k)(1)(D)(i), 34 C.F.R. § 300.530(d)(1)(i)

15 34 C.F.R. § 300.121(d)(3)(i), 34 C.F.R. § 300.530(d)(5)

16 34 C.F.R. § 300.520(b), 34 C.F.R. § 300.530(f)(i)

17 34 C.F.R. § 300.520(c), 34 C.F.R. § 300.530 (f)(1)(ii)

18 71 Fed. Reg. 46715 (August 14, 2006).

19 64 Fed. Reg. 12619 (March 12, 1999).

20 Although the phrase "continue to progress in the general curriculum" is used, that does not imply that the student must remain in the general education setting. On the contrary, the regulation includes the specific qualifier "although in another setting." 34 C.F.R. § 300.530(d)(1)(i)

21 71 Fed. Reg. 46715 (August 14, 2006).

22 *Id.*

23 34 C.F.R. § 300.530(f).

24 Because both the act (20 U.S.C. § 1415(k)(1)(ii)(I) and the regulation (34 C.F.R. § 300.530 (g)(1) use the phrase "carries a weapon to school or function," at least one court has ruled that a student possessing a weapon he obtained at school could not be placed in a forty-five-day interim alternative educational setting. The interpretation of the U.S. Department of Education is that congressional intent would call for a broader application to include a weapon the student found at school. 64 Fed. Reg. 12619 (March 12, 1999).

25 34 C.F.R. § 300.532(b).

26 18 U.S.C. 930(g)(2). (Note: The exception for a knife with a blade less than 2½ inches long would simply imply only that a school could not unilaterally impose a move to a forty-five-day interim alternative educational setting for possession of such a knife, it could still expel a student who brings it to or is in possession of it at school or a school function if the school's disciplinary code bans knives of any kind.)

27 34 C.F.R. § 300.530(2)

28 18 U.S.C. 1365(h).

29 34 C.F.R. § 300.531.

30 34 C.F.R. § 300.530(d)(2)

31 34 C.F.R. § 300.533.

32 34 C.F.R § 300.532.

33 C.F.R. § 300.532

34 34 C.F.R. § 300.531); Fed. Reg.: March 12, 1999 (Volume 64, Number 48) p. 12625.

35 *Honig*, 484 U.S. 305.

36 The procedures described in this section are specific only to children with disabilities and are in addition to those procedures (notice, hearing, etc.) required by state and local policy for any child facing expulsion.

37 34 C.F.R. § 300.530(h)

38 The "relevant members of the IEP Team are determined by the parent and local educational agency." 20 U.S.C. 1415(k)(1)(E)(i); 34 C.F.R. § 300.530(e).

39 34 C.F.R. § 300.530(e)

40 Farrin v. Maine Sch. Admin. Dist. No. 59, 165 F. Supp. 2d 37 (D. Me. 2001).

41 34 C.F.R. § 300.530(e)

42 34 C.F.R. § 300.530(e)(1)(i) and (ii)

43 20 U.S.C. 1415(k)(4)(C)(1997).

44 Prior to the 2004 amendments, the IEP team had to consider whether the child's IEP was appropriate at the time the misbehavior occurred. If the IEP or placement is found to be inappropriate in relation to the student's misbehavior, the expulsion or other disciplinary change of placement could not proceed. Note that the 2004 language only requires an examination of whether the IEP was properly implemented, not whether it was appropriate in the first place.

45 34 C.F.R. §300.530(e)(3).

46 34 C.F.R. § 300.530(f)

47 34 C.F.R. § 300.324(a)(2)(i)

48 34 C.F.R. § 300.530(c).

49 34 C.F.R. § 300.524(b).

50 34 C.F.R. § 300.530 (d)(i)

51 34 C.F.R. § 104.35.

52 OCR Senior Staff Memorandum, 16 EHLR 491, 493.

53 34 C.F.R. § 300.532(a) and (c).

54 34 C.F.R. § 300.532

55 Richland Sch. Dist. v. Thomas P., 2000 U.S. Dist LEXIS 15162 (W.D. Wis. 2000).

56 *Id.*

57 34 C.F.R. § 300.533.

58 34 C.F.R. § 300.534.

59 It is interesting to note that Congress eliminated a fourth category: "the behavior or performance of the child demonstrates the need for such services." 20 U.S.C. 1415(k)(8)(B)(ii)(1997).

60 34 C.F.R. § 300.534*b)(3).

61 Mr. & Mrs. R. v. W. Haven Bd. of Educ., 36 IDELR 211 (D. Conn. 2002).

62 Fed. Reg: March 12, 1999, (Volume 64, Number 48), p. 12629.

63 34 C.F.R. § 300.534(c)(2)

64 34 C.F.R. § 300.534(d)(2)(i).

65 *Id.*

66 34 C.F.R. § 300.534(d)(2)(iii)

67 Morgan v. Chris L., 106 F.3d 401 (6th Cir. 1997).

68 34 C.F.R. § 300.534

69 Valentino C. v. Sch. Dist. of Phila., 2004 U.S. Dist. LEXIS 2114 (E.D. Penn. 2004).

70 *Id.*

71 34 C.F.R. § 300.529(b).

72 34 C.F.R. § 99.30; 34 C.F.R. § 99.31(a)(9) and (10); 34 C.F.R. § 99.36.

73 This term, as used in the IDEA regulations, does not include in-school suspension as long as the student is afforded the opportunity to continue to appropriately progress in the general curriculum, receive services specified in the IEP, and participate with non-disabled students to the extent he/she would be in current placement. It includes bus suspension only if transportation is a related service in the student's IEP and the school provides no alternate transportation.

74 Also applies to suspension for more than ten consecutive school days or any other change of placement for disciplinary reasons.

75 20 U.S.C. 1415 (k)(1)(E)(2004); 34 C.F.R. § 300.530

76 34 C.F.R. § 300.530(f)

77 34 C.F.R. § 300.533

Chapter 19

Parental Rights

Susan Clark

Introduction

Principals are both building managers and instructional leaders. As instructional leaders, principals are charged with the development, implementation, and assessment of teaching and learning. As managers, principals are entrusted with the responsibility to ensure that the school functions well through efficient and effective operations and procedures. Both roles require the principal to assist staff—whose work with children and families brings meaning to those building policies and instructional practices—to understand their importance in a school-wide framework for high quality teaching and learning.

However, there may be impediments to effective organizational operations and to student access and opportunity to learn. One such obstacle can be the type, frequency, or quality of communication between administrators, teachers, and parents. The principal must develop and use effective interpersonal communication and relationship-building skills. By managing and nurturing relationships between and among staff and parents, a principal can improve instructional effectiveness. A hindrance to professional working relationships is often the lack of capacity that employees have in dealing with conflict and diminishing resources. Further complicating the work of the school is the increasing variance between and within students and the need to address those differences in a demanding political, social, and economic climate.

The federal education law crafted to protect students with disabilities was originally enacted in the 1970s in response to strong parent political and legal advocacy.[11] Since then, the law has evolved to include not only increased educational accountability, e.g., alignment with the No Child Left Behind Act,[22] but also to ensure that students with disabilities are prepared for participation as adults in the economic world of work. Today, the Individuals with Disabilities Education Act (IDEA), guarantees that all students with disabilities, no matter the nature and severity of the condition, will have a specially designed and individualized free appropriate public education (FAPE). Any denial of FAPE is a violation of federal law.

This FAPE is defined by the Supreme Court as both a substantive right and a procedural right. In *Board of Education of the Central Hudson School*

District v. Rowley,[33] the Supreme Court set forth the analysis for an alleged violation of the IDEA. The Court asked, *Did school district officials adhere to the procedural requirements of the Act* and *Was the individual educational program (IEP) reasonably calculated to confer meaningful educational benefit to the student?* If these two questions are answered in the affirmative, the state has met its obligation to provide FAPE. Hence, parental rights are procedural and process-oriented leading to the substantive right to FAPE as understood through the IEP and its implementation.

If a parent is denied an opportunity to be apprized of, and meaningfully participate in, the special educational process—a procedural violation—then the final *outcome*, the IEP and its implementation, may be legally flawed–an essential denial of the child's right to FAPE. Importantly, in 2006, the Supreme Court held that the IDEA grants to parents, not just procedural rights, but substantive rights of their own—a determination that now permits them to pursue federal FAPE claims in court without legal counsel.[44] The Court held that procedural rights, such as the right to pursue claims for procedural violations or to seek reimbursement and attorney fees, were "intertwined with the substantive adequacy" of a child's education. Parental rights to attend meetings, to participate in decision making, to request hearings, and to transfer their IDEA rights to their child upon reaching the age of majority all point to the Court's conclusion that parents have rights of their own under the statute. The Court stated:

> These provisions confirm that the IDEA (*sic*), through its text and structure, creates in parents an independent stake not only in the procedures and costs implicated by this process, but also in the substantive decisions to be made. *** We conclude that the IDEA does not differentiate, through isolated references to various procedures and remedies, between the rights accorded to children and the rights accorded to parents.

Consequently, the two elements of FAPE—procedural and substantive—are intertwined, as are the rights of the parent and child, along with the leadership and management roles of the principal. To protect a student's substantive rights, the principal must engage in strong instructional leadership skills, and to ensure that parents' procedural and substantive rights are safeguarded, the principal must utilize effective management tools, strong interpersonal communication skills, and conflict-resolution strategies.

Thus, the role of the principal is to identify policies, procedures, and practices that create barriers to effective communication, use of resources, and professional development, and to remove them. The other important role of the principal is to identify practices that support teaching and learning, including relationship building between home and school. Within this context, this chapter examines parental rights under the IDEA. The legal rights of which parents must be informed include rights to be notified of school district actions; rights to give consent before school officials may take certain actions; rights to meaningful participation in decision making about the child; rights to seek independent evaluation; rights to access records; and rights to file complaints and to seek dispute resolution. In each of the sections below, parental rights are identified and discussed. Notably, all parental rights under the IDEA transfer to the student at the age of majority, unless the student has been found to be incompetent under state law. The chapter concludes with recommendations for practice because principals are key to ensuring that parental and student rights are safeguarded.

Legal Issues

Rights to Notice of the Law

Parents have the right to know what federal law guarantees to them and to their children under the IDEA. The act requires that school districts provide parents with a written copy of the IDEA's procedural safeguards on numerous occasions. Procedural safeguards are the protections afforded to parents during the process in which school district officials engage to identify, evaluate, and educate children with disabilities. In essence, the procedural safeguards protect parental interests during the process. The procedures are so important that, under the first prong of the *Rowley* analysis, a court may find against a school district in a lawsuit if the parent is denied these rights.

The procedural safeguards are often included in a packet or booklet that explains all the legal rights available to a parent under the IDEA. These rights must be conveyed in easily understood language, even if the parent's mode of communication is not spoken English. In the event the parent uses another form of language, e.g., sign language or a foreign language, school officials must ensure that the notice is translated orally and that the parent understands its contents. Failure to give parents a copy of their procedural rights can result in a lawsuit and a finding of a denial of FAPE.[55] The procedural safeguards may be posted on the school district's webpage. However, written evidence must be kept to show that the parent received the procedural safeguards notice, such as a signed receipt, and should be considered if the district chooses to post the notice on the Internet.

The parents must be given a copy of their rights only once per school year, and whenever a parent so requests, but there are events that trigger the obligation to provide to them with still another copy. The notice of procedural rights must also be given to the parents the first time the student is referred for evaluation or the parent requests an evaluation, upon receipt of the first state complaint and first request for a due process hearing in a school year, and on the date a decision is made to remove a student from school that constitutes a change of placement for violating the student code of conduct.

A principal should procure a copy of the procedural safeguards and read them so as to be prepared to answer any questions a parent or teacher may have about them. Although there is nothing in the IDEA that requires a principal or any school official to explain the procedural safeguards to a parent, the regulations state that the explanation of these procedural rights must be "full." So either the writing should be self-explanatory for a parent or a principal should be prepared to discuss the procedural safeguards with a parent.

The principal should be aware of the duality of leadership regarding procedural safeguards. School district officials are charged with the duty to inform parents of their rights under the IDEA, including the right to sue the school district if a dispute should arise. Some educators may be uncomfortable telling parents the extent of their rights because doing so may expose the district to liability for failing to ensure FAPE. The school leader must recognize that due process is inherently about fairness. Assuring that building procedures and practices afford parents the process that is due to them is critical to creating a school culture in which partnership and communication are essential values to student success. Indeed, the process of understanding the reasons that students may not be making educational progress includes two-way discussions between teachers and parents. Identification of a student's educational needs is the heart of the evaluation process of special education and one in which parents play a role.

Rights Regarding Evaluation

The "child find" duty of school officials under the act requires that students with disabilities must be located, identified, and evaluated. This duty extends to public school students and to those enrolled in private schools that are located within the public school district's jurisdiction. An educational evaluation is required under the IDEA to determine the presence of a disability, identify the learning needs of the student, determine the content of an educational program, and determine the child's needs for involvement in and progress in the general education curriculum. Once a child who is suspected of having a disability is found, and before the district may proceed with an evaluation, the parent has the right to receive a copy of the procedural safeguards and to give informed consent to testing. Written consent to testing must be informed, which means that the parent has been made fully aware of all information pertinent to the evaluation process and its potential outcomes, including who will have access to the results. Notice of the tests that will be administered to the child is an element of informed consent. Such notice allows the parent to seek out additional information as to the content of the tests themselves and to the meaning of the results that will be obtained. Certainly, knowledge of the tests and the procedures in testing can help parents to prepare their children for the experience. Encouraging parents to explain to their child what to expect during the evaluation and to assuage any fears they may have can help make the process successful.

Informed consent also means that such consent may be revoked at any time. At times, district officials may experience difficulty obtaining parental consent. Generally, where consent is required, reasonable efforts to obtain it must be taken, and evidence that the parent failed to respond will be required if a dispute arises down the road. Reasonable efforts include telephone contacts, mailings, and home and workplace visits. A prudent principal will never permit an initial evaluation to proceed without prior written informed parental consent.

An evaluation must be conducted within sixty days after receipt of the parent's written consent. If the parent refuses to consent or revokes consent during the evaluation process, the principal may meet with the parents to listen to their concerns and to educate them about the need teachers have to understand how the student learns. Extensive knowledge of curriculum, assessment, and teaching is fundamental to the principal acting as an instructional leader in this situation. The willingness of the principal to openly communicate the importance of evaluation depends largely upon respect for the parent's feelings, fears, and rights.

With a refusal to consent to testing, the principal may offer parents an opportunity to participate in mediation in order to convince them of the need for testing. In mediation, a trained individual with no subjective interest in the outcome of the interest-based dialogue works with the parents and a representative from the school to come to a mutual decision about testing. If efforts to obtain written informed parental consent for testing have been unsuccessful, the school district has the option to seek a due process hearing to ask for a hearing officer to compel the evaluation.

Parental rights can be infringed upon by school officials' failure to find children with disabilities. For example, if a parent who removes the child from public school for inability to learn and places the child in private school later learns that the child had a disability, the district's failure to find, evaluate, and identify that child may be sufficient reason for that parent to receive reimbursement for the tuition paid to the private school.[66] Consequently, administrators should inform teachers to treat a parental request for testing as a referral and to proceed accordingly.

However, the duty to evaluate a student in order to make a determination as to the existence of a disability requires reasonable cause to suspect a disability. There is no parental right to have a child tested merely because a parent made such a request where educators do not believe there is evidence of a disability. Consequently, a request for testing made by a parent based on a child's problems that are evident only at home and not manifest at school may not be a sufficient reason to warrant a full, multi-factored evaluation in part because testing must result in a determination of the educational needs of the child. Recognizing that the student's problems must be schooling-related before evaluation is important because learning difficulties related to illegal drug use, juvenile delinquency, or family dysfunction may be considered social maladjustments, not disabilities, and any problems pursuant to either are certainly explainable by factors other than education. Educational problems stemming from limited English proficiency (LEP) or the lack of instruction may also constitute reasons for not testing as they are regarded as exclusion factors for some disability categories. Nevertheless, a drug-addicted student, one with LEP, or one who has not received adequate instruction may also have an undiagnosed disability. Recognizing that educators must ascertain the reasons for the child's inability to learn, the principal, as instructional leader, should facilitate a careful review of the child's schooling history including past performance, attendance, grades, parental input, and more before making the determination as to whether to evaluate for the existence disability.

In a case where the evaluation of a student is not appropriate, the principal should ensure that the parent received prior written notice of that decision and a copy of the district's procedural safeguards. A prudent administrator also would tell the family directly of the right to pursue a due process hearing because the parent who disagrees with the district's decision not to test the student has the right to appeal that decision through the due process procedures.

Interestingly, the parent of a student without an identified disability but who is being considered for suspension, expulsion, or placement in an interim alternative educational setting may assert the protections of the IDEA by alleging that school personnel knew or should have known that the child had a disability before the misconduct that triggered the disciplinary action occurred. A critical review of the student's file should be undertaken as soon as possible when a principal intends to act to protect the safety of the student or others.

Informal chats between teachers and other personnel about student learning problems that may or may not implicate a disability do not constitute school officials' knowledge that the child may need special educational services. Additionally, the protections of the IDEA do not apply to an unidentified student when an evaluation was conducted at some point in the student's schooling and the student was not found to have a disability or when it was determined that an evaluation was not necessary. Even in the case where the student was found eligible for services but where the parent denied consent for the services, under the IDEA, school officials do not have knowledge that the student is a student with a disability. In all of these situations, the parents were to have been included in the decision making and properly apprized of their rights to appeal those decisions through due process and were to have received a copy of the procedural safeguards. However, if evaluation is requested before the disciplinary action, and it is appropriate, it must be conducted in an expedited manner, and the parent is entitled to written notice of the procedures used to determine the existence of a disability and of their rights under the law.

Rights Regarding Identification

Once an evaluation is complete, the parent has the right to participate in the decision as to whether the student is eligible for special education and related services. Eligibility decisions are very important to the future of the child, yet many principals do not participate in those meetings. The principal should work closely with teachers to know the challenges they face in providing classroom instruction and the difficulties some students experience in learning.

Furthermore, the principal must manage all building resources in an effective manner. The human and other resources required to evaluate and examine a student's learning are evidence of a deep commitment to understanding the learner. The principal, therefore, should know and understand the testing process and the manner in which results are interpreted so as to be a leader who can ask and answer questions appropriate to the needs of both the teacher and the student.

Parental participation in decision making is an important component of evaluation, eligibility determinations, placement, and FAPE. The parent, however, does not have a right to guarantee that the child will, in fact, be found to be a student with a disability. To qualify for special education under the IDEA, the principal needs to know that the student must meet two tests. First, the student must meet the eligibility requirements under one or more of the disability categories listed in the IDEA. Second, the student must be in need of special education.

The two-pronged test is critical to the eligibility determination because a child may fall into one of the disability categories but not be in need of special education. For example, a student with an emotional disturbance may not require services because the student is achieving and is functioning appropriately in school. In one case, even assuming that a student with Attention Deficit Disorder did fall into the category of Other Health Impaired, the federal district court concluded that the student would not be in need of special education because he chose to not take his medication, to skip classes, to not complete homework, and to smoke marijuana. The court summed up its decision supporting the student's ineligibility by stating that what the student actually needed was to understand that the "responsibility for [his] actions" was his own and that "good choices usually open good doors and bad choices usually open, and often compel entry, through bad doors."[77]

Additionally, some students may have a medical diagnosis (e.g., seasonal allergies, high blood pressure) and not be legally disabled because they do not fall into one of the eligibility categories. Other students may be in need of related services, but do not "fit" a defined category of disability. Unless state law considers a related service—such as speech and language therapy—as a stand-alone special education program, a team may not find a student eligible for such a related service without a concomitant need for special education.

The key for the instructional leader is to help the team to pinpoint and to understand a student's success or lack of success in the classroom as a critical factor in the decision making as to whether the student is in need of special education. However, nothing in the IDEA requires that students must be served or classified in any one particular eligibility category as long as the student receives FAPE. For example, state law may provide that young children between the ages of three and nine who experience developmental delays and are in need of special education do not need to fit into one of eligibility categories and may be instead labeled developmentally delayed. In one case, even where the school district identified the student as Other Health Impaired, but recommended placement in a program for students with cognitive disabilities, the Seventh Circuit Court found no denial of FAPE because she received the services to which she was entitled.[88] Under the IDEA, the label is necessary only for the determination of eligibility because the category of disability does not dictate the type or level of services the student will receive. Rather, FAPE requires students to be provided with an education that is designed according to their unique needs, not according to their eligibility category.

Disagreement as to eligibility permits the decision-making team to determine what additional data, if any, may be necessary in order to fully consider the educational needs of the child. The principal should embrace disagreement and lead the team to consider a variety of sources in making the determination including ability, achievement, teacher recommendations, and parental input.

The parent's right to participate in the decision making as to whether the student falls into one of the disability categories or is in need of special education carries the additional right to an independent educational evaluation (IEE) at public expense. The right to an IEE is invoked when the parent disagrees with the school district's evaluation or eligibility determination. When this occurs, the school administrator may ask, but not require, the parent to explain what is the source of the disagreement.

In response to the parent's objection, school officials must either pay for the IEE or, after providing the parent with prior written notice, initiate a due process hearing to defend its evaluation. The hearing officer may deny the request for an IEE if the school district's evaluation is found to be appropriate. If inappropriate, the hearing officer may order the school district to pay for the IEE. If school officials authorize an IEE, they may provide payment for it in advance of the testing or reimburse the parent after the evaluation is completed without going to due process at all. The district's decision cannot prevent a parent from exercising the right to an IEE, and the parent has the right to have the results of any such independent evaluation considered by school officials.

Rights Regarding Decision Making

As discussed above, parents are entitled to be a member of any team assembled to make decisions about the identification, evaluation, and eligibility of their child. However, the decision-making process does not end with the evaluation and eligibility determination. Once eligibility has been determined, the parent has the right to participate in the development of the student's Individual Educational Plan (IEP). The written IEP commits the school district's resources to the student by defining the special instructional program and services the school district will provide to the student to ensure FAPE. A parent is entitled to attend and to participate in IEP decision making and to prior written notice of the purpose, time, location of IEP meetings, and who will be in attendance. In fact, the parent has the right to prior written notice of any change, or refusal to change, the evaluation or identification of the child.

Errors in assembling a properly constructed IEP team or failure to meaningfully consider parental input and suggestions may result in a procedural and substantive violation of the student's rights. Principals can model appropriate respect for parental opinion—no matter how unusual—and help the team to integrate what is important to the parent into the decision-making process. Principals should facilitate these decision-making meetings to ensure that voices are heard, ideas are explored, and data are used to substantiate student performance and to identify educational needs.

Additionally, the team should consider what the parent says about the home in developing the IEP. Some students that may need home programming. If home programming is necessary for the student to benefit from the special education provided in school, the team should be aware that parents may be eligible for related services. Parents, or classroom teachers for that matter, may need training or instruction in sign language or behavior modification, for example, so that they are equipped to implement the IEP goals if necessary to the provision of FAPE.

The right to participate in all decision making about the child does not extend to informal or unscheduled conversations involving any district personnel. Parents have no right to be privy to discussions between teachers who meet in the lunchroom or during planning periods to discuss a student. Nor does the right to participate confer upon the parent any claim to be a part of educators' professional determinations as to methodology, lesson planning, or coordination of services. Meetings scheduled for the purpose of planning meeting strategies or of working out a response to a parent proposal do not require parental participation to comply with the IDEA. In one case, parents of a ninth-grade student with Obsessive Compulsive Disorder, Tourette Syndrome, and Asperger's Syndrome sued the school district in part because they were not invited to a teacher in-service meeting during which the parents' consultant, hired by the district, worked to help teachers learn ways to better serve the child. The Sixth Circuit Court held that the parents were not denied meaningful participation in their child's education when they were not included in the meeting. The court found that they had shared what they wanted school officials to know when they met with teachers and administrators and when the district hired the consultant to work with staff.[99]

Rights to participate in decisions about the special education programming of the child do not include rights to choose the child's teacher, to select the teaching strategies or methodologies, or to any particular learning outcome or achievement level. While the IEP is required to contain a statement of the special education and related services and supplementary aids and services based on peer-reviewed research that will be provided to the child, the parent does not have the right to determine which services meet that requirement. The education and services to be provided should be researched-based to the extent practicable. Decisions about what the student needs are made by a careful consideration of the student's disability, its effect on learning, and curriculum and program expectations.

Principals should note that it is very important that educators do not predetermine the placement of a student. In one case, school district officials had invested a great deal of effort and money into training its staff in a particular autism methodology, and after they denied the parents' request for their preferred methodology, the parents successfully made a showing to the court that the educators had made their decision before the IEP team meeting. The IEP team meeting is the proper venue for decision making as to appropriateness based on an analysis of appropriate data, review of any independent evaluation reports, and meaningful consideration of parental input.

Although decisions about teaching content, methodology, and strategy are best made by professional educators with parental input, and the courts show great deference to such decisions when they are data-based and made in good faith, there is no requirement that the team reach a consensus. Certainly, consensus is desirable and the principal should work toward that end, but at some point, the school leader must ensure that FAPE is recommended for the student by making the offer in no uncertain terms. This practice may feel threatening to parents who may insist that the district is "forcing" a decision or is acting with complete disregard for their position. The fact that parents and school district officials may have principled disagreements between them does not mean that the district failed to take parental views seriously or that the district is not offering FAPE.[10] Any dispute the parent has with the school's recommendation may be taken to due process. During the meeting, the principal should ensure that the team articulates its rationale, that those implementing the IEP have the necessary experience and training to do so, and that the methodological approach taken by the district is at least adequate under the circumstances.[11]

If a student is identified as having a disability by a team that includes the parent, and the educational needs are ascertained, the informed written consent given by the parent for the initial evaluation does not imply consent for services. Informed written consent for the provision of services is separate from the informed consent required for the evaluation. Informed written consent is needed for the student's initial IEP. Should the parent deny such consent, school officials are prohibited from providing those services, from seeking mediation, or from initiating a due process hearing. In this case, the school district will not be in violation of the IDEA for failure to provide FAPE to the child.

However, once the initial IEP is written and services begin, no parent signature is required to continue services without a change in placement even though subsequent IEPs may be written. This is because the school district must offer FAPE to the child. If the parent refuses to sign an IEP for any reason, the district may continue the services under the last signed IEP, may implement that portion of the IEP with which the parent agrees, or may seek a due process hearing, all while continuing to work to resolve the disagreement.

If the school district offers a different placement or different services than those included in the previous IEP, parents are entitled to prior written notice of the change. When parents make a suggestion for a change to the child's program or FAPE and the district considered the recommendation but decided against it, parents must be given prior written notice of the refusal and reasons for it.

The Eighth Circuit Court of Appeals reviewed a case in which the parent brought suit against the school district for what was believed to be a denial of FAPE. The student with cerebral palsy had been on home instruction during his convalescence from surgery. After eleven months, although the parent insisted that the child continued to be unable to attend school, school district officials, believing home instruction to be inappropriate, offered the same program and the same IEP to the student but delivered in school, not home. The parents refused to bring the child to school until the district court weighed in on the matter. The court found that the school district changed the student's placement without prior written notice and violated the stay-put provision. The school district had argued that no program or placement change had occurred, merely the location of service changed. The district court disagreed, and the circuit court affirmed.[12] The appeals court averred that a transfer to a different school building for fiscal or other reasons unrelated to the child's disability is not a change in placement, whereas expulsion or other change in location made because of the student's disability or behavior is a change of placement.

Notably, a parent may revoke consent for evaluation or services at any time; however, all activity undertaken by the school district during the time the consent was in effect remains valid. For example, if a parent gives informed consent to testing to an IEP developed on the evaluation results and to a placement—even if she changes her mind, revokes consent, and demands that the child be returned to a full-time general education setting—the child would remain in the placement to which the parent consented until the dispute is resolved.[13] This right of the child to "stay-put" pending the outcome of any dispute will be discussed in the section below on due process rights.

Rights Regarding Re-evaluation

Once a student is deemed eligible for special education, an IEP is in effect before the start of the school year, placement determined, and services have been delivered, a parent has the right to written notice of a district decision concerning re-evaluation. The parent also has the right to request a re-evaluation and to be given a written copy of the procedural safeguards. A re-evaluation requires informed parental consent, unless the re-evaluation is merely a review of existing data. If a parent refuses consent for a reevaluation, school officials may initiate a due process hearing, but it is not required to do so. Should this situation arise, the school district will not be in violation of the IDEA for failing to provide FAPE. However, school officials must document all reasonable efforts taken to seek parental consent for the reevaluation. If a student is homeschooled or has been parentally placed in a private school, public school officials are prohibited from seeking mediation or initiating a due process hearing to resolve the dispute and are not required to consider those children eligible for special education when parents refuse to provide consent to an initial evaluation or reevaluation.

The purpose of a re-evaluation is to determine whether the student continues to be eligible for special education and to identify educational needs. The review of continued eligibility must occur at least every three years, unless agreed otherwise, but may not occur more than once each school year. Re-evaluation is necessary when the parent or teacher requests it or when school officials determine that additional data are needed to address the student's needs, including those needed to meet IEP goals and to improve academic achievement or functional performance. Importantly, no re-evaluation is needed when a student graduates from high school with a regular diploma or ages out of special education (i.e., reaches the age of twenty-two). Under those two circumstances, a parent only has the right to prior written notice of the change of placement unless the IEP team decides that re-evaluation is necessary, but the parent must be given a summary of the student's academic achievement and functional performance including recommendations as to how to assist the student to meet postsecondary goals.

Re-evaluation necessitates a review of existing data, which includes but is not limited to, current classroom-based assessments and observations, results of district or state tests given to all students, and teacher and related service providers' records of student performance. No parental permission is required for educators to review those existing data. In fact, parental consent is not required for school officials or teachers who choose to observe a student with a disability, to conduct ongoing classroom evaluations, or to conduct or to review any adapted or modified assessments of the sort given to all students in any class, grade, or school.

There is some question as to whether functional behavior assessment (FBA) is a new assessment requiring the parent's informed consent or is a classroom observation with no such requirement. An FBA is a process used most often in the context of student discipline after a violation of the code of conduct, but it can be utilized at any time. The FBA is a systematic method of identifying the antecedents and consequences of events that inform educators of the nature and purpose of student misconduct. If the process of FBA meets the requirement of a review of existing data or of an observation of behavior available to all students as explained above, then no parental consent is required.

Once the decision is made that the student's eligibility can be continued in special education based on a review of existing data and without any new assessment, the parent is entitled to written notice of that fact. The notice must explain to the parent that school officials believe all necessary data were available to make the decision as to continued eligibility and why no additional data are needed. Nevertheless, the notice must also inform the parent that the district will conduct further assessment irrespective of its decision that no new data were needed if the parent so requests.

Should school officials determine that a re-evaluation requiring additional testing is needed either through its own decision making or through parental request, the parent has the right to give informed consent to the process, but written consent is not necessary. Like the initial consent for evaluation, if a parent refuses to give consent for a re-evaluation involving new testing, the district may resort to mediation or the due process mechanism in order to obtain such consent, but to do so is not required. In that case, the school district will not be in violation of the IDEA.

Rights Regarding Educational Records

The IDEA comports with the Family Education Rights and Privacy Act (FERPA) right to inspect and review education records maintained by the school district and to protect records from third parties unless the parent consents to their disclosure. Educational records include any handwritten, typed, computer-generated, video or audio-taped record kept by the school and necessary for its business. All notice requirements under FERPA apply to the IDEA.

Under FERPA, records must be disclosed to parents, upon their request, no later than forty-five days of the request although the school's failure to do so does not provide the parent with a legal cause of action.[14] The time period allotted by law does not suggest that principals wait until the time is about to expire before making records available for parental review. Nor is the time to be spent "cleaning" the files or redacting any information contained in them. Rather, the time period affords the principal a reasonable time in which to review the records, to gather any information necessary to clarify their meaning, and to make time to sit with the parent during the review in order to answer questions and to protect the integrity of the file.

Under the IDEA, parental access to student records is a necessary component to the provision of FAPE because such access enables a parent to meaningfully participate in the process. In one case, the Ninth Circuit Court held that because the school district failed to disclose all of a student's records to her parents in a timely fashion, including records that indicated the child may have had autism and suggested that she be evaluated by a psychiatrist, her parents were not provided with sufficient notice of their child's condition. Because the parents did not have access to the full record of the child, the court held that they could not design an IEP that addressed the child's needs, and as such, the parents were denied meaningful participation in the special education process.[15] The circuit court stated that failure to provide the parents with the full educational record was a "particularly troubling" violation of the IDEA because the parents had no other way to know of the information contained in it and had no opportunity to give the child the care and treatment she needed.[16]

Special education records that may enable meaningful parental participation in the identification, evaluation, or placement decision making or in the provision of FAPE may include evaluation reports, testing protocols, disciplinary records, or nurse's files. There is no right under FERPA or the IDEA to records kept in the principal's or teacher's sole possession because such records are not considered to be education records and are instead considered to be personal notes for purposes of remembrance.[17] Nor is there a right to have the educational record amended unless the record contains information that is inaccurate, misleading, or violates the privacy or other rights of the child.

Logs must be kept by school officials to record the name, date, and purpose of those who access student records, except parents and authorized employees with legitimate educational interests. These logs constitute an educational record to which a parent may request access. Importantly, parents are entitled to not only inspect education records, but they are entitled to an explanation of them as well. Whenever a request for a records inspection is made, the principal should be prepared to answer any questions the parent may have.

Divorce, separation, and custody arrangements may alter which parent has access to school records, and it is important that the principal know the contents of any court order. For example, the Seventh Circuit Court held that a noncustodial parent had the right to seek a due process hearing based on the school district's failure to notify him of IEP meetings because the divorce decree permitted him to communicate with district personnel about the student's progress and to participate in school activities.[18]

In contrast, a divorced mother sought to be included as a member of the IEP team and to have access to all assessment and evaluation records including test protocols, testing reports, and eligibility determinations. She also sought to amend her child's special educational records by having all references to her ex-husband's wife changed from "mother" to "stepmother" and to obtain an IEE to contest the student's identification as emotionally disturbed. The Second Circuit Court examined whether she had standing as a noncustodial parent to assert those claims in the first place.[19] The court reasoned that the rights of a natural parent under the act were those identified by state law, and in the case of divorce, by the divorce decree. Because the divorce decree did not specifically revoke informational access, the parent was permitted to pursue her records-access claim under FERPA; she was entitled under state law to reasonable information regarding the child's progress in school. The court made clear, however, an entitlement to "reasonable" records did not mean access to every single cover letter, transmittal sheet, or scrap of paper that happened to be in the files. Nor did the entitlement necessitate access to more substantive original documents or notes if the information contained in them was substantially incorporated into reports or if the parent was otherwise informed of their content.

The court further held that the noncustodial parent had no rights to decision making or to an IEE. In so deciding, the Second Circuit Court noted that the implementing regulations of federal special education law established a wide range of persons who may be considered "the parent," including stepparents, grandparents, guardians, foster parents, and surrogates. The court opined that it was illogical that all those listed as "potential parents" would be expected to exercise the same parental rights under the act at the same time. Thus, the court concluded, parental rights under federal special education law are to be informed by applicable state law. The parent in this case lacked standing to make educational decisions; therefore, she had only the right to access information about the child's evaluation, identification, placement, and FAPE. Although the court decided that the parent could not seek a due process hearing to challenge the appropriateness of the identification, the court did not reach the question as to whether the noncustodial parent's right to reasonable information regarding the child's progress in school encompassed the federal right to notice of IEP meetings.[20] One interpretation of this unanswered question might be that the parent who has only access rights to information be given the results of the IEP meeting—the completed IEP—but the parent afforded decision-making authority be given prior notice and an opportunity to attend the meeting. Keep in mind that the focus of any decision-making meeting is the well-being and FAPE of the child, and the principal must keep the team focused to that end in accord with state law.

The IDEA, like FERPA, ensures that records are confidential unless parental consent is given to authorize their disclosure. Some parents may want the IEP itself kept confidential. Under the IDEA, the child's IEP must be made available to all staff members who are responsible for the implementation of the IEP. Consequently, all staff members must be informed of their duties and responsibilities related to IEP implementation irrespective of parental demands to keep the IEP confidential.

Furthermore, the principal can facilitate appropriate communication among staff members and families if some formal system of information sharing is adopted within the school. A few ways a principal can assist in this regard are by ensuring that teachers know a student's needs before that student enters the classroom; apprizing teachers and staff of their record-keeping duties; expecting data-based decision making; encouraging proactivity in keeping parents informed of student progress or lack of progress; valuing the importance of the IEP team as a decision-making body; and developing a method whereby the principal is made aware of problems, concerns, and questions that a teacher or parent may have regarding the education of the student with a disability. The importance of strong communication through reporting of progress and data collected as student records cannot be undervalued. Indeed, even where the parent does not want information shared, the principal may need to disclose information without their consent.

Records may be disclosed to third parties without parental consent under FERPA in the case of a health or safety emergency. Under FERPA and the IDEA, a parent does not have the right to prevent principals from sharing special educational records with police where the safety of the student or the school community is at stake. When a principal disclosed to the police the writings of a fifteen-year-old student with behavioral problems, the parents were unsuccessful in their attempt to include in their son's IEP a restriction on the authority of school officials to make reports to law enforcement.[21] In another case, the principal sent explanatory letters home to parents of children who were victims of, and witnesses to, the misconduct of a student with a disability. No FERPA violation was found because the court found it reasonable that school officials would notify parents that they were taking steps at school to ensure the safety of their children.[22]

Furthermore, when reporting criminal conduct to the police, the IDEA authorizes school officials to provide copies of disciplinary records to the authorities for their consideration. Additionally, records may be released without parental permission when state law permits disclosure to authorities in the juvenile justice system, to law enforcement personnel who keep records for law enforcement purposes, and with a court order or subpoena.

Although FERPA permits the school district to charge a reasonable fee for copies of records requested by parents, the IDEA requirement that education be at no cost to parents precludes school officials from charging parents for copies of the IEP. A reasonable fee may be charged for copies of other educational records, but the fee cannot preclude parental access. Generally, copies of the evaluation report, progress reports, and other records are provided to parents of children with disabilities should be at no cost to them.

Rights to Dispute District Practices

Parents have the right under the IDEA to complain to district officials about any special education services their children are, or should be, receiving. This right includes complaints about identification, evaluation, placement, and the provision of FAPE. The proper venues to resolve these student-based disputes are, first, with the IEP team, followed by mediation, and culminating at a due process hearing. A visit to the administrator's office should be encouraged at each step of the way, giving the principal an opportunity to defuse the situation, to clarify and articulate the various points of view, and to help the parents arrive at a decision, even if that decision is to go to due process. The principal should be careful to avoid interfering with the parent's right to invoke the due process mechanism.

An important distinction to be made is where parents are not disputing the child's placement, services, or program, but are complaining about the school district's policies, practices, or procedures. Problems with the operations, administrative hierarchy, and customs of the school or the school district itself are properly handled through the state complaint procedure, not due process. For example, parents who demanded that the public school provide special education to their son at a private school were not permitted to use due process proceedings to examine their claims; the court held that they needed to use the state complaint procedure because the state governed such entitlements, not the local school district.[23]

When a parent brings concerns about school district operations to the state, the state must conduct an on-site investigation and must issue a written decision with findings of fact along with its reasons.[24] When the principal is confronted by parental concerns about general school district operations and not the student's particular and individualized education, the parent is to be informed that the state complaint procedure is the appropriate venue for voicing such concerns.

Rights to Disagree Regarding Student's Program

When a dispute arises over the identification, evaluation, placement, or provision of FAPE to a particular student with a disability, the parents have the right to seek mediation, initiate a due process hearing, seek redress in civil court, and be reimbursed the costs of their attorney fees if they are prevailing parties. During any dispute, the parents have the right to ensure that their child remains in the current placement with the current services until the matter is settled. During the period of dispute resolution, the child's program or placement may not be changed until the matter is settled. This placement pending a decision is called "stay-put." Stay-put protects the child from unilateral actions taken by the school district by ensuring that the student "stays put" until the issues can be clarified and resolved. The stay-put provision can be altered if the parent and school district agree otherwise.

Mediation is voluntary between the parents and school officials and cannot be used to delay a due process hearing. During mediation, an objective third party attempts to guide each side to an understanding of each others' interests and to reach a settlement to which all can agree. Anything said during mediation may not be used in a subsequent due process hearing or in civil court; discussions are confidential and cannot be used as evidence. Because mediation is an option for parents, some states may require parents who refuse mediation to meet with a third party to encourage the use of mediation.

Any decisions reached through mediation are to be in writing. Oftentimes, mediation agreements contain a confidentiality provision in which both parties agree that neither party will discuss the settlement with others. However, there may be circumstances in which parents will inform other parents of the dispute and the result reached with school officials. This can happen when parents are pleased with the outcome and want to share their success with other parents or when parents are eager to help other parents who may present similar issues. Because of the confidentiality provision, this situation may be considered a breach of contract and may cause principals to have to respond to other families that may seek similar services. In that case, the appropriate response is to convene the IEP team to discuss the appropriateness of the current program of the complaining parents' child. Should the parent disagree with the decision, they, too, may seek mediation or a due process hearing. The principal should not breach the confidentiality agreement made during mediation.

The IDEA affords the parent the right to seek a due process hearing to have disputes resolved by an impartial hearing officer, usually assigned by the state, no later than forty-five days after the request for the hearing is made. The hearing can be likened to a mini-trial in which evidence is submitted, witnesses are called, testimony is heard, cross examinations are conducted, and a decision is rendered. The hearing officer's final decision is mailed to both parties, and the parent is entitled to a transcript of the proceedings.

The hearing may not proceed, however, until a mandatory resolution meeting is held or waived in writing by the parent and school officials. The resolution session must be conducted within fifteen days of the receipt of the parent's due process hearing request for the purpose of discussion of the complaint and the facts underlying it so that school officials have an opportunity to resolve it before the hearing. Information raised in the resolution session is confidential and may not be used at a due process hearing. Relevant members of the IEP team must attend the meeting and the determination as to who is relevant is made by both the parent and school officials. Only if the parent brings an attorney may the school district's attorney be present at the resolution session. If the matter remains unresolved, the due process hearing may be conducted.

A parent must comply with all IDEA procedural requirements relative to making a due process hearing request or risk the possibility of losing the opportunity to appeal the hearing officer's decision to civil court. A request for a due process hearing can be made anytime the school district proposes—or refuses—to initiate or change the identification, evaluation, or educational placement of the child or the provision of FAPE. The request must be in writing and must describe the name and address of the child, the child's school of attendance, a description of the nature of the problem of the child, and all related facts, as well as must propose a resolution. This required notice to the school district is to afford the district the opportunity to reconsider its decision, explore the parents' suggested solution, and to revise, if necessary, its offer. The party that chooses to bring forward a due process complaint bears the burden to persuade the hearing officer of the validity of its argument.[25]

If school district officials initiate a due process hearing, the parent is entitled to a written notice of the request. The written notice must inform the parent of the option for mediation and where to find free or low-cost legal representation; however, a resolution session is not required. As noted above, when the school district seeks to initiate or refuses to change the identification, evaluation, placement, or provision of FAPE, it must put its reasons in writing to the parent.

Additionally, parents must exhaust their due process privileges before filing suit in civil court. The exhaustion requirement means that in states with one tier of administrative review, the parent must go to due process and have a decision rendered in order to appeal to civil court. In states with two tiers of review, one local and the other at the state level, parents must take their dispute to both venues before the court will hear their complaint. There are some exceptions to the exhaustion requirement, especially when to take the matter to due process would be futile. The court will decide if one of the exceptions applies.

Rights Regarding Attorney Fees

A parent's right to attorney fees is not automatic. Rather, attorney fees are a discretionary award given to the prevailing party in an IDEA lawsuit. Additionally, if a settlement offer was already made during or after mediation or hearing and was rejected, the award of attorney fees to the parent, generally, will not be more favorable than the offer of settlement. Parents are not eligible for attorney fees accrued during an IEP team meeting, unless that meeting was convened as a result of an administrative hearing or judicial action. The costs of a parent's expert witness are not recoupable as attorney fees.[26]

School districts may be awarded attorney fees against the parent's attorney if the court finds that the attorney filed a complaint or subsequent cause of action that is frivolous, unreasonable, or without foundation, or if the attorney continued to litigate after the litigation clearly became frivolous, unreasonable, or without foundation. School districts also may be awarded such fees against the parent, if the parent's request for a due process hearing or subsequent cause of action was presented for any improper purpose, such as to harass, to cause unnecessary delay, or to needlessly increase the cost of litigation.

Rights Regarding Placement in Private Schools

Parents may remove their children from public schools at any time and enroll them in private schools, religious schools, or home schools. If the child has a disability, however, parents who remove their children without giving the school district prior notice of the decision to change schools and later seek public school funds for the costs assume a financial risk.

The public school has a duty to offer and to provide FAPE. If the parent disagrees with the school district's offer, the parent may resolve the dispute through mediation or through a due process hearing. Where FAPE is in dispute and the parent unilaterally removes the child and later sues the school district for tuition reimbursement, the court will not award tuition if FAPE was available in the public school. Tuition will be available if FAPE was not available at the time the child was removed or if it was not offered in a timely manner and the private school placement was appropriate, even if the school did not meet state standards.

The decision to award tuition reimbursement, however, is contingent upon several parental actions that must precede the removal from public school. First, parents must inform school officials at the last IEP meeting they attend before the removal of their rejection of the district's placement offer, including their concerns, and of their intent to enroll the child in a private school at public expense. Reimbursement may be denied if the parents did not give their reasons for rejecting the district's offer, their concerns, and put their notice of intent to withdraw in writing at least ten business days, including holidays that fall on business days, before they remove the child from public school. Additionally, the parents may not be eligible for reimbursement if the court finds that they behaved unreasonably or if they did not make the child available for a proper request for evaluation before they removed the child from public school.

There are exceptions to the parent written notice requirement. One obvious exception is when the parents are illiterate or do not speak English. Another is when the child may suffer physical or emotional harm by remaining in the public school and the parent must act swiftly in caring for the child's health and well-being. Recall that the procedural safeguards include notice to the parent that they must give notice prior to any withdrawal. Tuition, if appropriate, will not be denied to the parent who did not give the required notice to the school district if school officials did not give the parent a copy of the procedural safeguards when necessary. Occasionally, school officials will prevent the parent from giving the required notice if the relationship deteriorated during the decision making. Again, the court may overlook the notice requirement in that case.

When FAPE is not in dispute, that is to say, the parent chooses a private school for the child with a disability based on academic, social, philosophical, religious, or other reasons unrelated to special education, the parent has no right to expect that the public school will provide to the child some or all of the services the child would have received if enrolled in public school. In this case, the parent is not even entitled to a due process hearing. Due process hearings are available to parents of children parentally placed in private schools only for disputes over evaluation and child find.

Children placed in private schools by their parents where FAPE is not in dispute are not entitled to a FAPE; however, the school district must maintain records as to the number of students parentally placed in private schools that were evaluated, found eligible for special education, and were served. The only right under the IDEA these children have is equitable participation, not individual entitlement. These students may be eligible to participate in the services provided to the private school that are designated by the school district. To determine what services will be provided for private school students, if any, public school officials are required to consult with private school officials on how any available money will be spent; on whom to spend it; and on where, when, how, and what services to provide. Amounts expended for provision of services to students in private schools shall be equal to a proportionate amount of federal funds made available to the public school district for those students. The decision the public school district makes will be written as a service plan. The services, if any, can be provided on the premises of private schools, including those that are religious, to the extent that doing so is consistent with state law. If transportation is necessary, those costs can be taken from the amount allocated to the private school. If the school district fails to provide the services in the plan, parents then may file a state administrative complaint because a due process hearing is not available to them.

The situation changes when public school officials place the student in a private school because that placement offers a FAPE unavailable in the public school. Those students are entitled to a FAPE and their parents to all procedural safeguards discussed above because the rights belonging to the student and parent in that case are no different than they would have if the child were placed in public school.

Conclusion

Procedural and substantive parental rights of the kind identified above can result in a violation of the IDEA if the parent is unaware of them or is prevented from exercising them. In fact, the courts will not extend an inquiry to the second prong of *Rowley* to examine the IEP if the procedural violations found through the first-prong analysis alone deny the student's right to FAPE.[27] However, simple mistakes and oversights are not enough to violate the IDEA.[28] Procedural errors clearly violate the IDEA when they result in a compromise to the child's right to FAPE, when they seriously hamper the parent's opportunity to participate meaningfully in the IEP formulation process, or when they cause a deprivation of educational benefits to which the student was entitled.[29]

Recommendations for Practice

1. Parents have the right to be given a copy of their rights under the law. A written copy of the procedural safeguards must be given to parents at a minimum upon initial referral for evaluation, upon re-evaluation when new assessments are necessary, whenever a parent files the first request for due process or a state complaint during a school year, and before any disciplinary action that might result in a change of placement. Principals should have a record-keeping mechanism in place that gives them the assurance that parents did, in fact, receive a copy of procedural safeguards. Should the school

district go to due process, that information will be required for the district to prove it met its obligation under the law.

2. Before children are evaluated for a suspected disability, their parents have the right to a copy of the procedural safeguards, to written notice of the assessments the school district will use in order to identify the existence of any disability, and to give written informed consent to testing. Consent may be revoked at any time. In that case, should school officials desire to proceed with the evaluation, they may, but are not required to, seek mediation in order to convince the parent of the need for testing, or an order authorizing testing through the due process hearing mechanism.

3. A parent request to test a student may necessitate an evaluation; however, educators ultimately make the determination as to whether a disability is suspected through a careful analysis of student records, performance, behavior, and affect. If the team, including the parent, determines that testing is not necessary or is inappropriate, the decision and the team's rationale should be documented.

4. Parents are entitled to participate in the eligibility determination. Eligibility is based on a categorical definition accompanied by the child's need for special education as determined by the entire team. A parent may contest an eligibility decision through optional mediation or due process proceedings.

5. Parents who disagree with the school district's evaluation or eligibility determination have the right to request an independent educational evaluation at public expense. The principal may ask the parent to explain the reasoning behind the request, but the parent is under no obligation to discuss it. School district policy will dictate whether the district will issue an invoice for direct payment to the approved independent evaluator or whether the parent must pay for the evaluation and then be reimbursed. If the district believes that its evaluation is appropriate and refuses a request for an independent evaluation, the parent is entitled to prior written notice of that decision, including the reasons for the refusal, and the district must seek a due process hearing to defend its evaluation.

6. The results of any independent evaluation conducted, either paid for by the parent or by the school district, must be considered by the team. Failure to consider the results may result in a denial of FAPE.

7. Parents have the right to meaningful participation at any meeting regarding the provision of FAPE to the child, including the IEP meeting. Educators must plan the meeting and its purpose and be ready to explain their professional judgments and to answer questions. Consequently, parents are to be given prior written notice of the purpose of the meeting as well as the time, location, and who

will be in attendance. Decision-making meetings requiring parent attendance do not include business-related, organizational, in-service, strategic, or planning meetings of teachers. To allow otherwise would undermine the educators' need to engage in professional discussion and to give thoughtful consideration to a variety of organizational and staff concerns.

8. Any proposed changes to the child's identification, evaluation, placement, or provision of FAPE requires that the parent receive prior written notice of the school's proposal. Anytime the school refuses to change the identification, evaluation, placement, or provision of FAPE to the child, the parent is entitled to receive prior written notice of the district's decision. The notice must include the reasons for the school district's refusal. Such advance notice provides parents with the opportunity to consider the proposal and to seek advice if necessary.
9. Parents must provide written, informed consent before a child's placement may be changed. However, certain disciplinary removals do not require such consent, nor is consent required for conducting a re-evaluation or FBA that are merely reviews of existing data or of part of regular classroom observation available to all students.
10. Parents are entitled to inspect and review all educational records of their children and to receive copies of those records, but divorce, separation, or custody may alter participation and decision making rights, depending on state law. Principals should identify which parent(s) have access rights and which have decision-making rights and should communicate that information to those with a legitimate need to know.
11. Parents have no right to keep a child's records confidential where school employees have a legitimate need to know, where health or safety of student(s) or school community are at stake, or where law enforcement and juvenile justice authorities are to consider them. The overarching concern for the safety of the entire school community is of fundamental concern to the principal.
12. Parents have the right to present complaints about school district operations, policies, and procedures to the state through the state complaint procedure.
13. Parents have the right to review decisions and present complaints concerning their child's identification, evaluation, placement, and provision of FAPE, generally, first to the IEP team, then through optional mediation, and finally, in a due process hearing. Parents must exhaust administrative review before they may appeal an agency decision to civil court.

14. Parents have the right to attorney fees for the costs of a due process hearing and litigation if not limited by the court as long as they are prevailing parties and do not fail in the requirement to properly apprize school officials of their concerns before removing the child from public school.
15. Parents have the right to withdraw their children from public schools and to educate them in home schools, private, or religious schools. They may be entitled to reimbursement for those costs if the school district's placement is inappropriate, but only if they properly notify school officials of their intentions. This award ensures that the appropriate education to which their children are entitled is free and at no cost to them.

Endnotes

[1] Education for All Handicapped Children Act, P.L. 91-230, Title VI § 601, 84 Stat. 175 (1970), *amended* P.L. 93-380 (1974), 88 Stat. 579; *amended* P.L. 94-142, § 3(a), 89 Stat. 774 (1975), *amended* P.L. 95-49, 91 Stat. 230 (1977); *amended* P.L. 98-199, 97 Stat. 1357 (1983); *amended* P.L. 101-476 (1990), *renamed* Individuals with Disabilities Act, P.L. 102-119 § 25(b), 105 Stat. 587 (1991), *amended* 20 U.S.C. § 1400 *et seq.*(1997); *amended* P.L. 108-446, 118 Stat. 2647 (2004).

[2] Elementary and Secondary Education Act of 1965, *as amended*, 20 U.S.C. § 6301 *et seq.*

[3] Board of Educ. of Cent. Hudson Sch. Dist. v. Rowley, 458 U.S. 176 [5 Educ. L. Rep. 34] (1982).

[4] Winkleman *ex rel.* Winkelman v. Parma City Sch. Dist., 550 U.S. — (2007).

[5] Jaynes *ex rel.* Jaynes v. Newport News Sch. Bd., 2001 WL 788643 (4th Cir. July 10, 2001); Mason *ex rel.* Mason v. Schenectady City Sch. Dist., 879 F. Supp. 215 [99 Educ. L. Rep. 170] (N.D.N.Y. 1993).

[6] Doe v. Nashville Pub. Schs., 133 F.3d 384, 387-388 [123 Educ. L. Rep. 37] (6th Cir. 1998).

[7] Austin Indep. Sch. Dist. v. Robert M., 168 F. Supp. 2d 635, 640 [158 Educ. L. Rep. 352] (W.D. Tex. 2001), *aff'd*, 54 F. App'x 413 (5th Cir. 2002).

[8] Heather S. *ex rel.* Kathy S. v. Wisconsin, 125 F.3d 1045 [122 Educ. L. Rep. 493] (7th Cir. 1997).

[9] Kings Local Sch. Dist. Bd. of Educ., 325 F.3d 724 [175 Educ. L. Rep. 119] (6th Cir. 2003).

[10] Popson v. W. Clark Cmty. Schs., 230 F. Supp. 2d 910, 916 [172 Educ. L. Rep. 910] (S.D. Ind. 2002).

[11] *Popson*, 230 F. Supp. 2d at 936.

[12] Hale v. Poplar Bluff R-1 Sch. Dist., 280 F.3d 831 [161 Educ. L. Rep. 778] (8th Cir. 2002).

[13] Generally, in order to exit a child from special education, an assessment is required; however, the U.S. Department of Education intends to seek public comment as to whether a parent's revocation of consent for services is sufficient to relieve public schools from the duty of providing FAPE to the child.

[14] Gonzaga Univ. v. Doe, 536 U.S. 273 [165 Educ. L. Rep. 458] (2002).

[15] Amanda J. v. Clark County Sch. Dist., 267 F.3d 877 [157 Educ. L. Rep. 562] (9th Cir. 2001).

[16] *Amanda J.*, 267 F.3d at 893.

[17] Letter to Morgan County Sch. Dist. (FPCO 2001) (stating that the principal's handwritten notes concerning the discipline of a high school student were not education records).

[18] Navin v. Park Ridge Sch. Dist. 64, 270 F.3d 1147 [158 Educ. L. Rep. 576] (7th Cir. 2001).

[19] Taylor v. Vt. Dep't of Educ., 313 F.3d 768 [172 Educ. L. Rep. 871] (2d Cir. 2002).

[20]. *Taylor*, 313 F.3d at 781 n.10.
[21]. *Winner Sch. Dist.*, 36 IDELR 55 (SEA 2001).
[22]. Jensen *ex rel.* C.J. v. Reeves, 2001 WL 113829 (10th Cir. Feb. 9, 2001).
[23]. E.W. v. Sch. Bd. of Miami Dade County, 2004 WL 438322 (S.D. Fla., March 8, 2004).
[24] Gary S. v. Manchester Sch. Dist., 241 F. Supp. 2d 111, 115 [174 Educ. L. Rep. 229] (D.N.H. 2003).
[25]. Schaffer v. Weast, 546 U.S. 49 (2005).
[26]. Arlington Cent. Sch. Dist. Bd. of Educ. v. Murphy, 546 U.S. — (2006).
[27]. Amanda J. v. Clark County Sch. Dist., 267 F.3d 877 [157 Educ. L. Rep. 562] (9th Cir. 2001).
[28]. Burilovich v. Bd. of Educ., 208 F.3d 560, 566 [143 Educ. L. Rep. 437] (6th Cir. 2000).
[29]. *Amanda J.*, 267 F.3d at 892.

Chapter 20

Assessing Students with Disabilities under the IDEA and NCLB

Elizabeth Allen Borreca & Christopher P. Borreca

Introduction

Mr. Johnson, the principal of Jones Elementary School, is chairing an August IEP team meeting on Angie, a fifth-grader with an identified learning disability. The IEP team is discussing an annual goal for Angie in the area of reading. Angie enjoys reading and can respond to knowledge-level comprehension questions in fourth-grade material, but does not yet respond to higher level comprehension questions and cannot apply a variety of comprehension strategies in third or fourth-grade-level reading assignments. Her vocabulary skills, word recognition skills, and fluency rate, however, are at grade level. Because of her weak comprehension skills, however, on last year's statewide reading assessment, she scored "Does Not Meet Standards."

After much discussion, the IEP team still had not reached consensus on Angie's annual goal in the area of reading. Several members felt that Angie's goal could not possibly address grade-level content standards or grade-level academic achievement standards. Other members felt it could address grade level content standards, but with modified achievement standards. Still others felt unsure about how to make those decisions.

What does Mr. Johnson need to know and understand in order to lead the IEP team to make sound decisions for Angie, decisions that result in a standards-based IEP that provides access to the general education curriculum and high expectations for Angie as well as for all students? How do the team's decisions for Angie affect the way state or district-wide test scores are reported to parents, teachers, principals, and the public?

As this vignette illustrates, one of the critical challenges facing principals today is including students with disabilities in state and district accountability and standards systems. With increasing accountability for improving the academic achievement of all students with disabilities, principals must understand the unique assessment and accountability provisions of the Individuals with Disabilities Education Act (IDEA) and the No Child Left Behind Act

(NCLB), as well as the implications for implementation. These laws are two of the most significant federal laws related to the education and assessment of children. Together, they require states to hold schools accountable for the academic achievement of *all* students. While NCLB focuses on improving the education of all children, the IDEA focuses solely on improving the education of students with identified disabilities. Even though each law has a somewhat different focus related to assessment and accountability, as a result of recent changes, they are now much more closely aligned to work together to improve the educational performance of all students, including all students with disabilities. While there are differences in how the laws are implemented across states, there is a common framework for the development and implementation of assessment and accountability systems.

This chapter will focus on the assessment of students with disabilities under the IDEA and NCLB as it relates to what principals need to know and be able to do. The first section provides a brief overview of the historical development related to the evolution of assessment and accountability of students with disabilities under the IDEA and NCLB. The second section highlights the current legal requirements and issues related to this topic while the third section discusses decision-making guidelines for IEP teams related to participation of students with disabilities in state accountability systems. The fourth and final section provides recommendations for practice.

Historical Development: From Access to Accountability

1975 Education for All Handicapped Children Act

Prior to this law, many students with disabilities were excluded from mandatory attendance laws. The 1975 Education for All Handicapped Children Act (EAHCA) ensured that all children with disabilities would receive a free appropriate public education.[1] The EAHCA was later re-named the Individuals with Disabilities Education Act. Since the 1975 version of the law, where access to special education services was the primary focus, special education accountability has continued to increase and evolve in the IDEA as well as NCLB.

1997 IDEA Amendments

With the 1997 amendments to the IDEA, the focus on special education accountability took on a new meaning as it evolved from access to services to access to the general education curriculum as well as mandatory inclusion of all students with disabilities in state and district-wide assessment programs. "Under the IDEA, States have been required to include students with disabilities in regular assessments since 1997 and, beginning July 1, 2000, in alternate assessments."[2] These changes reflected a shift toward improving educational quality for students with disabilities.

No Child Left Behind Act of 2001

Accountability was again strengthened with the passage of the No Child Left Behind Act of 2001. "In particular, NCLB includes explicit requirements to ensure that students served by Title I are given the same opportunity to achieve high standards and are held to the same high expectations as all other students in each State."[3] Several elements of NCLB are designed to ensure that schools are held accountable for educational results so that all students can achieve to high standards. The purpose of the NCLB assessment requirements is, therefore, to establish accountability for student achievement at the school, district, and state levels.[4]

All public school students, including all IDEA-eligible students, are required to participate in their statewide assessment system. NCLB requires all students in grades 3-8 to be tested each year in both reading/language arts and math. High school students must also be tested at least once during tenth through twelfth grades in both reading/language arts and math. Beginning with the 2007–08 school year, all students must also be tested in science at least once in grades 3-5; once in grades 6-9; and once again in grades 10-12.[5] In addition, all students are to be proficient or higher in reading/English language arts, mathematics, and science by 2013–14.[6]

The above assessments are intended to measure student progress and hold states, districts, and schools accountable for adequately educating every student in critical core academic areas. The state assessments are based on each state's academic content standards and academic achievement standards in the core content areas and, as a result, vary from state to state. Because all students with disabilities are included in the statewide assessments and the statewide assessments must be based on each state's academic content standards and academic achievement standards, all students with disabilities must have access to the general education curriculum in order to perform well on the assessments.

As a part of the statewide testing program for all students, NCLB requires participating states to have challenging academic content standards and challenging academic achievement standards in place for reading/language arts, mathematics, and most recently, science. NCLB defines challenging academic content standards as "challenging academic standards in academic subjects that specify what children are expected to know and be able to do; contain coherent and rigorous content; and encourage the teaching of advanced skills."[7]

NCLB defines challenging achievement standards as "... academic achievement standards that are aligned with the State's academic content standards; describe two levels of high achievement (proficient and advanced) that determine how well children are mastering the material in the State academic content standards; and describe a third level of achievement (basic) to provide complete information about the progress of the lower-achieving children toward mastering the proficient and advanced levels of achievement."[8] States must determine which scores[9] differentiate among the achievement levels. The NCLB does not define the term "proficient." As a result, each state determines its own basic, proficient, and advanced levels of content mastery.

NCLB also requires all assessment methods to be aligned to, or based on, those standards. Having both types of standards and then aligning assessments to those standards is the cornerstone of NCLB's accountability system. Furthermore, it requires the aggregation, as well as disaggregation of assessment data for the four subgroups of economically disadvantaged students, students from major racial and ethnic minorities, students with disabilities, and students with limited English proficiency.[10]

2003 NCLB Regulations

Following the passage of NCLB in 2001, the next major development in the evolution of the accountability system for students with disabilities occurred in December of 2003 with promulgation of NCLB regulations that provided an additional option for including students with the most significant cognitive disabilities in statewide testing through alternate assessments linked to alternate academic achievement standards. Many felt that at least for this small group of students these regulations provided more reasonable and realistic performance expectations.[11]

2004 IDEA Reauthorization

In 2004, the IDEA was again reauthorized, and the accountability system for students with disabilities was further strengthened. This reauthorization made many of the requirements in NCLB applicable to special education. The term "modifications" was replaced in the IDEA 2004 with "appropriate accommodations" related to the administration of state or district-wide assessments for students with disabilities. This change in terminology now aligns more closely with the terminology used in NCLB, which is "adaptations and accommodations."[12]

In addition, in an effort to make assessments as accessible as possible, the definition of universal design was added[13] and defined as having the meaning given to the term in Section 3 of the Assistive Technology Act of 1998. The term "means a concept or philosophy for designing and delivering products and services that are usable by people with the widest possible range of functional capabilities, which include products and services that are directly accessible (without requiring assistive technologies) and products and services that are interoperable with assistive technologies."[14]

Another new IDEA provision also addresses universal design.[15] It states that "The State educational agency (or, in the case of a district-wide assessment, the local education agency) shall, to the extent feasible, use universal design principles in developing and administering any assessments under this paragraph."[16] This new IDEA requirement now aligns with a similar requirement in NCLB. The goal is to provide the most valid assessment possible for the greatest number of students. Universal design builds in accessibility for the greatest number of students during the development of the test. It does not change the standard of performance of assessments and is not intended to water down tests. It also does not replace accommodations as they may still be needed even when the elements of universal design are incorporated into a test.[17]

2007 Final Regulations Governing NCLB and the IDEA 2004

The most recent changes to the accountability provisions for students with disabilities are found in new regulations published on April 9, 2007. These final regulations amend the regulations governing the NCLB Act of 2001 and the IDEA 2004 and result in an even stronger alignment between the two laws.

> These regulations provide States with additional flexibility regarding State, local educational agency (LEA), and school accountability for the achievement of a small group of students with disabilities whose progress is such that, even after receiving appropriate instruction, including special education and related services designed to address the students' individual needs, the students' individualized education program (IEP) teams (IEP Teams) are reasonably certain that the students will not achieve grade-level proficiency within the year covered by the students' IEPs.[18]

These new regulations permit states to develop an additional alternate assessment option. This option is an alternate assessment based on modified academic achievement standards. With this additional option, states now have up to five allowable assessment options for including students with disabilities in the accountability system.

Legal Requirements and Issues Related to Assessment

As described above, the NCLB and IDEA assessment and accountability provisions are now designed to work together to reduce the achievement gap and improve the educational performance of all students, including all students with disabilities. This section will discuss the current legal requirements and issues related to the assessment and accountability of IDEA-eligible students under the IDEA and NCLB with a focus on the allowable assessment options, Adequate Yearly Progress (AYP), and reporting requirements and implications.

Allowable Assessment Options

As stated earlier, "under the IDEA, States have been required to include students with disabilities in regular assessments since 1997 and, beginning July 1, 2000, in alternate assessments."[19] States, however, have some choices in terms of allowable assessment options for including students with disabilities in their statewide assessment system. Following are the five allowable assessment options that states may include in their state and district-wide assessment systems:

Option 1: General grade-level state assessment (without accommodations)

Option 2: General grade-level state assessment (with accommodations)

Option 3: Alternate assessment judged against grade-level achievement standards

Option 4: Alternate assessment judged against modified achievement standards

Option 5: Alternate assessment judged against alternate achievement standards

It is expected that most students with disabilities will participate in a general grade-level state assessment with or without accommodations (options one and two). For students with disabilities who cannot participate in the general grade-level state assessment, a state must develop at least one alternate assessment but may choose to include up to three alternate assessment methods/options (Options 3 – 5).[20] See Table 1 for an overview of similarities and differences among the three allowable alternate assessments.

Characteristics of the Assessment Options

All of the assessment options are based on the same state academic content standards. In addition, all of the assessment options are increasingly being developed with universal design elements in mind, as required by the IDEA 2004 and discussed above. The universal design features result in more accurate scores that reflect actual student knowledge and skills. They are designed to increase access without changing the standard of performance of assessments. Examples of test elements that decrease accessibility and should be avoided include unnecessary use of graphics that cannot be presented in Braille and unnecessary linguistic complexity when language use/comprehension is not being assessed.[22]

Table 1: Characteristics of Allowable Alternate Assessments (Options 3 – 5) [21]

Characteristics of Alternate Assessments	**Method 3:** Alternate Assessment Based on Grade-Level Academic Achievement Standards	**Method 4:** Alternate Assessment Based on Modified Academic Achievement Standards	**Method 5:** Alternate Assessment Based on Alternate Academic Achievement Standards
Relationship to AYP Reporting	No cap on # of proficient & advanced scores counted toward AYP.	2% cap on # of proficient and advanced scores counted toward AYP.	1% cap on # of proficient and advanced scores counted toward AYP.
State Guide-lines Define who is Eligible	Student with a disability who cannot take the regular assessment with accommodations. IEP Team makes the decision regarding the appropriate assessment.	Student whose disability has precluded the student from achieving proficiency, as demonstrated by objective evidence of the student's performance and whose progress to date in response to appropriate instruction is such that, even if significant growth occurs, the student's IEP team is reasonably certain that the student will not achieve grade-level proficiency within the year covered by the IEP. IEP Team makes the decision regarding the appropriate assessment.	Student with the most significant cognitive disabilities. IEP Team makes the decision regarding the appropriate assessment.
Content Standards on which the Test is Based	Grade-level.	Grade-level.	A State may develop "extended standards" that substantially simplify content including pre-requisite skills.

Table 1: Characteristics of Allowable Alternate Assessments (Options 3 – 5) *(continued)*

Characteristics of Alternate Assessments	**Method 3:** Alternate Assessment Based on Grade-Level Academic Achievement Standards	**Method 4:** Alternate Assessment Based on Modified Academic Achievement Standards	**Method 5:** Alternate Assessment Based on Alternate Academic Achievement Standards
Achievement Standards	A grade-level academic achievement standard defines a level of "proficient" performance equivalent to grade-level achievement on the State's regular assessment. Achievement standards must include 3 levels of performance, cut scores that distinguish one level from another, and descriptions of the content-based competencies associated with each level. Must be defined grade-by-grade.	A modified academic achievement standard is aligned to grade-level content standards for the grade in which a student is enrolled and challenging for eligible students, but may be less difficult than grade-level achievement standards. Achievement standards must include 3 levels of performance, cut scores that distinguish one level from another, and descriptions of the content-based competencies associated with each level. Must be defined grade-by-grade.	An alternate academic achievement standard is an expectation of performance that differs in complexity from a grade-level achievement standard, usually based on a very limited sample of content that is linked to but does not fully represent grade-level content. May be defined for grade clusters, e.g., 3-5.
Assessment	Grade-level content.	Built on grade-level content but with easier items.	May include reduced coverage and/or simplification of grade-level content, based on "extended" standards. Format may permit variation in test content for individual students if results can be aggregated.
IEP	Must include annual measurable IEP goals.	Must include annual measurable IEP goals that are based on grade-level content standards.	Must include annual measurable IEP goals and benchmarks or short term objectives.

Adequate Yearly Progress (AYP)

Each of the five assessment methods, or options, must result in achievement scores that can be used in calculating AYP, a goal for annual improvement that states, school districts, and schools must meet each year in order to reach NCLB's requirement to demonstrate 100 percent student proficiency in reading and math by the year 2014. The goal is defined by each state and is based, in part, on school and district assessment results, not individual student results.[23] In order to meet AYP, schools need to have a minimum of 95 percent participation of all students and all subgroups, meet the state proficiency targets based on the number of proficient and advanced test scores, and meet at least one other "outside measure," as determined by the state. This measure is often attendance rates in elementary schools and graduation rates in high schools.[24]

One Percent Cap

In calculating AYP for local educational agencies (LEAs) and the state, the scores received by students with disabilities taking alternate assessments based on alternate achievement standards (Option 5) figure into the AYP calculation as long as the number of those who score at the proficient or advanced level on those alternate achievement standards at the LEA and state levels, separately, does not exceed 1 percent of all students in the grades assessed in reading/language arts and mathematics.[25] The 1 percent cap, however, does not limit access of students with disabilities to this assessment option when based on appropriate decision making. The 1 percent cap only addresses the inclusion of proficient/advanced scores for AYP calculations, unless an exception is granted by the U.S. Department of Education. In other words, the type of assessment appropriate for a given child must remain an individualized determination made by the IEP team.

Two Percent Cap

In addition to the 1 percent cap, a 2 percent cap is based on the proficient and advanced scores of students with disabilities on the alternate assessment judged against modified achievement standards (Option 4), "provided that the number of those scores at the LEA and at the State levels, separately, does not exceed 2.0 percent of all students in the grades assessed in reading/language arts and in mathematics."[26] The purpose of the 2 percent cap is to discourage schools from inappropriately holding students with disabilities to lower standards. States cannot permit LEAs to exceed the 2 percent cap, unless the number of proficient/advanced scores on alternate assessments judged against alternate achievement standards (Option 5) is less than 1 percent and the total percentage for both categories (alternate and modified) does not exceed 3 percent of all students in the grades assessed.[27]

Neither the 1 percent cap nor 2 percent cap applies to individual schools. These requirements only apply at the school district and state levels. States cannot request exceptions to caps on proficient/advanced scores based on alternate or modified achievement standards (Options 4 or 5). However, states may grant LEA exceptions to the 1 percent cap on proficient/advanced scores for alternate assessments judged against alternate achievement standards (Option 5) when the LEA has documentation to show that it has a higher incidence of students with the most significant cognitive disabilities that exceeds the 1 percent of all students in the combined grades assessed or cites other reasons to justify an exception.[28] In addition, the Secretary of Education may establish criteria to permit flexibility in accounting for the achievement of students with disabilities in AYP determinations for 2007-08 and 2008-09 for states moving expeditiously to adopt and administer alternate assessments judged against modified achievement standards.[29]

Reporting Requirements

Results of assessments are required to be reported to the public, to parents, and to federal agencies. States and districts must report on the participation and performance of students with disabilities for all of the assessment options. This public reporting is required by both the IDEA and NCLB. "The State must report to the public data on the number of students participating in each type of assessment and their performance, with the same frequency and in the same detail as it reports on students without disabilities (or for all students)."[30] States must also submit all assessment data to the U.S. Department of Education to facilitate national monitoring of student performance. The importance of communication with parents about assessment participation and results is emphasized in both the IDEA 2004 and NCLB. "NCLB requires schools to communicate with the parents of each child attending the school and to ensure that, regardless of the method or media used, it provides information in an understandable and uniform format including alternative formats on request. States are also required to provide individual student results for each student's assessment" [31]

Requirements and Guidelines for Assessing Students

The IEP team, which includes the student's parents, is responsible for determining how a student with a disability will participate in the statewide assessment system, not whether a student with a disability will participate. All students with disabilities who are unable to participate in the general assessment with or without accommodations (Options 1 and 2) must be provided with an alternate assessment. While IEP teams have ultimate responsibility for making assessment decisions for each student with a disability, states are required to have developed and implemented guidelines for appropriate accommodations and participation of children with disabilities in alternate assessments, including a list of accommodations approved for use with their statewide assessment system.[32]

An LEA is responsible for managing its IEP teams' decisions regarding who takes an alternate assessment. If an LEA permits schools to assess an inappropriately large number of students with Options 4 and/or 5, the LEA might exceed the 1 or 2 percent caps that have been established. This result would cause a number of non-proficient scores to be redistributed among the schools that administered these test options and would likely create negative consequences for schools that administered alternate assessments. To avoid this situation, LEAs must provide information and guidelines to school personnel and IEP teams regarding the decision-making process for selecting assessment options for students with disabilities.[33] When this result occurs, it is important to investigate to ensure that the assessment decisions are being made appropriately for each child and do not simply reflect misunderstandings about the assessment process.

Principals, therefore, need to understand the current assessment options found in NCLB and the IDEA and, even more importantly, those included in their state assessment system in order to make critical decisions. Likewise, principals need to assume leadership to train IEP teams to make critical decisions regarding the most appropriate assessment option(s) for each student with a disability. To those ends, principals need to be familiar with their state content and achievement standards in order to guide IEP teams in developing and aligning IEP goals to appropriate assessment options. To better understand and select the most appropriate assessment option(s) for including students with disabilities in the state assessment system, an overview of the five possible assessment options along with corresponding IEP team guidelines to consider when determining the most appropriate option(s) for each student with a disability is presented.

An overview of the options with corresponding IEP team guidelines is summarized by Table 2 below. This table lists the educational characteristics of students that IEP teams should consider when making recommendations about student participation in statewide assessments. States may specify additional considerations in their individual statewide assessment guidelines and guidance regarding the development of IEPs. Also, states that do not choose to use all of the assessment methods available in the regulations and summarized here should offer specific guidance about students with the most significant cognitive disabilities.

Table 2: A Decision Framework for IEP Teams Related to Methods for Individual Student Participation in State Accountability Assessments[34]

<table>
<tr><td colspan="3">Prerequisite Considerations
Before recommending an assessment other than the general statewide test, with or without accommodations, the IEP team should consider these three questions:</td><td colspan="3">• Has the student had access to grade-level content?
• Has the student had evidence-based instruction?
• Was instruction by a highly qualified teacher?</td></tr>
<tr><td colspan="6">If the answer to any of these questions is "No," then address access considerations and continue to apply grade-level achievement standards and evaluate response to intervention before considering an assessment method based on modified or alternate achievement standards.

If the answer to all three questions is "Yes," then consider the methods and questions below.</td></tr>
<tr><td>Questions to Consider</td><td colspan="5">Assessment Recommendation</td></tr>
<tr><td></td><td>Method 1. General Assessment</td><td>Method 2. General Assessment, with Accommodations</td><td>Method 3. Alternate Assessment, Grade-Level Achievement</td><td>Method 4. Alternate Assessment, Modified Achievement</td><td>Method 5. Alternate Assessment, Alternate Achievement</td></tr>
<tr><td>Question 1: In what way does the student access the general curriculum?</td><td colspan="3">Shows progress in the full scope and complexity of the grade-level curriculum but may not yet be on grade level (for the subject area assessment being considered).</td><td>Does not show grade-level achievement; needs changes in complexity and scope of curriculum to show progress in grade-level content.</td><td>Due to significant cognitive disabilities (e.g., memory, transfer of learning), needs extensive prioritization within grade-level content.</td></tr>
</table>

Table 2: A Decision Framework for IEP Teams Related to Methods for Individual Student Participation in State Accountability Assessments *(continued)*

Questions to Consider	Assessment Recommendation				
	Method 1. General Assessment	Method 2. General Assessment, with Accommodations	Method 3. Alternate Assessment, Grade-Level Achievement	Method 4. Alternate Assessment, Modified Achievement	Method 5. Alternate Assessment, Alternate Achievement
Question 2: What has been this student's response to academic interventions?	Responds to grade-level instruction but may not yet be on grade level. Shows progress in response to appropriate instruction and is likely to achieve grade-level proficiency or near grade-level proficiency within the school year covered by the IEP for the subject area assessment being considered.			Academic problems persist despite appropriate and intensive instruction; multiple years behind grade-level expectations. Progress is such that not likely to achieve grade-level proficiency within the school year covered by the IEP for the content assessment being considered.	Requires ongoing systematic instruction to learn prioritized skills; needs to focus on critical essence of content.
Question 3: How does this student interact with text?	On or near grade level in reading.			Needs controlled vocabulary/ reduced reading level; may also need text reader.	Needs key words, pictures, and auditory cues embedded in adapted or controlled text; may need text reader to use these cues; may have some emerging reading skills.

Table 2: A Decision Framework for IEP Teams Related to Methods for Individual Student Participation in State Accountability Assessments *(continued)*

Questions to Consider	Assessment Recommendation				
	Method 1. General Assessment	Method 2. General Assessment, with Accommodations	Method 3. Alternate Assessment, Grade-Level Achievement	Method 4. Alternate Assessment, Modified Achievement	Method 5. Alternate Assessment, Alternate Achievement
Question 4: Do the supports required by this student to perform or participate meaningfully and productively in the general education curriculum change the complexity or cognitive demand of the material?	None needed (for the subject area assessment being considered).	Needs accommodations (for the subject area assessment being considered).	Needs modified presentations and responses but on grade level (for the subject area assessment being considered).	Needs supports that reduce complexity or breadth of assessment items, such as aids that reduce judgment needed to do task or teacher scaffolding during assessment (for the subject area assessment being considered).	Needs extensive supports, such as simplified symbol system, peer model or motivation through choice making to retrieve response.
Question 5: What inferences can be made about the student's generalization/ transfer of learning?	Shows transfer of learning to the extent expected for the grade level during ongoing instruction.			Transfer of learning is more limited in scope than grade level; may only transfer to similar or familiar content or contexts.	Needs systematic instruction to generalize; because generalization is especially challenging during instruction, should not be assumed unless assessed.

Option 1: Participation in a General Grade-Level Assessment

This assessment measures student progress on the state grade-level content standards and grade-level achievement standards. It is the assessment option taken by students without disabilities, some section 504 students, and many IDEA-eligible students.

Implications: If a student with a disability shows progress in the full scope of the grade-level curriculum, responds to grade-level instruction without accommodations, and is on or near grade level in reading but may not yet be on grade level overall, this option may be the most appropriate.[35]

Option 2: Participation in a General Grade-Level Assessment with Accommodations

This assessment method also measures student progress on the state grade-level content standards and achievement standards. Many students with disabilities who receive accommodations under section 504, as well as the vast majority of IDEA-eligible students, participate in assessments by taking the same tests on the same content as students without disabilities, but with reasonable accommodations for their disabilities. Accommodations are addressed in both IDEA and NCLB regulations, but the term is not defined in either set of regulations. "Appropriate accommodations" are addressed in the regulations related to students eligible under the IDEA and section 504.[36] According to the regulations, a state's academic assessment system must provide appropriate accommodations for each IDEA-eligible student that the student's IEP team determines are necessary and for each section 504 student that the placement team "determines are necessary to measure the academic achievement of the student relative to the State's academic content and academic achievement standards for the grade in which the student is enrolled."[37] The regulations require that a state "develop, disseminate information on, and promote the use of appropriate accommodations to increase the number of students with disabilities who are tested against academic achievement standards for the grade in which the student is enrolled; and … ensure that regular and special education teachers and other appropriate staff know how to administer assessments, including making appropriate use of accommodations, for students with disabilities and students covered under section 504."[38]

Regulations also provide the following "accommodation guidelines" related to participation in assessments:

> (1) A State (or in the case of a district-wide assessment, an LEA) must develop guidelines for the provision of appropriate accommodations. (2) The State's (or in the case of a district-wide assessment, the LEA's) guidelines must (i) Identify only those accommodations for each assessment that do not invalidate the score; and (ii) Instruct IEP Teams

to select, for each assessment, only those accommodations that do not invalidate the score.[39]

Implications: This option should be considered for IDEA-eligible students with the same characteristics as those described under Option 1 above except that these students also need allowable accommodations to meet their unique needs.[40] As a result, principals and IEP team members need to have access to their state list of approved accommodations for use in the statewide assessment system and understand the purpose and appropriate use of the approved accommodations. In order to accomplish this, principals and all IEP team members need to be familiar with their state guidelines on how to select appropriate and allowable accommodations that do not change the test construct, retain test validity, and are necessary to measure the academic achievement of the student relative to the state's academic content and achievement standards for the grade in which the student is enrolled.

Option 3: Participation in an Alternate Assessment Judged against Grade-Level Academic Achievement Standards

The purpose of alternate assessments (Options 3-5), in general, is to measure how well students with disabilities know and can demonstrate their enrolled grade content standards, but the options differ as to how well and how much the student knows and can do. They also differ in terms of the target students for whom these assessments are intended. According to the National Education Association (NEA), "States must ensure that all students with disabilities are appropriately assessed and must provide at least *one* alternate assessment (unless all students with disabilities can be appropriately assessed with the general assessment that is used for all students)."[41] According to Quenemoen, "there is a small group of students who cannot show what they know on the regular assessment, even with the use of accommodations, and alternate assessments have been developed for many of these students."[42]

Option 3 is the first of three allowable alternate assessments. This method is meant to assess the same content standards and hold students to the same achievement standards as the regular assessments (Options 1 and 2). The assessment procedures, however, may differ from the regular assessments. For example, instead of multiple-choice questions, it may include performance tasks. AYP results from this option, however, should be treated in the same manner as results from the regular assessments.[43] Eligible students for this alternate assessment option may be from any of the IDEA disability categories; however, according to Quenemoen, "there are very few, if any, such alternate assessments in place in states now in part because of the very difficult measurement challenge of showing comparability to the regular assessment."[44]

Implications: As described in Table 2, before recommending an assessment other than the general statewide test, with or without accommodations for students with disabilities, the IEP team members need to be able to answer "Yes" to these prerequisite questions:

1.Has the student had access to grade-level content?

2. Has the student had appropriate instruction?

3. Was instruction by a highly qualified teacher?

If the answer to any of the above questions is "No," then the IEP team may want to address access considerations and recommend that a student's instructional program be changed before considering any of the alternate assessment options.[45]

If the answer to all of the above questions is "Yes," then consider the following questions.

1. Is this option included in your state assessment system?
2. Does the student being considered show progress in the full scope and complexity of the grade-level curriculum, but may not yet be on grade level?
3. Does the student respond to grade-level instruction, but may not yet be on grade level (for the subject area assessment being considered)?
4. Is the student on or near grade level in reading?
5. Does the student need modified presentations and responses, but on grade level (for the subject area assessment being considered)?
6. Does the student show transfer of learning to the extent expected for the grade level during ongoing instruction?[46]

If the answer to the above questions is "Yes," then this option may be appropriate as the student may need different assessment procedures from the regular assessments (i.e. performance tasks instead of multiple-choice questions) even though the student can be tested on grade-level content standards and grade-level achievement standards.[47]

Option 4. Participation in an Alternate Assessment Judged against Modified Academic Achievement Standards (2 percent cap)

This option, effective May 9, 2007, permits states to develop an alternate assessment based on modified academic achievement standards. "Modified academic achievement standards must be aligned with a State's academic content standards for the grade in which a student is enrolled. Thus, only the academic achievement standards are modified, not the content standards on which those modified academic achievement standards are based. Although the assessment and modified academic achievement standards for a particular grade must be challenging for eligible students, they may be less difficult when compared with the general test and grade-level academic achievement standards,"[48] but more demanding than alternate academic achievement standards (Option 5). Students must, however, have access to a curriculum based on grade-level content standards and, therefore, must be assessed with a measure that is also based on grade-level content standards.[49]

Eligible students for this assessment method may come from any of the IDEA disability categories, but this option is appropriate for only a small number of IDEA-eligible students "whose progress in response to appropriate instruction, including special education and related services designed to address the students' individual needs, is such that they are not likely to achieve grade-level proficiency within the school year covered by their IEPs."[50] In addition, an IEP team may decide that a student should take an assessment using this option in one subject and the general assessment in another subject. It is also expected that there will be students with disabilities who take this option one year, make considerable progress during the school year, and then take the general grade-level assessment the following year. As a result, an IEP team must consider a student's progress annually based on multiple, objective measures of the student's achievement before determining that the student should be assessed based on modified academic achievement standards.[51]

As stated earlier, when measuring AYP, states and LEAs have the flexibility to count the proficient and advanced scores of students who take alternate assessments based on modified academic achievement standards as long as the number of those proficient and advanced scores does not exceed 2 percent of all students in the grades assessed at the LEA and state levels. The 2 percent cap may be exceeded only if a state or LEA is below the 1 percent cap for students with the most significant cognitive disabilities who take alternate assessments based on alternate academic achievement standards and the total percentage for both categories (alternate and modified) does not exceed 3 percent of all students in the grades assessed.[52]

Implications: As discussed in Table 2, before recommending an assessment other than the general statewide test, with or without accommodations for students with disabilities, the IEP team members need to be able to answer "Yes" to the listed prerequisite questions. If the answer to any of those questions is "No," then the IEP team may want to recommend that a student's instructional program be changed before considering any of the alternate assessment options.[53]

If the answer to all of the above questions is "Yes," then the team should consider the following questions.

1. Is this option included in your state assessment system?
2. Is there objective evidence demonstrating that the student's disability has precluded the student from achieving grade-level proficiency? Such evidence may include the student's performance on state assessments or other assessments that can validly document academic achievement.
3. Is the student's progress in response to appropriate instruction, including special education and related services designed to address the student's individual needs, such that the student is not likely to

achieve grade-level proficiency within the school year covered by the student's IEP (for the subject area assessment being considered)? The IEP team must use multiple valid measures of the student's progress over time in making this determination.[54]

4. Does the student need controlled vocabulary, a reduced reading level, and/or may also need a text reader?
5. Does the student need supports that reduce the complexity or breadth of assessment items such as aids that reduce judgment needed to do tasks or teacher scaffolding during assessment?
6. Is the student's transfer of learning more limited in scope than grade level? Can the student only transfer to similar or familiar content or contexts?[55]
7. Does the student's IEP include goals that are based on the academic content standards for the grade in which the student is enrolled?[56]

If the answer to the above questions is "Yes," then this option may be appropriate as the student may need modified academic achievement standards for the subject area assessment being considered even though the student can be tested on grade-level content standards. Hopefully these guidelines will at least provide parameters to ensure that students are not assessed based on this option simply because of their disability category or racial or economic background.[57]

Option 5: Participation in an Alternate Assessment Judged against Alternate Academic Achievement Standards (1 percent cap)

This option permits states to develop an alternate assessment based on alternate academic achievement standards for students with the most significant cognitive disabilities. It is meant to assess the same content, but with a different definition of "how well" and "how much" of the content as is measured by the regular assessment. The achievement of these students on the content is very different from the achievement of students with disabilities taking the other assessment options, but these students are able to learn academic content with reduced complexity, breadth, and depth clearly linked to the same grade-level content as their peers.[58] "Post school outcomes for students with significant cognitive disabilities based on the functional curriculum as historically defined have been abysmal. It is not a great risk to assume their potential competence in academic content. Indeed there is much to gain."[59] The guidance from states, therefore, should emphasize that students with the most significant cognitive disabilities should have access to the general curriculum and that a totally functional curriculum will not serve these students well.[60]

> It is the State's responsibility to define which students have the most significant cognitive disabilities and to establish clear and appropriate guidelines for IEP teams to use when deciding if an alternate assessment based on alternate achievement standards is justified for an individual child. These guidelines should result in ensuring that students are not assessed based on this option simply because of their placement outside the regular classroom, their disability category or their racial or economic background.[61]

When achievement beyond the assessment items cannot be assumed, the student's performance should probably be assessed against modified or alternate achievement standards (Options 4 or 5).[62]

As discussed earlier, in calculating AYP for school districts and the state, a state may include the proficient and advanced scores of students with the most significant cognitive disabilities based on the alternate academic achievement standards, provided that the number of those scores at the LEA and at the state levels, separately, does not exceed 1 percent of all students in the grades assessed in reading/language arts and in mathematics.[63]

Implications: Again, as discussed in Table 2, before recommending an assessment other than the general statewide test, with or without accommodations for students with disabilities, the IEP team members need to be able to answer "Yes" to the three listed prerequisite questions. If the answer to any of the above questions is "No," then the IEP Team may want to recommend that a student's instructional program be changed before considering any of the alternate assessment options.[64]

If the answer to all of the above questions is "Yes," then the team should consider the following questions.

1. Is this option included in your state assessment system?
2. Due to significant cognitive disabilities (e.g., memory, transfer of learning) as defined by your state, does the student need extensive prioritization within grade-level content?
3. Does the student require ongoing systematic instruction to learn prioritized skills and need to focus on the critical essence of content?
4. Does the student need key words, pictures, and auditory cues embedded in adapted or controlled text, or a text reader, to use these cues and demonstrated some emerging reading skills?
5. Does the student need extensive supports, such as simplified symbol systems, peer models, or motivation through choice-making to retrieve responses?
6. Does the student need systematic instruction to generalize because generalization is especially challenging during instruction and should not be assumed unless assessed?[65]

If the answers to the above questions are "Yes," then this option may be appropriate as the student may need alternate academic achievement standards even though the student can be tested on content that is linked to grade-level standards.

Recommendations for Practice

Based on the requirements reviewed above, it is clear that assessment of children with disabilities, while complicated by the learning needs demonstrated by each child, requires both the knowledge of and a commitment to the legal requirements of NCLB and the IDEA by school leaders. To that end, the following are summary recommendations for principals as they lead their schools toward universal opportunity for all children.

1. Be thoroughly familiar with your state assessment system including allowable accommodations, implications for graduation, and the consequences for exceeding the applicable caps related to the calculation of AYP.
2. Be thoroughly familiar with the state grade-level content standards and grade level achievement standards.
3. Thoroughly understand the IDEA and NCLB assessment and accountability provisions.
4. Because all students will be assessed based on grade-level content standards, ensure that all students with disabilities receive instruction that is aligned to grade-level content in reading and math even though the content may be reduced in breadth, depth, and/or complexity for some students.[66]
5. Ensure that all IEP team members are thoroughly trained in the requirements of the statewide assessment system and the IEP decision-making process for determining appropriate assessment options for students with disabilities.

Endnotes

1 Public Law 94-142, codified at 20 U.S.C. 1400 *et seq.*

2 U.S. Department of Education, *Alternate Achievement Standards for Students with the Most Significant Cognitive Disabilities: Non-Regulatory Guidance*, at 9 (2005).

3 U.S. Department of Education, Office of Elementary and Secondary Education, *Standards and Assessments Peer Review Guidance: Information and Examples for Meeting Requirements of the No Child Left Behind Act of 2001*, at 1 (2007).

4 Miriam Kurtig Freedman, *Meeting NCLB's Mandates: Your Quick-Reference Guide to Assessments and Accountability*, at 7 (LRP Publications 2005).

5 34. C.F.R. 200.5(3)(b)(2002).

6 Freedman, *supra* note 4 at 6.

7 *Id.*

8 *Id.*
9 Sometimes referred to as "cut scores."
10 Freedman, *supra* note 4 at 2.
11 Sue Gamm, *Cracking the Code: IDEA and NCLB Alternate Assessment Rules Made Simple,* at vii (LRP Publications 2007).
12 Charles J. Russo, Allan G. Osborne, & Elizabeth Allen Borreca, *Individuals with Disabilities Education Improvement Act vs. IDEA '97: Charting the Changes*, at 224 (LRP Publications 2005).
13 20 U.S.C. §1402(35).
14 Russo, Osborne, & Borreca, *supra* note 12 at 46.
15 20 U.S.C. §1412(a)(16)(E).
16 Russo,. Osbourne, & Borreca, *supra* note 12 at 137 – 138.
17 Christopher J. Johnstone, Jason Altman, & Martha Thurlow, *A State Guide to the Development of Universally Designed Assessments*, at 3 (National Center on Educational Outcomes, 2006).
18 Improving the Academic Achievement of the Disadvantaged; Individuals with Disabilities Education Act (IDEA), 72 Fed. Reg, 17748 (April 9, 2007).
19 U.S. Department of Education, *supra* note 2.
20 U.S. Department of Education, *Modified Academic Achievement Standards: Non-Regulatory Guidance*, at 12 (2007).
21 Table adapted from: U.S. Department of Education, *Modified Academic Achievement Standards: Non-Regulatory Guidance*, Appendix A (2007).
22 Johnstone, Altman, & Thurlow, *supra* note 17 at 6.
23 Freedman, *supra* note 4 at 6.
24 *Id.* at 11.
25 34 C.F.R. §200.13(c)(2003).
26 34 C.F.R. §200.13(c)(2)(ii) (2007).
27 34 C.F.R. § 200.13 (c)(2007).
28 *Id.*
29 *Id.*
30 National Center on Educational Outcomes, *Fact Sheet: Reporting the Results of Alternate Assessments Based on Modified Achievement Standards*, at 2 (2007).
31 *Id.* at 6.
32 U.S. Department of Education, *supra* note 2 at 24.
33 *Id.* at 39.
34 Table adapted from: U.S. Department of Education, *Tool Kit on Teaching and Assessing Students with Disabilities: A Decision Framework for IEP Teams Related to Methods for Individual Student Participation in State Accountability Assessments*, at 15 (2006).
35 *Id.*
36 34 C.F.R. §200.6.
37 34 C.F.R. §200.6(a)(1)(i)(A).
38 34 C.F.R. §200.6(a)(1)(ii).
39 34 C.F.R. § 300.160(b).
40 U.S. Department of Education, *supra* note 34 at 15.
41 National Education Association, *NEA Summary/Analysis: U.S. Department of Education's Final Regulations on Assessing Students with Disabilities under the No Child Left Behind Act and the Individuals with Disabilities Education Act*, at 1 (2007).
42 Testimony of Rachel Quenemoen, Committee on Education and Labor, National Center on Educational Outcomes, *How NCLB Affects Students with Disabilities* (March 29, 2007) *available at* http://cehd.umn.edu/nceo/Presentations/EducationHearing2007/OralTestimony-29March2007html
43 U.S. Department of Education, *supra* note 2 at 12.
44 Testimony of Rachel Quenemoen, *supra* note 41.
45 U.S. Department of Education, *supra* note 34 at 8.

[46] *Id.* at 15.
[47] U.S. Department of Education, *supra* note 2 at 12.
[48] U.S. Department of Education, *supra* note 20 at14 – 15.
[49] *Id.* at 15.
[50] *Id.* at 16.
[51] *Id.* at 17 – 18.
[52] 34 C.F.R. §200.13.
[53] U.S. Department of Education, *supra* note 34 at 8.
[54] U.S. Department of Education, *supra* note 20 at 17.
[55] U.S. Department of Education, *supra* note 34 at15 - 16.
[56] U.S. Department of Education, *supra* note 20 at 17,
[57] *Id.*
[58] Testimony of Rachel Quenemoen, *supra* note 41.
[59] *Id.*
[60] U.S. Department of Education, *supra* note 2 at 25.
[61] *Id.* at 23.
[62] U.S. Department of Education, *supra* note 34 at 14.
[63] 34 C.F.R. § 200.13(c).
[64] U.S. Department of Education, *supra* note 34 at 8.
[65] *Id.* at 15 - 16.
[66] *Id.* at 3.

Section 3:

Teachers and the Law

Chapter 21

Teacher Dismissal

Dennis W. Van Berkum, Michael D. Richardson,
Karen-Ann Broe, & Kenneth E. Lane

Introduction

Because *education* was not mentioned in the United States Constitution, the governmental function was reserved for the states.[1] Consequently, each state has ultimate control over education, which makes education a game in the eyes of some politicians. Centralized control at the state level has appeal for many politicians, demonstrated by the dramatic growth of state control over education during the last two decades.[2] Since the *Nation At Risk* report in 1983, education has become the object of reform, reinvention, renewal, and revival, all without appreciable change.[3]

One of the many contentious issues often exploited by educational reformers is the concept of teacher quality. Teacher quality has been defined in numerous ways by many different associations, groups, researchers, and individuals.[4] However, the most important concept of teacher quality is how to deal with those who are not of sufficient quality to remain in the profession.[5] Although few agree on what constitutes good teaching, most educators and the public can agree on what constitutes poor teaching.[6] Such is the topic of this chapter: how to dismiss teachers.

Teacher dismissal has taken on the mantra of other educational concerns in the new century. Zero-tolerance policies for student behavior have been established. Schools are required to establish assessment plans to measure student progress. As school boards have become more concerned about being politically correct with student behavior, they have passed zero-tolerance policies. In addition, teacher evaluation is tied to student performance.[7] Accountability, as specified by state assessments and federal assessments under the No Child Left Behind Act (NCLB) demand that teachers and administrators alike demonstrate proficiency in the improvement of student learning. Evaluation systems are now being used to assess teacher and principal performance. A principal must address poor teaching and poor leadership, or student learning will suffer.[8] State legislatures have passed statutes that provide penalties and punishments for teachers who fail to meet specified targets of student performance.[9]

Legal Issues

Teacher Contracts and Dismissal

Corbin defines a contract as "a promise enforceable at law directly or indirectly."[10] The enforceable promise is important for local school districts as contracts may arise in two basic settings: employment and general services. Important to this discussion is the setting of employment. Principals are part of this setting and must be familiar with the state laws of certification, contract law, and the local rules for employment.

Employment of a teacher is generally governed in part by state licensure requirements and the local school's collective bargaining contract. The contract describes the duties and responsibilities of a teacher.[11] A lack of knowledge of contract language and expectations cannot be used as a defense in dismissal cases by teachers and principals alike. All are charged with the responsibility of knowing what is in the contract.[12]

Several elements of a contract must ordinarily be present in order to have a legally enforceable contract:

1. The parties must have the legal authority to enter into a contract;
2. There must be an offer and an acceptance of the contract;
3. The contract must contain valid and adequate consideration; and
4. The contract must generally be documented by a signed writing. [Note: In some cases, a verbal agreement may be enforceable as a contract, particularly if the term of performance is less than a year.]

The legal authority to enter contracts is typically found in state statutes that allow local districts to enter into agreements for employment. In most states, local boards of education have the legal authority to enter into contracts with individuals for educational services. Offer and acceptance are made in writing when a person is offered a position and he or she agrees to the terms of the offer and signs the contract.[13] Local schools offer salary, working conditions, and fringe benefits for consideration by the teacher. In return, the teacher promises to perform the requirements of the job for the length of the contract.[14] It is important to note that assignments of job duties made in addition to the regular contract may be governed by amendments or supplements to the regular contract.[15]

The failure of a teacher to fulfill a contractual duty may constitute a breach of contract. More specifically, a teacher has an absolute and immediate duty to perform substantial work obligations under the terms of the contract.[16] Failure of the teacher to meet the agreed obligation may be a breach of contract.[17] However, local school districts must consider the financial ramifications of pursuing an alleged breach of contract case through the court system because in breach of contract cases for wrongful dismissal and wrongful termination of contract, the non-breaching party may be entitled to both reinstatement and/or compensation.[18]

A contract is not valid unless the teacher holds a legal certificate of qualification at the time the contract period begins.[19] A contract must contain clear and definite language. In the case of teacher dismissal, most states' due process laws have been interpreted to include the identification of deficiencies and calls for methods of remediation. These identified deficiencies and remediation methods must be clear and in definitive language to ensure that the teacher understands the level of performance required to remain employed as a teacher in the local school district.

The standard written contract outlines the rights and duties of the teacher.[20] It is important to note, however, that a contract may be more than the expressed contractual writings. First, unwritten clauses or implied contract requirements may be inferred. Second, contracts often incorporate the language of other policies and documents, obligating employees under those contracts to also comply with the provisions of those otherwise external policies and documents. In other words, general rules and regulations adopted by the school board and the relevant state statutes may be included in the contract by implication.[21] In the case of implied requirements, contractual implications can be created "as a matter of reason and justice from the acts or conduct inferred from the intentions of the parties as evidenced by circumstances and ordinary course of dealing and common understanding...."[22] Alternatively, contracts may contain an "integration" clause stating that only the expressed contractual writings are included in the contract, absent a written amendment by the parties named in the contract.

The court case interpretations cited in the preceding paragraph should not be taken to mean that any additional requirements can be proclaimed as inferred contractual agreements. This is particularly true when a new requirement for a teacher's job duties seeks to void written contractual agreements and state requirements. For example, the continuation of work by a nontenured teacher for the remainder of one's contract, when that contract will not be renewed and the teacher has been so notified, does not constitute a change in contract.[23]

Termination

Typically, both the teacher and a school board can mutually terminate an employment contract. However, the termination of a contract is not always mutual and voluntary. For example, a teacher does not perform in accordance with the job duties described in the contract and without good reason. In such cases, the teacher's contract with the school may be terminated, nonrenewed, or suspended. In more serious cases, the teaching certificate or license may be revoked.[24] Three actions of discharge have been identified to address the permanent or temporary severance in employment:

1. Dismissal. This discharge refers to termination for cause of any school professional under contract. This includes both tenured and nontenured teachers.
2. Nonrenewal. This discharge refers to the decision not to renew a nontenured teacher, a tenured teacher who is not under some form of continuing contract law, or a teacher who fails to adequately improve on previously identified need for improvement.
3. Suspension. This discharge refers to the removal of a school professional from his or her duties for a limited period of time. This includes both tenured and nontenured contracts.[25]

Principals need an understanding of the implications of these actions and the appropriateness of these actions as they apply to the immediacy of a disciplinary action. They should not hesitate due to concerns of high legal cost.[26]

Legal Status of Dismissal for Tenured and Nontenured Teachers

The discharge of a teacher varies based upon the status of the teacher in tenure law. Generally, tenure is granted to a teacher, who has successfully completed a probationary period of one to three years in a school.[27] Tenured teachers are viewed as having a greater right to due process than nontenured teachers, thus giving rise to a greater expectation of procedural due process. However, due process has been viewed as a flexible concept, varying by seriousness of infraction and penalty more so than by contract status as tenured or nontenured. For example, both tenured teachers and nontenured teachers must be afforded notice and hearings before termination during the period of a contract. Once a teacher has received tenure, many assume that they cannot be dismissed. This is not true. A teacher, regardless of his or her tenure status, has an absolute and immediate duty to perform under the contract, and if such duty has not been discharged, then the failure of that party to meet the agreed-upon obligation may lead to dismissal.[28] A contract termination implicates both liberty and property rights, as recognized by the Fourteenth Amendment due process clause. Any violation of a teacher's constitutional rights may afford the teacher full due process rights under the law.[29] The amount of due process afforded depends on the level of deprivation of rights. In the case of a termination, liberty rights (in good name, reputation, honor, the right to enter into contract and to pursue professional work) and property rights (in the existing contract and its wages and benefits) are implicated. In the case of a nonrenewal of a nontenured teacher, only liberty interests are implicated, due to the fact that the contract, where a teacher will find his or her property interest, is expiring. It is here where the primary distinction between tenured and nontenured teachers can be made. Tenured teachers cannot have their contracts nonrenewed, while nontenured teachers can. Termination and suspension, however, apply to both tenured and nontenured teachers alike. In all discharge cases, a clear link should be established between the teacher's actions and the impact upon the school setting.

The Tenured Teacher

Tenure is a provision statutorily or contractually created to provide a teacher with certain rights and privileges. The purpose of tenure rights is to protect teachers from abuses or whims of principals and other administrators while protecting the public's interests in academic freedom in schools.[30] A broad purpose of tenure is to provide protection for teachers with a vested right in their employment, thus establishing a property right that ensures due process proceedings when dismissal actions occur. Most states have determined that teachers with tenure (also called continuing contract teachers) are entitled to full due process rights prior to termination.[31] Procedures are usually outlined in state tenure statutes and generally follow the pattern of:

1. Notice of the possible infraction and intention to terminate;
2. A written statement with specifics of the charges prior to dismissal;
3. A hearing on the charges;
4. Assistance of legal counsel;
5. Evidentiary procedures; and
6. The right to judicial review.[32]

Tenure is a status conferred upon a certified or licensed teacher who has served a probationary period, usually two to four years. Tenure is usually not transferable to another state or another school district.[33] Tenure guarantees a teacher a right to continued employment. Usually, the acquired tenure is in the area(s) of certification and the area of probation.[34] Tenure does not guarantee a particular position or indefinite employment. It does offer an expectation to employment if a teacher performs well and the position continues to exist. Many of the specific rights to tenure are found in the teacher's individual contract or local school district's collective bargaining agreement.

Causes for Termination

State statutes describe the causes for termination. Generally causes for termination are incompetency, insubordination, immorality, good cause, and reduction of force.

Incompetency. The courts have given a broad interpretation to incompetency. Because professional training and certification identify competent teachers, there exists a need for the school board to show incompetence of a teacher in the performance of one's duties in regard to parents, students, and supervisors. Incompetency is defined as the "lack of ability, legal qualification, or fitness to discharge the required duty."[35] Some situations where incompetency has been found include off-campus conduct that impacts the capacity of the teacher to conduct an effective classroom;[36] failure of students to make normal progress when compared to another classroom;[37] physical or psychological disabilities that threaten the health, safety, and welfare of students;[38] and the failure to maintain proper classroom discipline.[39] Some states have also used failure to meet continuing education or certification requirements as a component of incompetency.[40] Generally, a warning should precede charges for the dismissal of a teacher for incompetence, and the teacher should be given the opportunity to improve on the reason for the charges. Dismissal proceedings and time frames are identified in each state statute. In addition, it is vital the proper and precise documentation must be maintained to support any charges of incompetence. Incompetency has not been used frequently to dismiss teachers. Studies in Illinois found only two of 95,500 teachers were terminated on grounds of incompetence. Other studies in West Virginia and California produced similar results.[41]

Insubordination. Insubordination is the willful disregard of or refusal to obey reasonable directives.[42] Teachers who refuse to obey reasonable and rational rules, regulations, policies, and contractual provisions may be released from their position. In addition, teachers are expected to maintain a cooperative environment with other teachers, parents, students, and school officials to promote the goals of the school. These provisions may not be trivial and may not infringe on the legal rights of an individual. Cases of insubordination are often found in the form of teacher absenteeism from the classroom. Other forms of insubordination are seen in teacher actions where the teacher is late or absent from school for short periods of time;[43] refuses to supervise halls when ordered to do so;[44] fails to produce lesson plans or teach specific lessons ordered by the school board;[45] is excessively absent with adverse effect on student learning;[46] and strikes a student.[47] In most cases, the dismissal of a teacher for insubordination is the result of teacher actions that have not been corrected over a period of time.[48]

Dismissal for insubordination must be proven through the existence of a school rule or a superior's orders. In such a determination, consideration of several factors is important: the teacher's motive; whether harm occurred as it relates to the violation; whether the rule or order was valid and reasonable from the beginning; and whether the rule or order was enforced based upon bias or discrimination.[49] In most cases, the dismissal is the result of an established pattern of behavior(s) that has occurred over a period of time in one or more setting.[50]

Immorality. Immorality has been interpreted as "a course of conduct that offends the morals of the community and is a bad example to youth whose ideals a teacher is supposed to foster and elevate."[51] Standards for dismissal on the basis of immorality are vague. The courts have generally interpreted the statutes narrowly, indicating that the school board typically requires proof of violation before dismissal proceedings. Dismissal can occur if any teacher fails to meet the high standards of the profession. Sexual involvement with others is the most prevalent charge for immorality. Obviously, a teacher involved with a student is looked upon by the courts with disdain. Sexual activity with other adults may also be suspect when there is a logical nexus to performance of a teacher's duties in school. The courts have sustained other teacher dismissals on the grounds of immorality: the commitment of a felony, smoking marijuana with a student,[52] acquiescing in the growing of and sale of illegal drugs,[53] illegally receiving welfare benefits,[54] soliciting students to vandalize another's property,[55] inappropriate uses of school technology,[56] and theft of school property.[57]

Principals are often placed in a position to determine whether the school's personnel actions are immoral or not. The State of California offers a formula to determine immoral conduct measured by a seven-step criteria:

1. The likelihood that the conduct may have adversely affected students or fellow teachers.
2. The degree of adversity anticipated.
3. The proximity or remoteness in time of the conduct.
4. The type of teaching certificate held by the employee involved.
5. Extenuating or aggravating circumstances, if any.
6. The likelihood of recurrence of the questioned conduct.
7. The extent to which disciplinary action may inflict an adverse impact or chilling effect upon the constitutional rights of the teacher or other school employee.[58]

Good cause. Most state tenure statutes require specific causes for dismissal of a tenured teacher. However, it is obvious that no statute can cover all possible causes for discharge. "Good cause" statutes are used to address this void and cover a myriad of situations. Some of the situations may include and expand upon the identified causes for dismissal in statute. These areas include a decreased need for services, disloyalty, disobedience, financial liability, inefficiency, neglect of duty, conviction of a crime, fraud, and a re-alignment of school districts. These "good cause" provisions should not be construed as a "blank check" for principals to dismiss teachers.

Principals must maintain objective criteria for evaluating all personnel. For example, the values of a community should not be used in a good cause dismissal. Instead, the conduct should be measured against that of other teachers who are performing the same or similar duties.[59] Any dismissal, using the good cause standard, must be within the scope of the school's authority. Decisions must not be arbitrary and capricious, and all aspects of due process must be followed. It should be remembered that many of the examples of dismissal are not for instructional activities, but rather for incidents that occur before school, after school, or during non-instructional time.[60] The principal must be aware of his or her responsibility to all concerned in such situations.[61]

Some states also have nepotism laws that may be interpreted to include termination. These laws typically specify that a spouse or immediate family member cannot be the primary supervisor for another employee.[62]

Reduction-in-force. Reduction-in-force (RIF) is a special category of dismissal within the good clause portion of state teacher dismissal statutes. RIF is an action by a board of education that reduces staff due to financial constraints of the districts. If a school district claims financial hardship, the board is responsible for detailed documentation and reasons for the RIF actions.

Most state statutes do not identify a specific procedure for RIF. Most RIF procedures are written into a school master contract with the collective bargaining unit. Often, a last-on-first-off process is used for reduction. Several mutations of this process occur in contract language and relate to the contract language of tenure at the local level, e.g., tenure at the department level or in an area certified to teach.

Both tenured and nontenured teachers may be subject to an RIF dismissal. Generally, nontenured teachers are not considered to be part of a reduction action[63] because they have no entitlement to a continuing contract. However, several courts have indicated that if the action to dismiss a teacher is due to a reduction-in-force, a nontenured teacher may have rights to a job.[64] Often, principals are involved in the documentation of reasons for reduction-in-force. This places the principal in a difficult position. Many reasons may exist for an RIF. Principals need to know clearly the rationale for the reduction action and ensure that the reduction is based upon financial reasons, not a teacher performance issue.

The Nontenured Teacher

The nontenured teacher is one who has engaged in a contract to teach in a school and may be pursuing a tenure contract through a probationary period. This period typically varies from two to four years depending upon the state. The intent of the probationary period is to determine whether the nontenured teacher has the knowledge and skills a school is seeking for the purpose of continuing employment. In most states, tenure status is not transferable to another school district. Usually, an additional probationary period of one year is required to attain tenure. Nontenured teachers are required to maintain all of the rules and regulations and entitled to privileges of employment enjoyed by tenured teachers except the continuing contract provisions. Schools are not under any obligation to re-employ a nontenured teacher at the end of the contract period.[65]

Most states require schools to follow proper procedures in regard to a notice of intent to not offer an additional contract. The courts established that while nontenured teachers do not have the property right of tenure, they do have the right for employment.[66] Procedures for non-tenured teachers are found in state statutes. The basic element of procedure is a fair hearing.[67]

In some states, boards of education are required to review performance of nontenured teachers to determine developmental needs of the nontenured teacher. A prescribed number of evaluations must occur. If poor performance is identified, the nontenured teacher is to be placed on a developmental plan where reasonable time must be provided for the teacher to improve. Interestingly, the courts have not always held schools accountable for this process. Failure to adhere to the state's procedures may result in automatic tenure for the nontenured teacher. However, in a Massachusetts case, the court determined that the state statute placed greater emphasis on school officials' rights to determine the teacher's performance than on the required number of evaluations.[68]

Many courts have taken the position that a nontenured teacher who is challenging his or her employment contract termination or nonrenewal must demonstrate the denial of a property right. However, some courts have not adopted this position. Refusals by a school district to rehire a nontenured teacher, where the district does not make any charges that seriously damage the teacher's standing in the community or deny any opportunities for future employment, is not a liberty issue.[69]

Accountability in Teacher Dismissal

Recent federal mandates, such as NCLB, have also created possible avenues for teacher termination. The accountability legislation of NCLB specifies that teachers can be removed for non-performance and that even entire schools can be closed or reconstituted. Again, this piece of legislation is one of the first to address teacher quality and teacher accountability in terms of instructional performance and not moral or ethical considerations. Incompetence as a teacher is a difficult concept to prove, but this federal legislation specifies that teachers must be "highly qualified," meaning that they must be certified in the subject they teach.[70] These provisions are the first to hold principals accountable for placement and employment of teachers with appropriate credentials.[71] Whether the outcomes are beneficial or not will be proven over time, but there are new requirements for teacher quality.

Recommendations for Practice

1. Principals must understand that in most cases of teacher dismissal, they are the ones who are providing the evidence for dismissal. Obtaining appropriate documentation and systematically observing teachers is critical.
2. Teacher dismissal can have a negative impact upon a school. Principals, as instructional and school leaders, need to understand and use teacher performance appraisal as a means to improve the quality of education for all students.

3. All federal, state, and school policies should be reviewed in light of new federal requirements found in NCLB.
4. Principals need to stay abreast of case law governing the constitutional rights of teachers. Any acts that affect federal discrimination law may impact the decisions regarding tenure.
5. Principals must know federal, state, and local statutes pertaining to teacher qualifications, teacher dismissal, and their relationship to student and school performance.
6. Principals and teachers need to be cognizant of their contract, written and implied, and its relationship to teacher dismissal. Most formal evaluations are conducted in the classroom to identify the instructional abilities of a teacher. Teacher dismissal occurs more often in the implied duties.
7. Documentation of teacher performance is critical to the evaluation and dismissal of teachers. In all the cases reviewed, it is apparent that the principal must know what is going on in the classroom and have a record of teacher performance.
8. Evaluation, improvement, and teacher development should be systematized to ensure a qualified, effective teaching staff.
9. Current teacher certification and licensure statutes may be in conflict with NCLB requirements. This will require teachers, principals, and the school district to understand the law as they apply federal statutes to state and local requirements. Principals will need to stay fully abreast of the changes that occur at all levels and become involved in the development of new rulings.
10. In all aspects of dismissal, principals must not engage in any unreasonable, arbitrary, or capricious actions.

Endnotes

[1] H. G Good, A History of American Education (1962).

[2] M. Imber, *The Latest Chapter in Reform,* 190(4) Am. Sch. Bd. J. 62–63, 70 (2003).

[3] J. H. VanSciver, *Teacher Dismissals*, 72(4) Phi Delta Kappan 318–19 (1990).

[4] S.R. Painter, *Principals' Perceptions of Barriers to Teacher Dismissal,* 14(3) J. Personnel Evaluation Educ. 253–64 (2000).

[5] Painter, S.R. *Easing Dismissals and Non-renewals,* 57(9) Sch. Administrator 40–43 (2000).

[6] T. A. DeMitchell, *Competence, Documentation and Dismissal: A Legal Template,* 41 Int'l J. Educ. Reform 88–95 (1995).

[7] M.E. Ward, *Teacher Dismissal: The Impact of Tenure, Administrator Competence, and Other Factors,* 52 Sch. Administrator 16–19 (1995).

[8] Painter S. R., *supra* note 4.

[9] P. T. K. Daniel, *Personnel Evaluations in Education and the Law,* 69(7) Sch. Bus. Aff. 29–33(2003).

10 A. L. CORBIN, CORBIN ON CONTRACTS (1952). (Out-of-print; available from LexisNexis Revised edition, July 1993.)

11 Community Project for Students, Inc. v. Wilder, 298 S.E.2d 434 (N.C. Ct. App. 1982).

12 El Camino Cmty. Coll. Dist. v. Superior Court, 219 Cal. Rptr. 236 (Cal. Ct. App. 1985); Wolf v. Cuyahoga Falls City Sch. Dist. Bd. of Educ., 556 N.E.2d 511 (Ohio, 1990).

13 Reichert v. Draud, 701 F.2d 1168 (6th Cir. 1983).

14 California Teachers Ass'n v. Cory, 202 Cal. Rptr. 611 (Cal. Ct. App. 1984).

15 Cruciotti v. McNeel, 396 S.E. 2d 191 (W. Va 1990).

16 Franklin v. Ala. State Tenure Comm'n, 482 So. 2d 1214 (Ala. Civ. App. 1985).

17 N.D. CENT. CODE § 15–47–28 (1993 & Supp. 1995), TENN. CODE ANN § 49–5–508(b) (1996).

18 Lawson v. Wayne Cmty. Sch. Dist., 233 N.W.2d 713 (Mich. Ct. App. 1975).

19 MICH. COMP. LAWS ANN. § 380.1232 (West 1988).

20 MO. ANN. STAT. § 168.108 (West, 1991), *supra* note 29 and accompanying text.

21 Board of Educ. v. Jones, 823 S.W.2d 457 (Ky. 1992).

22 BLACK'S LAW DICTIONARY 323 (6th ed. 1990).

23 Kuta v. Joint Dist. No. 50(J), 799 P.2d 379 (Colo. 1990).

24 IND. CODE ANN. § 20–6, 1–4–10(a)(3) (Mich. 1996).

25 N.D. CENT. CODE § 15–47–28 (1993 & Supp. 1995); TENN. CODE ANN. § 49–5–508(b) (1996).

26 Reeder, S. *The hidden cost of tenure.* Small Newspaper Group. Retrieved from: http://thehiddencostsoftenure.com/stor.etc/press=displaytid=295712

27 Donvito v. Bd. of Educ. N. Valley Reg'l High Sch., 5877 C 646 03 SB 1 04 (ST Bd. of Educ. 2005)

28 N.D. CENT. CODE § 15–47–28 (1993 & Supp. 1995). TENN. CODE ANN. § 49–5–508(b) (1996).

29 Evans-Marshall v. Bd. of Educ. of the Tipp City Exempted Vill. Sch. Dist., 428 F.3d 223 (6th Cir. (2005).

30 Abrantes v. Bd. of Educ. of Norwood-Norfolk Cent. Sch. Dist., 630 N.Y.S.2d 220, 222 (N.Y. App. Div. 1995).

31 Kransdorf v. Bd. of Educ. of Northport-E. Northport Union Free Sch. Dist., 613 N.E.2d 537 (N.Y. 1993).

32 D. P. Witteman, *Procedural Due Process Under the Kansas Teacher Due Process Act: Going Through the Motions is Not Enough*, 29 WASHBURN L.J. 668 (1990).

33 IOWA CODE ANN. § 279.19 (West 1996) [two years]; COLO. REV. STAT. ANN. § 22–63–203.104 (West 1996) [three years]; MO. ANN. STAT. § 168 (West 1995).

34 Loftus v. Bd. of Educ. of Fairfield, 509 A.2d 500 (Conn. 1986); Dennery v. Bd. of Educ. of Passaic County Reg'l High Sch. Dist. No. 1, 622 A.2d 858 (N.J. 1993).

35 BLACK'S LAW DICTIONARY 688 (5th Ed. 1985).

36 Alabama State Tenure Comm'n v. Lee County Bd. of Educ., 595 So. 2d 479.

37 Belcourt v. Fort Totten Pub. Sch. Dist., 454 N.W.2d 703.

38 Clarke v. Shoreline Sch. Dist., 720 P.2d. 793 (Wash. 1986).

39 McKenqie v. Webster Parish Sch. Bd., 609 So. 2d 1028 (La. Ct. App. 1992).

40 Swanson v. Houston Indep. Sch. Dist., 800 S.W. 2d 630 (Tex. App. Houston 1990).

41 Reeder, S., *supra* note 26.

42 School Dist. No. 8, Pinal County v. Superior Court, 433 So.2d 28 (1967)

43 Hargis v. LaFourche Parish Sch. Bd., 593 So. 2d 400 (La. Ct. App. 1991).

44 Lockhart v. Bd. of Educ. Arapahoe County Sch. Dist., 735 P.2d 913 (Colo. Ct. App. 1986).

45 *In re* propose Termination of James E. Johnson's Teaching Contract, 451 N.W.2d 343 (Minn. Ct. App. 1990).

46 MacPherson v. Sch. Bd. of Monroe County, 505 So. 2d 682 (Fla. Dist. Ct. App. 1987).

47 Ketchersid v Rhea County Bd. of Ed., E2004 01153 COA R3 CV (Tenn. Ct. App. 2005).

48 Bellairs v. Beaverton Sch. Dist. FDA 04 01: A125893 (Or. Dist. Ct. App. 2006).

49 78 A.L.R. 3d 83–87.

[50] Horton v. Jefferson County - DuBois Area Voc'l Tech. Sch., 157 Pa. Commw. 424, 630 A.2d 481 (1993).

[51] Board of Educ. of Hopkins County v. Wood, 717 S.W.2d 837 (Ky. 1986).

[52] Jefferson County Sch. Dist. No. 509-J v. Fair Dismissal Appeals Bd., 812 P.2d 1284 (Or. 1991).

[53] Stelzer v. State Bd. of Educ., 595 N.E.2d 489 (Ohio Ct. App. 1991).

[54] Scheiber v. New York City Bd. of Educ., 593 N.Y.S.2d 653 (App. Div. 1993).

[55] E School News. *Teacher's Web: Site is grounds for dismissal.* Retrieved from www.eschoolnews.com/news/showstory.cfm?articleID=4430.

[56] Cochran v. Bd. of Educ. of Mex. Sch. Dist., 815 S.W.2d 55 (Mo. Ct. App. 1991).

[57] Governing Bd. of ABC Unified Sch. Dist. v. Haar, 33 Cal. Rptr. 2d 744, 751 (Cal. Ct. App. 1994).

[58] Ahmad v. The Bd. of Ed. of City of Chi., 03 CH 21482 (Ill. Ct. App. 2006)

[59] Schulz v. Bd. of Educ. of Sch. Dist. of Freemont, 315 N.W.2d 633 (Neb. 1982).

[60] C. P. Hooker, *Terminating Teachers and Revoking Their Licensure for Conduct Beyond the Schoolhouse Gate*, 4(2) Educ. L. Rep. 285–99 (1994).

[61] J. Matlock, *Solving the Problem of Problem Employees*, 14(10) Executive Educator 39–40 (1992).

[62] Cybyske v. Indep. Sch. Dist. No. 196, 347 N.W.2d 356 (Minn. 1984); Degnan v. Bering Strait Sch. Dist. 753 P.2d 146 (Alaska 1988).

[63] *See, e.g.*, Lezette v. Bd. of Educ., 319 N.E.2d 189 (N.Y. 1974); Hill v. Dayton Sch. Dist., 52 P.2d 1154 (Wash. 1975).

[64] Alexander v. Delano, 188 Cal. Rptr. 7095 (Ct. App 1983); Bonman v. Bd. of Educ. W. Clermont, 443 N.E.2d 176 (Ohio 1983); Carmody v. Bd. of Dirs., 453 A.2d 965 (Pa. 1982).

[65] Childer v. Indep. Sch. Dist. No. 1, 842 P.2d 355 (Okla. Ct. App. 1992).

[66] Board of Regents v. Roth, 408 U.S. 564 (1972).

[67] Stovall v. Huntsville City Bd. of Educ., 602 So. 2d 407 (Ala. Civ. App. 1992).

[68] Marotta v. Greater New Bedford Reg'l Vocational High Sch. Dist. Comm., 589 N.E.2d 334 (Mass. App. Ct. 1992).

[69] *Roth,* 408 U.S. at 573.

[70] L. E. Beyer, *The Politics of Standardization: Teacher Education in the U.S.A.*, 28(3) J. Educ. for Teaching 239–45 (2002).

[71] T. C. Dawson & K. L. Billingsley, Unsatisfactory Performance: How California's K-12 Education System Protects Mediocrity and How Teacher Quality can be Improved (2000).

Chapter 22

Teacher Certification

Tina Chang & William E. Sparkman

Introduction

Justice Louis Brandeis famously proffered, "To stay experimentation in things social and economic is a grave responsibility. Denial of the right to experiment may be fraught with serious consequences to the nation. It is one of the happy incidents of the federal system that a single courageous state may, if its citizens choose, serve as a laboratory; and try novel social and economic experiments without risk to the rest of the country."[1] The idea that states should serve as "laboratories of democracy" has historically resonated in the American public school system as well. Even today, teacher certification continues to be governed by state statutory dictates and administrative regulations. However, the passage of the No Child Left Behind Act of 2001 (NCLB)[2] and impending reauthorization in 2007 and 2008 plainly demonstrate the federal government's expanding role in teacher certification. At the same time that politicians and policy makers emphasize teacher quality and standards-based educational reform, there is a corresponding push in many regions for easing limitations on who may become a teacher. Expanded access to educator preparation, including alternative and emergency certification programs, has emerged in response to teacher shortages and other employment-related circumstances. Although it is premature to predict how this federal incursion into what has long been state enterprise will unfold, it can be said that the nation's educator certification landscape will not likely return to its more traditional roots.

As a result of the manifold demands arising from federal and state governments, principals have been entrusted with formidable responsibility in the area of teacher certification standards. In particular, principals should be very familiar with their respective state laws and regulations related to educator certification. In practice, many principals now review the status of teacher certification in their buildings on a yearly basis even though school district central offices generally monitor licensure and certification. This step is particularly apropos when a teacher on the staff is employed under a provisional endorsement or temporary certificate valid for only a year or two. A brief discussion of a few cases demonstrates the importance of monitoring the licensure of certified staff, including the principal. The cases illustrate how different state laws can lead to contradictory conclusions.

Although the statutes and regulations that govern teacher certification are state specific, there are some general principles that emerge from case law. Currently, there are three primary areas of concern in teacher certification: the basis of the state's authority and interest in teacher certification, the relation of certification to employment, and the reasons and processes necessary for the revocation of a certificate. Even though NCLB federal mandates are plenary, teacher certification is still primarily a state-specific concern. Therefore, principals should recognize statutory, regulatory, and case law specific to their individual state.

Legal Issues

State Authority and Interest in Certification

Teacher competency certification has been delegated to state regulatory agencies in all fifty states. The authority to regulate is described by a state court in Kansas as follows: "The State Board of Education is statutorily the only agency authorized to set standards for teacher certification. Certification by the State Board of Education, rather than subjective qualifications set up by each local school board, determines that a teacher is qualified to teach subjects endorsed on the teaching certificate."[3] Teaching certification is an acceptable method of satisfying a state constitutional mandate for the legislature to supply an education for youth.[4] According to an Illinois judge, "the predominate purpose in licensing a trade or profession is to prevent injury to the public by assuring that the occupation will be practiced with honesty and integrity and by excluding those who are incompetent or unworthy."[5] A Nevada court has held that the legislative intent behind the statutory procedures related to teacher certification was twofold: "First, the provisions were intended to provide an efficient procedure for finding and employing qualified teachers.... Second, the legislature wanted to protect qualified teachers from arbitrary decisions regarding their employment."[6]

State teacher performance requirements and related assessment instruments have generally been approved by various courts. A state appeals court upheld a requirement that individuals achieve passing scores on the National Teacher's Examination.[7] In an important en banc decision by a federal appeals court, a basic skills examination required for entry into the teaching profession was upheld. The court determined that, although the California Basic Education Skills Test (CBEST) is a basic skills test in reading, writing, and mathematics, it satisfied a three-step test for job-relatedness. The majority relied heavily on the fact that the CBEST had been validated on three separate occasions and had been partially written and developed by the Educational Testing Service (ETS).[8] A Massachusetts state board of education regulation requiring mathematics teachers in low-performing schools to take an assessment test prior to license renewal was upheld by the state supreme court as consistent with state school accountability measures.[9]

Legal challenges have been mounted in several states by churches operating private, sectarian schools. State authority over church schools and state interest over teacher certification are the major issues. These cases question whether such authority and interest are sufficient to allow the state to limit individual rights regarding the free exercise of religion. In Iowa, individuals involved in church-sponsored schools argued unsuccessfully in court that the state certification requirements burdened their First Amendment free exercise rights. In speaking about the relationship between the state's interest in education and teacher certification requirements, a federal judge wrote: "The importance lies, not in the piece of paper itself, but in the education a person must receive to become eligible for the certificate.… [T]his kind of knowledge is essential if one is to become a good teacher."[10] The court's conclusion was that Iowa's interest in requiring all teachers to be certified was sufficiently compelling to override the plaintiff's First Amendment claim that teachers in sectarian schools should not be subjected to such regulation.[11]

Actions related to certification must be neutral with respect to race, color, sex, religion, and national origin. Consequently, certification requirements must be applied in a nondiscriminatory manner.[12] The United States Supreme Court has sustained the authority of the states to enact laws requiring resident aliens to produce evidence of their intention to become naturalized citizens of the United States before they are issued a teaching certificate.[13] Certain types of loyalty oaths, such as "I solemnly swear or affirm that I will support the Constitution of the State of Colorado and of the United States of America and the laws of Colorado and the United States," have been upheld by the courts.[14]

Teacher Certification and Employment

A teaching certificate is a license and not a contract. A teaching license does not guarantee employment in a school district. It was established in the Seventh Circuit that teacher certification was merely a minimal threshold, and the school board had the salient authority to determine qualifications of employment.[15] Although the possession of a teaching certificate does not guarantee employment in a school district, it is required in order for the teacher to be a competent party to an employment contract and to be paid by the school board.[16] The certificate is an essential condition of an employment contract. For example, an Illinois court found that a school board was no longer bound by an employment contract where the teaching certificate of a substitute teacher had expired.[17] When California allowed waivers for credentials, a probationary employee had no statutory right to re-employment if the employee failed to make progress toward obtaining the required credential.[18] An Illinois court held that salary benefits under an employment contract may be calculated on the basis of the type of certification held rather than the actual position of employment.[19] Finally, the issue of timing in seeking an alternate certificate has arisen where teachers are required to obtain permanent certification to retain a position. At least one court has held that time requirements must be met and backdating after the expiration of a provisional certificate is not satisfactory.[20]

A question that is often troubling to educators is whether or not the state can change certification requirements. This point was highlighted in an Indiana case involving the revocation of a teacher's certificate. In upholding the revocation, the judge wrote that, "[a] license has none of the elements of a contract, and does not confer an absolute right, but only a personal privilege to be exercised under existing restrictions, and such as may thereafter be reasonably imposed."[21] Connecticut's Supreme Court also noted that a statute providing for exchange of permanent teaching certificates for five-year certificates renewable upon completion of continuing education courses did not violate teachers' procedural or substantive due process rights. The constitutional protection of the right to contract was not impaired.[22]

A related issue is whether the state can require all currently certified teachers and administrators to take and pass a competency examination in order to retain their teaching credentials. As part of the Texas school reform package enacted in 1984, the legislature required the examination of reading and writing skills of all persons certified prior to 1986.[23] This law caused a great deal of consternation among the state's educators and resulted in several lawsuits against the state. The Texas Supreme Court pronounced that the testing requirement was constitutional.[24] The court held that because a teaching certificate is not a contract, "the constitutional prohibition against impairment of contracts is not violated when the legislature imposes new conditions for the retention of the certificate."[25] The court also found that state law provided adequate due process protection for teachers who failed to pass the competency test. The court rejected the contention that the law was fundamentally unfair by holding that the test had "a rational relationship to the legitimate state objective of maintaining competent teachers in the public schools."[26]

A teacher in Oregon was dismissed by the local school board when it was reported that her certificate was no longer valid. The teacher received a renewal certificate from the state after her initial license had expired. She returned the renewal fee in the form of a personal check that was not honored by her bank. A letter was sent to her advising her of the problem with her check, but she did not pick up this letter. A subsequent letter was sent to her stating that the certificate was invalid because her check did not process. Ultimately, the teacher contested her dismissal in court, claiming that the board had not followed the procedures necessary to terminate her employment. Because she lacked a valid teacher's certificate, the court found that she was not "a teacher" within the meaning of the law.[27] This occurred even though her certificate had not been revoked, but merely nonrenewed.

A teacher in Alaska was required by state law to maintain current teacher certification. Her certificate expired during the school year and was not renewed until two months later. Neither she nor the school district was aware it had expired. A hearing board determined that she had lost her tenure status. On appeal, the court applied a statutory "substantial noncompliance standard." It found that the teacher had substantially complied with the Alaska statutory requirement. Applying the standard, it found that the certification lapse was of short duration. "She easily and promptly obtained renewal. Those requirements which would provide apparent protection of the public, i.e., continuing education, background check, and notification of arrest were not in issue."[28]

A teacher in New Mexico was terminated, and her contract was not renewed in spite of her tenure status after the school district superintendent informed the board that she lacked certification. The proceedings were complicated. It took two years before the court reversed the adverse employment action and ordered compensation. Problems were exposed about the state department of education concerning irregularities and delay. Among other things, the court found that the lack of certification was related to these difficulties.[29] A teacher in Maine had his application for recertification denied. The commissioner of education held that undue hardship related to personal problems including divorce and bankruptcy would excuse the untimely application. The school district appealed the commissioner's ruling, and the court upheld the decision stating the certification remained in effect until the application for recertification had been determined.[30]

A principal in Minnesota allowed his license to expire, and the school district entered into a new contract with him. The following year the school board, without citing cause and without a hearing, voted to not renew his contract for the next school year. The principal filed suit against the district. The major concern of the school district officials was that the principal had not supplied them with proof of a valid license. The court analyzed what should be a common sense duty that in Minnesota is a legal obligation:

> A school district has a duty to ascertain the licensure status of its teachers.... While a lapsed license would not be grounds for immediate discharge of a ... teacher, [a] two-year unlicensed status [is] a gross violation of a school district's obligation to ensure its teachers are qualified. The evident purpose of the filing requirement ... is to provide the school district with the information necessary to meet the obligation.... We conclude that under these circumstances the school district ... bore the burden of ensuring that the district's files were up to date.[31]

The court held that the district was precluded or estopped from asserting the licensure defect.[32]

The Revocation of a Teaching Certificate

With the right to certify teachers, a state has a collateral right to revoke certificates for just cause.[33] The suspension or revocation of a teaching certificate requires appropriate standards of due process as provided by law.[34] State statutes generally specify reasons for revocation of a certificate and provide the requisite due process procedures. A common reason in state statutes is the broad category of immorality. Several reasons that have been accepted by the courts as valid in revocation cases include wearing religious dress while performing teaching duties in contravention of state law,[35] possession of fifty-two marijuana plants,[36] conviction of perjury and extortion,[37] falsifying attendance records,[38] conviction of eight counts of indecent assault upon several male children,[39] mail fraud,[40] and failure to obtain satisfactory evaluations.[41] Many states provide that a teacher's certificate may be suspended or canceled for abandoning an existing contract without good cause and without consent of the board of education.[42] Unprofessional conduct permitting termination must relate to the fitness to act in his or her professional capacity.[43]

All applicable standards of due process must be observed.[44] This step would include offering proper notice and a hearing. A Florida court held that the failure by the state's education practices commission to give notice that a teacher was at risk of having his license permanently revoked was an error, even if the revocation action was otherwise justified and supported by the evidence.[45] Two terminated New York City teachers filed suit against the board of education arguing that an absence of pre-revocation license hearings violated their due process rights. The New York Court denied the board of education's motion to dismiss the plaintiffs' due process claims on the grounds that the plaintiffs had a right to offer evidence to support their claims regardless of whether or not they would ultimately prevail.[46]

A teaching certificate in South Carolina was canceled by the state board on the basis of a testing company invalidating a test score. Since the board did not disclose any evidence substantiating cancellation of the test scores, the court noted that a hearing granted to the teacher did not comport with procedural due process.[47] However, a New Jersey court ruled that due process did not require the testing service to prove actual wrongdoing by a teacher suspected of cheating on a licensure examination. The court concluded that the test scores could be cancelled upon an adequate showing of a substantial question as to their validity.[48]

An important point is once a teacher is certified by the state, that teacher is considered to be competent. The state bears the burden of proof in all revocation cases. A Florida court has made it clear that all forms and procedures must substantially comply with state law. The court noted that the prosecutor in revocation cases must prove a strong case, the record must substantiate the findings, and the hearing board must review contents of investigative files and actually accept such files into evidence.[49]

A California appeals court discussed hearsay evidence, stating, "[I]t is well settled that a board commits an abuse of discretion when it revokes a license to conduct a legitimate business without competent evidence establishing just cause of revocation, and that hearsay evidence alone is insufficient to support the revocation of such a license."[50] In contrast, an Oregon court rejected the position that hearsay evidence alone, even if inadmissible in a civil or criminal trial, is not capable of being "substantial evidence."[51] A Montana court emphasized that, although the rules of evidence in an administrative proceeding are generally relaxed, they are not so relaxed that they disregard due process and fundamental rights.[52]

Because of the increased importance of student academic assessments, many states have passed statutes and regulations to ensure integrity of the testing process, and teachers who violate examination procedures may be subject to termination or suspension.[53] A teacher in Georgia had his license revoked for improperly coaching his students on standardized tests.[54] Another teacher's certificate was suspended for six months for altering student responses on standardized examinations.[55]

The effect of criminal prosecution is another matter. In Indiana, trial testimony describing rape provided sufficient evidence of immorality and misconduct for revocation, even though the conviction for rape was reversed.[56] An admission from a New York teacher of inappropriate sexual conduct was admissible in an administrative proceeding, although the admission had been obtained following a false representation by a private investigator hired by the school.[57] Evidence of substantive charges for the distribution of drugs that were contained in an erased or expunged criminal record was held to be admissible in Utah.[58]

Finally, a number of cases have involved the issue of authority to revoke licenses. In Rhode Island, the court ruled that the board of regents exceeded its authority when it canceled certificates prior to the stated expiration dates.[59] While in Illinois, the appellate court held that the state superintendent lacked authority to revoke a license after the teacher certification board had voted not to revoke such license.[60] In Florida, the court stated that the education practices commission was not authorized to permanently revoke a teaching certificate when the administrative complaint sought only revocation with a possibility of reinstatement.[61]

Recommendations for Practice

It is clear that any person seeking state teacher certification has the responsibility to see that all requirements are met and that the appropriate paperwork is completed. It is also that person's responsibility to ensure that the certificate is current and that appropriate action is taken to renew the certificate upon its expiration.

1. School principals should carefully monitor the certification status of the staff to ensure that the certificates are current and in order.
2. Principals may find that they are more involved in the initial assignment of teachers or in their re-assignment because of fiscal problems or changing state curriculum regulations. Whether teachers may be assigned to teach outside of their area of certification is a question

to be determined by the individual state. Principals should be aware that states differ in their interpretation of this issue.

3. School principals may be called upon to provide documentation in a certificate revocation case. Such documentation must provide substantial evidence of the alleged wrongdoing.

Endnotes

[1] New State Ice Co. v. Liebmann, 285 U.S. 262, at 311 (1932).

[2] No Child Left Behind (NCLB). Conference report to accompany H.R. Rep. No., 107-334, 107th Cong., 1st Sess. (2001).

[3] Bauer v. Bd. of Educ., 765 P.2d 1129 at 1135 (Kan. 1988).

[4] Sheridan Road Baptist Church v. Dep't of Educ., 348 N.W.2d 263 (Mich. Ct. App. 1984).

[5] Trigg v. Sanders, 515 N.E.2d 1367 (Ill. App. Ct. 1987); *See also*, Howard v. Mo. State Bd. of Educ., 913 S.W.2d 887 (Mo. Ct. App. 1995).

[6] Clark Co. Sch. Dist. v. Harris, 913 P.2d 1268 (Nev. 1996); *See also*, State v. Rivinus, 328 N.W.2d 220 (N.D. 1982) and Picona v. Bd. of Educ., 671 A.2d 1035 (N.J. 1996).

[7] Feldman v. Bd. of Educ. of City Sch. Dist. of N.Y., 686 N.Y.S.2d 842 (N.Y. App. Div. 1999).

[8] Association of Mexican-Am. Educators v. California, 231 F.3d 572 (9th Cir. 2000), en banc. Note: The website for the Ninth Circuit Court of Appeals cites this decision as AMAE v. California.

[9] Massachusetts Fed'n of Teachers v. Bd. of Educ., 767 N.E.2d 549 (Mass. 2002).

[10] Fellow Baptist Church v. Benton, 620 F. Supp. 308 at 316 (S.D. Iowa 1985).

[11] *Id.*

[12] Hosford v. Sch. Comm. of Sandwich, 659 N.E.2d 1178 (Mass. 1996).

[13] Ambach v. Norwick, 441 U.S. 68 (1979).

[14] Hosack v. Smiley, 276 F. Supp. 876 (D. Colo. 1967), *aff'd,* 390 U.S. 744 (1968); *See also* Gough v. State, 667 A.2d 1057 (N.J. Super. Ct. App. Div. 1995).

[15] Epelbaum v. Chicago Bd. of Educ., 2001 U.S. App. LEXIS 20441 (2001).

[16] Bradford Cent. Sch. Dist. v. Ambach, 451 N.Y.S.2d 654, 656 (N.Y. 1982).

[17] Lewis-Connelly v. Bd. of Educ. of Deerfield Pub. Schs., Dist. 109, 660 N.E.2d 283 (Ill. App. Ct. 1996).

[18] Royster v. Cushman, 261 Cal. Rptr. 458 (Cal. Ct. App. 1989).

[19] Woods v. E. St. Louis Sch. Dist., 498 N.E.2d 801 (Ill. App. Ct. 1986).

[20] Smith v. Andrews, 504 N.Y.S.2d 286 (N.Y. App. Div. 1986).

[21] Stone v. Fritts, 82 N.E. 792, 794 (Ind. 1987).

[22] Conn. Educ. Ass'n v. Tirozzi, 554 A.2d 1065 (Conn. 1989).

[23] Tex. Educ. Code Ann. § 13.047 (West 1986).

[24] State v. Project-Principle, Inc., 724 S.W.2d 387 (Tex. 1987).

[25] *Id.* at 390.

[26] *Id.* at 391.

[27] Wagonblast v. Cook County Sch. Dist., 707 P.2d 69 (Or. Ct. App. 1985).

[28] Nenana City Sch. Dist. v. Coghill, 898 P.2d 929 at 934 (Alaska 1995).

[29] Board of Educ. of Taos v. Mun. Sch., 712 P.2d 1384 (N.M. Ct. App. 1985).

[30] Sabattus Sch. Comm. v. Dep't of Educ., 644 A.2d 1380 (Me. 1994).

[31] Lucio v. Sch. Bd. of Indep. Sch. Dist., 574 N.W. 2d 737 at 740 (Minn. Ct. App. 1998).

[32] *Id.*

[33] *See* Nev. Rev. Stat, § 391.330, which states:

The state board may suspend or revoke [a teacher's certification] for: 1) Immoral or unprofessional conduct. 2) Evident unfitness for service. 3) Physical or mental incapacity which renders the teacher, administrator or other licensed employee unfit for service. 4) Conviction for a felony or crime involving moral turpitude. 5) Conviction of a sex offense … in which a pupil enrolled in a school of a county school district was the victim. 6) Knowingly advocating the overthrow of the Federal Government or of the State of Nevada by force, violence or unlawful means. 7) Persistent defiance of or refusal to obey the regulations of the state board, the commission or the superintendent of public instruction, defining and governing the duties of teachers, administrators and other licensed employees.

[34] Greenwald v. Cmty. Sch. Bd. No. 27, 329 N.Y.S.2d 203 (N.Y. App. Div. 1972).

[35] Cooper v. Eugene Sch. Dist. No. 4J, 723 P.2d 298 (Or. 1986).

[36] Adams v. State Prof'l Practices Council, 406 So. 2d 1170 (Fla. Dist. Ct. App. 1981).

[37] Homer v. Commw. Dep't of Educ., 458 A.2d 1059 (Pa. Commw. Ct. 1983).

[38] Balentine v. Ark. State Bd. of Educ., 684 S.W.2d 246 (Ark. 1985).

[39] Couch v. Turlington, 465 So. 2d 557 (Fla. Dist. Ct. App. 1985).

[40] Startzel v. Cmmw. Dep't of Educ., 562 A.2d 1005 (Pa. Commw. Ct. 1989).

[41] Eiche v. La. Bd. of Elementary and Secondary Educ., 582 So. 2d 186 (La. 1991).

[42] *See, e.g.,* Nev. Rev. Stat. § 391.350 ("Any teacher or other licensed employee employed by any board for a specified time who willfully refuses or fails to fulfill his employment … or to comply with the provisions of his contract may be found guilty of unprofessional conduct. The board shall not unreasonably withhold its consent.") *See also* Nev. Rev. Stat. § 391.330 (which lists "unprofessional" conduct as a ground for suspension or revocation of a license to teach).

[43] Boss v. Fillmore County Sch. Dist. No. 441, 559 N.W.2d 448 (Neb. 1997). *See* Hoffman v. State Bd. of Educ., 763 N.E.2d 210 (Ohio App. 8 Dist. Cuyahoga 2001).

[44] Brayton v. Monson Pub. Sch., 950 F. Supp. 33 (D. Mass. 1997).

[45] Longenecker v. Turlington, 464 So. 2d 557 (Fla. Dist. Ct. App. 1985).

[46] Behrend v. Klein, 2006 U.S. Dist. LEXIS 68652 (E.D.N.Y. 2006).

[47] Brown v. State Bd. of Educ., 391 S.E.2d 866 (S.C. 1990).

[48] Scott v. Educ. Testing Serv., 600 A.2d 500 at 504 (N.J. Sup. App. Ct. 1991).

[49] Fields v. Turlington, 481 So. 2d 960 (Fla. Dist. Ct. App. 1986).

[50] Carl S. v. Comm. for Teacher Preparation and Licensing, 126 Cal. App. 3d 365 (Cal. Ct. App. 1991).

[51] *Supra* note 35.

[52] *In re* Thompson, 893 P.2d 301 (Mont. 1995).

[53] For example, Nev. Rev. Stats. § 391.312 (q), (r).

[54] Professional Standards Comm'n v. Smith, 571 S.E.2d 443 (Ga. App. 2002).

[55] Professional Standards Comm'n v. Denham, 556 S.E.2d 920 (Ga. Ct. App. 2001).

[56] Ulrich v. State, 555 N.E.2d 172 (Ind. Ct. App. 1990).

[57] Stedronsky v. Sobol, 572 N.Y.S.2d 445 (N.Y. App. Div. 1991).

[58] Ambus v. State Bd. of Educ., 800 P.2d 811 (Utah 1990).

[59] Reback v. R.I. Bd. of Regents for Elementary and Secondary Educ., 560 A.2d 357 (R.I. 1989).

[60] Hunt v. Sanders, 554 N.E.2d.285 (Ill. App. Ct. 1990).

[61] Williams v. Turlington, 498 So. 2d 468 (Fla. Dist. Ct. App. 1986).

Chapter 23

Academic Freedom and Censorship

Ralph Sharp

Introduction

The concept of academic freedom originated at the university level and is more often associated with the university professor's role than with that of the public school teacher. While initially the term was used to describe the professor's right to decide what should be taught, through the years, the term has taken on broader meanings. Today, even at the university level, different views exist as to its nature and its legal status.[1] Although some legal scholars and many academicians adhere to the position that academic freedom is an "inalienable" right of the professor or teacher to select both content and method of instruction, others deny that academic freedom has any sort of independent existence beyond the First Amendment rights possessed by all citizens.

Censorship refers to the suppression of speech or other forms of expression and to any disciplinary action taken by government or governmental agencies such as public schools. The extensive case law on censorship is applicable to all public employees, including teachers. Although the Supreme Court has rendered a series of landmark decisions on this issue involving both students and teachers over the past four decades, disputes continue. When the terms *censorship* and *academic freedom* are linked, the primary focus is teachers' speech related to the curriculum.

Legal Issues

The United States Supreme Court first recognized academic freedom in the 1950s and 1960s in cases resulting from attempts to rid schools of Communist influences.[2] It was not until 1968, in *Pickering v. Board of Education of Township High School District 205*,[3] that the Court ruled that teachers' speech in the form of a letter to a newspaper was entitled to First Amendment protection. The Court held that a teacher cannot be discharged or otherwise punished for speaking out on issues of "public" concern. The following year, in *Tinker v. Des Moines Independent Community School District*,[4] the Court proclaimed that neither students nor teachers "shed their constitutional rights to freedom of speech or expression at the schoolhouse gate" and declared that interference with those rights could be justified only on the basis of "material and substantial disruption."

In *Mt. Healthy City School District Board of Education v. Doyle*,[5] the Supreme Court expressly recognized that other legitimate reasons can exist for disciplining teachers who at the same time are exercising their constitutional rights. This 1977 decision established the required approach for deciding such cases. First, the teacher has the burden of showing that constitutionally protected conduct was a motivating factor in the teacher's discharge or other school disciplinary action. Assuming that the teacher successfully makes that showing, the burden shifts to the school officials to prove that they would have followed the same course of action in the absence of the protected conduct. On the heels of that decision, the Court made it clear that speech of public concern is protected speech even though it may be expressed privately by an employee to a supervisor.[6] In 1983, the Court reinforced its *Pickering* standard by upholding the employer's right to dismiss an employee whose speech was of a private rather than a public concern.[7] And in 2006, the Court ruled that the First Amendment does not protect a public employee whose statements are made pursuant to official duties rather than as a private citizen.[8]

Until the 2007 opinion in *Morse v. Frederick*,[9] the Supreme Court had rendered its most recent decisions on free speech in schools in the second half of the 1980s. In its 1986 decision, *Bethel School District No. 403 v. Fraser*,[10] the Court found no First Amendment protection for obscene or vulgar speech. Two years later, the Court upheld the authority of school officials to control the curriculum in *Hazelwood School District v. Kuhlmeier*[11] when it permitted administrators to delete objectionable articles from the school newspaper. Even though these cases pertained to students' speech, they have profoundly affected the subsequent rulings of the lower courts in their rulings on teachers' speech, especially those cases in which the teacher claimed to be protected by academic freedom.

Following the precedents represented by the Supreme Court decisions, the lower courts in subsequent cases became more supportive of school officials in disputes with teachers stemming from the choice of instructional materials and methods. In fact, two state supreme courts had adopted the rationale established in *Hazelwood* three years before the high court ruled. In 1985, the Alaska Supreme Court upheld the dismissal of a teacher who violated a school policy requiring administrative approval of supplementary materials used in classes.[12] The materials in question included a book on gay rights. The court stated that the First Amendment does not "eliminate the school board's right to control the curriculum."[13] Similarly, the Maine Supreme Court rejected the claims of a teacher who charged that the school board had violated his right to academic freedom under the First Amendment by canceling a symposium he had planned.[14] This program, referred to as "tolerance day," was arranged by the teacher in response to the drowning of a homosexual by three high school students. The court stated: "However broad the protections of academic freedom may be, they do not permit a teacher to insist upon a given curriculum for the whole school where he teaches."[15]

Beginning in the late 1980s, a series of federal circuit courts decided a number of First Amendment speech cases involving schools. The Sixth Circuit refused to overturn the dismissal of a teacher who had shown an "R" rated movie to high school students on the last day of school.[16] The court's majority, applying the *Mt. Healthy* approach, found that since the movie was not "expressive or communicative" it did not qualify as speech protected by the First Amendment. In a concurring opinion, agreeing with the outcome, another judge relied on *Bethel*, pointing out the vulgar content of the tape that was shown to a captive audience justified the teacher's dismissal.

The Fifth Circuit in 1989 upheld the nonrenewal of a teacher who substituted, without administrative approval, his own supplemental reading list in a world history class for the school's official list.[17] The appellate court determined that the issue of supplemental reading lists did not present a matter of public concern and was rather "nothing more than an ordinary employment dispute."[18] The following year the Third Circuit reviewed a decision in a very complicated case in which a teacher sought an injunction to prevent school officials from banning a teaching methodology she favored and barring them from interfering with her use and advocacy of the method.[19] Although the appellate court agreed with the district court's denial of the injunction, it observed that if the teacher were disciplined for the advocacy of the methodology outside the school, her First Amendment rights would be violated.

In 1991, the Tenth Circuit considered an appeal of a teacher who was punished with a four-day suspension and a letter of reprimand for remarks made in class during an informal discussion.[20] The offensive remark repeated a rumor about two students "making out" on the tennis courts. The teacher filed suit charging that the disciplinary action "chilled" his free speech rights and violated his academic freedom. Beginning with the first step of the *Mt. Healthy* analysis, asking whether the teacher's comments were constitutionally protected, the court looked to the analysis in *Hazelwood.* Relying on *Hazelwood*, the court reasoned that the teacher's comments were "school sponsored expression" in a nonpublic forum;[21] therefore, school officials need only show "a legitimate pedagogical interest" in controlling the teacher's speech. The school officials' burden was met because the school was justified in insisting that a teacher "exhibit professionalism and sound judgment" and not "make statements about students that embarrass those students among their peers."[22] Lastly, in rejecting the other claim, the court said: "[T]he case law does not support [his] position that a secondary school teacher has a constitutional right to academic freedom."[23]

By the end of the decade, the Fourth and Eighth Circuits had ruled in cases that clearly involved disputed authority to control curriculum. In *Boring v. Buncombe County Board of Education*,[24] the court affirmed the transfer of a drama teacher who selected a play that administrators later decided was inappropriate for her students. A divided Fourth Circuit, in considering the issue of "[w]hether a public high school teacher had a right to participate in the makeup of the school curriculum through the selection and production of a play" ruled that she did not. Finding that the board had "legitimate pedagogical reasons" for its actions, the appellate court sustained the district court's judgment for the school district. In *Lacks v. Ferguson Reorganized School District R-2*,[25] the Eighth Circuit permitted the board to dismiss a tenured high school teacher after she allowed students to use vulgar language in plays they wrote and performed as an assignment in her creative writing class. This decision turned on the court's findings that the board had established a legitimate pedagogical concern in prohibiting profanity in the classroom, that the principal had warned her of violations of a board policy on profanity, and that she had been dismissed for violating board policy as provided by state law. The Supreme Court declined to review either of these decisions.

The beginning of the twenty-first century saw courts affirm district authority over the curriculum. In 2000, a federal district court in Virginia upheld the administrative removal of a banned books pamphlet posted by an English teacher on the outside of his classroom door.[26] The court found that the posted pamphlet, as part of the curriculum, was not protected speech; and if it were considered protected, the posting of the pamphlet could still be censored because it "impedes on the school district's ability to teach the selected curriculum based on community values that previously had been approved by the school board."[27] In another Virginia dispute, the Fourth Circuit ruled in 2007 that a Spanish teacher did not have a right to post religious materials on his classroom bulletin board. Citing *Boring*, the appellate court found that the items were curricular in nature since they were posted on school-owned and controlled bulletin boards and designed to impart knowledge to students; therefore, the conflict was simply an employment dispute.[28]

Other decisions since 2000 have upheld district authority to prohibit controversial or inappropriate language in the classroom. *In re Bernstein*[29] saw New York's highest court rule that a district could punish (fine and reprimand) a previously warned English teacher who used sexually explicit language to describe a theory of literary criticism involving phallic symbolism. In *Erskine v. Board of Education*,[30] a federal district court in Maryland (later affirmed by the Fourth Circuit in an unpublished per curiam opinion) upheld the transfer of a teacher who wrote *negro*, the Spanish word for black, on the board when teaching a lesson on Spanish words for color. The court found that the teacher had no protected First Amendment interest in his speech. In 2003, the Sixth Circuit in *Lautermilch v. Findlay City Schools*[31] held that none of a substitute teacher's alleged speech dealt with a matter of public concern, and consequently was not protected by the First Amendment, where the substitute had told inappropriate jokes in an Ohio public school classroom. The Seventh Circuit in 2007 held that an elementary teacher did not have a First Amendment right to insert her personal opinions on political controversies into classroom current events discussions.[32] The principal had instructed the teacher that she could teach about the U.S. policies toward Iraq and use arguments for the different perspectives, but she had to keep her personal opinions to herself. The court declared: "The Constitution does not entitle teachers to present personal views to captive audiences against the instructions of elected officials."[33]

Two federal circuit courts rejected the claims of repeatedly insubordinate educators that they were terminated or nonrenewed for protected speech. In *Vukadinovich v. Board of School Trustees of North Newton School Corp.*,[34] an Indiana technology teacher, unhappy about his proposed extra-duty compensation for coaching a basketball team, criticized the superintendent and school board in numerous letters to local newspapers. The Seventh Circuit found that the school district had lawfully terminated the teacher for insubordination and neglect of duty, not for his expression. The teacher refused, failed, or half-heartedly attempted on five occasions to comply with his principal's specific instructions to submit his lesson plan book and identify how it addressed the state technology qualifications that his program failed to meet. An Oklahoma elementary teacher similarly failed to comply with reasonable administrative directions in *Greenshields v. Independent School District I-1016 of Payne County, Oklahoma.*[35] The second-grade teacher repeatedly refused to follow her district's science curriculum that incorporated learning modules because she favored traditional science methods and materials. The Tenth Circuit in 2006 found that she was nonrenewed for willful neglect of duty and other statutory grounds (insubordination is not a statutory ground for dismissal or nonrenewal of tenured teachers in Oklahoma), based upon her refusal to follow district curriculum and policies and to comply with administrative directives, not for criticizing the district's curriculum, generating public controversy, and bringing suit against the district.

An exception to the pattern of decisions in favor of school districts came in 2001 in *Cockrel v. Shelby County School District.*[36] The Sixth Circuit reviewed the termination of a Kentucky fifth-grade teacher who had invited actor Woody Harrelson and several farmers to speak on the environmental benefits of industrial hemp, an illegal substance in the state. In remanding the case for a determination of whether termination would have occurred absent the controversial activity,[37] the appellate court found that selection of speakers for a class presentation constituted speech that touched on a matter of public concern and in this situation passed *Pickering*'s balancing test, despite evidence of some disruption to the work environment.

Recommendations for Practice

Principals of the twenty-first century have the guidance of a line of cases in which the courts, with notable consistency for more than two decades, have supported the authority of the public schools to control curriculum.[38] Nonetheless, school administrators must realize that censorship of teachers' speech still carries with it the risk of a lawsuit[39] with the possibility of the assessment of damages should the teacher win. Principals should know and respect teachers' rights. They should approach personnel problems with a spirit of fairness and attempt to resolve them by doing what is in the best interest of the students. Finally, they should recognize potential legal implications and act under the guidance of competent legal counsel before—and not wait until after—such problems develop. The lessons of the cases reviewed serve as the basis for additional suggestions that follow:

1. Be aware that outside the classroom, teachers have a First Amendment right to express opinions about matters of public concern even though those views may be controversial and unpopular. The only justification for interfering or punishing teachers for such speech is material and substantial disruption of the educational process.
2. Exercise extreme caution when recommending the release of inferior or otherwise undesirable teachers who at the same time may be engaged in protected speech or other constitutional rights. The evidence documenting the legitimate reasons for the action must convince the courts that those reasons alone would have resulted in the dismissal or other disciplinary action.
3. Do not base a recommendation for dismissal or other disciplinary action on what teachers may have said in a private conference because if the statements are about matters of public concern, they are protected speech.
4. If teachers are to be disciplined for what they say in the classroom or for the subject matter or methods they use, make certain that the school has and can show some legitimate pedagogical justification for the actions.

The twenty-first century began with public school administrators having broad judicial support for their authority to control the curriculum. In the near future, there is little indication that this authority will be eroded by elementary and secondary school teachers' claims of academic freedom. However, few would question the desirability of teacher involvement in curriculum decisions. Communication between principal and teacher about what is taught and how it is taught is essential.

Endnotes

1 For an example of current higher education issues involving academic freedom, see Urofsky v. Gilmore, 216 F.3d 401 (4th Cir. 2000), *cert. denied,* 531 U.S. 1070 (2001), where the Fourth Circuit in 2000 ruled that public university professors do not have a First Amendment right of academic freedom to access sexually explicit materials on state owned or leased computers. *See also* Loving v. Boren, 133 F.3d 771 (10th Cir. 1998).

2 *See, e.g.*, Keyishian v. Bd. of Regents of Univ. of State of N.Y., 385 U.S. 589 (1967).

3 Pickering v. Bd. of Educ. of Tp. High Sch. Dist. 205, 391 U.S. 563 (1968).

4 Tinker v. Des Moines Indep. Cmty. Sch. Dist., 393 U.S. 503 (1969).

5 Mt. Healthy City Sch. Dist. Bd. of Educ. v. Doyle, 429 U.S. 274 (1977).

6 Givhan v. W. Line Consol. Sch. Dist., 439 U.S. 410 (1979).

7 Connick v. Myers, 461 U.S. 138 (1983).

8 Garcetti v. Ceballos, 547 U.S. 410 (2006).

9 127 S. Ct. 2618 (2007).
10 Bethel Sch. Dist. No. 403 v. Fraser, 478 U.S. 675 (1986).
11 Hazelwood Sch. Dist. v. Kuhlmeier, 484 U.S. 260 (1988).
12 Fisher v. Fairbanks N. Star Borough Sch. Dist., 704 P.2d 213 (Alaska 1985).
13 *Id.* at 217.
14 Solmitz v. Me. Sch. Admin. Dist. No. 59, 495 A.2d 812 (Me. 1985).
15 *Id.* at 817.
16 Fowler v. Bd. of Educ. of Lincoln County, Ky., 819 F.2d 657 (6th Cir. 1987).
17 Kirkland v. Northside Indep. Sch. Dist., 890 F.2d 794 (5th Cir. 1989), *cert. denied*, 496 U.S. 926 (1990).
18 *Id.* at 802.
19 Bradley v. Pittsburgh Bd. of Educ., 910 F.2d 1172 (3d Cir. 1990).
20 Miles v. Denver Pub. Sch., 944 F.2d 773 (10th Cir. 1991).
21 *Id.* at 776.
22 *Id.* at 778.
23 *Id.* at 779.
24 Boring v. Buncombe County Bd. of Educ., 136 F.3d 364 (4th Cir. 1998), *cert. denied*, 525 U.S. 813 (1998).
25 Lacks v. Ferguson Reorg. Sch. Dist. R-2, 147 F.3d 718 (8th Cir. 1998), *cert. denied*, 526 U.S. 1012 (1999).
26 Newton v. Slye, 116 F. Supp. 2d 677 (W.D. Va. 2000) (the court denied an injunction).
27 *Id.* at 685.
28 Lee v. York County Sch. Div., 484 F.3d 687 (4th Cir. 2007).
29 *In re* Bernstein, 726 N.Y.S.2d 474 (N.Y. App.Div. 2001).
30 Erskine v. Bd. of Educ., 207 F. Supp. 2d 407 (D. Md. 2002), *aff'd,* 56 F. App'x 615 (4th Cir. 2003).
31 Lautermilch v. Findlay City Sch., 314 F.3d 271 (6th Cir. 2003) (the substitute had also allegedly commented on the size of a female teacher's breasts and acted inappropriately with young people).
32 Mayer v. Monroe County Cmty. Sch. Corp., 474 F.3d 477 (7th Cir. 2007).
33 *Id.* at 480.
34 Vukadinovich v. Bd. of Sch. Trs. of N. Newton Sch. Corp., 278 F.3d 693 (7th Cir. 2002).
35 Greenshields v. Indep. Sch. Dist. I-1016 of Payne County, Okla., 174 F. App'x 426 (10th Cir. 2006).
36 Cockrel v. Shelby County Sch. Dist., 270 F.3d 1036 (6th Cir. 2001).
37 The district cited Cockrel's alleged failure to teach the school's curriculum, calling the principal names in front of students and staff, and failure to cooperate with faculty members and staff at her elementary school. *Id.* at 1041.
38 Higher education case law involving employees' use of sexually and racially offensive language in the job setting has yielded mixed results in the past decade. While the Sixth Circuit upheld the disciplining of two employees where objectionable language was involved (*see* Bonnell v. Lorenzo, 241 F.3d 800 (6th Cir. 2001) and Dambrot v. Cent. Mich. Univ., 55 F.3d 1177 (6th Cir. 1995)), two other appellate court decisions favored faculty who used, or allowed to be used, offensive and disparaging language in their classrooms (*see* Vanderhurst v. Colorado Mt. Coll. Dist., 208 F.3d 908 (10th Cir. 2000), and Hardy v. Jefferson Cmty. Coll., 260 F.3d 671 (6th Cir. 2001)).
39 *See, e.g.*, Harris v. Victoria Indep. Sch. Dist., 168 F.3d 216 (5th Cir. 1999), *cert. denied,* 528 U.S. 1022 (1999) (which was initiated by teachers who were transferred to other schools in the district after they criticized the school principal).

Chapter 24

Sexual Harassment in the Workplace

M. David Alexander & Jennifer A. Sughrue

Introduction

Sexual harassment in the workplace is viewed under the law as a form of sexual discrimination and, therefore, a civil rights violation. Sexual harassment results when someone in a position of power or influence uses his or her status to extort sexual favor from a subordinate or when an employee's job performance deteriorates due to extensive or abusive sexual innuendo or behavior in the workplace.[1]

Prior to the Civil Rights Act of 1991, the law limited the damages that victims could collect in sexual harassment cases basically to equitable relief that included back pay and attorney fees, but it did not allow for punitive damages or for other substantial monetary relief. These limitations were ameliorated with the amended Civil Rights Act, extending the rights of sexual discrimination victims to sue for damages ranging from $50,000 for companies with 100 or fewer workers to $300,000 for employers with more than 500 workers.[2]

Starting in the 1970s,[3] litigation and the feminist movement prompted various studies, including Catherine MacKinnon's book, *Sexual Harassment of Working Women*. As a result, sexual harassment became recognized as a serious problem within the workplace.[4]

Legal Issues

Despite the clarity of the legal language, sexual harassment is not easily defined, and its incidence is difficult to measure. It may range from verbal innuendo to an overt act, and the definition must be broad enough to encompass a diversity of behavior.[5]

Sexual harassment is uniformly cast as a gender issue. The overwhelming majority of cases involve female workers being harassed by male colleagues or supervisors.[6] In recent years, however, litigation has brought attention to the issue of same-sex harassment.[7] The Supreme Court has ruled that both males and females enjoy protection from sexual discrimination under Title VII, which includes protection from same-sex harassment.

> As some courts have observed, male-on-male sexual harassment in the workplace was assuredly not the principal evil Congress was concerned with when it enacted Title VII. But statutory prohibitions often go beyond the principal evil to cover reasonably comparable evils, and it is ultimately the provisions of our laws rather than the principal concerns of our legislators by which we are governed. Title VII prohibits "discriminat[ion] ... because of ... sex" in the "terms" or "conditions" of employment. Our holding that this includes sexual harassment must extend to sexual harassment of any kind that meets the statutory requirements.[8]

Sexual harassment violations are not exclusively a function of the workplace. Students may be victims of sexual harassment, both by persons in positions of authority, such as teachers, or by peers. The law regarding sexual harassment of students is explored in another chapter of this book. The focus of this chapter is on employee-to-employee sexual harassment.

Title VII

Employees are protected from sexual harassment in the workplace by Title VII of the Civil Rights Act of 1964 and by the Civil Rights Act of 1991, which, together, provide for damages in cases of intentional employment discrimination. Title VII makes it "an unlawful employment practice for an employer ... to discriminate against any individual with respect to his compensation, terms, conditions or privileges of employment, because of such individual's race, color, religion, sex, or national origin."[9] Court cases concerning sex discrimination in the 1970s started recognizing sexual harassment, but it was not until 1980 that the Equal Employment Opportunity Commission (EEOC) promulgated regulations prohibiting sexual harassment. These regulations provide that:

> Unwelcome sexual advances, request for sexual favors, and other verbal or physical conduct of a sexual nature constitute harassment when (1) submission to such conduct is made explicitly or implicitly a term or condition of an individual's employment, (2) submission to or rejection of such conduct by an individual is used as a basis for employment decisions affecting such individual, (3) such conduct has the purpose or effect of unreasonably interfering with an individual's work performance or creating a intimidating, hostile, or offensive working environment.[10]

Quid Pro Quo and Hostile Environment

According to earlier EEOC guidelines, there were two types of sexual harassment, *quid pro quo* and *hostile work environment*. The first type, *quid pro quo*, referred to those situations in which employment opportunity or benefit was dependent upon compliance with or acceptance of sexual advances. The second type of sexual harassment, *hostile work environment*, referred to abusive conditions in the workplace. These conditions could be the result of the sexual nature of comments, stares, jokes, innuendo, and other similar occurrences.

> The guidelines provide that sexual conduct constitutes prohibited "sexual harassment," whether or not it is directly linked to the grant or denial of an economic *quid pro quo*, where such conduct has the purpose or effect of unreasonably interfering with an individual's work performance or creating an intimidating, hostile, or offensive working environment.[11]

In *Meritor Savings Bank, FSB v. Vinson*, the Supreme Court determined that an employee's coerced participation in a sexual relation creates a hostile environment. Vinson, an employee of the bank, was promoted from teller-trainee to assistant branch manager in four years. The advancements were based on merit. Shortly after Vinson was employed, however, her supervisor made sexual advances toward her. Out of fear of losing her job, Vinson consented to having sexual intercourse with Taylor, Vinson's supervisor. They engaged in sexual intercourse approximately forty to fifty times over the next four years. At the end of this period, Vinson told Taylor she was taking indefinite sick leave. Two months later, she was discharged for excessive use of leave.

In the *Vinson* ruling, the Supreme Court upheld the EEOC guidelines and emphasized the concept of the hostile environment in the workplace. Her supervisor claimed that Vinson's participation had been voluntary, but the Court ruled that the concept of voluntary participation could not be used as a defense if the sexual advances were unwelcome. The Court said that the "correct inquiry was whether the bank employee, by her conduct, indicated that sexual advances were unwelcome, not whether her actual participation in sexual intercourse was voluntary."[12]

Employer liability

The organization for which the offending supervisor works can be held accountable if no action is taken to discourage sexual harassment. In a 1998 case, *Burlington Industries, Inc. v. Ellerth*,[13] the Supreme Court determined a single test of employer liability for harassment by supervisors under Title VII. The Court ruled that even where the employee suffered no tangible retaliation in employment opportunity or benefit, an employer has vicarious liability for a hostile environment created by the severe or pervasive conduct of a supervisor.

Ellerth was a salesperson for Burlington Industries, but she quit her job after fifteen months. She alleged she had been sexually harassed by one of her supervisors. Ellerth suffered no adverse employment consequences as a result of rejecting her supervisor's sexual advances, but she claimed the hostile work environment forced her constructive discharge. The Court ruled that "[a]n employer is subject to vicarious liability to a victimized employee for an actionable hostile environment created by a supervisor with immediate (or successively higher) authority over the employee."[14]

In a companion case to *Ellerth*, the Court determined that employers should expect the potential for sexual harassment.[15] Ocean lifeguard Faragher resigned her position with the City of Boca Raton and brought suit, claiming that her two supervisors "had created a 'sexually hostile atmosphere' at work by repeatedly subjecting Faragher and other female lifeguards to 'uninvited and offensive touching,' by making lewd remarks, and by speaking of women in offensive terms."[16] A lower court ruled that the city did not have vicarious liability because it did not have actual or constructive knowledge of the supervisors' inappropriate behavior. The Supreme Court disagreed, noting that sexual harassment is "one of the normal risks of doing business" and that an employer "can reasonably anticipate the possibility of sexual harassment occurring in the workplace."[17]

Employers can assert an affirmative defense in cases where no adverse employment action results from the harassment. An affirmative defense must comprise "a preponderance of evidence" that "(a) the employer exercised reasonable care to prevent and correct promptly any sexually harassing behavior and (b) that the plaintiff employee unreasonably failed to take advantage of any preventive or corrective opportunities provided by the employer or to avoid harm otherwise."[18]

Burlington Industries had a policy against sexual harassment with guidelines for submitting a complaint, but Ellerth did not avail herself of these procedures. In fact, she admitted she did not inform her immediate supervisor because he would have been obligated to report the incidents. Noting these circumstances in its remand to the lower court, the Supreme Court held that Burlington was subject to vicarious liability for the supervisor's actions, but that it should have the opportunity to offer an affirmative defense to its liability.

The City of Boca Raton also had a sexual harassment policy, yet information provided to the Court indicated that the city did not distribute its policy among the beach employees, did not provide adequate oversight of its supervisors' conduct, and did not provide any assurances in its policy that the offending supervisors could be bypassed in registering complaints. The Court held that the city "could not be found to have exercised reasonable care to prevent the supervisors' harassing behavior"[19] and, therefore, questioned the city's ability to offer an affirmative defense. It is important to emphasize that the City of Boca Raton lost the opportunity to establish an affirmative defense partially because "it officially made no attempt to keep track of the conduct of [its] supervisors."[20]

As a result of these two cases, the early distinction between *quid pro quo* and *hostile environment* harassment has been modified by the Supreme Court and since by updated EEOC guidelines. The modification reflects the Supreme Court's creation of a single test (the existence of severe and pervasive conduct) for an employer's vicarious liability and whether an employer will have an opportunity to raise a defense (when there is no evidence of adverse effect on employment) to an ascribed vicarious liability. It is now more accurate to distinguish between "harassment *that results in a tangible employment action* [emphasis added] and harassment that creates a hostile work environment, since that difference determines whether the employer can raise the affirmative defense to vicarious liability."[21]

The Court has made a point of distinguishing between severe and pervasive conduct and the occasional isolated remark. In a 2001 case, *Clark County School District v. Breeden*, the Court ruled that a single comment during a review of job applicant profiles did not constitute sexual harassment.[22] Furthermore, the Court has provided guidance to lower courts in weighing the nature and degree of harassment:

> [D]etermine whether an environment is sufficiently hostile or abusive by "looking at all the circumstances," including the "frequency of the discriminatory conduct; its severity; whether it is physically threatening or humiliating, or a mere offensive utterance; and whether it unreasonably interferes with an employee's work performance."[23]

In 2006 the Supreme Court again addressed a sexual harassment issue, that of retaliation. The Civil Rights Act of 1964 forbids "employment discrimination based on race, color, religion, sex or national origin" whereas the anti-retaliation provision prohibits "discrimination against" an employee or job applicant. Burlington Northern and Santa Fe Railway Co. wanted the narrow language or limiting words applied to the retaliation section. The court, in giving a broader interpretation to the retaliation section, said that a plaintiff needs to show the action "well might have dissuaded a reasonable worker from making or supporting a charge of discrimination."[24]

In a 1999 education case brought under Title VII, Scrivner, an elementary school teacher, alleged that she was sexually harassed by her principal, Cardenas, and suffered job retaliation. She sued her employer, Socorro Independent School District (SISD), for vicarious liability. The school district conceded that a hostile work environment was created by Cardenas's behavior. However, SISD was allowed to offer an affirmative defense because Scrivner could not substantiate her claim she suffered a tangible adverse effect in her employment.

The facts of the case indicate that SISD received an anonymous letter in 1994 complaining about Cardenas's harassing behavior. In response, the district launched an investigation during which Scrivner was interviewed, along with sixty-three other faculty and staff. Although she later detailed incidents in which Cardenas harassed her, she denied in the interview that his behavior was harassing or vulgar. Based on its investigation, SISD found no tangible evidence of sexual harassment, but it warned Cardenas to "refrain from making unprofessional '[j]okes, innuendoes, and pointed comments.'"[25]

Frustrated that Cardenas's behavior worsened after the investigation, Scrivner filed a formal complaint in 1996 with the district against Cardenas, claiming that he had called her a lesbian among other sexual harassing behaviors. The district again promptly initiated and published the results of an investigation and concluded that the principal's behavior created a hostile environment. Cardenas was removed from his position, and he soon resigned from the district.

In its affirmative defense to vicarious liability, the district was able to demonstrate that it had promulgated an anti-discrimination policy, that it had responded reasonably and vigorously to the two harassment complaints filed against Cardenas, and that Scrivner had "unreasonably failed to take advantage of any preventive or corrective opportunities provided by [SISD] or to avoid harm otherwise."[26] As a result, the Fifth Circuit Court of Appeals upheld the lower court's summary judgment for the defendant district.

Title IX

Title IX of the Education Amendments of 1972 also addresses sex discrimination and sexual harassment. The sexual harassment prohibition of Title IX is not as clear as in Title VII. Title IX specifies: "No person in the United States shall on the basis of sex, be excluded from participation in, be denied the benefits of, or be subjected to discrimination under any education program or activity receiving federal financial assistance."[27] Since Title IX was patterned after Title VI of the Civil Rights Act of 1964 and covers students in educational institutions, some courts initially ruled that Title IX does not cover school employees. In 1982, however, the Supreme Court stated that "while section 901(a) does not expressly include [or exclude] employees within its scope or expressly exclude them, its broad directive that 'no person' may be discriminated against on the basis of gender … includes employees as well as students."[28]

The Office of Civil Rights (OCR) of the United States Department of Education (DOE) is the primary administrative agency charged with enforcing Title IX. The Department of Health and Human Services (HHS) also has some jurisdiction over Title IX for those programs under the jurisdiction. Both DOE and HHS have promulgated identical regulation for Title IX. Both offices have Offices of Civil Rights for enforcement.[29]

The debate over whether Title IX covers sexual harassment was settled by the Supreme Court in 1992. In *Franklin v. Gwinnett County Public Schools*,[30] the Court ruled that a damage remedy is available for a sexual harassment action brought to enforce Title IX. Although this case did not involve a complaint by an employee, the judicial standard is applicable all the same. Enforceability was available through an implied right of action.

In *Franklin v Gwinnett*, a female student had been subjected to continual sexual harassment from a high school coach/teacher. School officials, after becoming aware of the harassment, discouraged the student from pressing charges against the teacher. Subsequently, the teacher resigned on the condition all matters relating to him be dropped. The school agreed and closed the investigation. The district court dismissed the student's complaint, ruling that Title IX did not provide for damages. In determining that Title IX did allow damages, the Supreme Court opined:

> The assertion that Title IX remedies should nevertheless be limited to back pay and prospective relief diverges from this court's traditional approach to deciding what remedies are available for violations of a federal right. Both suggested remedies are equitable in nature, and it is axiomatic that a court should determine the adequacy of damages of law before resorting to equitable relief. Moreover, both suggested remedies are clearly inadequate in that they would provide Franklin no relief: back pay because she was a student when the alleged discrimination occurred, and prospective relief because she no longer attends school in respondent system and Hill no longer teaches there.[31]

Institutional liability under Title IX was addressed in an earlier case. In *Lipsett v. University of Puerto Rico*,[32] the First Circuit Court of Appeals stated that in a Title IX case an educational institution is absolutely liable for *quid pro quo* sexual harassment and discriminatory discharge regardless of whether it knew, or should have known, or approved of the actions of the supervisor involved.

The educational institution is liable also for *hostile environment* sexual harassment unless it can demonstrate that appropriate steps were taken to dissipate the hostile environment. Among specific behaviors (that are unwanted and sexual in nature) that could constitute hostile environment sexual harassment includes touching, verbal comments, sexual name calling, spreading sexual rumors, gestures, jokes/cartoons/pictures, too personal a conversation, cornering/blocking movements, pulling at clothes, attempted rape, and rape.[33] School districts that do not have a sexual harassment policy and grievance procedure are in violation of Title IX.[34]

In 2005, in *Jackson v. Birmingham Board of Education*,[35] the Supreme Court ruled that Title IX included a right to assert a retaliation claim. A girl's basketball coach at a public high school complained that girls did not receive equal funding or equal access to facilities or equipment. After his complaints, he started receiving negative work evaluations and was removed as the girls' coach. Although Title IX does not mention retaliation, as does Title VII of the 1964 Civil Rights Act, Title IX implies a right to assert a retaliation claim while Title VII gives express authority to do so.

While the Supreme Court has decided that Title IX protection extends to employees as well as students, litigation for sexual harassment under Title IX has remained primarily the domain for student complaints. There is no substantial body of Title IX claims brought by school employees on which federal courts have ruled.[36] The majority of school employee cases are litigated under Title VII.

Equal Protection

The Seventh Circuit Court of Appeals, in *Bohen v. City of East Chicago*,[37] was the first federal court to recognize a sexual harassment claim under the equal protection clause of the Fourteenth Amendment. This action opens another legal avenue for public employees.[38] To be successful, the plaintiff must show that the discrimination was intentional. The plaintiff's claim must demonstrate that the sexual harassment was "inten[ded] to discriminate because of her status as a female and not 'because of' characteristics of her gender which are personal to her."[39] This discrimination may be shown by a single event, but it is unlikely that one event will constitute denial of equal protection. In *Bohen*, the court said, "Forcing women and not men to work in an environment of sexual harassment is no different than forcing women to work in a dirtier or more hazardous environment than men simply because they were women."[40]

Recommendations for Practice

Standards for sexual harassment in the workplace are the same for both public and private employers. As evinced in *Ellerth* and *Faragher*, the employer may have vicarious liability for severe or pervasive conduct of employees in supervisory positions but may offer an affirmative defense if the plaintiff employee has suffered no tangible adverse effect on his or her employment. An important component of the affirmative defense is demonstrating the existence and dissemination of an anti-sexual harassment policy. With this in mind, the following recommendations are made. The local school board should:

1. Develop, review, and disseminate a strong workplace policy prohibiting sexual harassment. Preferably there should be a mechanism for the faculty and staff to contribute to and ultimately endorse the policy and to help monitor it.

a. The policy should contain a statement explaining why it is important to prevent sexual harassment.
b. Included in this policy should be a clear description or explanation of the prohibited behaviors. Generally speaking, these behaviors are unwarranted or unwanted sexual attention from peers, subordinates, supervisors, customers, clients, or anyone the employee must interact with in order to fulfill the duties of the job or school where the employee's responses might be restrained by fear of reprisals. The range of behaviors includes but is not limited to leering, pinching, unnecessary touching or patting, verbal comments, subtle pressure for sexual activity, rape, and attempted rape.
c. There should be clear assurances in the policy that an employee who files a harassment complaint or who provides information related to such a complaint will be protected from retaliation. There should also be assurances that to the degree possible the employer will protect the confidentiality of those who file harassment complaints.
d. The policy should outline procedures for filing a complaint and should describe the employer's process for investigating and responding to a complaint. The process should include the following: the timeline for the investigation; suggestions for possible informal resolution of the problem; and assignment of complaint managers who are respected by the employees, are sensitive to the issue, and able to empathize with the victim.[41]

2. The school board should adopt, publicize, and enforce penalties for violations of the policy.[42]
3. The board should keep written records. However, it should take precautions to protect confidentiality.[43]
4. The school board should publish results of resolved complaints but should protect the identity of the individuals involved.[44]
5. Measures should be taken to facilitate employees' awareness of the EEOC sexual harassment guidelines and alertness to the problem.
   a. It is advisable that employers conduct periodic training for administrators and others in supervisory positions, teachers, and staff to ensure all employees understand and comply with the policy.
   b. Orientation programs for new faculty and staff should include discussion of the sexual harassment policy and EEOC guidelines.
6. The school board should include all policies related to sexual harassment in faculty, staff, and student handbooks.

Endnotes

1 Sexual harassment in the workplace was raised to national prominence during the Senate confirmation hearings for United States Supreme Court nominee Clarence Thomas when Anita Hill, a law professor from the University of Oklahoma and a former employee under Thomas, testified of alleged acts of sexual harassment by Thomas. From testimony of Anita Hill and Clarence Thomas on nationally televised Senate confirmation hearings for United States Supreme Court nominee, Clarence Thomas, October 10-13, 1991.

2 United States Congress passed Public Law 102-166, the 1991 Civil Rights Act, in November 1991.

3 Ingulli, *Sexual Harassment in Education*, 18 RUTGERS L. J. 281, 282 (Winter 1987).

4 *See* Mondschein & Greene, *Sexual Harassment in Employment and Educational Practices*, SCH. L. UPDATE 1986 (ERIC Document No. ED 272996).

5 Schneider, *Sexual Harassment and Higher Education*, 65 TEX. L. REV. 525 (Feb. 1987).

6 Gibbs, *Sex, Lies, and Politics: America's Watershed Debate on Sexual Harassment*, TIME 138, no. 15 (October 21, 1991).

7 In *Oncale v. Sundowner Offshore Services, Inc.*, 523 U.S. 75, 118 S. Ct. 998 (1998), Joseph Oncale, a male worker on an offshore rig, alleged that he had been "forcibly subjected to sex-related, humiliating actions ... physically assaulted ... in a sexual manner, and ... threatened with rape." 118 S. Ct. 998, 1001. It is interesting to note that this is the only majority opinion that ruled in favor of the victim of sexual harassment in which Justice Thomas concurred. In the other key post-1991 Title VII cases discussed above, Justice Thomas submitted dissenting opinions.

8 *Id.* at 1002.

9 42 U.S.C. § 2000e-2(a)(1).

10 29 C.F.R. § 1604.11(a) (1986).

11 Meritor Sav. Bank, FSB v. Vinson, 106 S. Ct. 2399, 2404-2405 (1986).

12 *Id.* at 2406.

13 118 S. Ct. 2257 (1998).

14 *Id.* at 2261.

15 Faragher v. City of Boca Raton, 118 S. Ct. 2275 (1998).

16 *Id.* at 2277.

17 *Id.* at 2278.

18 *Id.* at 2279.

19 *Id.*

20 *Id.* at 2293.

21 EEOC, *Enforcement Guidance: Vicarious Employer Liability for Unlawful Harassment by Supervisors*, no. 915.002, endnote 7 (June 18, 1999).

22 121 S. Ct. 1508.

23 Harris v. Forklift Sys., Inc., 114 S. Ct. 367 (1993), quoted in *Faragher*, 118 S. Ct. at 2283.

24 Burlington N. & Santa Fe Railway Co. v. White, 126 S. Ct. 2405, 2407 (2006).

25 Scrivner v. Socorro Indep. Sch. Dist., 169 F.3d 969, 970 (5th Cir. 1999).

26 *Id.* at 971.

27 20 U.S.C. § 1681.

28 North Haven Bd. of Educ. v. Bell, 102 S. Ct. 1912, 1914 (1982).

29 34 C.F.R. Part 106; Title IX Legal Manual, U.S. Department of Justice, Civil Rights Division (2001).

30 112 S. Ct. 1028 (1992).

31 *Id.* at 1030-1031.

32 864 F.2d 881, 882 (1st Cir. 1988).

33 Strauss, *Sexual Harassment in the School: Legal Implications for Principals*, NASSP BULLETIN: 93-97, 94 (March, 1988).

34 *Id.*

35 Jackson v. Birmingham Bd. of Educ. 125 S. Ct. 1497 (2005).

[36] Singleton v. Chi. Sch. Reform Bd. of Trs. of the City of Chi., 2002 WL 2017082 (N.D. Ill.) (concerning a teacher's claim under Title VII, Title IX, First Amendment, and Equal Protection. Summary judgment was granted the school board on all counts).

[37] 799 F.2d 1180 (7th Cir. 1986).

[38] In *Bohen*, the plaintiff was a fire department dispatcher. Her coworkers and supervisor subjected her to repeated acts of sexual harassment.

[39] Trautvetter v. Quick, 916 F.2d 1140, 1151 (7th Cir. 1990).

[40] *Bohen*, 799 F.2d at 1185.

[41] *Strauss*, *supra* note 33, at 97.

[42] Nebraska Association of School Boards, *12 Steps to Deal with Sexual Harassment in Schools*, NASB EMPLOYEE QUARTERLY, (Summer 1993), on-line: http://www.nebr-schoolboards.org/12steps.htm.

[43] *Id.*

[44] *Id.*

Chapter 25

Evaluations

Lynn Rossi Scott

Introduction

A principal is often charged, whether under state statute, regulation, or some negotiated agreement, with the responsibility to evaluate the individuals he or she supervises. Unfortunately, and somewhat ironically, the evaluation of campus employees is perhaps the most difficult job function of the campus principal. Since most campus principals are former classroom educators, they tend to adhere to one of the basic philosophical beliefs of an educator, that "All Children Can Learn." A dedicated educator believes that if a child has not learned something, it is more a reflection of the teacher's ability to teach than it is a reflection on the student's ability to learn. Therefore, the dedicated educator will reteach, repeat, or try different manipulations of the environment, different instructional strategies, or different presentation methods, all in an effort to ensure that a child will learn. The evaluation of employees requires, at least to some degree, the same mindset since evaluation is, at its fundamental level, a form of teaching. However, it is not the responsibility of the supervisor, evaluator, or administrator to manipulate the environment, to change the employee's job description, or to reteach the employee until the employee learns how to master his or her job. At some point, after the supervisor has given the employee full notice of job expectations and performance deficiencies, it is the employee's responsibility to perform that job at an acceptable level; it is not the supervisor's responsibility to change the job so that the employee is successful.

Conversely, educators who correct and guide students every work day sometimes react negatively to correction and guidance from their supervisors. What must be communicated to these reluctant learners is that constructive evaluations enable employees to become even better at their jobs. Evaluations allow employees to better understand the expectations on which they are judged. Most professionals would not knowingly continue doing things that disturb their supervisors. Only through evaluations or some other remediation attempts, however, can professionals know what their supervisors find disturbing.

Without open and honest evaluation of job performance, the possibility exists that a professional will continue to act in a manner that is intolerable to a supervisor, ultimately and ignorantly destroying their working relationship.

This chapter will discuss statutory and judicial guidance regarding the elements of appropriate evaluation systems and practical advice to avoid legal claims.

Legal Issues

Goals and Functions of Evaluation

An appropriately conducted evaluation process opens the way for open, honest, and effective communication between the supervisor and the employee, making clear the supervisor's expectations for job performance and the supervisor's methods of evaluating that job performance. The evaluation process then provides the employee with notice of strengths, weaknesses, and required improvements in job performance. It may also provide timelines for corrections of behavior and methods by which behavior must be corrected. This notice then becomes an effective tool to manage employee behavior. In the vast majority of cases, the outcome of an appropriate evaluation system is improved employee performance.

Legal Intervention

In the rare situations when improved performance does not occur, however, the ultimate outcome of an evaluation process is the termination or nonrenewal of an employee's employment or the recognition by the employee that it is time to seek other employment. Adverse employment decisions are often litigated. At the time that a state or federal judge steps in to review an employer's actions regarding an employee's job performance, the judge is not in a position to view a teacher in a classroom or a custodian in a hallway. Rather, the judge must rely on complete written evaluation documents drafted by the supervisor and others with responsibility to inform employees of necessary remediation of their job performance. Evaluations, therefore, become critical evidence when employers must justify adverse employment decisions. Judicial intervention in employee evaluation or termination often requires that the court interpret statutory language, regulatory provisions, board policies, collective bargaining agreements, contract language, and the evaluation instruments themselves. Therefore, it is essential that these potential pieces of evidence be understandable to non-educators and be direct, clear, and capable of withstanding such judicial scrutiny.

Indeed, it is becoming more and more common for state statutes to require that employment termination and contract nonrenewal decisions be based on written evaluations that point out specific job performance deficiencies and for courts to overturn employment termination decisions when evaluations are either not provided or are improperly provided.[1] For example, West Virginia's statute states:

> Every employee is entitled to know how well he/she is performing his/her job, and should be offered the opportunity of open and honest evaluation of his/her performance on a regular basis. Any decision concerning promotion, demotion, transfer or termination of employment should be based upon such evaluation, and not upon factors extraneous thereto. Every employee is entitled to the opportunity to improve his/her job performance, prior to the terminating or transferring of his/her services, and can only do so with the assistance of regular evaluation.[2]

Statutory mandatory notice of performance deficiencies prior to adverse employment action is becoming more common, for the simple reason that it looks and feels fair to employees and to the legislatures who create such laws.

That is not to say that the absence of a poor evaluation grade on a specific termination reason will necessarily destroy an employment termination case. In fact, even in some states in which performance evaluations or written records of notice of unsatisfactory work performance are required by law, there is an acknowledgment that certain conduct is nonremediable or uncorrectable and, therefore, does not require a remediation attempt. Such nonremediable conduct can include intentionally harmful conduct, insubordination, intemperance, dishonesty, immorality, misrepresentation, fraud, and other intentional misconduct such as abuse or battery.[3] Evaluations are also typically unnecessary when employment is terminated for budgetary or financial exigency reasons unrelated to an employee's job performance.[4] Finally, evaluations are often unnecessary for employees who are at-will employees who can be fired or who can resign for any reason.[5] In the majority of cases, however, a proper evaluation system, correctly implemented, is essential.

The Importance of Appropriate Evaluation Systems

A proper evaluation can make a termination or nonrenewal case pass judicial muster. On the contrary, a poorly drafted evaluation, or the lack of an evaluation, can sometimes doom a termination or nonrenewal case. For example, consider two adverse employment actions, which after judicial review, resulted in very different consequences, based on the evaluations provided by supervisors.

The Supreme Court of Appeals in West Virginia reviewed a termination action of a thirteen-year employee of a school district, who had an exemplary record until her campus got a new principal.[6] After their relationship quickly became strained, the principal started keeping records, ultimately listing ten incidents of the teacher's improper behavior, involving such things as the teacher throwing bookbags; crying and stating that she wished she would die when she was upset about a classroom scheduling issue; telling the principal that if she was having a bad day, she might jump out a window and give the proceeds to her children; calling her principal "Napoleon"; failing to maintain classroom discipline; taking all of her students with her on an out-of-class errand; moving a heavy locker by herself; and falling to her knees during a parent-teacher conference in which she was explaining how the parent's special education student received red marks around his neck. However, the principal did not share any of his written documentation or any warning, criticism, or concern with the teacher until he wrote five of the incidents on the teacher's otherwise excellent classroom observation a number of months later. The principal then presented the evaluation to the teacher with a needs assessment and asked her to sign it, without allowing any meaningful discussion. She refused because she did not understand his needs assessment. Four months later, he again observed her classroom performance, again noting exemplary classroom teaching, and again attached his criticisms regarding the teacher's prior acts. At the summative evaluation conference, after the principal read his criticisms, he again did not allow discussion. Instead, he asked the teacher to immediately sign the evaluation documents because he had to leave to serve lunch duty. She refused; there was a gust of wind; and the paper landed on the floor, where she either stepped or "stomped" on it. Two days later, the principal again asked her to sign the evaluation, again without giving her an opportunity to discuss his comments. When she refused to sign a second time, her principal told her that she would be called to appear before the board in Welch, West Virginia, regarding her refusal. She responded by telling her principal that she would draw a map for him to get to Welch. Then the situation really went downhill. Days later, the teacher, without prior warning, was driven to the superintendent's office to discuss the principal's concerns about her job performance and her refusal to sign her evaluation. Again, however, in the meeting with the superintendent, assistant superintendent, and the principal, she was not given an opportunity to respond to her principal's criticisms but was just asked to sign the documents or face discipline. Feeling like a "caged animal," she told the principal that she should have blown his head off with a shotgun. After hearing the teacher's comment, the superintendent called 911 and told her that he was recommending termination of her employment because her comment confirmed that the principal's allegations were legitimate and she was insubordinate.[7]

The teacher filed suit after her employment was terminated for insubordination, which by that state's statute, does not require remediation. The West Virginia Supreme Court of Appeals ultimately remanded the case for further consideration under West Virginia law, which requires employee evaluations and a remediation opportunity, except for situations such as insubordination. Describing the situation as a personality conflict that "escalated grievously," the court characterized the teacher's conduct as performance-related rather than insubordinate and then criticized the principal as lacking in constructive communication. The court was highly critical of the principal, whose apparent fear of confrontation resulted in limited communication and a failure to constructively address what were legitimate job-performance concerns. The court held that the teacher's job performance and communication with her supervisor should have been "meaningfully deliberated upon" and the district should have analyzed whether or not the teacher's conduct was correctable before terminating her employment. Because neither occurred, the court, without sanctioning the teacher's behavior, determined that she should have been given a remediation attempt and an improvement period, if her behavior was remediable. Therefore, in spite of clearly unprofessional conduct by the teacher, the case was remanded to determine whether or not the teacher's conduct was correctable, with the likelihood being that the teacher would reclaim her job.[8]

On the other hand, consider the teacher in the Houston Independent School District in Texas who had a continuing contract with the district and whose performance was evaluated numerous times during two school years. Evaluations of the teacher's performance included both written assessments and videotapes of the teacher's classroom performance. The videotapes were used so that the teacher could more easily follow and understand the evaluation team's observations and criticisms. At the termination hearing, the school board heard testimony from the teacher's supervisors and reviewed approximately one hundred documents regarding the teacher's classroom performance. The board also viewed a thirty-minute videotape, which included excerpts from five separate videotapes made of the teacher's classroom performance. The court held that both the written evaluation and the videotapes revealed numerous problems with the teacher's performance. The teacher was told of these problems but did not correct and improve her performance. Therefore, the court upheld the board's employment termination decision.[9]

Judges are not educators, nor are they education evaluators. As such, when there is the existence of an evaluation or assessment procedure, when that procedure appears to have been followed, and when there is concrete evidence of an evaluation or other evaluative materials, judges have shown a great deal of deference to educational administrators in determining the appropriate standards of performance of education professionals and other school employees. As stated by one court, public schools need not be "married to mediocrity" when setting standards for the evaluation of professional employees.[10] What school administrators must do, however, is communicate those standards and notify those who do not meet the standards. Where evaluations are mandatory under state statute, regulations, local policies, or contracts, the courts appear to afford a great deal of protection to employees, requiring that the employees be properly evaluated and informed regarding job performance problems so that their deficient performance can be corrected.[11]

Furthermore, when those evaluations are statutorily required, and those evaluations are properly performed, courts are much more likely to conclude that an employee "cannot complain" about notice of job performance concerns and the remediation opportunity that notice provides, even when the employee fails to understand the remediation required or the consequences of a failure or refusal to remediate job performance.[12]

It is incumbent upon a board to develop sound policies with regard to evaluations. It is further incumbent upon the campus administrator to follow the evaluation policies and procedures that are developed. It is then necessary that specific job-related performance criteria, those that are valid and observable, be used in the evaluation of an employee's performance so that it is clear to the employee that the performance level expected by a supervisor will enable the employee to achieve success in that workplace. Further, it is highly recommended that employees be given advance notice of performance criteria, the priorities and expectations of the administrator, and the procedures that will be followed, in order to minimize the degree of uncertainty in the process and to make clear that the process is as objective and nondiscriminatory as possible.

Implementation of Evaluation Policies

A number of cases have considered whether a failure to comply with evaluation procedures is a constitutional defect. These cases tend to reflect that problems with an evaluation do not rise to the level of a constitutional violation. While courts often find property rights to employment, there is seldom found a property right to a certain evaluation. A statutory right to an evaluation does not normally create a protected property right to continued employment, although at least one court has held that a teacher is entitled to a hearing, complete with cross examination, regarding whether the statutory criteria were followed in assessing a teacher.[13] The typical due process notion of notice and a hearing before deprivation of a property right, therefore, seldom applies to an evaluation. Courts have held that federal procedural due process does not entitle any employee to an evaluation or any related procedures, although that may be required under state law or board policy.[14] Even if a statutory evaluation process creates a protected property interest, however, an "unsatisfactory" evaluation does not normally constitute egregious official misconduct sufficient to trigger a violation of substantive due process.[15] In addition, stigmatizing comments on a performance evaluation do not normally implicate an employee's liberty interests because evaluation comments are not normally made public and, therefore, do not impair an employee's rights to a good name, reputation, honor, or integrity, as required to support a liberty interest due process claim.[16] The courts have even held that an evaluation policy that is established by a school district board of education does not create a right to re-employment by a nontenured teacher,[17] although the evaluation procedure itself may be subject to mandatory negotiation in a collective bargaining state.[18]

That does not mean, however, that those conducting evaluations need not follow procedures. The responsibility to implement evaluation policies and to document compliance with those policies is typically the responsibility of the campus principal. In general, the courts adopt a standard called "substantial compliance" in determining whether or not a campus principal complied with required procedures.[19] This standard of "substantial compliance," as opposed to "full and complete compliance," attempts to avoid placing an undue burden on a school administrator.[20] Supervising administrators are not required to ensure that every employee fully understands every suggestion for improvement or the means by which an employee might obtain assistance in making required improvements.[21] However, failures to comply with essential elements of evaluation policies can result in reinstatements for school employees when it is determined those employees have been improperly subjected to inadequate, incomplete, or prejudicial performance evaluations, or when an essential criterion for assessment, such as student performance, has not been considered.[22] Furthermore, a violation of an evaluation statute has, in at least one situation, resulted in reinstatement of a school employee, when it was impossible to evaluate the employee because she was off work on approved medical leave.[23]

Elements of Appropriate Evaluation Systems

In order to avoid later contentions that an evaluation system is arbitrary or capricious, it is essential that evaluation criteria be valid and observable and directly related to the job. These job-related criteria must be relevant to the job performance and validly related to the requirements of the position.[24]

While not always essential, employees should also receive advance notice of potential consequences of good and of bad evaluations.[25] While it can certainly be argued that professional employees know the consequences of good and bad evaluations, because different systems result in different management decisions based on evaluations, employees should understand the consequences of failing to improve job performance after receipt of evaluations in their school systems.

The most effective evaluation environment is that in which the supervisor develops a pattern of continual feedback regarding the employee's job performance so that nothing on a summative performance evaluation comes as a surprise to the employee. This can be done informally, by discussing situations as they arise, or on a more formal basis, through appropriate documentation.

A good evaluation system starts with a pre-observation conference, at which a supervisor informs the employee of the supervisor's criteria, the supervisor's priorities and expectations, and the procedure that will be used for the evaluation. This conference should be documented so that it is clear that the pre-observation conference occurred. At this point, it is appropriate for the employee to have input into that evaluation process. This participation can come in the form of a pre-observation discussion of expectations, plans and goals, or warnings and should give the employee the opportunity to inform the evaluator of any special circumstances that the evaluator may observe. The pre-observation conference can also help to insure that an employee understands what conduct will be assessed and how it will be assessed so that both the evaluator and the employee can focus on the appropriate elements of the employee's performance.[26]

After the supervisor has observed employee performance, timely notice of specific performance deficiencies that are related to the employee's job performance should be provided to the employee. Those deficiencies should be consistent with the job-related evaluation criteria that were originally established. If they are not, then either those deficiencies do not hinge upon appropriate job performance, or the criteria upon which the evaluation is based should be revised.[27] This timely notice should be in written form but should also be presented orally to the employee so that frank person-to-person communication can occur, misunderstandings can be corrected, and expectations can be clarified.[28]

The written document should be closely edited to insure that there are no typographical, factual, or other embarrassing errors that could take the focus off of the purpose of the evaluation, discredit the evaluator, or be used as evidence in any administrative or judicial proceeding or made public through some other means. A post-observation evaluation conference should also provide an employee an opportunity to respond to the comments that were made by the evaluator. After the conference, the employee should be provided with an opportunity to respond in writing to an unsatisfactory performance evaluation, and the supervisor should review that response so that errors can be corrected and all sides of a story can be considered.[29] In some jurisdictions, the employee is allowed to grieve that performance evaluation to the board or beyond, or to have some other measure of oversight.[30]

If a campus principal is concerned that an employee will allege that the principal has shown bias in the evaluation of the employee, it is always a good idea for the campus principal to bring in objective third parties to also observe the teacher's performance. These observation evaluations by trained evaluators can confirm deficiencies discovered by the principal and can provide additional assistance to the employee in remediating improper job performance. Further, these outside evaluators will not be perceived as having the same alleged bias as an on-campus professional. They, therefore, strengthen evidence that may be presented in any later proceeding.[31] It is likely that a school board or a court would rely to a greater degree on multiple reports by different evaluators that confirm a specific performance deficiency of an employee. Of course, the supervisor does run the risk that a different evaluator may find an employee's performance to be satisfactory, which could jeopardize any future remediation attempts or adverse employment actions contemplated by the supervisor. Should such an evaluation occur, it is incumbent upon the campus administrator to seriously review his or her evaluation of the employee's performance to determine whether or not bias does, in fact, exist.

Remediation of Employee Job Performance

It is essential that all employees be evaluated in a uniform manner and that all employees be given an opportunity to remediate perceived correctable performance deficiencies. In a Fifth Circuit termination case, an employer was held liable for race discrimination against a minority employee who was given consistently good evaluations and pay raises, in spite of performance deficiencies. The employee's supervisor stated that the good evaluations were given in an effort to avoid any confrontations with the employee about her work. The supervisor further admitted that he instructed other employees to give her good evaluations in order to avoid charges of race discrimination by the employee. The Fifth Circuit held that by ignoring its own evaluation procedures, the employer discriminated against the employee by not giving her the same opportunity to improve her job performance as the employer did of white employees who received honest evaluations.[32]

A remediation plan for the improvement of an employee's job performance should be developed in cooperation with the employee. The remediation plan should note the specific deficiencies that are being targeted, methods by which the employee can remediate the specific job performance areas, and objective criteria for determining whether or not the employee has accomplished the goal of remediating his or her job performance. Finally, a remediation plan should include a timeline for remediation of the performance.[33] A reasonable time period for an employee to complete a remediation plan should be allowed. The nature of the performance deficiencies, the nature of the employment, the extent of the person's education and experience, and the egregiousness of the conduct all factor into the amount of time that is required for remediation of performance.[34] For example, it may only take one day to learn to stand at the classroom door and greet students with a smile when they enter. On the contrary, it may take a year to perfect implementation of a new computer curriculum.

What if an employee refuses to cooperate in the development of a growth plan or objects to the supervisor's expectations? As long as the supervisor is consistent in his or her expectations, it is within the supervisor's discretion to require certain job performance standards. Therefore, while a certain amount of "give and take" is to be expected in the development of a growth plan, a supervisor ultimately can, and should, set job-performance standards and expect those standards to be consistently met.

Prior to making an adverse employment decision to nonrenew, nonextend, terminate or demote an employee, it is recommended that all anecdotal records regarding all previous job performance issues, including classroom observations and complaints by parents or fellow workers, be compiled. These anecdotal records and formal and informal reports contribute to the overall weight of the evidence to be accorded an unsatisfactory job evaluation.[35] They will form the basis of any adverse employment action.

Avoiding Legal Claims

Courts have frequently considered whether poor performance evaluations constitute "adverse employment actions" sufficient to present discrimination or retaliation claims in court, most often requiring tangible changes in working conditions or duties, or material changes in salary or position before an actionable adverse employment action is found.[36] On the other hand, a negative evaluation that results in denial of a raise could constitute an adverse employment action sufficient to maintain a discrimination or retaliation claim.[37]

The very nature of an employee evaluation system requires that the supervisor discriminate between effective and noneffective employees. It is very important, however, that a supervisor be careful to not illegally discriminate against any employee. Furthermore, it is incumbent upon a supervisor to refrain from any sort of retaliation, especially when an employee has exercised a constitutional or statutory right.

Federal protections against illegal discrimination and retaliation include free speech on matters of public concern;[38] illegal discrimination on the basis of race, national origin, religion, and/or sex;[39] illegal discrimination on the basis of age;[40] or illegal discrimination on the basis of disability.[41] The supervisor must also avoid discrimination or retaliation on the basis of pension interests,[42] wage and hour complaints,[43] workplace safety,[44] garnishment of indebtedness,[45] refusal to submit to a polygraph test,[46] union membership or political party membership,[47] or medical leave for family or self,[48] among others. Depending on the state, numerous state protections and common law protections also exist to protect an employee against illegal discrimination or retaliation.

To avoid potential state defamation claims, evaluations must also be truthful and accurate, and the negative comments made in evaluations should be kept confidential from all except the employee being evaluated. As long as comments in an evaluation are truthful and are not made public to third parties, an employee will not be able to claim that he or she was defamed or that his or her good name and reputation was impaired.[49] In fact, in some states, teacher evaluations are expressly made confidential by law.[50]

Recommendations for Practice

1. Develop sound evaluation policies and procedures and follow them.
2. Apply specific job-related performance criteria that are valid, observable, and related to an employee's job performance.
3. Give advance notice of performance criteria, priorities, and expectations and the procedures that will be used.
4. Give advance notice of potential consequences of good and bad evaluations.

5. Consider employee input into the process.
6. Develop a pattern of continual feedback regarding job performance.
7. Proofread all documentation before presentation to the employee.
8. Timely inform the employee of specific evaluation problems orally and in writing.
9. Allow the employee to respond to evaluations, either orally; in writing; or through a grievance, appeal, or arbitration process.
10. Evaluate all employees in a uniform manner to avoid the inference of discrimination.
11. Ensure that evaluations are truthful and accurate.
12. Keep evaluations confidential from all except the employee being evaluated.
13. Do not use an evaluation to retaliate against any employee for any legally protected conduct or to discriminate based on any legally protected status.
14. Develop a remediation plan in cooperation with the employee, if necessary. Follow-up on the remediation plan with periodic check ups.
15. Provide a reasonable time for the employee to correct deficiencies, with activities actually designed to correct performance problem areas.
16. Allow more than one evaluator to observe an employee if there are concerns regarding objectivity or bias.
17. Make all employment decisions based on job performance as a whole, using all available documents, including evaluations.
18. If making an adverse employment decision, follow all constitutional, statutory, and contractual procedures.

Endnotes

[1] Simmons v. New Pub. Sch. Dist. No. 8, 574 N.W.2d 561 (N.D. 1999); WEST FLA. STAT. §1012.34.

[2] 9 W.VA. C.S.R. § 126–141–2.6 (2007); West Virginia Board of Education Policy § 5300(6)(a).

[3] West v. San Jon Bd. of Educ., 79 P.3d 842 (N.M. Ct. App. 2003); Harjo v. Bd. of Educ. of Indep. Sch. Dist. No. 7 of Seminole Co., 976 P.2d 1096 (Okla. Civ. App. 1999); W. VA. CODE § 18A–2–8 (Repl. Vol. 2007).

[4] Savre v. Indep. Sch. Dist. No. 283, 642 N.W.2d 467 (Minn. App. 2002).

[5] Gonzalez v. State Operated Sch. Dist. of Newark, 784 A.2d 101 (N.J. Super. Ct. App. Div. 2001).

[6] Maxey v. McDowell Co. Bd. of Educ., 575 S.E.2d 278 (W. Va. 2002); *see also* Boss v. Filmore Co. Sch. Dist. No. 19, 559 N.W.2d 448 (Neb. 1997).

[7] *Id.*

[8] *Id.*

[9] Roberts v. Houston Indep. Sch. Dist., 788 S.W.2d 107 (Tex. App. 1990).

[10] Briggs v. Bd. of Dirs. of Hinton Comm. Sch. Dist., 282 N.W.2d 740, 743 (Iowa 1979).

[11] Chicago Bd. of Educ. v. Smith, 664 N.E.2d 113 (Ill. Ct. App. 1996); Farmer v. Kelleys Island Bd. of Educ., 630 N.E.2d 721 (Ohio 1994) (opinion clarified by 638 N.E.2d 79) (Ohio 1994); Hellman v. Union Sch. Dist., 170 S.W. 3d 52 (Mo. App. E.D. 2005).

[12] Hoffner v. Bismarck Pub. Sch. Dist., 589 N.W.2d 195 (N.D. 1999); Dakos v. Lorain City Sch. Dist. Bd. of Educ., No. 01–CA–007888, 2002 WL 57977 (Ohio Ct. App. Jan. 16, 2002).

[13] Yates v. District of Columbia, 224 F. Supp. 2d 68 (D.D.C. 2002), *aff'd on other grounds,* 324 F.3d 724 (D.C. Cir. 2003); Witgenstein v. Sch. Bd. of Leon County, 347 So.2d 1069 (Fla. App. 1 Dist 1977).

[14] Atencio v. Bd. of Educ. of Penasco Indep. Sch. Dist. No. 4, 658 F.2d 774, 779 (10th Cir. 1981); Wood v. Indep. Sch. Dist. No. 141 of Pottawatomie County, 661 P.2d 892 (Okla. 1983); and Goodrich v. Newport News Sch. Bd., 743 F.2d 225 (4th Cir. 1984).

[15] Yates v. District of Columbia, 324 F.3d 724 (D.C. Cir. 2003).

[16] Echtenkamp v. Loudon County Pub. Schs., 263 F. Supp. 2d 1043 (E.D. Va. 2003).

[17] King v. Jefferson County Bd. of Educ., 659 So. 2d 686 (Ala. Civ. App. 1995).

[18] *In re* Pittsfield Sch. Dist., 744 A.2d 594 (N.H. 1999).

[19] McKenzie v. Webster Parish Sch. Bd., 653 So. 2d 215 (La. Ct. App. 1995); Thomas v. Bd. of Educ. of Newark City Sch. Dist., 643 N.E.2d 131 (Ohio 1994); White Mountain Reg'l Sch. Dist., 154 N.H. 136, 908 A. 2d 790 (N.H. 2006).

[20] *Thomas*, 643 N.E.2d 131, 134 (Ohio 1994).

[21] *Dakos*, 2002 WL 57977 (Ohio Ct. App. 2002).

[22] Snyder v. Mendon-Union Local Sch. Dist. Bd. of Educ., 661 N.E.2d 717 (Ohio 1996); Sherrod v. Palm Beach Co. Sch. Bd., 2006 WL 3207981 (Fla. App. 4 Dist. 2006).

[23] Skilton v. Perry Local Sch. Dist. Bd. of Educ., No. 2001–L–140, 2002 WL 31744700 (Ohio Ct. App. Dec. 6, 2002), *aff'd by* 807 N.E.2d 919 (Ohio 2004).

[24] Meyer v. Bd. of Educ. of Charlotte Valley Cent. Sch. Dist., 581 N.Y.S.2d 920 (N.Y. App. Div. 1992).

[25] McQuinn v. Douglas County Sch. Dist. No. 66, 612 N.W.2d 198 (Neb. 2000).

[26] Crump v. Durham County Bd. of Educ., 327 S.E.2d 599 (N.C. Ct. App. 1985).

[27] Iversen v. Wall Bd. of Educ., 522 N.W.2d 188 (S.D. 1994); Hendrickson v. Spartanburg Co. Sch. Dist. No. 5, 413 S.E.2d 871 (S.C. Ct. App. 1992).

[28] *Maxey*, 575 S.E.2d 278 (W. Va. 2002).

[29] *In re* Lincoln-Woodstock Coop Sch. Dist., 731 A.2d 992 (N.H. 1999).

[30] Homan v. Blue Ridge Sch. Dist., 405 A.2d 572 (Pa. Commw. Ct. 1979).

[31] Cliff v. Bd. of Sch. Comm'rs of Indianapolis, 42 F.3d 403 (7th Cir. 1994); Spry v. Winston-Salem-Forsyth County Bd. of Educ., 412 S.E.2d 687 (N.C. Ct. App. 1992), *aff'd* 422 S.E.2d 575 (N.C. 1992).

[32] Vaughn v. Edel, 918 F.2d 517, 523 (5th Cir. 1990).

[33] Kurey v. New York State Sch. for the Deaf, 642 N.Y.S.2d 415 (N.Y. App. Div. 1996); Newcomb v. Humansville R-IV Sch. Dist., 908 S.W.2d 821 (Mo. Ct. App. 1995); Thomas v. Bd. of Educ. of Newark City Sch. Dist., 643 N.E.2d 131 (Ohio 1994).

[34] Gayno v. Indep. Sch. Dist. No. 832, 311 N.W.2d 497 (Minn. 1981); Mason County Bd. of Educ. v. State Superintendent of Schs., 274 S.E.2d 435 (W. Va. 1980).

[35] Seifert v. Lingleville Indep. Sch. Dist., 692 S.W.2d 461 (Tex. 1985); Aigner v. Cass Sch. Township of LaPorte County, 577 N.E.2d 983 (Ind. Ct. App. 1991); and Beck v. James, 793 S.W.2d 416 (Mo. Ct. App. 1990).

[36] Weimann v. Indianola Cmty. Sch. Dist., 278 F. Supp. 2d 968 (S.D. Iowa 2003).

[37] Sprenger v. Fed. Home Loan Bank of Des Moines, 253 F.3d 1106 (8th Cir. 2001).

[38] Pickering v. Bd. of Educ. of Township High Sch. Dist. 205, 391 U.S. 563 (1968); Levich v. Liberty Cent. Sch. Dist, 361 F. Supp. 2d 151 (S.D. N.Y. 2004).

[39] 42 U.S.C. § 2000e *et seq.* (2007); 42 U.S.C. § 1981 (2007); Burlington N. & Santa Fe Railway Co. v. White, 126 S. Ct. 2405 (2006).

[40] 29 U.S.C. § 631 *et seq.* (2007).

[41] 29 U.S.C. § 793 *et seq.* (2007); 42 U.S.C. § 12101 *et seq.* (2007).

[42] 29 U.S.C. § 1140 *et seq.* (2007).

[43] 29 U.S.C. § 215 (2007).

[44] 29 U.S.C. § 660 (2007).

[45] 15 U.S.C. § 1674(a) (2007).

[46] 29 U.S.C. § 2001 *et seq.* (2007).

[47] 29 U.S.C. § 158 (2007); Alaniz v. San Isidro Indep. Sch. Dist., 742 F.2d 207 (5th Cir. 1984).

[48] 29 U.S.C. § 2601 *et seq.* (2007).

[49] *Echtenkamp*, 263 F. Supp. 2d 1043 (E.D. Va. 2003).

[50] Tex. Educ. Code § 21.355 (West 2007).

Chapter 26

Student Injury

Suzanne Eckes & Jesulon Gibbs

Introduction

School districts have become increasingly concerned about legal liability resulting from student injury. This concern is justifiable considering that legal problems in this area are increasing in number and are becoming more complex.[1] In order to avoid litigation, it is imperative that educators become familiar with laws involving student tort liability. Liability stemming from student injury generally occurs in one of two ways. Either parents, on behalf of the injured student, bring a negligence or other tort claim against the school district under state tort law, or parents pursue relief under federal and state civil rights acts. This chapter will focus on the former, tort law.

Torts are civil wrongs resulting in personal injury and/or injury to one's property or reputation.[2] Tort law offers civil remedies to individuals who are harmed by the unreasonable conduct of others. Educators are held to a high duty of care and, therefore, must be conscious of potential liability. Negligence occurs when the conduct of school personnel unintentionally fails to meet an acceptable standard of care. Oftentimes, negligence in schools focuses on whether a reasonable person in the school official's position could have anticipated the harm. In contrast to negligence, in intentional tort cases, liability is imposed due to an individual's conscious decision to cause the particular harm.[3] Intentional torts include assault and battery, false imprisonment, and intentional infliction of emotional distress. Defamation is also considered a tort. Defamation involves an injury to one's reputation, generally through libel and/or slander. Most tort actions are heard in state court. Generally, punitive damages are not available in tort cases, and a plaintiff must affirmatively prove actual compensatory damages.

Legal Issues

Elements Needed to Establish Negligence

There are four elements that must be proven to prevail on a negligence claim: (1) the plaintiff must demonstrate that the school owes a particular duty to the injured student(s); (2) the duty must be breached by the failure to exercise an appropriate standard of care; (3) the negligent conduct must be the proximate cause of the injury; and (4) an actual injury must occur.[4]

It is also important to note that if the student injury that occurred was not foreseeable, there is no liability. In other words, in order for school personnel to be found liable, school personnel must have knowledge or notice of the particular dangerous practice or activity with respect to which the injury occurred.[5] The courts have often held that school personnel are not required to anticipate all acts that occur in schools.[6]

Duty of Care. School personnel acting within the scope of their employment have a duty to supervise students. In general, regarding teachers, the teacher has a duty to act as a reasonable and prudent teacher. Courts have adopted the common law standard for determining reasonableness.[7] This objective standard requires that teachers provide the same level of care as reasonably prudent professionals of similar education and background. Some factors that may be taken into consideration when determining such a standard include age, training, education, and experience.[8] Consistent with this reasoning is that when students are adequately supervised, school personnel should prevent students from being injured by reasonably foreseeable dangers. In the classroom, the teacher is responsible for supervising the students. In one case, when a ninth-grade student hit another student with a pencil, causing an eye injury, the teacher was held liable because evidence demonstrated that the teacher had poor classroom management.[9] In this case, the court noted that the teacher owed a duty to her students in providing a safe learning environment.[10]

A duty to supervise also extends to extracurricular activities or field trips sponsored by the school. One court did not find a school district liable when a young student was injured on a hay ride during a school field trip.[11] Although the student's parents alleged that the district did not provide adequate supervision on the trip, the court found that the district met its duty in supervising the students because there were plenty of adults present.[12] In another case, the court reasoned that the degree of supervision required on a field trip depends on the degree of the foreseeable danger.[13] Specifically, the court noted that teachers were not responsible for the assault on a student who was beaten by local juveniles with no connection to the school while on a field trip to a museum.[14] While the students had been released by teachers to tour the museum without direct supervision, the court found that it was nearly impossible for a teacher to have a duty to watch every student at all times in a large museum.[15]

School officials may also have a duty before or after school. For example, once school officials know, or should know, that students are present before or after school, they must take the necessary steps to supervise the students.[16] The requisite level of supervision may decrease during these non-school hours if school officials are not aware that students are on school property. Further, a school district has a duty to protect students walking to and from school in certain situations. For example, when a student walking home from school was struck by a truck as she crossed a street, the school district was liable because of the negligence of the crossing guard, the district's failure to provide adequate safety precautions, and the district's failure to provide instructions for the students.[17] In another case, a student was injured when he was struck by a car on his way home from school on an early dismissal day. The school district's motion for summary judgment was denied because the court needed to consider whether the school had adopted a reasonable early dismissal policy.[18]

Finally, the amount of duty one must provide often depends on the age of the student. Some states have recognized that a different set of criteria are used when considering the tortious acts of minors. When determining the negligence of a minor defendant, courts often consider the following: minors under the age of seven years are conclusively presumed incapable of negligence; minors over the age of fourteen years are presumptively capable of negligence; minors between the ages of seven and fourteen are presumed incapable of negligence; however, such presumption is rebuttable and grows weaker as students approach age fourteen.[19]

Breach of Duty. School officials are expected to use ordinary care in controlling and disciplining students.[20] Teachers are considered to have breached their duty of care when they fail to conform to this standard of care. A breach of duty could occur when a teacher omitted or failed to be reasonable under the circumstances. For example, when a student was injured after another student hit him with a piece of beef jerky during study hall, the school district did not prevail because evidence demonstrated that the injury may have been foreseeable.[21] In this case, school officials were aware of students throwing objects during study hall on previous occasions. The court also noted that school officials had a duty to properly monitor the fifty students in the study hall and may have breached their duty in failing to provide adequate supervision.[22]

In contrast, when a seventeen-year-old student was injured during a woodshop class, the court held that the teacher was not responsible for the accident.[23] The student in this case was injured when she attempted to remove a piece of wood from an operating machine and severed two of her fingers.[24] When deciding this case, the court considered the age and maturity of the student and whether the teacher had provided adequate supervision and instruction.[25] The court noted that before the student used the saw, the teacher had demonstrated how to safely operate the saw and had issued a safety booklet.[26] The court also considered that the teacher had been adequately assisting this student and that the accident occurred only when the teacher turned his attention to another student.[27] Considering these facts, combined with the maturity of this student, the court found that the teacher did not breach his duty to this student.[28]

Causation. It must also be proven that the defendant's conduct was the "cause in fact" of the injury. Several tests exist to demonstrate cause in fact; the most well-known is the "but for" test. Under this test, the plaintiff must show that the injury would not have occurred "but for" the defendant's act. In addition to proving cause in fact, the defendant's conduct must also be a proximate cause of the injury. Specifically, there must be a causal connection between the defendant's alleged misconduct and the resulting injury. A component of breach and causation is the foreseeability of the incident. In deciding the issue of proximate cause, courts will consider whether the defendant could or should have seen the potentially dangerous consequences of the action (or inaction, in some situations) when it was taken. In one example, an elementary school student was injured after she fell off a cement barrel that was part of the playground equipment.[29] The students' parents alleged that school officials were negligent in supervising the playground.[30] The court ruled in favor of the district, finding that the playground monitors had warned the student not to play on the top of the cement barrel.[31]

Injury. Even if the above three elements are met, there must also be evidence of an actual injury to prevail on a negligence claim. For example, if a student falls off a swing during recess because the swing was broken, the student must have an actual injury in order to bring a negligence claim. A scraped knee, for example, would probably not suffice.

Defenses to Negligence

Four principal defenses that are frequently interposed by school districts in actions based on negligence are the doctrines of immunity, assumption of risk, contributory negligence, and comparative negligence.

Immunity. Under the doctrine of sovereign or governmental immunity, adopted by several states, usually through legislation, the state (including the public school district) is immune from tort liability, unless it has assumed such liability by constitutional provision or legislative enactment.[32] The theory of immunity is based on the premise that public schools are funded with taxpayer dollars, and as a result, private individuals who are suing a school would actually be suing themselves. In order to avoid bankrupting the state, a state can grant school districts immunity from negligence claims. Immunity statutes vary widely among states. One court accepted the immunity defense when a student sustained injuries after a mini-trampoline accident at school.[33] The court relied on a state code that insulated school districts from liability when a defendant did not act in a "willful or wanton" manner.[34] In this case, the court found that school officials acted reasonably and that the state's immunity law therefore protected the school district from liability.

Similarly, in another case, immunity protected a teacher supervising the physical education class from a negligence action brought by an injured student. The court reasoned that if school teachers performing everyday functions were hauled into court for similar conduct, fewer individuals will aspire to be teachers.[35] The court stated more specifically that those who have embarked on a career in education will be reluctant to act, and the orderly administration of the school systems (and, by extension, an important arm of the government) will suffer, all to the detriment of our youth and public at large.[36]

Many states have repudiated sovereign immunity; thus, school districts tend to focus on the remaining three defenses.[37] While some school districts still use immunity, courts are moving toward requiring school districts to be responsible for their actions.[38]

Contributory Negligence. School districts use the defense of contributory negligence when the student contributed to his or her own injuries. Contributory negligence is a strict rule because a plaintiff who is 1 percent negligent can be prohibited from recovery. The plaintiff's contributory negligence bars recovery against a defendant whose negligent conduct would otherwise make him liable to the plaintiff for the harm sustained by him. In other words, when the defendant has violated his duty, has been negligent, and would otherwise be liable, the plaintiff is denied recovery because his or her own conduct in conjunction with the defendant's disentitles him or her to maintain the action. Under this defense, both parties are at fault, and the defense is one of the plaintiff's disability rather than the defendant's innocence.[39]

In one case, a student brought an action against a teacher and the school district for injuries stemming from an explosion after another student took potassium chlorate from an unattended chemical storage room without the teacher's knowledge or consent.[40] The court held that the fifteen-year-old student and the student who took the chemical knew that the chemical formula was powerful, dangerous, and risky. Given their knowledge of the danger involved, the court concluded that the students were contributorily negligent in this situation.[41] In another case, a man fell off a set of bleachers and was injured during a high school basketball game. The man filed a negligence action against the school district because there was no back rail on the bleachers. The school district argued that the man was contributorily negligent. The court agreed, reasoning that the man could see that the bleachers had no back rail and that he therefore contributed to his own injuries.[42]

Assumption of Risk. Assumption of risk occurs when school officials argue that the student knew of the risk involved yet still participated in the activity. While assumption of risk is somewhat related to contributory negligence, the two doctrines are not synonymous. In contrast to contributory negligence, assumption of risk means that the plaintiff, in advance, has given his or her express consent to relieve the defendant of responsibility for injuries common to the activity.[43] Similar to contributory negligence, a plaintiff who voluntarily assumes a risk of harm rising from the negligent or reckless conduct of the defendant cannot recover for such harm.

Specifically, to satisfy the assumption of risk defense, the evidence must show that the victim had general knowledge of a possible danger or harm and that he or she understood the specific risk confronting him or her. For example, when a student was injured while playing in a varsity high school football game, one court held that the possibility of injury to a voluntary participant in a varsity high school tackle football game was a normal, obvious, and usual incident of the activity.[44] The court reasoned that participants in athletics accept the normal physical contact of the particular sport.[45] The school district's use of the assumption of risk defense was successful in this case. In another case, however, the court found that the assumption of risk defense was not a valid argument.[46] In this case, an injured student and her mother sued the school district and an instructor for negligence after her daughter was struck in the head by a golf ball during golf class. The parent had signed an enrollment contract agreeing that the school would not be liable for all damages arising from personal injury. They also signed an athletic form stating that the guardians assume the risk of injuries in interscholastic activities. The court denied the school district's motion for summary judgment because the student's claims were related to the negligent supervision of a school activity.[47]

Comparative Negligence. The comparative negligence defense divides the damages between the parties who are at fault. Under comparative negligence, there is a reduction of damages to be recovered by the negligent plaintiff in proportion to his or her fault. "Pure" comparative negligence is used to apportion the costs of an accident based on the relative fault of both the plaintiff and the defendant.[48] For example, an elementary school student was injured when she fell at school. The parent alleged that the school district was negligent because the teacher did not provide proper supervision in the bathroom and because the slippery floor was unreasonably dangerous. The court found that the school board was 75 percent liable and the student was 25 percent liable in this case.[49]

The most common legislative approach for apportioning fault is the modified or "50 percent" system, under which a plaintiff's contributory negligence does not bar recovery as long as it remains below a specified proportion of the total fault. There are two varieties of the 50 percent comparative negligence approach. Under the "equal fault bar" approach, a plaintiff cannot recover anything if his fault is equal to or greater than that of the defendant.[50] Under the "greater fault bar" system, the plaintiff is prevented from all recovery only if his or her fault exceeds the defendant's; he or she is therefore allowed to recover if his or her negligence is equal to or less than that of the defendant.[51]

The rise of comparative negligence has forced the courts and commentators to reconsider the role of assumption of risk and contributory negligence. In several states, general statutes applicable to all negligence actions have annulled the contributory negligence rule and have created the doctrine of comparative negligence. Bearing this in mind, it is important for educators to be aware of the legal trend in their respective state.

Intentional Torts

An intentional tort requires a deliberate act toward another individual. As mentioned, liability is imposed without fault in intentional tort cases. For school districts, the most common types of intentional torts include assault, battery, false imprisonment, and intentional infliction of emotional distress.

Assault and Battery. Assault occurs when someone is placed in apprehension of immediate harm. Generally, an assault must contain not only threatening words but also an offer of physical violence. Assault is often considered a mental attack. In order to be successful in an assault claim, the plaintiff must feel reasonable apprehension. An example would be a student threatening another student with a toy knife. If the student being threatened believed that the knife was real and was fearful, the student with the knife could be liable for assault. In contrast, battery is an actual physical attack. In the example just cited, the student with the toy knife would actually need to physically strike the other student for the injured student to have a battery claim.

In the past, students have made battery claims against school personnel. In one case, a student was unsuccessful when she accused the assistant principal of assault and battery when he physically restrained the student for failing to present her hall pass.[52] The court reasoned that the assistant principal was reasonably carrying out his duties.[53] In other cases, students have also claimed that corporal punishment constitutes battery, but courts have generally not agreed with this claim unless the educator acted with malice.[54]

False Imprisonment. False imprisonment may be claimed when students are unjustifiably restrained against their will. While the student must be aware of the restraint, the student does not need to demonstrate specific damages. Generally, school authorities could be liable for false imprisonment if the student is confined within certain fixed boundaries, the teacher's action directly or indirectly results in such a confinement of the student, and the student is conscious of the confinement or is harmed by it.[55] For example, there was enough evidence for a successful false imprisonment claim when a teacher chained a student to a tree while the rest of the students in the class were painting troughs around the trees.[56] The teacher chained the student to the tree for approximately twenty-five minutes in order to prevent him from leaving the class early.[57]

Intentional Infliction of Emotional Distress. Intentional infliction of emotional distress is available to individuals who have suffered from severe mental anguish. In order to prevail on such a claim, the plaintiff must prove that the extreme and outrageous conduct occurred intentionally or recklessly and caused severe emotional distress. When a superintendent re-assigned a teacher from her administrator's position at a substantially lower salary, the teacher was unsuccessful in her claim for intentional infliction of emotional distress.[58] The court held that such a re-assignment of duties does not support a claim of intentional infliction of emotional distress because there was no proof of extreme and outrageous conduct by the superintendent.[59] Although this standard has been hard to meet, there have been a few plaintiffs that have prevailed on a claim of intentional infliction of emotional distress.[60] In *Baird v. Rose*, for example, a middle school student sustained a claim for intentional infliction of emotional distress against her music teacher after the teacher humiliated the student in class. The teacher singled her out for application of an absence policy, which prevented the student from performing with the choir. The student suffered from depression and missed school often, and the evidence pointed to the teacher using the disability against the student, to further emotional, psychological, and physical injury.[61]

Defamation

Defamation is also considered a tort. Defamation is an injury to one's reputation. It involves the intentional or negligent unprivileged communication of a false statement to a third party about the plaintiff. Written defamation is known as libel, while spoken defamation is known as slander. In one case, an elementary school principal brought a defamation action against parents who wrote a letter critical of her official conduct.[62] The court held that a public elementary school principal was a public official who could not recover for defamation without proving actual malice. Actual malice means the defendant acted with knowledge that the statements were false or with reckless disregard of whether the statements were true or false.[63] When considering whether defamation has occurred, courts consider whether the targeted person is a public or private individual.[64] While private individuals need to prove only that the statement was false, public individuals (i.e., public officials or public figures) must also demonstrate that the statement was made with malice or reckless disregard for the truth. Definitions of who constitutes a public official or public figure vary by state.[65]

Recommendations for Practice

1. The student handbook should include all policies and expectations regarding appropriate behavior.
2. Rules and expectations of students should be reviewed with all students and staff.
3. School personnel should routinely inspect facilities to reduce potential hazards.
4. School personnel should be trained on the elements of negligence instead of just being told to "never leave your classroom" for fear of negligence lawsuits.
5. If an item is in disrepair on the playground or in the school, appropriate school personnel should be immediately notified, and the problem should be rectified.
6. School personnel should eliminate potential hazards to students, such as faulty equipment or other protruding objects in and around the school building.
7. Parents should be informed of any major change in the school climate that is potentially hazardous. The school should discuss how it will remedy the problem.

8. When physical restraints are necessary, school authorities need to document the circumstances detailing why such actions were necessary.
9. School personnel should establish supervision responsibilities for events and extracurricular activities.
10. School personnel should be reminded that permission slips do not negate negligent supervision.
11. Educators should be aware whether their state has adopted the comparative negligence defense.

Endnotes

1 Susan D. Looney, *Education and the Legal System*, *in* TORTS AND SCH. LIABILITY 23, 44 (2004).
2 THOMAS R. MCDANIEL, SCHOOL LAW FOR SOUTH CAROLINA ADMINISTRATORS 101 (2007).
3 NELDA H. CAMBRON-MCCABE, ET AL., PUBLIC SCHOOL LAW: TEACHERS' AND STUDENTS' RIGHTS 102 (5th ed. 2004).
4 Bill Evans & Suzanne Eckes, *Tort Law and Public Schools*, *in* THE YEARBOOK OF EDUCATION LAW 142-165 (Charles Russo ed., 2006).
5 Rodriguez v. Bd. of Educ. of N.Y., 480 N.Y.S.2d 717 (N.Y. App. Div. 1984); Santee v. Orleans Parish Sch. Bd. 430 So. 2d 254 (La. Ct. App. 1983).
6 *See* Morris v. Ortiz, 437 P.2d 652 (Ariz. 1968).
7 *See* CHARLES J. RUSSO, REUTTER'S, THE LAW OF PUBLIC EDUCATION (5th ed. 2004).
8 *See id.*
9 Maynard v. Bd. of Educ. of Massena Sch. Dist., 663 N.Y.S.2d 717 (N.Y. App. Div. 1997).
10 *See id.*
11 David v. City of New York, 835 N.Y.S.2d 377 (N.Y. App. Div. 2007).
12 *Id.*
13 Mancha v. Field Museum of Natural History, 283 N.E.2d 899 (Ill. App. Ct. 1972).
14 *See id.*
15 *See id.*
16 *See* RUSSO, *supra* note 7 at 414–15.
17 Robin C. Miller, Annotation, *Tort Liability of Public Schools and Institutions of Higher Learning for Injury to Student Walking To Or From School*, 72 A.L.R. 5th 469 (2004).
18 Jerkins *ex rel.* Jerkins v. Anderson, 922 A.2d 1279 (N.J. 2007).
19 Berman v. Phila. Bd. of Educ., 456 A.2d 545 (Pa. 1983).
20 L.W. v. McComb Separate Mun. Sch. Dist., 754 So. 2d 1136 (Miss. 1999).
21 Schirmer v. Bd. of Educ. of the Spencerport Cent. Sch. Dist., 824 N.Y.S.2d 697 (N.Y. App. Div. 2006).
22 *See id.*
23 Miles v. Sch. Dist. No. 138 of Cheyenne County, 281 N.W.2d 396 (Neb. 1979).
24 *See id.*
25 *See id.*
26 *See id.*
27 *See id.*
28 *See id.*
29 Rodriguez v. Elmont Sch. Dist., 829 N.Y.S.2d 221 (N.Y. App. Div. 2007).
30 *Id.*
31 *Id.*

[32] 33 A.L.R. 3d 703 (58).
[33] Murray v. Chi. Youth Ctr., 864 N.E.2d 176 (Ill. 2007).
[34] *See id.*
[35] Lentz v. Morris, 372 S.E.2d 608 (Va. 1988).
[36] *See id.*
[37] Paul Thurston & Donna Metzler, *Student Injury*, *in* PRINCIPAL'S LEGAL HANDBOOK 213, 219 (William E. Camp et al. eds., 2000).
[38] Susan D. Looney, *Education and the Legal System*, *in* TORTS AND SCHOOL LIABILITY 23, 44 (2004).
[39] PROSSER AND KEATON, ON THE LAW OF TORTS 131 at 481 (W. Page Keeton ed. 5th ed. 1984).
[40] Hutchison v. Toews, 476 P.2d 811 (Or. Ct. App. 1970).
[41] *See id.*
[42] Funston v. Sch. Town of Munster, 849 N.E.2d 595 (Ind. 2006).
[43] *See* PROSSER & KEETON, *supra* note 39 at 481.
[44] Hammond v. Bd. of Educ. of Carrol County, 639 A.2d 223 (Md. Ct. Spec. App. 1994).
[45] *See id.*
[46] Wu v. Shattuck-St. Mary's Sch., 393 F.Supp.2d 831 (D. Minn. 2005).
[47] *Id.*
[48] Jean W. Sexton, *Tort Law—Assumption of Risk and Pennsylvania's Comparative Negligence Statute*—Howell v. Clyde, 67 TEMP. L. REV. 903, 922 (1994).
[49] Agnor v. Caddo Parish Sch. Bd., 936 So. 2d 865 (La. Ct. App. 2006).
[50] *See* PROSSER & KEETON, *supra* note 39, at 473.
[51] *See id.*
[52] *Ex parte* Turner, 840 So. 2d 132 (Ala. 2002).
[53] *See id.*
[54] Hinson v. Holt, 776 So. 2d 804 (Ala. Civ. App. 1998).
[55] *See* CAMBRON-MCCABE, *supra* note 3, at 488–89.
[56] Banks v. Fritsch, 39 S.W.3d 474 (Ky. Ct. App. 2001).
[57] *See id.*
[58] *See* Wallace v. Casa Grande Union High Sch., Dist. No. 82, 909 P.2d 486 (Ariz. Ct. App. 1995).
[59] *See id.*
[60] Nims v. Harrison, 768 So. 2d 1198 (Fla. Dist. Ct. App. 2000).
[61] 192 F.3d 462 (4th Cir. 1999).
[62] Johnson v. Robbinsdale Indep. Sch. Dist. No. 281, 827 F. Supp. 1439 (D. Minn. 1993).
[63] *See id.*
[64] *See* CAMBRON-MCCABE, *supra* note 3, at 491.
[65] *See id.*

Chapter 27

Documentation

Kelly Frels

Introduction

The primary objective of a school district's employee evaluation system is to improve employees' performance so they can become successful and contribute to achieving the district's goals. If the evaluation process does not produce this positive result, the employee must be replaced, either by resignation or termination. The district's evaluation system thus serves a secondary function—the removal of the unsatisfactory employee.

Depending upon the nature of the employee's relationship or contract status with a school district, the district must observe various degrees of procedural due process before relieving a person of a position. In many situations, this process culminates with a hearing before the board of education or a hearing officer to determine whether cause exists to terminate the employee.

In school employee termination hearings, principals are often faced with the claim that there is too little documentation or evidence that assistance has been given to the employee and, as such, the principal has not done a sufficient job in working with the employee to remediate weaknesses. In other cases, the aggrieved employee claims that the principal has developed so much documentation that the employee has been harassed. At other employee termination hearings, the employee complains that the process is unfair and that he or she did not know what was expected in the performance of his or her duties. As a result of these assertions, there has been a noticeable unwillingness on the part of principals and other supervisors to bring a recommendation for termination to the superintendent or the board of education. In most situations, the supervisor recognizes that the supervisor, rather than the employee, will be put on trial at a hearing.

In an effort to provide support for the supervisor, especially principals, and to help ensure the fair treatment of employees who are evaluated, a simple but effective system of communication founded in documentation has been developed. This system can be used in conjunction with virtually any school district's evaluation system, as well as with a variety of contractual schemes authorized by state statutes. This documentation system is founded on the concept of communication, and its goal is to humanize the evaluation and documentation process with the ultimate objective of improving an employee's performance to an acceptable level. If an employee's performance does not improve, the system is designed to provide an incentive for voluntary resignation or, if voluntary resignation is not received, to provide the necessary documentation for the supervisor to have confidence in recommending the employee's termination.

For simplicity and to provide a focus, this chapter will use teachers as the representative employee group. Although this monograph refers to the teacher/principal relationship, the content is equally applicable to the relationship between a school employee and supervisor at any level, including colleges and universities. This chapter will also refer to memoranda with the intention that the comments are equally, if not more emphatically, applicable to emails, with which there is often less opportunity to analyze the impact of what one has written.[1]

Legal Issues

This communication and documentation system becomes an essential ingredient in preparing the district's principals and supervisors, not only for a hearing before a hearing officer or the board of education, but for appeals and lawsuits filed with a state commissioner of education, an arbitrator, or a court. This system can also provide the necessary documentation to sustain the termination if the employee files a discrimination complaint with the Equal Employment Opportunity Commission or the Department of Education. Furthermore, adherence to a system of this nature can help avoid First Amendment or whistleblower problems from becoming significant issues. If there is systematic documentation of poor performance before an employee engages in a protected speech activity, the performance deficiency may continue to be addressed as needed and termination recommended if required. In contrast, the absence of such documentation prior to an employee's engaging in a protected speech activity could brand the employee as legally untouchable because the documentation may appear to be retaliation for the employee's speech.[2]

Much has been written about the due process requirements involved in the termination process. Because that process varies by state and the nature of the employment relationship with a district, this monograph will not include a review of the procedural requirements necessary to effect a termination. Instead, it will provide practical advice to principals and other supervisors concerning the documentation that should be generated and used in the evaluation process and presented at any required hearing to support a recommendation for termination. It is important to remember that the due process rights of employees do not shield them from termination. Incapable or insubordinate employees can and should be terminated. Due process requirements simply prescribe procedures that must be followed in effectuating those terminations. Of course, the allowable grounds for termination will usually be enunciated in state law, an employment contract, and/or a collective bargaining agreement.

Thus, these sources must be examined to determine the criteria under which employees should be judged and evaluated.

The Documentation System

The documentation contemplated in a teacher evaluation system involves the use of several types of written memoranda. First, *memoranda to the file* should be sparingly used to serve as a supervisor's memory keys for less-significant infractions or deviations by a teacher. Second, *specific incident memoranda* should be used to record conferences with a teacher concerning a more significant event. Third, *summary memoranda* should be used to record conferences with a teacher in which several incidents, problems, or deficiencies are discussed. Fourth, *visitation memoranda* should record observations made of a teacher's on-the-job performance. Fifth, an *assessment instrument* should be used to evaluate the teacher's overall performance.

Documentation concerning a teacher can and should be used for several purposes. First, it allows the principal to follow a teacher's actions and performance, thus enabling the principal to pinpoint weaknesses and problem areas. Second, it informs the teacher of any problems or deficiencies and provides valuable information concerning the necessary corrective steps the teacher must take to improve. Third, if a teacher's performance does not improve, it serves as concrete evidence to support a recommendation for termination.

The process outlined below should keep the volume of documents to a minimum, yet meet the need for full and complete documentation. This documentation system anticipates that a district has an evaluation system and that the system attempts to take into account the practicalities of the time constraints placed on school principals and other supervisors. By following the suggested documentation process below, the goals of improving employee performance or removing an unsatisfactory teacher should be attainable. Care must be taken, however, to ensure that this process conforms with state law, school board policies, and/or a collective bargaining agreement.

Memoranda to the File

Whenever a principal observes an incident or behavior that is not of such a significantly serious nature to require an immediate conference with the teacher, but which should ultimately be considered in the teacher's evaluation or discussed at a general conference with the teacher, the principal should prepare a short *memorandum to the file*. These *file memoranda* can be in various forms, such as a notation on a calendar, in a notebook with separate pages designated for specific individuals, or in a teacher's folder in an electronic data system. These file memoranda should include the name of the teacher, the name or initials of the principal, the date of the occurrence, and the facts of the event observed. These file memoranda can be used as memory keys generally for the following limited purposes:

1. Conference with the teacher concerning the incident or incidents;
2. Assessment of the teacher's performance; and
3. Refreshing the memory of the principal for testimony at any proceeding or hearing relative to the teacher's performance if the memos have not been incorporated into *summary memoranda* or the evaluation documents.

Most administrators find it counterproductive to keep the existence of these file memoranda secret from the teachers. In fact, most administrators find it helpful to make all employees aware that these memoranda are kept and actually encourage the employees to review any file memoranda made concerning their performance. Openness is important to successful communication.

Copies of these file memoranda normally need not be given to the teacher unless the teacher requests them under a state's freedom of information act. However, if the copies are not given to the teacher upon request, they should not normally be used in a subsequent hearing as evidentiary documentation to establish facts. In fact, in some states, documents not shown to the teacher may not be considered in that state's formal evaluation process. The best practice is to incorporate the contents of these file memoranda into a summary memorandum or evaluation that is given to the teacher after a conference. If a summary memorandum includes the information contained in the file memoranda, the file memoranda should never have to be used again. (Whether these documents must be retained, and if so, for how long, are controlled by each state's records retention laws.)

Even though it may not be the intention of the principal to use these documents as future evidence or to share the file memoranda with the teacher, the memoranda should be written with the knowledge that copies may actually be introduced into a future proceeding or made available to the teacher through a request under most states' freedom of information acts. For example, if file memoranda are being used to refresh a principal's memory at a hearing, most state laws entitle the attorney for the teacher to see copies of the documents. Thus, a principal should exercise care not to write or record anything in a manner that could cause future embarrassment. A good practice is to record facts rather than conclusions or opinions in file memoranda.

These file memoranda should be used sparingly and only for minor matters. If an incident is in any way serious, the *specific incident memorandum* following a conference with the teacher should be used.

Specific Incident Memoranda

If the principal observes an incident or behavior, or has a significant complaint from a third party, the principal should consider sending the teacher a memorandum concerning the specific incident. This memorandum should be sent only *after* the principal holds a conference with the teacher at which the incident is discussed and the teacher's viewpoint is considered. The specific incident memorandum should summarize the complaint, whether the complaint is from a third party or from the principal's observation(s); the teacher's response; the principal's decision regarding the matter; and any directives, corrective action, or reprimands to the teacher. If the incident is so serious that termination is to be recommended immediately, the memorandum should so state. While many administrators might like to avoid talking with a teacher about an incident in the hope that it will go away, such an attitude is self-defeating and naive. These incidents should be faced head-on as they occur. Teachers generally want to know of problems immediately to avoid their reoccurrence. Thirty minutes spent when the incident occurs may provide the spark to help the teacher improve or may avoid a two-day hearing or a week-long trial at some later date.

Moreover, the failure to confront problems, infractions, and deficiencies at the time they occur can weaken a later case for termination. For example, suppose several incidents occur in the fall of a school year, but they are not mentioned to the teacher by the principal. An attempt to use those incidents to support a proposed termination in the spring of that school year may prove difficult. The teacher will claim that he or she is being treated unfairly or that the reasons are a pretext for discriminatory motives because the reason(s) for termination were not discussed with the teacher earlier in the school year when they occurred. Not dealing with the problems as they occur makes the principal appear to be arbitrary or devious and may taint a proposal to terminate.

If the specific incident concerning the teacher comes from a third party such as a parent or student, the principal must fully examine the facts and determine whether the third party's information is correct. It is improper and potentially disastrous to base a decision to terminate on information from a third party when the truthfulness of the allegation has not been established. Upon receiving a third-party complaint, the principal should request the informant to submit the complaint in writing and conduct an investigation. Some school district policies or collective bargaining agreements require that third-party complaints be in writing before any action can be taken. On the other hand, many states' laws require that suspected child abuse or neglect be reported within certain time limits, regardless of whether the information is received in writing.

The principal should arrange a conference with the teacher to obtain the teacher's side of the story. If there is a discrepancy between the third party's allegations and the teacher's explanations, the principal should interview any witnesses and attempt to determine what occurred. It may be necessary to have the teacher confront the complainant in an informal conference to determine what actually occurred. Although the results of a polygraph test cannot be used in a termination proceeding in most states, in really serious situations a district may permit a teacher to voluntarily take a polygraph test as a means to aid in establishing his or her innocence. The district should approve the examiner and approach used. The principal should advise the third party if adverse action may be taken against the teacher based on the incident, and the third party must be available to testify before the board, a hearing officer, an arbitrator, or a court. If the third party will not agree to appear as a witness, other independent evidence must be available to establish the relevant facts at a hearing. Otherwise, action adverse to the teacher should not be taken because there will be no evidence to support the reason(s) for the action.

In many cases, it simply will not be possible for the principal to have everyone agree on what happened, so the principal has to act as a judge and decide whose story to believe. If the parties can eventually reach agreement, or if the principal has enough information to make a factual determination, a specific incident memorandum can be prepared. Such a memorandum should explain the findings made by the principal and the reasons for those findings. Specific directives or suggestions to the teacher should be included in the memorandum as appropriate.

It is important to establish on the face of the specific incident memorandum that the teacher received a copy of the document. In teacher termination hearings, disputes often arise over whether the teacher ever received a copy of a particular document. It is essential, therefore, to have the teacher sign the memorandum acknowledging its receipt. If a teacher refuses to sign, the principal should have an adult witness other than the principal sign and date a copy of the document verifying that the teacher was given a copy of the memorandum but refused to sign an acknowledgement of its receipt. It should be made clear to the teacher (either on the face of the document or orally) that the teacher's signature, verifying that a copy of the memorandum has been received, does not constitute agreement with its contents.

It is important that the teacher has the opportunity to respond to any memorandum. This can be accomplished by inviting the teacher to make a written statement concerning any differences of fact or opinion expressed by the principal in the memorandum by a certain date or within a given number of days. For example, the final paragraph of a memorandum might conclude, "If you disagree with the facts or conclusions stated in this memorandum, please advice me in writing no later than (date) so we can meet and work out any differences." By so doing, any disagreement can be noted and the differences hopefully resolved immediately. In serious situations where the employee has proven to be recalcitrant or is of questionable veracity, one might consider a final sentence such as "If you do not respond, I can only assume you agree with the facts stated in this memorandum." A statement of this nature should be used sparingly because it tends to polarize the positions of the administrator and the employee, thus making future communications more difficult.

Giving the teacher an opportunity to submit a written response disagreeing with the contents of the memorandum puts the teacher on notice of the facts and findings stated in the memorandum. If no disagreement is noted in writing by the teacher, most reasonable people presume that the contents of the memorandum accurately reflect the facts. Members of a jury, a hearing officer or a judge examining this situation will normally take the view that a reasonable person who received such a memorandum, and who disagreed with the facts, would prepare a written response to the items with which the individual disagreed. If the teacher does not respond within the time stated in the memorandum, it becomes difficult to argue at a termination hearing that the teacher now disagrees with the content of the memorandum or disagreed when the memorandum was written.[3]

Visitation Memoranda

In some school districts, it is a common practice of principals to summarize a visit to a teacher's classroom. If visitation forms or checklists are used, or if *visitation memoranda* are prepared, their contents should be reviewed with the teacher, and the teacher should be given a copy. Suggestions for improvement or any specific directives should be made in a conference and noted in the memorandum. A visitation memorandum may be used in a termination proceeding, but the results of a visitation are normally reviewed in a summary memorandum or in the evaluation document.

Summary Memoranda

Summary memoranda are ideal ways to outline the results of conferences concerning several incidents, of classroom visitations, or of a conference regarding general teacher performance. Through such memoranda, the principal may incorporate matters referred to in the file memoranda (which may not have been given to or discussed with the teacher previously) and matters not reflected in other memoranda. The summary memorandum should be used to issue directives to the teacher, reach understanding, establish standards, provide evidence that a conference was held, and confirm the subjects discussed. A copy of each summary memorandum should be given to the teacher, and the teacher should acknowledge receipt by signing a copy.

The teacher should also be given an opportunity to offer any written responses disputing the facts and conclusions stated in the memorandum. If a teacher disagrees with the facts stated in the memorandum and files a response, a subsequent conference should be held with a follow-up memorandum to try to resolve any differences that may exist. The same comments applicable to the specific incident memoranda reviewed above are also applicable to summary memoranda, with the major difference being that summary memoranda are designed to cover general conferences with the teacher on several matters rather than on only a specific incident.

The Assessment or Evaluation Document

The *assessment or evaluation document* should be completed as prescribed by the policies and procedures of the district and by any state laws or regulations. A summary narrative should be considered for each negative assessment noted in the document. This can be done on the assessment document or on an attachment to the evaluation itself. If the assessment is such that the teacher might be terminated if no improvement is shown, the teacher should be advised that failure to improve could result in a recommendation for termination. Furthermore, it is wise to include instructions or specific directives for improvement. Such a practice is not only helpful to the teacher, but it also strengthens the argument that the teacher has been treated fairly, if the principal's actions are later questioned. Through the use of such evaluation documents, the teacher will be put on notice that there are deficiencies that could result in a proposal to terminate should those deficiencies not be remedied according to the instructions given for improvement. All identified deficiencies of the teacher, as well as any problems that have been encountered during the assessment period, should be included in the assessment document. If the teacher has not remedied a deficiency from previous years, it should be noted on the assessment. A deficiency once identified and not corrected never becomes stale if the deficiency is appropriately carried forward in documentation.

In order to avoid difficulties with ratings on the evaluation, a teacher should not be rated too highly or too positively when he or she is initially employed or assigned to a school and before the administrator has an in-depth and accurate picture of the teacher's skill, talent, and capability. Rather, a straightforward and truthful evaluation should be made. It is much easier to raise evaluation scores in subsequent years than it is to lower previous inflated assessments. Furthermore, a fair system of evaluation requires the setting of standards and expectations at the beginning of the school year with the principal following through with the implementation of those standards through the evaluation process.

The Close-Out Memorandum

Occasionally, a teacher will write a response to the administrator's memorandum if he or she disagrees with the facts, conclusions, or directives in it. If a teacher does respond to the memorandum, it is essential that the administrator carefully review the response. If the teacher disagrees with the principal's statement of facts in the original memorandum and offers specific information in his or her defense, the principal may need to investigate the matter further. Sometimes a teacher may accuse the administrator of discriminatory conduct or motives in the teacher's response. Such accusations should not be ignored but should be addressed specifically by the principal. A teacher's response may also indicate that he or she is confused about a directive or corrective action. After reading the response, the administrator should not hesitate to hold another conference with the teacher to resolve any issues created by the teacher's response.

The results of this follow-up conference should be memorialized in a specific incident or summary memorandum sent from the principal to the teacher. If the communication in the conference is effective and is properly reflected in the memorandum, a teacher will rarely have reason to respond again. However, a second response from the teacher sometimes does occur, and another conference may be necessary. At some point, however, the memorandum writing must be brought to a close. In normal circumstances, the sending of the follow-up memorandum to this conference may be an appropriate time to close out the memoranda exchange. A close-out memorandum may be written. The language inviting a response from the teacher used in prior memoranda is deleted, and the teacher is advised that the matter should be considered closed.

Recommendations for Practice

1. Any memorandum should be sent only after a conference with the teacher.
2. In preparing any memorandum, reliance should be on the facts. Conclusionary statements not supported by the facts should be avoided. For example, in a classroom visitation memorandum, a statement that the teacher's classroom was disorderly, without any explanation, is not very specific or effective. Rather, the principal should note that three children were observed in the classroom talking during class and one child was playing in the back of the room. The principal should note that these acts were unnoticed by the teacher and were not corrected by the teacher.
3. In preparing a memorandum, inflammatory words should not be used. For example, rather than characterize an action as insubordination, the action should be factually described and the teacher's action referred to as a failure to comply with specific official directives or school board policy.
4. Directives given in a memorandum should be positive and specific, and educational jargon should be avoided. For example, when directing a sometimes tardy teacher to arrive at school on time, state, "You are required to be at school by (a specific time), and you will be expected to have signed in by that time," rather than, "You are required to be at school on time." Instead of directing, "Your lesson plans are due once a week," one might state, "Your lesson plans must be emailed to me or placed in my box by 4:00 p.m. on each Friday, and I expect you to have them there beginning this Friday." When written in a constructive manner, precise directives like these tend to avoid real or imagined confusion about what is expected.
5. The specific incident memorandum, the summary memorandum, the visitation memorandum, and the assessment document should be personalized as much as possible. The use of "we" or "they" should be avoided unless two or more people are involved, in which

case each individual should be identified by name. The key to the success of this documentation system is to provide an opportunity for the principal and the teacher to sit down and mutually work out the problem and determine the future actions of the teacher.

6. Care should be taken to treat all teachers alike, especially when dealing with absences and tardiness. It is embarrassing and potentially destructive to have a teacher's attorney present a school's sign-in sheet at a hearing to show that other teachers have more tardies and more absences than the teacher who is being proposed for termination for excessive tardiness and absences.
7. An administrator should never send a memorandum to a teacher when the administrator is upset or angry. It is much better to reflect for a day or so or to call in a third party to review a memorandum prior to sending it. By doing so, the principal can avoid writing statements that might be regretted later. This admonition is especially relevant when the method of communication is electronic rather than by paper memorandum.
8. In order to be effective, any memorandum must be prepared and sent to the teacher soon after the incident and the subsequent conference occur. Under no circumstances should a memorandum be prepared after the decision to terminate has been made and backdated to reflect the incident upon which the proposed termination will be based.
9. Warn the teacher verbally and in the memorandum if adverse employment action, such as termination, may occur if corrective action is not taken.
10. Have the teacher sign to acknowledge receipt of the memorandum without requiring agreement with its contents. Invite a written response and set a specific time for the response to be provided. If the teacher refuses to sign for receipt, have an adult witness sign a copy of the memorandum noting that it was provided to the teacher, and indicate the person who provided it and the date provided.
11. The evaluator should be careful to ensure that the teacher believes he or she has been treated fairly. One should remember that if the teacher's performance does not improve and a recommendation for termination is made, the fairness of the process will be judged by the members of the board or a hearing officer and, possibly, by the state's commissioner of education, an arbitrator, a judge, or even a jury. In ensuring that a teacher has been treated fairly, one should attempt to conduct an evaluation from the perspective of a reasonable person who, after receiving all the facts, determines that the process was fair. Another helpful standard for judging fairness is for the principal to treat the teacher as the principal would like to be treated if he or she were in the same circumstances.

12. Normally the only documents that would be used as documentary evidence at a termination hearing would be the summary memoranda and the evaluation or assessment instruments. Occasionally, specific incident and visitation memoranda would be included; however, these specific incident and visitation memoranda should be reviewed and included in a subsequent summary memorandum or evaluation instrument. If the teacher does not receive a copy of a memorandum to the file, it should not be used as evidence at a hearing but should be used only when necessary to refresh the principal's memory while testifying concerning the specific facts of an event.

Conclusion

Like all other personnel-related activities, this simple system of communication and documentation is not fail safe. It must be implemented by humans, and it is subject to error. This system does, however, provide an opportunity for a principal to demonstrate leadership and to communicate effectively with teachers while developing the proper documentation for improvement or termination. In working with this system, the members of the board of education, hearing officers, the state commissioner of education, arbitrators, judges, or juries will evaluate the termination recommendation on the basis of fairness and reasonableness. In the implementation of this system, a principal should be guided by the standard of treating the teacher as the principal would like to be treated if the principal were in the teacher's position. The principal should also strive to establish and maintain a climate where the employee can maintain his or her personal dignity. The use of this fair and effective documentation system should result in the improvement of most personnel problems and promote the efficient resolution of major or persistent problems through termination.

Endnotes

[1] For a more complete treatment of documentation, including sample memoranda and a checklist, see K. Frels & J.L. Horton, A Documentation System for Teacher Improvement or Termination, (6th ed. 2007).

[2] For a more complete review of how to prevent First Amendment problems, see K. Frels & M. Schneider-Vogel, The First Amendment and School Employees: A Practical Management Guide (1986).

[3] For more detailed treatment of investigating alleged wrongdoing by employees, see R.E. Bump, K. Frels & J. Horner, Investigating Alleged Misconduct by Employees (2007).

Chapter 28

Educational Curriculum

Brenda Kallio & Rick Geisel

Introduction

The term *curriculum* generally refers to the courses mandated by the state and offered by local school boards, as well as the content of those courses and the materials used to teach them. As a rule, state and federal courts are reluctant to interfere with the instructional programming offered in schools. This is due, in part, to the fact that per the Tenth Amendment, individual states have jurisdiction over public education. Abiding by the constitutional principles of federalism and separation of powers, courts usually refrain from substituting their judgment for that of the state legislatures and educational policy makers. As a result, curriculum may differ from state to state, a direct reflection of the diversity produced by state and local control.

While most courts acknowledge the authority of the states over public education and the importance of leaving matters of curriculum and pedagogy to the professional expertise of educators, the courts have been called upon to scrutinize the instructional program when fundamental, constitutional rights may be implicated. For example, in *Meyer v. Nebraska*,[1] the first curriculum-related case decided by the United States Supreme Court, a teacher was convicted under a Nebraska law that made it illegal for a teacher to teach any subject in a language other than English or to teach a foreign language to any public or private school student who had not completed the eighth grade. Essentially, the state of Nebraska made a curricular decision that prohibited foreign language instruction prior to the eighth grade. However, the U.S. Supreme Court ultimately held that the Nebraska law was a violation of the right to liberty guaranteed by the Fourteenth Amendment of the U.S. Constitution as applied to both the private school teacher convicted under the law, as well as the parents who engaged the teacher to instruct their children.

Over the years, the courts have been called upon to address a variety of objections to the "curriculum." The remainder of this chapter addresses some of the most frequent areas of the instructional program challenged in the courts, including removal of books from the school library, classroom curriculum, evolution versus creationism, sex-education programs, the inclusion of service learning requirements for graduation, and obscenity in the curriculum.

Legal Issues

School Libraries

Courts have long recognized that boards of education have broad discretion in the management of school affairs[2] and have repeatedly affirmed that school boards have the discretionary powers to control the schools[3] and to inculcate the fundamental values necessary to maintain a democratic political system.[4] However, courts have also recognized that removing books from school libraries "may offend the First Amendment by restricting access to discussion, debate, and the dissemination of information and ideas."[5]

In *Board of Education, Island Trees Union Free School District v. Pico,*[6] a 1982 case involving removal of books from school libraries, the court stated that "students must always remain free to inquire, to study and to evaluate [in order] to gain new maturity and understanding;"[7] thus, the court limited a board of education's right to remove books from school libraries. However, in the 1972 U.S. Court of Appeals case, *President's Council v. Community School Board,*[8] the court ruled that boards of education do have discretionary powers to remove books from school libraries if the books are without merit either as works of art or science. In addition, this same appellate court stated that when faced with financial or architectural realities, boards of education should be allowed to winnow books from school libraries without fear of violating constitutional freedom of speech. Similarly, the court in *Zykan v. Warsaw Community School Corporation*[9] extended board of education powers to include "prohibit[ing] the use of texts, remov[ing] library books, and delet[ing] courses from the curriculum as a part of the effort to shape students into good citizens."[10]

In 1980, the *Bicknell v. Vergennes Union High School Board of Directors*[11] court ruled that boards of education have the discretion to remove and to screen book acquisitions if the books are considered to be vulgar, obscene, or sexually explicit. However, this court admonished that books could not be removed from school libraries based solely on the book's ideological content. While some courts felt the *Bicknell* decision was a step in the right direction, the ruling, as applied, seemingly allowed for the arbitrary standards and tastes of school board members to overly influence the removal of books. Two years later, the *Sheck v. Baileyville*[12] court required boards of education to adopt procedural safeguards to ensure books were removed for legitimate pedagogical concerns and not because of conflict over the book's ideological content.

In 1982, the U.S. Supreme Court ruled on the benchmark book-removal case, *Board of Education, Island Trees Union Free School District No. 26 v. Pico.*[13] The primary issue before the *Pico* court was whether the First Amendment imposes limitations on the book-removal process for high school and junior high school libraries. In *Pico*, members of the board of education had attended a conference presented by a politically conservative parent organization that was involved with New York educational legislation. At this conference, members of the board of education obtained a list of books described as objectionable and improper for school students. After returning from the conference, the board of education gave an "unofficial directive" that the books identified at the conference be removed from the school's libraries. Facing criticism from the community, the board of education responded by labeling the nine books in question as "anti-American, anti-Christian, anti-Semitic and just plain filthy."[14] The board of education stated, "[I]t is our duty, our moral obligation, to protect the children in our schools from this moral danger as surely as from physical and medical dangers."[15] A lawsuit was filed alleging that the board of education ordered the removal of the books from school libraries based on board member's personal social, political, and moral values.

The Supreme Court's *Pico* decision was a plurality vote with seven of the nine justices writing opinions. These seven opinions outlined a wide range of viewpoints on the ability of boards of education to retract the spectrum of knowledge in school libraries. Several Justices noted that boards of education must be allowed to create curriculum consistent with community values, which includes permitting school districts to decide on the type of books that remain in school libraries.

Other Justices posited that while boards of education have direct control over curriculum, the school board should assert less control over school libraries. These Justices' assumptions were that boards of education should not be permitted to establish procedures that inhibit students' legitimate exercise of academic inquiry and that schools should not be allowed to "strangle the free mind."

In the end, the court's consensus was that "school officials may not remove school books based on orthodoxy or narrow political purposes or deny students access to ideas to which authorities simply disagree"[16] and that school districts may not remove books to aid the partisan or political ideology of the board of education. "Books should be judged on suitability for relevance to curriculum and appropriateness for an age level."[17]

One would assume the Supreme Court's *Pico* ruling would have put an end to the controversy of book removal from school libraries, but that has not proven to be the case. In 1990, a court was asked to decide whether a Holy Bible could be removed from a classroom library,[18] and in 1995, the U.S. District Court of Kansas was asked to determine whether a school district could remove the book, *Voodoo and Hoodoo,* from the school's library without contracting the spectrum of knowledge.[19] The court responded that the school was not allowed to remove the book and specifically noted that the 'board's motivation' is a critical factor in determining whether book removals from school libraries are constitutional.[20]

Once again, it seemed as though the issue of book removals from school libraries had been clearly and completely resolved, but the debate continues, as exemplified by a 2006 case wherein a Florida district court was asked to issue an injunction that would prevent the Miami-Dade County School Board from removing the book, *Vamos a Cuba!,* from its school's library shelves because a Cuban refugee denounced the book us unrepresentative of the living conditions in Cuba.[21] At trial, the school district claimed the book qualified as curriculum; therefore, it fell under the school board's discretion to either make the book available to students or to remove the book from the school's curriculum. As a part of its opinion, this court determined that because no teacher used the book as part of any academic units and because the book was not part of any assigned readings, the book could not be classified as curriculum but rather as library materials. As a result, the book in question was subject to a higher level of scrutiny before it could be removed from the school library.

Community and Parental Challenges to Curriculum

In addition to the removal of books from school libraries, community and parental challenges to the curricular content of classrooms have been (and remain) an important curricular issue for public schools. Historically, many of the requests to alter curriculum have originated from members of religious groups who seek to remove curriculum that portrays ideologies other than those held by their religious sect. The primary legal argument advanced by such groups is that requiring students to read or be subjected to readings and discussions of topics that conflict with the parents' religious views is tantamount to coercion and as such is a violation of the First Amendment.

The issue of whether parental and community values should guide the content of classroom curriculum is not new. Throughout recent history, various groups have sought to ban works such as Orwell's *Animal Farm*, Pasternak's *Doctor Zhivago*, Paine's *The Rights of Man*, and Beecher Stowe's *Uncle Tom's Cabin*. Other books that various groups of citizens have been deemed as inappropriate for inclusion as classroom readings include *The Age of Reason* by Thomas Payne; *Oliver Twist* by Charles Dickens; *On the Origin of the Species* by Charles Darwin;, *Jude the Obscure* by Thomas Hardy; various translations of the *Bible, the Koran, the Talmud;* and most recently, *Harry Potter* by J.K. Rowling.[22] As demonstrated by the examples that follow, the courts have, in large part, allowed communities to maintain their values by granting control of curriculum to the local communities.[23]

In one of the first cases to deal with a school's prerogative to direct curriculum, a father wanted his son to take additional math and science classes in lieu of participation in the school's mandatory music program. The court ruled the legislature had delegated sufficient discretionary powers to public school trustees to allow the school board to establish and direct the content and curricular requirements of the school.[24] Similarly, in 1927, an Arizona court ruled that the state may require students to participate in physical education classes.[25]

Decades later, the courts continued to be asked to resolve curricular issues. For example, in *Mozert v. Hawkins County Board of Education,*[26] the school district offered a separate reading program for students whose parents felt the reading materials used in the regular class contained content that was in opposition to parental religious beliefs. Subsequently, the separate reading program was canceled, and the district required all students to read from the same board-adopted readers. The plaintiff refused to allow her child to attend the regular reading classes and vowed she would not be tolerant of the public school teaching her child material she deemed counter to her religious beliefs. This parent filed suit and challenged the court to decide whether a governmental requirement that exposes a child to ideas parents find religiously objectionable constitutes a burden to the free exercise of that parent's religion.

The court ruled that, in this case, the school was merely attempting to acquaint students with a variety of ideas and there was no evidence that the mandatory readings would sway children to a belief other than that held by their parents. The court posited that had the parents demonstrated the students had been disciplined for disputing assigned materials, the court would have been compelled to investigate the element of compulsion. Since the case, as pled, had only required students to participate in reading and discussing the divergent ideas, the First and Fourteenth Amendments were not violated.

The impact of the *Mozert* decision can be seen in *Fleischfresser v. Directors of School District 200*[27] where the court stated that stories with ghosts, goblins, and witches did not foster any religion; that the stories were not promoting paganism; and that these types of curricular decisions were best left for state and local districts to decide.[28] Similarly, in *Brown v. Woodland Joint Unified School District,*[29] the court ruled that it is not illegal to ask students to read curriculum that is contrary to their religious beliefs.

The Sixth Circuit Court of Appeals' position in *Mozert* that teaching fundamental values is essential to a democratic society and that such teaching includes tolerance of divergent political and religious views[30] mirrored the sentiments of the Supreme Court's decision in *Everson v. Board of Education,*[31] where the Court stated the following:

> Our public schools [are] … organized on the premise that secular education can be isolated from all religious teaching so that the school can inculcate all needed temporal knowledge and also maintain a strict and lofty neutrality as to religion. The assumption is that after the individual has been instructed in worldly wisdom he will be better fitted to choose his religion.[32]

In *Smith v. Board of School Commissioners of Mobile County,*[33] parents claimed the texts used in home economics, history, and social studies classes advanced secular humanism and inhibited theistic religion, thus violating the Establishment Clause. In 1989, in a Florida case, a group of parents complained that several stories in an English text contained inappropriate sexual content. The school withdrew the texts and placed them in locked storage. Other members of the community filed suit claiming the district had contracted the spectrum of knowledge based on the religious preferences of one denomination.[34] The school leaders testified they found the content of the stories sufficiently vulgar and obscene. The court ruled that since schools are allowed to tailor curriculum and texts (provided there is a legitimate pedagogical concern), there had been no constitutional violations and that the district was free to add or delete curricular materials as it saw fit. A California appeals court applied the same reasoning used in *McCarthy v. Fletcher*[35] when it ruled educational unsuitability, not religious preference, must be the reason for removal of curricular materials and that school boards have wide discretion in determining educational benefit. To date, parents have had limited success removing content from a school's curriculum.

Teaching Evolution

Ever since the Scopes "monkey trial" of 1927, the manner in which the public school science curriculum addresses the origin of life has been the subject of several court challenges. In *Scopes v. State,*[36] the Tennessee Supreme Court upheld the constitutionality of a state statute that prohibited public school teachers from teaching any theory that denied the story of the divine creation of man as taught in the Bible, including any theory that man descended from a lower order of animals. More than forty years later, the United States Supreme Court weighed in on the issue of whether state laws could restrict the teaching of evolution. In *Epperson v. Arkansas,*[37] the Court struck down an Arkansas law that prohibited the teaching of evolution, reasoning that the law was meant to prohibit a body of knowledge from the public school curriculum solely because it conflicted with a particular religious doctrine. The Court acknowledged the right of the states to prescribe the curriculum of their public schools but held that Arkansas' anti-evolution statute was an unconstitutional exercise of power under the Establishment Clause of the First Amendment because it favored one religious interpretation of the origin of life over other interpretations.

The next battlefront in the "science wars" involved a state statute that required the equal treatment of evolution and creationism in the science curriculum. In the 1987 case of *Edwards v. Aguillard,*[38] the United States Supreme Court considered a Louisiana statute that required equal time for creation science and evolution, as well as mandated that school boards make curriculum guides and other resource materials on creation science available to the students. The Court struck down the statute as a violation of the First Amendment's Establishment Clause because it had no secular purpose. Rather, the Court concluded that the main purpose of the statute was the advancement of one particular religion. Subsequent to the Supreme Court's decision in *Edwards*, the Ninth Circuit Court of Appeals was called upon to determine whether a school district's requirement that evolution be taught was also a violation of the Establishment Clause.[39] In this case, a biology teacher challenged the school district's policy that he teach evolution as part of the high school biology curriculum, arguing that evolution was a religious belief system that he was being required to teach as valid scientific theory. The Ninth Circuit held that evolution defines a biological concept, namely, that higher forms of life evolve from lower forms of life. The court argued that the concept has nothing to do with how the universe was created and whether there was a divine Creator. Consequently, the Ninth Circuit held that evolution was not a religion. Thus, the school district's mandate that evolution be part of the curriculum did not violate the Establishment Clause of the First Amendment.

The latest battlefront in the "science wars" involves the promotion of "intelligent design" as an alternative to Darwin's theory of evolution. In 2004, the little town of Dover, Pennsylvania, made national headlines when its local school board adopted a resolution that required the following statement be read in all ninth-grade biology classes:

> The Pennsylvania Academic Standards require students to learn about Darwin's Theory of Evolution and eventually to take a standardized test of which evolution is a part.
>
> Because Darwin's Theory is a theory, it continues to be tested as new evidence is discovered. The Theory is not a fact. Gaps in the Theory exist for which there is no evidence. A theory is defined as a well-tested explanation that unifies a broad range of observations.
>
> Intelligent Design is an explanation of the origin of life that differs from Darwin's view. The reference book, *Of Pandas and People*, is available for students who might be interested in gaining an understanding of what Intelligent Design actually involves.
>
> With respect to any theory, students are encouraged to keep an open mind. The school leaves the discussion of the Origins of Life to individual students and their families. As a Standards-driven district, class instruction focuses upon preparing students to achieve proficiency on Standards-based assessments.[40]

Subsequently, several parents and teachers sued the Dover Area School District, arguing that the district's intelligent design resolution was an unconstitutional violation of the First Amendment's Establishment clause.[41] In a rather sweeping opinion, the federal district court for the middle district of Pennsylvania held that "it is unconstitutional to teach ID [intelligent design] as an alternative to evolution in a public school science classroom."[42]

According to the court, the "overwhelming evidence at trial established that ID is a religious view, a mere re-labeling of creationism, and not a scientific theory."[43] As a result, the court found that the district's intelligent design policy amounted to a government advancement of a religious viewpoint regarding the origins of life and was therefore unconstitutional.[44]

There is ample evidence that the controversy over evolution and creationism in the science curriculum will continue to be a matter debated in both courtrooms and classrooms for the foreseeable future.[45] Various state legislatures, state boards of education, and local school boards continue to debate the role of evolution in the science curriculum and to what extent alternative theories should be considered.

Sex Education

The vast majority of states either require or encourage the inclusion of sex education in the public school curriculum.[46] While such requirements have generated legal challenges asserting that mandatory sex education programs violate various individual rights, courts have universally upheld the authority of public schools to teach sex education,[47] especially when school districts routinely allow parents to exempt their children from certain controversial aspects of a sex education program.[48] The right to exempt one's child from a health education course or family life course, however, is not absolute and may be limited to those areas of the course curriculum that have the potential to directly impinge on parental rights. At least one court has ruled against parents who attempted to exempt their child from an entire health education course rather than only those lessons that clearly raised issues of privacy and religious freedom.[49]

Many of the parental challenges to sex education programs have been argued, at least in part, on the grounds that sex education in the public school context violates the free exercise of religion. The courts, however, have not accepted this position as sufficient grounds to prohibit the teaching of sex education. For example, when a parent group tried to obtain an injunction against several California school districts to prevent the implementation of family life and sex education programs on the basis that the programs violated their religious rights, the court denied injunctive relief, reasoning that the state is required to plan its curriculum on the basis of educational needs without reference to religious considerations.[50]

Thirty years ago, the legal battles over sex education largely centered on the issue of whether the states had the right to offer or require sex education classes in public schools. With those challenges decided in favor of the states and the public schools, the more recent legal battles appear to focus on the content of the sex education curricula. To date, the courts have given schools a great deal of latitude in creating course content for sex education programs[51] but have intervened when the components of the curriculum are not supported by fact or when the court deems the program violates the

Establishment Clause of the First Amendment.[52] This was the case when the Maryland federal district court granted a temporary restraining order preventing the Montgomery School District from launching a pilot sex education program, which the court deemed as promoting one set of religious beliefs and "disseminat[ing] one-sided information on a controversial topic."[53] However, in 2006 and again in 2007, the district courts in Kentucky[54] and Massachusetts,[55] respectively, acknowledged that parents have the right to raise their children in a manner they see fit but ultimately ruled that parents do not have the rights to prescribe curricular content. In addition to legal guidance from the courts, the *No Child Left Behind Act of 2001*[56] (NCLB) prohibits the use of federal money to develop materials that are designed to promote or encourage sexual activity, distribute legally obscene materials to minors on school grounds, provide sex education or HIV education unless such education is age appropriate and includes the health benefits of abstinence, and distribute contraceptives in schools.[57] The area of sex education in the curriculum will no doubt continue to produce litigation as various philosophies of acceptable content compete for curricular dominance.

Community Service Learning Requirements

In 1919, Justice Oliver Wendell Holmes coined the phrase "marketplace of ideas" and posited that in order for a democratic society to prevail, students must be given the tools to produce the right answers to complex problems.[58] In an effort to provide students with the opportunity to create a wide base of information from which to draw, a number of American school districts have established community service requirements. The addition of a community service requirement to the school's curriculum has led several parent groups and students to file suits in which they claim the mandatory community service programs violate portions of the Constitution.

In one such case, *Steirer by Steirer v. Bethlehem Area School District,*[59] the school district required students to complete a community service half credit as a graduation requirement. The purpose of the requirement was to "help students acquire life skills and learn the significance of rendering services to the community … [and to] gain a sense of worth and pride as they understand and appreciate the functions of community organizations."[60] To meet this curricular mandate, students could use one of the school's established service plans or could create a personal plan that met the district's requirements.

Some students and their parents claimed the mandatory participation in community service forced the students to declare a belief in the value of altruism and that the Fourteenth Amendment protected the students from being required to accept and express governmental views of citizenship. The students also claimed the mandatory community service requirement was *prima-facie* coercion (threat of no diploma) that elevated the graduation requirement to the level of involuntary servitude and thereby violated the Thirteenth Amendment.

In its ruling, the court stated that the constitutional line would be crossed only when instead of using the community service requirement as a teaching tool, the educators demanded the students express agreement with the educator's view. Citing *West Virginia State Board of Education v. Barnette*,[61] the court noted there was no evidence that students "were obliged to express their belief, either orally or in writing, in the value of community service."[62] Furthermore courts have posited that not every situation in which an individual faces a choice between labor or legal sanction constitutes involuntary servitude.[63]

Three years after *Steirer*, the courts heard two similar cases. In the first case, *Herndon v. Chapel-Hill-Carrboro City Board of Education*,[64] students and parents filed suit claiming the school district's fifty-hour community service requirement was the equivalent of involuntary servitude, violated personal liberties, and deprived parents of their constitutional right to direct the upbringing and education of their children. In its deliberation, the court recognized the implications of *Meyer v. Nebraska*[65] and *Pierce v. Society of Sisters*[66] (both of which confirmed parents' rights to direct the education of their children) but affirmed the school's responsibility to educate students to become good citizens. As for the claim of Thirteenth Amendment violations, the court stated that mandatory community service was not sufficiently "akin to African slavery" to warrant prohibition of the program. The court also stated that the "involuntary servitude" prohibited by the Thirteenth Amendment is not necessarily the same as service that is not voluntary.[67]

Similar to the school districts involved in the decisions in *Steirer* and *Herndon,* the Rye Neck School District required its 275 students to complete forty hours of community service before graduation. As with the other districts, the students were allowed to choose from service plans designed by the district, or the students could create a plan with the caveats that students could not receive pay for services rendered, nor could they displace a paid employee. Students were allowed to meet the requirements of the program by working for religious organizations involved in charitable work, but students were not given credit for service that involved proselytizing activities. The suit filed against this district claimed the district's curricular requirement violated the students' Thirteenth and Fourteenth Amendment rights and the parents' Fourteenth Amendment right to direct the education of their child. The court found the service requirement was a legitimate curricular requirement and not in violation of the Constitution. The court reiterated that the requirement was not "akin to slavery" and would not become a constitutional issue unless students were made to wash teachers' cars and paint teachers' houses and that until those types of situations occurred, the curricular requirement was not exploitive. The court further stated that while the government may not unreasonably interfere with parental rights, community service programs easily meet the rational basis test as it is in the government's interest to instill the values and habits of good citizenship and to introduce students to their social responsibilities.[68]

Obscenity and the Curriculum

By 1957, courts were in general consensus that obscenity, defined as material or speech that is "utterly without redeeming social importance,"[69] was not protected by the First Amendment. However, by the late 1960s, the courts were being asked to more clearly define obscenity. In *Ginsberg v. New York*,[70] one of the first cases to deal with obscenity and children, the court was more definitive and upheld a state statute prohibiting the sale of sexually explicit magazines to young children. In its decision, the court established a "variable obscenity" standard when it stated that it is not a violation of children's free expression rights when states adjust obscenity standards to reflect a child's age and mental maturity. As justification for its position, the Court concluded that the state has the power to promote a societal value of morality and that controlling the degree of obscenity available to children falls within the state's authority. *Ginsberg*, however, did not provide a bright line for obscenity in public schools. In *Parducci v. Rutland,*[71] an Alabama court was asked to determine whether a teacher could be fired for assigning an allegedly obscene story. In reaching its decision, the Alabama court applied *Roth*'s "utterly without redeeming social importance" and *Ginsberg*'s stricter "variable obscenity" and determined that while the story contained several vulgar words and a reference to a sexual act, the court could not find where the story met established guidelines for obscenity, especially since the reading of the story had not caused a significant disruption in the educational process.

Three years later, in *Miller v. California*,[72] the court affirmed previous legal interpretations of obscenity and established questions designed to aid in the identification of obscene materials. These questions revolved around whether the material dealt with sex in a manner appealing to the prurient interest; whether the work depicted or described, in an offensive manner, sexual conduct specifically defined by applicable state law; whether the material portrayed sexual conduct in a patently offensive way; or when taken as a whole, the material lacked serious literary, artistic, political, or scientific value. Similar to the judicial findings in *Parducci*, the court in *Brubaker v. Board of Education*[73] ruled that while brochures regarding a movie on Woodstock contained questionable language, the use of the brochure was not so offensive that its classroom use was "obviously improper." The court's addition of the "obviously improper" standard made it increasingly difficult for schools to adequately determine whether materials or speech met the obscenity guidelines.

The Supreme Court's decision in *Bethel School District No. 403 v. Fraser*[74] took a major step toward identifying the school's role in establishing and enforcing school obscenity procedures. In *Bethel,* the school district sought to discipline a student for his use of obscene language in a speech presented to the student body. The student's parents filed suit claiming the school violated the student's First Amendment right of free speech when the school disciplined the student for the content of his speech. The Supreme Court determined that public schools have the responsibility to inculcate societal values, manners, and civility in students and that to meet this level of responsibility, schools must have the authority to determine whether student expression interferes with the educational purpose of the school. The decision in *Bethel* gave schools the authority to regulate vulgar, indecent, or offensive behavior.

During 1986, the lower courts were also hearing obscenity cases. In *Martin v. Parrish,*[75] a college professor was sued for repeatedly used tirades of "four letter words" in the classroom. In this case, the court determined that the Constitution does not automatically guarantee the right to use questionable language in the classroom and reiterated that the "rights of the speaker [are] always tempered by a consideration of the rights of the audience and the public purpose served."[76] Thus, the court continued to reinforce that school speech does not extend to language that is offensive and unnecessary to accomplish the educational objectives. In *Broussard v. School Board of Norfolk,*[77] a student was suspended for wearing a T-shirt that said "Drugs Suck." The court expanded *Bethel* and stated that school authority is broad and that schools may ban speech "even if the audience is not offended … or the speaker honestly believed the speech was inoffensive."[78]

To date, the courts generally look to the following questions when determining whether material is obscene within the context of the educational setting. Does the material or speech tend to excite lustful thoughts as determined by how the average person reflecting the attitudes of a common community standard would adjudge the material? Does the material or speech provide representations or descriptions of ultimate sexual acts, normal or perverted, actual or simulated? Does the speech or educational material have an educational purpose, and if so, is it relevant to the educational purpose? And finally, is the material age appropriate? Taken in its totality, the courts appear to agree that obscenity has no definitive definition and is relative to factors such as the age and sophistication of the students. The courts have, however, have given the schools broad authority to determine whether verbal and/or non-verbal speech is considered obscene.

Recommendations for Practice

The American educational system is premised on the basis that individual states are responsible for the education of their citizenry and that local communities also have rights and responsibilities in this area. While the courts continue to uphold the right for local communities to shape educational curriculum, they have placed limits on those rights by mandating that curricular decisions (to include or exclude ideas and materials) must be based on appropriate educational pedagogy and not on the ideological or religious tenets of a particular political or religious group.

When making decisions pertinent to educational curriculum educators are encouraged to remember the following:

1. Boards of education have broad discretion in the management of school affairs.[79]
2. The courts have charged schools with the responsibility of inculcating the fundamental values of manners and civility necessary to maintain a democratic political system.[80]
3. Students must always remain free to inquire, to study, and to evaluate.[81]
4. Boards of education have the discretion to remove books that are considered to be vulgar, obscene, or sexually explicit and to screen future library acquisitions without being guilty of suppressing the First Amendment.[82]
5. Books may not be removed from school libraries simply based on the book's ideological [or religious] content;[83] however, some states or local school boards may require that reasonable accommodations or exemptions be made for students with religious objections.
6. It is legal to ask students to read content and participate in discussions of materials that may not coincide with their religious or political beliefs.[84]
7. Teaching evolution as part of the curriculum is not a violation of the Establishment Clause of the First Amendment.[85]
8. The right to exempt one's child from a health education course or family life course is not absolute, and the exemption may be limited to those areas of the curriculum that have the potential to directly impinge on parental rights.
9. Community service programs required by school districts as partial requirements for graduation do not constitute involuntary servitude.[86]
10. The courts have provided guidelines as to what constitutes obscenity but schools are given considerable leeway in regulating what constitutes vulgar, indecent and offensive behavior.[87]

Endnotes

1 Meyer v. Nebraska, 262 U.S. 390 (1923).

2 *See, e.g.,* Meyer v. Nebraska, 262 U.S. 390 (1923); Pierce v. Soc'y of Sisters, 268 U.S. 510 (1925).

3 Tinker v. Des Moines Indep. Cmty. Sch. Dist., 393 U.S. 503 (1969).

4 *Id.*

5 First Nat'l Bank of Boston v. Bellotti, 435 U.S. 765, 783 (1978).
6 457 U.S. 853 (1982).
7 *Id.* at 868 (quoting Keyishian v. Bd. of Regents, 385 U.S. 589, 603 (1967)).
8 President's Council, Dist. 25 v. Cmty. Sch. Bd. No. 25, 457 F.2d 289 (2d Cir. 1972).
9 Zykan v. Warsaw Cmty. Sch. Corp., 631 F.2d 1300 (7th Cir. 1980).
10 *Id.* at 1303.
11 Bicknell v. Vergennes Union High Sch. Bd. of Dirs., 638 F.2d 438 (2d Cir. 1980).
12 Sheck v. Baileyville Sch. Comm., 530 F. Supp. 679 (D.C. Me. 1982).
13 Board of Educ., Island Trees Union Free Sch. Dist., No. 26 v. Pico, 457 U.S. 853 (1982).
14 *Id.* at 857.
15 *Id.*
16 Stephen Goldstein, E. Gordon Gee, & Philip T.K. Daniel, LAW AND PUBLIC EDUCATION: CASES AND MATERIALS 735 (3d ed. Michie 1995).
17 Michael LaMorte, SCHOOL LAW: CASES AND CONCEPTS 219 (2d ed. Prentice-Hall 1987).
18 Roberts v. Madigan, 702 F. Supp. 1505 (D. Colo. 1989), *aff'd*, 921 F.2d 1047 (10th Cir. 1990).
19 Case v. Unified Sch. Dist. No. 233, 908 F. Supp. 864 (D. Kan. 1995).
20 *Id.*
21 American Civil Liberties Union of Fla., Inc v. Miami-Dade County Sch. Bd., 439 F. Supp. 2d 1242 (S.D. Fla. 2006).
22 Kern Alexander & M. David Alexander, THE LAW OF SCHOOLS, STUDENTS AND TEACHERS 56 (Thomson 2003).
23 State *ex rel.* Andrews v. Weber, 8 N.E. 708 (Ind. 1886).
24 *Id.*
25 Alexander v. Phillips, 254 P. 1056 (Ariz. 1927).
26 Mozert v. Hawkins County Bd. of Educ., 827 F.2d 1058 (6th Cir. 1987), *cert. denied*, 484 U.S. 1066 (1988).
27 Fleischfresser v. Dirs. of Sch. Dist. 200, 15 F.3d 680 (7th Cir. 1994).
28 *Id.*
29 Brown v. Woodland Joint Unified Sch. Dist., 27 F.3d 1373 (9th Cir, 1994).
30 Mozert v. Hawkins County Bd. of Educ., 827 F.2d 1058 (6th Cir. 1987).
31 Everson v. Bd. of Educ., 330 U.S. 1 (1947).
32 *Id.* at 23-24.
33 Smith v. Bd. of Sch. Comm'rs of Mobile County, 655 F. Supp. 939 (S.D. Ala. 1987).
34 Virgil v. Sch. Bd. of Columbia County, Fla., 677 F. Supp. 1547 (11th Cir. 1989).
35 McCarthy v. Fletcher, 207 Cal. App. 3d 130 (1989).
36 Scopes v. State, 289 S.W. 363, 364 (Tenn. 1927).
37 Epperson v. Arkansas, 393 U.S. 97 (1968).
38 Edwards v. Aguillard, 482 U.S. 578 (1987).
39 Peloza v. Capistrano Unified Sch. Dist., 37 F.3d 517 (9th Cir. 1994).
40 Kitzmiller v. Dover Area Sch. Dist., 400 F. Supp. 2d 707, 708-709 (M.D. Pa. 2005).
41 *Id.* at 709.
42 *Id.* at 765.
43 *Id.* at 726.
44 *Id.* at 764.
45 *See* Freiler v. Tangipahoa Parish Bd. of Educ., 185 F.3d 337 (5th Cir. 1999) (striking down a school board policy that required a disclaimer to be read in elementary and secondary classrooms prior to evolution being taught); Daugherty v. Vanguard Charter Sch. Acad., 116 F. Supp. 2d 897, 916 (W.D. Mich. 2000) (teachers' incidental references to God and creationism in response to student questions did not rise to the level of an Establishment Clause violation); and Moeller v. Schrenko, 554 S.E.2d 198 (Ga. Ct. App. 2001) (references to creationism in high school biology text did not violate the Establishment Clause).
46 Edward A. Wynne & Kevin Ryan, RECLAIMING OUR SCHOOLS: A HANDBOOK ON TEACHING CHARACTER, ACADEMICS, AND DISCIPLINE 223 (2d ed. 1997).

[47] Cornwell v. State Bd. of Educ., 428 F.2d 471 (3d Cir. 1970); Hobolth v. Greenway, 218 N.W.2d 98 (Mich. Ct. App. 1974).
[48] Hopkins v. Hamden Bd. of Educ., 289 A.2d 914 (Conn. Ct. Com. Pl. 1971); Medeiros v. Kiyosaki, 478 P.2d 314 (Haw. 1970); Smith v. Ricci, 446 A.2d 501 (N.J. 1982).
[49] Leebaert v. Harrington, 332 F.3d 134 (2d Cir. Conn. 2003).
[50] Citizens for Parental Rights v. San Mateo County Bd. of Educ., 124 Cal. Rptr. 68 (Cal. App. 1975).
[51] Medeiros v. Kiyosaki, 478 P.2d 314 (Haw. 1970).
[52] Coleman v. Caddo Parish Sch. Bd., 635 So. 2d 1238 (La.App. 2 Cir. 1994).
[53] Citizens for a Responsible Curriculum v. Montgomery County Pub. Schs., 2005 WL 1075634, at *13 (D. Md. 2005).
[54] Morrison *ex rel.* Morrison v. BOE of Boyd County, Ky., 419 F. Supp. 2d 937 (E.D. Ky. 2006).
[55] Parker v. Hurley, 474 F. Supp. 2d 261 (D. Mass. 2007).
[56] No Child Left Behind Act of 2001, U.S.C. § 9526 (2001).
[57] *Id.*
[58] Abrams v. United States, 250 U.S. 616 (1919, Holmes, J., dissenting).
[59] Steirer by Steirer v. Bethlehem Area Sch. Dist., 987 F.2d 989 (3d Cir. 1993).
[60] *Id.* at 990.
[61] West Virginia State Bd. of Educ. v. Barnette, 319 U.S. 624 (1943).
[62] 987 F.2d at 996.
[63] Steirer by Steirer v. Bethlehem Area Sch. Dist., 987 F.2d 989 (3d Cir. 1993).
[64] Herndon v. Chapel-Hill-Carrboro City Bd. of Educ., 89 F.3d 174 (4th Cir. 1996).
[65] Meyer v. Nebraska, 262 U.S. 390 (1923).
[66] Pierce v. Soc'y of Sisters, 268 U.S. 510, 530 (1925).
[67] Herndon v. Chapel-Hill-Carrboro City Bd. of Educ., 89 F.3d 174 (4th Cir. 1996).
[68] Immediato v. Rye Neck Sch. Dist., 73 F.3d 454 (2d Cir. 1996).
[69] Roth v. United States, 354 U.S. 476, 484 (1957).
[70] Ginsberg v. New York 390 U.S. 629 (1968).
[71] Parducci v. Rutland, 316 F. Supp. 352 (C.D. Ala. 1970).
[72] Miller v. California, 413 U.S. 15, 24 (1973).
[73] Brubaker v. Bd. of Educ., Sch. Dist. 149, Cook County, Ill., 421 F.2d 965 (7th Cir. 1974).
[74] Bethel Sch. Dist. No. 403 v. Fraser, 478 U.S. 675 (1986).
[75] Martin v. Parrish, 805 F.2d 583 (5th Cir. 1986).
[76] *Id.* at 584.
[77] Broussard v. Sch. Bd. of Norfolk, 801 F. Supp. 1526 (E.D. Va. 1992).
[78] *Id.* at 1536.
[79] Meyer v. Nebraska, 262 U.S. 390 (1923).
[80] Tinker v. Des Moines Indep. Cmty. Sch. Dist., 393 U.S. 503 (1969). Bethel Sch. Dist. No. 403 v. Fraser, 478 U.S. 675 (1986).
[81] Keyishian v. Bd. of Regents, 385 U.S. 589 (1967).
[82] Bicknell v. Vergennes Union High Sch. Bd. of Dirs., 638 F.2d 438 (2d Cir. 1980).
[83] Sheck v. Baileyville Sch. Comm., 530 F. Supp. 679 (D. Me. 1982).
[84] Mozert v. Hawkins County Bd. of Educ., 827 F.2d 1058 (6th Cir. 1987).
[85] Peloza v. Capistrano Unified Sch. Dist., 37 F.3d 517 (9th Cir. 1994).
[86] Steirer by Steirer v. Bethlehem, 987 F.2d 989 (3d Cir. 1993); Herndon v. Chapel-Hill-Carrboro City Bd. of Educ., 89 F.3d 174 (4th Cir. 1996).
[87] Bethel Sch. Dist. No. 403 v. Fraser, 478 U.S. 675 (1986).

Section 4:

Schools and the Law

Chapter 29

The No Child Left Behind Act

Mario S. Torres, Jr. & R. Lance Potter

Introduction

The passage of the No Child Left Behind Act[1] in January of 2002 signified a pivotal change in the relationship that the states and the United States federal government share in the administration of public education. The No Child Left Behind Act (NCLB)[2] requires both minimum levels of performance and the integration of empirically proven models of practice and participation in exchange for legitimacy and federal financial support. This degree of federal involvement signifies a departure from the traditional assumption that public education is a matter for state and local governments to decide. Even though the U.S. Constitution makes no mention of education, the federal government has clearly altered its posture with respect to its role and responsibility in educating tomorrow's citizenry. Following this introduction, this chapter is divided into four parts. Part one provides an overview and background on movements leading up to NCLB. The second and largest section describes the legal requirements of the act. The third section discusses significant changes to the rules and regulations affecting the implementation of the act since its inception. The fourth section offers some brief conclusions on the positive aspects of the act and potential difficulties with its implementation.

Overview

Rewards and sanctions for school productivity form the core of NCLB.[3] State and local school reform initiatives, past and present, have attempted to respond to critics' assertions that public schools perpetuate academic mediocrity. However, these efforts have had mixed results and pale in both scope and magnitude when compared to NCLB. First wave reform efforts in the 1980s produced state legislation tightening academic curriculum, graduation requirements, and teacher certification, to name a few. Second wave reforms of the early 1990s sought decentralization of management and operation in the hope that a diminished bureaucratic educational administration structure would create greater efficiency and effectiveness. Most recently, a third wave touting school choice and other alternatives has gained political strength, particularly among critical consumers. School choice continues to gain strength and is partly a stimulus for the enactment of NCLB.

Legal Requirements

NCLB frames school improvement through the integration of a myriad of programming and accountability policies to meet specific needs and objectives. The federal government has identified four guiding principles it considers essential to student and school success, which underlie these policies. First, states, local education agencies (LEAs), and schools must be held "accountable" for productivity in students and systemic results in exchange for greater local control and federal support.[4] Second, parents must be given a greater degree of "choice" and decision-making power in determining the best fit for individual family and student educational needs.[5] Third, the selection of academic, intervention, and professional development programming must be based on scientifically researched evidence demonstrating effectiveness.[6] Fourth, states and LEAs must be afforded added "flexibility and local control" to both facilitate funding acquisition and allocation and to use funds in a manner that best addresses specific educational needs locally.[7] The degree to which NCLB achieves its objectives will depend in large part on the successful application of these four guiding principles identified by the U.S. Department of Education.

Accountability

The most likely to have a far-reaching impact on all state and local educational stakeholders are the accountability pieces of NCLB.[8] As expressed in Title I, the primary purpose for accountability is to "ensure that all children have a fair, equal, and significant opportunity to obtain a high-quality education and reach, at a minimum, proficiency on challenging State academic achievement standards and State academic assessments."[9]

Title I, part A enlists states to adopt a challenging body of standards in reading or the language arts, mathematics, and science, which in effect mandates LEAs and schools to adopt and abide by such academic standards. Such standards-based educational delivery creates two conditions. First, it sets forth a specific body of challenging academic content, which students are expected to master and teachers are expected to deliver. Second, it creates both an evaluative framework from which academic outcomes of students are gauged and a means to cross check student achievement with academic content standards.[10]

States are required by law to establish unitary systems of accountability. The purpose expressed by the act is to "[determine] the yearly performance of the State and of each local educational agency and school in the State in enabling all children to meet the State's challenging student achievement standards. . . ."[11] The act specifies that the given assessment be the same for all students, that it be aligned with the state's content and achievement standards, and that it provide meaningful and "coherent" data to inform instruction and remediation.[12]

To comply, systems must include and implement rigorous academic standards. Such standards include yearly academic assessments of students between grades 3 and 8 in reading, mathematics, and science; adequate yearly progress targets; and rewards and sanctions based on performance.[13] States and LEAs are additionally required to establish data monitoring and tracking systems to not only ensure that all groups are meeting minimum levels of performance standards, but also to serve as a data delivery system to disclose assessment results to the public.[14]

Adequate Yearly Progress

States, LEAs, and schools must make "adequate yearly progress" on uniform statewide academic performance assessment by meeting or exceeding minimum levels of performance for aggregate and disaggregated populations set forth by the state.[15] The primary purpose is to ensure that all states, LEAs, and students are making "continuous and substantial" improvement on statewide assessments, graduation rates, and other indicators.[16] The starting point for adequate yearly progress is determined by the greater of two indicators drawn from the 2001–02 state-assessment data. These indicators are either (a) the lowest-achieving percentage for either racial, ethnic, limited English proficient, low income, or disability subgroup, or (b) the school at the twentieth percentile in the percentage of students meeting the proficient level. The act requires states to create an improvement timeline spanning twelve years or fewer to ensure that all students in the four major subgroups are meeting or exceeding the level of proficiency on the state assessment.[17]

Although adequate yearly progress benchmarks are identical for all schools in the state for reading/language arts and mathematics' assessments, separate adequate yearly progress targets are established and must be met or exceeded for each of the four major subgroups, which include minority, economically disadvantaged, limited English proficient students, and students with disabilities.[18] Fulfilling adequate yearly progress requirements is determined by percentages of groups meeting yearly improvement objectives established by the state and the percentage of students within subgroups participating in the assessment.[19] States, LEAs, and schools must meet the adequate yearly progress criteria for each subgroup to maintain an acceptable standard of performance.

Highly Qualified Teachers and Paraprofessionals

NCLB addresses the importance of instructional capacity and quality through various mandates and programming. Perhaps one of the more notable features of the act is the "highly qualified teacher" requirement. Here, the act requires that all school personnel teaching core academic subjects to have earned highly qualified status by the 2005–06 calendar year.[20] In order for schools to be eligible for Title I funding, core subject teachers must possess at minimum a bachelor's degree, state educator certification, and demonstrate competency in the subject area they teach. States and LEAs are responsible for having created a plan of objectives to meet the highly qualified teacher requirement by the 2005–06 school year. In addition, school administrators are required by NCLB to formally attest each year that their respective schools are in full compliance with the highly qualified teacher mandate.

LEAs and schools must also comply with new paraprofessional qualification and duty requirements. For employment eligibility, paraprofessionals must either hold an associate's degree, have completed two years of higher education study, or hold a high school diploma along with successful completion of a state or district paraprofessional certification program. Paraprofessionals hired prior to January 8, 2002, are required to attain these paraprofessional qualifications within four years of this date. In addition, NCLB specifies that paraprofessionals may only act in supplementary tutoring and assistance capacities and may not engage in direct instructional service unless under the supervision of a teacher.[21]

Disclosure

Disclosure of assessment outcomes serves as another key dimension to the act. Title I, part A requires schools to adopt measures to ensure effective communication of information to parents. Assessment outcomes and school improvement actions must be articulated and disseminated in a manner that is "understandable" and "practicable."[22] In addition to the requirement that states issue outcomes in a prompt manner, assessment results must be presented in a report format that is "descriptive, interpretative, and diagnostic" and allow school officials to comprehend and use data to address students' academic needs and modify instruction.[23]

States are mandated to create a "concise" and "understandable" statewide report card system containing both aggregate and disaggregate statewide assessment data.[24] To comply, states must, at a minimum, report performance data subdivided by race, ethnicity, gender, disability status, migrant status, English proficiency, and economically disadvantaged status. States must disclose this information when comparing subgroup performance with statewide measurable objectives for subgroup performance. Statewide report cards must additionally include percentages of students untested (aggregate and disaggregate), trend performance data, adequate yearly progress indicators, graduation rates, school performance indicators for LEAs (i.e., identification of schools in need of improvement), and teacher qualifications.[25]

LEAs, at a minimum, are obligated to report the frequency and percentage of schools needing improvement, comparison indicators showing how the LEA performed in contrast to the state, whether a school has been designated as needing improvement, and comparison indicators showing how some schools performed in contrast to other schools in the LEA and the state.

NCLB also requires states and LEAs to report statewide assessment information and results to the public. LEAs must disseminate report card data to all schools within the district as well as parents of students in a manner that is both "understandable" and "practicable."[26] Means of data disclosure might include, but are not limited to, the Internet, local media outlets, and other public agencies.[27]

Sanctions

If adequate yearly progress targets are not met for two consecutive years, the LEA must afford students enrolled in schools that are identified as needing improvement the opportunity to transfer to a school residing within the same LEA.[28] Provision of transportation is the fiscal responsibility of the LEA in cases when students elect to transfer to another school. The act requires the LEA to afford schools a period of time not to exceed thirty days to review and challenge all pertinent evidence serving as the basis for identification, including corrective action and restructuring. After this time, identification will be made to the public.[29]

After the review process, schools have a period of three months to develop a two-year plan to address areas in need of improvement. The plan must involve the adoption of scientifically researched strategies found to be effective through whole school reform models and core curriculum coverage to "directly [address]"[30] the problem of low achievement and possible deficits in professional capacity. Furthermore, the plan must include measurable objectives for each subgroup of students to meet the proficiency requirements designated by the state. Schools identified at any level of improvement are released from requirements when adequate yearly progress is met for two consecutive years.[31] If adequate yearly progress targets go unmet beyond the initial school-improvement phase for two additional years, corrective action is taken to stimulate change and improvement. This occurs when schools, per results from state assessments, have failed to respond to first-level school-improvement intervention and thus have demonstrated "consistent academic failure"[32] in meeting adequate yearly progress requirements. Corrective action involves more aggressive changes to school structure. In addition to the same types of interventions called for in schools identified as needing improvement, corrective action requires the additional institution of, at minimum, one of the following actions: (a) replacement of school staff, (b) selection of a new curriculum and professional development, (c) establishment of a decentralized management model, (d) extension of the school day or school year, (e) appointment of an external expert to oversee improvement plan implementation, or (f) restructuring the school organization. Schools are required to inform parents and the public of their proposed actions.[33]

Restructuring, the most drastic of the corrective actions, occurs when schools, after having been identified for correction for one year, fail to make adequate yearly progress. LEAs subject to restructuring could modify the failing schools into charter schools, privatize the schools, replace staff, submit to complete state control, or institute other fundamental changes in school leadership and governance.[34]

Programming Accountability

Aside from the more notable accountability mechanisms in Title I, part A, LEAs and schools are held more accountable for results than other federally supported programs throughout the act. For instance, grantees are typically required to submit a yearly report to the U.S. Secretary of Education and the U.S. Department of Education detailing programming goals and objectives, criteria for judging program effectiveness, and objective data indicating whether the programming initiative met its goals. For instance, for the Reading First, Early Reading First, Goodling Even Start, and Improving Literacy through School Library programs, states and LEAs must report and demonstrate evidence of program effectiveness and/or provide plans for improvement to retain funding.[35] Agencies receiving grants for the Early Childhood Educator Professional Development[36] and Mathematics and Science Partnership[37] programs also must submit reports describing program impact and progress in meeting goals.

Parental Choice

Recognizing the need for greater parental participation and involvement, NCLB broadly underscores the role of parents and the local community in the educational process. First, the act clearly empowers parents with greater decision-making power over school choice and supplementary educational services.[38] Second, the act has established basic "right to know" provisions requiring schools to communicate information to parents and the community in language that is both "practicable" and "understandable."[39]

Parents of students have the option of selecting school placement for their children when neighborhood schools are identified as needing school improvement, corrective action, or restructuring status (i.e., schools failing to meet adequate yearly progress targets for two or more years).[40] Depending on the extent of school improvement status, parents' school choice options can range from district school selections to public charter schools to privatized schools.

NCLB clearly states that the educational needs of children in high need areas can be met outside the school, which, in effect, creates more parental options. In cases where schools fail to meet adequate yearly progress targets one year after being given the school improvement identification, the act requires schools to arrange for and afford parents the right to choose and select from an approved list of supplemental educational service providers.[41] Broader eligibility requirements have expanded the list of possible grant recipients for supplementary learning services extending beyond the public school realm. For example, the act grants parents greater latitude in selecting from a variety of after-school tutorial, enrichment, counseling, and prevention services through the creation of 21st Century Community Learning Centers. Faith-based organizations, local government social agencies, as well as private and public entities are eligible for program funding in addition to public school agencies, which, in effect, expands the pool of services.[42]

NCLB's financial support of charter school systems and voluntary school choice programming creates even more options for parents. Aside from the mandatory charter school provision for students in schools requiring corrective action, the act provides competitive funding opportunities for the implementation, support, and facilities acquisition/funding assistance of charter schools.[43] Funding incentives made available through Voluntary School Choice Programs, described in Title V, also encourage eligible state, local, public, profit, and nonprofit entities to compete for funding to offset charter school planning, tuition transfer logistics, student transportation, and public relations support.[44]

Another unique feature of the act requires schools to notify parents of teacher qualifications prior to the beginning of the school year. For example, NCLB entitles parents of limited English proficiency children to notice of placement in, and the right to remove their children from, limited English proficiency classes.[45]

A final, significant piece of the NCLB agenda is school safety, addressed in the Unsafe School Choice Option of Title IX.[46] This provision gives parents of children in "persistently dangerous" schools the option to remove and place their children in another school or charter school within the school district.[47]

Focus on What Works

NCLB offers states, LEAs, and schools, as well as nonpublic school-related entities, competitive and noncompetitive funding opportunities to support programming goals the federal government has determined as critical to bringing about positive academic experiences for all children. Consistent with the overall press for efficient resource investment, NCLB places greater emphasis on selection and implementation of scientifically researched and proven programming. The act identifies several high priority areas, including assistance to appropriate target areas, addressing the needs of historically underserved populations, building instructional capacity, providing early childhood intervention, and ensuring school safety.

Targeting Assistance

Schools may allocate funds directly to students with the greatest academic needs. Eligibility is determined by failure to meet expectations on statewide assessment, students demonstrating a high probability for failure, or through performance levels deemed less than proficient according to local assessments.

Schools having concentrations of economically disadvantaged, migrant, and limited English proficient students as well as students with disabilities are eligible for targeted assistance. Also included are neglected, delinquent, or homeless children or children in Head Start or other similar programs.

Resources are expected to maximize the opportunities for marginalized and underperforming populations to meet high academic content and performance standards. These resources should include extended instructional and learning opportunities for students to meet objectives, opportunities for applied learning, highly qualified teacher instruction, greater coordination and utilization of social services, and increased parental involvement. Targeted assistance programming must entail an ongoing review process, which regularly determines when intervention and assistance are required and/or whether the situation warrants extended time before or after school, during the summer, and/or nontraditional school year formats.

Addressing Needs of Underperforming and Underrepresented Populations

NCLB addresses the instructional delivery to and performance of underrepresented populations. Formula grants make funding available to assist schools in providing and coordinating services, programming, and challenging academic content to migrant and limited English proficient (Title III) children.[48] Formula and competitive grants also provide support for the Indian Education,[49] Native Hawaiian Education,[50] and the Alaska Native Education[51] programs to meet these populations' unique cultural needs and to ensure that rigorous academic content and performance standards are provided to all children.

NCLB also makes funding available to support programming for educational experiences of delinquent, at-risk, neglected, and homeless children and youth. For instance, the Prevention and Intervention Programs for Children and Youth Who are Neglected, Delinquent, or At-Risk[52] provide formula funding to schools to assist juvenile offenders and other students in making state institution-to-school, school-to-work, or school-to-school transitions. The Dropout Prevention program[53] makes grants available to schools experiencing higher than average dropout rates to establish effective intervention programming. NCLB's McKinney-Vento Homeless Education Assistance Improvement program allows LEAs to compete for funding to allay the hardship and effect of homelessness on children and youth through provisions such as supplementary educational assistance, social and health service referral assistance, and transportation services to name a few.[54]

Building Instructional Capacity

Other features of NCLB place extra emphasis on professional development, preparation, and recruitment. For example, programs such as School Leadership[55] and Advanced Certification and Advanced Credentialing[56] provide both discretionary and competitive funding opportunities to high-need school districts to create infrastructures to retain, recruit, and prepare administrators and teachers for unique educational challenges. NCLB additionally supports curricular and instructional enrichment by making competitive and noncompetitive grants available for partnerships between educational agencies and nonprofit entities. Examples include the Mathematics and Science Partnership[57] sponsored jointly by the U.S. Department of Education and the National Science Foundation and the National Writing Project,[58] which supports professional development in effective teaching of writing.

NCLB underscores the importance of better integrating technology to more effectively transmit curriculum and instruction. For instance, the Educational Technology State Grants Program provides formula funding to support the use of technology to improve academic experiences for children in high-need schools.[59] Other programs such as Ready-To-Teach[60] make competitive grants available to nonprofit telecommunications institutions to enhance curriculum and instruction via media such as the Internet and public broadcasting.

Other NCLB programs are designed to recruit teachers by creating alternative routes into the teaching profession. Transition to Teaching[61] provides competitive funding opportunities to state education agencies, high-need school districts, higher education institutions, and other applicable agencies to create and implement incentives, support and induction services, and other strategies to enlist and retain non-education-certified college graduates and other career professionals. Similar in purpose, Troops-to-Teachers (administered by the Department of Defense) facilitates the entry of highly skilled, former military personnel into the teaching profession.[62]

Creating a Solid Learning Foundation

NCLB clearly stresses the importance of programming aimed at giving children and youth a strong foundation for future academic success. Programs such as Reading First, Early Reading First, and Reading is Fundamental provide a systematic framework emphasizing the acquisition of critical reading elements such as phonics, phonemic awareness, vocabulary, fluency, and reading comprehension, as well as instructional readiness and children's access to books.[63]

Competitive funding programs, such as the William F. Goodling Even Start Family Literacy Program[64] and Improving Literacy Through Libraries,[65] affirm the importance of early childhood, adult education, parental education, and parent-child activities in minimizing the deleterious impact of socioeconomics on literacy acquisition. Other programs give added attention to children's early cognitive, psychological, and emotional development. For instance, programs such as Early Childhood Educator Professional Development,[66] Elementary and Secondary School Counseling,[67] Early Reading First,[68] Ready-to-Learn Television,[69] and Foreign Language Assistance[70] all provide capacity-building opportunities for personnel to more effectively intervene in critical early childhood development stages.

Funding is also available to support greater parental and community involvement in educating children, especially in high-need communities. For example, adult education, parenting education, and parent-child activities are three major components guiding the William F. Goodling Even Start programs for preschool youth.[71] The Community Technology Centers programs also make available funding for profit and nonprofit entities, public schools, and higher education institutions to provide high-need areas access to technology and opportunities to acquire technological skills.[72]

Creating a Safe Learning Environment

NCLB clearly underscores the critical link between school safety and student learning through various requirements and programming. Through the Paul D. Coverdell Teacher Protection Act of 2001, NCLB shields teachers, administrators, and other school professional personnel from excessive financial liability when comporting with federal, state, and local law in student disciplinary matters.[73] Programming and regulations made available through Title IV also facilitate efforts at building and maintaining school order.[74] Through a combination of formulas and discretionary funding opportunities, the Safe and Drug Free Schools and Communities Act supports the creation of drug and violence prevention programming focused on more effectively providing services using objective sources of data and information to guide intervention.[75]

Other features of Title IV such as the Gun Free Schools Act[76] and Pro-Children Act of 2001[77] set forth and clarify minimum levels of compliance for weapons possession and tobacco use offenses, respectively. For the former, NCLB requires states to pass laws mandating students bringing or possessing a gun on school property to be expelled for no less than one year.[78] The latter prohibits the use of tobacco smoke products in healthcare, childcare, library, and school facilities providing services to children under the age of eighteen.[79]

Flexibility and Local Control

NCLB provides states and LEAs greater flexibility and control over funding allocation and administrative decision making in exchange for more extensive accountability. Added flexibility and control comes in the form of four key aspects: (a) broader eligibility requirements for program recipients and grantees; (b) enhanced data systems for delivering student information to schools and parents; (c) greater authority and discretion over programming; and (d) funding, program, application, and report consolidation.

Eligibility

In addition to widening the pool of potential supplemental education providers, NCLB creates more flexibility with respect to eligible program recipients and supplementary service providers. First, the act makes it possible for a greater number of students to benefit from Title I programming. Because NCLB reduces the poverty threshold from 50 percent to 40 percent for schoolwide program eligibility, more LEAs and schools have the liberty to use Title I funds in ways benefiting both at-risk children and the general student population. The act affords LEAs opportunities to adopt schoolwide improvement programs (made possible through a consolidation of federal, state, and local dollars) if at least one of two criteria are satisfied: (a) at least 40 percent of the children enrolled must come from low income families, or (b) at least 40 percent of the children within the school attendance area must come from low income families.[80]

Under the act, schoolwide programs are unique because they do not target student subgroups for intervention. These programs generally involve administering whole-school need assessments; selecting research-based reform strategies to guide curriculum, instruction, and assessment standards; allowing opportunities for professional development and growth; providing greater involvement in decision making to meet students' post-secondary needs; involving parents at a greater level; implementing effective remediation strategies for academically struggling students; and coordinating social service delivery systems.[81] Development of schoolwide plans is a collaborative approach involving school officials and external constituencies. Eligible schools also have the freedom to use schoolwide funds to create pre-kindergarten programs.[82]

A greater number of children within the community are now eligible to benefit from various funding opportunities. Programs such as Elementary and Secondary School Counseling[83] may provide a greater number of children with social service intervention provisions when funding permits. Goodling Even Start[84] and Partnerships in Character Education[85] make services available to school-aged children enrolled in both public and private school settings.

Also, more public and private entities are now eligible to receive funding through various programming initiatives. The range of eligible entities depends largely on the nature of the program. For instance, nonprofit entities specializing in advanced placement coursework are now eligible to receive grants and provide services to children.[86] Programs such as Goodling Even Start,[87] the Safe and Drug Free Schools and Communities Act,[88] and the 21st Century Community Learning Center Act[89] permit LEAs, nonprofit community-based organizations, private and public nonprofit entities, and institutions of higher learning to apply and compete for financial assistance and support. Moreover, local and state government entities in addition to private nonprofit entities are eligible to compete for charter school acquisition, construction, and renovation funding assistance to defray costs.[90]

Enhanced Data Monitoring and Communication Systems

NCLB makes efforts to improve the availability and access to both student and school information. Specific initiatives within the act focus on maintaining and utilizing data to assist in decisions concerning student academic and social needs. For instance, in conjunction with the Prevention and Intervention Programming for Vulnerable Youth,[91] data regarding neglected and delinquent youth will be centralized in a state database to both facilitate correctional capability to school transition and monitor academic progress. Addressing the high frequency of missing information for migratory children requires creation of a national information system centralizing health and educational information for all migratory children.[92] State and local agencies will be able to provide records to other state educational agencies at no cost. Other programs, such as Parental Assistance Information Centers,[93] will operate as communication hubs serving both as a center for disseminating information to parents regarding Title I policies and a means to facilitate greater parental involvement.

Greater Authority and Discretion over Programming

As a condition for greater accountability, NCLB affords state and local agencies greater freedom and control over service, administration, and instructional facets of programming than previously permitted under earlier versions of the Elementary and Secondary Education Act. This increase in latitude is clearly evident in many areas of the act. In Title III for instance, LEAs are given greater discretion over selection of instructional methods for limited English proficient students. In addition, state educational agencies are required to distribute 95 percent of Title III (i.e., Language Instruction for Limited English Proficient and Immigrant Students) funding to the local level, giving LEAs and schools added discretion over selection of resources. Similarly, through programs made possible by the Jacob K. Javits Gifted and Talented Students Education Act[94] and the Magnet Schools Assistance Program,[95] NCLB provides LEAs added flexibility in funding expenditures and program design. Programs such as Advanced Placement[96] and 21st Century Community Learning Centers[97] shift authorization and administrative responsibilities to other government agencies to enable more effective coordination and integration of services.

Consolidation

An additional goal of NCLB is to reduce the bureaucratic burden commonly associated with meeting programming, funding, and reporting requirements. For instance, former initiatives such as the Eisenhower Professional Development and Class Size Reduction programs are now supported through formula grants made available through the Improving Teacher Quality State Grants Program.[98] Other programs such as the State-Flexibility Authority[99] and Local-Flexibility Demonstration[100] provide funding opportunities to states and LEAs to create and support unique innovative educational systems that best meet the priorities and needs of students within their authority. The bureaucratic and programming process for American Indians,[101] Native Hawaiian Americans,[102] and Alaska Natives[103] has also been significantly streamlined to more effectively meet cultural and academic needs.

NCLB has made funding expenditure, application, and reporting requirements less rigid as well. For instance, in Title VI, the section on Funding Transferability for State and LEAs[104] allows states and LEAs the discretion to shift up to 50 percent of funds from identified programs to other programs, such as Title I, which best address situational needs. More flexibility is also given to investments in innovative programming. Programs such as Enhancing Education Through Technology[105] and Magnet Schools Assistance[106] permit funds to be used to create distant-learning partnerships between states and innovative school programming, respectively. The act has also greatly simplified reporting and grant application processes. Through Title IX, states can now apply for funding for numerous programs in one application. As for accountability and program effectiveness reports, states and LEAs are now required to submit one annual report to the U.S. Department of Education instead of submitting separate reports for each program.[107]

Changes in Rules and Regulations

The No Child Left Behind Act is up for reauthorization in 2008, and changes to the present structure are likely. This section reflects changes made to the rules and regulations since the original bill was enacted in 2001 that impact how NCLB is put into practice.

One change concerns the participation rate requirement. The original rule required that 95 percent of the students in a school must take the state assessment that year in order for a school to meet AYP. This includes subgroups of students such as ethnicity, poverty, disability, or English language proficiency, if the subgroup has sufficient numbers of students. As "part of the department's ongoing effort to develop policies that are right for students and fair for schools,"[108] in March, 2004, the Department of Education issued a new policy that allows districts to average the participation rate over a period of up to three years. If this two- or three-year average meets or exceeds 95 percent, the school will still meet the AYP requirement. The new policy also permits schools increased flexibility to omit students from inclusion in the participation calculation for certain medical emergencies such as car accidents. [109]

Highly Qualified Teachers

The Highly Qualified Teachers (HQT) requirements were revised in March of 2004. The Department of Education added three areas of flexibility so that more teachers could meet the highly qualified requirement. This flexibility was added to "benefit teachers, local and state administrators, and most importantly—students."[110] The changes applied to rural teachers, science teachers, and current multi-subject teachers.

First, teachers in eligible rural districts who were already highly qualified in at least one subject were given three years to become highly qualified in the additional subjects they teach. Part of this process required "professional development, intense supervision or structured mentoring to become high qualified in those additional subjects."[111]

Next, the Department of Education recognized that science teacher certification requirements vary significantly from a broad general science certification to subject-specific certification. New flexibility allows states to determine whether science teachers "demonstrate that they are highly qualified either in 'broad field' science or individual fields of science (such as physics, biology or chemistry)."[112]

Finally, the Department of Education realized, under NCLB, that current multi-subject teachers could face a long and repetitive process to certify mastery of the subject taught. With the revised guidelines, under a state's HOUSSE (High, Objective, Uniform State Standard of Evaluation) framework, states may develop "a method for current, multi-subject teachers to demonstrate through one process that they are highly qualified in each of their subjects and maintain the same high standards in subject matter mastery."[113]

Limited English Proficiency/English Language Learner Rules

The Department of Education amended regulations in September of 2006 relating to the assessment and accountability requirements for limited English proficient (LEP) students under NCLB.[114] Under the regulations, newly arriving limited English proficient students to the United States enrolled in school for fewer than twelve months are exempt from one administration of the reading/language arts assessment.[115] These LEP students still need to take the English language proficiency assessment, in order to be counted toward meeting the 95 percent assessment participation requirement for AYP determinations for reading/language arts.[116] Additionally, the state and local education authorities must report the number of students exempted from taking the reading/language arts assessment.[117]

While newly arriving LEP students still must take the mathematics assessment, their scores are not required to be included for AYP purposes.[118] Beginning in the 2007-08 school year, newly arriving LEP students must also take state science assessments.[119] On the other end of the LEP spectrum, students who no longer receive LEP services may continue to have their scores count for AYP purposes for two years after they no longer meet the state's definition for limited English proficient.[120]

Testing Students with Disabilities

Two changes have occurred with regard to the testing of students with disabilities. The earlier change concerns students with the most significant cognitive disabilities. The more recent change concerns students with less-severe disabilities who nonetheless are not able to progress to grade-level and successfully take the regular state assessment.

Alternate Academic Achievement Standards

In December of 2003, the U.S. Department of Education issued a rule change that allows students with significant cognitive disabilities to take an alternative assessment. The department wanted to ensure that students with the most significant cognitive disabilities are fully included in state accountability systems and have access to challenging instruction linked to state content standards.[121] The regulations consist of three main components. First, the regulations allow the administration of an alternate assessment. Second, the assessment does not have to be at grade-level. Third, there is a one percent cap on the reporting of students taking alternative assessments as proficient or higher.

The Department of Education considers an alternate assessment:

> an assessment designed for the small number of students with disabilities who are unable to participate in the regular State assessment, even with appropriate accommodations. An alternate assessment may include materials collected under several circumstances, including (1) teacher observation of the student, (2) samples of student work produced during regular classroom instruction that demonstrate mastery of specific instructional strategies in place of performance on a computer-scored multiple-choice test covering the same content and skills, or (3) standardized performance tasks produced in an "on-demand" setting, such as completion of an assigned task on test day.[122]

The department also stipulates that, depending on the disabling condition of the participating students, a range of alternative assessments may be used as long as they have a defined structure, clear guidelines for participation, scoring criteria and procedures, and a reporting format aligned with the academic achievement standards defined by the particular state.[123]

In the case of students with the most significant cognitive disabilities, an alternate assessment may be scored against alternate achievement standards rather than at grade level. The regulations further require that parents of children taking alternative assessments be informed that "their child's achievement will be based on alternate achievement standards."[124] Additionally, the state or LEA must report both the number and the percentage of students taking the alternative assessments as well as students with disabilities taking regular assessments with appropriate accommodations.[125]

Even if students take an alternate assessment evaluated under alternate academic achievement standards, their achievement is still calculated within AYP. The regulations allow LEAs to include proficient and advanced scores of students with the most significant cognitive disabilities based on alternate academic achievement standards up to one percent of all students assessed.[126] The state or LEA may also request an exemption to the temporarily exceed the one percent cap with a showing of special circumstances that justify such an exception.[127] More than one percent of the students may take the alternative assessments and achieve proficient or advanced scores on alternative academic achievement standards. However, unless the aforementioned exception is granted, all scores above the one percent cap must be counted as non-proficient. It is up to the LEA to decide which scores to count.[128]

Modified Academic Achievement Standards

The second change concerning the testing of children with disabilities involves what the department calls "modified academic achievement standards." In response to the changes that permit alternate assessments, the experiences of many states, and recent research, the department realized that a small group of students exists "whose disability has precluded them from achieving grade-level proficiency and whose progress is such that they will not reach grade-level proficiency in the same time frame as other students."[129] Accordingly, the Department of Education acknowledged that for these students, the current assessment options do not provide an accurate gauge of these students' abilities. The regular grade-level assessment is too difficult, and the alternative assessment is too easy. Neither type of assessment gives teachers and parents the type of information useful in helping this student group progress toward grade-level.[130]

To remedy this assessment gap, the Department of Education changed the regulations concerning NCLB to permit states to develop an assessment that is "appropriately challenging for this group of students as part of their State accountability and assessment systems …"[131] The regulations require that such an assessment be based on modified academic achievement standards that cover grade-level content so that students can work toward grade-level achievement.[132]

The department is intentionally silent on which students are eligible to be assessed using modified academic achievement standards as long as the students are in any of the disabilities categories listed in the Individuals with Disabilities Education Act (IDEA). However, the state must develop eligibility criteria that at least considers the following: (a) objective evidence that a student is unable to achieve grade-level proficiency because of the student's disability; (b) the student's progress, even with special education services is such that the student will not achieve grade-level proficiency within the year;

and (c) the student's individualized education program (IEP) goals are based on academic content standards for the student's enrolled grade. Pursuant to the state criteria, determination of eligibility is left up to a particular student's IEP team, which includes the student's parents.[133]

The Department of Education assumes that many of the students who will be assessed under the modified academic achievement standards are in the regular education classroom with students their own age and will represent only "a small portion of students with disabilities."[134] Like the earlier alternate assessment regulations for students with significant cognitive disabilities, the Department of Education imposes a cap on the percentage of advanced or proficient scores that an LEA or state may count toward AYP. Unlike the one percent cap for assessments based on "alternate" academic achievement standards, the cap for assessments based on "modified" academic achievement standards is 2 percent of all students in the grades assessed.[135] Also, states and LEAs may not ask for an exception to this cap,[136] but they may exceed the 2 percent cap if the number of "proficient and advanced scores based on alternate academic achievement standards" is less than 1 percent and the "number of proficient and advanced scores based on alternate or modified academic achievement standards combined does not exceed 3 percent of all students in the grades assessed" (emphasis added).[137]

The assessment that states may develop based on modified academic achievement standards must adhere to the same grade-level standards for the grade in which the student is enrolled. The state may use different strategies to create the assessment, such as simplifying the answers or providing an audio or visual format, as long as the assessment satisfies requirements for high technical quality including validity, reliability, accessibility, objectivity, and consistency with nationally recognized and technical standards.[138]

Other Recent Changes in the Regulations

Several other changes to the NCLB regulations were published in the Federal Register on April 9, 2007, that do not concern modified academic achievement standards for students with disabilities. Each will be described briefly here.

One change requires states to establish that all separate subgroups have the same minimum number of students.[139] If a state previously permitted different sized subgroups, it does not have to adopt the smallest group size it used. It just must use the same group size for all subgroups starting on AYP determinations for the 2007-08 school year.[140]

Another change in the regulations permits multiple assessment administrations for all students. This decision to permit students to take an assessment more than once is up to the states. Usually this situation concerns graduation tests or other high-stakes assessments.[141]

A third change allows states to include the scores of students who were previously identified with disabilities under the IDEA, but no longer receive special education services. States may permit such students' scores to count when making AYP determinations in the IEP subgroup for up to two years after they no longer receive services. If states choose to include some former students with disabilities, they must include all of them, not just students who achieve "proficient" or "advanced" on the state assessment.[142]

Growth Models

Responding to requests by states and educators, Secretary of Education Margaret Spellings announced a program for qualified states to request the use of growth-based accountability models in November, 2005. Such models offer "greater flexibility in tracking individual students' annual progress [and] provide states with more options for a nuanced accountability system, while adhering to the core principles of No Child Left Behind."[143] What distinguishes a growth model from the standard state assessment model is that the assessment system must produce comparable results from grade to grade and year to year and track student progress as part of the state data system.[144]

The Department of Education set several principles that all growth model proposals had to meet. For example, any growth model must measure achievement based on meeting grade-level proficiency, not on student background or school characteristics. Any model must also hold schools accountable for student achievement in reading/language arts and mathematics, ensure that all students in tested grades are included in the assessment and accountability system, hold schools and districts accountable for the performance of each student subgroup, and include all schools and districts in a given state. A model must assess each of grades 3-8 and in high school for both reading/language arts and mathematics, as well as include student participation rates and student achievement on a separate academic indicator in the state accountability system.[145]

Finally, a state's model had to receive approval through a "rigorous" NCLB peer review process, which was instituted to "ensure that the selection process was fair and transparent for all participating states."[146] The peer review process consisted of states submitting their proposed growth models to a review board made up of nationally recognized education experts who then made recommendations on states' proposals. Thirteen states reached the peer review stage and nine states received either full approval or conditional approval of their models.[147]

In December of 2007 Secretary of Education Margaret Spellings announced that the growth model would be open to all states noting that there is "broad bipartisan support for growth models and now, many states have improved data systems so they can track individual student growth over time."[148] Any state that wanted to submit a growth model proposal to the U.S. Department of Education had to do so by February 1, 2008. New proposals would be subject to a similar peer review process as previous proposals.[149]

Conclusion

In summary, NCLB is perhaps one of the most extensive pieces of education legislation in recent history. It is also certainly one of the most demanding. It contains very specific built-in accountability features while presumably creating more leeway for state and local agencies by way of consolidating programs and paperwork. Recent changes to the legislation, although minor, suggest it will likely encounter further compliance and implementation challenges in the future. With the realization that schools demonstrate varying strengths and weaknesses when it comes to teaching and learning, an ongoing evaluation of the legislation will seemingly be necessary, which may lead to even greater flexibility being afforded to local units. Although the capacity of schools to adhere to the legislation's core mandates is important, the intent of motivating schools to excel and providing opportunities for children to reach their potential is equally paramount. While NCLB promises much for underachieving students and provides remediation as well as sanctions for noncompliant schools, the act has had its critics, many of whom are concerned about lack of funding to implement the law as well as a draining of resources from schools serving poor children. Clearly, NCLB is a bold attempt to improve education in this country. Whether it ultimately meets its goals will depend on the level of commitment, communication, and support from all its key stakeholders.

Endnotes

1 20 U.S.C. § 6301 *et seq.,* Pub. L. No. 107–10, 115 Stat. 1425 (2002).
2 Hereafter referred to as NCLB or "the Act."
3 *Id.*
4 U.S. Department of Education, Office of Elementary and Secondary Education, No Child Left Behind: A Desktop Reference (2002).
5 *Id.*
6 *Id.*
7 *Id.*
8 115 Stat. 1425, Title I, Part A
9 Title I, § 1001, at 1439.
10 Title I, Part A, Subpart 1, § 1111 (b)(1)(D).
11 *Id.* at § 1111(b)(3)(A), 115 Stat. 1449.
12 *Id.*
13 By the 2005–06 school year, states are required to institute, at minimum, a statewide assessment in reading and mathematics. If needed, a language arts assessment may be substituted for a reading assessment. In addition, states are required no later than the 2005–06 school year to establish a unitary body of science standards. States are required by the 2007–08 school year to integrate the science assessment. Other requirements specify minimum testing for students. For instance, students must be assessed in reading or mathematics at least once between grades 3 and 5, 6 and 9, and 10 and 12. The same periods apply to science assessments beginning in 2007–08.
14 *Id.*
15 Title I, Part A.
16 Title I, Part A, subpart 1, 115 Stat. 1446.

[17] The act specifies that no later than twelve years after the 2001–02 school year, all children will be required to meet or exceed the proficiency standards on the state assessment according to each state's adequate yearly progress timeline. Although adequate yearly progress targets may be the same targets for more than one year, intermediate adequate yearly progress targets must increase at least every third year or less.

[18] Students with special needs must be provided accommodations and adaptations in a manner consistent with the Individual with Disabilities Education Act. Students identified as limited English proficient must be provided an "assessment in the language and form most likely to yield accurate data on what students know and can do in academic content areas" (Title I, Part A, Subpart 1, § 1111 (b) (3) (C) (ix)). In addition, LEAs are currently required to administer yearly English proficiency examinations to limited English proficient students. The act specifies that students attending a school within the United States for three or more consecutive years are required to take English written examinations unless deemed unreliable on a case by case basis.

[19] The method for measuring adequate yearly progress must also be valid and reliable. As the law states, "not less than 95 percent of each group of students [in all groups] who are enrolled in the school [is] required to take the test" (*Id.* at 1448). However, the act concedes that the 95 percent rule does not apply in situations when either the statistical measure is deemed unreliable or when it discloses "personally identifiable" information regarding particular students. Also, if a subgroup's performance on the state assessment diminishes by 10 percent in one year but yields progress in at least one alternate indicator (e.g., graduation rate, locally administered assessments, attendance rates), a school can still fulfill the adequate yearly progress requirements.

[20] Title I, Part A, subpart 1, § 1119.

[21] Title I, Part A, § 1119, 115 Stat. 1505.

[22] *Id.*

[23] *Id.*

[24] *Id.*

[25] *Id.*

[26] *Id.* at 1460.

[27] *Id.*

[28] Student transportation to the school of choice and supplementary services is funded by the local educational agency through funding made available through Title I, Part A. If funds are exhausted, lowest achieving children classified as low income are given priority. Transferring students may remain at an alternate school until the student has completed the highest grade the school offers. For instance, if a student transfers to a middle school at sixth grade but the student's former school is no longer identified as needing improvement, the local educational agency is no longer obligated to provide school choice (*Id.* at 1487). LEAs, such as schools failing to meet adequate yearly progress for two consecutive years, are also subject to improvement action (*Id.* at 1488).

[29] *Id.* at 1488.

[30] *Id.* at 1481.

[31] *Id.* at 1487.

[32] *Id.* at 1483.

[33] *Id.* at 1483–84.

[34] *Id.*

[35] Title I, Part B.

[36] Title II, Part A.

[37] Title II, Part B.

[38] Title IV, Part A.

[39] 115 Stat. 1461.

[40] Schools are required to expend at least 20 percent of funding accorded through Title I, Part A on school choice option programs and supplementary education service programs.

[41] Title I, Part A, Subpart 1, § 1116(e). Potential providers as defined in the legislation include profit, nonprofit, and LEAs.
[42] Title IV, Part B.
[43] Title V, Part B, Subparts 1 & 2.
[44] Title V, Part B, Subpart 3.
[45] With respect to identification, the act requires that parents of limited English proficient students be afforded information within thirty days from the beginning of the school year regarding reasons for placement, means of assessment employed, utilized methods of instruction, individualized progress, and program exit criteria to name a few.
[46] Title IX, Part E, Subpart 2, § 9532.
[47] Criteria defining "persistently dangerous" status are determined by the state along with "a representative sample" of LEAs.
[48] Title I, Part C.
[49] Title VII, Part A.
[50] Title VII, Part B.
[51] Title VII, Part C.
[52] Title I, Part D.
[53] Title I, Part H.
[54] Part C of Title X.
[55] Title II, Part A, Subpart 5, § 2151 (B).
[56] Title II, Part A, Subpart 5, § 2151 (C).
[57] Title II, Part B.
[58] Title II, Part C, Subpart 2.
[59] Title II, Part D, Subparts 1 & 2.
[60] Title V, Part D, Subpart 8.
[61] Title II, Part C, Subpart 1, Chapter B.
[62] Title II, Part C, Subpart 1, Chapter A.
[63] 115 Stat. 1550.
[64] Title I, Part B, Subpart 3.
[65] Title I, Part B, Subpart 4.
[66] Title II, Part A, Subpart 5, § 2151 (E).
[67] Title V, Part D, Subpart 2.
[68] Title I, Part B, Subpart 2.
[69] Title II, Part D, Subpart 3.
[70] Title V, Part D, Subpart 9.
[71] Title I, Part B, subpart 3.
[72] Title V, Part D, Subpart 11.
[73] Title II, Part C, Subpart 5.
[74] Title IV, Part A.
[75] *Id.*
[76] Title IV, Part A, Subpart 3.
[77] Title IV, Part C.
[78] Title IV, Part A, Subpart 3.
[79] Title IV, Part C.
[80] Title I, §§1113–14.
[81] Title I, §§1113–19.
[82] Title I, Part A, § 1114, 115 Stat. 1475.
[83] Title V, Part D, Subpart 2.
[84] Title I, Part B, Subpart 3.
[85] Title V, Part D, Subpart 3.
[86] Title I, Part G.
[87] Title I, Part B, Subpart 3.
[88] Title IV, Part A.
[89] Title IV, Part B.

[90] Title V, Part B, Subpart2.
[91] Title I, Part D.
[92] Title I, Part C.
[93] Title V, Part D, Subpart 16.
[94] Title V, Part D, Subpart 6.
[95] Title V, Part C.
[96] Title I, Part G.
[97] Title IV, Part B.
[98] Title II, Part A.
[99] Title IV, Part A, Subpart 3 (a).
[100] Title IV, Part A, Subpart 3 (b).
[101] Title VII, Part A.
[102] Title VII, Part B.
[103] Title VII, Part C.
[104] Title VI, Part A, Subpart 2.
[105] Title II, Part D, Subparts 1 & 2.
[106] Title V, Part C.
[107] Title IX, Part B.
[108] Department of Education. (2004, March 29) *Secretary Paige Issues New Policy for Calculating Participation Rates Under No Child Left Behind.* Retrieved September 20, 2007, from http://www.ed.gov/news/pressreleases/2004/03/03292004.html.
[109] *Id.*
[110] U.S. Department of Education. (2004, March). *New No Child Left Behind Flexibility: Highly Qualified Teachers, Fact Sheet.* Retrieved September 20, 2007, from http://www.ed.gov/nclb/methods/teachers/hqtflexibility.html.
[111] *Id.*
[112] *Id.*
[113] *Id.*
[114] Office of Elementary and Secondary Education, U.S. Department of Education. (2007, May) *Assessment and Accountability for Recently Arrived and Former Limited English Proficient (LEP) Students: Non-Regulatory Guidance.* Retrieved September 20, 2007, from http://www.ed.gov/policy/elsec/guid/edpicks.jhtml?src=ln.
[115] U.S. Department of Education, 71 Fed. Reg. 54,187 (September 13, 2006)(to be codified at 34 C.F.R. pt. 200) Retrieved September 20, 2007, from: http://www.ed.gov/legislation/FedRegister/finrule/2006-3/091306a.html.
[116] U.S. Department of Education, *supra* note 8.
[117] U.S. Department of Education, *supra* note 9.
[118] *Id.*
[119] U.S. Department of Education, *supra* note 8.
[120] *Id.*
[121] U.S. Department of Education, 68 Fed. Reg. 68,697, 68,698 (December 9, 2003)(to be codified at 34 C.F.R. pt. 200). Retrieved September 20, 2007, from http://www.ed.gov/legislation/FedRegister/finrule/2003-4/120903a.html.
[122] *Id.* at p. 68699.
[123] *Id.*
[124] *Id.* at p. 68702 (to be codified at 34 CFR 200.6(a)(2)(iii)(A)(2)).
[125] *Id.* (to be codified at 34 CFR 200.6(a)(2)(iii)(B)).
[126] *Id.* at p. 68703 (to be codified at 34 CFR 200.13(c)(1)(ii)).
[127] *Id.* (to be codified at 34 CFR 200.13(c)(2) &(3)).
[128] *Id.* (to be codified at 34 CFR 200.13(c)(4)).
[129] U.S. Department of Education 72 Fed. Reg. 17,747, 17,748 (April 9, 2007). Retrieved September 25, 2007, from: http://www.ed.gov/legislation/FedRegister/finrule/2007-2/040907a.html.
[130] *Id.*
[131] *Id.*

[132] *Id.*

[133] *Id.* at p. 17749.

[134] *Id.*

[135] *Id.* at p. 17779 (to be codified at 34 CFR 200.13(c)(2)(ii)).

[136] *Id.* (to be codified at 34 CFR 200.13(c)(4)).

[137] *Id.* (to be codified at 34 CFR 200.13 (c)(3)).

[138] *Id.* at p. 17750.

[139] U.S. Department of Education. (2007, July 20). *Additional Title I Provisions Included in the Regulations Package on Modified Academic Achievement Standards Published in the Federal Register on April 9, 2007: Non-regulatory Guidance.* Retrieved on September 25, 2007, from: http://www.ed.gov/policy/speced/guid/modachieve-summary.html. (This change is to 34 C.F.R. pt. 200.7(a)(2)).

[140] *Id.*

[141] *Id.* (change is to 34 C.F.R. pt. 200.20(c)(3)).

[142] *Id.* (change is to 34 C.F.R. pt. 200.20(f)).

[143] Growth Models: Ensuring Grade-Level Proficiency for All Students by 2014. July 2007. Retrieved October 25, 2007, from http://www.ed.gov/admins/lead/account/growthmodel/proficiency.html.

[144] *Id.*

[145] *Id.*

[146] *Id.*

[147] Alaska, Arizona, Arkansas, Delaware, Florida, Iowa, North Carolina, Ohio, and Tennessee.

[148] Secretary Spellings Invites Eligible States to Submit Innovative Models for Expanded Growth Model Pilot. December 7, 2007. Retrieved December 17, 2007, from http://www.ed.gov/news/pressreleases/2007/12/12072007.html.

[149] *Id.*

Chapter 30

Religious Influences and Accommodations in Public Schools

Martha M. McCarthy

Introduction

Religious—primarily Protestant—influences in American public education were common from colonial times through the 1950s. Then, in the early 1960s, these religious observances in public schools were significantly curtailed by two landmark Supreme Court decisions that relied on the Establishment Clause of the First Amendment to bar school-sponsored daily prayer and Bible reading from public schools.[1] The Court reasoned that voluntary participation of students in the religious activities was irrelevant; school sponsorship of such devotionals abridged the First Amendment. Instead of resolving all the controversial issues regarding devotional activities in public education, these decisions catapulted school prayer into the political realm, spawning more than four decades of litigation and legislative responses.[2]

From the mid-twentieth century through the 1980s, the Supreme Court generally supported church/state separation in education cases. Starting in 1971, for about two decades the Court consistently applied the stringent three-part test articulated in *Lemon v. Kurtzman* to evaluate Establishment Clause claims.[3] For government action to satisfy the *Lemon* test, it must have a secular purpose and a primary effect that neither advances nor impedes religion, and it must avoid excessive governmental entanglement with religion. Recently, however, the federal judiciary seems to be shifting away from this separationist stance and moving toward support for greater government accommodation of religion, especially in cases involving government aid to private schools.[4] Even in public school cases, courts seem more likely to uphold student-initiated religious expression than they were a quarter century ago.[5] The "wall of separation" between church and state has given way to the notion of equal treatment and equal access for religious and secular groups and expression. The current Supreme Court seems to favor flexibility in selecting criteria to assess Establishment Clause claims in individual cases, employing an endorsement standard,[6] a coercion test,[7] a modified *Lemon* analysis,[8] or perhaps all three, depending on the circumstances. Cases often pit Establishment Clause restrictions against rights guaranteed by the Free Speech and Free Exercise Clauses, which further complicates the judiciary's task.[9] This chapter explores recent legal developments in connection with various types of religious influences and accommodations in public education, highlighting recent changes in legal doctrine.

Legal Issues

Silent Prayer

Students can pray silently in public schools; indeed, it would be impossible to know whether such silent devotionals were taking place. The legal challenges have focused on state laws or school board policies that authorize a period of silent meditation or prayer in public schools (usually one minute at the beginning of the day). In 1985, the Supreme Court rendered its only opinion to date on this issue, *Wallace v. Jaffree*, in which it relied on the Establishment Clause to invalidate a 1981 Alabama silent prayer law.[10] The Court carefully reviewed the legislative history of the amended law that added "or voluntary prayer" to a silent meditation provision, concluding that the law was designed to advance religion. The Court indicated, however, that laws calling for silent meditation or prayer in public schools *without* a legislative intent to compel prayer might survive an Establishment Clause challenge.

In a more recent case, the Eleventh Circuit found no Establishment Clause violation in a Georgia law requiring a moment for silent reflection in all public school classrooms at the beginning of the school day.[11] The law specified that the moment of silence was not to be a religious observance (although students can choose to pray silently). The law's provision stipulating that nothing in the statute would be construed to interfere with permissible voluntary student devotional activities was contested as authorizing voluntary verbal prayer. The court reasoned that this provision simply stated that other parts of the Georgia law should not be interpreted as prohibiting such voluntary prayer.

The Fourth Circuit subsequently upheld a Virginia law stipulating that each school board shall provide for the daily observance of one minute of silence in all classrooms so pupils may "meditate, pray, or engage in other silent activity."[12] The appeals court found that the law was religiously neutral and intended to provide time for quiet reflection, which is an appropriate way to start the school day. Given these rulings, it appears that challenges to silent prayer provisions will continue to be treated on a case-by-case basis.

Voluntary Spoken Devotionals

Following the Supreme Court decisions barring daily Bible reading and prayer sponsored by public schools in the 1960s,[13] federal courts struck down several state laws and school board policies authorizing voluntary student participation in prayers in public school assemblies and classrooms, reasoning that such actions represented the public school.[14] The status of graduation devotionals was unclear until the Supreme Court rendered *Lee v. Weisman* in 1992, invalidating a Rhode Island school district's policy that permitted principals to invite clergy members to deliver invocations and benedictions at middle and high school graduation ceremonies.[15] The Court held that the policy had a coercive effect in that students felt peer pressure to participate in the devotionals during the school-sponsored graduation ceremony. The Court was not convinced that the Establishment Clause violation was diminished because participation in the graduation ceremony was optional, reasoning that students should not have to miss this important event because of their religious faith.

Weisman was a controversial decision, generating widespread negative reactions across school districts, especially in the South. A number of school districts that had not held baccalaureate programs for more than two decades reinstated them, although these religious services must be sponsored by churches or other outside groups, which can rent space from the school district to hold the programs.[16]

Devotionals Initiated by Private Actors. Some school districts responded to *Weisman* by designating the graduation ceremony a forum for student expression. Under such circumstances, advocates assert that the student-led devotionals do not represent the public school. The Ninth Circuit upheld an Idaho school district's policy that prohibited school authorities from censoring students' graduation speeches in this forum created for student speakers to select "an address, poem, reading, song, musical presentation, prayer, or any other pronouncement" of their choosing.[17] The court reasoned that the policy was permissible since student speakers were selected based on secular criteria (academic standing) and were not encouraged by school personnel to include devotionals in their remarks.[18]

However, the Ninth Circuit in two other cases upheld school districts in refusing to allow students to deliver proselytizing graduation speeches. School policies in these districts required students' speeches to be submitted to the school principals for review.[19] In one case, the student plaintiff had been informed that proselytizing parts of his graduation speech would have to be removed to respect the Establishment Clause, but that he could keep references to his own beliefs. The school rejected the student's request for a notation to be put in the graduation program disclaiming sponsorship of the speech but did allow him to announce that his speech had been involuntarily altered and that copies of the original version would be available following the ceremony. School authorities in this district clearly maintained control of the graduation ceremony, and the court agreed that censorship of proposed religious speeches was necessary to avoid an Establishment Clause violation.[20] In such cases, the key concern is whether the school has explicitly established a forum for student expression in the graduation ceremony; if not, school personnel can review students' graduation speeches, and they may have a duty to censor religiously proselytizing speeches.

The most controversial post-*Weisman* strategy to return devotionals to public schools has been to allow students to vote whether to include student-delivered invocations and benedictions in the graduation ceremony. The

Fifth Circuit has upheld such graduation devotionals, reasoning that allowing students to decide by election whether to have nonsectarian, nonproselytizing graduation prayers removed the school's sponsorship of the religious expression.[21] Subsequently, the Third and Ninth Circuit appellate courts reached an opposite conclusion, concluding that school authorities cannot delegate to students decisions that the First Amendment forbids school districts from making in the first place.[22]

Although the Supreme Court has not directly addressed student-led graduation prayers, in 2000 it struck down a Texas school district's policy authorizing student elections to determine whether to have student-led devotionals before public school football games.[23] The Court majority in *Santa Fe Independent School District v. Doe* declared that student religious expression at a school event on school property and representing the student body under the supervision of school personnel could not be considered private speech.[24] Even though students made the ultimate choice of speakers and content, the school authorized the school election in the first place, giving the impression that the devotionals represented the school. Thus, the Court majority concluded that the practice entailed both perceived and actual endorsement of religion and that the policy at issue had a sham secular purpose like the district's previous initiatives to promote Christian observances in school-related events.[25] However, the majority emphasized that the Constitution does not prohibit public school students from voluntarily praying at school if the devotionals are not school sponsored.[26]

The *Santa Fe* ruling left unanswered questions about student-initiated devotionals in public schools, especially in graduation ceremonies. *Santa Fe* was rendered soon after two Eleventh Circuit decisions in which the appeals court took a strong stand in protecting student-initiated religious expression in public schools.[27] In one case, the appellate court in an *en banc* decision upheld a Florida school district's policy that authorizes public school seniors to select classmates to give graduation messages and allows the speakers to choose the content, which can be sectarian.[28] In the second decision, the Eleventh Circuit lifted the portion of an injunction that had prohibited students from publicly expressing religious views in most school settings in an Alabama school district.[29] The appeals court declared that the Establishment Clause does not require and the Free Speech Clause does not permit suppression of student-initiated religious expression in public schools. The Supreme Court vacated both Eleventh Circuit decisions and remanded the cases for further consideration in light of *Santa Fe*, and the appeals court subsequently reaffirmed its earlier rulings.[30] The Eleventh Circuit declared that all student religious speech in public schools is not sponsored by the public school.[31] Thus, despite *Weisman* and *Santa Fe*, the federal judiciary continues to expand the protection of student religious expression in public schools, as long as the expression does not clearly represent the school.

The Eighth Circuit broadly interpreted what constitutes private in contrast to school-sponsored religious expression, finding no Establishment Clause violation in a board member's unscheduled recitation of the Lord's Prayer in the graduation ceremony.[32] The district allowed board member Scheer to deliver a short message during the ceremony, given the district's practice of allowing school board members whose children were graduating to address the class. After brief remarks, Scheer recited the Lord's Prayer and encouraged others to join him. Even though the expression took place at a school-sponsored event and Scheer was on the governing board of the school district, the appeals court found the expression to be private and thus constitutionally protected.[33] The court found no affirmative school sponsorship of the board member's prayer.

In addition to guidelines from courts, the federal No Child Left Behind Act (NCLB) of 2001 directs the U.S. Department of Education to advise school districts regarding permissible religious activities. Under NCLB, for the first time federal aid is conditioned on school districts certifying to the state educational agency that no school policy prevents or denies participation in constitutionally protected prayer in public elementary and secondary schools.[34] The U.S. Department of Education's *Guidance on Constitutionally Protected Prayer in Public Elementary and Secondary Schools* is intended to identify religious activities that must be allowed in public schools, and for topics without a clear Supreme Court precedent, the *Guidance* supports conservative citizen groups' expansive interpretation of permissible religious activities.[35]

Other Devotional Expression in the Classroom. Most of the recent legal activity has focused on the distinction between private and school-sponsored devotionals, but other issues have also generated controversies. For example, while well established that students cannot be compelled to recite the Pledge of Allegiance to the American Flag,[36] controversy surrounds whether the Pledge can be said at all in public schools, because it contains the phrase, "Under God." The Seventh Circuit reasoned that the phrase, which was added to the Pledge in 1954, did not change this patriotic observance into a prayer, so it rejected an Establishment Clause challenge to an Illinois law requiring students to recite the Pledge.[37] This court concluded that the "ceremonial deism" in the Pledge "has lost through rote repetition any significant religious content."[38] Similarly, a Virginia federal district court found the Pledge's reference to God to be "theologically benign."[39] The court further ruled that nonparticipating students were not punished, even though recitation of the Pledge was considered in a citizenship reward program.

In contrast, the Ninth Circuit attracted national attention in 2002 when it declared that saying the Pledge in public schools abridges the Establishment Clause by endorsing a belief in monotheism.[40] Rejecting the "ceremonial deism" justification, the court found the coercive impact particularly harmful in school settings, given the age and impressionability of children who "are required to adhere to the norms set by their school, their teacher, and their fellow students."[41] The appellate panel applied the *Lemon,* coercion, and endorsement standards in finding an Establishment Clause violation and emphasized that the words "under God" had been inserted in the Pledge to promote religion rather than to advance the legitimate secular goal of encouraging patriotism.

The Supreme Court reversed the Ninth Circuit's decision in 2004 without addressing the constitutional claim in *Elk Grove Unified School District v. Newdow.* The majority reasoned that under California law, the noncustodial parent, Newdow, lacked standing to challenge his daughter's participation in the Pledge.[42] Observing that Newdow retained the right to instruct his daughter regarding his religious views, the Court ruled that this right does not extend to curtailing his daughter's exposure to religious beliefs endorsed by her mother. In a subsequent suit, a California federal district court again ruled that the classroom recitation of the Pledge violates the Establishment Clause,[43] so the Supreme Court soon could have another opportunity to address the substantive issue. If the Supreme Court should strike down the practice, the political reactions would likely be significant.

Allegations that public schools are proselytizing students also have been raised in other contexts. For example, federal appellate courts have ordered teachers to remove religiously oriented materials from their classrooms[44] and to refrain from classroom devotionals[45] or religious references in the instructional program.[46] A federal district court also held that school authorities properly instructed a teacher to cover a proselytizing shirt at school.[47]

Courts have upheld the dismissal of teachers who were proselytizing students or disregarding selected aspects of the curriculum that conflicted with their religious values. To illustrate, the Seventh Circuit upheld a school board's dismissal of a kindergarten teacher who literally interpreted the Biblical prohibition against worshiping graven images and thus refused to teach about the American flag, the observance of patriotic holidays, and the importance of historical figures such as Abraham Lincoln.[48] More recently, the Fourth Circuit rejected a teacher's claim that he had a constitutional right to display in his classroom several news articles promoting Christianity and a poster publicizing the National Day of Prayer.[49]

Proselytization of students by public school teachers clearly violates the Establishment Clause, but the Supreme Court has emphasized that it is permissible, even desirable, to teach the Bible and other religious documents from a literary, cultural, or historical perspective.[50] Many public schools across two-thirds of the states use the Bible as a textbook in academic courses.[51] Yet, the linc is not always clear between teaching about religion and instilling religious tenets. Some Bible study courses, particularly at the elementary school level, have been challenged as a ploy to advance sectarian beliefs. Courts have struck down programs where private groups have controlled the hiring and supervision of personnel or the selection of curricular materials.[52] While most challenges have involved instruction pertaining to the Bible and the Christian faith, the Ninth Circuit upheld a school's use of role-playing to teach seventh-grade world history students about Islam, reasoning that learning about the five pillars of Islam did not entail the practice of a religion.[53]

Several controversies since the 1990s have focused on students' decisions to use religious materials or topics in academic classes, and federal courts consistently have ruled that the public school instructional program is state-sponsored and subject to Establishment Clause restrictions. Students have not yet been successful in claiming a free exercise or free speech right to express their religious views in class assignments. Courts have reasoned that school projects can be censored to ensure that the school is not perceived as endorsing religious content.[54] Nonetheless, students seem likely to continue to assert that religious views should be treated like other views in the classroom (as they are during noninstructional time). Also, the Department of Education's *Guidance* stipulates that students may express their religious views in their homework, artwork, and other written and oral assignments,[55] despite the judicial rulings to the contrary.

Religious Displays and Holiday Observances

The observance of religious holidays and the display of religious documents in public schools also remain contentious. In 1980, the Supreme Court declined to hear an appeal of an Establishment Clause case in which the Eighth Circuit allowed the prudent and objective observance of the Christmas holiday in public schools, even though songs such as "Silent Night" were sung and the nativity scene was displayed.[56] A week later, however, the divided Supreme Court rendered *Stone v. Graham*, striking down a Kentucky law calling for the display of the Ten Commandments in public school classrooms.[57] The Court majority held that the purpose of the Kentucky legislation was to advance a particular religious faith in violation of the Establishment Clause.

Other religious displays also have been challenged under the First Amendment. The Sixth Circuit invalidated the display of a portrait of Jesus in a public secondary school,[58] and the Eleventh Circuit upheld school authorities in ordering removal of religious words and symbols from murals painted for a school beautification project because the murals represented the school.[59] However, the New Jersey federal district court found that inclusion of religious holidays (e.g., Christmas and Hanukkah) on school district calendars satisfied the *Lemon* test because it was designed to broaden students' sensitivity towards diversity and knowledge of the role of religion in the development of civilization.[60] And a Virginia federal district court rejected an Establishment Clause challenge to the application of a state law requiring the posting of "In God We Trust" in public schools, reasoning that the motto's reference to God to symbolize the historic role of religion in our society.[61]

A Pennsylvania federal district court rejected an Establishment Clause challenge to a school district's winter display and program including a menorah, Kwanzaa candelabra and cloth, books about Kwanzaa and Hanukkah, a "giving" tree, books on holidays, a banner with "Happy Holidays," Hanukkah songs, a Kwanzaa chant, and secular Christmas songs (e.g., Frosty the Snowman).[62] The thrust of the complaint was that the display and program were not "Christian enough." Disagreeing, the court reasoned that the intent of the program and display was to celebrate religious diversity and the freedom for individuals to choose their own beliefs, and the program did not promote a particular faith.[63]

There has also been renewed interest in posting the Ten Commandments in public schools despite the 1980 Supreme Court precedent. A number of states and even Congress are considering legislation that would authorize posting the Ten Commandments with other historical documents in public buildings including schools, and some school boards have authorized these displays. The Supreme Court rendered two companion decisions pertaining to displays of the Ten Commandments in government buildings or on courthouse lawns in 2005. The Court upheld the longstanding display of a Ten Commandments monument on the Texas state capitol grounds along with other monuments and artifacts that reflect the secular purpose of paying tribute to the state's history.[64] In contrast, the Court struck down the display of framed copies of the Ten Commandments in two Kentucky county courthouses, noting that several attempts to add items to the displays did not eliminate their initial religious purpose.[65] Although *school* displays of the Ten Commandments were not at issue in these cases, the Supreme Court indicated that it still supports the *Stone v. Graham* decision.

Several other Supreme Court decisions outside the school domain since the 1990s have condoned the use of public funds or property for certain religious displays.[66] Notwithstanding these decisions, courts seem likely to continue to strike down sectarian displays in public schools. However, the objective recognition of religious holidays will presumably withstand judicial scrutiny as long as particular faiths are not being promoted.

Student and Community Devotional Meetings During Noninstructional Time

The issue of student and community groups holding devotional meetings in public school facilities before or after school involves competing First Amendment rights: free speech, free exercise, and association rights versus Establishment Clause restrictions.[67] While community groups requesting such access must rely on the First Amendment, high school students have federal statutory rights as well.

The Equal Access Act. In 1984, Congress passed the Equal Access Act (EAA) stipulating that if a federally assisted public secondary school provides a limited open forum for noncurriulum student groups to meet during noninstructional time, it cannot deny access to specific student groups because of the religious, political, or philosophical content of their meetings.[68] If the meetings have a religious orientation, school employees can attend only in a "nonparticipatory capacity" to maintain discipline.[69] Public high schools can comply with the EAA by not establishing a limited open forum for student expression and, thus, confining school access during noninstructional time to curriculum-related student groups.[70] Even if a limited open forum is created, school authorities can curtail meetings that would disrupt educational activities.

The Supreme Court in 1990 rejected an Establishment Clause challenge to the EAA in *Board of Education of the Westside Community Schools v. Mergens.*[71] The Court declared that a public secondary school allowing even one noncurriculum student group to meet is subject to the EAA and, thus, must grant school access to all nondisruptive student groups. The majority concluded that secondary schools would be exempt from the act's coverage only if all student groups are related to the curriculum in that their subject matter is currently or soon to be taught in the curriculum, they pertain to the body of courses as a whole, or participation in the groups is required as a part of courses.[72] But, the Court acknowledged the difficulties associated with determining whether specific groups are curriculum related.

Federal appellate courts in subsequent cases have ruled that the EAA prevails over state law calling for greater separation of church and state than demanded by the Establishment Clause[73] and that the EAA allows a student religious group to ensure the spiritual content of its meetings by requiring certain officers to be Christians.[74] A California appeals court held that clubs organized by adults, such as the Fellowship of Christian Athletes, could use the EAA to meet in public schools, as long as their on-campus meetings were initiated by students.[75]

The Third Circuit expansively interpreted the EAA's protection of student religious expression, holding that a student religious group was allowed to meet during the district's activity period, which was considered noninstructional time, even though attendance was taken.[76] The Ninth Circuit disagreed, concluding that a student/staff period—when student clubs were allowed to meet—was instructional time because students were expected to be present and attendance was taken.[77] Nonetheless, the Ninth Circuit broadly interpreted the EAA as entitling a student religious club to be treated like secular clubs in being featured in the school yearbook free of charge and using the public address system and bulletin boards.[78] The religious club also used the First Amendment to secure access to the student/staff period as well as other school resources available to secular clubs, even though these entitlements were not covered by the EAA.

Meetings of Community Groups. Since the EAA protects only student meetings during noninstructional time in secondary schools, community religious groups must rely on the First Amendment to gain access to public schools when classes are not in session. In *Lamb's Chapel v. Center Moriches Union Free School District*, the Supreme Court held in 1993 that a religious group was entitled to use the public school in the evening to show religious films pertaining to family life because school districts cannot enforce policies governing community facility use that entail viewpoint discrimination against sectarian groups.[79] In short, the Free Speech Clause demands that religious views be allowed on topics that are addressed in the forum from secular perspectives.

In 2001, the Supreme Court in *Good News Club v. Milford Central School* echoed this reasoning in allowing a private Christian organization to conduct its meetings in a New York public school.[80] The Milford School District had denied the Good News Club's request to hold afternoon meetings at the school, citing its community-use policy that allowed various civic and recreational groups to use the school but not for religious purposes. The Second Circuit reasoned that since the club meetings involved religious worship and instruction targeting children ages six to twelve, meetings immediately after school violated the Establishment Clause.[81]

Reversing the Second Circuit, the Supreme Court majority held that the school district's policy discriminated against religious viewpoints in violation of the Free Speech Clause.[82] The Court found it constitutionally irrelevant whether moral lessons are taught through films, as in *Lamb's Chapel,* or live storytelling and prayers.[83] The majority further declared that the Court has never barred private religious conduct during nonschool hours simply because elementary school children might be involved. Thus, under *Milford,* if a public school creates a limited forum for community meetings during nonschool hours, it cannot deny access to religious groups, even though students attending the school are the central participants in the groups' devotional activities.

Recently, student religious clubs also have relied in part on the First Amendment to challenge their discriminatory treatment in public schools.[84] The federal judiciary's broad interpretation of the First Amendment's protection of private speech, including religious expression, in public schools calls into question the continued need for the Equal Access Act. Since First Amendment protections are not confined to federally funded schools or to the secondary school level as is the EAA, this may suggest that there will be fewer EAA suits and more First Amendment claims involving student devotional meetings as well as community religious activities in public schools.

Distribution of Religious Literature

Most courts have prohibited school personnel[85] and religious groups[86] from distributing Bibles and other sectarian materials to captive public school audiences. Departing from this trend, however, the Fourth Circuit in 1998 upheld the distribution of Bibles at the high school level in a West Virginia school district.[87] The court considered the Gideons to be *private* citizens, not representatives of the school, and thus upheld the district's policy designating a day that private groups could make religious or political materials available to secondary students during noninstructional time. Yet, such distribution was not allowed in elementary schools due to concerns about whether younger children would misperceive the materials as sponsored by the public school.[88]

Courts have been more receptive to the distribution of religious publications by *students*, in contrast to religious *organizations*. Several courts have concluded that the same legal principles govern students' distribution of religious and nonreligious literature.[89] In 2004, the Supreme Court declined to review a decision in which the Ninth Circuit found viewpoint discrimination in a school district's refusal to allow the distribution of flyers for a summer camp because two of the camp's offerings were religious in nature.[90] But the federal district court ruled that the district's prohibition on selected perspectives violated the Free Speech Clause and did not implicate the Establishment Clause. The court reasoned that the school district had created a forum with the broad purpose of notifying students and their parents about community activities of interest. The court recognized, however, that the school district could require proselytizing language to be eliminated.[91]

Conflicting opinions have been rendered regarding student distribution of gifts with religious messages to classmates. A Massachusetts federal district court issued an injunction against school authorities who were prohibiting members of a high school religious club from distributing candy canes with religious messages during noninstructional time.[92] The court reasoned that the distribution did not represent the school and was thus protected private expression under the First Amendment. Yet, the Third Circuit upheld school officials in prohibiting elementary school students from distributing pencils and candy canes with religious messages during classroom holiday parties.[93] The court concluded that reasonable accommodations were made in that religious materials could be distributed before and after school and during recess. The court noted the difficulty young children would have in distinguishing school sponsorship from private religious expression during school activities.

The key factors in the constitutional assessment are *when* and *where* the religious materials are distributed (e.g., during class or noninstructional time) and *who* distributes the materials (e.g., students or school personnel). The age of the students is also a concern, since older children have greater ability to comprehend that materials distributed by classmates do not represent the school. Even if it is established that religious materials can be distributed, the students must comply with reasonable time, place, and manner regulations that are applied to the distribution of secular materials.[94]

Accommodations for Religious Beliefs

Some controversies have focused on the extent that public schools must provide accommodations to enable individuals to practice their religious beliefs. Legal developments involving release-time programs for sectarian education and religious exemptions from secular public school observances and activities are briefly reviewed below.

Release-Time Programs. The Supreme Court has invalidated the practice of using public school classrooms for clergy to provide religious training to public school students during the instructional day,[95] but the Court has held that the school can accommodate religion by releasing students to receive such religious training off public school grounds.[96] A release-time program was even upheld in a school district where students received an hour of religious instruction each week in a mobile unit parked at the edge of school property.[97] While it might seem easier to defend releasing all students early one day a week to broaden their choices, courts to date have not concluded that the single option of attending sectarian instruction or remaining in the public school advances religion or impairs nonparticipating pupils' state-created right to an education.

In a Utah case, the Tenth Circuit held that time spent by public school students in a release-time program at a Mormon seminary program could be counted toward satisfying compulsory school attendance and in calculating the school's state aid.[98] However, the court enjoined the school's practice of awarding high school credit for the secular aspects of daily instruction received at the seminary because the monitoring required to determine which parts of the course were sectarian would unconstitutionally entangle school officials with the church.

An Indiana federal district court also enjoined several features of a nondenominational Christian release-time program that was held in trailers located on public school property. Utilities for the trailers were supported by the school district, and nonparticipating students were required to read silently when their classmates participated in the religious instruction.[99] The court found Establishment Clause violations in the school district's effort to encourage participation in the program and in the use of school property for the religious classes.

Religious Exemptions from Secular Activities. Students and their parents often seek exemptions from public school observances and requirements that allegedly impair the practice of their religious tenets. As noted, the Supreme Court in *West Virginia State Board of Education v. Barnette* relied on the First Amendment in 1943 to strike down required student participation in the Pledge of Allegiance,[100] overturning a precedent it established only three years earlier.[101] However, the nature of required exemptions from the Pledge continues to be litigated. Courts have struck down laws or policies requiring students to stand during the Pledge or mandating parental notification of nonparticipating students, reasoning that such requirements coerce students into reciting the Pledge.[102]

An Alabama student brought suit after he was paddled by his teacher and principal because he silently raised his fist during the Pledge to protest the public chastisement of a classmate for not reciting the Pledge. The Eleventh Circuit concluded that the disciplinary action was an unwarranted infringement on the student's expression rights and that the principal and teacher were not entitled to summary judgment on qualified immunity grounds.[103] The court emphasized that the student's protest was not disruptive; nonparticipating students can be disciplined if they create a disturbance while others are reciting the Pledge.

In addition to excusal from participating in the Pledge, religious exemptions also have been requested from curriculum components. Whereas teachers cannot assert a free exercise right to disregard aspects of the state-prescribed curriculum,[104] the judiciary has been more inclined to support students' requests for exemptions from instructional requirements because students are required to attend school. School authorities must have a compelling justification to deny students an exemption from a requirement that impairs the exercise of sincere religious beliefs.

Requests for religious exemptions usually are handled at the classroom or school level and do not evoke legal controversies. Students often have secured religious exemptions from instructional activities, such as drug education, sex education, coeducational physical education, dancing instruction, officers' training programs, and specific course assignments, if alternatives can satisfy the instructional objectives.[105] Although specific children are excused, the secular activities themselves are not disturbed. When controversies have evoked litigation, some courts have ordered exemptions where the student's educational program is not adversely affected. For example, an Illinois federal district court upheld a parent in keeping her children home on "opposite sex day" because students dressing as members of the opposite sex had a coercive effect on the practice of her religious beliefs.[106]

Religious exemptions have not been honored if considered unnecessary to accommodate the practice of religious tenets or if the exemptions would substantially disrupt the school or students' academic progress. In an illustrative case, the Second Circuit rejected a parent's request for his son to be exempted from a Connecticut school district's mandatory health curriculum, finding such attendance rationally related to the legitimate governmental goal of providing students important health information.[107] However, the offended student was allowed to be excused from certain lessons, including those on family life, physical growth, and AIDS instruction. The Sixth Circuit rejected fundamentalist Christian parents' request that their children be excused from exposure to the basal reading series used in elementary grades in a Tennessee school district.[108] Reversing the lower court's grant of the exemption, the Sixth Circuit reasoned that the books did not burden the students' exercise of their religious beliefs because the students were not required to profess a creed or perform religious exercises. Courts also have denied religious exemptions for student athletes if an excusal from specific regulations might pose a safety hazard or interfere with the management of athletic teams.[109]

Conservative parent organizations have been successful in getting federal and state laws enacted that allow students to be excused from certain public school activities and components of the curriculum for religious and other reasons.[110] For example, more than half of the states currently allow students to opt out of sex education instruction or require parental consent for children to participate in such instruction in public schools.[111] Thus, parents may be able to use legislation to secure exemptions for their children under such laws, even if they cannot substantiate that particular instructional activities impair free exercise rights.

Religious Challenges to the Curriculum

Unlike its receptivity to reasonable exemptions for individual students, the federal judiciary has not condoned requests for various courses, activities, and instructional materials to be eliminated from public schools to satisfy parents' religious preferences. The Supreme Court has recognized that "'the state has no legitimate interest in protecting any or all religions from views distasteful to them.'"[112]

Instruction about Evolution. Instruction pertaining to the origin of human life on earth has generated legal disputes since the famous *Scopes* "monkey trial," in which the Tennessee Supreme Court in 1927 upheld a law that prohibited the teaching of any theory that denies the Genesis version of creation or suggests "that man has descended from a lower order of animals."[113] In 1968, however, the United States Supreme Court struck down an Arkansas anti-evolution statute under the Establishment Clause, concluding that evolution is science rather than a secular religion and holding that a state cannot restrict student access to such information simply to satisfy religious preferences.[114] Subsequently, the Supreme Court in 1987 invalidated a Louisiana statute that mandated "equal time" for creation science and evolution and required school boards to make available curriculum guides, teaching aids, and resource materials on creation science.[115] The Court concluded that the law was intended to discredit scientific information and advance religious beliefs in violation of the Establishment Clause.

Notwithstanding two Supreme Court decisions, the origin of humanity continues to generate legal activity. Courts have rejected teachers' claims that they have a right to disregard directives to teach evolution[116] and assertions that biology texts should be dropped for allegedly treating evolution as fact instead of theory.[117] Federal courts also have struck down efforts to include disclaimers (indicating that evolution is not a fact) in instruction or texts as a ploy to convey support of fundamentalist Christian doctrine.[118]

There has been political activity at the school district or state level pertaining to teaching evolution and alternative theories in forty states during the past decade, and developments in some states, such as Kansas, have made front-page news.[119] Much of the recent controversy has focused on teaching intelligent design (ID), which supporters distinguish from creationism because ID doctrine contends that human beings are too complex to have evolved randomly by natural selection, but it does not mention God.[120] In 2004, a Pennsylvania school district became the first to require high school biology teachers to introduce students to ID as an alternative to evolution. After some teachers complained, the school board dropped the requirement and instead instructed administrators to read a statement that evolution is a theory and to refer students to a book explaining ID as an alternative theory. Several families challenged the resolution, and the federal district court struck down the policy, reasoning that it was a ploy to infuse religious beliefs in the public school science curriculum.[121] Nonetheless, controversies over teaching evolution and alternative theories continue in legislative and judicial forums.

Other Curriculum Components. Allegations also are being made that other components of the public school curriculum violate the Establishment Clause because they advance "secular humanism" or "New Age theology," which critics claim denies God and exalts humans as masters of their own destinies.[122] Central targets, in addition to evolution, have been sex education, values clarification, and outcome-based education, but few aspects of the curriculum have escaped such claims. Recently, inclusion of the popular *Harry Potter* series in public school libraries has been challenged because the books deal with wizardry and magic that allegedly advance the occult/Satanism.[123]

Even courts that have considered nontheistic creeds to be "religions" for First Amendment purposes have not ruled that challenged public school courses and materials advance such creeds. In 1987, the Eleventh Circuit reversed an Alabama federal judge's conclusion that a school district's use of several dozen home economics, history, and social studies books unconstitutionally advanced secular humanism, finding instead that the books instilled in students values such as "independent thought, tolerance of diverse views, self-respect, maturity, self-reliance, and logical decision-making."[124]

More recently, the Second Circuit also found no constitutional violations in celebrating Earth Day or in role playing as part of a drug prevention program using peer facilitators.[125] However, it ruled that one teacher's assignment for students to construct images of a Hindu deity abridged the First Amendment and that making worry dolls amounted to preference of superstition over religion in violation of the Establishment Clause. Also, the Eighth Circuit ruled that a Missouri teacher's contract was impermissibly not renewed after she sent a "magic rock" home with each student.[126] The court found community complaints that the letter and rock advanced New Ageism to be the basis for the board's action rather than the asserted concerns about the teacher's grading practices.

Though sex education classes have often been challenged as advancing an antitheistic faith, courts consistently have found that these courses do not denounce Christianity and instead present public health information that furthers legitimate educational objectives.[127] In 2006, the Ninth Circuit reiterated that parents do not have the exclusive right to be the sole provider of sex education and that parental interests do not prevail over the state's interests in giving students important health information.[128] The judiciary has ruled that the Establishment Clause precludes the state from barring sex education simply to conform to the religious beliefs of some parents. However, courts have acknowledged that students have a free exercise right to be excused from sex education classes if such instruction conflicts with their sectarian beliefs.[129]

Some sex education programs that stress abstinence between unmarried people have been challenged. A Louisiana appeals court found that one of these abstinence-only programs violated state law by promoting Christian doctrine and including some false information.[130] The court required the school district to delete passages that were factually inaccurate or that dealt with the moral and spiritual implications of premarital sex, contraceptives, and sexually transmitted diseases.

Curricular materials designed to promote tolerance for alternative lifestyles also have generated litigation. A Massachusetts federal district court held that an elementary curriculum encouraging respect for gay persons and same-sex marriage did not abridge the free exercise rights of students or parental rights to direct the upbringing of their children.[131] However, a Maryland federal district court enjoined implementation of a school district's pilot sex education programs that address "sexual variation," reasoning that additional investigation was needed to ascertain whether the program constitutes viewpoint discrimination by presenting only the perspective that homosexuality is natural and a morally correct lifestyle and implying that certain religious beliefs about homosexuality are unenlightened and misguided.[132]

Allegations that curricular materials advance the Wicca religion have not been successful. For example, the Impressions reading series, employing the whole-language approach to teaching reading, was challenged in the late 1980s and early 1990s as being morbid and depressing and promoting witchcraft based on Wicca. Both the Seventh and Ninth Circuits ruled that reading stories about witches or even creating poetic chants does not constitute the practice of witchcraft or advance a pagan cult.[133] More recently, an Arkansas federal district court struck down a school district's policy requiring parental permission for students to check out certain library books dealing with witchcraft and the occult. The court found insufficient justification for the policy that stigmatized the books in question and impaired students' First Amendment rights to have access to the materials without parental permission.[134] Also, a Florida appeals court ruled that the display of witches to celebrate Halloween does not promote a nontheistic religion or give an impression that the public school endorses Wicca.[135]

Courts have not condoned parental attacks on various aspects of the public school curriculum that allegedly conflict with their religious values, but more difficult legal questions are raised when policymakers support curriculum restrictions for religious reasons. Courts show considerable deference to legislatures and school boards in educational matters, unless their actions clearly violate protected rights. To illustrate, the Eleventh Circuit upheld a Florida school board's decision to ban a humanities book because it included Aristophanes's *Lysistrata* and Chaucer's *The Miller's Tale*, which board members considered vulgar and immoral. Although the court did not condone the board basing its decision on fundamentalist religious views, it nonetheless deferred to the board's broad discretion in curricular matters.[136] Conservative parent organizations have had more success in influencing school board elections than in challenging components of the public school curriculum in court.

Recommendations for Practice

Lower courts continue to render decisions all along the separation/accommodation continuum, even though the U.S. Department of Education is supporting greater government accommodation of religion in public schools than it was in the 1970s and 1980s. The Supreme Court has espoused a separationist position in a few cases since 1990,[137] but it seems to be redefining the notion of governmental neutrality toward religion with an emphasis on the protection of private religious expression and equal treatment of sectarian and secular expression and groups.[138]

Public schools are experiencing some effects of the doctrine shift toward religious accommodation, and there may be significant future implications. Observable religious activities in public schools will likely increase and reflect preferences of the community's dominant religious group. This, in turn, may stimulate additional Establishment Clause challenges from members of minority sects, asserting that they are unconstitutionally being subjected to the will of the religious majority. Although the exact nature of the controversies cannot be predicted, it seems assured that church/state disputes involving schools will continue to generate a steady stream of litigation in the foreseeable future.

Notwithstanding the evolving nature of the law in this domain, legal developments to date provide some guidance for school personnel as they make daily decisions regarding permissible and impermissible religious activities in public schools.

1. School-sanctioned prayer during the public school day violates the Establishment Clause, regardless of whether student participation is voluntary.
2. Students can engage in silent prayer in public schools, but school personnel cannot promote such silent devotionals.
3. Public schools cannot sponsor religious observances in school events including graduation exercises and extracurricular activities.
4. Graduation ceremonies can be (but do not have to be) a designated forum for student expression, where content-based restrictions are not placed on students' speeches, including religious messages.
5. If school authorities maintain control of the graduation ceremony and review students' speeches, students would have to eliminate proselytizing content from their remarks.
6. Public schools cannot allow students to determine by election to have student-led prayers before athletic events.
7. Public schools cannot permanently display sectarian documents, but they can recognize religious holidays in an objective manner.

8. If a federally assisted secondary school has created a limited forum for noncurriculum student groups to meet during noninstructional time, all student groups, including religious groups, must be allowed equal access.
9. Public schools cannot discriminate against religious viewpoints in creating a forum for community groups to use school facilities when classes are not in session, even if a religious group targets children attending the school.
10. School authorities would be wise to bar religious organizations from distributing sectarian literature in public schools, whereas individual students have a free expression right to distribute such literature during noninstructional time in conformance with reasonable school regulations.
11. Teachers cannot proselytize students, but they can teach *about* religion.
12. Release-time programs in which students receive religious instruction off public school grounds during the school day do not violate the Establishment Clause.
13. Students can be excused from observances and instructional assignments in public schools for religious reasons if the exemption does not interfere with their educational progress or management of the school.
14. Teaching creationism or intelligent design in public school science classes advances religious beliefs.
15. Although the Establishment Clause restricts the promotion of theistic and antitheistic religious beliefs, most claims that secular public school instruction advances antitheistic doctrine have not been successful.

Endnotes

1 School Dist. of Abington Twp. v. Schempp, 374 U.S. 203 (1963); Engel v. Vitale, 370 U.S. 421 (1962). A few historical parts of this chapter build on Stephen Thomas, Nelda Cambron-McCabe, and Martha McCarthy, PUBLIC SCHOOL LAW: TEACHERS' AND STUDENTS' RIGHTS, 6TH ed. (Boston: Allyn & Bacon, in press).

2 *See* Ira C. Lupu, *The Lingering Death of Separationism*, 62 GEO. WASH. L. REV. 230, 234 (1994).

3 403 U.S. 602 (1971).

4 *See* Zelman v. Simmons-Harris, 536 U.S. 639 (2002) (rejecting an Establishment Clause challenge to a state-supported voucher program under which public funds flow to religious schools); Mitchell v. Helms, 530 U.S. 793 (2000) (upholding federal aid program under which computers and other instructional materials and equipment are provided for students in private schools); Agostini v. Felton, 521 U.S. 203 (1997) (lifting injunction and rejecting Establishment Clause challenge to the use of public school personnel to provide remedial

services in parochial schools); Zobrest v. Catalina Foothills Sch. Dist., 509 U.S. 1 (1993) (finding no Establishment Clause violation in the use of public funds to provide sign language interpreters for hearing-deficient children in parochial schools).

5 *See, e.g.,* Good News Club v. Milford Cent. Sch., 533 U.S. 98 (2001) (requiring equal school access for devotional meetings aimed toward elementary school children attending the school if other community groups are allowed access during nonschool hours); *infra* text accompanying note 80.

6 Under the endorsement standard, government action will be invalidated if an objective observer would view the actions as endorsing or disapproving religion. *See* Lynch v. Donnelly, 465 U.S. 668, 687 (1984) (O'Connor, J., concurring).

7 The coercion standard requires direct or indirect government coercion on individuals to adopt a religious belief. See Lee v. Weisman, 505 U.S. 577, 587 (1992).

8 See Mitchell v. Helms, 530 U.S. 793, 807-808 (2000); Agostini v. Felton, 521 U.S. 203, 232-234 (1997) (making it explicit that consideration of excessive entanglement is simply part of the policy's primary effect, thus modifying the *Lemon* test).

9 *See, e.g.*, Locke v. Davey, 540 U.S. 712 (2004); Good News Club v. Milford Cent. Sch., 533 U.S. 98 (2001); Santa Fe Indep. Sch. Dist. v. Doe, 530 U.S. 290 (2000).

10 472 U.S. 38 (1985).

11 Bown v. Gwinnett County Sch. Dist., 112 F.3d 1464 (11th Cir. 1997).

12 Brown v. Gilmore, 258 F.3d 265, 270 (4th Cir. 2001), *interpreting* VA. CODE ANN. § 22.1-203 (Michie 2000).

13 School Dist. of Abington Twp. v. Schempp, 374 U.S. 203 (1963); Engel v. Vitale, 370 U.S. 421 (1962).

14 *See* Thomas, et al., *supra* note 1, Chapter 2.

15 505 U.S. 577 (1992).

16 *See* Shumway v. Albany County Sch. Dist. No. One, 826 F. Supp. 1320 (D. Wyo. 1993) (upholding a baccalaureate program as not sponsored by the school, even though students rented the high school gym for the event, the school band performed, and graduation announcements included the baccalaureate); Verbena United Methodist Church v. Chilton County Bd. of Educ., 765 F. Supp. 704 (M.D. Ala. 1991) (holding that a school board must take all reasonable measures to disassociate itself from a baccalaureate service sponsored by a religious organization and held in space rented from the school district).

17 Doe v. Madison Sch. Dist. No. 321, 147 F.3d 832 (9th Cir. 1998), *vacated and remanded en banc*, 177 F.3d 789 (9th Cir. 1999) (vacating the panel decision because the plaintiff had graduated, but the contested policy was not invalidated).

18 *Doe*, 147 F.3d at 835.

19 Lassonde v. Pleasanton Unified Sch. Dist., 320 F.3d 979 (9th Cir. 2003); Cole v. Oroville Union High Sch. Dist., 228 F.3d 1092 (9th Cir. 2000).

20 *Lassonde*, 320 F.3d at 984.

21 Jones v. Clear Creek Indep. Sch. Dist., 930 F.2d 416 (5th Cir. 1991), *vacated and remanded*, 505 U.S. 1215 (1992), *on remand*, 977 F.2d 963 (5th Cir. 1992).

22 ACLU of N.J. v. Black Horse Pike Reg'l Bd. of Educ., 84 F.3d 1471 (3d Cir. 1996); Harris v. Joint Sch. Dist. No. 241, 41 F.3d 447 (9th Cir. 1994), *vacated,* 515 U.S. 1155 (1995).

23 Santa Fe Indep. Sch. Dist. v. Doe, 168 F.3d 806 (5th Cir. 1999), *aff'd*, 530 U.S. 290 (2000). Courts consistently have struck down prayers led or encouraged by school personnel during athletic contests or other extracurricular events. *See e. g.,* Doe v. Duncanville Indep. Sch. Dist., 70 F.3d 402 (5th Cir. 1995) (prohibiting public school employees from leading or encouraging prayers during school-related activities, but upholding the school's choir use of a religious theme song).

24 *Santa Fe*, 530 U.S. at 310.

25 *Id.* at 308-310.

26 *Id.* at 313.

27 *See* Adler v. Duval County, 206 F.3d 1070 (11th Cir. 2000), *vacated and remanded* (for reconsideration in light of Santa Fe v. Doe), 531 U.S. 801 (2000), *reinstated on remand,* 250

F.3d 1330 (11th Cir. 2001); Chandler v. James, 180 F.3d 1254 (11th Cir. 1999), *vacated and remanded* (for reconsideration in light of Santa Fe v. Doe), 530 U.S. 1256 (2000), *reinstated on remand sub nom.* Chandler v. Siegelman, 230 F.3d 1313 (11th Cir. 2000).

[28] *Adler,* 206 F.3d 1070.

[29] *Chandler,* 180 F.3d 1254.

[30] *Adler,* 250 F.3d 1330; *Chandler,* 230 F.3d at 1313.

[31] *Chandler,* 230 F.3d at 1316.

[32] Doe v. Sch. Dist., 340 F.3d 605 (8th Cir. 2003).

[33] *Id.* at 612-613.

[34] 20 U.S.C. § 7904 (2007).

[35] 68 Fed. Reg. 9645-01 (Feb. 28, 2003).

[36] West Va. State Bd. of Educ. v. Barnette, 319 U.S. 624 (1943).

[37] Sherman v. Cmty. Consol. Sch. Dist. 21, 980 F.2d 437 (7th Cir. 1992).

[38] *Id.* at 446 (citing Brennan, J., dissenting, in Lynch v. Donnelly, 465 U.S. 668, 716 (1984)).

[39] Myers v. Loudoun County Sch. Bd., 251 F. Supp. 2d 1262, 1268 (E.D. Va. 2003).

[40] Newdow v. U.S. Cong., 292 F.3d 597 (9th Cir. 2002), *judgment stayed,* No. 00-16423, 2002 U.S. App. LEXIS 12826 (9th Cir. June 27, 2002), *opinion amended and superseded by* 328 F.3d 466 (2003), *rev'd sub nom.* Elk Grove Unified Sch. Dist. v. Newdow, 542 U.S. 1 (2004). When President Eisenhower signed the law adding "under God" to the Pledge, he observed that from that day forward, schoolchildren would proclaim "the dedication of our nation and our people to the Almighty." *See* James Piereson, *Under God,* WEEKLY STANDARD, Oct. 27, 2003.

[41] *Newdow,* 328 F.3d at 488.

[42] *Newdow,* 542 U.S. at 17-18 (2004).

[43] Newdow v. U.S. Cong., 383 F. Supp. 2d 1229 (E.D. Cal. 2005).

[44] However, the court enjoined the school board from removing the Bible from the school library, noting that the Bible has significant literary and historical significance. Roberts v. Madigan, 921 F.2d 1047 (10th Cir. 1990).

[45] *See* Jaffree v. Bd. of Sch. Comm'rs, 705 F.2d 1526 (11th Cir. 1983).

[46] Marchi v. Bd. of Coop. Educ. Servs., 173 F.3d 469 (2d Cir. 1999).

[47] The shirt read "Jesus 2000, J2K." Downing v. W. Haven Bd. of Educ., 162 F. Supp. 2d 19 (D. Conn. 2001). *See also* Hennessy v. City of Melrose, 194 F.3d 237 (1st Cir. 1999) (upholding termination of a Fundamentalist Christian student teacher for criticizing the district's curriculum and school activities and vilifying the principal; religious beliefs cannot override compliance with reasonable school directives).

[48] Palmer v. Bd. of Educ., 603 F.2d 1271 (7th Cir. 1979).

[49] Lee v. York County Sch. Div., 484 F.3d 687 (4th Cir. 2007), *cert. denied,* No. 07-140, 2007 U.S. LEXIS 11244 (Oct. 9, 2007) (holding that the expression was curricular in nature, so it constituted an employment dispute and not protected expression). *But see* Williams v. Vidmar, 367 F. Supp. 2d 1265 (N.D. Cal. 2005) (recognizing the legitimate pedagogical concern that teachers not promote religion in their classrooms in violation of the Establishment Clause, but allowing the teacher to proceed with his equal protection claim that he was treated differently because of his religion since his lesson plans required prior administrative approval whereas other teachers' plans did not).

[50] *See* School Dist. of Abington Twp. v. Schempp, 374 U.S. 203, 225 (1963).

[51] *See* THE BIBLE AND ITS INFLUENCE (Cullen Schippe & Chuck Stetson, eds., Front Royal, VA: Bible Literacy Project, 2005); Brenda Goodman, *Teaching the Bible in Georgia's Public Schools,* N. Y. TIMES, March 29, 2006, at 7; David J. Hoff, *Alabama Lawmakers Push Elective on Bible's Role in History, Literature,* EDUC. WEEK, Jan. 18, 2006, at 21; National School Boards Association, *Curriculum,* LEGAL CLIPS, Jan. 11, 2007, at 7.

[52] *See, e.g.,* Doe v. Human, 725 F. Supp. 1499 (W.D. Ark. 1989), *aff'd mem.,* 923 F.2d 2d 857 (8th Cir. 1990); Hall v. Bd. of Sch. Comm'rs, 707 F.2d 464 (11th Cir. 1983); Herdahl v. Pontotoc County Sch. Dist., 933 F. Supp. 582 (N.D. Miss. 1996). *See also* Doe v. Beaumont Indep. Sch. Dist., 240 F.3d 462 (5th Cir. 2001) (*en banc*), *on remand sub nom.* Oxford v. Beaumont

Indep. Sch. Dist., 224 F. Supp. 2d 1099 (E.D. Tex. 2002) (invalidating school district's "clergy in schools" counseling program under the Establishment Clause).

53 Eklund v. Byron Union Sch. Dist., 154 F. App'x 648 (9th Cir. 2005), *cert. denied,* 127 S. Ct. 86 (2006).

54 *See, e. g.,* Peck v. Baldwinsville Cent. Sch. Dist., 426 F.3d 617 (2d Cir. 2005) (holding that censorship of a student's poster with religious phrases and pictures did not violate the student's free exercise rights); C.H. v. Oliva, 166 F.3d 1204 (3d Cir. 1998) (rejecting the claim that the school district abridged First Amendment rights by preventing a student from reading a Bible story to classmates; holding that teachers can exercise viewpoint-neutral regulations reasonably related to legitimate educational purposes to govern classroom activities); Settle v. Dickson County Sch. Bd., 53 F.3d 152 (6th Cir. 1995) (upholding a teacher who gave a student a zero on a report because the student had cleared a different topic and then wrote the paper on the life of Jesus Christ); DeNooyer v. Livonia Pub. Schs., 12 F.3d 211 (6th Cir. 1993) (upholding a school district's denial of an elementary school student's request to show a videotape of herself singing a proselytizing religious song as part of a religious presentation); Duran v. Nitsche, 780 F. Supp. 1048 (E.D. Pa. 1991) (upholding school personnel in prohibiting a student in a class for the gifted from distributing a religious survey to classmates), *appeal dismissed and vacated,* 972 F.2d 1331 (3d Cir. 1992).

55 U.S. Department of Education, Guidance on Constitutionally Protected Prayer in Public Elementary and Secondary Schools, 68 Fed. Reg. 9645-01 (Feb. 28, 2003).

56 Florey v. Sioux Falls Sch. Dist. 49-5, 619 F.2d 1311 (8th Cir. 1980).

57 Stone v. Graham, 449 U.S. 39 (1980). The Court rejected the state judiciary's conclusion that the constitutional impairment was neutralized because the copies were purchased with private donations and carried a disclaimer emphasizing the secular application of the Ten Commandments. *Id.* at 41.

58 Washegesic v. Bloomingdale Pub. Schs., 33 F.3d 679 (6th Cir. 1994).

59 Bannon v. Sch. Dist., 387 F.3d 1208 (11th Cir. 2004).

60 Clever v. Cherry Hill Twp. Bd. of Educ., 838 F. Supp. 929 (D.N.J. 1993). *See* Ralph Mawdsley, *Clever v. Cherry Hill Township Board of Education: Recognition of Religious Diversity in Public Schools,* 90 Educ. L. Rep. 533 (1994).

61 Myers v. Loudoun County Sch. Bd., 251 F. Supp. 2d 1262 (E.D. Va. 2003).

62 Sechler v. State Coll. Area Sch. Dist., 121 F. Supp. 2d 439 (M.D. Pa. 2000).

63 *Id.* at 451.

64 The monument was donated by the Fraternal Order of Eagles in 1961. Van Orden v. Perry, 545 U.S. 677 (2005).

65 McCreary County, Ky. v. ACLU, 545 U.S. 844 (2005).

66 *See, e. g.,* Capitol Square Review and Advisory Bd. v. Pinette, 515 U.S. 753 (1995) (upholding the right of the Ku Klux Klan to place an unattended cross on the Ohio capitol square during the Christmas season); County of Allegheny v. ACLU, 492 U.S. 573 (1989) (upholding the public display of a Menorah along with a Christmas tree and a sign declaring the city's salute to liberty, but striking down a display of the Nativity Scene with a banner proclaiming "Gloria in Excelsis Deo" in the county courthouse).

67 *See* Widmar v. Vincent, 454 U.S. 263 (1981) (holding that student groups cannot be disadvantaged in access to college facilities to hold religious meetings).

68 20 U.S.C. § 4071 (2007).

69 *Id.* at § 4071(c)(3). The Equal Access Act stipulates that "nothing in this subchapter shall be construed to limit the authority of the school, its agents or employees, to maintain order and discipline on school premises, to protect the well-being of students and faculty, and to assure that attendance of students at meetings is voluntary," 20 U.S.C. at § 4071(f).

70 Some controversies have focused on what constitutes curriculum-related clubs, and many of these cases have dealt with requests by the Gay/Straight Alliance to meet in public schools. *See, e.g.,* Caudillo v. Lubbock Indep. Sch. Dist., 311 F. Supp. 2d 550 (N.D. Tex. 2004); Boyd County High Sch. Gay/Straight Alliance v. Bd. of Educ., 258 F. Supp. 2d 667 (E.D. Ky.

2003); Colin v. Orange Unified Sch. Dist., 83 F. Supp. 2d 1135 (C.D. Cal. 2000); East High Gay/Straight Alliance v. Bd. of Educ., 81 F. Supp. 2d 1166 (D. Utah 1999).

71 496 U.S. 226 (1990).

72 *Id.* at 239-40.

73 *See* Ceniceros v. Bd. of Trs., 66 F.3d 1535 (9th Cir. 1995), *opinion withdrawn, substituted opinion on remand,* 106 F.3d 878 (9th Cir. 1997) (also interpreting the EAA as allowing student religious groups to meet during the lunch period since it was noninstructional time and other student groups were allowed to meet); Garnett v. Renton Sch. Dist. No. 403, 987 F.2d 641 (9th Cir. 1993).

74 *See* Hsu v. Roslyn Union Free Sch. Dist., 85 F.3d 839 (2d Cir. 1996) (holding that the club could require its president, vice president, and musical coordinator to be Christians, but that this restriction could not be applied to other officers whose responsibilities do not impact religious speech).

75 Van Schoick v. Saddleback Valley Unified Sch. Dist., 104 Cal. Rptr. 2d 562 (Ct. App. 2001) (finding triable issues regarding whether the school had established a limited forum for noncurriculum student groups to meet).

76 Donovan v. Punxsutawney Area Sch. Bd., 336 F.3d 211 (3d Cir. 2003).

77 Prince v. Jacoby, 303 F.3d 1074, 1088 (9th Cir. 2002); *infra* text accompanying note 84.

78 *Id.* at 1087-1090.

79 508 U.S. 384 (1993).

80 533 U.S. 98 (2001). The club is affiliated with a national organization, Child Evangelism Fellowship, which has more than 3,400 clubs nationwide. *See also* Culbertson v. Oakridge Sch. Dist. No. 76, 258 F.3d 1061 (9th Cir. 2001) (upholding the Good News Club's right to meet in the public school after school hours, but prohibiting teachers from distributing permission slips for the meetings because such action would unconstitutionally promote the club).

81 *Good News Club*, 533 U.S. at 112-113.

82 *Id.*

83 *Id.* at 108-110. *See also* Wigg v. Sioux Falls Sch. Dist. 49-5, 383 F.3d 807 (8th Cir. 2004) (holding that a teacher could participate in Good News Club meetings immediately after school at the school where she taught; such participation entailed private speech and would not be viewed as the public school's endorsement of religion).

84 *See* Donovan v. Punxsutawney Area Sch. Bd., 336 F.3d 211, 227 (3d Cir. 2003); Prince v. Jacoby, 303 F.3d 1074 (9th Cir. 2002). *See supra* text accompanying notes 76-77.

85 *See* Jabr v. Rapides Parish Sch. Bd., 171 F. Supp. 2d 653 (W.D. La. 2001) (holding that the principal's distribution of Bibles to elementary students in his office violated the Establishment Clause).

86 *See, e. g.,* Doe v. S. Iron R-1 Sch. Dist., 498 F.3d 878 (8th Cir. 2007); Doe v. Duncanville Indep. Sch. Dist., 70 F.3d 402 (5th Cir. 1995); Berger v. Rensselaer Cent. Sch. Corp., 982 F.2d 1160 (7th Cir. 1993).

87 Peck v. Upshur County Bd. of Educ, 155 F.3d 274 (4th Cir. 1998). *See also* Schanou v. Lancaster County Sch. Dist. No. 160, 863 F. Supp. 1048 (D. Neb. 1994), *vacated*, 62 F.3d 1040 (8th Cir. 1995) (instructing the lower court, which had upheld board policy allowing Bible distribution outside school, to dismiss challenge to the policy and to the single incident of Bible distribution in the public school hallway in violation of the policy); Bacon v. Bradley-Bourbonnais High Sch. Dist. No. 307, 707 F. Supp. 1005 (C.D. III 1989) (upholding distribution of Gideon Bibles on the school-owned sidewalk in front of high school because it was considered a public forum for use by the general public).

88 *Peck*, 155 F.3d at 288.

89 *See, e. g.,* Muller v. Jefferson Lighthouse Sch., 98 F.3d 1530 (7th Cir. 1996); Hedges v. Wauconda Cmty. Unit Sch. Dist., 9 F.3d 1295 (7th Cir. 1993); Slotterback v. Interboro Sch. Dist., 766 F. Supp. 280 (E.D. Pa. 1991).

90 Hills v. Scottsdale Unified Sch. Dist., 329 F.3d 1044 (9th Cir. 2003).

[91] *Id.* at 1052-1053. *See also* Rosenberger v. Rector & Visitors of the Univ. of Va., 515 U.S. 819 (1995) (holding that a public university could not withhold support from a student group desiring to use student activity funds to publish religious materials).

[92] Westfield High Sch. L.I.F.E. Club v. City of Westfield, 249 F. Supp. 2d 98 (D. Mass. 2003).

[93] Walz v. Egg Harbor Twp. Bd. of Educ., 342 F.3d 271 (3d Cir. 2003).

[94] *Compare* Harless v. Darr, 937 F. Supp. 1351 (S.D. Ind. 1996) (supporting a school policy requiring students to give the principal advance warning of the distribution and to submit a copy of the literature to the superintendent, but not for approval purposes; the policy was not an unconstitutional prior restraint on a student's distribution of religious tracts) *with* Johnston-Loehner v. O'Brien, 859 F. Supp. 575 (M.D. Fla. 1994) (striking down a policy requiring students to get the superintendent's approval before distributing any materials on campus; this prior restraint on distributing religious invitations and pamphlets inhibited religion in violation of the Establishment Clause).

[95] McCollum v. Bd. of Educ., 333 U.S. 203 (1948).

[96] Zorach v. Clauson, 343 U.S. 306, 313-14 (1952).

[97] Smith v. Smith, 523 F.2d 121 (4th Cir. 1975).

[98] Lanner v. Wimmer, 662 F.2d 1349 (10th Cir. 1981). However, South Carolina adopted a law in 2006 allowing students to receive up to two credits for off-campus religious study. *See* S.C. Code Ann. § 59-39-112 (2006).

[99] Moore v. Metro. Sch. Dist., No. IP 00-1859-C-M/S, 2001 U.S. Dist. LEXIS 2722 (S.D. Ind. Feb. 7, 2001). *See also* Doe v. Shenandoah County Sch. Bd., 737 F. Supp. 913 (W.D. Va. 1990) (granting a temporary restraining order against Weekday Religious Education classes being held in buses—almost identical to public school buses—parked in front of the school, with instructors going into the school to recruit students).

[100] 319 U.S. 624 (1943). As discussed previously, controversy surrounds whether "under God" can be said in the Pledge *at all* in public schools. *See supra* text accompanying note 36.

[101] Minersville Sch. Dist. v. Gobitis, 310 U.S. 586 (1940).

[102] *See, e.g.,* Lipp v. Morris, 579 F.2d 834, 836 (3d Cir. 1978) (striking down part of a New Jersey law requiring all students to stand during the Pledge); Frazier v. Alexandre, 434 F. Supp. 2d 1350 (S.D. Fla. 2006) (enjoining the school district's unconstitutional practices and awarding damages to a student who was publicly reprimanded for not participating in the Pledge and told he would have to get parental permission to opt out and would have to stand when others recited the Pledge); Circle Sch. v. Phillips, 270 F. Supp. 2d 616, 626 (E.D. Pa. 2003) (holding that a state law requiring parental notification of nonparticipating students violated the First Amendment).

[103] Holloman v. Harland, 370 F.3d 1252 (11th Cir. 2004) (also allowing the student's Establishment Clause claim that the teacher encouraged students to pray during the daily moment of silence to proceed against the teacher and the school board).

[104] *See* Palmer v. Bd. of Educ., 603 F.2d 1721 (7th Cir. 1979).

[105] *See* Thomas, et al., *supra* note 1.

[106] The court also denied the school district's motion to dismiss the parent's defamation claim, her claim of retaliation against her and her children (for her stance regarding opposite sex day), and her claim for harassment based on opposite sex day and published jokes that were offensive to women. But the court held that the parent lacked standing to seek a preliminary injunction because the family had moved from the school district so there was no threat of continued harm. Stanley v. Carrier Mills-Stonefort Sch. Dist. No. 2, 459 F. Supp. 2d 766 (S.D. Ill. 2006).

[107] Leebaert v. Harrington, 332 F.3d 134 (2d Cir. 2003).

[108] Mozert v. Hawkins County Bd. of Educ., 827 F.2d 1058 (6th Cir. 1987).

[109] *See, e.g.,* Menora v. Ill. High Sch. Ass'n, 683 F.2d 1030 (7th Cir. 1982); Keller v. Gardner Cmty. Consol. Grade Sch. Dist. 72C, 552 F. Supp. 512 (N.D. Ill. 1982).

[110] *See* Protection of Pupil Rights Amendment to the NCLB Act of 2001, 20 U.S.C. § 1232h (2007).

[111] *See* David Rigsby, *Education Law Chapter: Sex Education in Schools*, 7 GEO. J. GENDER & L. 895, 898 (2006).

[112] Epperson v. Arkansas, 393 U.S. 97, 107 (1968) (quoting Joseph Burstyn, Inc. v. Wilson, 343 U.S. 495, 505 (1952)).

[113] Scopes v. State, 289 S.W. 363, 364 (Tenn. 1927).

[114] *Epperson*, 393 U.S. 97.

[115] Edwards v. Aguillard, 482 U.S. 578 (1987).

[116] *See* Peloza v. Capistrano Unified Sch. Dist., 37 F.3d 517 (9th Cir. 1994); LeVake v. Indep. Sch. Dist. No. 656, 625 N.W.2d 502 (Minn. Ct. App. 2001). *See also* Webster v. New Lenox Sch. Dist. No. 122, 917 F.2d 1004 (7th Cir. 1990) (upholding the school board's prohibition on teaching nonevolutionary theory).

[117] *See* Moeller v. Schrenko, 554 S.E.2d 198 (Ga. Ct. App. 2001); Johnson v. Chesapeake City Sch. Bd., 52 Va. Cir. 252 (Va. Cir. Ct. 2000).

[118] *See* Selman v. Cobb County Sch. Dist., 390 F. Supp. 2d 1286, 1312 (N.D. Ga. 2005), *vacated with instructions for the district court to conduct new evidentiary proceedings,* 449 F.3d 1320 (11th Cir. 2006); Freiler v. Tangipahoa Parish Bd. of Educ., 185 F.3d 337, 344-47 (5th Cir. 1999).

[119] *See* National Center for Science Education, "News Archive," *Events of 2005-2007*, Sept. 8, 2007, *available at* http://www.ncseweb.org/pressroom.asp?branch=statement.

[120] *See* Martha McCarthy, *Instruction About the Origin of Humanity: Legal Controversies Evolve*, 203 EDUC. L. REP. 453 (2006).

[121] *See* Kitzmiller v. Dover Area Sch. Dist., 400 F. Supp. 2d 707, 747 (M.D. Pa. 2005). The board members who championed the policy were voted out of office, and the policy had been rescinded before the decision was rendered.

[122] *See* Thomas, et al., *supra* note 1.

[123] *See* Kathleen K. Manzo, *Charmed and Challenged*, EDUC. WK., Nov. 14, 2001, at 14-15.

[124] Smith v. Bd. of Sch. Comm'rs, 655 F. Supp. 939 (S.D. Ala. 1987), *rev'd*, 827 F.2d 684, 692 (11th Cir. 1987) (also rejecting the contention that the mere omission of Christian religious facts in the curriculum represented unconstitutional hostility toward theistic beliefs). *See also* Grove v. Mead Sch. Dist. No. 354, 753 F.2d 1528 (9th Cir. 1985) (reasoning that the book, *The Learning Tree,* does not advance an antitheistic faith).

[125] Altman v. Bedford Cent. Sch. Dist., 245 F.3d 49 (2d Cir. 2001).

[126] Cowan v. Strafford R-VI Sch. Dist., 140 F.3d 1153, 1156 (8th Cir. 1998).

[127] *See, e.g.*, Citizens for Parental Rights v. San Mateo County Bd. of Educ., 124 Cal. Rptr. 68 (Ct. App. 1975); Smith v. Ricci, 446 A.2d 501 (N.J. 1982).

[128] Fields v. Palmdale Sch. Dist., 447 F.3d 1187 (9th Cir. 2006), *cert. denied,* 127 S. Ct. 725 (2006) (upholding school district's administration of a psychological assessment questionnaire with several questions pertaining to topics of a sexual nature).

[129] *See, e.g.,* Brown v. Hot, Sexy and Safer Prods., Inc., 68 F.3d 525 (1st Cir. 1995).

[130] Coleman v. Caddo Parish Sch. Bd., 635 So. 2d 1238 (La. Ct. App. 1994). *See also* ACLU v. Foster, No. 02-1440, 2002 U.S. Dist. LEXIS 13778 (E.D. La. July 25, 2002) (ordering state officials to ensure that federal funds are not used to promote religious beliefs under the Governor's Program on Abstinence).

[131] Parker v. Hurley, 474 F. Supp. 2d 261 (D. Mass. 2007) (dismissing state law claims without prejudice and instructing such claims to be reinstituted in state courts).

[132] Citizens for a Responsible Curriculum v. Montgomery County Pub. Schs., No. AW-05-1194, 2005 U.S. Dist. LEXIS 8130 (S.D. Md. May 5, 2005).

[133] Fleischfresser v. Dirs. of Sch. Dist. 200, 15 F.3d 680 (7th Cir. 1994); Brown v. Woodland Joint Unified Sch. Dist., 27 F.3d 1373 (9th Cir. 1994). This series was discontinued in 1994 because of the controversies generated over its whole language approach to teaching reading and the nature of the content selected.

[134] Counts v. Cedarville Sch. Dist., 295 F. Supp. 2d 996 (W.D. Ark. 2003).

[135] Guyer v. Sch. Bd., 634 So. 2d 806 (Fla. Dist. Ct. App. 1994).

[136] Virgil v. Sch. Bd., 862 F.2d 1517 (11th Cir. 1989).

[137] *See* Lee v. Weisman, 505 U.S. 577 (1992); Santa Fe Indep. Sch. Dist. v. Doe, 530 U.S. 290 (2000).

[138] *See* Good News Club v. Milford Cent. Sch., 533 U.S. 98 (2001); Rosenberger v. Rector & Visitors of the Univ. of Va., 515 U.S. 819, 839 (1995).

Chapter 31

Copyright Laws in the Age of Technology and Their Applicability to the K-12 Environment

Philip T.K. Daniel & Patrick Pauken

Introduction

With the advent of Internet technology, and its exponential growth over the past three decades, copyright laws have been extended to encompass the myriad concerns these technological innovations have created. The Technology, Education, and Copyright Harmonization Act (TEACH), The Digital Millennium Copyright Act (DMCA), and Copyright Term Extension Act ([CTEA] also known as the "Sonny Bono" Act) represent the activities of the United States Congress to update copyright law with tomorrow's advances in mind. This chapter will provide an analysis of copyright issues for education officials and school administrators faced with the complexities of this rapidly changing area of jurisprudence. Emphasis will be placed first on a basic understanding of copyright law including "fair use" and the significance of this exception to copyright infringement for school administrators. This will be followed by a description and explanation of the amendments to copyright law extending the life of a copyright or accentuating technology. All of the topics will be discussed in terms of how changes in intellectual property have the potential for affecting the school environment.

Legal Issues

The Exclusive Rights and Limitations of Copyright

Exclusive Rights. Copyright law protects against unauthorized copying, performance, or distribution of copyrighted works, and the unauthorized creation of derivative works.[1] The copyright statute grants the following exclusive rights to copyright holders and anyone acting under their authority:

1. the reproduction of the copyrighted work in copies or phonorecords;
2. the preparation of derivative works based on the work;
3. the distribution of copies or phonorecords to the public by sale or transfer;

4. public performances of the work (including by audio transmission); and

5. displays of the work.[2]

In a school setting, the copying of material or the public performance of a musical or drama has copyright implications. The copyright holders (authors, composers, and distributors) may authorize schools to reproduce materials or to perform their work. If a profit motive is involved, or if the copyright holder stands to lose commercial value for his or her creation, use of that creation will require permission usually by contract or the payment of royalties. If the use is one involving nonprofit activity, such as is the case in most educational settings, those who desire to utilize protected materials must either obtain permission or exercise *fair use* (discussed below) of said materials. If permission is required, but not obtained, the legal or beneficial owner of a copyright may sue for infringement of that copyright.[3]

Fair Use. As broad as a copyright holder's exclusive rights are, the copyright laws do impose several limits.[4] Of those laws, the most important for public schools is fair use. Under Section 107 of the Copyright Act, the fair use of a copyrighted work, "for purposes such as criticism, comment, news reporting, *teaching (including multiple copies for classroom use)* [authors' emphasis], scholarship, or research, is not an infringement of copyright."[5] Fair use recognizes that there are circumstances in which the goals of the Copyright Act are better served by allowing the reasonable use of a copyrighted work than by prohibiting the use.[6] The intent behind this provision is to balance the otherwise exclusive rights of creators with the needs of users to obtain, use, and disseminate information.

Because the facts in alleged infringement cases vary widely, the fair use doctrine is designed as an equitable rule of reason to be applied flexibly, on a case-by-case basis.[7] The statute provides four factors to examine for determining whether the use made of a copyrighted work in a particular case is fair:

1. the purpose and the character of the use, including whether such use is of a commercial nature or is for nonprofit educational purposes;

2. the nature of the copyrighted work;

3. the amount and substantiality of the portion used in relation to the copyrighted work as a whole; and

4. the effect of the use upon the potential market for or value of the copyrighted work.[8]

These factors are not exhaustive and should be balanced flexibly, with no one factor determinative.[9] If the use of the work is primarily commercial, then damages are presumed because such use may evidence some meaningful likelihood of future harm.[10] If the use is noncommercial (e.g., educational), then the copyright holder must show by either actual or present harm that if the use becomes widespread, the market for the work would be adversely affected.[11] The question in factor one is not the profit motive of the alleged infringer, but the possibility that the alleged infringer stands to profit from use of the work without paying the customary price. Typically, courts consider two sub-factors when examining the character of the use: (1) productivity of the use (for the broader useful arts versus private use)[12] and (2) good faith of the alleged infringer (fair use presupposes good faith and fair dealing).[13]

Ideally, the four factors are to be applied flexibly to the facts of each case. However, the Supreme Court has suggested that the effect of the use on the work's value or potential market is the single most important factor.[14] Once the copyright holder establishes, with reasonable probability, that the infringement caused a loss in revenue, the burden shifts to the defendant to show that the loss would have occurred anyway.

Although few intellectual property disputes discuss fair use in the public school context, *Marcus v. Rowley* is instructive for all school personnel designing instructional packets for students. In that case, a teacher prepared a "learning activity package" on cake decorating that incorporated some pages from a copyrighted booklet on the same subject.[15] Applying the four factors mentioned above, the court found that the copying constituted an unfair use of a copyrighted work. On factor one, the court held in favor of the copyright holder. While the court found an educational use, it further noted that the teacher was using the copyrighted booklet for the same purposes as would the copyright owner and that the teacher made no attempt to secure the owner's permission. Factor two was inconclusive: the work copied had both factual and expressive features. On factor three, eleven out of twenty-four pages of the packet were taken verbatim from the owner's work; the court weighed this factor against the teacher. Finally, the court noted that even if the teacher's copying had no effect on the owner's market, this did not preclude a finding of infringement.

Although important, this is an unusual decision in the school context. Most educators may invoke the fair use doctrine successfully since most uses by school personnel will be neither commercial nor infringing. In fact, the wording of the fair use section of the law is actually the result of a long controversy over the problems of fair use and the reproduction of copyrighted works for educational and scholarly purposes.[16] In addition to the above factors, the Ad Hoc Committee of Educational Institutions and Organizations on the Copyright Law Revision of 1976 saw the need for greater certainty and protection for teachers and published guidelines for educational classroom copying of books and periodicals.[17] These guidelines are paraphrased as follows:

Permissible single copies for teachers (for use in teaching or preparation to teach a class):

1. a chapter from a book;
2. an article from a newspaper or periodical;
3. a short story, essay, or poem; and
4. a chart, diagram, graph, or picture from a book, periodical, or newspaper.

Moreover, an extremely important limitation on the exclusive rights of copyright holders is the allowance of certain performances and displays of copyrighted works in classroom activities.[18] Section 110(1) of the Copyright Act provides important information to be applied to the traditional K-12 classroom. The section permits the performance or display of a copyrighted work by instructors or students "in the course of face-to-face teaching activities" of a nonprofit educational institution, in a classroom, or similar place devoted to instruction. In the case of a motion picture or other audiovisual work, the performance, or the display of individual images, the copy used must be lawfully made, and the person responsible for the performance must not know or have reason to know that the copy is not lawful.

Notwithstanding the deference to instructional activity, there are other constraints that may apply to the types of works covered by this provision. Teachers and students may well be free to read aloud from texts, act in plays, sing or play musical instruments, show movies, or display text or pictures by way of audio-visual equipment. These activities may be circumscribed, however, by additional legal requirements that could include, for example, permission from the copyright holder to use the materials. Moreover, both teachers and students may need to receive permission from school officials to engage in the activities listed above, especially if the pursuits are not part of the formal subject matter or if such information would not be suitable for the particular class or would negatively impact the sensibilities of students. Note also that with the advent of distance education and online education, the definition of *classroom* is broadened in scope, and recent developments in copyright legislation discussed below define that scope.

Recent Copyright Legislation

The Technology, Education and Copyright Harmonization Act (TEACH). The recent Technology, Education, and Copyright Harmonization Act of 2002[19] significantly broadens the definition of the classroom. Codified in section 110(2), the TEACH Act permits the following educational activities in distance education and/or online settings:[20]

1. Performance of a nondramatic literary or musical work.
2. Performance of reasonable and limited portions of dramatic literary works.
3. Display of any work in an amount comparable to that which is typically displayed in the course of a live classroom session, by or in the course of a transmission.

In essence, the TEACH Act permits in distance education or online environments the same activities as would be permitted in traditional classroom environments.[21] There are, however, several institutional requirements. First, the performance or display must be made at the direction of or under the actual supervision of an instructor. Second, it must be an integral part of a class session offered as a regular part of the "systematic mediated instructional activities" of an accredited nonprofit educational institution.[22] Third, the performance or display must be directly related and of material assistance to the teaching content of the transmission. Fourth, and particularly important, the transmission must be made solely for—to the extent technologically feasible—students officially enrolled in the course and officers or employees of the educational institution as part of their official duties. Fifth, the school or other educational institution must institute policies regarding copyright; provide informational materials to teachers, students, and relevant staff members that accurately describe and promote compliance with copyright law; and provide notice to students that materials used may be subject to copyright law. Finally, the school or school district must apply technological measures that reasonably prevent the retention and accessibility of the copyrighted work for longer than the class session; must reasonably prevent the unauthorized further dissemination of the copyrighted work to others; and must not engage in conduct that could reasonably be expected to interfere with technological measures used by copyright owners to prevent such retention or unauthorized further dissemination.[23]

The new exemptions, however, apply only to "mediated instructional activities," defined as "activities that use copyrighted materials … integral to the class experience, controlled by or under the actual supervision of the instructor and analogous to the type of performance and display that would take place in a live classroom."[24] The exemptions involving fair use explained above do not apply to copyrighted works produced or marketed primarily for distance education. These materials (e.g., distance education courses for sale) have their own market and must be legally acquired. Similarly, course reserves or reserves placed in the school library are not applicable to these exemptions; their use must be approved elsewhere in copyright law. Violations of the TEACH Act do carry severe penalties, including an award of actual civil damages for using another's copyrighted work without permission. These remedies are similar to those under trademark law and may result in a treble damages award.[25]

The Digital Millennium Copyright Act (DMCA). Passed in 1998 and effective in October of 2000, the Digital Millennium Copyright Act[26] updated United States copyright law to meet the demands of the digital age, combat copyright infringement on the Internet, and conform United States law to the requirements of the World Intellectual Property Organization (WIPO). The DMCA contains within it two central pieces of legislation. First, the WIPO Copyright and Performances and Phonograms Treaties Implementation Act prohibits the circumvention of technologies that have been installed to prevent online infringement.[27] With some exceptions, the act also prohibits the manufacture and distribution of circumvention devices. Second, the Online Copyright Infringement Liability Limitation Act primarily creates a safe harbor for online service providers against infringement liability of the provider's subscribers.[28] This act includes a special provision for libraries, archives, and nonprofit educational institutions such as public schools.[29]

Each of the WIPO treaties obligates the United States to prevent circumvention of technological measures used to protect copyrighted works. As such, the DMCA prohibits the circumvention of any effective "technological protection measure" (e.g., a password or form of encryption) used by a copyright holder to restrict access to its material.[30] Section 1201 divides technological measures into two categories: those for the *restriction of access* to copyrighted works and those for the *restriction of copying* of those works. This categorization was fashioned to assure that fair use continues. In some cases, copying a copyrighted work will be considered fair use. Therefore, circumvention of a technological measure that prevents copying may not be an infringement. Gaining unauthorized access to a work, however, will not be supported by a fair use defense. This is obviously an important consideration for school personnel in an era where a preponderance of school students have more than a pedestrian acquaintance with computers and the Internet. Unauthorized access to websites or impermissible downloading, when the school or school district is the Internet service provider, may attract unnecessary outside attention or sanctions to schools and school districts, especially if commercial value is affected.

Fair use is not a privilege completely eliminated within the DMCA, and school personnel should be cognizant of this issue. While the DMCA targets computer programs that are commercially limited and primarily designed and marketed for circumvention, there are exceptions. The following circumvention activities are not prohibited by the DMCA and are, therefore, fair uses of copyrighted works:

1. Circumvention by nonprofit library, archive, and educational institutions solely for the purpose of determining, in good faith, whether or not they wish to obtain *authorized* access to the work. [This provision applies only when the library is open to the public and, therefore, would likely not include public school libraries.]

2. Encryption research.

3. Testing technological devices that are designed to prevent access by minors [such as school students] to certain material on the Internet.

4. Testing the security of a computer, computer system, or computer network with the permission of its owner or operator.[31]

A person injured by a violation of the DMCA may bring a civil action for equitable and monetary damages.[32] Special protection is given to nonprofit libraries, archives, and educational institutions, which may be entitled to complete remission of damages in circumstances where the violator proves that he or she was unaware and had no reason to believe the alleged acts were infringing.

An analysis of WESTLAW indicates to date that no cases have been litigated at the K-12 level involving the DMCA; however, case law involving private entities may have implications for the school environment. Any entity that provides access to the Internet through a mainframe computer system can be considered an Internet service provider (ISP); this could include colleges, universities, and school districts. Such institutions, therefore, are open to limited liability for copyright infringement.

In most circumstances, the ISP will not be liable for the infringing acts of users—acts that include transitory network communication of infringing conduct, intermediate or temporary storage of infringing text or images, and long-term storage of infringing text or images stored at the direction of the user and not the service provider. As long as the Internet service provider plays no substantive roles in the content, direction, or communication of the infringing material, liability will be limited. The provider must establish that it did not have actual knowledge or awareness that the infringing activity was occurring.[33]

Litigation under the DMCA, to date, has not involved educational institutions directly. Some coverage of the recent developments is instructive, however. Case law involves First Amendment challenges to the DMCA, particularly the anti-circumvention provisions; infringement lawsuits challenging the service provider's knowledge of the users' infringing conduct; fair use defenses; and the safe harbor limitations on liability for service providers. The free speech defenses from the alleged circumventers have, by and large, failed. While the courts have generally agreed that the circumvention software developed, used, and distributed by the defendants constituted speech, they have held that the DMCA is a valid content-neutral restriction on that speech. For example, in *Universal City Studios, Inc. v. Corley*, the movie industry sued a number of individuals and organizations that distributed a computer program (DeCSS) designed to circumvent the content scramble system (CSS), an encryption system that prevents copying DVDs.[34] The Court of Appeals for the Second Circuit upheld the district court's grant of a permanent injunction prohibiting defendants from posting the DeCSS program on their website and from posting hyperlinks to other websites containing DeCSS. The court held that the DMCA was designed to target the program's functional attributes, not its expressive ones. The DMCA does not prohibit making lawful copies of DVDs; it simply prohibits the decryption method of copying.[35] According to the court in *DVD Copy Control Association v. Bunner*, a case with facts similar to those in *Corley*, such an injunction against the distribution of DeCSS "burdens no more speech than is necessary to serve the government's important interest in maintaining commercial ethics."[36]

Online copyright infringement is most certainly a concern for schools whether or not they are aware of the infringing conduct. The Internet access provisions and prevalence of Internet music and movie downloads among the student population have put educational administrators and students on notice. More recent cases involve file sharing, an issue very germane to students and staff in schools in this age of cyberspace. The case of *In re Aimster Copyright Litigation*[37] is instructive for school audiences. Aimster, a file-sharing operation, was accused by record industry owners of vicarious and contributory copyright violations. The Court of Appeals for the Seventh Circuit ruled that Aimster had knowledge that it was a contributory infringer based on the amount of the infringement and the fact that it could have eliminated the file sharing from its site after several warnings. Specifically, Aimster was making its site available to users even though it provided no space for storing and offered no files for those who gained access to its site. According to the court, this cyberspace brokerage role was enough to substantiate a violation since its service was designed such that its site-based encryption system eviscerated any hope of ascertaining which users were transferring which files.

Equally instructive to educators, and more recent than *Aimster*, is the unanimous Supreme Court decision in *Metro-Goldwin-Mayer Studios, Inc. v. Grokster.*[38] In *Grokster*, the Court held that software distributors could be liable for indirect copyright infringement when they market software with the intention and the knowledge that computer users will infringe copyrights by downloading and sharing protected works. The fact that the software was capable of noninfringing uses was not helpful to the defendant software distributors, primarily because of the substantial evidence that the defendants knew about and encouraged the infringing uses. For example, there was evidence that the defendants offered guidance to users who contacted them for help in downloading files. Additionally, they marketed themselves as the alternative to Napster, an unsuccessful defendant in a similar file-sharing copyright-infringement case. Finally, the fact that it is nearly impossible for the defendants to track down and prevent the numerous infringers who use their software did not help them. In fact, it helped the plaintiffs. The Court held a finding of contributory or vicarious infringement is necessary in cases where the direct infringers are too numerous, quick, mysterious, and constant to catch, especially in the face of defendants who knew and encouraged such infringement. The application of *Grokster* to educational settings is not direct, as schools are extremely rare software distributors. However, the fact that evidence of a defendant's knowledge and encouragement of infringement can lead to contributory or vicarious liability under copyright law ought to convince schools and school leaders to be very vigilant in their policy formation and enforcement when they allow teachers, staff, and students to use their computer systems.

Even with the passage of laws like the Digital Millennium Copyright Act, copyright law does not fit neatly in the digital age. The challenge is to see how traditional, long-standing law can apply to new media. Publication and distribution of education-related copyrighted works is a diurnal occurrence. With the Internet, publication and distribution are made even easier, with less time and expense required. This also means that the subsequent distribution (and perhaps alteration) of these publications cannot always be controlled or monitored by the copyright holder. In other words, publication, distribution, and infringement are easy, while detection and enforcement are difficult.[39] While it occurs often, unfortunately, "authors who would be granted full exclusive rights in their hard paper copies of works off the Net may lose or be forced to share those rights if the same works are posted and distributed [and even altered] on the Net."[40] This is the challenge for school personnel since much computer activity by students and staff could go on for some time undetected. If infringement is discovered by the copyright holders or their agents, however, the consequences for school districts could be substantial and subject the districts to stiff civil penalties.

Copyright Term Extension Act (The CTEA, The "Sonny Bono" Act). School districts must be vigilant in understanding changes in copyright law—such changes have occurred more recently relative to the length of time a creation is protected from unregulated public use. Over the years, the Copyright Act amendments have changed the terms of copyright protection; as a result, the length of a copyright term depends largely on when the work was created and/or published. The most recent legislation, the Sonny Bono Copyright Term Extension Act, retroactively extended the duration of copyright from the life of the author plus fifty years to the life of the author plus seventy years, in the case of individual works, and from seventy-five years to ninety-five years in the case of works of corporate authorship and works first published before January 1, 1978. It also extended copyright protection by twenty years for both new works and pre-existing works not yet in the public domain.[41] Works in the public domain are those works that are not protected by copyright law and may be used freely by everyone. The reasons a work may not be protected include the following: (1) the term of copyright has expired; (2) the author failed to satisfy statutory formalities to perfect the copyright; or (3) the work is a work of the United States Government. The table below outlines copyright durations.[42]

Challenges to these changes emanated from those using works thought to be subject to unfettered public use or works whose protection was about to expire based on previous law. In 2003, in *Eldred v. Ashcroft*, the Supreme Court upheld the CTEA against constitutional challenges.[43] The plaintiffs in *Eldred* alleged that the CTEA violated the First Amendment and the "limited times" provision of the Constitution, particularly for existing copyrightable works created within the Copyright Act of 1976. In declaring that the CTEA was rationally related to a legitimate government purpose, the Court majority was deferential to the judgments of Congress.

Congress articulated that the reason for the extension of years to copyright holders was to bring United States law into harmony with internationally recognized principles. A 1993 agreement by the European Union (EU) established a copyright term of life plus seventy years, and the agreement directed EU members to deny this term to the works of non-EU countries whose laws did not secure that same protection. Adding to this motivation, Congress also passed the CTEA in light of demographic, economic, and technological changes. Longer terms will "encourage copyright holders to invest in the restoration and public distribution of their works.'"[44] In addition, greater terms of protection and longer personal life spans will allow families of authors to reap the benefits of their relatives' creations. Finally, the increased commercial life of copyrightable works can now be protected in an age of vast and rapid communications media and technological change. Therefore, according to the Supreme Court majority in the case, the CTEA is well within the congressional authority to "promote Science and the Useful Arts.'"[45]

This legislation, though promulgated after more recent technology amendments, works in concert with those laws in protecting copyright holders in an increasingly electronic environment. School personnel must investigate all materials that involve copyright, even those thought, heretofore, to be in the public domain. This message must also be conveyed to staff and students since the Supreme Court has indicated that the First Amendment right to free expression will not be heard as a defense to inappropriate use of materials.

Copyright Durations

Date of Work	Protected From	Term
Published before 1923	In public domain	None
Published from 1923–1963	When published with notice	28 years + could be renewed for 47 years, now extended by 20 years for a total of 67 years; if not so renewed, now in public domain
Published from 1964–1977	When published with notice	28 years from first term; now an automatic extension of 67 years for second term
Created before 1–1–1978 but not published	1–1–1978, the effective date of the Copyright Act of 1976, which eliminated common law copyright	Life of author + 70 years or 12–31–2002, whichever is greater
Created before 1–1–1978 but published between then and 12–31–2002	1–1–1978, the effective date of the Copyright Act of 1976, which eliminated common law copyright	Life of author + 70 years or 12–31–2047, whichever is greater
Created 1-1-78 or After	When work is fixed in a tangible medium of Expression	Life + 70 years (or if work of corporate Authorship, the shorter of 95 years from publication, or 120 years from creation)

Conclusion

It can be assumed that educators are still protected in their pursuits involving copyrighted materials in the information age, but vigilance involving teachers, staff, and students must be a hallmark of any decision making and any policy. Providing the school population with access to the Internet or having knowledge that students are using or sending information through the school's mainframe raises legal issues; hence, instruction on proper Internet behavior is important. Educators should assume any work placed on the Internet could be protected. Even if not on the Internet, recent changes in intellectual property law extend the life of any copyrighted work by several years. It would be prudent for readers to take special precautions as penalties, if applied, could be costly and profound. While criminal penalties would likely not be applied in an educational context, this is not true of civil remedies. Copyright owners, for example, may seek actual or statutory damages. The copyright owner is entitled to recover any actual damages suffered by him or her as a result of the infringing action, plus any additional profits attributable to the infringement that are not taken into account in computing the actual damages.[46] The copyright owner may also elect, at any time before final judgment is rendered, to recover, instead of actual damages, an award of statutory damages for all infringements involved in the action. Statutory damages must not be less than $750 or more than $30,000 with respect to the infringement of any one work.[47] In cases where the copyright owner has the burden of proof and the court finds that infringement was committed willfully, the court may increase the award of statutory damages to a sum of not more than $150,000. In a case where the infringer has the burden of proof and the court finds that such infringer was not aware and had no reason to believe that his or her acts constituted an infringement, the court may reduce the award of statutory damages to a sum of not less than $200.[48] Please note that only statutory damages can be the remedy, if one is warranted, in cases involving an infringer who is an employee or agent of a nonprofit educational institution acting within the scope of his or her employment who reasonably believed that the infringing use was a fair use.

Recommendations for Practice

1. Online access to copyrighted materials opens schools to limited liability; these institutions need to be proactive and unambiguous in their policies about institutional responsibilities.
2. Students and staff must observe and adhere to the fact that there are restrictions on the use of copyrighted materials whether in hardcopy or online.

3. Additional copyright protections may be available to creators of materials used in distance education, and this information must also be listed in any school policy.
4. Copyrighted materials may now have additional years of protection, and school personnel may need to apply for continued permission to employ such creations or ensure that fair use is applicable.
5. Assume that Internet-based material is copyrighted, and investigate to make sure it is not.
6. Prepare acceptable use policies for online and hardcopy materials that offer proper guidance for copyright restrictions and provide sanctions for inappropriate activity.

Endnotes

1 Progressive Animal Welfare Soc'y v. Univ. of Wash., 125 Wash. 2d 243, 884 P.2d 592 [95 Educ. L. Rep. 711] (1994).

2 17 U.S.C.A. §§ 102–03.

3 The copyright statute examines the scope of these exclusive rights according to the nature of the work: pictorial, graphic, and cultural works (17 U.S.C.A. § 113); sound recordings (§ 114); distribution and performance of non-dramatic musical works (§§ 115, 116); and non-commercial broadcasting (§ 118).

4 17 U.S.C.A. §§ 107–12, 117, 119.

5 17 U.S.C.A. § 107.

6 Robinson v. Random House, Inc., 877 F. Supp. 830 (S.D.N.Y.1995). Note that this use, if fair, does not require advance consent from the copyright holder. Hustler Magazine, Inc. v. Moral Majority, Inc., 796 F.2d 1148 (9th Cir.1986).

7 Twin Peaks Prods., Inc. v. Publ'ns Intern., 778 F. Supp. 1247 (S.D.N.Y.1991); Iowa State Univ. Research Found., Inc. v. Am. Broad. Cos., Inc., 621 F.2d 57 (2d Cir.1980).

8 17 U.S.C.A. § 107.

9 Sony Corp. of Am. v. Universal City Studios, Inc., 464 U.S. 417, 104 S. Ct. 774, 78 L. Ed. 2d 574 (1984).

10 The fact that the ultimate users of the copies are students does not preclude a finding that the use of the copies is primarily commercial. A commercial copying service that compiles and repackages several copyrighted works into packets for university students to purchase may be guilty of infringement unless it pays royalties or permission fees. Princeton Univ. Press v. Mich. Document Servs., 99 F.3d 1381 [114 Educ. L. Rep. 34] (6th Cir.1996). *But see,* Basic Books, Inc. v. Kinko's Graphics Corp., 758 F. Supp. 1522 [66 Educ. L. Rep. 983] (S.D.N.Y.1991). Although the federal district court in *Kinko's* found a copyright violation because college student course packets were packaged and sold without the original publisher's permission, the judge in the case did not proscribe all unconsented anthology copying. The court determined that this is to be decided on a case-by-case basis, looking at both the need for protecting the author's intellectual property and the necessary flexibility for extending ideas to students and teachers.

11 A finding of educational use does not automatically dictate a "fair" use. Campbell v. Acuff-Rose Music, Inc., 510 U.S. 569, 114 S. Ct. 1164, 127 L. Ed. 2d 500 (1994).

12 Basic Books, Inc. v. Kinko's Graphics Corp., 758 F. Supp. 1522 (S.D.N.Y.1991).

13 Rubin v. Brooks/Cole Publ'g Co., 836 F. Supp. 909 (D. Mass.1993).

14 Harper & Row Publishers, Inc. v. Nation Enters., 471 U.S. 539, 105 S. Ct. 2218, 85 L. Ed. 2d 588 (1985). In *Harper & Row,* Nation magazine printed part of former President Gerald

Ford's memoirs in an attempt to scoop a TIME magazine article. TIME had agreed with the memoir publisher, Harper & Row, to print pre-publication excerpts. As a result of the NATION article, TIME canceled its agreement with Harper & Row, and Harper & Row sued Nation Enterprises. With respect to factor four, Harper & Row directly lost $12,500 that it would have received from TIME. *See also* Salinger v. Random House, Inc., 811 F.2d 90 (2d Cir.), *cert. denied,* 484 U.S. 890, 108 S. Ct. 213, 98 L. Ed. 2d 177 (1987).

[15] 695 F.2d 1171 [8 EDUC. L. REP. 258] (9th Cir.1983).

[16] Notes of Committee on the Judiciary, House Report No. 94–1476 (1976).

[17] *Id. See also* NATIONAL ASSOCIATION OF COLLEGE STORES ET AL., QUESTIONS AND ANSWERS ON COPYRIGHT FOR THE CAMPUS COMMUNITY (1991).

[18] 17 U.S.C. § 110.

[19] 17 U.S.C. § § 110–12.

[20] 17 U.S.C. § 110(A)(B)(C)(D).

[21] *Id.*

[22] Mediated instructional activities are defined as "activities that use copyrighted materials ... integral to the class experience, controlled by or under the actual supervision of the instructor and analogous to the type of performance and display that would take place in a live classroom."

[23] Examples of protections universities can implement are passwords, PINs, and time-sensitive access.

[24] 17 U.S.C. § 110(2).

[25] 15 U.S.C. § 1117.

[26] 17 U.S.C. § 101.

[27] 17 U.S.C. §§ 1201–04.

[28] 17 U.S.C. § 512.

[29] 17 U.S.C. § 512(e).

[30] 17 U.S.C. § 1201.

[31] 17 U.S.C. § 1201(d)-(j).

[32] 17 U.S.C. §§ 1203–04. Criminal liability exists, as well. But nonprofit libraries, archives, and educational institutions are exempt from criminal liability under the DMCA.

[33] Hendrickson v. Ebay, Inc., 165 F. Supp. 2d 1082 (C.D. Cal. 2001).

[34] 273 F.3d 429 (2d Cir. 2001).

[35] *See also* United States v. Elcom Ltd., 203 F. Supp. 2d 1111 (N.D. Cal. 2002).

[36] 1 Cal. 4th 864, 878, 75 P.3d 1, 11 (2003).

[37] 334 F.3d 643 (7th Cir. 2003).

[38] 545 U.S. 913 (2005).

[39] *See also* P.T.K. Daniel & P.D. Pauken, *The Impact of the Electronic Media on Instructor Creativity and Institutional Ownership Within Copyright Law,* 132 EDUC. L. REP. 1 (1999).

[40] Daniel and Pauken propose that the Copyright Act offers at least three protections to authors whose works are manipulated and linked to others in cyberspace: joint authorship, collective authorship, and derivative work authorship *Id.* at 15.

[41] 17 U.S.C. §§ 301–04.

[42] Lolly Gasaway, *When U.S. Works Pass into the Public Domain, available at* http://www.unc.edu/~unclng/public-d.htm. Per Gasaway, the chart may be freely duplicated or linked to for nonprofit purposes. No permission needed. Please include web address on all reproductions of chart so recipients know where to find any updates.

[43] 537 U.S. 186 (2003).

[44] *Id.* at 187.

[45] *Id.* at 223.

[46] 17 U.S.C. § 504.

[47] *Id.*

[48] *Id.*

Chapter 32

Charter Schools

Preston C. Green, III

Introduction

Since 1992, forty states and the District of Columbia have enacted legislation for charter schools. As of September, 2006, there are 4,000 charter schools serving more than one million students.[1] Charter schools are public schools that are created by a charter between a chartering authority and those individuals who wish to run a school. Charter schools receive much autonomy from regulations pertaining to traditional public schools. In return, the schools must meet the educational goals established in the charter or face possible closure.[2]

This interplay between autonomy and accountability has given rise to a great deal of litigation. This chapter examines several types of legal issues. The first section analyzes state constitutional challenges to the creation of charter schools. The second section explores some of the legal issues surrounding the establishment of charter schools. The third section examines litigation surrounding charter school renewals and revocations. The fourth section examines judicial review of charter schools. The fifth section addresses litigation that has arisen during the operation of the charter. The sixth section analyzes the legal issues pertaining to race. This chapter closes with an analysis of the legal issues that charter schools have faced with respect to students with disabilities.

State Constitutional Challenges to Charter Schools

Critics have alleged in state courts that charter schools should not be permitted to exist because they violate state constitutional principles regarding public schools. One category of constitutional challenge asserts that charter schools are undeserving of public funding because they are not under the sufficient control of public school system officers. In *Council of Organizations and Others for Education about Parochiaid v. Governor*,[3] the Supreme Court of Michigan ruled that the state constitution did not require charter schools to be under the exclusive control of the state. However, the court noted that the charter schools statute could have still satisfied this requirement. The authorizing bodies, which were public institutions, exercised control over charter schools through the application and revocation process. The state also exercised control over charter schools through funding. Finally, other sections of the school code applied to charter schools.

The second category of state constitutional challenge is that charter schools violate the requirement that they must be part of a system of common schools. In *State ex rel. Ohio Congress of Parents & Teachers v. State Board of Education*,[4] for example, the Supreme Court of Ohio held that the state's charter schools were part of a thorough and efficient system of public schools. Although charter schools were exempt from a number of state standards, many of these standards were picayune in nature. Moreover, charter schools were still required to comply with other standards that were applicable to traditional public schools. For example, charter school students had to satisfy the graduation test requirements as if they attended traditional public schools. Further, Ohio charter schools had to administer proficiency, achievement, and diagnostic tests; maintain adequate facilities; comply with all health and safety requirements; and abide by numerous school code provisions as though they were traditional public schools.

The third category of constitutional challenge is that charter school statutes divest authority over public education from entities designated by state constitutions. In *Board of Education of School District No. 1 in the City and County of Denver v. Booth*,[5] the Supreme Court of Colorado analyzed whether the charter school statute's second-appeal provision unconstitutionally divested control of instruction from local school boards. This provision authorized the state board to remand a local board's decision to deny a charter with directions to approve the application if the board found that the decision was "contrary to the best interests of the pupils, school district, or community."[6] The court found that the second-appeal provision did not infringe upon the local board's control of instruction because it did not require the "approved application to serve as a binding contract."[7] Instead, the legislature intended the second-appeal provision to serve as "interim step toward creation of that contract."[8] Accordingly, a local school board could abide by the state board order "and still expect resolution of its initial grounds for denial in a satisfactory final agreement with the charter school applicants."[9]

The fourth type of constitutional challenge is that charter school statutes have unconstitutionally delegated authority to operate charter schools. In *Utah School Board Association v. Utah State Board of Education*,[10] a school board asserted that the state's charter school law unconstitutionally delegated authority over charter schools to the state board of education. Specifically, the association contended that because the state constitution vested the state board with only general control and supervision of the public school system, the legislature could empower the state board only to take actions affecting the entire school system. The Supreme Court of Utah rejected this argument, finding that the vesting general control and supervision of the public education system included the authority to direct and manage specific components within the educational system.

The fifth category of constitutional challenge is that charter schools have a negative impact on traditional public schools. In the *Ohio Congress of Parents & Teachers* case, the appellants argued that the state's charter school law violated the state constitution's requirement that the legislature provide a thorough and efficient system of common schools by making urban school districts more reliant on local property taxation. This was the case because the state reduced state funding for every student who leaves a district to attend a charter school. In rejecting this argument, the court distinguished the charter school funding provisions from *DeRolph v. State*,[11] a case in which the court invalidated the school finance system for its overreliance on local property taxation. As the court explained:

> What the *DeRolph* majority found so egregious was Ohio's public schools' heavy dependence upon local property taxes for their support. That simply is not the case here. [Charter] schools do not rely on local property taxes…. [Charter] schools cannot levy or spend local taxes…. The state treats [charter-school] students in the same way it has treated any student who has ever left a school district. It reduces its per-pupil funding to the school district, just as it does when students leave for private schools, for other school districts, or for home schooling.[12]

Criteria for Granting a Charter

All charter school statutes have developed an application process in which individuals who are interested in establishing a charter school must apply to a chartering authority that may grant or reject the application. Each charter school statute lays out a number of criteria that the chartering authority must consider in deciding whether to grant the application. A number of cases have dealt with the following criteria: (1) support for the charter school, (2) the educational soundness of the proposal, and (3) the appropriateness of the facilities.

In several cases, the Pennsylvania courts have held that the criterion in the charter school law requiring the chartering authority to examine the existence of "demonstrated, sustainable support" from "teachers, parents, other community members and students"[13] did not require the charter school applicant to provide support from each individual category. Instead, the charter school applicant may satisfy this criterion by providing evidence in the aggregate.[14] For instance, in *Carbondale Area School District v. Fell Charter School*, the Commonwealth Court of Pennsylvania ruled that the applicants established sustainable support for the charter school proposal even though there was limited support from teachers. The court found that there was sustainable support for the proposal in light of the fact that the petition included 554 signatures, more than $10,000 in donations from eighty-one donors, and $40,000 in extra pledges.

The Pennsylvania courts have also examined the meaning of the criterion that charter schools must provide "comprehensive learning experiences."[15] In *McKeesport Area School District v. Propel Charter School McKeesport*,[16] the Commonwealth Court of Pennsylvania found that the charter school proposal had satisfied this requirement. Even though the charter school proposal would have one less report card than other schools within the school district, the court concluded that the charter school would adequately measure student progress through a variety of strategies including weekly progress reports, regular literacy assessments, and annual standardized testing. The court further noted that the charter school statute did not require the charter school to exceed other programs within the district in order to provide a comprehensive learning environment.

It is important to recognize that other statutes may require applications to demonstrate that students attending the proposed charter schools will perform better than students attending traditional public schools. In *Board of Education of the Roosevelt Union Free School District v. Board of Trustees of the State University of New York*,[17] a school district challenged the granting of a charter to a school that would have been located within the district. A New York appellate court remitted the case back to the school district because the chartering authority failed to make a statutorily required finding that the charter school was likely to improve student learning and achievement.[18]

A number of charter school statutes require the chartering authority to consider the economic soundness of the proposal with respect to the charter school and the surrounding school district. In *Comprehensive Community Solutions, Inc. v. Rockford School District No. 205*,[19] the Supreme Court of Illinois upheld a state board's denial of a charter school application, which would have provided academic instruction and on-the-job training to students between the ages of seventeen and twenty-one because the proposal failed to provide "[e]vidence that the terms of the charter as proposed are economically sound for both the charter and the school district."[20] The proposed charter school would have provided stipends ranging from $4,998 in 2002 to $6,426 in 2006. Further, the proposal called for the charter school to receive 100 percent of the district per-pupil-expenditure for each student attending the school.

The state board of education denied the application on the grounds that it was not in compliance with the charter school law and not in the best interest of students. The Supreme Court of Illinois found that these conclusions were not clearly erroneous. The court observed that even at the rate of 75 percent per capita funding and 85 percent attendance proposed by school district, it stood to lose $30,717 during the five-year period of the charter. If the charter school received funding at 100 percent per capita and 90 percent attendance, the school district would have lost at least $1.03 million over five years. Further, an independent audit found that the district might have had to close schools, shorten school days at the remaining schools, and eliminate staff and programs.

Three state courts have analyzed whether a chartering authority may deny a charter application because of its potentially negative impact on school districts in the absence of an express provision. In *Keystone Central School District v. Sugar Valley Concerned Citizens*, the Commonwealth Court of Pennsylvania ruled that a chartering authority may not act in this manner because "[t]he General Assembly specifically provided that the funding for charter schools shall come from school district revenues. To deny the charter school because it may deplete school district revenues is inconsistent with the purpose of the [charter school law]."[21]

In contrast, the Supreme Court of New Jersey ruled that the state commissioner of education must analyze the economic impact upon a district when determining whether to grant a charter even though the charter school statute did not expressly mandate such a consideration. The court acknowledged that the statute placed the commissioner's focus on determining the per-pupil funding amount on the charter school's needs. However, the court explained that the commissioner could not make such a determination without considering the effect of the charter on the district's ability to meet its constitutional mandate of providing a thorough and efficient education to its remaining students.[22]

In *State Board of Osceola County v. UCP of Central Florida*,[23] a school board asserted that even though Florida's charter school statute did not contain an express provision authorizing chartering authorities to deny an application on fiscal grounds, it did permit chartering authorities to deny an application for "good cause." The board maintained that there was good cause for denial of the application because the proposed charter school would dilute capital funding from all other charter schools within the district. The board also claimed that the charter application's reliance on operational funding to pay for capital expenditures would negatively affect the school district's capacity to provide all students with an adequate education. In making its case, the board pointed out that Florida law required school boards to ensure that all students had adequate facilities and instructional materials. Further, the charter school law required chartering authorities to monitor charter school revenue and expenditures and to review the financial plan of each application. The board maintained that these general legislative directives and the school district's financial problems constituted good cause for denial of the charter school application.

The Florida District Court of Appeal rejected the board's assertion that there was good cause to deny the charter on fiscal grounds. The court found that the district did not qualify for capital funding, and if the application was approved, the charter school would have no impact on the capital funding provided to other charter schools for at least three years. As to the second argument, the court found that the board proffered no empirical evidence demonstrating that approval of the application would result in other schools in the district receiving an inferior education.

In a series of cases, the Commonwealth Court of Pennsylvania has examined whether the loss or potential loss of a proposed facility may result in a denial of the application. In *Souderton Area School District v. Souderton Charter School Collaborative*,[24] a school district claimed that the Charter Appeal Board (CAB) acted arbitrarily by finding that the charter school facilities did not have to be reviewed and approved by the school board prior to the opening of the school. The district complained that the CAB order required it to grant the application without ever reviewing the site. The court acknowledged that if the district was correct in its interpretation of the CAB order, then CAB had violated the charter school law. However, the board found that the district had misinterpreted CAB's intent. CAB had found that the proposed site was appropriate, but that the application was two years out of date. Thus, the CAB order applied only if the approved facility was available. If the facility was not available, then the proposers would have to submit a new application and provide the district with the opportunity to determine whether the new facility was in compliance with the charter school law.

In *Brackbill v. Ron Brown Charter School*, the school district argued that CAB was incorrect to grant a charter because the proposed facilities were no longer available. In this case, CAB required the applicant to provide the district and CAB with the information prior to the opening of the school. The district argued that CAB's action was contrary to public policy because charter schools could wait until an application was approved before proposing a location. Further, the district asserted that the CAB order did not consider a remedy in case the building chosen after the granting of the charter was unacceptable. The Commonwealth Court of Pennsylvania rejected this argument, pointing out that "[w]hat the School District fails to recognize is that any loss of authority to react in the first instance to the proposed facility is a deprivation of its own making."[25] The applicant had listed two facilities in its application in accordance with the charter school law. However, the school district's inaction caused the charter school to lose rights in these proposed facilities. By failing to act on the revised application, the court held that the district surrendered to CAB the right to review the relevant criteria.

In *Montour School District v. Propel Charter School-Montour*,[26] a district denied a charter school petition in part because of questions regarding the leasing and renovation of the proposed facility. The charter school applicant then appealed to CAB. At oral argument, the applicant told the district and CAB that the proposed facility was no longer available and that the applicant was pursuing a lease for another building, which would need improvements and zoning modifications to be used as a charter school. CAB found that at the time of the application and ruling by the school board, the proposed facility was in compliance with the charter school law. CAB believed that the charter school law did not require all elements of the school's facilities in order for the charter to be approved. Citing *Souderton* and *Brackbill*, CAB held that the loss of a facility was not fatal to the application. CAB then ordered the district to grant the charter and that prior to the opening of the school, the applicant was to provide CAB and the district with information regarding the facility to be used for the charter school.

The Commonwealth Court of Pennsylvania vacated CAB's order and remanded to CAB for the purpose of determining whether the new facilities were in compliance with the charter school law. The court distinguished the instant case from *Brackbill*, noting that the proposed facility was unavailable because of the district's delay. The court also observed that in both *Souderton* and *Brackbill*, the charter schools would be allowed to open only if they had found suitable facilities.

Revocation and Nonrenewals of Charter Schools

Charter school statutes generally include provisions for determining the circumstances under which a sponsor may revoke or refuse to renew a charter. Grounds for revocation or nonrenewal may include material violations of charter provisions, failure to achieve reasonable progress to the educational goals established in the charter, failure to abide by fiscal accountability procedures, or violations of laws not excused by the charter.[27]

State ex rel. School District of Kansas City v. Williamson[28] illustrates the potential damage that unclear statutory language, with respect to renewals and revocations, may cause for charter schools and charter school authorizers. In this case, a Missouri appellate court addressed the question of whether a school district had revoked a charter before the end of the charter term or merely had decided against renewing the charter. This distinction was significant because the charter school statute provided detailed procedures for the revocation of charters. For example, a chartering entity could revoke a charter on certain grounds, including material breach of the charter, failure to fulfill academic performance standards, failure to satisfy fiscal management standards, or violation of law. The statute also provided for judicial review of revocations. By contrast, the charter school law was silent regarding the criteria to be used for renewals of charters or whether there was judicial review of a chartering entity's decision not to renew a charter.

Determining whether the chartering entity's decision was a revocation or nonrenewal depended upon the length of the charter term. Although the charter school law required the charter to state the length of the term, the charter at issue failed to include such a provision. This failure compelled the court to determine the legislature's intent regarding charter duration. The court observed that the legislature set a five-year minimum in order to give the charter experiment a valid chance for success. The legislature also stipulated in the statute that the charter could last for no more than ten years in order to give charter schools and potential chartering authorities more flexibility to evaluate their effectiveness. In light of these policy considerations, the court found that in the absence of a specific term, the charter was limited to a five-year term—which just so happened to be the length of time that the charter school was in operation. Thus, the court concluded that the decision was deciding whether to renew the charter instead of whether to revoke the charter.

The next stage of the court's examination was to determine the standards and procedures that were applicable to charter school renewals. In the absence of a statutory right to renewal, the application had to be treated like a new charter application. The court found that the school district had met the procedures for new charter school applications because the district had requested the charter school to submit a renewal application and provided written notice within sixty days of receiving the application that the charter would not be renewed.

Judicial Review of Applications, Renewals, and Revocations

In a number of instances, aggrieved parties have sought judicial review of application, renewal, or revocation decisions. In *Comprehensive Community Solutions, Inc. v. Rockford School District No. 205*, the Supreme Court of Illinois explained that according to the state's administrative review law, the standard of review depended on whether the administrative agency addressed a question of law, a question of fact, or a mixed question of law and fact. The standard of review for questions of law was *de novo* review. In those cases, the reviewing court was not bound by the administrative body's interpretation of the statute. The standard of review for questions of fact was more deferential to the agency. In such cases, the court examines whether "the agency's decision is against the manifest weight of the evidence."[29] A mixed question of law and fact requires the court to decide "whether established facts satisfy applicable legal rules."[30] The standard of review for mixed questions of law and fact was also deferential, and such cases would be overturned only where the agency's decision was "clearly erroneous."

The primary issue in the *Comprehensive Community Solutions* case was whether the state board of education was correct to affirm the local board's decision to deny the charter proposal on the ground that it was not "economically sound for both the charter school and the school district" in accordance with the charter school statute.[31] The Supreme Court of Illinois found that this question required a two-part inquiry. First, the court would have to determine the statutory requirement. The standard of review for this part of the inquiry was *de novo*. Second, the court had to determine whether the charter school proposal satisfied the statutory requirement. The standard of review for the inquiry was the "clearly erroneous" standard. With respect to the first part of the inquiry, the court found that the economic soundness provision required both the charter school and the school district to be financially secure and solvent if the charter were granted. The court then found that the state board of education's decision to uphold the local board's decision to deny the charter was not clearly erroneous because there was evidence that the proposed charter school would exacerbate the financial problems faced by the school district.

In *State ex rel. School District of Kansas City v. Williamson*, a Missouri appellate court held that a charter school was prohibited from attaining any judicial review of a school district's refusal to renew its charter. The court determined that the charter applicant did not have a right to a contested case review, which would have entitled the applicant to judicial review. The applicant also tried to seek judicial review through noncontested case review. According to Missouri law, judicial review through noncontested case review is available in situations where the administrative decision determines a person's legal rights, duties, or privileges. However, the charter school could not obtain judicial review of the chartering authority's decision to deny a charter because the charter school law provided no right to the renewal of a charter. Noncontested case review was available with regard to whether the chartering authority followed proper procedures in deciding whether to renew the charter. The charter school was not entitled to such review on this issue because there was a dispute on the record.

The Operation of the Charter School

Several charter school cases have dealt with the operational issues. One area of concern for charter schools is the availability and quality of facilities. Charter schools often have a difficult time obtaining facilities because they generally do not receive funding for facilities and cannot raise taxes for facilities through taxation. California's charter school law has attempted to address this problem by requiring a school district to provide a charter school located in that district with facilities at no charge. The facilities must be reasonably equivalent to other public schools, contiguous, and fully equipped. To qualify for such facilities, the charter school must demonstrate a reasonably projected enrollment of "[eighty] units of average daily classroom attendance."[32]

In *Sequoia Union High School District v. Aurora Charter School*,[33] a California appellate court determined that while a charter school must provide some explanation for its projection, it was not required to establish its projection with "arithmetical precision." The charter school met its burden in *Sequoia Union* by basing its projection on the school's historical attendance rates, its current enrollment, and the expressed interest of current and prospective pupils. By contrast, in *Environmental Charter High School v. Centinela Valley Union School District*,[34] the state appellate court found that the school district did not arbitrarily or capriciously deny a charter school's facilities request where the charter school submitted an incomplete application after the deadline. Finally, in *Ridgecrest Charter School v. Sierra Sands Unified School District*,[35] a state court held that a school district abused its discretion by offering to provide a charter school with classrooms from five different sites separated by sixty-five miles. The district abused its discretion because it failed to fairly balance the needs of the charter schools with the needs of district-operated schools.

Charter schools commonly lease facilities from religious institutions. In *Porta v. Klagholz*,[36] a federal district court examined whether one such arrangement in New Jersey violated the Establishment Clause. The court determined that leasing agreements between charter schools and religious institutions did not facially violate the Establishment Clause. Such agreements had a legitimate, secular purpose of providing charter schools with suitable space for operating classes. Lease agreements between religious institutions and school districts did not advance or inhibit religion because charter schools are exclusively secular. The court found no entanglement because lease agreements between religious institutions and schools are no different from other types of landlord-tenant agreements.

The court also found that the specific leasing arrangement did not violate the Establishment Clause as applied. There was no evidence of religious indoctrination because religious iconography on the school site was kept to a minimum. The leasing agreement was religiously neutral because the charter school leased the church after conducting an extensive search for affordable housing. Finally, there was no entanglement between the parties because the leasing arrangement was a typical landlord-tenant arrangement.

Charter Schools and Race

Critics of charter schools have worried that whites and minorities might use these schools to segregate themselves from each other. One manifestation of this concern was that white parents and teachers might use charter schools to circumvent court-ordered desegregation decrees. Several states expressly require charter schools to abide by such decrees. Charter schools might violate desegregation decrees by being more segregated than other public schools within the school district. Charter schools might also make it difficult for school districts to satisfy school desegregation decrees by attracting a disproportionately high percentage of students and faculty of one race away from other public schools within the districts.

Charter school applications must explain how they would be in compliance with school desegregation decrees to avoid having their proposals rejected. In *Berry v. School District of the City of Benton Harbor*,[37] a federal district court permitted the funding of the Benton Harbor Charter School because the applicant provided evidence that the school's faculty and staff recruitment policies, curricular requirements, and diversity training of faculty, staff, and board of directors would comply with a desegregation decree. On the other hand, the court disallowed the funding of the Benton Harbor Community Academy because the proposal provided insufficient information about the racial composition of the student body. Therefore, the court could not determine whether the charter school would have hindered the district's ability to comply with the decree.

Racial balancing provisions are another strategy for preventing charter schools from becoming racially segregated. Several states require the racial composition of charter schools to be reflective of that of the surrounding school districts. For instance, North Carolina's charter school law states:

> [w]ithin one year after the charter school begins operation, the population of the school shall reasonably reflect the racial and ethnic composition of the general population residing within the local school administrative unit in which the school is located or the racial and ethnic composition of the special population that the school seeks to serve residing within the local school administrative unit in which the school is located.[38]

In *Beaufort County Board of Education v. Lighthouse Charter School Committee*,[39] a South Carolina trial court determined that the state's racial balancing provision, which required the racial composition of charter schools to be within 10 percent of the surrounding school district, violated the Equal Protection Clause. Because the enrollment policy employed a race-based classification, the court determined that strict scrutiny applied. Thus, the policy had to be narrowly tailored to satisfy a compelling interest. Applying strict scrutiny, the court ruled that the racial-balancing provision violated the Equal Protection Clause. It rejected the claim that the provision satisfied the compelling interest of encouraging student diversity among charter schools. The court took notice of Supreme Court Justice Lewis Powell's opinion in *Regents of the University of California v. Bakke*[40] that universities may use race as a factor in their admissions decisions to attain diversity, but rejected the legal meaning of this decision, noting that "[n]either of the two major opinions [in *Bakke*] shared Powell's view of the law."[41] The racial-balancing provision was also constitutionally lacking because, "[w]hile a charter school may not even use race as a factor in its admissions decisions, race becomes the *only* factor when a certain racial make-up is reached."[42]

The court further held that even if diversity were a compelling governmental interest, the state's racial balancing provision violated the Equal Protection Clause because it was not narrowly tailored. One weakness was that the charter school would have to satisfy the racial balancing requirement in perpetuity. A second problem with the racial-balancing provision was that there was a relationship between the numerical goal and the charter school's pool of students. Moreover, the racial-balancing provision was too inflexible and excessively burdensome on innocent third parities because the charter school would have been forced to recruit students from fifty miles away in order to comply with the racial-balancing provision. Because the provision was not severable from the charter school law, the court determined that the entire statute was unconstitutional.

The case was appealed to the Supreme Court of South Carolina. In the meantime, the state legislature responded to the trial court's decision by amending the racial-balancing provision to require the racial composition of a charter school to be within 20 percent of the surrounding school district's population.[43] The amended statute also provided that a charter school must be approved, even if it failed to satisfy the racial-balancing requirement, if the applicant made a good faith effort to recruit other racial groups and the "application is acceptable in all other aspects."[44] Because of these amendments, the Supreme Court of South Carolina vacated the trial court's opinion and dismissed the appeal as moot. The court further ruled that the new provisions had substantially "changed the character of the racial composition requirement by injecting a fact-based determination regarding discrimination rather than mandating a straightforward racial quota."[45]

Since the *Beaufort* decision, the Supreme Court held in *Grutter v. Bollinger*,[46] which endorsed Justice Powell's opinion in *Bakke,* that diversity was a compelling governmental interest that could justify the University of Michigan Law School's race-conscious admissions policy. With regard to the compelling interest inquiry, the Court observed that the concept of diversity was grounded in a university's academic freedom under the First Amendment to choose its student population. Moreover, the law school's admission policy was narrowly tailored because race was a "plus" in a particular applicant's file instead of a quota, there was serious consideration about the ways that each applicant might contribute to the diversity of the law school, and the law school meaningfully considered diversity factors other than race. The Court was satisfied that the law school had adequately considered all available alternatives. The Court also observed that race-conscious policies must be limited in time and that the law school promised that it would terminate the race-conscious admissions policy as soon as possible.

In 2007, the Supreme Court addressed the constitutionality of race-based student assignment plans in *Parents Involved in Community Schools v. Seattle School District No. 1.*[47] This case has serious implications for charter school racial-balancing provisions. In a 5-4 judgment, the Court held that the use of racial classifications to achieve racial balancing is unconstitutional under the Equal Protection Clause. While the Court appeared to rule out the use of racial-balancing provisions, the opinions did suggest that charter school statutes may use other means to obtain a racially diverse student body. While the plurality of Justices Alito, Scalia, Thomas, and Chief Justice Roberts would apply traditional strict scrutiny to all race-based classifications, even the plurality opinion does not foreclose all future uses of race. In this respect, Chief Justice Roberts specifically stated:

> other means—*e.g.,* where to construct new schools, how to allocate resources among schools, and which academic offerings, to provide to attract students to certain schools—implicate different considerations than the explicit racial classifications at issue in these cases, and we express no opinion on their validity—not even in dicta. Rather, we employ the familiar and well-established approach of strict scrutiny to evaluate the plans at issue today.[48]

In his concurrence, Justice Kennedy stated that school districts can constitutionally pursue an interest in providing equal educational opportunity.[49] Kennedy also seems to support the idea that charter schools can attain a racially diverse student body through other means. For instance, Justice Kennedy noted that "[i]f school authorities are concerned that the student-body compositions of certain schools interfere with the objective of offering an equal educational opportunity to all of their students, they are *free to devise race-conscious measures* to address the problem in a general way."[50] An indication of his willingness to permit race-conscious measures is also evident in his following statement:

> School boards may pursue the goal of bringing together students of diverse backgrounds and races through other means, including strategic site selection of new schools; drawing attendance zones with general recognition of the demographics of neighborhoods; allocating resources for special programs; recruiting students and faculty in a targeted fashion; and tracking enrollments, performance, and other statistics by race. These mechanisms are race conscious but do not lead to different treatment based on a classification that tells each student he or she is to be defined by race, so it is unlikely any of them would demand strict scrutiny to be found permissible.[51]

Charter Schools and Students with Disabilities

In the beginning of the charter school movement, there was much confusion about the responsibilities of charter schools to students with disabilities. Indeed, the responsibilities that charter schools have with respect to this group of students are complex. Charter schools must understand the interplay among federal law, state law, and charter contracts in order to completely comprehend their responsibilities with respect to this student group.[52]

Section 504 of the Rehabilitation Act of 1973 (Section 504) and the Americans with Disabilities Act (ADA) provide part of this legal foundation.[53] Section 504 is a civil rights statute that forbids discrimination based on disability by any recipient of federal funding. The ADA extends these restrictions to the workplace regardless of whether the employer receives federal financial assistance. The requirements of Title II of the ADA, which deals with the schools' treatment of children with disabilities, mirror those of section 504 in public school contexts.

To be in compliance with section 504 and the ADA, charter schools must ensure that students with disabilities have meaningful physical and programmatic access. The *TOVAS Charter School*[54] case illustrates the problems that a charter school could face for failure to comply with section 504 and the ADA. While examining a complaint for wrongful discharge, the Office for

Civil Rights discovered irregularities in the school's compliance with section 504. Specifically, the school had failed to put into practice procedures to identify and serve children with disabilities, to adopt a proper notice of non-discrimination, or to establish complaint procedures.

Charter schools must also be cognizant of the Individuals with Disabilities Education Act (IDEA). The IDEA provides funding to serve those children with disabilities whose impairments "adversely affect educational performance" such that they require special education. In 1997, the amendments to the IDEA included specific provisions regarding charter schools. The first section states that for "charter schools that are public schools of the local educational agency [LEA]," the LEA must serve students attending those schools in the same manner that it serves students in its other schools and must provide funds received through the IDEA to the charter schools in a like manner to its other schools.[55] Additionally, the IDEA makes provisions for charter schools that are designated as LEAs independent of any larger district.[56] The regulations further note that a third kind of charter school may exist that is neither an LEA nor part of another LEA. In such a case, "the SEA [state educational agency] is responsible for ensuring that the requirements of this part are met."[57] States have generally dealt with the LEA issues in three ways: (1) the charter school in which the district is located may serve as the LEA; (2) the charter school may be designated as the LEA; or (3) the state may create a mixture of categories of charter schools for special education purposes. An additional layer of complexity is added by each charter contract. The specific terms of the contract may define further how the IDEA is implemented in a given charter school.

As previously noted above, the first charter school type named in the IDEA is the charter school that is part of a larger LEA, usually a school district. In that instance, the school district serves as the LEA for IDEA purposes and owes the same obligation to charter school students as it does for its students in more traditional schools. Charter schools that fall into this category will need to work with their parent school district to develop their special education delivery pattern.

The second charter school type named in the IDEA is the LEA charter school, a charter school that is independent of any larger district and serves as its own LEA. These independent charter schools have the same obligations as larger school districts that serve as LEAs. Being an independent charter school does not, however, necessarily mean that the charter school is its own LEA. Independent charter schools should first consult with state law to be certain they are LEA charter schools. This step is necessary because states may designate another entity to assume this responsibility for independent charter schools.

Some states through statutes may require local or resident school districts to serve as LEAs, even for those charter schools that are otherwise independent of a school district. LEA charter schools must consider the same questions raised above for district charters and may wish to consider entering into agreements on those issues with the serving LEA or LEAs. However, if state law has not designated the LEA for independent charter schools, each individual charter school bears those LEA responsibilities.

An interesting issue that arises in the LEA charter school context might be termed the state statute conundrum. A number of states relieve charter schools from compliance with state statutes and rules regarding special education. This relief creates an interesting situation for those charter schools. These sources of state authority typically define how a state will implement the IDEA. They often create more detailed eligibility definitions and criteria for determining whether a child qualifies as a child with a disability beyond what is delineated in the federal statute and regulations. Whatever is contained within those exempted state provisions, according to federal law, an LEA charter school must adopt written policies and procedures to implement the mandates of the IDEA that must meet with the satisfaction of the state educational agency.

Consequently, LEA charter schools are faced with a choice. They must choose between creating their own independent policies and procedures based solely on federal law and following the state's rules and regulations despite being technically relieved from them.[58] Many charter schools may decide that the most practical route may be the latter, given the myriad other issues involved in charter school operation. Moreover, because the SEA must be satisfied with whatever is developed and the state statutes and regulations effectively create an existing template, voluntary compliance may be the simplest way to assure SEA satisfaction.

Conclusion

As this chapter has demonstrated, charter schools have sparked a wide variety of litigation. There has been litigation regarding the constitutionality of charter schools, the establishment process, and revocations and renewals of charter schools. Plaintiffs have also made legal challenges over issues of race and students with disabilities. Many of these challenges are the result of the interplay between the concepts of accountability and autonomy.

Endnotes

1 *National Charter School Data*, Center for Education Reform, *at* http://www.edreform.com/_upload/CER_charter_numbers.pdf (visited Sep. 30, 2007).

2 Preston C. Green & Julie F. Mead, Charter Schools and the Law: Establishing New Legal Relationships (2003).

3 566 N.W.2d 208 (Mich. 1997).

4 857 N.E.2d 1148 (Ohio 2006).

5 984 P.2d 639 (Colo. 1999).

6 Colo. Rev. Stat. § 22-30.5-108(3)(d) (2007).

7 *Booth*, 984 P.2d at 654.

8 *Id.*

[9] *Id.*
[10] 17 P.3d 1125 (Utah 2001).
[11] 780 N.E. 259 (Ohio 1997).
[12] *Ohio. Cong. of Parents & Teachers*, 857 N.E.2d at 1160.
[13] PA. STAT. ANN. tit. 24, §§ 17-1717-A (West 2007).
[14] Brackbill v. Ron Brown Charter Sch., 777 A.2d 131 (Pa. 2001); Carbondale Area Sch. Dist. v. Fell Charter Sch., 829 A.2d 400 (Pa. 2003); McKeesport Area Sch. Dist. v. Propel Charter Sch. McKeesport, 888 A.2d 912 (Pa. Cmwlth. 2005); Montour Sch. Dist. v. Propel Charter Sch. Montour, 889 A.2d 682 (Pa. Cmwlth. 2006).
[15] PA. STAT. ANN. tit. 24, § 17-1717-A (West 2007).
[16] 888 A.2d 912 (Pa. Cmwlth. 2005).
[17] 731 N.Y.S.2d 524 (App. Div. 2001).
[18] N.Y. EDUC. LAW § 2852 (McKinney 2007).
[19] 837 N.E. 1 (Ill. 2005).
[20] ILL. COMP. STAT. ANN. § 5/27A-7(a)(9) (West 2007).
[21] Keystone Cent. Sch. Dist. v. Sugar Valley Concerned Citizens, 799 A.2d 209, 218 (Pa. Cmwlth 2002).
[22] *In re* Grant of Charter Sch. Application of Englewood on the Palisades Charter Sch., 753 A.2d 687 (N.J. 2000).
[23] 905 So. 2d 909 (Fla. App. 2000).
[24] 764 A.2d 688 (Pa. Cmwlth. 2000).
[25] Brackbill v. Ron Brown Charter Sch., 777 A.2d 131, 139 (Pa. 2001).
[26] 889 A.2d 682 (Pa. Cmwlth. 2006).
[27] Suzanne Eckes et al., *Charter School Accountability: Legal Considerations Concerning Non-renewal and Revocation Procedures*, 2006 BRIGHAM YOUNG U. EDUC. & L. J. 551 (2006).
[28] 141 S.W.2d 418 (Mo. App. 2004).
[29] Comprehensive Cmty. Solut., Inc. v. Rockford School District No. 205, 837 N.E. 1, 11 (2005).
[30] *Id.*
[31] *Id.*
[32] CAL. EDUC. CODE § 47614 (2007).
[33] 5 Cal. Rptr. 3d 86 (Cal. Ct. App. 2003).
[34] 18 Cal. Rptr. 3d 417 (Cal. Ct. App. 2004).
[35] 30 Cal.Rptr.3d 648 (Cal. Ct. App. 2005).
[36] 19 F. Supp. 2d 290 (D.N.J. 1998).
[37] 56 F. Supp. 2d 866 (W.D.Mich. 1999).
[38] N.C. GEN. STAT. § 115C.238.92F(g)(5)(ii) (2007).
[39] No. 97-CP-7-794 (S.C. Ct. Com. Pleas May 8, 2000).
[40] 438 U.S. 265 (1978).
[41] *Beaufort*, No. 97-CP-7-794, at 3.
[42] *Id.* (emphasis added).
[43] S.C. CODE ANN. § 59-40-50 (Law. Co-op. 2007).
[44] *Id.* § 59-40-70D.
[45] Beaufort County Bd. of Educ. v. Lighthouse Charter Sch. Comm., 576 S.E.2d 180 (S.C. 2003).
[46] 539 U.S. 306 (2003).
[47] 127 S.Ct. 2738 (2007).
[48] *Id.* at 2766.
[49] *Id.* at 2792.
[50] *Id.* (emphasis added).
[51] *Id.*
[52] Julie F. Mead, *Determining Charter Schools' Responsibilities for Children With Disabilities: A Guide Through the Legal Labyrinth*, 11 B.U. PUB. INT. L.J. 167 (2002).
[53] 29 U.S.C. § 794 (2007).

[54] TOVAS Charter School, 37 IDELR 290 (OCR 2002).
[55] 20 U.S.C. § 1413(a)(5) (2007).
[56] *Id.* § 1413(e)(1)(B).
[57] 34 C.F.R. § 300.312(d)(1) (2007).
[58] See Green & Mead, *supra* note 2.

Chapter 33

Collective Bargaining in Public Schools

Justin M. Bathon

Introduction

For the past fifty years, collective bargaining of teachers and other school personnel has been an integral part of public school employment in the United States. This collective bargaining of school employees generally serves to strengthen the bargaining position of the employees against their employer, typically the school board. Given the unique nature of the relationship between public employees and their governmentally based employers, many states have enacted individual state laws to govern this relationship when it comes to collectively negotiating employment contracts. While there are many potential benefits and detriments of collective bargaining in the public schools,[1] the process is better served when individuals in the process are clearly aware of the established legal framework within which they are operating.

This chapter outlines the legal framework within which most public school collective bargaining occurs. First, this chapter examines the statutory and case law frameworks that either permit or deny collective bargaining of school employees in the United States. Also included in this section is a brief historical perspective on the development of the right to bargain in the United States and the specific development of teachers' unions. Second, the chapter examines various issues related to the bargaining process. These legal aspects of the bargaining process include the definition of the bargaining unit, good faith bargaining and unfair labor practices, and the acceptable subjects of collective bargaining. Third, this chapter examines the procedures that are allowed or mandated when the collective bargaining process breaks down, including an examination of strikes. Fourth, after an agreement is in place, most disputes cumulate in a grievance; therefore, the chapter examines the grievance procedure. Finally, some recommendations for practicing principals with respect to the collective bargaining process are provided.

This examination of collective bargaining is just an introduction. Principals finding themselves involved in legal issues related to collective bargaining in education should consult more detailed sources specific with state-related information or their legal counsel for more information.

Legal Issues

The Right to Bargain

The right to bargain collectively has not always been guaranteed in the United States. Although collective bargaining entities have existed nearly since the creation of the country, they had little rights and little effect on the workplace until the 1930s.[2] During this time, important federal legislation was passed that set the framework for collective bargaining of employees to this day. While these federal acts were substantial steps toward the legitimacy of collective bargaining, these laws applied only to the private sector and did not address state or other governmental employees, including public school teachers. In 1960, Wisconsin was the first state to mandate bargaining by public employees.[3] These types of state laws, combined with increasing teacher activism such as a strike by teachers in New York City, led to a drastic increase in the unionization of teachers in the United States in the 1960s.[4]

Although the private-sector legislation that emerged out of this contentious period of labor formation does not apply directly to public sector bargaining, many of the ideas and basic principles of these early acts still serve as the fundamental principles of all labor relations in the United States. Thus, knowing a little about these statutes helps in understanding the basic requirements of collective bargaining.

The first act Congress passed in relation to collective bargaining was the Norris-LaGuardia Act of 1932.[5] This act limited courts from using injunctions to stop collective actions by employees against employers and was an important first step toward the legitimization of collective bargaining. The second and more important act passed by Congress was the Wagner Act in 1935.[6] Also known as the National Labor Relations Act (NLRA), this statute created the National Labor Relations Board, which safeguarded the basic rights of employees in their collective activities.[7] These new protections included a limitation on employer interference with union activities, limits on discrimination against unions in hiring, and also a requirement that employers bargain in good faith. If employers violated any of these new union protections, the union could file an unfair labor practice claim against the employer with the National Labor Relations Board.[8] More than ten years later, the Taft-Hartley Act was passed as an attempt to balance the collective bargaining field by placing many of the same requirements on labor unions as were placed on employers.[9] Over the years, the basic foundation laid out by these important acts have been amended numerous times. However, the basic provisions established by these statutes still not only form the foundation for private sector collective bargaining, but have also been relied upon to varying degrees by public sector collective bargaining laws across the states.

While public sector collective bargaining is similar to private sector collective bargaining in many ways, there are some important fundamental differences. The most significant difference is that rather than a collectively bargained contract between two private individuals or corporations, in public sector bargaining, one of the parties to the contract is the government itself. Governments have several powers that private companies do not have, one of which is the power to make many of the rules.[10] In many cases the governmental employer retains more managerial rights than private companies; the public employer must work within a more structured time and budgetary framework, and the public employer retains greater control to limit the union's primary negotiating weapon, the strike.[11]

An important ruling by the U.S. Supreme Court in 1967, in the case of *Keyishian v. Board of Regents of the University of the State of New York,* found that a public employer cannot force employees to give away their right to join a union.[12] Subsequent court cases have followed the *Keyishian* decision in protecting teachers' constitutional rights to join and participate in union activities. Even where a state legislature attempted to prohibit public employees from joining a union, it was found to be unconstitutional.[13] Thus, all public employees have, at a minimum, the right to join a union. However, while public employees may join unions, this does not mean that such unions have a right to be the recognized collective bargaining agent for the membership. Such a right has been legislatively recognized in more than thirty states,[14] and courts have found collective bargaining units recognizable in other states.[15] Some states, though, have enacted legislation prohibiting collective contracts between public employers and employees, and in other states, the courts have ruled that such bargaining cannot occur without enabling legislation from the state legislature.

Thus, school administrators must be aware of the legal status of collective bargaining rights in their state before engaging in the collective bargaining process at all. For those states that prohibit or have not enabled collective bargaining of school employees, schools do not have to collectively bargain employee contracts. Instead, each school employee functions only with an individual employment contract. The remainder of this chapter will focus solely on states that permit collective bargaining of public employees.

Legal Issues in the Bargaining Process

In states that allow collective bargaining of teachers and other school employees, there are several similarities in terms of defining the bargaining unit, good faith negotiation and unfair labor practices, and the permissible subjects of collective bargaining. The next sections review each of these general similarities. However, it is important to keep in mind that these provisions may vary slightly from state to state depending on the specific provisions contained in the different state collective bargaining laws.

Defining the Bargaining Unit

The definition of the bargaining unit is a crucial step in the collective bargaining process. First, local employees must form a union and certify that union with the state labor relations board. Once a union is certified as a representative of a particular bargaining unit, such units become the exclusive bargaining agent for the entire population of the defined bargaining unit, regardless of whether each individual employee is a member of the union. Thus, unions represent even non-union employees within the bargaining unit. Second, state laws provide some clarity on who may be included in the bargaining unit. Typically, a bargaining unit must share some characteristics like similar working skills, wages, and conditions, as well as fit within a similar operative and administrative structure of the employer.[16] In schools, this typically translates into a distinct collective bargaining unit for teachers and a distinct collective bargaining unit for other staff such as custodial and central office staff.[17] In some cases, all non-administrative employees of a public school can be within a single bargaining unit. When this happens, the unit is called a wall-to-wall bargaining unit. However, wall-to-wall bargaining units occur much less frequently than distinct units for professional employees and classified employees.

Administrative employees typically may not be included in the bargaining unit. Specifically, exclusions to a bargaining unit have been made when employees are considered managerial, supervisory, or have access to confidential information regarding the employer's labor practices.[18] When principals or assistant principals have managerial and supervisory roles within the school, they are excluded from the bargaining unit.[19] There has also been controversy surrounding other school personnel, such as department chairs[20] and superintendent secretaries;[21] however, the central test remains whether such employees are managerial, supervisory, or have access to confidential information.

Good Faith and Unfair Labor Practices

Although there are multiple rights each party holds in the collective bargaining process, two specific rights are important for an understanding of public sector collective bargaining. First, there is a duty to bargain in good faith, which is necessary for parties to work together toward an agreement. If a party does not bargain in good faith or commits one of a multitude of other collective bargaining violations, they can be charged with committing an unfair labor practice, the primary mechanism for remedying disputes in the bargaining process.

Once a bargaining unit is established and defined, it becomes the exclusive bargaining representative for the population of individuals contained within the definition of the bargaining unit. To ensure a productive bargaining process between the exclusive representation agent and the public sector employer, the law places a duty to bargain in good faith on both parties.[22] In public sector collective bargaining, the duty to bargain in good faith is not always exactly akin to the private sector NLRA definition,[23] but it is frequently similar. Because of the contentious nature of the good faith bargaining provision, some states have added further clarity to their public employee good faith bargaining requirement. For example, the following is the good faith bargaining requirement in California:

> Meet and confer in good faith means that a public agency, or such representatives as it may designate, and representatives of recognized employee organizations, shall have the mutual obligation personally to meet and confer promptly upon request by either party and continue for a reasonable period of time in order to exchange freely information, opinions, and proposals, and to endeavor to reach agreement on matters within the scope of representation prior to the adoption by the public agency of its final budget for the ensuing year. The process should include adequate time for the resolution of impasses where specific procedures for such resolution are contained in local rule, regulation, or ordinance, or when such procedures are utilized by mutual consent.[24]

Although good faith bargaining does not require the parties to reach an agreement, the failure to bargain in good faith results in an unfair labor practice. Unfair labor practices are the primary remedy for disputes arising around the formation of the collectively bargained agreement and cover not only failures to bargain in good faith, but the majority of all other illegal activities related to the formation of the union and the collectively bargained agreement. In the private sector, unfair labor practice charges are heard by the National Labor Relations Board.[25] However, in public sector collective bargaining, these unfair labor disputes are heard by the state agency with authority for oversight of collective bargaining. If a dispute arises, a complaint is typically filed with the relevant state labor relations board. The board then investigates, and if it finds sufficient evidence of an unfair labor practice, the labor relations board will file a complaint against the violating party. This complaint is then typically first heard by an administrative law judge employed by the state labor relations board with subsequent rights to appeal to the judicial system.[26]

A charge of an unfair labor practice may be filed with the relevant state agency by either the employer or the employee. For the most part, what constitutes an unfair labor practice is not well defined in statutes. However, some statutes have attempted to provide greater definition as to what constitutes an unfair labor practice in regard to education. For example, Illinois law states that educational employers shall not interfere with employees in the exercise of their union rights, interfere with the formation of a union, discriminate against union members in hiring practices, refuse to bargain in good faith, or refuse to comply with a binding arbitration agreement, among others.[27]

In addition to statutory definitions of unfair labor practices, such as the ones mentioned above, courts frequently rule on charges of unfair labor practices. Courts have found that subcontracting bargaining unit work,[28] failing to promote to a non-union position,[29] and refusing to provide information to the union[30] can be unfair labor practices along with many other employer actions.[31] While used less frequently, unfair labor practices against employee unions include intentionally coercing employees to join the union, refusing to bargain in good faith, and refusing to comply with a binding arbitration agreement, among others.[32]

Subjects of Collective Bargaining

One of the frequently contested aspects of collective bargaining in schools is the different topics that can be the subject of collectively bargained contracts. The relationship between employers' right to manage their business and employees' right to bargain elements of their employment has led to three different classifications for possible topics of collective bargaining: unlawful subjects of bargaining, mandatory subjects of bargaining, and permissive subjects of bargaining.

First, topics that are inherently managerial in nature cannot be bargained. These managerial topics are considered an essential part of the government's role in determining the policy and direction of schools and as such cannot be bargained away, even if the school board wanted to. Policy decisions that cannot be bargained include school curricular matters and school staffing needs. Additionally, some courts have interpreted tenure decisions, the school calendar, dismissal procedures, and the choice of department heads and chairs as unlawful subjects of bargaining.[33]

Alternatively, some subjects must be bargained. State statutes that are modeled on the National Labor Relations Act use the general guideline that "wages, hours and other terms and conditions of employment" must be bargained in the formation of the collective bargaining agreement.[34] Clearly, then, subjects such as the salary of teachers and employees, their hourly responsibilities, and other fringe benefits must be bargained. Other topics that have been found in some cases to be mandatory subjects of bargaining include reimbursement for education and professional development, holiday and overtime pay, vacation and sick leave, early retirement incentives, reduction-in-force plans, and teacher evaluation procedures.[35]

Those subjects of bargaining, which are neither unlawful nor mandatory, are considered permissive subjects of bargaining. These subjects may become elements of the collective bargaining agreement if both parties agree. Permissive subjects of bargaining have included mid-contract renegotiation, drug testing, and the implementation dates of layoffs.[36]

Some provisions of contracts frequently generate litigation to determine their status in the bargaining process. Among these especially contested subjects are class size, the school calendar, evaluations, and dismissals. While some may naturally consider class size a condition of employment and thus a mandatory subject of bargaining,[37] most courts have not found this to be the case and have found a managerial prerogative regarding class size because of the essential personnel and facilities issues underlying class size decisions.[38]

Similarly, the school calendar has been found to be both an unlawful subject of bargaining[39] and a mandatory subject of bargaining,[40] with a majority considering it either an unlawful or permissive subject of bargaining.[41] For some subjects of bargaining, there is a distinction in the courts between bargaining the item itself and bargaining the impact of the subject. For instance, the impact of class size determinations has been found to be bargainable, even if the actual class size determination is solely a managerial decision.[42] This is the same for teacher evaluations. With some exceptions,[43] courts have found that the evaluation criteria of teachers are non-negotiable, while the procedures and practices administrators engage in when evaluating teachers may be permissive or mandatory subjects of bargaining.[44] Finally, teacher termination is a frequently contested subject of bargaining.[45] Teachers' unions want to have the maximum amount of control over the processes and timing of employment decisions while school administrators contend that employment decisions are solely matters of educational policy and thus non-negotiable. In situations where dismissal decisions are predicated on financial concerns, commonly called reductions-in-force, courts have found that while the decision to eliminate positions was one solely for the board of education, the notice and timing of the job terminations could be negotiated.[46]

Other subjects of bargaining that also frequently cause controversy are provisions intended to benefit the union itself. The most well known of these provisions in education are fair-share provisions. A fair-share provision is a requirement that all non-union members of the collective bargaining unit be required to pay a substantial service fee to cover the costs of the union in representing that individual.[47] The Supreme Court has upheld the constitutionality of the fair-share provision if the non-union member's dues do not go to cover the political activities of the union.[48] While these fair-share provisions are permissible, more than twenty states have enacted "right to work" laws, which attempt to prevent this type of union security clause.[49] Also, unions attempt to negotiate provisions that aid them directly within the school context such as direct payroll deductions for dues and access to school mailboxes and other communication outlets. Courts have generally found these provisions to be acceptable permissive subjects of bargaining because of their function of promoting labor peace and stability within the school.[50]

Implications of Non-Agreement in the Bargaining Process

When collective bargaining negotiations fail there are a variety of procedures that must take place. When negotiations become stale and there is no longer any progress toward an agreement, the negotiations are said to have reached an impasse. Once at an impasse, mediation, fact finding, and arbitration may be triggered. At least in the private sector if none of the impasse procedures succeed in restarting negotiations toward an agreement, private sector employees may begin the series of steps that leads to a strike.

In public sector collective bargaining, many states have legislatively removed the unions' ability to strike.

Occasionally, negotiations between certified unions and school boards do not produce an agreement. If the parties cannot reach an agreement and all progress and conversations toward agreement have stopped, the negotiations are said to have reached an impasse. In most states, once negotiations reach an impasse there are a variety of procedures that the parties must engage in. Typically, the first step to engage in once parties have reached impasse is mediation. Mediation is a process where an outside, noninterested party is brought in to restart the bargaining process. Mediators will often make findings and suggest possible resolutions to parties, but will not make those findings or recommendations public. Fact finding, on the other hand, makes the findings of the third-party mediator public to add outside pressure to the collective bargaining process to encourage further negotiation toward resolution. Fact finding is required in some states and permissive in many more.[51] In both fact finding and mediation, the recommendations of the third party may be accepted or rejected by the parties. That is in contrast to arbitration, which is required in a few states[52] and permissive in many more, where the third party's decisions are binding on the parties. If all the required impasse procedures have been tried and there is still not an agreement, the parties may move toward a strike or a final offer, depending what is permitted under state law.

The most intimidating implication of a failure to agree are strikes. Strikes are the primary weapon of unions, particularly in the private sector. In the public sector, most states prohibit strikes by employees, including school employees. Where there is not a specific state law prohibiting strikes, courts have generally found that strikes are not permissible for the public welfare of the state,[53] although a few states have found that public employees may strike.[54] Thus, usually only when strikes are specifically provided for in state law are they found to be legal in public school collective bargaining. Fewer than ten states legislatively allow for teachers to strike.[55] In the states that do legislatively permit teachers to strike, there are usually a set of requirements that must be met before a strike can occur. These requirements include the expiration of the contract, filing an intent to strike document with the state labor relations board, and evidence that the strike will not pose a danger to the public health and safety.[56] If these requirements have been met, teachers' unions in these states only may engage in a strike that may force the temporary closure of the school.

In the more numerous states where strikes are not permitted, the union occasionally decides to engage in a strike illegally.[57] When this happens, there are a variety of penalties for the union and the teachers. First, a school will usually immediately seek an injunction from the court to stop the union's activities. The union and its leaders can be found in contempt of court if an injunction to stop the strike is violated and eventually imprisoned if the violations continue. Also, unions may face fines and a loss of privileges previously acquired in the collective bargaining agreement. Teachers that join an illegal strike may face a loss of pay, reimbursement to the board for costs of the strike, or even the loss of their job.[58] Keep in mind, however, that a strike can be more than a total work stoppage. Actions such as work slowdowns, sick-outs, and refusing to perform duties under contract also can be a strike and can trigger penalties. However, when teachers continue to work but engage in informational picketing, this practice is usually upheld unless the picketing creates an obstruction or disruption.[59]

Post-Agreement Grievances

After a contract has been agreed upon and it takes effect, disputes under the contract typically evolve into grievances. A grievance is typically defined as an allegation that there has been a violation of the contract on the part of the board.[60] Although courts have the ultimate authority to decide on grievances, arbitration has become the primary form of grievance resolution. Unless a statute expressly forbids schools from entering into arbitration agreements, courts have found the grievance arbitration clauses to be enforceable.[61] These grievance arbitration clauses largely remove the courts from the process of resolving disputes under the contract because the arbitration is binding on both of the parties and will typically not be overturned except if the arbitration award is not based on the contractual provisions or if the arbitration award concerns an illegal provision such as taking inherent managerial rights from the school.[62] Because of this lack of oversight on the part of courts, arbiters have greater flexibility in crafting remedies to grievances.

One area related to grievance arbitration that has spurned litigation is the subjects that are capable of being arbitrated. Typically, when crafting a grievance arbitration provision, the school will seek to make it as narrow as possible, including time limitations for filing, and the union will seek to make it as broad as possible.[63] Also contained in the collective bargaining agreement are a series of steps for processing a grievance once it has been submitted by an employee to management. These steps typically provide management an opportunity to resolve the grievance to the satisfaction of the employee before the matter is sent to binding arbitration.[64]

Recommendations for Practice

1. Collective bargaining can become a contentious and frustrating process within a school. Given their position as the middle-manager between school boards and school employees, principals should take care before unnecessarily getting involved too deeply in the process on either side of the issue.

2. It is important to understand that much of the collective bargaining process between schools and school employees are governed by state

laws. Therefore, before participating in collective bargaining in any capacity, principals need to familiarize themselves with the specific rules governing collective bargaining in their state.

3. Also important is to understand the distinctions between unlawful, mandatory, and permissive subjects of bargaining. Parties may seek to include provisions in the contract that are unnecessary or illegal under the law. Principals must keep in mind the classification of topics of bargaining and have a plan concerning which permissive topics of bargaining the school is willing to engage in.
4. Perhaps most importantly, principals and other school administrators should be open minded regarding collective bargaining and should approach contract negotiations from a positive perspective. Because many state laws mandate such negotiation to occur once a union is recognized, approaching the bargaining from a negative or stonewalling position can cause more harm to the school in the long run. Collective bargaining, in most cases, can be a helpful process for both parties by providing clarity and consistency in school-employee relations.

Endnotes

1 *See* James Rapp, Education Law § 7.01(2007) (providing an extended list of benefit and detriments of collective bargaining in education).

2 Martha M. McCarthy, Nelda H. Cambron-McCabe & Stephen B. Thomas, Public School Law: Teachers' and Students' Rights 406 (4th. ed. 1998).

3 Charles J. Russo, Reutter's: The Law of Public Education, 586 (5th ed. 2004).

4 Todd A. DeMitchell & Casey D. Cobb, *Teachers: Their Union and Their Profession. A Tangled Relationship.* 212 Educ. L. Rep. 1, 3 (2006).

5 29 U.S.C. §§ 101-115 (2007).

6 Pub. L. No. 74-198, 49 Stat. 449 (1935). *See also,* Theodore J. St. Antoine, *How the Wagner Act Came to Be: A Prospectus.* 96 Mich. L. Rev. 2201 (1998).

7 29 U.S.C. § 153 (2007).

8 29 U.S.C. § 158 (2007).

9 Pub. L. No. 80-101, 61 Stat. 136 (1947).

10 Kern Alexander & M. David Alexander, American Public School Law 847 (5th ed. 2001).

11 McCarthy, *supra* note 2, at 407.

12 385 U.S. 589 (1967).

13 Atkins v. City of Charlotte, 296 F. Supp. 1068 (W.D.N.C. 1969).

14 Carl Krueger, *State Collective Bargaining Policies for Teachers,* Education Commission of the States (2002).

15 Board of Trs. of Univ. of Ky. v. Pub. Employees Council No. 51, 571 S.W.2d 616 (Ken. 1978).

16 McCarthy, *supra* note 2, at 411.

17 Russo, *supra* note 3, at 587.

18 Rapp, *supra* note 1, at § 7.02.

19 Chicago Principals Ass'n v. Educ. Labor Relations Bd., 543 N.E.2d 166 (1989); *But see* Wellesley Sch. Comm., 376 Mass. 112 (1978) (finding principals and assistant principals

were not managerial); Chicago Teachers Union, IFT/AFT, AFL-CIO v. IELRB, 695 N.E.2d 1332 (1998) (assistant principals who had fulltime teaching responsibilities were not managerial).

20 Parkway Sch. Dist. v. Local 902/MNEA, 807 S.W.2d 63 (Mo. 1991) (department heads can be members of bargaining unit because they are not confidential employees).

21 North Hills Sch. Dist. v. Pa. Labor Relations Bd., 762 A.2d 1153 (Pa. Commw. Ct. 2000) (secretary who participated in negotiations was a confidential employee and excluded from the bargaining unit); Barrington Sch. Comm. v. R.I. State Labor Relations Bd., 608 A.2d 1126 (R.I. 1992) (finding secretary to business manager excluded from the bargaining unit).

22 Rapp, *supra* note 1, at § 7.03.

23 29 U.S.C. § 158 (2007) ("For the purposes of this section, to bargain collectively is the performance of the mutual obligation of the employer and the representative of the employees to meet at reasonable times and confer in good faith with respect to wages, hours, and other terms and conditions of employment, or the negotiation of an agreement, or any question arising thereunder, and the execution of a written contract incorporating any agreement reached if requested by either party, but such obligation does not compel either party to agree to a proposal or require the making of a concession").

24 Cal. Government Code § 3505 (2007).

25 29 U.S.C. § 153 (2007).

26 Rapp, *supra* note 1, at 7.09.

27 115 Ill. Comp. Stat. 5/14(a) (2007).

28 Vestal Employees Ass'n v. Pub. Employment Relations Bd. of the State of N.Y., 94 N.Y.2d 409 (2000).

29 School Bd. of Martin County v. Martin County Educ. Ass'n, 613 So. 2d 521 (Fla. Dist. Ct. App. 1993).

30 Chicago Sch. Reform Bd. of Trs. v. Ill. Educ. Labor Relations Bd., 734 N.E.2d 69 (App. Ct. 1st Dist. 2000).

31 *See* Rapp, *supra* note 1, at 7.09.

32 115 Ill. Comp. Stat. 5/14(b) (2007).

33 Russo, *supra* note 3, at 587, 589; Alexander, *supra* note 10, at 863.

34 29 U.S.C. § 158(d) (2007).

35 Russo, *supra* note 3, at 588; McCarthy, *supra* note 2, at 416; Alexander, *supra* note 10, at 863.

36 Russo, *supra* note 3, at 590.

37 This was the finding of an Illinois Appellate Case, (Decatur Bd. of Educ. v. Ill. Educ. Labor Relations Bd., 536 N.E.2d 743 (Ill. App. Ct. 1989).

38 Kenai Peninsula Borough Sch. Dist. v. Kenai Peninsula Educ. Ass'n, 572 P.2d 416 (Alaska 1977); Tualatin Valley Bargaining Council v. Tigard Sch. Dist. 23J, 840 P.2d 657 (1992).

39 City of Biddeford v. Biddeford Teachers Ass'n, 304 A.2d 387, 421 (Me. 1973).

40 City of Beloit v. Employment Relations Comm'n, 242 N.W.2d 231 (Wis. 1976).

41 West Cent. Educ. Ass'n v. W. Cent. Sch. Dist., 655 N.W.2d 916, 923 (S.D. 2002).

42 *In re* West Irondequoit Teachers Ass'n, 315 N.E.2d 775 (N.Y. 1974).

43 *See,* Aplington Cmty. Sch. Dist. v. Iowa Pub. Employment Relations Bd., 392 N.W.2d 495 (Iowa 1986).

44 Board of Educ. U.S.D. No. 352, Goodland v. NEA-Goodland, 785 P.2d 993 (Kan. 1990).

45 *See,* McCarthy, *supra* note 2, at 417-18.

46 Central City Educ. Ass'n v. Ill. Educ. Labor Relations Bd., 599 N.E.2d 892 (Ill. 1992); Township of Old Bridge Bd. of Educ. v. Old Bridge Educ. Ass'n, 489 A.2d 159 (N.J. 1985).

47 Brian A. Braun, Illinois School Law Survey 253 (9th ed. 2006) (A fair-share provision is also called an agency shop provision).

48 Abood v. Detroit Bd. of Educ., 431 U.S. 209 (1977); *See also* Chicago Teacher's Union Local No. 1 v. Hudson, 475 U.S. 292 (1986); Lehnert v. Ferris Faculty Ass'n, 500 U.S. 507 (1991).

[49] Krueger, *supra* note 14 (Most of these right to work states are in the southern United States).

[50] McCarthy, *supra* note 2, at 424.

[51] McCarthy, *supra* note 2, at 429.

[52] *See* N.Y. Civ. Serv. Law § 209 (2007); Or. Rev. Stat. § 243.742 (2007).

[53] Norwalk Teachers' Ass'n v. Bd. of Educ., 83 A.2d 482 (Conn. 1951); Anchorage Educ. Ass'n v. Anchorage Sch. Dist., 648 P.2d 993 (Alaska 1982); Board of Educ. v. N.J. Educ. Ass'n, 247 A.2d 867 (N.J. 1968); Jefferson County Bd. of Educ. v. Jefferson County Educ. Ass'n, 393 S.E.2d 653 (W. Va. 1990).

[54] County Sanitation Dist. No. 2, Los Angeles County v. Los Angeles County Employees' Ass'n, 699 P.2d 835 (Cal. 1985); Davis v. Henry, 555 So. 2d 457 (La. 1990).

[55] Krueger, *supra* note 14 (Alaska, Illinois, Montana, Ohio, Oregon, Pennsylvania, Rhode Island, Vermont, Wisconsin).

[56] McCarthy, *supra* note 2, at 431.

[57] For instance, even though strikes are illegal in Michigan, the teachers in Detroit Public Schools have engaged in strikes in 1999 and 2006. Catherine Jun, *Detroit Teachers Strike, Pickets Begin as Union Rejects Pay Cut, Parents Worry about School Year,* The Detroit News, Aug. 28, 2006.

[58] Russo, *supra* note 3, at 599-600.

[59] *Id.*

[60] Braun, *supra* note 47, at 257.

[61] Norwalk Teachers' Ass'n v. Bd. of Educ., 83 A.2d 482 (Conn. 1951).

[62] Holmes v. Orleans Parish Sch. Bd., 698 So. 2d 429 (La. Ct. App. 1997).

[63] Rapp, *supra* note 1, at § 7.04.

[64] *Id.*

Chapter 34

School Funding Litigation

R. Craig Wood & John Dayton

Introduction

Since the Supreme Court of California's 1971 decision in *Serrano,*[1] the highest courts in at least thirty-six states have issued opinions on the merits of school funding suits, with nineteen courts upholding state funding systems and seventeen courts declaring the state systems unconstitutional.[2] All fifty states have experienced post-*Serrano* school funding reform efforts ranging from informal, grass roots funding reform movements to highly organized, intense, and protracted litigation, sometimes extending over decades.[3] School funding litigation continues with no end in sight, and every new suit has the potential to spark significant changes not only in education funding, but also in education programs, policy, taxation, and politics.

The decades long battles over school funding are nothing less than battles over defining the future of education, who will receive what educational opportunities, and who will pay for them. In legal battles over state school funding systems, the educational futures of millions of children may be impacted, billions of dollars in educational resources and tax burdens may be re-allocated, and nearly everyone in the state may be affected as either students, parents, educators, property owners, or taxpayers.

The study of education finance litigation is actually the study of the litigation of state aid distribution formulas and the results of those formulas in terms of the expenditure and revenue patterns to school districts.[4] Education finance as an academic discipline has only emerged since the early 1900s. This academic discipline is distinctly different from economics and the study of broader areas of public policy but encompasses aspects of both. Further, the issue of financing public elementary and secondary education is such an integral part of the social, fiscal, and legal fabric of our society that it is only a small step to move the financing of public education into that stream of political and legal activity within every state. This is especially true when the wider implications of education finance are considered, such as equality of educational opportunity as it relates to matters of discrimination and equal opportunity.

This chapter reviews the critically important role of federal law and litigation in establishing the legal, social, and political foundation for school funding litigation, the resulting shift to state court venues, and the possible future of this litigation based on a logical extrapolation from where this litigation has been to where it is likely going.

Litigation Based on Federal Law

While no federal school finance lawsuits existed before the mid-twentieth century, the foundations were laid by American ideals concerning equality. From the nation's first formal statement in the Declaration of Independence proclaiming that "all men are created equal"[5] to the adoption of the Fourteenth Amendment,[6] and through the litigation in *Brown v. Board of Education,*[7] and the school funding equity movement spawned by *Brown*, the struggle toward greater equality has engendered long and difficult battles in American courtrooms.

The Fourteenth Amendment's equality provision led to three litigation strands[8] that were to have a powerful impact on education finance. The first strand was a series of lawsuits under the concept of desegregation, in which enforcement of equality before the law for all persons was sought.[9] The second strand was a series of cases known as the re-apportionment decisions, establishing the principle of "one man, one vote."[10] The third strand emerged from lawsuits that became known as the indigent defendants and administration of criminal justice cases, which established that defendants may not be denied the right of appeal simply because of inability to pay for a transcript of trial proceedings because such denial is tantamount to wealth discrimination.[11] Although seemingly unrelated to education finance, these strands were to lay a framework for equal protection in resource distribution.

Desegregation cases had an enormous impact on public schools and the way that people viewed educational opportunities. Desegregation cases were fervently litigated for decades, with significant impacts on the costs and structure of public elementary and secondary education. The question of whether differential wealth, under certain circumstances, could lawfully be a barrier to equality under the law began to emerge over time, generating new visions of what states were required to provide in terms of equal educational opportunity.

These strands were actually the expression and extension of judicial sympathy to a fairly liberal construction of the meaning of equality that had already resulted in the establishment of certain fundamental rights under the law. In addition to the rights and liberties specifically guaranteed by the Federal Constitution, the U.S. Supreme Court had at various times enumerated several other rights that it found to be so fundamental that these rights could not be abridged or denied except by the most exacting due process of law. Several of these rights were established in the cases that formed the strands (e.g., the Court had found a fundamental right to interstate travel,[12] procreation,[13] voting,[14] and the right to criminal appeal[15]). The essence of fundamental rights was to ensure the fundamental equality of each citizen so that arbitrary abridgment of certain freedoms could never be countenanced in a democratic nation.

The effect of the Fourteenth Amendment's equality clause was to create two distinct lines of litigation. The first line resulted from unequal treatment of a suspect class. As defined by the courts, various conditions might lead to the establishment of a suspect class wherein "prejudice against discrete and insular minorities may be a special condition, which tends seriously to curtail the operation of those political processes ordinarily to be relied upon to protect minorities and which may call for a correspondingly more searching judicial inquiry."[16] Subsequent litigation was to create suspect classes for race,[17] national origin,[18] and alienage,[19] with special judicial concern for guarding fundamental rights under the Constitution.

The concepts of suspect class and fundamental right were vitally important to equal protection litigation because if a court were persuaded that differential treatment was premised on a fundamental right or suspect class, courts would evaluate an act or a law with strict scrutiny. This would require the government to prove that any differential treatment was necessary to a compelling interest and narrowly tailored to achieving that interest, a very difficult burden of proof, making a victory for plaintiffs likely. In contrast, if plaintiffs failed to establish that inequalities were premised on differential treatment of a suspect class or a fundamental right, courts generally apply a rational basis test only, requiring government officials to establish that the differential treatment is justified as reasonably related to some rational basis, a very easy burden of proof, making a victory for government defendants likely.

As Kurland noted, the concepts derived from these three broader strands were quickly applied to education,[20] wherein litigants launched concerted efforts to establish suspect class status and that education was a fundamental right. Although the origins of equality in American law are more complex than briefly stated within this paper, these strands illustrate why it was ultimately sensible in a historical context to first bring lawsuits involving public elementary and secondary education to the federal level. Regardless of whether the topics were race discrimination or fiscal resources, the goal of any such lawsuit would be to seek federal protection wherein inequality would be alleged and from which it would be argued that equal educational opportunity was denied. Thus, from a simple hierarchical perspective, if education were found in some way to merit the protections of the Fourteenth Amendment, especially in areas where abridgment would be severely proscribed, new federal precedents would also be controlling on the states. Winning a federal lawsuit was thus critical.

The Federal Response

Although federal litigation regarding racial equality spanned many decades,[21] it was in 1954 in *Brown v. Board of Education*[22] where equality of educational opportunity under the law received its greatest impetus. In an often-quoted passage, the Court proclaimed:

> [E]ducation is perhaps the most important function of state and local governments. Compulsory school attendance laws and the great expenditures for education demonstrate our recognition of the importance of education to our democratic society. It is required in the performance of our most basic public responsibilities, even service in the armed forces. It is the very foundation of good citizenship. Today it is a principal instrument in awakening the child to cultural values, in preparing him for later professional training, and in helping him to adjust normally to his environment. In these days, it is doubtful that any child may reasonably be expected to succeed in life if he is denied the opportunity of an education. Such an opportunity where the state has undertaken to provide it, is a right which must be made available to all on equal terms.[23]

Invoking the equal protection clause of the Fourteenth Amendment, *Brown* spoke strongly to the value of education, calling it one of the most important functions of government and noting its central role to the preservation of a literate and free people. The Supreme Court in *Brown* declared that education was a right that must be made available on equal terms.

It could be argued that if the Court's apparent mandate in *Brown* were to be fully satisfied, equal educational opportunity would have strong application to fiscal resources since uneven revenues are at the root of most other forms of inequality. Although it had not been a simple matter to force legal condemnation of racial inequality, at least there had been a long record of discrimination lawsuits against which concepts and theories could be empirically tested. In comparison, in education finance inequality there was no similar rich data driven empirical history on which to rely. The question first became one of a conceptual nature, rather than a formal legal and research standard, from which litigants would develop and demonstrate their arguments. The other alternative was to make analogy to the strands cited earlier, bolstered by the strong language and mandate of *Brown*.

The first strand of unequal treatment under the law seemed well established in *Brown* because school children must be provided equal opportunity. The second strand also seemed viable because it was reasonable to draw an equal protection analogy to geographic discrimination since it was widely known that educational opportunity varied greatly based on residence. The third strand also seemed applicable, as there was sufficient case law to argue that wealth may not serve to bar equality under the law. Of particular support to the latter theory was the belief that school district wealth could be the basis of wealth discrimination, i.e., leading to establishment of a new suspect class. Funding equity, the plaintiffs believed wealth suspectness was grounded in case law and it was simply a matter of transferring the *Brown* logic condemning racial inequality to fiscal inequality. The plaintiffs relied on the fact that the Supreme Court had long ago said in *United States v. Carolene* that "[p]rejudice against discrete and insular minorities may be a special condition, which tends seriously to curtail the operation of those political processes ordinarily ... relied upon to protect minorities, and which may call for a correspondingly more searching judicial inquiry."[24] In addition, there were the voting rights and criminal appeals cases cited earlier in which the Court had held that classifications based on wealth were to be strictly scrutinized.[25]

These conditions seemed ripe for a federal decision extending equality of educational opportunity to include fiscal equality. The first suit to be filed was *Burruss v. Wilkerson*[26] that was brought in Virginia in 1968. The plaintiffs in *Burruss* based their claims on the Fourteenth Amendment, arguing that inequality in the school division's (district's) physical and instructional facilities resulted in a lack of equal protection of the law because the quality varied among school divisions. An examination of the arguments made by the plaintiffs at trial does not reveal very much quantitative discussion. Largely, the plaintiffs relied on anecdotal stories of the conditions of buildings and curriculum in attempting to prove their contentions. Issues of test scores or any robust statistical evidence appeared lacking. Of course, it should also be noted that in 1968, such standards were largely undeveloped within the realm of education finance analysis.[27]

A three-judge United States District Court, which heard oral arguments, rendered a decision in May of 1969, stating that while "[t]he existence of such deficiencies and differences is forcefully put by plaintiffs' counsel ... we do not believe they are creatures of discrimination by the State ... our reexamination of the Act confirms that the cities and counties receive State funds under a uniform and consistent plan ... we can only see to it that the outlays on one group are not invidiously greater or less than that of another ... no such arbitrariness is manifest here."[28] The court added that although the "plaintiffs seek to obtain allocations of State funds among the cities and counties so that the pupil in each of them will enjoy the same educational opportunities ... the courts have neither the knowledge, nor means, nor the power to tailor the public monies to fit the varying needs of these students throughout the state."[29]

A second federal case, *McInnis v. Shapiro,*[30] was decided in Illinois in the same year. Heard in a United States District Court and later affirmed by the U.S. Supreme Court,[31] *McInnis* was also a Fourteenth Amendment equal protection suit seeking to overturn the state education funding formula on the grounds that unequal educational expenditures based on variable property values as tax rates of local districts were arbitrary and an unreasonable denial of equal protection of the law. The plaintiffs' evidence consisted largely of descriptive data concerning tax rates and related information. The court ruled for the defendant state.

The court noted several features that were to become summative of the federal position in school finance litigation. While the court acknowledged wide variations in expenditures per pupil based on wealth, the court stated its vulnerability before the question in several respects. First, variations in revenue were not on the face invidious and arbitrary. Second, the legislature's decision to allow local choice and experimentation was reasonable, particularly since the common school fund placed, at that time, a $400 minimum base under each student. Third, the court ruled that there was no constitutional requirement establishing rigid guidelines for equal dollar expenditures under the Fourteenth Amendment's equal protection provisions. The plaintiffs had shown descriptive data regarding tax rates yet never adequately demonstrated the nexus between tax rates and achievement or tax rates and a variety of input variables. And fourth, the court was clear in stating that allocation of revenue was a policy decision better suited to legislatures.

In both instances, federal courts had uniformly refused to intervene on three importantly consistent grounds. The first rationale was a plain reading of the Fourteenth Amendment, noting no equal protection mandate for equal revenues. The second rationale was equally important, as the court deferred to the legislative branch by relying on the separation of powers doctrine in the absence of blatant invidious discrimination. The third rationale applied to the court's lack of judicially manageable standards, even if it were to rule for the plaintiffs.

These issues would finally make it to the U.S. Supreme Court for review on the merits in *San Antonio Independent School District v. Rodriguez*.[32] The case had actually been filed in 1968, and a three-judge panel had rendered a decision in 1971, holding the Texas system of school finance unconstitutional under the Fourteenth Amendment.[33] The case was then accepted on appeal by the United States Supreme Court. The plaintiffs argued key points taken from previously successful, broader litigation. The plaintiffs contended that the Texas funding system violated the federal equal protection clause by discriminating against a suspect class based on poverty and that poorer students were denied a fundamental right to an education.

The Supreme Court, however, refused to accept the plaintiffs' arguments since it found no class of persons who were identifiably suspect. The plaintiffs argued that the injured class should be comprised of all students living in poor school districts, rather than poor students themselves. Justice Powell, writing for the majority, noted that wealth discrimination in prior cases had historically been confined by the Court to personal wealth, and that the class in *Rodriguez* was not one for which special protection is usually provided, i.e., it was neither politically powerless, discrete, or an insular minority.[34] The Court further noted that individual income did not necessarily correlate with district wealth and that even if the correlation were strong, the Court's historic application of wealth discrimination under strict scrutiny had been limited to absolute deprivation rather than relative differences.[35] Under these conditions, the Court found no distinct suspect class.

The Court in *Rodriguez* then turned to the plaintiffs' claims for fundamentality, claiming that education was a fundamental right, before again refusing to accept the plaintiffs' arguments. The plaintiffs had recognized the difficulty of this argument and had based their claims on the relationship of education to other extant fundamental rights in an effort to establish a clear nexus.[36] In this concept, public education was inextricably tied to other existing fundamental rights, wherein the intelligent exercise of the right to vote and the right to free speech were said to depend on education. The Supreme Court rejected these arguments, however, stating that it saw no more connection between public education and these rights than it could find between housing, food, or other subsistence and the right to vote.[37] The Supreme Court especially noted a difference between hindering a child from a public education and the state education finance distribution formula that, in its view, instead sought to improve available offerings.[38] Although the Supreme Court noted wide disparities among Texas school districts, it rejected the standard of strict scrutiny, stating that a rational relationship was all that was required to defend a state distribution formula where no invidious discrimination could be found. In *Rodriguez*, a rational basis could be found in the state's goal of promoting local control of schools — a view supported by the Supreme Court's own words:

> Education, perhaps even more than welfare, presents a myriad of intractable economic, social, and even philosophical problems. The very complexity of the problems of financing and managing a statewide public school system suggests that there will be more than one constitutionally permissible method of solving them, and that, within the limits of rationality, the legislature's efforts to tackle the problems should be entitled to respect.[39]

In a 5-4 decision in *Rodriguez*, the Court had delivered a significant defeat to school funding reformers by holding that education was not a fundamental right protected under the U.S. Constitution[40] and that the Texas system of school finance did not disadvantage any suspect class.[41] Since education was not a fundamental right and the challenged system did not disadvantage any suspect class, the Court reversed the district court's judgment for the plaintiffs, finding that the Texas system of school funding need only meet the Court's rational basis test instead of the strict scrutiny test applied by the district court. Under the rational basis test, challenged state actions need only bear a rational relationship to a legitimate state purpose, and the Court held that the defendant's asserted interest in promoting local control of public schools was sufficient under rational basis scrutiny.

Litigation Based on State Law

The Supreme Court ruling in *Rodriguez* had one primary effect concerning education finance litigation: to turn litigants' attention to the state courts. At the state level, litigation has been focused on state constitutional language as well as statutory provisions of the individual states. In 1971, the California Supreme Court issued its decision in the landmark case of *Serrano v. Priest*.[42] The plaintiffs in *Serrano* were Los Angeles County children and their parents. They represented all public school children in the state of California and the parents of those children who pay real property taxes, except those in the most privileged district.[43] *Serrano* was the first successful challenge to a state aid system of public school finance.[44] Additionally, *Serrano* was the first case to establish a judicially manageable standard for courts in addressing inequities in school funding,[45] the *Serrano* principle,[46] which declared that the quality of a child's education cannot be a function of the wealth of the local community. Instead, under the *Serrano* principle, public school funding must be a function of the wealth of the state as a whole.[47]

State courts' analyses of equal protection challenges in school funding cases have been largely uniform because of the pervasive influence of the federal model of equal protection analysis. The issues generally considered are 1) whether education is a fundamental right; 2) whether the plaintiffs constitute a suspect class; 3) what level of judicial scrutiny is appropriate in reviewing the state's system of funding; and 4) whether the state has an appropriate justification for inequities in the public school funding system.

Whether premised on federal or state provisions, this litigation has generally proven complex, difficult, and often protracted. Historically, education finance litigation has focused its efforts on issues of equal opportunity. More recently, however, cases have addressed the adequacy of education finance distribution formulas in terms of meeting state constitutional and statutory guidelines. The vast majority of state court examinations are filtered through a social/interpretive filter, regardless of the nature of the presentations. This filtering process has led to judicial translations of phrases like *sound basic education* (NY) into "meaningful high school education, one which prepares them to function productively as civic participants"[48] or *thorough and efficient education* (WV) into "preparation for useful and happy occupations, recreation and citizenship."[49] Increasingly, attempts are being made to further operationalize these translations and empirically estimate the costs of achieving the stated goals, assuming those goals to be both robust and measurable.

Several states have ruled that portions of the state education finance distribution formula were unconstitutional (e.g., in Idaho) regarding the distribution of capital outlay financial assistance,[50] and the methodology of funding classes for English language learners in Arizona.[51] Several state supreme courts have issued rulings wherein the then presiding state high court has overruled a previous state high court decision, which has had the effect of changing the state education finance distribution formula. These include Arizona,[52] North Carolina,[53] South Carolina,[54] Ohio,[55] and Texas.[56]

From this overall litigation, significant features have emerged. First, the high courts in a number of states have declared that education is a fundamental right based on the state constitution. Second, based on the state constitution, there are many states in which the highest court has declared that education is not a fundamental right. Third, there has been no perfect pattern whereby establishing fundamentality has automatically invalidated a state finance distribution formula by virtue of invoking coveted strict scrutiny. For example, the Supreme Court of Arizona found that education was a fundamental right but nonetheless ruled for the state in *Shoftstall v. Hollins* in 1973. Similarly, the Wisconsin high court declared in *Buse v. Smith*[57] that education was a fundamental right, but later noted in *Kukor* that a rational basis was all that was required to uphold the state aid distribution formula when absolute denial of education is not at question. Fourth, the harshness of this reality has been somewhat softened by the New Jersey High Court's logic of *Robinson*, as several state high courts have ruled for the plaintiffs by finding equality a requirement, even absent the one feature of fundamentality that would invoke strict scrutiny analysis.[58] Only one state other than California has declared wealth a suspect class, as the Supreme Court of Wyoming in *Washakie*[59] invalidated its education finance distribution formula, establishing that no equality could exist until funding was also equal.

Although federal law and litigation, from *Brown* through *Rodriguez,* formed the critically important historical foundation of school funding litigation, the Court's decision in *Rodriguez* had the effect of turning this litigation from federal to state courts, where this battle continues. Much has been written about the history of state court litigation to date.[60] But state courts are likely venues for future litigation. Accordingly, the remainder of this chapter focuses on the likely future of school funding litigation in the states.

Examining School Funding Litigation's Fiscal Horizon

In contemplating the potential future of school funding litigation, a useful place to start is an examination of the likely availability of fiscal resources.[61] When fiscal resources are very limited, additional resources for school funding reform simply may not be available, making it difficult or impossible to provide plaintiffs with requested remedies.[62] No court, however, has expressly acknowledged that state fiscal difficulties affected its ruling in a school funding case.[63] Nonetheless, the status of the economy in the state may influence judges in practically assessing remedial options in school funding cases.[64] Further, fiscal realities will certainly affect the legislative response to any judicially ordered remedy.[65] As La Morte and Williams recognized:

> [E]conomic recessions, can act to thwart plaintiffs' hopes since the unavailability of revenue makes change more difficult and bolsters defendants' contention that workable solutions do not exist. When the fiscal condition of state governments is relatively healthy, equity may well enjoy popularity: state revenue is available for a "leveling up" process, which is clearly a more palatable task for both courts and legislatures than requiring a "leveling down."[66]

It is difficult to imagine that elected state court judges are not to some degree influenced by the financial and political realities in their state, or that they are unaware that fully funding costly school funding reforms may be politically difficult or impossible in times of severely limited resources. State court judges are not immune from political realities in their state. They generally do not enjoy the protections of life-time tenure granted to federal judges and instead may be periodically subject to voter approval or recall.[67] To remain on the bench, most state court judges must be reasonably sensitive to political circumstances in their state. Given this reality, few state court judges would want to knowingly invite legislative non-compliance with their judicial orders and the politically costly public embarrassment that legislative non-compliance presents.

Healthy fiscal circumstances are advantageous to school funding reform advocates, making the provision of the requested remedies easier to achieve and, in times of large surpluses, relatively painless. But because the contrary is also true, the fiscal horizon in the U.S. may give future school funding reform advocates some cause for concern. Although the fiscal future of the U.S. cannot be predicted with any great certainty, and there are nearly always many good reasons for future hope, there are also some long-term reasons for serious concern.[68] In addition to concerns about the falling dollar, rising energy costs, interest rates, trade imbalances, an aging work force, rising costs of health and retirement benefits, and very low national savings rates, federal spending deficits are creating a darkening shadow on the future of the U.S. economy. There are warnings that if hard choices are not made to bring federal spending under control "we would see widening and eventually unsustainable budget deficits, which would impede capital accumulation, slow economic growth, threaten financial stability, and put a heavy burden of debt on our children and grandchildren."[69]

Although the financial situations of the individual states are varied, a financially sinking federal government would likely continue to act as a dead weight on state economies. To varying degrees, many states have been struggling economically for decades now, and all states face an uncertain economic future with growing global competition for jobs and resources.[70] All of these factors could make it more difficult for future school funding reform advocates to obtain additional new funds and long-term financial and political support for school funding reforms. In times of budget surpluses and political stability, it is relatively easy to address school funding inadequacies by simply making the fiscal pie bigger for everyone. In contrast, school funding reform advocates will likely have greater difficulties obtaining additional resources if funds are limited and political support for funding reform is diminished by serious fiscal concerns among legislators.

Examining School Funding Litigation's Political Horizon

State politics can be a complex subject not given to easy prediction. Further, basing future projections in school funding cases on political explanations may be especially problematic, as judges have a duty to make objective, non-partisan decisions regardless of political circumstances or their personal political views. Nonetheless, politics and political motivations seem to permeate nearly every realm of human interaction, so it might be more surprising if political ideology and affiliation did not play a role in school funding cases, as these cases can dramatically impact the politically volatile issues of public education, resource distribution, and taxation.[71]

There is, however, some evidence that political affiliation may sometimes be a factor in judicial decision making.[72] Either consciously or subconsciously, judges may be influenced in their decisions by their political views and affiliations.[73] Not surprisingly, most judges are unlikely to openly admit to any political predisposition and resulting bias. The general public, however, seems to tacitly accept that judges, like most everyone else, may be influenced by their foundational political views and political affiliations. Most voters assume that judges with a more conservative political philosophy, for example, may behave differently on the bench than judges with a more liberal political philosophy.[74] It may very well be that in school funding disputes, more conservative judges tend to favor the state's status quo, judicial deference, and local control, while more liberal judges may lean more toward the cause of funding equity reform, judicial duty to enforce constitutional mandates, and state-level accountability for providing equal educational opportunity.

The effects of judges' political orientations may be most evident in their views about the fundamental role of courts in school funding cases. Individual judge's views on the proper role of courts in school funding disputes differ significantly across the resulting activism-deference continuum, with left-leaning judges advocating more active judicial intervention in school funding reform efforts and right-leaning judges supporting greater judicial deference to the political branches in school funding cases.[75]

Even if judicial decisions were not affected by judges' political perspectives, decisions in the political branches are highly sensitive to political orientations and circumstances. And before finance reform can become law, legislative action is required, and that legislation generally must be signed by the state's governor. Like their judicial branch counterparts, however, more conservative legislators and governors tend to favor the state's status quo, while more liberal-leaning legislators and governors may be more receptive to the cause of school funding equity reform. The greatest potential for intergovernmental conflict and protracted litigation may exist in those states that have, for example, a majority of more activist, liberal-leaning judges, and a conservative majority in the political branches. Plaintiffs may find themselves with a strong mandate for school funding reform from the court, but very limited prospects of getting the political branches to actually deliver the ordered reform, resulting in a protracted procession from the court to the legislature and back again, indefinitely.[76]

In some states facing judicial mandates for school funding reform, more conservative legislators have become increasingly aggressive in responding to what they perceive as activist judicial intrusions on the legislative domain. For example, in response to a 2005 court order in Kansas requiring the general assembly to appropriate an additional $143 million for school funding reform, legislators instead proposed constitutional amendments limiting the authority of the courts in school funding cases.[77] Similarly, while a funding challenge was still pending in Missouri, a bill was introduced in the state senate that would amend the state constitution to grant full authority over school funding expressly to the legislature and to prohibit any future judicial intervention in school funding disputes.[78]

To date, these sorts of legislative restraints on judicial authority have failed to become law. Nonetheless, they may indicate growing and increasingly open opposition to what some legislators perceive as activist mandates from the judiciary in some states. Even when these legislative efforts to limit judicial authority in the area of school funding fail, they may make judges much less enthusiastic about initiating another judicial-legislative battle over school funding in the future.[79]

Examining the Evolving Landscape Affecting School Funding Litigation

In addition to fiscal and political shifts that could affect the future of school funding litigation, there are significant legal, institutional, and demographic changes underway that could also have a dramatic impact on future school funding reform efforts. School funding litigation occurs in an environment that is affected not only by fiscal and political factors, but also by evolving legal theories, new judicial decisions, statutory changes, programmatic and educational changes, demographic shifts, and other elements that may impact school funding and public education. For decades, these ever-changing factors have driven the ongoing evolution of school funding litigation.[80]

The Impact of the NCLB

The evolution of school funding litigation continues with a recent major development being driven by the No Child Left Behind Act (NCLB).[81] School funding reform advocates appear to have become the beneficiaries of some unintended consequences under the NCLB.[82] The NCLB is increasingly controversial, and even its staunchest defenders would likely acknowledge that its sweeping legislation contains some flaws.[83]

Critics contend that the NCLB is premised on seriously flawed assumptions,[84] including the assumption that children in schools may be assumed to act as raw materials functioning in a manufacturing process. [85] As with the processing of other fungible commodities, the NCLB seems to assume that the final result can be controlled as a function of the process. But as every experienced educator knows, to the contrary, children are not a fungible commodity. Every child is unique and brings to the educational experience unique strengths and weaknesses. For example, even with the same instruction, academically advantaged children will likely achieve higher scores on standardized tests than their more academically challenged peers.[86] The state clearly does not, as the NCLB seems to assume, have complete control over student achievement. Many of the factors that affect student achievement are controlled by the child, the parents, and other non-school factors.[87]

The NCLB also assumes that standardized exams provide an accurate measure of the quality of the educational experience and learning, an assumption that is flawed for at least two reasons. First, as noted above, academically advantaged children are likely to score higher on standardized exams largely independent of the quality of the school they attend, while the test scores of academically challenged students may show only marginal gains even with high quality instruction. Second, standardized tests cannot measure the totality of the educational experience or the broader array of learning that may occur in the individual student. While standardized tests present the advantages of cost effectiveness in administration and ease of comparison across schools, whatever they are measuring, it is not the total quality of the educational experience and all valuable learning by children.[88]

School funding plaintiffs appear to be the unintended beneficiaries of the NCLB's acceptance of state responsibility for student achievement and standardized tests as the proper measure of that achievement. Prior to the passage of the NCLB, funding reform plaintiffs faced a significant challenge in proving their claims that the state had failed to comply with the mandates of the state's education clause. To make their case, the plaintiffs had to first establish that the state constitution's education clause could be translated into a measurable duty for the state to provide educational opportunity. Second, the plaintiffs had to prove that the state had failed to meet the standard established by the education clause.[89] Due to the difficulty in establishing both of these elements, plaintiffs had achieved mixed results in litigation, until more recently when plaintiffs began taking advantage of the "accountability" standards in the NCLB.[90]

The NCLB and similar state accountability legislation has proven extremely useful to school funding plaintiffs.[91] This accountability legislation in many cases defines adequate public school performance in producing what the state itself considers adequate educational achievement. Further, the state's own student testing data helps plaintiffs to prove that students in many of the state's poorest schools are failing to achieve at state-established levels of competence on state-adopted standardized tests.[92] When the state itself defines adequate educational achievement, and then the state's own test data confirms that the children in the plaintiffs' state-controlled schools are failing, it then becomes relatively easy for the plaintiffs to successfully make their case.

States are facing a very difficult scenario. By accepting the premise under the NCLB and similar state-level accountability legislation that state schools are responsible for student achievement and that standardized test scores are the proper measure of that achievement, states have made it much easier for plaintiffs to prove their cases in challenging school funding systems. If plaintiffs can convince the court that the proper remedy for poor performance on state tests of adequate yearly progress is more funding, then continued poor performance on these tests is then further evidence that still more remedial resources are required. States may be exposed to potentially open-ended financial liability in these cases.[93]

In contrast to plaintiffs' more recent claims supported by evidence based on accountability legislation and student testing data, claims based on more traditional equity and adequacy challenges were tied to measures of inputs and had clearer limits on state financial liability. The ceiling for state financial liability in equity suits is generally limited by the level of reaching equity in per-pupil expenditures. Similarly, adequacy suits are limited by a demonstration that the state support for all schools was at least minimally adequate. But the model of state accountability embedded in the NCLB and similar state legislation presents no definite upper limit on state financial responsibility when plaintiffs' students consistently fail to meet state-established standards. This scenario presents tremendous potential future advantages to school funding plaintiffs, and some serious problems for state defendants.[94]

The Emergence of Voucher Remedy Plaintiffs

In the current economic and political climate, there also appears to be an emerging movement by school voucher advocates to advance their cause by piggybacking on the present momentum of school funding suits.[95] In a lawsuit in Georgia, the first of its kind in the nation, voucher advocates sought to have their case consolidated with another, more traditional school funding suit brought by advocates for poorer rural schools.[96] Plaintiffs in the school funding suit and the voucher remedy suit agreed that many children were receiving an inadequate education and that when the state fails to meet its constitutional obligation to provide an adequate education, courts should order a proper remedy. They disagreed, however, concerning what constitutes a proper remedy.

The "voucher remedy" plaintiffs assert that because the right to an adequate education belongs to the child and not to the school district, the remedy also belongs to the child and not to the school district.[97] A proper remedy, they argue, would be a school voucher that could be used at any public or private school selected by students and their parents. Further, they argue that the residence-based method of assigning students should be abolished, giving parents the ability to choose any school in the state for their children.[98]

Although the first of these suits was filed in Georgia, these "voucher remedy" plaintiffs have a much larger national agenda.[99] They seek two goals, including making "the funding equity suits more child-centered, with more realistic remedies" and "to provide an opportunity for school choice supporters in states where legislative prospects are not bright."[100] The group identified New Jersey as a promising arena for these suits, and in July 2006 they filed a suit in *Crawford v. Davey*, requesting that students be provided with a state funded voucher to be used for tuition at public or private schools of their choice.[101]

These voucher remedy cases, however, face some significant legal obstacles: 1) It may be difficult or impossible to square some states' constitutional mandates to provide free public education with vouchers for private schools; 2) It may be difficult or impossible to reconcile vouchers for private, religious schools with constitutional mandates in states with "Blain Amendments" prohibiting transfers of state funds to sectarian institutions; 3) State and federal accountability measures must follow state and federal money, even in private schools; and 4) Because of the constitutional separation of powers, it is doubtful that courts could legitimately order a funding remedy as specific as school vouchers.[102] A court may order school funding reform if the school funding system is ruled unconstitutional, but the specific means of reform, including whether to use state funded vouchers as a remedy, is a decision for legislators not judges.[103]

Nonetheless, in filing these "voucher remedy" lawsuits, advocates for vouchers are gaining significant national attention. Even if they are not ultimately successful in litigation, the remedies they propose may appeal to some legislators either as an alternative to simply allocating more money to some schools or, more ominously, as a means of putting funding reform advocates on notice that they should be careful what they ask for, as the remedy the legislature provides could be vouchers instead of additional school funding. If the voucher movement gains a firm political footing, it could give parents another way to choose to educate their children outside of public schools and would be yet another disincentive for parents to elect to pay higher taxes for public schools.[104]

Serrano's Continuing Legacy

Events in California continue to be instructive concerning the possible future of school funding litigation. Despite the acclaim afforded to the Supreme

Court of California's 1971 decision in *Serrano v. Priest,* some scholars argue that the unintended consequences of *Serrano* were actually quite harmful to public education in California, ultimately resulting in diminished resources and educational quality.[105] Whatever the cause, many schools in California appear to lack needed resources, prompting continued litigation.[106]

In *Williams v. State*, plaintiffs in California were seeking remedies for conditions in schools that were "so grossly inferior that the conditions simply shock the conscience."[107] In *Williams* and several other recent cases in other states, plaintiffs were attempting to force the creation of a state-wide commission to review education quality and recommend improvements, establish statewide preschools, and overhaul school funding systems.[108] The *Williams* plaintiffs introduced evidence of embarrassingly poor conditions in their schools, eventually prompting the state to settle the case with a promise of nearly a billion dollars in new funding.[109] No doubt most parties hoped the dispute was resolved, but an important lesson from *Williams*, and many other streams of school funding litigation since *Serrano*, is that it's never really over. Among the repercussions of the *Williams* case were that "[t]he State claimed that if the conditions were as the plaintiffs alleged, the school districts themselves had violated California statutes and regulations and their constitutional duties and obligations. The State sought to enjoin the school districts from continuing these violations, and recover from them financially for any costs from the litigation."[110] Further, concerning the proposed Quality Education Committee, Governor Schwarzenegger "refused to appoint the final member, preventing the commission from meeting. Then-Secretary of Education Richard Riordan announced in January 2005 the governor's intent to eliminate the commission entirely and replace it with a Governor's Commission on Education Excellence, which was to look at a broad range of issues and would not have been required to address adequacy."[111] One of the lessons from *Williams* may be that calling for more state-level responsibility in funding schools may also be accompanied by more state-level authority in governing local schools and that state officials may not be willing to simply send more money without also asserting more state-level control.

The Push for Preschool Programs as a Remedy

School funding plaintiffs' calls for preschool programs, however, do appear to be gaining some traction in many states, although it is not clear that litigation will prove to be the most effective means of promoting these programs. A recent study found:

> [S]tates spent at least $3.3 billion last year on pre-kindergarten. That doesn't include money from federal and local governments, which contribute to the state programs. The state funding is up from $2.8 billion in 2005 … In all, nearly 1 million children, or 20 percent of the country's 4-year-

> olds, were in state pre-kindergarten last year—up from 17 percent the previous year.[112]

Advocates for preschool programs appear to have strong research supporting the utility of these programs.[113] Utility arguments, however, are arguments properly made to the political branches, not the courts. Because a program may have value does not mean that there is a constitutional right to that program.

Universal state-funded pre-kindergarten programs are generally politically popular. The catch is that they are also very costly. And when these programs are scaled back to include only low-income children, political support diminishes. This political dynamic is what prompted the plaintiffs to push for court-ordered pre-kindergarten programs in some states as part of the broader remedial effort in school funding reform cases: "By recognizing a right to preschool, courts could provide cover for risk-averse legislators who would like to increase access but fear repercussions from raising taxes or cutting other programs. This is precisely how some successful school finance cases have played out in the legislatures."[114]

Nonetheless, plaintiffs appear to be on shaky legal ground in many states when arguing for a constitutional right to pre-kindergarten. Opponents of state funding for these programs will likely argue that even if some state courts and legislators find a judicial order for a state-funded pre-kindergarten program a convenient vehicle for achieving their desired policy goals, a judicial order for such programs raises serious separation of powers concerns. Courts do not have the constitutional charge of weighing the relative costs and benefits of proposed social and educational programs, even if they are endorsed by social science research. Nor is it a legitimate function of courts to grant new property rights to citizens, an intrusion into the legislative domain, even if welcomed by some faint-hearted legislators seeking political cover for the increased taxes necessary to fund these new programs.

The Elusive National-Level Remedy

Two issues that seem to have become perennial causes in school funding reform are efforts to overturn the U.S. Supreme Court's decision in *San Antonio v. Rodriguez*[115] and efforts to address interstate inequalities in school funding.[116] Given the direction of the U.S. Supreme Court since its 1973 decision in *Rodriguez,* it is highly improbable that the Court will overturn *Rodriguez* and embrace any broad new federal right to education in the near future.[117] Further, without a federal right to education, it is difficult to see how federal courts could issue an order for greater interstate equity in education. Also unclear is where the money to fund such a massive undertaking would come from.

The Continuing Legacy of *Brown*

Despite many challenges, plaintiffs in school funding cases have enjoyed significant successes in recent years.[118] In coming full circle, one still-promising line of argument that is likely to remain prominent on the school funding litigation horizon traces its roots back before *Serrano* to the initial catalyst in the modern school funding revolution, *Brown v. Board of Education.*[119] Advocates for children in economically disadvantaged schools read the Court's statement in *Brown* as broad enough to include the rights of all children to an equal educational opportunity.[120] By the late 1960s, civil rights advocates began to press for judicial mandates for school funding equity, focusing on the critical issue left unaddressed in *Brown*: inequities in public school funding.[121] Citing *Brown,*[122] the *Serrano* court stated:

> We have determined that [the state's school funding] scheme invidiously discriminates against the poor because it makes the quality of a child's education a function of the wealth of his parents and neighbors. Recognizing as we must that the right to an education in our public schools is a fundamental interest which cannot be conditioned on wealth, we can discern no compelling state purpose necessitating the present method of financing. We have concluded, therefore, that such a system cannot withstand constitutional challenge and must fall before the equal protection clause.[123]

Some judges see in school funding litigation the last ghost of *Brown*, and the last hope of helping disadvantaged children to obtain equal educational opportunity. In viewing the state's education clause through this particularly historical and ideological lens, these judges may see not only the plain text of the constitution, but also the state's social and educational history, as well as the intent of the state constitution's founders in creating a state -level right to education. In so doing, courts have the opportunity to promote greater social equity and further extrapolate to determine how that intent would manifest under contemporary circumstances, including current efforts to realize the yet unrealized goals of *Brown*.

Critics of this approach to adjudicating school funding cases suggest that this judicial approach is ungrounded in law, represents an activist intrusion into the legislative domain, and is dangerously overreaching by creating a vehicle for judges to impose their personal social views on others through the power of the court, even when these views may be contrary to the political will of the majority. In contrast, others argue that because of historical denials of full citizenship rights to minorities, linked to systematic denials of equal educational opportunity, there is a constitutional duty for judges to provide a remedy to disadvantaged children that have been so consistently denied access to equitable opportunities, even when these remedies may be contrary to the will of the majority.[124]

Conclusion

Since *Brown*, the courtroom has become the arena of choice for an ongoing dialogue over equal access to educational opportunities. The line of litigation begun in *Serrano* is now in its fourth decade with no discernible end in sight, and it is likely to continue into the indefinite future. Regardless of the difficulties of successfully navigating the long road through the courthouse and the statehouse to achieve school funding reform, school funding reform advocates will likely continue to use litigation as an important tool in their efforts to promote greater school funding equity.

Endnotes

1 487 P.2d 1241 (Cal 1971).

2 *See* John Dayton, Anne Dupre, & Christine Kiracofe, *Education Finance Litigation: A Review of Recent State High Court Decisions and Their Likely Impact on Future Litigation,* 186 Educ. L. Rep. 1, 1 (2004) (listing state high court opinions on the merits of school funding challenges since *Serrano*).

3 *See, e.g.,* Abbott v. Burke (Abbott II), 575 A.2d 359 (N.J. 1990); Abbott v. Burke (Abbott I), 495 A.2d 376 (N.J. 1985); Robinson v. Cahill (Robinson VII), 360 A.2d 400 (N.J. 1976); Robinson v. Cahill (Robinson VI), 358 A.2d 457 (N.J. 1976); Robinson v. Cahill (Robinson V), 355 A.2d 129 (N.J. 1976); Robinson v. Cahill (Robinson IV), 351 A.2d 713 (N.J. 1975); Robinson v. Cahill (Robinson III), 335 A.2d 6 (N.J. 1975); Robinson v. Cahill (Robinson II), 306 A.2d 65 (N.J. 1973); Robinson v. Cahill (Robinson I), 303 A.2d 273 (N.J. 1973).

4 For a thorough discussion of education finance litigation see, R. C. Wood & D. C. Thompson, Education Finance Law: Constitutional Challenges to State Aid Plans, An Analysis of Strategy, 2d Ed, (Dayton Ohio, Educ. Law Ass'n), 1996.

5 U.S. Declaration of Independence (1776).

6 U.S. Const. amend. XIV (1868).

7 347 U.S. 483 (1954).

8 Phillip Kurland, *Equal Educational Opportunity: The Limits of Constitutional Jurisprudence Undefined*, u. chi. l. rev. 35 (1968), 583-600.

9 The history of racial equality is too complex to fully describe herein. In an educational context, it is obvious that *Brown v. Board of Education,* 374 U.S. 483 (1954), was the most critical. However, this analysis is aided by recognition of a long history of such. *See Brown* which in an educational context included, e.g., Gong Lum v. Rice, (275 U.S. 78 (1927); Missouri ex. rel. Gaines v. Canada, 305 U.S. 337 (1938); Freeman v. County Sch. Bd., 82 F. Supp. 167 (E.D. Va. 1948); Butler v. Wilemon, 86 F. Supp. 397 (N.D. Tex. 1949); Pitts v. Bd. of Trs., 84 F. Supp. 975 (E.D. Ark. 1949); McLaurin v. Okla. State Regents, 339 U.S. 637 (1950); Sweatt v. Painter, 339 U.S. 629 (1950); Carter v. Sch. Bd., 182 F.2d 531 (4th Cir. 1950); and Davis v. County Sch. Bd., 103 F. Supp. 337 (E.D. Va. 1952).

10 These cases are also multiple and meaningful. *See* Baker v. Carr, 369 U.S. 186 (1962), where accident of geography and arbitrary boundaries of governments may not be a basis for discrimination among otherwise equal citizens, in this instance forbidding the requirement that one must pay property taxes in order to vote; Gray v. Sanders, 372 U.S. 368 (1963); Wesberry v. Sanders, 276 U.S. 1 (1964); Reynolds v. Sims, 377 U.S. 533 (1964); Davis v. Mann, 377 U.S. 678 (1964).

11 These cases are also multiple and far ranging. *But see, e.g.,* Shapiro v. Thompson, 394 U.S. 618 (1969), where a law against bringing indigents into a state violated the right to interstate travel; *see also* Lubin v. Panish, 415 U.S. 706 (1974), where a filing fee as prerequisite to the right to vote is wealth discrimination; *see also* Harper v. Va. Bd. of Elections, 383 U.S. 663

(1966), where a state poll tax was wealth discrimination; and Griffin v. Illinois, 351 U.S. 12 (1956), where denying an indigent defendant a transcript of trial for appeal was wealth discrimination.

12 *See, e.g.*, Shapiro v. Thompson, 394 U.S. 618 (1969).

13 *See, e.g.*, Skinner v. Oklahoma, 316 U.S. 535 (1942).

14 *See, e.g.*, Reynolds v. Sims, 377 U.S. 533 (1964).

15 *See, e.g.*, Griffin v. Illinois, 351 U.S. 12 (1956).

16 United States v. Carolene Prods. Co., 304 U.S. 144 at 153 (1938).

17 *See, e.g.*, Loving v. Virginia, 388 U.S. 1 (1967).

18 *See, e.g.*, Oyama v. California, 332 U.S. 633 (1948).

19 *See, e.g.*, Graham v. Richardson, 403 U.S. 365 371 (1971).

20 Kurland, *supra* note 8.

21 Litigation regarding this issue is longstanding, e.g., a Massachusetts court in 1850 addressed school segregation under Massachusetts' 1780 equality statute in 59 Mass. (5 Cush.) 198 (1850).

22 Brown v. Bd. of Educ., 374 U.S. 483 (1954).

23 *Brown,* at 493 (1954).

24 United States v. Carolene, 304 U.S. 144 at 153 (1938) n.4 (dictum).

25 *See e.g.*, Griffin v. Illinois, 351 U.S. 12 (1956); Douglas v. California, 372 U.S. 353 (1963); and Harper v. Virginia Bd. of Elections, 383 U.S. 663 (1966). This logic was especially supported as the Court had stated in *Harper*, in ruling against a poll tax, that "[l]ines drawn on the basis of wealth or property, like those of race, are disfavored."(at 668).

26 Burruss v. Wilkerson, 310 F. Supp. 572 *affirmed mem.*, 397 U.S. 44 (1970).

27 However, what is critical to note is how much this approach has not changed in numerous other cases and more than thirty-five years.

28 Burruss v. Wilkerson, 310 at 574 (1969).

29 *Id.*

30 McInnis v. Shapiro, 293 F. Supp. 327 (N.D. Ill. 1968).

31 *Aff'd sub nom.* McInnis v. Ogilvie, 394 U.S. 322 (1969).

32 San Antonio Indep. Sch. Dist. v. Rodriguez, 411 U.S. 1 (1973).

33 337 F. Supp. 280 (W.D. Tex. 1971).

34 *San Antonio,* 411 U.S. 1 at 27-28 (1973).

35 *San Antonio,* 411 U.S. 1 at 20-22 (1973); noting Griffin v. Illinois, 351 U.S. 12 (1956) on transcripts; Douglas v. California, 372 U.S. 353 (1963) on hiring counsel.

36 It will be seen under state review later that this claim was not entirely novel, as it had been successfully utilized in *Serrano v. Priest,* 487 P.2d 1241 (1971), in California. It had not, however, been tried at the federal level even though the state court in *Serrano* invoked the Fourteenth Amendment in its decision. The lack of demarcation between overlapping federal and state chronology should be noted, as state litigation had already begun following *McInnis* and *Burruss*, but prior to *Rodriguez.*

37 *San Antonio,* 411 U.S. at 37 (1973).

38 *Id.* at 39.

39 *Id.* at 42.

40 *Id.* at 37.

41 *Id.* at 28.

42 487 P.2d 1241 (Cal. 1971). *See also* Note, *The Serrano Documents*, 2 YALE REV. L. & SOC. ACTION 77 (1971).

43 *Id.* at 1244.

44 D. FRANKLIN, THE CONSTITUTIONALITY OF THE K-12 FUNDING SYSTEM OF ILLINOIS 19 (Vol. I, 1987).

45 MICHAEL LA MORTE, SCHOOL LAW 353 (3rd ed. 1990).

46 The *Serrano* principle is one of fiscal neutrality. *See* NATIONAL EDUCATION ASSOCIATION, UNDERSTANDING STATE SCHOOL FINANCE FORMULAS 5 (1987).

47 Serrano v. Priest, 487 P.2d 1241, 1244 (Cal. 1971).

[48] Campaign for Fiscal Equity v. State, 295 A.D.2d 1, 744 N.Y.S.2d 130, 2002 N.Y. App. Div

[49] Pauley v. Kelly, 255 S.E.2d 859, 877 (W. Va. 1979)

[50] Idaho Schs. for Equal Educ. Opportunity v. State of Idaho, 976 P.2d 913.

[51] Flores v. Arizona, 48 F. Supp. 2d 939 (1999), in which the court ordered an adequacy study.

[52] *Roosevelt Elementary Sch. Dist. v. Bishop*, 877 P.2d 806, effectively overturned the previous Arizona State Supreme Court ruling in *Shofstal v. Hollins*, 515 P.2d 590 (Ariz. 1973). *See also*, Roosevelt Elementary School Dist. v. State, -- Ariz. ---- [179 Educ. L. Rep. 900], 406 Ariz. Adv. Rep. 33m (2003).

[53] Leandro v. State, 488 S.E.2d 249 (N.C. 1997).

[54] Abbeville v. State, 515 S.E.2d 535.

[55] DeRolph v. State, 677 N.E.2d 733 (Ohio 1997): 728 N.E.2d 993 (Ohio 2000) overturned *Board of Educ. v. Walter*, 390 N.E.2d 813.

[56] Edgewood Indep. Sch. Dist. v. Kirby, 777 S.W.2d 391.

[57] Buse v. Smith, 247 N.W.2d 141 (Wis. 1976).

[58] Robinson v. Cahill (Robinson VII), 360 A.2d 400 (N.J. 1976); Robinson v. Cahill (Robinson VI), 358 A.2d 457 (N.J. 1976); Robinson v. Cahill (Robinson V), 355 A.2d 129 (N.J. 1976); Robinson v. Cahill (Robinson IV), 351 A.2d 713 (N.J. 1975); Robinson v. Cahill (Robinson III), 335 A.2d 6 (N.J. 1975); Robinson v. Cahill (Robinson II), 306 A.2d 65 (N.J. 1973); Robinson v. Cahill (Robinson I), 303 A.2d 273 (N.J. 1973)

[59] Washakie County Sch. Dist. V. Herschler, 606 P.2d 310 at 334 (Wyo. 1980).

[60] *See,* John Dayton & Anne Dupre, *School Funding Litigation: Who's Winning the War?,* 57 Vand. L. Rev. 2351 (2004).

[61] This section updates sections from a previous article, *see* John Dayton & R. Craig Wood, *School Funding Litigation: Scanning the Event Horizon,* Educ. L. Rep. (in press).

[62] Nonetheless, some courts have held that state fiscal difficulties do not excuse failure to comply with constitutional mandates to support education, with one court declaring that financial difficulties "do not trump the Constitution ...We realize that the General Assembly cannot spend money it does not have. Nevertheless, we reiterate that the constitutional mandate must be met. The Constitution protects us whether the state is flush or destitute." DeRolph v. State, 780 N.E.2d 529, 530-532 (Ohio 2002). Similarly, in declaring the entire public education system of Kentucky unconstitutional, the Supreme Court of Kentucky stated: "The taxpayers of this state must pay for the system, no matter how large, even to the point of being unexpectedly large or even onerous." Rose v. Council for Better Educ., 790 S.W.2d 186, 208 (Ky. 1989). The Supreme Court of Texas stated: "The legislature must establish priorities according to constitutional mandates; equalizing educational opportunity cannot be relegated to an 'if funds are left over' basis." Edgewood v. Kirby, 777 S.W.2d 391, 397-398 (Tex. 1989).

[63] *See* John Dayton & Anne Dupre, *School Funding Litigation: Who's Winning the War?,* 57 Vand. L. Rev. 2351, 2403 (2004) ("Although no court has explicitly stated that state fiscal difficulties affected its ruling, the status of the economy in the state may have some effect on how the court views the evidence that is presented in the case ... State court judges are likely aware that if the General Assembly cannot, or will not, comply with a judicial mandate for greater equity in funding, this noncompliance will constitute an open threat to the continuing authority of the court. There is some evidence to support the notion that judicial decisions concerning school funding litigation may be influenced by perceptions of the status of the economy").

[64] *Id.*

[65] Richard Briffault, *Public Finance in the American Federal System: Basic Patterns and Current Issues,* 2 Colum. J. Eur. L. 533, 553 ("most state constitutions require balanced state budgets").

[66] Michael W. La Morte & Jeffrey D. Williams, *Court Decisions and School Finance Reform,* 21 Educ. Admin. Q. 59, 81 (1985).

[67] Steven P. Croley. *The Majoritarian Difficulty: Elective Judiciaries and the Rule of Law,* 62 U. CHI. L. REV. 689, 725 (1995) ("in only twelve states are most judges not electorally accountable to the citizenry: Connecticut, Delaware, Hawaii, Maine, Massachusetts, New Hampshire, New Jersey, New York, Rhode Island, South Carolina, Vermont, and Virginia. These states choose judges largely through executive nomination and legislative confirmation (or, in a few, through legislative election). Many of these states choose lower or local judges electorally, however. This is true in New York, for example. In the remaining thirty-eight states in which judges are elected, twenty-three have elections to select judges, who thereafter stand for reelection periodically. Of these, ten have partisan judicial elections—Alabama, Arkansas, Illinois, Mississippi, New Mexico, North Carolina, Pennsylvania, Tennessee, Texas, and West Virginia—and thirteen have nonpartisan elections—Georgia, Idaho, Kentucky, Louisiana, Michigan, Minnesota, Montana, Nevada, North Dakota, Ohio, Oregon, Washington, and Wisconsin. Judges in the fifteen states that have adopted some version of the "merit plan" are initially appointed by a state's governor and thereafter stand for periodic reelection. These fifteen include Alaska, Arizona, California, Colorado, Florida, Indiana, Iowa, Kansas, Maryland, Missouri, Nebraska, Oklahoma, South Dakota, Utah, and Wyoming").

[68] *Outlook for the U.S. Economy: Hearing Before the Joint Economic Committee,* 109th Cong. (April 27, 2006) (statement of Federal Reserve Board Chairman Ben S. Bernanke) ("Although recent economic developments have been positive, the nation still faces some significant longer-term economic challenges. One such challenge is putting the federal budget on a trajectory that will be sustainable as our society ages. Under current law, federal spending for retirement and health programs will grow substantially in coming decades–both as a share of overall federal spending and relative to the size of the economy–especially if health costs continue to climb rapidly. Slower growth in the workforce may also reduce growth in economic activity and thus in tax revenues ... The resolution of the nation's long-run fiscal challenge will require hard choices"). Also, given the heavy reliance on property-based taxes in current school funding systems, any disruption to the value of taxable property raises special concerns in adequately funding schools. *See, Semiannual Monetary Policy Report to Congress: Hearing Before the Senate Committee on Banking, Housing, and Urban Affairs,* 110th Cong. (Feb. 14, 2007) (statement of Federal Reserve Board Chairman Ben S. Bernanke) ("the ultimate extent of the housing market correction is difficult to forecast and may prove greater than we anticipate. Similarly, spillover effects from developments in the housing market onto consumer spending and employment in housing-related industries may be more pronounced than expected").

[69] *Outlook for the U.S. Economy: Hearing Before the Joint Economic Committee,* 109th Cong. (April 27, 2006) (statement of Federal Reserve Board Chairman Ben S. Bernanke).

[70] *See* Iris J. Lav & Andrew Brecher, *Passing Down the Deficit: Federal Policies Contribute to the Severity of the State Fiscal Crisis,* Center on Budget and Policy Priorities, *available at* www.cbpp.org/5-12-04sfp.htm (Aug. 18, 2004) ("The state fiscal crisis has been deep and prolonged ... Federal policies, which have reduced state revenues and imposed additional costs on states, have played a significant role in enlarging these deficits and are impeding states' fiscal recovery").

[71] Debra H. Dawahare, *Public School Reform: Kentucky's Solution,* 27 U. ARK. LITTLE ROCK L. REV. 27, 27 (2004), *citing* Rose v. Council for Better Education, 790 S.W.2d 186, 215 (Ky. 1989), and providing a review of the impact of the decision ("Lest there be any doubt, the result of our decision is that Kentucky's entire system of common schools is unconstitutional. There is no allegation that only part of the common school system is invalid, and we find no such circumstance. This decision applies to the entire sweep of the system—all its parts and parcels. This decision applies to the statutes creating, implementing, and financing the system and to all regulations, etc., pertaining thereto. This decision covers the creation of local school districts, school boards, and the Kentucky Department of Education to the Minimum Foundation Program and Power Equalization Program. It covers school construction and maintenance, teacher certification—the whole gamut of the common school system in Kentucky").

[72] The Supreme Court of Ohio's eleventh hour decision terminating the school funding litigation just weeks before two Republicans were to be seated on the court seems to support the view that political affiliation may influence decision making in school finance litigation. Although the Ohio Supreme Court presumably ended *DeRolph* litigation with its December 2002 decision, plaintiffs continued to petition the courts for remedy. On March 4, 2003 *DeRolph* plaintiffs petitioned the trial court "to schedule and conduct a conference to address the defendants' compliance with the orders of the common pleas court and this [supreme] court". *See* State ex rel. State v. Lewis, 789 N.E.2d 195, 199 (Ohio 2003). After a series of state and plaintiff actions (including an attempt by the Ohio Coalition for Equity & Adequacy of School Funding to "intervene as additional respondents"), the Supreme Court reaffirmed its December 2002 decision by issuing a *writ of prohibition* "prohibiting Perry County Common Pleas Court Judge Linton D. Lewis Jr. from exercising further jurisdiction in *DeRolph v. State*" *State ex rel. State v. Lewis. Id.* at 195. *See also* William S. Koski, *The Politics of Judicial Decision-Making in Educational Policy Reform,* 55 HASTINGS L.J. 1077 (2004) (providing a detailed analysis of the political dynamics in the *DeRolph* litigation).

[73] Some scholars argue that every constitutional opinion "is sensitive [to the judge's] political conviction." RONALD DWORKIN, FREEDOM'S LAW: THE MORAL READING OF THE AMERICAN CONSTITUTION 2-3; 36-37 (1996).

[74] *See* DAVID M. BEATTY, THE ULTIMATE RULE OF LAW 31 (2004) *(*"[judges who] draw inspiration from different legal and political philosophers will read the same cases, even pivotal cases, quite differently").

[75] *See* DeRolph v. State, 574 N.E.2d 1184, 1188 (Ohio 2001) ("Since it was first docketed in this court in 1995, this dispute has produced from this court no fewer than three signed majority opinions, a per curiam opinion, eleven separate concurrences and dissents, and a number of rulings on motions filed by plaintiffs and defendants. Every justice of the court has expressed her and his views regarding the constitutional issue that once again is presented for our disposition nearly six years after the court exercised its discretionary jurisdiction to review the merits. The written opinions of the justices reflect deeply held beliefs regarding the responsibility of the court as an institution and the principles that define the framework by which each justice decides issues brought to the court. The informal and formal discussions among the justices regarding the jurisdictional and merit issues have been of an intensity and duration unmatched by any other case").

[76] Some states have experienced decades of serial litigation in school funding cases. *See* Abbott v. Burke (Abbott II), 575 A.2d 359 (N.J. 1990); Abbott v. Burke (Abbott I), 495 A.2d 376 (N.J. 1985); Robinson v. Cahill (Robinson VII), 360 A.2d 400 (N.J. 1976); Robinson v. Cahill (Robinson VI), 358 A.2d 457 (N.J. 1976); Robinson v. Cahill (Robinson V), 355 A.2d 129 (N.J. 1976); Robinson v. Cahill (Robinson IV), 351 A.2d 713 (N.J. 1975); Robinson v. Cahill (Robinson III), 335 A.2d 6 (N.J. 1975); Robinson v. Cahill (Robinson II), 306 A.2d 65 (N.J. 1973); Robinson v. Cahill (Robinson I), 303 A.2d 273 (N.J. 1973); *see also* San Antonio Indep. Sch. Dist. v. Rodriguez, 411 U.S. 1 (1973); Carrollton-Farmers Branch v. Edgewood Indep. Sch. Dist., 826 S.W.2d 489 (Tex. 1992); Edgewood Indep. Sch. Dist. v. Kirby, 804 S.W.2d 491 (Tex. 1991); Edgewood Indep. Sch. Dist. v. Kirby, 777 S.W.2d 391 (Tex. 1989).

[77] David J. Hoff, *Kansas Lawmakers Agree on Spending Plan,* 24 EDUC. WEEK 23 (July 13, 2005). *See also,* Richard E. Levy, *Gunfight at the K-12 Corral: Legislative vs. Judicial Power in the Kansas School Finance Litigation*, 54 U. KAN. L. REV. 1021 (2006).

[78] Robert C. Johnston, *Bar on Finance Cases Sought,* 24 EDUC. WEEK 17 (March 2, 2005).

[79] *See* Arthur D. Hellman, *Judicial Activism: The Good, the Bad, and the Ugly,* 21 MISS. C. L. REV. 253, 253-254 (2002) ("in recent years some of the boldest ventures in judicial activism have come in the decisions of state judges. Many of the examples are familiar: State courts in California, Tennessee, Texas, and more than a dozen other states have struck down the state's system of financing education as violating state constitution equal protection clauses or other provisions of the state constitution").

[80] *See* John Dayton & Anne Dupre, *School Funding Litigation: Who's Winning the War?*, 57 VAND. L. REV. 2351, 2409 (2004) (discussing legal history and evolving strategies in school funding litigation).

[81] 20 U.S.C. § 6301 (2002). *See also*, Philip T.K. Daniel, *No Child Left Behind: The Balm of Gilead Has Arrived in American Education*, 206 EDUC. L. REP. 791 (2006).

[82] John Dayton, Anne Dupre, & Christine Kiracofe, *Education Finance Litigation: A Review of Recent State High Court Decisions and Their Likely Impact on Future Litigation*, 186 EDUC. L. REP. 1, 11 (2004) ("Accountability legislation, from the NCLB Act to similar state legislation could become fertile new grounds for funding litigation").

[83] Brandi M. Powell, *Take the Money or Run?: The Dilemna of the No Child Left Behind Act for State and Local Governments*, 6 LOY. J. PUB. INT. L. 153, 153 (2005) ("The No Child Left Behind Act … was hailed as a successful effort at bipartisan education reform. Ironically, after two years of implementation efforts, the NCLBA has succeeded in dividing educators, parents, and legislators on the local, state, and national levels. While there is agreement as to the importance of the purpose of the NCLBA, which is to 'ensure that all children have a fair, equal, and significant opportunity to obtain a high-quality education,' and to close the 'achievement gaps between minority and non-minority students, and between disadvantaged children and their more advantaged peers,' few agree on the manner in which the NCLBA seeks to bring about these goals").

[84] *See* James E. Ryan, *The Perverse Incentives of the No Child Left Behind Act*, 79 N.Y.U. L. REV. 932, 934 (2004) ("the Act's fatal flaw is that it creates incentives that work against the Act's goals"). There is growing dissatisfaction with the NCLB Act. *See* Steve Meade, *The Growing State Resistance to NCLB*, 48 NOV ADVOCATE (Idaho) 16, 16 (2005) (discussing pending law suits contesting provisions in the NCLB Act and stating "a number of school districts and states across the nation have begun calculating the cost of complying with the NCLB and are looking at ways to 'opt out'"). *See also* James W. Guthrie, *American Education Reform: What is Needed is 'National' Not Federal*, 17 ST. LOUIS U. PUB. L. REV. 125, 138-139 (1997) ("federal authority when invoked for education is too clumsy, too heavy handed. The apparent need for one-size-fits-all regulations is harmful when applied to the extraordinary span and diversity of America's 100,000 schools … A more sensitive, flexible, and less politicized institution is now needed"). Professor Guthrie suggests as an alternative either a "National Education Foundation" or a "National Education Trust" and notes that: "Each offers the prospect of providing states and school districts with inducements for change without imposing a heavy regulatory hand which, in the past, has proved counter productive." *Id.* at 139.

[85] Many of the factors that affect student achievement are controlled by the child, the parents, and other non-school factors. *See* Eric A. Hanushek, *When School Finance "Reform" May Not Be Good Policy*, 28 HARV. J. ON LEGIS. 423, 431-432 (1991) (*citing* the "Coleman Report" as finding "that schools are not very important in determining student achievement. Families, and to a lesser extent peers, were the primary determinants of variations in performance … Policymakers directly control some [educational inputs] such as the characteristics of the schools, teachers, and curricula. Other inputs such as those of family and friends, plus innate endowments of the students, generally cannot be affected by public policy").

[86] *See* Alex Duran, *Factors to Consider When Evaluating School Accountability Results*, 34 J.L. & EDUC. 73, 98 (2005) ("The validity of interpretations and uses of AYP results is questionable when school outcomes, home income, and student achievement are highly correlated with one another. It may be that home income factors are the most direct causes of academic achievement. If accountability systems determine school effectiveness on the basis of academic achievement results without the inclusion of added contextual variables, then one must question the validity of the results because school populations are not created through a process of random selection and random assignment. The contextual reality may be that the challenges that are encountered by high poverty schools are more difficult and greater in number than the ones encountered by affluent schools").

87 *See* Eric A. Hanushek, *When School Finance "Reform" May Not Be Good Policy,* 28 HARV. J. ON LEGIS. 423, 431-432 (1991) (*citing* the "Coleman Report" as finding "that schools are not very important in determining student achievement. Families, and to a lesser extent peers, were the primary determinants of variations in performance ... Policymakers directly control some [educational inputs] such as the characteristics of the schools, teachers, and curricula. Other inputs such as those of family and friends, plus innate endowments of the students, generally cannot be affected by public policy").

88 Using schools' standardized exam scores to measure educational quality is like using a tape measure to judge the quality of automobiles. The longest vehicle is not necessarily the best quality vehicle, anymore than the school with the highest test scores is necessarily providing the best educational experiences for its students. *See also,* Gerald W. Bracey, *The 16th Bracey Report on the Condition of Public Education*, 88 PHI DELTA KAPPAN 151 (Oct. 2006) (comparing political claims concerning the NCLB and statistical data, and stating: "When political considerations define the agenda for or shape the findings of research, the results may seem frustrating or silly–but often the losers are students and teachers").

89 *See* John Dayton, *Serrano and Its Progeny: An Analysis of 30 Years of School Funding Litigation,* 157 EDUC. L. REP. 447 (2001).

90 *See* Campaign for Fiscal Equity v. State, 801 N.E.2d 326 (N.Y. 2003); Lake View v. Huckabee, 91 S.W.3d 472 (Ark. 2002); Claremont v. Governor, 794 A.2d 744 (N.H. 2002). *See also* Michael Heise, *Educational Jujitsu*, EDUCATION NEXT, Fall 2002, p. 3.

91 *Id.*

92 School funding reform advocates have increasing found that "accountability" litigation is proving successful. This is not a completely new approach, but it was elevated in prominence in Claremont v. Governor. *See* Claremont v. Governor, 794 A.2d 744, 751-752 (N.H. 2002) (the highest courts in Massachusetts, Ohio, New Jersey and Tennessee had discussed accountability legislation as setting the level of state duty before *Claremont III* was decided, listing other states that have recognized "accountability as a logical corollary to the State's duty to provide a constitutionally adequate education"). But the New Hampshire high went further in 2002, making accountability a central issue in the case. *Id.* at 745. In keeping with that same tone, the Supreme Court of Arkansas also recognized a state duty of accountability under this same theory in Lake View v. Huckabee, 91 S.W.3d 472 (Ark. 2002), as did the high court in New York, in Campaign for Fiscal Equity v. State, 801 N.E.2d 326 (N.Y. 2003).

93 *See* Michael Heise, *Educational Jujitsu*, EDUCATION NEXT, Fall 2002, p. 3 ("Such policy changes seek to shift school regulation away from the traditional focus on inputs—teacher-to-student ratios, per-pupil spending, number of certified teachers—and toward a focus on performance as the basic metric of education quality. However, in an ironic twist, this output-driven movement has made it easier for activists to appeal to the courts for more inputs. The standards movement enables activists to define adequacy as that level of funding necessary for a school district and its students to meet state education standards. Thus a new wave of litigation may be upon us, one that turns the states' efforts to improve achievement through standards against the state and enables school districts to gain financially from their inability to perform at desired levels. These failures are used in court to bolster legal claims that such schools underachieve because their resources are inadequate and, therefore, unconstitutional").

94 *See generally* Thomas Rentschler, *No Child Left Behind: Admirable Goals, Disastrous Outcomes,* 12 WIDENER L. REV. 637 (2006).

95 David J. Hoff, *Movement Afoot to Reframe Finance-Adequacy Suits*, 25 EDUC. WEEK 25 (Oct. 26, 2005) (reporting on a 2005 conference focusing on vouchers and charter schools as remedies in school funding litigation cases, and quoting Kenneth W. Starr, former judge, special prosecutor, and current Dean of the Pepperdine University School of Law, as saying about current school funding suits: "It appears to me that the bloom is off the *Rose* [a reference to the Supreme Court of Kentucky's 1989 decision in *Rose*] ... It's time to be reflecting on other options and different ways to think [about school funding remedies]" and Clint Bolick, president and general counsel of the Alliance for School Choice as saying: "School

districts do not have the guarantee of an education, children do ... [s]chool districts are not the victims [of inadequate funding]. They are the violators").

[96] *See* Williams v. State, 2005 WL 2156135 (N.D. Ga. Aug. 11, 2005) (defendant's motion to dismiss); *see also,* Consortium for Adequate School Funding in Georgia v. State, No. 2004CV91004 (Super. Ct. Fulton Co., Ga. Oct. 28, 2005) (ruling that plaintiffs' representing poorer rural schools challenging the state's system of school funding may proceed on claims that the system is inadequate under the state constitution's education clause, but that equal protection claims are barred by McDaniel v. Thomas, 285 S.E.2d 156 (Ga. 1981)).

[97] Caroline Hendrie, *Georgia Lawsuit Seeks Vouchers as Remedy to School Aid Disparities,* 24 EDUC. WEEK 17 (Oct. 26, 2005).

[98] *See* Glenn Delk, attorney at law, representing plaintiffs in Williams v. State, No. 1:05-CV-0427 at 9-10 (N.D. Ga. Apr. 27, 2005) (plaintiffs' response to motion to dismiss of state defendants) ("the State of Georgia is still operating a dual system of public education half a century after the Supreme Court said that black children should be given equal opportunities 'with all deliberate speed.' If parents have sufficient funds to purchase a house in a district with good schools, they receive a public education with teachers qualified to teach their subject matter, with academically rigorous courses, including advanced placement courses, and with high expectations. However, Plaintiffs do not have sufficient funds to purchase a home [in a district with good schools]. Therefore, their children must attend the school assigned to them [by the State]. Plaintiffs' children are, or will be, taught by the unqualified teachers denied access to the rigorous courses and lose their chance at a college education and are otherwise being denied their constitutional rights").

[99] *Id.* According to the general counsel for the Alliance for School Choice: "There is active discussion of the voucher remedy in about a half-dozen states." (quoting Clint Bolick, president and general counsel for the Alliance for School Choice).

[100] *Id.*

[101] David J. Hoff, *Lawsuit Seeks Vouchers for N.J. Students*, 25 EDUC. WEEK 22, 24 (July 26, 2006).

[102] *See* Brian L. White, *Potential Federal and State Constitutional Barriers to the Success of School Vouchers,* 49 U. KAN. L. REV. 889 (2001). *See also,* James Forman, Jr., *The Rise and Fall of School Vouchers: A Story of Religion, Race, and Politics,* 54 U.C.L.A. L. REV. 547 (2007).

[103] Jonathan Feldman, *Separation of Powers and the Judicial Review of Positive Rights Claims: The Role of State Courts in an Era of Positive Government,* 24 RUTGERS L.J. 1057, 1091 (1993) ("in the context of school finance, a court could well impose a remedy which required the legislature to increase state funding of education. It would be inappropriate, however, for the court to decree how the funds must be raised (e.g., by ordering the legislature to impose an income tax) or to mandate the funding levels owed to specific educational programs (e.g., by ordering that a certain sum be spent on art or mathematics). The legislative and executive branches are better equipped to address these policy questions").

[104] Mark G. Yudof, *School Finance Reform: Don't Worry, Be Happy*, NOLPE NOTES, May 1992, at 3 ("Affluent parents may even opt to minimize taxes in order to free up income for tuition expenses at private schools").

[105] *See* Isaac Martin, *Does School Finance Litigation Cause Taxpayer Revolt? Serrano and Proposition 13,* 40 LAW & SOC'Y REV. 525, 526 (2006) ("Proponents [of the finance litigation backlash theory] argue that court-ordered school finance equalization undermined popular support for schools and ultimately triggered a backlash that crippled public education. Voters who had happily paid heavy taxes to support their local schools were unwilling to pay the same taxes for schools outside of their own communities. When courts mandated equalization, voters responded by demanding laws to limit the property tax levy. An unnamed legislator interviewed by Kozol (1991) summarized the theory succinctly: 'This [property tax limitation] is the revenge of wealth against the poor. 'If the schools must actually be equal,' they are saying, 'then we'll undercut them all.' This theory originated in California, which was home to both the most widely cited school finance equalization decision [Serrano] and the

most dramatic and well-known antitax backlash initiative, Proposition 13." Note, however, that Martin concluded that evidence did not support the common assumption that *Serrano* caused the tax payer revolt in California).

[106] Lisa Lopez Trifiletti, *The Role of Litigation in Education Reform: Holding California Responsible, While Preserving Local Control,* 38 Loy. L.A. L. Rev. 967, 967 (2004) ("California policy perpetuates educational inequity that too frequently condemns California's children to unequal lives. Millions of children are forced to attend California public schools that lack qualified teachers, necessary instructional materials, and clean, safe, and educationally appropriate facilities. In classrooms that lack proper ventilation or comfortable climates and in schools riddled with vandalism, pealing paint, mold, vermin, and filthy restrooms, students struggle to learn without textbooks, basic supplies, and sometimes without permanent teachers").

[107] Filed as case No. 312236 in San Francisco Superior Court on May 17, 2000. *See* Christopher R. Lockard, *In the Wake of Williams v. State: The Past, Present, and Future of Education Finance in California,* 57 Hastings L.J. 385, 403 (2005), *citing* First Amended Complaint for Injunctive and Declaratory Relief at 1, Williams v. State, No. 312236 (S.F. Super. Ct. May 17, 2000), available at: http://www.decentschools.org/courtdocs/01FirstAmendedComplaint.pdf.

[108] *Id.* 385.

[109] *Id.* at 411.

[110] *Id.* at 408.

[111] *Id.* at 414-415.

[112] *States Stress Benefits of Pre-Kindergarten Programs,* CNN, March 15, 2007, *available* at http://www.cnn.com/2007/EDUCATION/03/14/paying.for.pre.kindergarden.ap/index.html (citing a March 14, 2007 report by the National Institute for Early Education Research at New Jersey's Rutgers University).

[113] *See* James E. Ryan, *A Constitutional Right to Preschool?,* 94 Cal. L. Rev. 49, 56 (2006).

[114] *Id.* at 53.

[115] 411 U.S. 1 (1973) (holding that poverty was not a suspect class, and that there is no fundamental right to education under the U.S. Constitution, effectively removing challenges to school funding from the federal courts to state courts).

[116] *See* Goodwin Liu, *Interstate Inequality in Educational Opportunity,* 81 N.Y.U. L. Rev. 2044 (2006).

[117] *See* Christopher R. Lockard, *In the Wake of Williams v. State: The Past, Present, and Future of Education Finance in California,* 57 Hastings L.J. 385, 420-421 (2005) ("A group of professors at the University of California at Berkeley, Boalt Hall School of Law have formed a project called 'Rethinking Rodriguez.' The group is considering mounting a school finance lawsuit based on federal constitutional rights with the hope of overruling Rodriguez. Their goal is to make education a fundamental right, that is, 'a right belonging to all children, protected by an enforceable guarantee of 'adequacy' or 'equality' or both.' They will have an uphill battle").

[118] *See* John Dayton, Anne Dupre, & Christine Kiracofe, *Education Finance Litigation: A Review of Recent State High Court Decisions and Their Likely Impact on Future Litigation,* 186 Educ. L. Rep. 1 (2004).

[119] 347 U.S. 483 (1954). The Court's decision in *Brown* served as the ideological foundation for the modern school funding equity movement, however, school funding litigation in the United States can be traced back nearly two centuries. In 1819, in Commonwealth v. Dedham, the town of Dedham was charged with failing to provide an adequate education, and the Supreme Judicial Court of Massachusetts stated, "The schools required by the statute are to be maintained for the benefit of the whole town, as it is the wise policy of the law to give all the inhabitants equal privileges, for the education of their children in the public schools. Nor is it in the power of the majority to deprive the minority of this privilege." 16 Mass. 141, 146 (1819).

[120] *Id. See also,* Joseph T. Henke, *Financing Public Schools in California*, 21 U.S.F. L. Rev. 1, 5 (1986) ("The language of the *Brown* case sounded broad enough to apply to unequal expenditures on children's education even when racial discrimination was not involved").

[121] *See* Sheryll D. Cashin, *American Public Schools Fifty Years After Brown: A Separate and Unequal Reality,* 47 How. L.J. 341, 347 (2004) ("The battle for equal or adequate funding would be left to a later generation of civil rights lawyers and it would be fought in state courts based upon state constitutions").

[122] 487 P.2d 1241, 1256 (Cal. 1971).

[123] *Id.* at 1244.

[124] *See also* R. Craig Wood & George Lange, *Selected State Education Finance Constitutional Litigation in the Context of Judicial Review,* 207 Educ. L. Rep. 1 (2006) (discussing "Ely's 'representative-reinforcing' theory of judicial review. Ely constructed a rationale premised on the responsibility of the judiciary to insist that the legislature provide citizens the rights essential to the operation of a democratic political process. To Ely, 'unblocking stoppages in the democratic process is what judicial review ought preeminently to be about.' In a similar approach, Dworkin argued that the function of judges was to secure the 'democratic conditions,' necessary for a democracy to exist. Key to this appreciation of judicial review, evidenced in the recent case record, is the right of all citizens in a democracy to be informed participants; thus imposing upon the state the responsibility to ensure that they are provided the opportunity to achieve what Dahl characterized as 'enlightened understanding.' This aggressive affirmation of the nexus between education and the fundamental rights of citizenry, dismissed in *Rodriquez* in a judicial treatment utilized subsequently in courts presented as restrained, has become an integral principle characteristic of an activist state judiciary in the realm of education finance").

Chapter 35

Affirmative Action

Jay Cummings, Bill Camp, Richard Fossey, & Doug Otto

Introduction

The concept of affirmative action programs as an acceptable instrument to advance the notion of voluntary preferences in education and employment has promoted a contentious debate in the United States. Affirmative action developed as a voluntary preference plan in hiring or selecting students in response to a statistical disparity in representation of people of specific races or genders or for past discrimination. Specifically, these policies and programs increased employment or educational opportunities for both under-represented groups as well as those who faced historic discrimination. Drawing heavily from the standards articulated in a variety of court decisions, affirmative action programs continue to polarize different factions. Prevailing standards of strict scrutiny, compelling state interest, and narrowly tailored plans serve as parameters for determining the constitutionality of affirmative action plans.

The constantly changing political landscape surrounding affirmative action continues to be based on court challenges and decisions which turn on typical legal interpretations of the Fifth and Fourteenth Amendments and Title VI or VII of the Civil Rights Act. Although affirmative action plans are often successful in combating discrimination in education and employment, they sometimes trigger resentment which occasionally leads to litigation. In determining whether affirmative action plans could pass constitutional muster, the courts have considered whether the plans could be justified based on a compelling governmental interest and whether the plans were narrowly tailored such that they could withstand strict scrutiny. The plans must be temporary in nature and terminate upon successful integration of workers or students.

Legal Issues

With the advent of the U.S. Supreme Court's recent rulings regarding race-conscious admissions policies in public schools of Louisville, Kentucky, and Seattle, Washington, the policy environment witnessed an ideological shift toward the conservative majority of Justices. What was a contentious policy environment has been enveloped by a shift in partisan policies, wherein five to four rulings are predicted to continue with the conservative judges in the majority and are now able to impact public policies that are linked directly to social justice practices. An example of this not-so-subtle reality change is *Grutter v. Bollinger,*[11] wherein the Supreme Court upheld the use of race in university admissions because the affirmative action plan for the law school met standards of compelling interest, narrow definition, and strict scrutiny. Then, only four years later, the Court struck down voluntary affirmative action programs in two public school systems.

Education

Public Schools (K-12)

The Supreme Court issued its long-awaited decision in *Parents Involved in Community Schools v. Seattle School District No. 1,*[22] which will surely stand as one of the Supreme Court's landmark decisions in the area of school desegregation and affirmative action. In June of 2007, the Supreme Court rejected race-based student assignment plans in schools not legally required to remedy past segregation. In a five to four decision, the Court struck down student assignment plans in two school districts—Seattle, Washington, and Jefferson County, Kentucky. Reversing rulings by the Sixth and Ninth Circuits, the Court ruled that both plans violated the Equal Protection Clause of the Fourteenth Amendment. Chief Justice Roberts wrote the plurality opinion, in which Justices Alito, Scalia, and Thomas joined in full, while Justice Kennedy joined only in part.

The Court addressed a crucial issue for public school districts in this seminal decision—whether a district can operate race-based student assignment plans when it is not under a legal obligation to remedy past segregation. The Seattle schools had never operated legally segregated schools and had never been subject to court-ordered desegregation. The Jefferson County school system had once been subject to a federal desegregation order, but the district had been declared unitary in 2000; thus, it too had no legal obligation to take race into account in assigning students to schools.

Under established Equal Protection Clause jurisprudence, the Court said, the school districts had not shown a compelling governmental interest that would justify race-based decision making in the cases before it. The Court identified only two reasons that could justify the extreme measure of assigning students to schools based on race—a form of racial discrimination. First, such a course of action might be justified as a means of remedying past segregation of students. Second, an interest in student diversity might justify racial discrimination in some instances—at least at the college and university level. However, according to the Court, neither justification was applicable to the student assignment plans that had been challenged in Seattle and Jefferson County.

In striking down the two plans, the Court distinguished the school districts' race-conscious student assignment plans from the University of Michigan's law school admissions plan, which the Supreme Court had approved in *Grutter v. Bollinger.*[33] In the *Grutter case*, the University of Michigan had taken race into account as one factor among many in achieving the goal of student diversity. In contrast, for both Seattle and Jefferson County, race, when it came into play in student assignment plans, was "decisive by itself."

The Court noted that the parties to the Seattle and Jefferson County cases disputed whether racial diversity had a positive impact on test scores or provided other social benefits. But this was a debate that the Court need not resolve, Justice Roberts wrote, because the racial classifications used by both school districts were not "narrowly tailored" to achieve their educational and social goals. "In design and operation, the plans are directed only to racial balance, pure and simple, an objective this Court has repeatedly condemned as illegitimate."[44]

In addition, the Court expressed skepticism about the purported goals that would be met by the school district's race-conscious student assignment plans. The Court pointed out that neither district had considered alternatives before resorting to "explicit racial classifications to achieve their stated goals," and both plans would have only a minimal impact on the racial makeup of schools, which "casts doubt on the necessity of using racial classifications."[55]

Finally, Chief Justice Roberts's plurality ruling devoted a considerable part of the opinion to criticizing the dissenting Justices' views. The plurality opinion made clear that it believed its views were more in harmony with *Brown v. Board of Education*[66] than the ones expressed by the dissent. *Brown*, the plurality opinion pointed out, prohibited assigning students to schools on the basis of race. "What do the racial classifications do in these cases, if not determine admission to a public school on a racial basis?"[77]

Justice Kennedy's concurring opinion differed from Chief Justice Roberts's opinion in that Justice Kennedy recognized that diversity could be a compelling interest that would justify race-based decision-making by school leaders in some circumstances. Justice Kennedy also wrote that schools should be free to devise race-conscious measures to address the racial composition of student bodies "in a general way and without treating each student in a different fashion solely on the basis of a systematic, individual typing by race."[88]

In particular, Justice Kennedy said that schools can address racial composition of student bodies by "strategic site selection of new schools; drawing attendance zones with general recognition of the demographics of neighborhoods; allocating resources for special programs; recruiting students and faculty in a targeted fashion; and tracking enrollments, performance, and other statistics by race."[99] Justice Thomas filed a concurring opinion, affirming his belief in a "color-blind interpretation of the Constitution" and chided the dissenters for indulging in reasoning that would give "school boards a free hand to make decisions on the basis of race, an approach reminiscent of that advocated by the segregationists in *Brown*."[10]

Justice Breyer wrote a lengthy dissent, which was joined by Justices Stevens, Souter, and Ginsburg. Drawing on historical events and statistics, Breyer articulated his belief that the Seattle and Jefferson County school assignment plans satisfied the strict scrutiny test for constitutionality under the Equal Protection Clause. In a separate dissenting opinion, Justice Stevens decried what he considered to be the plurality's departure from *Brown*. "It is my firm conviction," Justice Stevens concluded, "that no Member of the Court that I joined in 1975 would have agreed with today's decision."[11]

In a 2007 decision, the United States District Court for the District of Arizona reviewed the request of unitary status for Tucson Unified School District and required defendants to file a comprehensive report to show that any vestiges of *de jure* segregation related to student assignments had been eliminated.[12] The court found Tucson's student assignment transfer policy to be race-based and violated equal protection. The court stated that Policy 5090 was unconstitutional based on recent rulings in Seattle. In this case, the court determined that the policy was unconstitutional unless it was required to remedy intentional discrimination. The district states it has a new policy to replace Policy 5090 that would allow students to take greater advantage of student choice.

The principles of an admissions policy that was narrowly tailored and addressed a compelling state interest were illustrated by the Ninth Circuit in *Hunter Ex. Rel. Brandt v. Regents of University of California*, where a university elementary school was operated as a research laboratory by UCLA's Graduate School of Education and Information Studies.[13] The *Hunter* case was one of a only a few K-12 decisions that were decided before the *Grutter v. Bollinger* or *Gratz v. Bollinger* decisions. In this case, the older daughter of the Hunter family was admitted to the elementary school through the admissions policy. In 1995, a year after the older daughter graduated, the Hunters attempted to enroll their younger daughter. When she was not selected to be admitted, the parents sued the Regents of the University of California under Title VI of the Civil Rights Act of 1964, challenging the constitutionality of the admissions process. The federal trial court entered judgment for the defendants, and the parents appealed. On appeal, the Ninth Circuit held that the state's interest in operating a research-oriented elementary school dedicated to improving the quality of education in urban public schools was a compelling state interest, and the use of race and ethnicity as a factor in admissions met the state's interest in providing effective education. The educational purpose of the university elementary school was one of the few examples of a narrowly tailored plan that satisfied the Equal Protection Clause of the Fourteenth Amendment with a compelling state interest in remedying past discrimination and improving the quality of public urban education. It is important to note for this case, as well as for some of the subsequent cases that are discussed in this chapter, that this decision was decided before the Michigan affirmative action decisions or the recent K-12 student assignment Supreme Court decisions.

Earlier concerns with student assignment plans containing race as a factor were debated in previous appellate court cases. These events resulted in other factors gaining importance in the policy environment where the Equal Protection Clause was regarded as a guarantee for all citizens and not just the protected groups under affirmative action demands. In *Wessman v. Gittens*, the First Circuit held that the admissions policy of the Boston Latin School violated the equal protection rights of Sarah Wessman, a white applicant who was not admitted.[14] Fifty percent of the available openings for the school's entering class was determined by composite score rank. The remaining fifty percent of admissions was determined on the basis of a formula that included race as a factor. From 1974 until 1987, the Boston Public Schools were under federal desegregation court orders. In 1987, the First Circuit held that student assignment had eliminated segregation. The admission policy, which was designed originally to foster diversity in the student population at the Boston Latin School, resulted in the district court ruling that student diversity was no longer a compelling government interest that justified a race-based admissions policy. The First Circuit reversed the judgment of the district court, ruling that Sarah Wessman was entitled to be admitted to the Boston Latin School. Since the Boston Public Schools had gained unitary status from the federal court in 1987, the ability to use race as a compelling governmental interest had been eliminated as a compliance instrument to foster desegregation.

In *Boston's Children First v. City of Boston*, the plaintiffs challenged the constitutionality of the Boston Public Schools' student assignment plan, which was called the Controlled Student Assignment Plan.[15] In 1985, the First Circuit required the Boston School Committee to maintain specific racial percentages in the city's schools through student assignments. In 1987, the First Circuit vacated the orders addressing the student assignment process. However, a permanent injunction remained in place, enjoining the Boston School Committee from creating, promoting, or maintaining racial segregation in any school or facility in the Boston Public Schools. On March 10, 1999, John O'Toole, Jr.'s parents were informed that his six choices for kindergarten had been denied, and he would be placed on a waiting list with other unassigned students. On June 28, 1999, Boston's Children First joined the plaintiff in filing a complaint. The plaintiffs argued that the violation of equal protection rights under the Fourteenth Amendment constituted irreparable harm, and they sought a preliminary injunction of the policy. The district court held that the record was insufficient to predict whether the plaintiffs were likely to prevail on merits and hardship, and the motion was denied.[16] Approximately three weeks after the filing of the plaintiffs' complaint, the Boston School Committee voted 5-2 to change the student assignment plan by removing race as a factor starting in the 2000-01 school year.

In actions subsequent to the change in the student assignment plan, the school district adopted a plan that considered race as a factor in evaluating the transfer of students from neighborhood schools. Parents sued, stating the plan violated the state and federal constitutions. The federal trial court granted summary judgment to the district, stating the plan did not violate the Equal Protection Clause since the race-conscious element was narrowly tailored to achieve a compelling state interest and did not violate state provisions.[17] Another case from Massachusetts challenged a district transfer plan since the plan considered racial imbalance as a factor.[18] The federal trial court rejected the parents' claim for relief, stating that the parents did not demonstrate irreparable injury as they were satisfied with the current placement of their children.

In 1999, the Fourth Circuit ruled that the use of a weighted lottery to create a diverse student population violated the Equal Protection Clause. In *Tuttle v. Arlington County School Board,* the district weighted the selection of students to enter the Arlington Traditional School to match the district population, allowing minority groups an increased chance of selection.[19] The policy was not developed to remedy past discrimination, but the court deferred stating diversity could be a compelling interest. The court then found that the policy did not have a stated ending date, favored minority applicants, and burdened other groups. The policy was found unconstitutional since it was not narrowly tailored.

The tenor of the times, from the years of Supreme Court Justice Warren to the years of Supreme Court Justice Roberts, blurred what was once clearly visible, as the courts shifted from embracing judicial activism in support of affirmative action remedies to a stronger adherence to conservative ideology in their interpretations. The best admissions policies utilized factors that were race neutral, contained multiple criteria, and were narrowly tailored. In the rulings, the admirable intent of creating a student population rich in diversity was rejected equally on the rationale that it could result in racial discrimination, thereby not meeting the standard of a compelling governmental interest, as well as violating the Equal Protection Clause of the Fourteenth Amendment.

Higher Education

Higher education strategies presented a less confrontational approach, heralding the potential results of dismantling the disparate effect of past discriminatory practices in admissions as a worthy strategy supporting a compelling state interest. Although the Supreme Court in the *Regents of the University of California v. Bakke* decision ruled the special admissions program at the University of California at Davis Medical School to be unconstitutional, a legal perspective by Justice Lewis F. Powell was transformed into an affirmative action doctrine when the goal of achieving a diverse student body in a state school was compelling enough to justify the permissible use of racial classifications as one factor in an admissions policy.[20] Thus, the *Bakke* decision addressed two critical components. Initially, the medical school's admissions program was ruled unconstitutional as it failed to withstand strict scrutiny because race was the sole criteria. Secondly, the Court determined that race, as one factor in decision-making, could be constitutionally considered in college admission decisions. In the discussion, Harvard and Princeton's admission policies were cited as examples of legal affirmative action plans because they used race as a "plus" factor instead of the only factor in admitting students.

The Sixth Circuit upheld a race-sensitive admissions policy at the University of Michigan Law School.[21] The faculty had developed a policy that admitted not only the most capable applicants, but also sought to admit a diverse student body with varied experiences and backgrounds. The policy included a commitment to ethnic and racial diversity and specified inclusion of students from groups who had experienced discrimination historically. The law school expressed a goal of admitting a "critical mass" of racial and ethnic minorities including, but not limited to, African Americans, Native Americans, and Hispanics. "Critical mass" was defined as a level that minority students would not feel isolated or view themselves as token representatives. In 2003, the Supreme Court in *Grutter v. Bollinger* upheld this affirmative action program at the University of Michigan Law School.[22] The Court determined that the law school's program was sufficiently flexible, used race as a plus, imposed no quotas, reserved no places, considered individual applicants, and was sufficiently narrowly tailored. Justice Sandra Day O'Conner wrote for the Court that "the program is flexible enough to ensure that each applicant is evaluated as an individual and not in a way that makes race or ethnicity the defining feature of the application."[23]

However, the Supreme Court struck down the undergraduate affirmative action program at the University of Michigan in *Gratz v. Bollinger*.[24] Under the program, applicants were awarded specified points toward admission. Points could be given based on high school grade point average, standardized test scores, personal essay, rank of high school attended, legacy, and other categories. For example, an applicant from an under-represented minority group was automatically awarded twenty points toward admission. Other applicants were awarded twenty points for athletic ability, low-income status, or attendance at a socioeconomically disadvantaged high school. Applicants were also awarded ten points for state residency in Michigan, five points for artistic skills, five points for leadership and community involvement, and more. The Court's majority objected to the automatic distribution of twenty points to every applicant from an under-represented minority group, indicating that the practice had the impact of making the factor of race a decisive one. The fundamental distinction appeared to have been that the use of numbers, rather than a system of individualized consideration, was so rigid that it violated the Equal Protection Clause of the Fourteenth Amendment to the U.S. Constitution.

Following the ruling in the *Grutter* case permitting the use of race in law school admissions, the Michigan Civil Rights Initiative took form as a vehicle to pass a state referendum to overturn what had been gained through the Supreme Court's decision.[25] Michigan voters voted to eliminate affirmative action by 58 percent to 42 percent margin in November of 2006. This action essentially eliminated race-conscious affirmative action in Michigan. The Sixth Circuit granted a stay pending an appeal of a district court's preliminary injunction.[26] The court stated that there was little chance of invalidating Proposal 2 on federal grounds.

On the heels of the recent decisions in Louisville and Seattle court cases, the Washington-based Project on Fair Representation is suing the University of Texas over the second-tier portion of its school admissions process, which considers many factors beyond class rank including race. This continues the spirited opposition to race-conscious school admission plans and suggests strongly that the policy environment has shifted toward anti-affirmative action positions.

Employment

Race-Based Issues

In *United Steelworkers of America v. Weber*, the Supreme Court determined that Title VII did not prohibit all affirmative action plans.[27] These voluntary plans must be carefully scrutinized, justified by a compelling governmental interest, and developed to overcome historic patterns of discrimination. In *Weber*, a white male worker was denied a promotion and filed suit. The Supreme Court determined the private, voluntary affirmative action plan was permissible since white workers were not discharged, the plan did not bar future promotions to white workers, and it was a temporary plan remedying a pre-existing racial imbalance. The principles currently associated with judging the constitutionality of affirmative action programs emanated from this case and embraced the following: the program must be justified by a compelling government interest, tailored narrowly to overcome historic patterns of discrimination, and developed to withstand careful scrutiny.

A United States federal court granted summary judgment to the Department of Defense and the Department of the Air Force when a contractor challenged the 2006 reauthorization of Section 1207 of the National Defense Authorization Act of 1987.[28] Section 1207 provides a "goal" that 5 percent of defense contracts be awarded to businesses that are small or controlled by socially and economically disadvantaged individuals. The court determined that Congress had a compelling interest in the reauthorization of this federal affirmative action program, and the program met the requirements of strict scrutiny by being narrowly tailored.

These principles were used as a foundation for the court decision in *Adarand v. Pena*, when the Supreme Court repealed race-based preferences in state contracts finding race-based governmental action was suspect.[29] Race-based decision making could be used only to address the lingering effects of discrimination. The Court held that all governmental levels that imposed racial classifications must be reviewed under strict scrutiny. In this case, Adarand Constructors, Inc. sued the Federal Department of Transportation after its lowest bid was rejected, and a minority-owned company was awarded the construction contract. When the Court applied the strict scrutiny review principle, the federal practice was ruled unconstitutional because it did not serve a compelling governmental interest, nor was it narrowly tailored.

Government set-asides for minority business enterprises were struck down in *Richmond v. J.A. Crosson Co.*[30] The Supreme Court invalidated a city ordinance designed to increase minority-owned businesses by requiring general contractors to reserve and award 30 percent of their city contracts to minority-owned businesses as sub-contractors. The Court determined this affirmative action plan was remedial since no evidence of past discrimination was found. The Court determined that the plan was not narrowly tailored, as the policy had no logical stopping point. The Court used the strict scrutiny analysis to conclude that the standards for being narrowly tailored and meeting a compelling state interest had not been met. In *United States v. Paradise*, the Court specified four factors necessary for an affirmative action policy to be considered narrowly tailored.[31] This evaluative test considered the necessity, flexibility, and duration of the proposed relief; the potential effectiveness of alternative remedies; the goals and their relationship to the relevant market; and the impact of the relief of those impacted by the policy.

The evaluative test became more interpretively useful in *Wygant v. Jackson Board of Education*, when the United States Supreme Court determined that a layoff plan favoring minority teachers with less seniority than nonminority teachers was too intrusive and drastic to survive a challenge under the Equal Protection Clause.[32] The Court struck down a role model theory where the district stated that these minority teachers served as important role models for minority students. The Court ruled that the decision must be justified by a "compelling government interest" and the program or policy must be "narrowly tailored to achieve that goal."[33] Specifically, the Court reasoned that clear and convincing evidence must be demonstrated that the district had engaged in past racial discrimination to support such a layoff plan. However, the Court did state that hiring goals favorable to minority teachers could be acceptable because the "denial of future employment opportunity was not as intrusive as loss of an existing job."[34]

In *Taxman v. Board of Education of the Township of Piscataway*, the court reviewed a challenge under Title VII of the Civil Rights Act and again stated that affirmative action plans were permissible under Title VII as long as they did not infringe on the rights of nonminority teachers.[35] The Third Circuit held that the school board violated Title VII by laying off an equally qualified white teacher while retaining a black teacher. The board retained the black teacher to preserve racial diversity on the faculty. Since the decision was based on race and was not remedial, the Third Circuit ruled the decision was not justified. In this case, the district had implemented an affirmative action plan that did not demonstrate a remedial purpose, nor were minority teachers under-represented in the district's faculty. The court ruled that the district's affirmative action plan to create a more racially diverse educational environment violated Title VII since the purpose was to promote diversity, and not to eliminate discrimination. The case was then settled out of court, leaving the Third Circuit decision intact, and again demonstrating that courts viewed the layoff of individuals as an intrusive step that required a compelling reason.

In a Tenth Circuit case, the court stated that strict scrutiny must be used for review of racial preference programs and intermediate scrutiny for gender preference programs.[36] In this case, Denver used a set-aside program in public contracting to remedy racial discrimination in the Denver construction industry. The program defined participation goals for racial minorities and women for certain city projects. The court determined that the city had a compelling interest in offering the affirmative action programs and that the programs were narrowly tailored. The Supreme Court denied a *writ of certiorari*, but Justice Scalia dissented, stating the decision was based on evidence of racial discrimination that patently did not measure up to the standards set forth in *Croson*.[37]

In a Ninth Circuit case, university faculty sued Northern Arizona University and the university president, asserting equal protection violations and Title VII claims.[38] The university president granted pay adjustments to minority faculty under a federally approved affirmative action plan. The plan was based on a flawed regression analysis and did not allow nonminority faculty to compete for the adjustments. The Ninth Circuit determined that the equity pay adjustments did not trammel the rights of the university's white male professors since they retained their current salaries and were eligible for future promotions. The court remanded the case to determine if the adjustments were more than remedial. On remand, the court reasoned that it was remedial only if it eliminated a manifest race- or gender-based pay imbalance.

A military class action claimed a violation of the Equal Protection Clause of the Fifth Amendment when instructions for involuntary termination of officers provided different treatment for officers based on their race and gender.[39] The United States Court of Federal Claims used a rational basis analysis stating the Air Force Secretary's Memorandum of Instruction (MOI) had not used a racial or gender-based classification. The court ruled for the government, reasoning that an intermediate level of review was required. The appellate court determined that strict scrutiny was the appropriate level of review since the MOI included a racial and gender-based classification, and the court reversed the grant of summary judgment and remanded the case.[40] The United States Court of Federal Claims approved a settlement agreement in 2004.[41]

Gender-Based Issues

Gender classifications, while "suspect," have typically been reviewed with intermediate scrutiny, which has allowed many of these plans to survive.[42] In *Johnson v. Transportation Agency, Santa Clara County*, the Court reviewed an example in which a female was promoted over a more highly qualified male.[43] The Court upheld the affirmative action plan and promotion due to a "manifest imbalance" demonstrating under-representation of women in the job category. The Court noted that gender was only one basis for the hiring decision. In *Pivirrotto v. Innovative Systems, Inc.*, a female director was fired and a male employee assumed her duties.[44] She claimed she was fired because she was a woman. Though the Court determined the company had a legitimate business reason for the action, the case illustrated that a plaintiff did not have to demonstrate that she was replaced with someone outside the protected class to show a *prima facie* case of discrimination. In this case, the Court examined whether the person has been treated less favorably than similarly situated employees due to race or gender.

A decision in *Desert Palace, Inc. v. Costa* revealed how the court's actions had been modified over time when considering mixed-motive cases.[45] The only woman in a work unit covered by a collective bargaining agreement was involved in a physical altercation with a male coworker. The employer fired the woman but only suspended the male for five days. The female filed a grievance, and an arbitrator determined that the employer had just cause to fire her. The employee sued the former employer, claiming gender discrimination under Title VII. At trial, a jury found in her favor and awarded back pay and compensatory and punitive damages. The employer appealed the jury's finding, and the court of appeals ruled that the employee could establish a mixed-motive case. The two necessary steps for a mixed-motive case were met when proof that an impermissible motive played a motivating part in an adverse employment decision, and the employer did not demonstrate that the same decision would have been made if the impermissible motive had not influenced the decision. Amendments to Title VII, which included a provision stating that "an unlawful employment practice is established when the complaining party demonstrates that race, color, religion, sex, or national origin was a motivating factor for any employment practice, even though other factors also motivated the practice," served as the rationale for the Supreme Court's ruling in agreement with the appellate court.[46]

Recommendations for Practice

Close examination of the policy environment surrounding the concept of affirmative action relating to education and employment show that many affirmative action disputes are unlikely to be settled without court intervention. Competing forces vie for either more expedient race-based remedies or more conservative, status-quo positions. These differences are difficult to accommodate in the policy environment. Differences in employment and admissions standards are affected by past discrimination and racially biased practices. Remedies, to be judicially successful, must be narrowly tailored in promoting compelling state interests. The prevailing standard of strict scrutiny, compelling state interest, and narrowly tailored plans continues to serve as a parameter for determining the constitutionality of affirmative action plans. When considering race-conscious programs:

1. The plans should be temporary in nature and terminate upon successful integration of workers or students.
2. A layoff plan favoring minority employees with less seniority than nonminority employees may be too intrusive and drastic to survive a legal challenge. Hiring goals favorable to minority employees may be acceptable where past discrimination has not been remedied since denial of future employment opportunity is not as intrusive as the loss of an existing job.
3. Districts under court orders to desegregate have more latitude to use race in student assignments than districts not operating under federal court desegregation orders. If the purpose of a school's admissions process is narrowly tailored to serve the compelling interest of improving the quality of education and remedying past discrimination, the use of race or ethnicity can be a factor.
4. Admissions policies built on a race-neutral basis and multiple criteria can be applied fairly and equitably, thereby constituting a proven policy development direction. In developing race-neutral criteria for public state university admissions policies, the use of multiple criteria such as class rank or social economic status, instead of race, could prove legally permissible.
5. School administrators need to immediately review and update admissions and student-assignment plans designed to remedy past discrimination in school districts no longer under desegregation court orders.

Endnotes

1. 539 U.S. 306 (2003).
2. 127 S. Ct. 2738 (2007).
3. 539 U.S. 306 (2003).
4. Parents Involved in Cmty. Schs., 127 S. Ct. at 2755.
5. *Id.* at 2760.
6. 347 U.S. 483 (1954).
7. Parents Involved in Cmty. Schs., 127 S. Ct. at 2768.
8. *Id.* at 2792.
9. *Id.*
10. *Id.* at 2768.
11. *Id.* at 2800.
12. Fisher v. United States, 2007 U.S. Dist. LEXIS 61679 (D. Ariz. Aug. 21, 2007).
13. 190 F.3d 1061 (9th Cir. 1999), *cert. denied*, 2000 U.S. LEXIS 5928 (2000).
14. 160 F.3d 790 (1st Cir. 1998).
15. 62 F. Supp. 2d 247 (D. Mass. 1999).
16. *In re* Boston's Children First, 244 F.3d 164 (1st Cir. 2001).
17. Boston's Children First v. Boston Sch. Comm., 260 F. Supp. 2d 318 (D. Mass. 2003).

18. Comfort v. Lynn Sch. Comm., 100 F. Supp. 2d 57 (D. Mass. 2000).
19. 189 F.3d 431 (4th Cir. 1999).
20. 438 U.S. 265 (1978).
21. Grutter v. Bollinger, 288 F.3d 732 (6th Cir 2002), *aff'd*, 539 U.S. 306 (2003), *rehearing denied*, 2003 LEXIS 5357 (U.S., 2003).
22. Grutter v. Bollinger, 539 U.S. 306 (2003).
23. *Id.* at 311.
24. 539 U.S. 244 (2003), *on remand*, 2003 U.S. App. LEXIS 22468 (6th Cir. Mich., Oct. 29, 2003).
25. Proposal 2 amending Michigan Constitution, article I, § 26.
26. Coalition to Defend Affirmative Action v. Granholm, 473 F.3d 237 (6th Cir. 2006).
27. 443 U.S. 193 (1979).
28. Rothe Dev. Corp. v. DOD, 499 F. Supp. 2d 775 (W.D. Tex. 2007).
29. 515 U.S. 200 (1995).
30. 488 U.S. 469 (1989).
31. 480 U.S. 149 (1987).
32. 476 U.S. 267 (1986).
33. *Id.* at 274.
34. *Id.* at 283.
35. 91 F.3d 1547 (3d Cir. 1996), *cert. granted*, 521 U.S. 1117 (1997), *cert. dismissed*, 522 U.S. 1010 (1997).
36. Concrete Works of Colo., Inc. v. City and County of Denver, 321 F.3d 950 (10th Cir. 2003), *cert. denied*, 124 S. Ct. 556 (2003).
37. Concrete Works of Colo., Inc. v. City and County of Denver, 124 S. Ct. 556 (2003).
38. Rudebusch v. Hughes, 313 F.3d 506 (9th Cir. 2002).
39. Berkley v. United States, 48 Fed. Cl. 361 (2000).
40. Berkley v. United States, 287 F.3d 1076 (Fed. Cir 2002).
41. Berkley v. United States, 2004 U.S. Claims LEXIS 32.
42. Califano v. Webster, 430 U.S. 313 (1977).
43. 480 U.S. 616 (1987).
44. 191 F.3d 344 (3d Cir. 1999).
45. 539 U.S. 90 (2003).
46. 42 U.S.C. § 2000e-2(m).

Chapter 36

School Desegregation during an Era of Judicial Disengagement

Charles J. Russo

Introduction

The United States Supreme Court decided its most important education case, perhaps its most significant ruling, on May 17, 1954. In a unanimous opinion in *Brown v. Board of Education of Topeka, Kansas* (*Brown I*),[1] the Court held that the de jure segregation of public schools based on race deprived minority children of equal educational opportunities in violation of the Equal Protection Clause of the Fourteenth Amendment. A year later, in *Brown v. Board of Education of Topeka, Kansas* (*Brown II*),[2] the Court set about dismantling segregated school systems. Later cases attacked de facto and de jure segregation in schools as well as the wider arena of American society. Even so, *Brown I* remains the unchallenged catalyst for judicially initiated systemic change. Beginning with school desegregation and culminating in the Civil Rights Movement, *Brown* spawned an era of equal educational opportunities by heightening consciousness for protecting the rights of other disenfranchised groups, most notably women and students with disabilities.[3]

In the initial quarter of a century after *Brown*, the Supreme Court resolved more than thirty cases involving desegregation of public school systems alone.[4] Yet, since then, the Court has consciously adopted a diminished role in ensuring educational equity, resolving only six cases. The Court's lack of involvement in desegregation efforts has undoubtedly contributed to the fact that many school boards act as if *Brown* never occurred. One can only hope that the Court will remain true to the spirit of this landmark case and its progeny by returning to take a more active approach in safeguarding equal educational opportunities for all students.

The first, and larger, part of this chapter reviews litigation in the federal courts dealing with school desegregation. This initial section reviews Supreme Court cases from the 1990s and then examines lower federal court cases, focusing on disputes over whether formerly segregated school systems achieved unitary status. The latter part of the chapter highlights cases on unitary status because only by creating school systems that function by serving all children, without regard to segregation by race, can educators create the necessary pre-conditions for academic success.

After reflecting on the status of school desegregation, the chapter concludes that although the Supreme Court and lower federal courts have contributed a great deal toward the dismantling of segregated school systems in the first twenty-five years after *Brown*, their actions in the following years have resulted in the Court taking one step forward and half a step backward. Indeed, the very conditions that *Brown* sought to eliminate appear to be returning in many public school systems today.

Litigation Involving School Desegregation

Supreme Court Cases

Background

After a busy twenty-year period during which it resolved more than two dozen cases on school desegregation, the first twenty-two of which resulted in unanimous rulings in favor of proponents of equal educational opportunities, the Supreme Court's attitude underwent a dramatic shift beginning in the mid-1970s. The Court's judgment in *Milliken v. Bradley (Milliken I)*[5] (1974), a case from Detroit, Michigan, dealing with interdistrict remedies, evidenced two major changes in its perspective. First, *Milliken I* was the first major defeat for supporters of school desegregation since *Brown I*, as the Court concluded that an interdistrict remedy was constitutionally impermissible absent proof that the state or the surrounding school systems were involved in discriminatory acts. Second, although it was not readily apparent at the time, *Milliken I* was a harbinger of the Court's growing disinterest and disengagement in disputes involving school desegregation.

Milliken I involved a federal trial court's order calling for a multidistrict, area wide desegregation remedy, which would have required fifty-three suburban school systems to take part in the process of desegregating schools in Detroit. The trial court found that since Detroit's schools were already segregated, and proposed remedies would have exacerbated the situation, it had no choice but to look beyond district boundaries in attempting to solve the problem. A closely divided Supreme Court reversed the decision in declaring the interdistrict remedy inappropriate. The Court contended that, absent evidence that the schools were segregated or that district boundaries were created in order to promote segregation, the suburban boards were not accountable, especially since they did not even have a chance to present their case or to participate in creating the proposed remedy.

On remand in *Milliken I*, the federal trial court called for a remedy that created a pupil assignment plan and remedial plans for the Detroit schools while directing the state to share funds equally in the cost of these programs. On further review in *Milliken v. Bradley II* (*Milliken II*),[6] the Supreme Court affirmed that the remedy was appropriate since the trial court based its judgment on substantial evidence aimed at eradicating the vestiges of de jure segregation. Affording a measure of vindication for supporters of school desegregation, the Court reasoned that the trial court acted within its jurisdiction in calling for prospective relief and requiring the state to share fiscal responsibility for implementing the remedy.

Including one case it resolved during the same term that it decided *Milliken II*,[7] the Supreme Court only addressed two additional disputes, from Dayton[8] and Columbus,[9] Ohio, on school desegregation during the remainder of the 1970s. Further, the Court examined a scant two cases on the issue in the 1980s, both decided on the same day, in what remains its least active decade since it took on desegregation in *Brown I*. Clearly, the Court indicated that its interest in school desegregation was waning and it had become a backburner issue at best. In the 1982 *Washington v. Seattle School District* case,[10] the Court struck down a state-approved voter initiative from Washington calling for busing that would have permitted school boards to assign students to schools that may not have been closest to their homes. In *Crawford v. Board of Education of the City of Los Angeles*,[11] the Court upheld an amendment to the California constitution that prohibited state courts from mandating pupil assignments or busing unless a federal court ordered such a remedy for a violation of equal protection.

The 1990s: Half A Step Backward

The 1990s opened on a promising note from the point of view of proponents of school desegregation when the Court agreed to review the long-running case from the Kansas City, Missouri, School District. In *Missouri v. Jenkins (Jenkins I)*,[12] a divided Supreme Court surprised many in upholding the authority of a federal trial court judge to increase taxes to pay for desegregating Kansas City's public schools. However, the ray of hope was short-lived, as the Court's decisions were significantly less favorable to desegregation efforts in the other three cases that it would address in the remainder of the decade: *Board of Education of the Oklahoma City Public Schools v. Dowell*,[13] *Freeman v. Pitts*,[14] and *Missouri v. Jenkins (Jenkins II)*.[15]

After an eight-year layoff in this area, the Supreme Court agreed to hear a case involving school desegregation. The first of the four cases that the Court resolved in the 1990s, *Jenkins I*, was more concerned with the authority of the federal judiciary to impose a tax increase to fund a remedy in a formerly dual system than it was with the substantive aspects of school desegregation.

As part of a thirteen-year court struggle, lower courts agreed that the state of Missouri and the Kansas City Public School District maintained a segregated school system. Yet, since the state constitution placed a cap on property tax increases, the lower federal court imposed a tax increase to pay for implementing a desegregation order. In *Jenkins*, a divided Supreme Court surprised many observers in upholding the authority of federal judges to increase taxes to pay for the cost of desegregating the public schools in Kansas City. The Court essentially reasoned that since the other branches of government refused to act, the judiciary had no choice but to enforce the constitutional mandate of ensuring equal educational opportunities for students, even if it meant ordering an increase in property taxes used to fund public schools.

The next two cases in the 1990s examined substantive issues in school desegregation. *Board of Education of the Oklahoma City Public Schools v. Dowell* (*Dowell*),[16] the last desegregation case in which Justice Thurgood Marshall participated, addressed the appropriate standards for determining whether a formerly segregated school system had achieved unitary status. In reversing and remanding the Tenth Circuit's judgment for further consideration, by a five to three decision with Justice Souter not participating, the Court dissolved the desegregation order that had been in place since 1972.

In *Dowell*, the Supreme Court pointed out that since desegregation orders "are not intended to operate in perpetuity,"[17] federal trial courts can terminate such decrees if school board officials satisfied a three-part test. According to the Court, school boards can be released from judicial oversight if officials prove that they complied in good faith with the desegregation decree since it was entered, eliminated the vestiges of past discrimination, and exhibited a commitment to future desegregation efforts coupled with the promise not to return to their former ways.[18] Once school boards prove that they meet these three conditions, the Court can declare that the school district has achieved unitary status and that it no longer operates dual or segregated school systems. The Court added that in making such a finding, a judge should not view a board's adoption of a particular plan as a breach of good faith, even if it was technically flawed, as long as the plan was accepted in reliance on the express language of a judicial order decreeing that a system achieved unitary status.[19]

In the Supreme Court's consideration of whether the vestiges of segregation were eradicated, it continued to rely on the principles enunciated in *Green v. County School Board of New Kent County (Green).*[20] The six so-called *Green* factors that must be taken into account in determining whether a school system has achieved unitary status are the composition of the student body, faculty, and staff; transportation; extracurricular activities; and facilities. These principles have been applied in a plethora of school desegregation cases since *Green* in 1968. Consequently, since the Court was satisfied that the board achieved unitary status with regard to student assignments, transportation, physical facilities, and extracurricular activities, it agreed that the trial court properly returned control to the school board even though all six *Green* factors were not fulfilled. In an earlier iteration of this litigation, *Dowell v. Board of Education of the Oklahoma City Public Schools*,[21] the Court vacated the Tenth Circuit's reversal of a school board's proposal to further desegregate a school system by revising attendance boundaries.

In 1992, *Freeman v. Pitts* considered whether judicial supervision of a desegregation order can be terminated incrementally before achieving full compliance. After a federal trial court in Georgia relinquished control incrementally, the Eleventh Circuit reversed and reinstated the entire plan.

The Supreme Court, in turn, reversed the Eleventh Circuit's decision without any dissenting opinions. Justice Thomas did not participate in the case. The Court, also relying on the *Green* factors, ruled that a federal trial court has the authority to relinquish supervision and control over a school district in stages while retaining limited jurisdiction as long as it is satisfied that educational leaders made a good-faith commitment to comply with the dictates of its order, especially where demographic changes occurred that were beyond the ability of school officials to control.

In *Missouri v. Jenkins (Jenkins II),* the Supreme Court revisited the ongoing litigation in Kansas City. This time, in a five-to-four opinion spearheaded by the dissent in *Jenkins I,* the Court reversed an earlier judgment in favor of the plaintiffs, thereby signaling a further retrenchment in the struggle to end racially segregated schooling. In *Jenkins II,* the Justices found that a federal trial court exceeded its discretion in calling for a desegregation remedy that required the state to pay for both across-the-board salary increases and the quality education programs in Kansas City—at a total cost of more than $1.3 billion dollars—since student-achievement levels were still at or below national norms at many grade levels. *Jenkins II* is noteworthy because it is the last Supreme Court case on the issue of desegregation. As noted, this is the longest period the Court has gone without addressing the issue of desegregation it handed down in *Brown I,* clearly reiterating the message that it is simply not interested in this important arena any longer.

Lower Court Cases

After *Jenkins II,* lower federal courts continue to consider an array of issues arising in conjunction with desegregation plans and other racial classifications in America's elementary and secondary schools. Among the key issues that the courts have addressed are student admissions and transfers based on race, teacher assignments based on race, teacher rights, and attorney fees. However, as noted in the introduction to this chapter, the remainder of this section focuses on the issue of unitary status, since it is crucial to the development of schools where all children can learn under equitable conditions.

This part of the chapter also reviews two disputes that involve the related question of consolidation and deconsolidation in school systems that operate under desegregation orders. It is worth noting that the courts continue to address the so-called *Green* factors when evaluating whether judicially declared segregated school systems have achieved unitary status. This judicial activity has taken place largely in light of a recent report from the Civil Rights Division of the Office of the Assistant Attorney General of the United States, indicating that it continues to monitor approximately 308 school systems that continue to operate under desegregation orders nationwide.[22]

In a case from Mississippi that was consistent with *Dowell* and *Pitts,* the Eleventh Circuit affirmed that a school system achieved unitary status when the board proved that remaining racial imbalances were caused by uncontrollable demographic changes.[23] The court maintained that the district achieved unitary status since board officials acted in good faith to eliminate the vestiges of de jure segregation to the extent practicable through a good-faith commitment to and compliance with the desegregation plan. During the same year, a federal trial court in Florida court reached a like result in ending twenty-seven years of jurisdiction over a school district.[24] During the course of a desegregation plan, some school systems have attempted to carry out both consolidation and deconsolidation. Similarly, the Eighth Circuit, in a consolidation of two disputes from Arkansas, affirmed that since it was not clearly erroneous that districts achieved substantial compliance with their long-running desegregation orders, they were correctly released from judicial supervision.[25]

As illustrated by a case from Louisiana, a federal trial court denied a school board's request to divide into independent districts because the system was under a desegregation plan and had failed to achieve unitary status. The court pointed out that deconsolidation would have resulted in one district becoming slightly more black than white and the other new districts becoming overwhelmingly white. The court determined that the division would have harmed efforts to desegregate the existing school system.[26] The Fifth Circuit then vacated the trial court's judgment on the ground that the dispute was not ripe for review, commenting that there was no imminent threat of harm to the district or the desegregation decrees, only potential harm.[27] About a year later, the Fifth Circuit remanded the dispute to the trial court with the instructions that the new district select a board of trustees and conduct more hearings to allow the state and the new board the opportunity to show that the new district will not adversely impact the desegregation plan that was in place in the school system.[28]

In the first of two later cases from Louisiana to reach the Fifth Circuit, albeit in a dispute involving private rather than public education, the court refused to release the school from a thirty-year-old desegregation order.[29] Insofar as the court was not satisfied that officials at the school demonstrated a good-faith effort to eliminate the vestiges of past discrimination or make meaningful progress toward becoming fully integrated, it could not participate in a scholarship program to assist its students.

Where an association that was formed to encourage students to attend neighborhood schools sought to intervene in a forty-year-old lawsuit that sought to end de jure segregation, it appealed the denial of its application to do so. The Fifth Circuit affirmed that the association could not intervene as a matter of right because it was unable to demonstrate that it had a legally cognizable interest that would have been impeded or impaired in response to the school board's remediation consolidation plan for its schools.[30]

Earlier, in a similar action, a county board of education in Alabama obtained judicial approval to consolidate a school district that was under a desegregation order and to relocate students within the system after a fire destroyed one school and it was not economically feasible for the district to build another.[31] The court was of the opinion that the consolidation plan was acceptable since it neither perpetuated nor re-established a racially segregated district.

In a long-running suit from Texas, a federal trial court was satisfied that a school system achieved unitary status with regard to student assignments despite an increase in the number of single race and primarily minority schools since its initial desegregation decree in 1971.[32] The court stated that there were no other reasonable measures that the board could have taken to achieve racial balance, as officials implemented remedial measures such as redrawing attendance zones, implementing majority-to-minority transfer policies, creating magnet schools, allowing curriculum transfers, and developing an honors program. Even though the court declared the school system unitary, it retained jurisdiction over the case for three years. Three years later, the court maintained that a proposed system for teacher assignment satisfied the requirement that the school board achieve the maximum desegregation practicable in faculty assignment.[33] More recently, in noting that the board had already obtained a declaration of unitary status, a federal trial court granted its motion to be released from judicial supervision on the basis that it made sufficient progress in providing equal educational opportunities for students.[34]

A civil rights organization in Florida unsuccessfully challenged a declaration that a school district achieved unitary status. Relying largely on the *Green* factors and *Pitts*, the Eleventh Circuit affirmed that since the existence of identifiably black schools in the district was the result of white flight and voluntary residential isolation, and not a vestige of de jure segregation, the board was properly entitled to an order terminating judicial oversight.[35]

Parents in Louisiana unsuccessfully attempted to intervene in a long-standing desegregation case by questioning a school board's plan to adjust attendance zones to meet educational needs and academically restructure some schools. In dismissing the parents' motion, a federal trial court decided that they could neither intervene as a right nor by permissive intervention since the district had achieved unitary status eleven years earlier.[36]

In an almost forty-year-old school desegregation case from Alabama, a school board sought a declaration of unitary status and dismissal of litigation. A federal trial court granted the board's motions since it was content that officials fully and satisfactorily complied with its decrees and that officials eliminated vestiges of past discrimination to the extent practicable.[37]

Where a school board in Michigan, in another long-running case, entered a motion seeking unitary status, a federal trial court granted its request even though student achievement scores in the district remained slightly below the state average.[38] Relying largely on the *Green* factors and *Pitts*, the court was satisfied that since board officials complied in good faith with raising the level of minority student achievement, they did what they could to eliminate the vestiges of segregation and so were entitled to have their motion granted. At the same time, the court ordered state officials to continue to provide funding for transportation for students to attend other school systems and to reimburse the local board for state funding lost by student transfers during the phase-out period for the programs.

A federal trial court in Arkansas, in yet another ongoing school desegregation case, partially granted a school board's motion for unitary status.[39] The court was satisfied that school officials substantially and satisfactorily complied with its obligations in five of the six challenged areas of the school desegregation plan, namely good faith, student discipline, extracurricular activities, advanced placement courses, and guidance counseling. The court decided that the board was therefore entitled to a declaration of unitary status in those five challenged areas, releasing them from judicial oversight in these matters. However, because the court did not think that school officials substantially complied with their obligations to assess academic programs annually in order to evaluate the effectiveness of the academic programs in improving African American achievement, it retained supervision and monitoring over the board's compliance with this section of the plan.

When another school board in Arkansas sought a declaration of unitary status, the Eighth Circuit affirmed that it had only partially achieved its goal.[40] The court noted that insofar as the school board failed to comply with a provision in the consent decree that required it to conduct an annual assessment of its academic programs in order to evaluate whether they helped the achievement of minority students, it was not entitled to a full release from judicial oversight.

In a thirty-year-old case from Pennsylvania, a federal trial court granted a school board's motion that it achieved unitary status.[41] In language echoing *Dowell* and *Green*, the court agreed to end judicial oversight, in light of the good-faith efforts of school officials to comply with prior court orders and in recognition that they had made gains over the lengthy history of the case.

Another lower court case in one of the highest profile cases on unitary status reflects the trend set by the Supreme Court. *Belk v. Charlotte-Mecklenburg Board of Education* (*Belk*)[42] was a continuation of *Swann v. Charlotte-Mecklenburg Board of Education (Swann).*[43] The original case marked the entry of busing into the national debate on achieving unitary status, thrusting the question to center stage for the better part of a decade. *Swann* is also notable because it was simultaneously the first major desegregation claim reviewed on its merits by the Burger Court and the last unanimous ruling in a major desegregation case.

In *Swann's* latest iteration, an en banc panel of the Fourth Circuit, after vacating an earlier judgment from a federal trial court, affirmed that part of the opinion granting the board's motion to be released from judicial supervision was because it had achieved unitary status. In addition, the court dissolved an injunction that would have required the board to refrain from race-based lotteries and other mechanisms since it observed that nothing in the record suggested that school officials would have used race in an unconstitutional manner. Although the Supreme Court's refusal to hear an appeal is of no precedential value other than to the parties, the Court's response clearly shows that it no longer views school desegregation as a priority.[44]

A second case from North Carolina dealt with a plaintiff's request for attorney fees. A federal trial court, in rejecting the board's claim that it was in precarious financial condition, rejected its argument that this was a sufficient basis on which to excuse it from paying the fees.[45] At the same time, however, the court did reduce the amount of fees by 15 percent in light of the plaintiff's limited success.

Discussion

In the more than half-century that has passed since the Supreme Court struck down segregation based on race in public education in *Brown v. Board of Education*, school officials and the judiciary have made progress in eradicating educational inequities. Yet, a great amount of work remains to be done. Since the late 1970s, especially during the 1990s and beyond, the Supreme Court has not remained vigilant in the fight to ensure educational equity in segregated schools.

The Supreme Court's disengagement in school desegregation is evident in the fact that since *Missouri v. Jenkins II* in 1995, it has now gone longer than it has at any time in its history since *Brown* without addressing a desegregation case. Moreover, even though this author does not categorize the Court's recent decision in *Parents Involved for Community Schools v. Seattle School District* (PICS),[46] it clearly evidences an intent in this direction. This author chose not to identify PICS as a desegregation case because Seattle had never been under a desegregation order, and Louisville had been released from judicial oversight. Also, PICS is discussed in the affirmative action chapter of this book.

A full discussion of the extent to which this judicial inactivity has been caused by the change in the composition of the Court, political factors in Washington, a difference in societal attitudes, or a combination of these elements is beyond the scope of this analysis. Clearly, though, all of these elements have contributed to the present situation. Even so, the Court's less-than-enthusiastic role, coupled with the increasing number of lower federal court cases wherein formerly segregated school systems are being declared unitary, thereby relieving them of judicial oversight, is worthy of some discussion because it has opened the door to the troublesome emergence of racially resegregated schooling.

When reflecting on the Court's growing disengagement with regard to desegregation over the past thirty years or so, two seemingly divergent points of view emerge. On one hand, based on the need for constitutional separation of powers, an argument can be made that the courts should not be given the unfettered ability to usurp the authority of the other branches of government. To this end, once courts have issued desegregation decrees, state and local educational officials, including local school boards, should be free to resolve matters on their own without ongoing judicial oversight. On the other hand, when educational leaders and others refuse to act to provide equitable learning opportunities for all children, either by inertia or by design, it is imperative that the courts, as a matter of last resort, intervene. Although this author prefers judicial restraint, it is time for the Court to adopt more of an activist role in providing leadership to ensure educational equity for all students because the other branches of government have failed to do so.

As witnessed by the long, ugly history of segregation, it is essential that in the absence of initiatives undertaken by the legislative and/or executive branches, the federal courts (led by the Supreme Court) must act unequivocally to ensure compliance with constitutional dictates. This being said, and giving the Court the benefit of the doubt that it hoped—and trusted—that educational officials in segregated systems would comply in good faith with judicial orders, it is difficult to understand why, in light of the data on resegregation reflected in the Orfield studies[47] and other indicators, the Court has disengaged from the fight to ensure equal educational opportunities for all students.

Faced with what can, at best, be described as mixed judicial messages with regard to desegregation over the past quarter of a century, it should not be entirely surprising that state and local educational officials have failed to adopt proactive stances in implementing *Brown* and its progeny. Thus, it may be that many locations throughout the nation act as if *Brown* had never been decided because judicial indifference, beginning with the Supreme Court, has sent out the unmistakable signal that desegregation is no longer a priority among national goals and objectives.[48] Moreover, as clear evidence of ongoing disputes with regard to school segregation, the Department of Justice's Fiscal Year 2008 Performance Budget for its Civil Rights Division, reports that about 308 school systems continue to operate under desegregation orders nationwide.[49]

The continuing struggle to provide equitable schooling by desegregating public education is nowhere better reflected than in Orfield's ongoing study of the resegregation of urban American schools.[50] In a recent study, based on data from the 2001–02 school year, Orfield reported that in many locales, when court-ordered desegregation ended over the past decade, there was a dramatic increase in resegregation.[51] Even conceding that some conditions are beyond the ability of educators to control, such a turn of events belies the judiciary's apparently unspoken assumption that state and local educational officials will act in good faith to comply with court-ordered remedies, especially where educational inequities can be linked to insufficient funding. Among other key findings in this study are that there has been a significant slippage toward segregation in most states that were desegregated in 1991, that nearly one-fourth of students live in states with a majority of non-whites, and that the vast majority of heavily segregated minority schools are in areas of poverty, thereby exacerbating inequities in educational opportunities.

One can only hope that the Court remains true to the spirit of *Brown* and its progeny by working to guarantee equal educational opportunities for all students. Having taken a major step forward in *Brown I*, the Nation cannot allow the progress that was achieved to slip by returning to a time when many children suffered due to inequitable educational opportunities.

Endnotes

1 347 U.S. 483 (1954).

2 349 U.S. 294 (1955).

3 For a review of the first forty years of litigation, see Charles J. Russo, J. John Harris & Rosetta Sandidge. Brown v. Board of Education *at 40: A Legal History of Equal Educational Opportunities in American Public Education,* 63 The J. of Negro Educ. 297–309 (1994).

4 Following its seminal decisions in *Sweatt v. Painter*, 339 U.S. 629 (1950), and *McLaurin v. Oklahoma State Regents for Higher Education*, 339 U.S. 637 (1950), both of which helped to pave the way for *Brown,* the Court repudiated inter- and intra-institution segregation, respectively, in higher education, the Court turned its attention to elementary and secondary education beginning with *Brown I.*

5 Milliken v. Bradley, 418 U.S. 717 (1974).

6 Milliken v. Bradley, 433 U.S. 267 (1977).

7 Dayton Bd. of Educ. v. Brinkman, 433 U.S. 406 (1977).

8 Dayton Bd. of Educ. v. Brinkman, 443 U.S. 526 (1979).

9 Columbus Bd. of Educ. v. Penick, 443 U.S. 449 (1979).

10 458 U.S. 457 (1982).

11 Crawford v. Bd. of Educ. of L.A., 458 U.S. 527 (1982) (upholding an amendment to the California constitution that prohibited state courts from mandating pupil assignments or busing unless a federal court ordered such a remedy for a violation of equal protection).

12 Missouri v. Jenkins, 495 U.S. 33 (1990), *on subsequent appeal, sub nom.* Jenkins by Agyei v. State of Mo., 949 F.2d 1052 (8th Cir. 1991).

13 Board of Educ. of the Okla. City Pub. Sch. v. Dowell, 498 U.S. 237 (1991), on remand, 778 F. Supp. 1144 (W.D. Okla. 1991), *aff'd,* 8 F.3d 1501 (10th Cir. 1993).

14 Freeman v. Pitts, 503 U.S. 467 (1992), *on remand,* 979 F.2d 1472 (11th Cir. 1992), *on remand sub nom.* Mills v. Freeman, 942 F. Supp. 1449 (N.D. Ga. 1996), *appeal after remand,* 118 F.3d 727 (11th Cir. 1997).

15 Missouri v. Jenkins II, 515 U.S. 70 (1995), *appeal after remand,* 103 F.3d 731 (8th Cir. 1997), *reh'g and suggestion for reh'g en banc denied.*

16 Board of Educ. of the Okla. City Pub. Sch. v. Dowell, 498 U.S. 237 (1991), *on remand,* 778 F. Supp. 1144 (W.D. Okla. 1991), *aff'd,* 8 F.3d 1501 (10th Cir. 1993).

17 *Id.* at 248.

18 *See id.* at 261.

19 *See id.*

20 Green v. County Sch. Bd. of New Kent County, 391 U.S. 430 (1968).

21 Dowell v. Bd. of Educ. of the Okla. City Pub. Sch., 396 U.S. 269 (1969).

22 United States Department of Justice, FY 2008 Performance Budget, Civil Rights Division, Congressional Budget Submission http://www.usdoj.gov/jmd/2008justification/pdf/18_crt.pdf

23 Lockett v. Bd. of Educ. of Muscogee County Sch. Dist., 111 F.3d 839 (11th Cir. 1997), *reh'g en banc denied,* 121 F.3d 724 (11th Cir. 1997).

24 United States v. Bd. of Pub. Instruction of St. Lucie County, 977 F. Supp. 1202 (S.D. Fla. 1997).

25 Little Rock. Sch. Dist. v. Armstrong, 359 F.3d 957 (8th Cir. 2004).

26 Valley v. Rapides Parish Sch. Bd., 960 F. Supp. 96 (W.D. La. 1997), 145 F. 3d 329 (5th Cir. 1998), 173 F. 3d 944 (5th Cir. 1999).

27 *Id.*

28 *Id.*

[29] Moses v. Washington Parish Sch. Bd, 379 F.3d 319 (5th Cir. 2004).
[30] Graham v. Evangeline Parish Sch. Bd., 132 F. App'x 507 (5th Cir. 2005).
[31] Lee v. Geneva County Bd. of Educ., 892 F. Supp. 1387 (M.D. Ala. 1995).
[32] Tasby v. Woolery, 869 F. Supp. 454 (N.D. Tex. 1994).
[33] Tasby v. Gonzalez, 972 F. Supp. 1065 (N.D. Tex. 1997).
[34] Tasby v. Moses, 265 F. Supp. 2d 757 (N.D. Tex. 2003).
[35] N.A.A.C.P. v. Duval County Sch., 273 F.3d 960 (11th Cir. 2001), *reh'g denied en banc,* 31 F. App'x 943 (11th Cir. 2002).
[36] Jones v. Caddo Parrish Sch. Bd., 204 F.R.D. 97 (W.D. La. 2001).
[37] Lee v. Butler County Bd. of Educ., 183 F. Supp. 2d 1359 (M.D. Ala. 2002).
[38] Berry v. Sch. Dist., 195 F. Supp. 2d 971 (W.D. Mich. 2002), *clarified,* 206 F. Supp. 2d 899 (W.D. Mich. 2002).
[39] Little Rock Sch. Dist. v. Pulaski County Spec. Sch. Dist. No. 1, 237 F. Supp. 2d 988 (E.D. Ark. 2002).
[40] Little Rock Sch. Dist. v. N. Little Rock Sch. Dist., 451 F.3d 528 (8th Cir. 2006).
[41] Hoots v. Commonwealth, 272 F. Supp. 2d 539 (W.D. Pa. 2003).
[42] Belk v. Charlotte-Mecklenburg Bd. of Educ., 233 F.3d 232 (4th Cir. 2000), *reh'g en banc,* 269 F.3d 305 (4th Cir. 2001), *reconsideration denied sub nom.* Belk v. Capacchione, 274 F.3d 814 (4th Cir. 2001), *cert. denied, sub nom.* Capacchione v. Charlotte-Mecklenburg Bd. of Educ., 535 U.S. 986 (2002).
[43] Swann v. Charlotte-Mecklenburg Bd. of Educ., 402 U.S. 1 (1971), *reh'g denied,* 403 U.S. 912 (1971).
[44] *Cert. denied, sub nom.* Capacchione v. Charlotte-Mecklenburg Bd. of Educ., 535 U.S. 986 (2002).
[45] Coippedge v. Franklin County Bd. of Educ., 345 F. Supp. 2d 567 (E.D.N.C. 2004).
[46] 127 S. Ct. 2738 (2007).
[47] Gary Orfield, The Growth of Segregation in American Schools: Changing Patterns of Separation and Poverty Since 1968 (1993).
[48] Gary Orfield & Chungmei Lee, *Brown* at 50: King's Dream or Plessy's Nightmare? (2004) *available at* http://www.civilrightsproject.harvard.edu/research/ reseg04/resegregation04.php.
[49] United States Department of Justice, FY 2008 Performance Budget, Civil Rights Division, Congressional Budget Submission http://www.usdoj.gov/jmd/2008justification/pdf/18_crt.pdf
[50] Gary Orfield, The Growth of Segregation in American Schools: Changing Patterns of Separation and Poverty Since 1968 (1993); Gary Orfield & J.T. Yun, Resegregation in American Schools (1999) *available at* http://www.law.harvard.edu/groups/.../publications/resegregation99.html.
[51] Orfield, *supra* note 47.

Chapter 37

English Language Learners

Scott Ellis Ferrin

Introduction

The needs of language-minority or English language learner (ELL) students have become highly politicized in America, affecting how educational leaders at all levels respond to English language learners' needs and rights. This chapter defines some of the programs used to meet ELLs' needs, including noting that program labels are not always monolithic but comprise a host of practices within discrete program label categories. Foundational legal rights and duties surrounding ELLs are discussed, including the impact and requirements of No Child Left Behind, current referenda intended to outlaw bilingual education, and some important reminders of the rights of ELL students who are also exceptional because of potential disability status. The Individuals with Disabilities Education Act (IDEA) and its requirements regarding individualized education as it relates to ELLs is discussed, and some best practices are suggested. Finally, guidelines and findings from the Teachers of English to Speakers of Other Languages board are appended as a reminder of the important factors to consider when developing programs for ELL students.

America is currently divided politically and culturally over the needs of language-minority students, or English language learners. Recently, politicians and interest groups have indulged in energetic theoretical debates regarding bilingual education's efficacy and the issue of whether English should be established as the "official" language of the United States. However, while the debates rage, principals, because of their close relationship with their communities, parents, and students, cannot afford to ignore the realities of the linguistic and educational needs of all the children served in their schools. Such building level leaders will need to comply with the law, and will also need to determine what practices are most successful with their own unique mix of language learners. In most instances, the new federal mandate known as No Child Left Behind will hold leaders accountable for language learners' attainment of language and academic skills. As building-level leaders consider the rights of such students, there are some methodological terms to consider and some bedrock fundamental legal rights to note—rights that are being affected by current legal and political issues.

Legal Issues

Methodological Definitions

First, it is important to clarify terms used to describe language policies, methodologies, and programs, as they are known by different names to different groups. Beyond language discrepancies in naming programs, referring to programs is further complicated by the fact that the current administration seems to disfavor bilingual education programs. In fiscal year (FY) 2001, the Department of Education provided Program Development Implementation Grants for "discretionary grants to support the development and implementation of comprehensive, coherent, and successful bilingual or English as a second language programs and other special alternative instructional programs for limited English proficient students."[1] Such programs were funded at $44,271,207 in FY 2001, which was dropped to $37,193,585 in FY 2002 and $23,027,739 in FY 2003, and no new awards are currently anticipated. The authors of the No Child Left Behind legislation have avoided even using the term "bilingual education" at all when referring to English language learners and the programs available to teach them. A basic set of the most common program definitions, including the seemingly illicit term, "bilingual education," follow.

Bilingual education. This program definition can be divided by some into "maintenance" or "developmental bilingual education" and "transitional bilingual education." Recently, under the executive branch and most state guidelines, most bilingual education programs focus on transitional bilingual education with an emphasis on rapid transition to English. The labels on any of these programs do not perfectly predict the wide variation of practice within programs called the same thing. Though there are many variations on the theory when it is applied in practice, the basic idea of transitional bilingual education is that while students are preparing to transition to fully mainstream English classes, students should learn core academic subjects in their native language so that when English is fully acquired, they are not behind in other subjects such as math, science, etc. There are few, if any "maintenance bilingual education" programs currently in the United States. Such programs value the social, sociolinguistic, and cognitive benefits that bilingualism provides for students. Since maintenance programs are currently politically unpopular, and rarely seen or advocated for by principals, the above will suffice as a brief definition.

English as a Second Language, or ESL. ESL is used most often when there are only a few students of a specific language group in a school, or when the community that comprises a school district's political climate believes it is less expensive than other programs. Generally ESL programs are done through "pull out" classes where kids leave their normal academic classrooms for separate classes a few times a week. There is no other assistance usually provided to these students in their normal academic classroom. In ESL basic theory, it is posited that the teacher need not have any facility with a student's native language to provide instruction in the target language of English. Methods include group memorization, mimicry, and some grammar-based training. Simplified speech and verbal contextual clues in speech situations are often utilized. There are many types of practices and practitioners within the field of ESL. ESL theory and methodology continue to adapt and advance, and the theories and practices of ESL and bilingual education are beginning to blend as practitioners react to new research on second-language acquisition. Within some ESL programs, para-educators, or classroom aides who speak students' native language, may be involved in providing vocabulary and other language supports to students in both the ESL and the mainstream classroom. There are far more ESL-trained teachers than bilingual-trained teachers available in many school districts, which may account for the popularity of ESL programs. Although ESL is often presented as less expensive than bilingual education, school leaders would be well served to analyze this claim in their own settings. ESL may require separate staffs and classrooms, while bilingual programs may only require trained teachers with similar salaries to other teachers, with just one classroom.

Immersion or Structured Immersion. This methodology is also sometimes called "sheltered English." The major mode of instruction is in the target language of English, and academic subject matter is taught in the target language. However, contextual clues and other helps are given to aid students in acquiring clues necessary to gain English, but this assistance lasts only for a transitional period of time, such as one year. Lesson materials are often simplified while awaiting students' advances in English language competence. Immersion tends to be most successful in gaining the more accessible BICS (basic interpersonal communication skills) types of skills in language, since such proficiency is often highly contextualized, and can be embedded in visual clues such as pointing to a door while saying the word "door." Deeper levels of language proficiency or CALPS (cognitive academic language proficiency skills) are not as easily developed through immersion since it is difficult to provide contextual clues or point to more abstract or academic terms such as "implicit" or "nuanced" or "unified field theory."

Dual Immersion. As in all the other programs, the label describes a number of different actual practices, but *dual immersion,* also know as *two-way bilingual* or *bilingual immersion,* essentially brings in native speakers of two languages, such as Spanish and English, and instructs them in the same classroom with the intent that they learn each other's language while also receiving academic instruction in both languages. There are different models, such as half days with two teachers, with one language being utilized for one half of the day and the other for the second half. Such courses can also be team-taught, mixing the languages throughout the entire school day. Research has tended to favor such programs, as has public opinion. Because these programs intermix native language speakers, acquisition is in a high quality, language-rich environment, in which sociolinguistic barriers to acquisition of both languages are lowered. Research shows that the native English speakers are affected and benefited by the courses as well as the non-native English speakers. Unfortunately, some models of dual immersion favor treating these classes as high status academic classes with entrance requirements, blocking the access of English language learners who might benefit the most, since their overall grades might be too low to enter the program.

The above section is far from exhaustive in defining and describing program models and practices for instructing ELLs, but it does include simplified descriptions of some of the most common classifications of language programs. There are many others, and the labels hide a host of differences in actual practices among same-labeled programs. In fact, this discrepancy in labeling has been part of the controversy over whether bilingual education hurts or helps students. Many programs labeled *immersion* and touted as *successful* by researchers seem like bilingual programs to other researchers, and likewise programs labeled bilingual that researchers have evaluated as *not excellent* resemble immersion programs to other researchers. Thus, it is difficult to answer such a broad research question as "Does bilingual education hurt or help children?" by looking at many programs labeled *bilingual* by researchers across several states. A more fruitful and "answerable" question might be to study basic language acquisition research to determine what types of programs might be of the most benefit to the different types of language learners in schools. Certainly, students come with many diverse language backgrounds and skills. Trying to determine whether one approach works for all children across diverse backgrounds, while taking into account differences in funding and practices in the programs themselves, seems relatively sterile and unhelpful for building level administrators.

Foundational Legal Rights of English Language Learners

No matter what program is followed, principals and other educational leaders should note that language-minority children's rights are based on a well-established line of cases and statutes. In the foundational case, *Lau v. Nichols,*[2] the Supreme Court made it clear that language-minority children who lack proficiency in English are entitled to some sort of language intervention or program that will enable them to benefit from the educational program of their school. The *Lau* Court avoided the constitutional questions raised by the case because there was a clear controlling statutory authority and cited instead Section 601 of the Civil Rights Act of 1964, 42 U.S.C.A. Section 2000d, which bans discrimination based on "the grounds of race, color, or national origin," in "any program or activity receiving Federal financial assistance." The court also cited guidelines promulgated by the U.S. Department of Health Education and Welfare:

> Where inability to speak and understand the English language excludes national origin-minority group children from effective participation in the educational program

> offered by a school district, the district must take affirmative steps to rectify the language deficiency in order to open its instructional program to these students. Any ability grouping or tracking system employed by the school system to deal with the special language skill needs of national origin-minority group children must be designed to meet such language skill needs as soon as possible.[3]

These guidelines, and well-accepted case and statutory law, require that "affirmative steps" be taken to rectify language deficiencies to open a district's instructional program to language-minority children. It also requires that any grouping or tracking of ELL students be designed to meet students' "language skill needs as soon as possible." Although these guidelines do not require a specific program—and this was clear even before California's Proposition 227 outlawing bilingual education was passed—they do set a standard of affirmative, active, and speedy programmatic intervention.

Referenda Outlawing Bilingual Education

Where do Proposition 227 in California, Proposition 203 in Arizona, and Question 2 in Massachusetts—and all state laws that outlaw bilingual education—leave these standards? The *Lau* Court neglected to mandate a specific program of any type, such as bilingual education or ESL education. California's law at the time required that "English shall be the basic language of instruction in all schools" and that the "policy of the state" was to "insure the mastery of English by all pupils in the schools."[4] Also, and perhaps most importantly, the *Lau* plaintiffs did not request any specific bilingual or language program as a remedy. The court noted:

> No specific remedy is urged upon us. Teaching English to the students of Chinese ancestry who do not speak the language is one choice. Giving instructions to this group in Chinese is another. There may be others. Petitioners ask only that the Board of Education be directed to apply its expertise to the problem and rectify the situation.[5]

The lower court and the school board defendants were only required to do *something* to "rectify the language deficiency" of the language-minority students.[6]

The court did note that Section 602 of the Civil Rights Act of 1964 states that a federal fund recipient (in this case a school) "may not … utilize criteria or methods of administration which have the effect of subjecting individuals to discrimination or have the effect of defeating or *substantially impairing accomplishment of the objectives of the program as respect individuals of a particular race, color, or national origin*"[7] (emphasis added). After noting this standard, the court remanded the case and ordered the educational agency to develop appropriate relief. The court noted that a school district may not use methods that defeat or "substantially [impair] accomplishment of the objectives of the program as respect individuals of a particular race, color or national origin."[8]

Under the current set of statutes established by referenda in California, Arizona, and Massachusetts outlawing bilingual education, educational leaders need to develop programs that can effectuate the core purposes defined above. If immersion is used as the only educational method to meet the needs of ELLs, and it is a low-cost method generally, it seems likely that community advocates and language-minority group representatives may at some future time be motivated to seek legal intervention to require an evaluation of English submersion programs to determine whether or not, as applied to language-minority students after an appropriate trial period, they have become unconstitutional because they have served to impair "accomplishment of the objectives of the program."[9] No Child Left Behind (NCLB) will tend to provide discrete data that can be used to outline the educational attainment, or lack thereof, of English language learners. This will necessarily involve a metric that a court, perhaps through the services of a court-appointed master, would find reliable. The new provisions of NCLB legislation may perhaps be used as a yardstick, or as an indicator, to measure the effectiveness of these various programs for ELL students. If substantial numbers of language-minority students fail to make adequate yearly progress over time, particularly in states that have outlawed bilingual education and have applied English immersion with some minimal waivers, this data could potentially be enough to find the outlawing of bilingual education unconstitutional under the basic constitutional guidelines established by the Court in *Lau*. While such an eventuality may be remote, building-level leaders should ensure that sufficient and appropriate teacher and para-educator resources are made available, no matter what language program is used, to provide appropriate educational attainment for English language learners. Such proactive steps will lessen the vulnerability of educational leaders, schools, and school systems to legal challenges based on *Lau* and other civil rights acts.

Currently, California's Proposition 227 has been upheld against constitutional challenges in the Ninth Circuit. However, the basis for those challenges have been on constitutional theories regarding the facial unconstitutionality of the proposition or statute. Such a standard ignores the actual educational attainment and "ability to participate" standard that is more fundamental. In *Valeria v. Davis*,[10] the constitutionality of Proposition 227 under the Fourteenth Amendment's Equal Protection Clause was challenged in the Ninth Circuit. The court rejected the "political structure" equal protection analysis urged by petitioners under the doctrines of *Hunter v. Erickson*[11] and *Washington v. Seattle School District No. 1*.[12] The court held that when otherwise facially neutral legislation is challenged under the Fourteenth Amendment, there must be both inquiry and proof regarding whether the legislation was designed to cause disparate treatment on the basis of racial considerations.[13] This intent or "design" standard presents an extremely difficult hurdle for plaintiffs to surmount.

However, once a track record has been established for a statute *as applied*, it appears that advocates for minority-language children may properly begin to consider legal challenges based upon the Fourteenth Amendment and civil rights statutes regarding English submersion and the statutes that require it, *as applied.* A challenge of a statute as *applied,* as opposed to on its face, or a *facial challenge* is a completely different review. It may indeed be easier to prove, especially with the federal government apparently poised to show through NCLB that language-minority students and the schools that contain them will fail to meet adequate yearly progress standards. Although *Lau* never required bilingual education, it can clearly be read to require that some appropriate and effective action be taken in favor of language-minority students. Educational leaders who select immersion or other less intensive programs should not relax, simply because there is legal precedent allowing the adoption of programs other than bilingual education. A vital concern for building-level leaders should be to demonstrate the educational attainment of language-learner students in any program, especially if it is the relatively less ambitious choice of immersion.

The Equal Educational Opportunities Act and *Castaneda:* Defining Appropriate Action

The question becomes: What is appropriate action to allow language-minority students to participate in federally supported educational programs? If the great majority of language-minority students are shown to be failing to achieve strict standards under NCLB, a violation of fundamental equal protection law could then be established. What are the standards for establishing programs to meet the needs, and respond to the rights, of language-minority students to participate in and benefit from public education?

Equal Educational Opportunities Act

In 1974, Congress passed the Equal Educational Opportunities Act, following the *Lau* decision, requiring that school systems develop programs for limited English proficiency students. It states: "No state shall deny educational opportunity to an individual on account of his or her race, color, sex or national origin, by … the failure by an educational agency to take appropriate action to overcome language barriers that impede equal participation by its students in its instructional programs."[14] Congress was not clear, however, on what constitutes "appropriate action to overcome language barriers."

In the 1986 case of *Castaneda v. Pickard*[15] and its 1981 predecessor, *Castaneda I,*[16] the Fifth Circuit gave a great deal of deference to state and local educational authorities to determine "appropriate action to overcome language barriers" in their educational setting. The *Castaneda* court said:

> We by no means imply … that a state must provide a program of bilingual education to all limited English speaking

> students in order to satisfy § 1703 (f) of the EEOA. We hold fast to our conviction, voiced in *Castaneda I*, that in enacting § 1703 (f) Congress intended to leave state and local educational authorities a substantial amount of latitude in choosing the programs and techniques they would use.[17]

However, this substantial latitude has limits, and statistical and standardized test metrics showing a consistent lack of success should be used to limit local latitude to simply impose English submersion on ELL students. Courts have continued the deference to state and local authorities begun in *Lau*, continued in *Castaneda I* and *Castaneda*, and reiterated and clarified in *Keyes v. School District No 1.*[18] The *Keyes* court found *Castaneda I* "very instructive" and stated the *Castaneda* test as a series of three questions used to determine whether "appropriate action" is being pursued to overcome language barriers:

1. Is the school system pursuing a program based on an educational theory recognized as sound or at least as a legitimate experimental strategy by some of the experts in the field?
2. Is the program reasonably calculated to implement that theory?
3. After being used for enough time to be a legitimate trial, has the program produced satisfactory results?[19]

The *Keyes* court also analyzed 20 U.S.C. Section 1703 and noted:

> Congress' use of the less specific term, "appropriate action," rather than "bilingual education" indicates that Congress intended to leave state and local educational authorities a substantial amount of latitude in choosing the programs and techniques they would use to meet their obligations under the Equal Education Opportunity Act [EEOA].[20]

The *Keyes* court suggested that Congress did not intend to constrain local educational authorities to use bilingual education because they used the less specific term *appropriate action*. However, the *Keyes* court *did* note that Congress created an enforceable duty in the EEOA, including a private right of action, that requires state and local educational authorities to make appropriate programs available to language-minority students:

> By including an obligation to address the problem of language barriers in the EEOA and granting limited English speaking students a private right of action to enforce that obligation in S 1706, Congress also must have intended to insure that schools made a genuine and good faith effort, consistent with local circumstances and resources, to remedy the language deficiencies of their students and deliberately placed on federal courts the difficult responsibility of determining whether that obligation had been met.[21]

In *Keyes,* the court was willing to investigate the adequacy of the program of instruction. The court noted:

> The emphasis on the acquisition of oral English skills for LEP students is another cause for concern. The record indicates that on the average, ESL instruction by a teacher or tutor is limited to 40 minutes per day of remedial English instruction using an audiolingual approach. While there is no doubt that acquisition of oral English skills is vital for the students' participation in classroom work, it is equally obvious that reading and writing skills are also necessary if it is expected that "parity in participation" in the total academic experience will be achieved.[22]

The specific weaknesses of the program in *Keyes* is not as important as is the willingness of the court to investigate the program. If a standard of "parity in participation" is used, and if courts are willing to investigate student outcomes and the relationship between educational methodology and outcomes, it may be possible that statutes outlawing bilingual education may become unconstitutional over time based on their programs' track records with language-minority students and their student outcomes. Similarly, the decision to use low-cost programs such as "immersion" may become inappropriate over time if students are not showing appropriate educational attainment.

Since NCLB requires that state educational agencies (SEAs) hold local educational agencies (LEAs) accountable to meet annual measurable benchmarks in academic achievement and the achievement of English proficiency, LEAs must assess ELL or LEP (Limited English Proficient, in the statute's terms) children annually in five specific domains: speaking, reading, writing, listening, and comprehension. Most significantly, Title III of NCLB (the section dealing with language learners) requires LEAs to report on the progress made by LEP children after they are no longer receiving services as language learners under Title III. Specifically they must report on progress in meeting state academic content and achievement standards for the two years after they leave language-minority student services. Thus, in states that have outlawed bilingual education, or that may yet outlaw bilingual education, the academic achievement of students who have exited the abbreviated one-year sheltered immersion or transitional bilingual English program will be measured and compared to non-limited English proficient (LEP) students. After this data is collected, a comparable difference in performance may be legally significant. Although, under the reasoning of *Valeria v. Davis,* such quantitative statistical data is problematic in establishing a facial Fourteenth Amendment challenge, it is possible that after an appropriate time of collecting data and evaluating language programs, or the lack thereof, in states that have outlawed bilingual education, such data could form the basis for an "as applied" challenge based on the standards of *Lau.* These standards include civil rights statutes and equal protection foundations. Under the reasoning of *Castaneda,* and also that of

Keyes, it seems appropriate to set as a standard the answer to the question: "After being used for enough time to be a legitimate trial, has the program produced satisfactory results?"[23]

The Equal Educational Opportunities Act, 20 U.S.C. Section 1703 (f), commands that no state shall deny equal educational opportunity to an individual by "failure by an educational agency to take appropriate action to overcome language barriers that impede equal participation by its students in its instructional programs." In *Keyes*, the court clearly stopped its analysis at the second "prong" of the *Castaneda* test because the court found that the school district did not implement its chosen program adequately when it allowed, under its reduction-in-force policy, unqualified, monolingual teachers to teach the transitional bilingual program they had adopted. The third prong, regarding results, should be rigorously analyzed in a decision regarding the constitutionality of language programs that are failing children.

Scientifically Based Research

NCLB mandates, in fact reiterates more than 120 times, that programs must be based on "scientifically based research." It specifically requires that programs to assist LEP language-minority students must be based on "scientifically based evidence,"[24] and funding recipients must develop language instruction educational programs and curricula that are based on scientifically based research on teaching limited English proficient children.

States are required to submit a plan that describes:

> How eligible entities in the State will be given the flexibility to teach limited English proficient children—(A) using a language instruction curriculum that is tied to scientifically based research on teaching limited English proficient children and that has been demonstrated to be effective; and (B) in the manner the eligible entities determine to be the most effective.[25]

This language seems to echo the concerns of the first prong of *Castaneda*: "Is the school system pursuing a program based on an educational theory recognized as sound or at least as a legitimate experimental strategy by an educational theory recognized as sound or at least as a legitimate experimental strategy by some of the experts in the field?"[26] The statute defines scientifically based research as:

> Research that—(A) applies rigorous, systematic, and OBJECTIVE PROCEDURES to obtain valid knowledge relevant to reading development, reading instruction, and reading difficulties; and (B) includes research that—(i) employs systematic, empirical methods that draw on observation or experiment; (ii) involves rigorous data analyses that are adequate to test the stated hypotheses and justify

> the general conclusions drawn; (iii) relies on measurements or observational methods that provide valid data across evaluators and observers and across multiple measurements and observations; and (iv) has been accepted by a peer-reviewed journal or approved by a panel of independent experts through a comparably rigorous, objective, and scientific review.[27]

To advocates of bilingual education, the requirement that a plan must be based on "scientifically based research" sounds like the statute is intended to make it difficult to choose bilingual education as a teaching methodology. This fear, in the minds of such advocates, is also manifested by the removal of the term *bilingual education* from the current administration's statutes and regulations. However, such an intention is difficult to prove, and there is a large body of research regarding bilingual education that can be used to justify, even laud, various bilingual education methodologies. It is possible that a war of words regarding research methodologies and quality could be our future under the statute.

Massachusetts' Statute as an Example of Current Referenda on Language Rights

There are some unusual features in the current referendum espoused by Ron Unz and other "English Only" advocates that attempts to outlaw bilingual education in several states. The new referendum was promoted and defeated in Colorado, but was successfully used in Massachusetts, where it passed as Question 2, and included some powerful language regarding enforcement and teachers. Because of a perception that teachers in California and other settings are unwilling to implement such a draconian statute outlawing any bilingual assistance when they see individual students needing or seeking assistance, the statute creates a private right of action in parents to sue teachers, school board members, elected officials, and others directly for failure to fully implement the statute. The statute also seeks to make it illegal for any immunity, indemnification, or third-party assistance to be provided to teachers or school board members who are said to violate the statute.

Any teachers, employees, school board members, or any other elected officials who fail to provide a strictly English education beyond the waiver years of the statute must also be fired or impeached and cannot be considered for rehire or re-election for five years. This personal liability and exposure for individual educators is highly unusual, as is the limitation on the rights of the ballot and the apparent impeachment provision. The statute states:

> Section 6. Legal standing and parental enforcement
>
> (a) As set forth in Section 4 of this chapter, all school children are to be provided at their assigned school with an English language public education. The parent or legal

> guardian of any school child shall have legal standing to sue for enforcement of the provisions of this chapter, and if successful shall be awarded reasonable attorney's fees, costs and compensatory damages.
>
> (b) Any school district employee, school committee member or other elected official or administrator who willfully and repeatedly refuses to implement the terms of this chapter may be held personally liable for reasonable attorney's fees, costs and compensatory damages by the child's parents or legal guardian, and shall not be subsequently indemnified for such monetary judgment by any public or private third party. Any individual found so liable shall be barred from election or reelection to any school committee and from employment in any public school district for a period of five years following the entry of final judgment.[28]

Whether this feature of the statute is enforceable and constitutional remains to be seen. It even prohibits private third parties from indemnifying teachers. Presumably, private insurers cannot develop insurance programs for teachers in this area. This raises questions under the Commerce and Supremacy Clauses of the U.S. Constitution, as well as due process issues under the Fourteenth Amendment. Before educational institutions discharge teachers under these provisions, a very full hearing procedure with exacting standards of proof must be employed.

The practical effects of these provisions in Question 2 will be a chilling effect, making it likely that teachers, school board members, and others will avoid developing innovative programs for language-minority students or even avoid working with them based on the specter of defending themselves personally from parent lawsuits. The cost of answering even one frivolous lawsuit tends to outstrip the financial resources of most individual educators. Can teachers' unions be constitutionally prohibited from providing insurance to their members in this area? Will prepaid legal service plans in teachers' unions be seen as indemnification under this statute? Many questions abound surrounding the severe provisions of the statute.

Use of Referenda

Perhaps the central question, though, has to do with the use of referenda to determine the rights of language minorities. Obviously, referenda, or direct democratic structures, tend to put minorities at the mercy of majoritarian values and processes. In Massachusetts, for example, note the reported disconnect between Latino voters and the majority. Although Question 2 passed by a vote of about 70 percent of the states voters, exit polling in Massachusetts found that 93 percent of Latinos voted in favor of bilingual education, rejecting Question 2.[29] Obviously, the voters at large did not have the viewpoint that the minority voters had. Nevertheless, direct democracy and the majority's understanding fundamentally affected the interest of the minority.

A large body of experience and political science research tends to indicate that whenever direct democracy, such as referenda, advantages a majority over a minority, such referenda have a tendency to pass. Ron Unz's utilization of referenda to impact language-minority rights in education are prime examples. Researchers such as David Magelby and important democratic documents such as the *Federalist Papers,* offer a critical view of referenda and direct democracy in establishing "reforms" that implicate minorities' interests.[30] They are highlighted because such reforms will affect principals' abilities in the near future to provide appropriate language programs for English language learners in various states as the referenda process and these campaigns continue throughout the United States. Principals and other educational leaders cannot afford to be passive in the face of referenda campaigns. Experience shows that referenda dealing with limiting language program choices, as minority issues, tend to pass absent a very massive and concerted effort to educate the electorate on the issues. If principals and educational leaders do nothing in the face of such referenda, recent history indicates that their programmatic choices to serve English language learners will be limited by such statutes. Such limitations are based more on political forces than on research. A statement from the Teachers of English to Speakers of Other Languages is appended as a statement by experienced teachers and researchers in this area regarding effective practices in developing literacy and language skills in English language learners.

Rights of Parents of ELLs, Including Issues under the IDEA

Although groups opposed to bilingual education and other language programs for English language learners may limit programmatic approaches for students, language-minority parents and students continue to have rights that should be protected by building-level educational leaders. Principals must not forget the nexus between language-minority students' needs and student rights under the IDEA and other statutes to help students with disabilities. In the findings section of the IDEA as reauthorized in 1997, Congress found:

> (F) The limited English proficient population is the fastest growing in our Nation, and the growth is occurring in many parts of our Nation. In the Nation's 2 largest school districts, limited English proficient students make up almost half of all students initially entering school at the kindergarten level. Studies have documented apparent discrepancies in the levels of referral and placement of limited English proficient children in special education. The Department of Education has found that services provided to limited English proficient students often do not respond primarily to the pupil's academic needs. These trends pose special

> challenges for special education in the referral, assessment, and services for our Nation's students from non-English language backgrounds. (IDEA Part A section 601 (c) (7) (F))

There are two problems that occur in the disproportionate referral and replacement of ELL students in special education. They include the more well-known problem of overreferral of language-minority students to special education simply based on inability to provide for their language needs. However, there is also a potential problem if a building-level leader notes that there is a large ELL population in the school population, and too low a percentage of that population is being served in special education. This may occur because it is often difficult to bring together the expertise of the staffs serving ELLs with the staffs serving special education populations. Every cultural and language group should have some percentage of children who have disabilities that might require special educational services. Leaders would do well to monitor not only overreferral, but also be sensitive to the underreferral of ELLs to special education.

As an individualized education plan (IEP) is developed for students with special education needs, principals should be sure that IEP teams do not assume that the primary mode of instruction should be in English. An IEP is required to be individualized, and in order to meet individualized needs, there may be need for native language instruction or some other type of language methodology. It is not certain under the IDEA that a young student with disabilities and an IQ of forty whose only language is one other than English would best be served by providing all services in English, with the first goal being the acquisition of English. In addition, establishing functioning levels of cognitive abilities and IQ baselines may be problematic if primary language concerns are not addressed in testing.

Best practices in fulfilling the IDEA's requirements would include making sure that parents are given the required notices of their rights under the IDEA in the "home language" of the parents, if there are indications that the primary language in the home might be other than English. If there are indications that there is a language other than English used in the student's home, assessment for IDEA and other services may be required in that home or native language, depending on the student's language capabilities.

Basic Steps or Guidelines in Assessing ELLs with Potential Special Education Needs

The basic steps educational leaders should consider when assessing exceptional students needs who are also ELLs include the following:

1. assess the primary language used in the student's home;
2. determine the student's proficiency in the student's first or home language and English using assessment instruments and assessing personnel in both languages, even if this requires the use of aides or

para-educators to assist in assessment for students from relatively rare language backgrounds;

3. decide which language will be used for making the complete assessment for special education needs;
4. administer all complete assessments and diagnostic tools for special education purposes in both languages if necessary;
5. report to the IEP team;
6. notify and support parents in their home language of decisions regarding language of instruction and language needs in student's IEP team without assuming that the primary method of instruction will be English based on availability or lack of teachers or resources; and
7. provide parents attending IEP team meetings with language assistance and/or translation, including the right to have bilingual representatives attend to assist parents.

Recommendations for Practice

Based on research in early literacy development and second-language acquisition, the following features of effective early literacy programs are recommended for young ESOL students.

1. *Oral language and literacy development is supported by the student's native language.*

   Development and learning begin at an early age, and the language young children have heard since birth is the language they have used to begin to construct their knowledge and form meaningful communicative relationships. All young children come to school with knowledge and learning from home. Successful early childhood programs acknowledge and build upon this prior knowledge. Wherever possible, young ESOL learners should receive their initial reading instruction in their native language. The body of research in second-language acquisition shows that literacy learning is easiest when the initial instruction is in the student's native language because literacy skills are easily transferred from the first to the second language. Moreover, use of the native language builds a connection between the home and school. ESOL students' families should be encouraged to read and talk to their children in the family's native language if this is their strongest language. ESOL students' interaction with their families in their native language will give them the richest possible language foundation, advancing the learning of their first language, as well as English, in both academic and social situations. These experiences will allow young children to associate reading with meaning from the very beginning so that they do not word call, that is, pronounce words from print when they do not understand them.

2. *Adequate time is provided for students to acquire literacy skills in English.*

   It is well documented that all children learn at different rates. This principle is especially true for young ESOL learners, who follow developmental patterns that are distinctly different from those of native English speakers. Young ESOL learners should not be hurried prematurely into formal literacy instruction in any language or into moving from reading in their native language to reading in English. Oral or social language proficiency, which can be achieved within two to three years, should not be equated with academic proficiency or literacy in a language. Literacy as well as cognitive and conceptual development of ESOL students should be interlaced. Research shows that for young children in particular, the stronger the native language foundation, especially when learned in formal schooling environments, the greater the academic success in English literacy development. Of course, not all new English language learners or their families have had formal schooling opportunities. Therefore, accountability systems that hold teachers and schools responsible for English literacy development for ESOL learners in an unrealistic time frame may, in the long run, hinder the students' chances for academic success.

3. *Instruction and materials are developmentally appropriate.*

   ESOL students who are at early stages of schooling (pre-K through grade 2) need to experience developmentally appropriate instruction that will help them develop oral and written language proficiency in one or more languages. This kind of instruction engages children in meaningful interactions with adults, other children, concrete materials, and print materials. Moreover, the materials that are used need to be comprehensible to the learner and meet their developmental, cognitive, social, and cultural needs, which for young ESOL learners include language proficiency. In developmentally appropriate classrooms, students spend most of their time in rich language environments in which they observe, touch, listen, talk, and interact. Early reading and writing instruction is largely informal, playful, and based on oral language activities and personal experiences. Activities that typically challenge the attention span of young learners, such as sitting quietly and listening for long periods or printing neatly on fine-lined paper, should be limited. Standards-based instruction, as described in *ESL Standards for Pre-K-12 Students* (TESOL, 1997) and *Integrating the ESL Standards Into Classroom Practice: Grades*

Pre-K-2 (TESOL, 2001), should be incorporated into developmentally appropriate practices.

4. *Literacy programs are meaning-based and balanced.*

   ESOL learners need to understand why people read and write in order to be motivated to excel in their own literacy development. A preponderance of isolated skills, such as an intensive phonics program that is not firmly grounded in books and stories, does not foster overall reading comprehension. A balanced literacy program will teach skills within the context of meaningful interactions with texts that elicit students' emotional and intellectual responses to ideas, characters, and events. Using children's literature, preferably from a wide variety of cultural backgrounds, will be a key part of any such program. Effective literacy programs seek both literacy and content development, assert that students within the program are learning the same content as native-English-speaking children, and look beyond the classroom for literacy experiences.

5. *Assessment is reliable, valid, and ongoing.*

   Many young children cannot demonstrate the knowledge and skills they possess if they are assessed with methods more appropriate to older learners or those designed for native English speakers. In order to more accurately assess the literacy development of young ESOL learners, a variety of formal and informal tools should be used. Assessments that only focus on phonics, spelling skills, and writing content and style may be vulnerable to linguistic interference from the native language. Teachers should be aware that errors on assessments of English literacy skills can be developmental in nature and will disappear over time as students acquire English language proficiency. By continually using reliable, valid, and fair assessments, teachers are able to modify their instruction and tailor it to the individual needs of ESOL learners. Gathering classroom data on an ongoing basis, as described in *Scenarios for ESL Standards-based Assessment* (TESOL, 2001) keeps teachers apprised of student progress toward the attainment of ESL standards.

6. *Professional preparation and development is continually provided for educators regarding linguistic and cultural diversity.*

   The presence of English language learners and culturally diverse classrooms—long a characteristic only of major cities—is more and more becoming the norm throughout the country. In order to face the challenges that come with a diverse classroom, all educators and administrators need to have both pre- and in-service training opportunities in linguistic and cultural diversity and in principles of first and second-language development. It is also critical for the early childhood educator to understand the linguistic and cultural backgrounds of their students in order to facilitate learning and build cross-cultural understandings with their families.

Conclusion

For young children, the quality of education they receive in their first years of schooling is often a critical indicator of their long-term academic success. Early literacy and language development are interlaced with social and cognitive development and are vital elements in the education of young children. For young ESOL learners, the complexities involved with literacy and language development are compounded by the fact that they must be achieved in a language other than their native language and often before they are literate in that language. Successful early childhood programs build upon the knowledge that young learners bring from home, and for young ESOL learners, this knowledge is learned and expressed in their native language.

Research in second-language development has shown that literacy in a second language is much more easily achieved when literacy is developed first in the native language, as literacy skills are more easily transferred from the first language to the second language. Differences between social and academic language need to be recognized and addressed by all teachers that ESOL students encounter. In other words, all teachers need to understand that social language is based principally on familiar and often concrete concepts, whereas academic language is more linguistically complex, often involving abstract concepts, and is embedded into new cognitive information and topics. As a result, teachers, administrators, and families should understand that social language skills may develop within two to three years, as compared to full academic proficiency in a second language, which is more literacy dependent and can take five to seven years to develop. Arbitrary time limits for mainstreaming ESOL learners should not be placed on programs, nor should educators be encouraged to move young students hastily into literacy programs before they are capable of performing successfully.

Instruction and materials should be appropriate in terms of developmental characteristics and language proficiency. Effective literacy programs maintain a balanced focus on both literacy and content development. In order to measure young learners' progress, a variety of formal and informal tools should be used that are reliable, valid, and fair. Most importantly, early childhood educators, just as their peers in K-12 education, need to receive pre- and in-service training on the importance of linguistic and cultural diversity, as well as the foundations of second language learning for young children, so that they can meet the needs and challenges of their diverse classrooms.

Endnotes

1 http://www.ed.gov/programs/pdi/funding.html?exp=0.
2 414 U.S. 563, 94 S. Ct. 786 (1974).
3 Lau v. Nichols, 94 S. Ct. 786, 789 (1974), *see also* 35 Fed. Reg. 11595 (1970).
4 West's ANN. CAL. EDUC. CODE § 71 (1973).
5 *Lau* at 567.
6 *Id.*
7 *Id.* at 68.
8 *Id.*
9 *Id.*
10 307 F.3d 1036 (9th Cir. 2002).
11 393 U.S. 385, 89 S. Ct. 557 (1969).
12 458 U.S. 457, 102 S. Ct. 3187 (1982).
13 *Id.* at 1040.
14 20 U.S.C.A. § 1703 (f).
15 781 F. 2d 456 (5th Cir. 1986).
16 Castaneda v. Pickard, 648 F. 2d 989 (5th Cir. 1981).
17 *Id.* at 1009.
18 Keyes v. Sch. Dist. No. 1, Denver, Colo., 576 F. Supp. 1503 (D. Colo. 1983).
19 *Id.* at 1510 (citing Castaneda v. Pickard, 648 F.2d 989, 1009 (5th Cir.1981)).
20 *Id.*
21 *Id.*
22 *Id.* at 1517.
23 *Id.* at 1510 (citing Castaneda v. Pickard, 648 F.2d 989, 1009 (5th Cir.1981)).
24 Based on a rough count by the author.
25 No Child Left Behind Act of 2001, 20 U.S.C.A. § 6823 § 3116 (B)(6).
26 Castaneda v. Pickard, 648 F.2d 989, 1009 (5th Cir.1981).
27 No Child Left Behind Act of 2001, 20 U.S.C.A. § 6368 § 1208 6 (B) (iv).
28 From the Official Massachusetts Voter Information Site, citing the text of the statute, *available at* http://www.state.ma.us/sec/ele/elebq02/bq02full.htm#q2anc.
29 From the Mauricio Gaston Institute, which conducted the research, citing an article and presentation at the Institute by Jorge Capetillo-Ponce, Ph.D., *available at* http://www.gaston.umb.edu/.
30 James Madison, 10 *The Federalist* 58 (The Modern Library 1941). As James Madison wrote:

[A] pure democracy … can admit of no cure for the mischiefs of faction. A common passion or interest will, in almost every case, be felt by a majority of the whole; a communication and concert result from the form of government itself; and there is nothing to check the inducements to sacrifice the weaker party or an obnoxious individual. Hence it is that such democracies have ever been spectacles of turbulence and contention; have ever been found incompatible with personal security or the rights of property; and have in general been as short in their lives as they have been violent in their deaths.

See also David Magleby, *Let the Voters Decide?: An Assessment of the Initiative and Referendum Process,* 66 COLO. L. REV. 13, 31–34 (1995); DAVID B. MAGLEBY, DIRECT LEGISLATION: VOTING ON BALLOT PROPOSITIONS IN THE UNITED STATES 77–99 (1984), which describes empirical evidence on ballot issue voting patterns. *See also* Sherman J. Clark, *A Populist Critique of Direct Democracy,* 112 HARV. L. REV. 434 (1998).

Chapter 38

Responsibility for Education Law

Kenneth E. Lane

Introduction

One of the advantages of writing the concluding chapter is the opportunity to gaze into the proverbial crystal ball. Thus, the predictions that follow are those of the author and do not necessarily reflect the views of the Education Law Association. Hopefully, what follows will incite some spirited discussion of education law and the future.

The chapter authors for this handbook are comprised of attorneys, professors who teach educational law, and school administrators. They have addressed legal issues that confront school personnel including school boards, superintendents, district office staff, teachers, and administrators—in particular, school principals. The legal issues addressed are current, but not exhaustive. Additionally, the law is subject to change in its interpretations and applications based upon new or amended federal and state laws, rules, and regulations as well as new decisions by the judicial system from the state courts through the United States Supreme Court. Educational law is a flexible concept due to the impact of these laws and court decisions. It is incumbent upon the school principal to stay abreast of these changes in order to stay within the legal parameters of operating the schools and working with the students in those schools.

The future for school administrators and teachers is most likely a continuation of new laws and new decisions. The recent change in the philosophical make-up of some of our courts, notably the Supreme Court, will give rise to concern that some of the decisions of the past may be reversed. Therefore, it is safe to predict that litigation will continue on many of the issues identified by the chapter authors. However, it is probably safe to predict that some issues are fairly stable including search and seizure rights, freedom of students for religious expression, substantive and procedural due process rights, protections of student and personnel records, certification of teachers, and desegregation. However, some issues have been in the court systems for many years, and one never knows when a court of jurisdiction will move forward on the law case. A primary example is the ongoing litigation in the states regarding financial issues as they pertain to education.

Specifically, decisions handed down by the United States Supreme Court will be more conservative than previous decisions of the Warren and Burger eras. The interpretation of the U.S. Constitution may well be more restrictive than past court decisions. The outcome of any election, especially the presidential election as well as the congressional elections, may indicate a change in what issues are addressed by the new legislative branch and the interpretations of the laws by the judicial branch. The Supreme Court currently headed by Chief Justice John G. Roberts, Jr. is considered a conservative court. If Associate Justices John Paul Stevens or Ruth Bader Ginsberg leaves the bench soon, the new President will have considerable choice in deciding whether to strengthen the conservatism of the Supreme Court or to maintain the current balance in judicial philosophy. It is important to note, however, that the philosophical perspective of a justice may change upon appointment by the President to and approval by the Senate for the Supreme Court. A prime example is Earl Warren who was thought to be a conservative, but is considered one of the most liberal justices of the past century.

Predictions

To take the crystal gazing a step further, an informal listserv question was posed to the school administrators, attorneys who practice education law, and professors who teach education law. The question simply asked what issues in education law they expected the courts to address in the next few years. The issues articulated by the groups include the following:

1. Bilingual Education
2. Church and State - Religious accommodation beyond the traditional ones raised by Christians
3. Continued church and state disputes
4. Creationism - Continued suits about states trying to mandate the teaching of it
5. Discipline - School discipline and potential Patriot Act issues
6. Drug Testing of students and teachers
7. First Amendment rights of students - Legal status of student non-verbal First Amendment rights and the Second, Sixth, and Ninth Circuits' interpretations of the application of educational mission; Limits to students' free speech rights
8. Gender - Including trans-gender equity
9. Immigration - Educational issues arising from *Plyler v. Doe*/local and state ordinances/DREAM Act matters
10. NCLB - Opponents will try to have certain provisions of it declared unconstitutional; Impact of not making AYP; Educational malpractice tied to NCLB & AYB.

11. Safe Campuses - Securing schools and protecting them from terrorist threat and mass violence
12. School Choice
13. School Finance - At the state level and intra-district inequities; Challenges to lack of adequacy of funding
14. Search & Seizure - Schools' abilities to search communications equipment including cell phones, iPods, Blackberrys, even personal computers that use the school's WiFi system
15. Special Education - Accommodations and especially those concerning testing and ADD diagnoses; Inclusion issues; Parents removing their children from schools for private placement and asking for tuition reimbursement; Exceptional student education cases will continue to be heard as the parents will not be satisfied with programs provided to their children
16. Student Harassment
17. Technology - Use of "MySpace" as related to school activities and students; Cyber-bullying particularly when the action is initiated from an off-site computer but infringes on school activity; Issues of whether any privacy rights for a student or an employee regarding the use of any technology provided by the school or school district
18. Zero Tolerance Policies - Mandatory suspension and expulsion for student misbehavior will be challenged, especially in the Ninth Circuit.

The range of predicted issues before the courts correlates well to what is currently being litigated. The list will be no surprise to principals facing these issues.

Challenges for School Principals

School principals will continue to face the issues raised in the above list in their schools and making decisions based on the law is of utmost importance. Some issues faced are not as well settled in the law, which requires school administrators to remain current on federal and state court rulings as well as local decisions, rules, and regulations. Additionally, legislation enacted by both the U.S. Congress and state legislatures will need to be reviewed to ensure appropriate procedures are followed in working with students and teachers. Ignorance of these issues will not serve as a defense.

Recommendations for Practice

School principals are faced with a wide range of legal issues on a daily basis. To this end, the following recommendations are made to principals to enable them to be current in the area of educational law and how it impacts their schools, students, teachers, and community.

1. Use this Handbook as a source when faced with legal issues.

2. Principals need to avail themselves of good school law courses, legal conferences and in-service workshops that address these issues.

3. Principals are strongly encouraged to use the Internet to locate legal information so that they and their teachers and staff stay apprised of current legal developments.

4. The courts have sent a clear message that they will support administrators and teachers who act in a fair and reasonable manner.

5. Watch the U.S. Supreme Court for any move toward narrowly defined decisions on the issues raised in the above list.

6. Principals should arrange for education law information to be presented to teachers and staff at least once a year, preferably prior to the beginning of a new school year. An in-service workshop offered through attorneys whose practice is in education law and university professors who teach education law will provide needed information on recent changes in laws as well as current changes in rules and regulations.

7. Join a professional organization like the Education Law Association to receive monthly information on education law issues, legal conferences, newsletters, websites, and books The Education Law Association (ELA) has a wealth of books, monographs, and a monthly *School Law Reporter* to enable the principal to stay current on legal issues in education.

Index

R

S